Print and publishing:
Lulu, Inc.
ISBN 978-1-300-55258-1

For Alwin († 2012)

冬季には	*tōki ni wa*	This winter,
刀の見納め	*tō no mi-osame*	a final glance at the sword,
旅に暮る	*tabi ni kuru*	and so the journey ends.

Preface

An unavoidable difficulty with books that deal with Japanese swords in general is that the workmanship of a smith has to be reduced to its most important characteristics which can be seen on the majority of his works. The more extensive the publication is the more deviating interpretations, certain peculiarities, stylistic changes and the schools context may be incorporated. But the problem is that it still remains generalized theoretical information. This problem in turn might be supplemented or compensated by comparing the information with the descriptions of concrete examples. So you will end up with more or less detailed characteristics of a smith which match more or less with his actual works.

It is here that this work comes into play, with the motive to provide more concretely described reference examples. For this purpose, the *kantei* blades from „*Tōken-Bijutsu*" issued by the NBTHK are ideal. In „*Tōken-Bijutsu*", the five blades and accompanying *oshigata* which were provided in the previous month´s *kantei* meetings are namely described in detail. Unique is that – depending on the blade – the participant's *kantei* bids are also addressed. This means that one's own approach and attempt at attributing a blade may also be comprehended.

With the 189 introduced *kotō* blades from altogether 19 provinces (including the five *gokaden*) this volume constitutes an extensive reference work. The order starts in the classical way, namely with the *gokaden* Yamato, Yamashiro, Bizen, Sōshū and Mino. Regarding the numbering, the first number is a serial number and the second number refers to the issue in which the blade was published in the „*Tōken-Bujutsu*". A „k" at the end means that the blade was a *kantei* riddle in that particular issue. For example, the *tantō* of Uda Kunimune with the number „163.666k" is the 163rd blade of this volume and was the *kantei* riddle in issue 666. For the sake of a uniform format, meaning the *oshigata* on the verso and the description on the recto, a blank page had to be sometimes added. This page is marked with the placeholder ❋. Finally it should be noted that both volumes, i.e. „Kotō-kantei" and „Shintō-Shinshintō-kantei" contain all of the five *kantei* blades from the „*Tōken-Bijutsu*" issued between the years 2006-2012.

Winter 2012
Markus Sesko

Contents

[Years in angular brackets refer to a date signature]

Yamato

Yamashiro

Bizen

Sōshū

Mino

Bitchū

Bingo

Hōki

Wakasa

Suruga

Etchū

Kaga

Ise

Ôshū

Dewa

Chikuzen

Bungo

Higo

Satsuma

Yamato

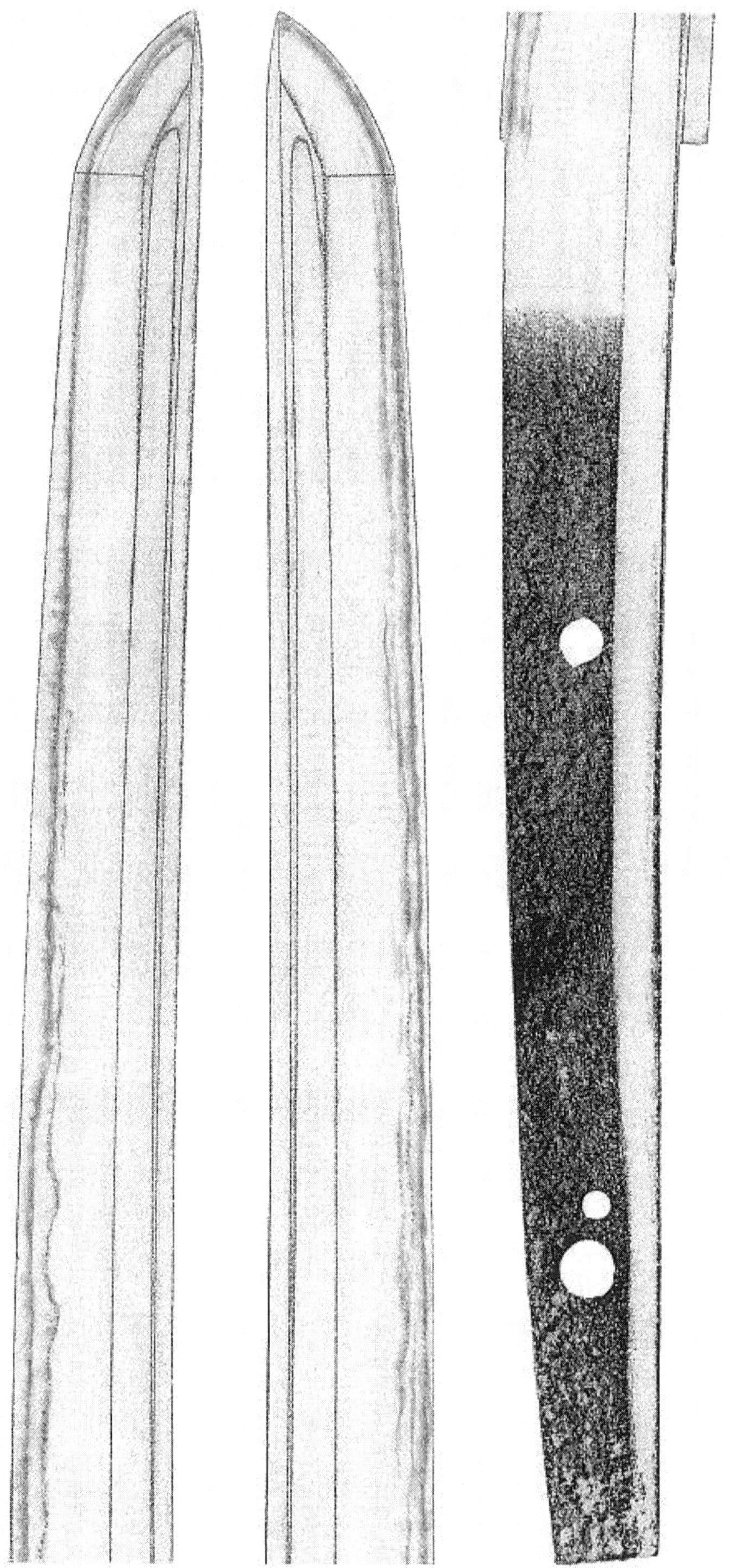

1.639 *katana*
mumei: Ko-Senjū'in (古千手院)
nagasa 67,3 cm, *sori* 1,8 cm, *shinogi-zukuri*, *iori-mune*

ji: dense *itame*, partially mixed with *masame*, fine *ji-nie*, *chikei*
hamon: *hoso-suguha* mixed with some *ko-chōji*-like elements, *nijūba*, *kuichigaiba*, *hotsure* and *uchinoke* along the *habuchi*, plentiful of *nie*, *kinsuji* and *sunagashi*
bōshi: on both sides *sugu* with a *ko-maru-kaeri* and some *hakikake*
horimono: on both sides a *bōhi* which runs with *kake-nagashi* into the tang

This is a *jūyō-tōken ō-suriage mumei katana* which is attributed to the Ko-Senjū'in school. There are only very few signed Senjū'in works extant. Most of the blades of this school going round today are *mumei* and bear „only" an attribution to „Senjū'in". When we look at these blades we learn that they have a relative slender or normal wide *mihaba*, they taper noticeably towards the tip and the *hamon* is a Yamato-typical *suguha-chō* with *hataraki* like *nijūba*, *kuichigaiba*, *uchinoke* and/or *hotsure*. This Senjū'in-*suguha* shows the most classical interpretation of all the five Yamato schools and the *habuchi* is rich in *hataraki*.

There were some bids on Ko-Naminohira (古波平). From the point of view of production time this bid is quite good because we are in the late Heian and early Kamakura period. But the *jigane* of Ko-Naminohira works – which is an offshoot of the Yamato tradition – is a dense, „sticky" looking *itame* mixed with *masame* or an *itame* which shows large areas of *masame-nagare*. The *hada* is also standing out, the steel is blackish and a *shirake-utsuri* appears at Naminohira.

Incidentally, not all works of the Yamato tradition show such a varied *habuchi* like the *kantei* blade and many are much more unobtrusive.

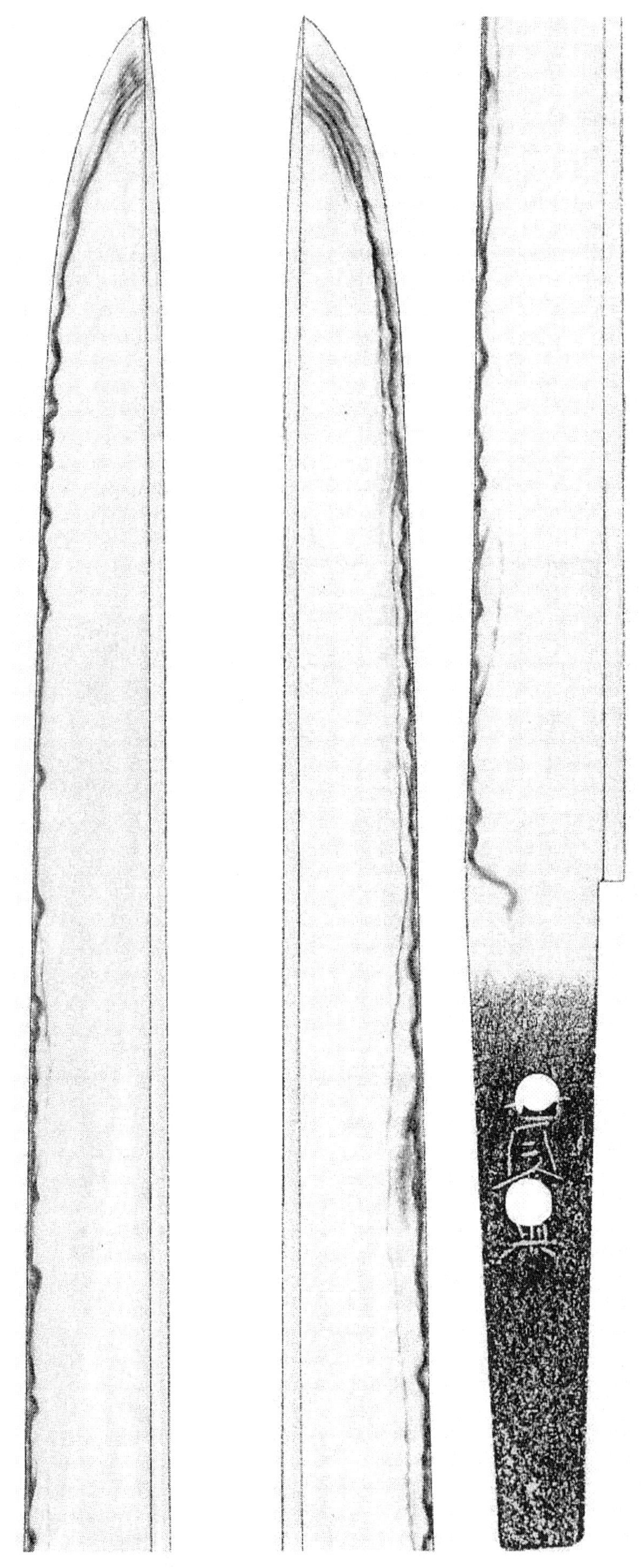

2.654k *tantō*
mei: Sadaoki (貞興)
nagasa 25,9 cm *uchizori*
moto-haba 2,0 cm *moto-kasane* 0,6 cm
nakago-nagasa 9,7 cm no *nakago-sori*

hira-zukuri, *iori-mune*, normal *mihaba*, about standard length (*jōsun*), relative thick *kasane* in proportion to the *mihaba*, *uchizori*. The *jigane* is an excellently forged *masame* with plentiful of *ji-nie*, *chikei*, and *nie-utsuri*. The steel is clear. The *hamon* and the *bōshi* can be seen on the *oshigata*. In addition, *hotsure*, *nijūba*, *kuichigai-ba*, many *nie*, as well as fine *kinsuji* and *sunagashi* appear. The *hamon* is bright and clear. The tang is *ubu*, has a *kirijiri*, the typical *yasurime* of this school, two *mekugi-ana* and is signed on the *sashi-omote* side.

The blade has a normal *mihaba*, about standard length (*jōsun*) and *uchizori*, that means it can be attributed to the middle or late Kamakura period on the basis of its shape. The *jigane* of the Hoshō school is a pure *masame* which is mostly excellently forged, covered in thick *ji-nie*, shows plentiful of *chikei* and is altogether bright and clear. But there are also some Hoshō works like the *kantei* blade which show a *nie-utsuri*. This *nie-utsuri* differs from the *nie-utsuri* of the Rai school because the latter occurs at an *itame-hada*. Induced by the *masame* structure, the *ji-nie* of the Hoshō school appears clearly distinguished from the areas where it does not occur, i.e. there is no smooth transition. That means it runs parallel to the *masame* which gives the *nie-utsuri* a striped appearance.

The *hamon* of the Hoshō school is a *suguha* with some *notare*. The *habuchi* shows *hotsure*, *nijūba* and *sanjūba*, is *nie*-loaden and bright and clear. Also *kinsuji* and *sunagashi* appear and the *deki* corresponds exactly to the style of the Yamato tradition. The *bōshi* is mostly *yakitsume* with plentiful of *hakikake*. At some Hoshō blades, many large *nie* appear from the *habuchi* towards the *ha* and especially bright shining *kinsuji* and *sunagashi* can be seen. But from time to time, we also find more quiet interpretations like the *kantei* blade which have relative unobtrusive *nie* and fewer *kinsuji*, *sunagashi* and *hakikake*.

The tip of the tang of Hoshō blades is *kiri* and the signature is chiselled on the *sashi-omote* side. The *yasurime* are distinctive *higaki*. This was pointed out in the description of the *kantei* by „typical *yasurime* of this school".

Allmost all bids were on Sadaoki, followed by Sadayoshi (貞吉), Sadakiyo (貞清), Sadamune (貞宗) and other Hoshō smiths. The workmanship of all of them is quite close and without a signature, a definite attribution is often difficult. In this sense, all bids on Hoshō were counted as *atari*. From the point of view of shape, we find relative many larger dimensioned blades by Sadayoshi, and Sadaoki made in comparison more smaller blades. Sadakiyo on the other hand works in both ways. Sadamune is regarded as the most representative Hoshō smith but there are hardly any works going round which can be definitely attributed to him. So it is better at a *kantei* not to go for Sasamune.

By the way, there are actually not that many signed Hoshō-*tachi*, -*tantō* and -*katana* available which show a pure *masame* like here. If you add up all existing signed Hoshō blades designated as *kokuhō*, *jūyō-bunkazai*, *jūyō-bijutsuhin*, *tokubetsu-jūyō-tōken* and *jūyō-tōken*, you arrive at only 23 pieces! Unsigned blades with an attribution to Hoshō which bear one of the mentioned designations count aroand 45. That means it is quite a rarety to study such a textbook-like work.

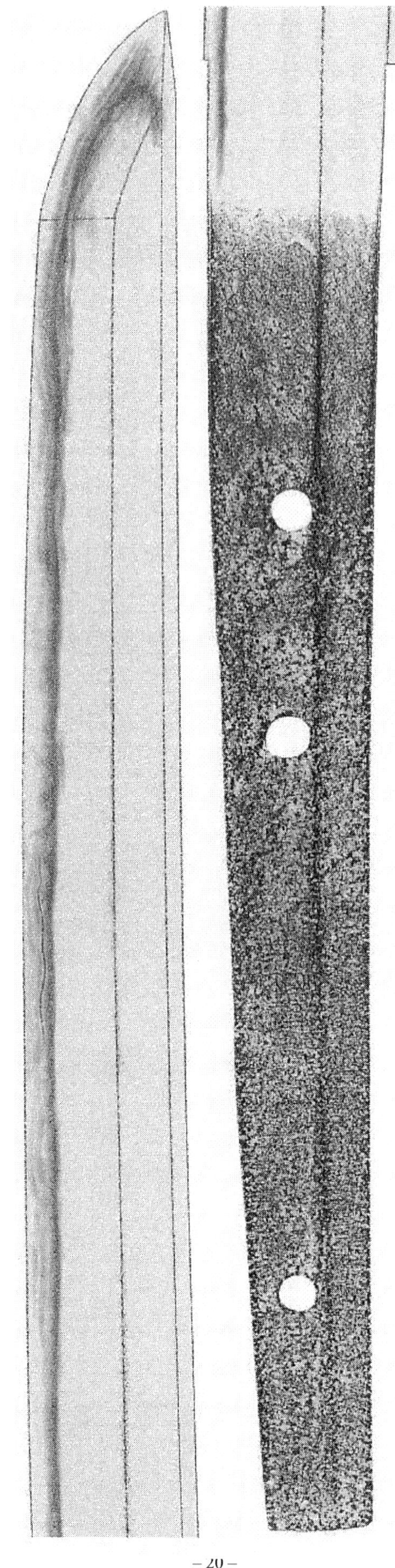

3.595 *katana*
mumei: Kanenaga (包永)
nagasa 68,6 cm, *sori* 1,2 cm, *shinogi-zukuri*, *iori-mune*

ji: dense *ko-itame*, partially mixed with *nagare* and *masame*, fine *ji-nie* and *chikei*
hamon: *suguha-chō* mixed with *ko-gunome*, *hotsure*, *nijūba*, *kuichigaiba*, *ashi*, *yō*, *kinsuji* and *sunagashi*, there are plentiful of *nie*, some of them sparkle a lot and tend towards *ara-nie*, the *yakiba* is bright and clear
bōshi: *sugu* with a *ko-maru-kaeri* and plentiful of *hakikake*

This is an *ō-suriage-mumei* blade with an old attribution to Tegai Kanenaga (手掻包永). That it is shortened can be recognized by the hardly remaining *funbari*, but when you „reconstruct" the original form, you arrive at a normal *mihaba*, a noticeably tapering, a *chū-kissaki* and a *sori* which increases again towards the tip. That means we have a typical *sugata* of the mid or late Kamakura period.

The *shinogi* is high and the *shinogi-ji* wide, that means we are in the Yamato tradition. When we combine this with the production time and the fine and beautifully forged *ko-itame* mixed with *masame*, the *suguha-chō* with its *hotsure*, *kuichigaiba* and *nijūba*, and the sparkling *ha-nie*, then we inevitably end up at the Tegai school. The attribution to Kanenaga goes probably back to the fact that some of his signed works show a quite bright *habuchi* like here and usually not seen at other Tegai-*mono*. In addition, Kanenaga´s works are already described in old sword texts with „the *nie* are beautifully sparkling like the stars" and the like. And the *kantei* blade is truly *nie*-loaden and shows also a considerable amount of *ara-nie*.

That means most of the bids were *atari* on Kanenaga but some also reckoned it as a work of Taima Kuniyuki (当麻国行). This is matching from the point of view of production time and quality but all extant signed works of Kuniyuki show much more calm *nie*. On the other hand, the *ō-suriage-mumei* blades attributed to Kuniyuki are quite *nie*-loaden, even more than the *kantei* blade, and show wilder *kinsuji* and *sunagashi*. This work is thus somewhere in between and because we see some Tegai characteristics, the attribution to Kanenaga is the most consistent.

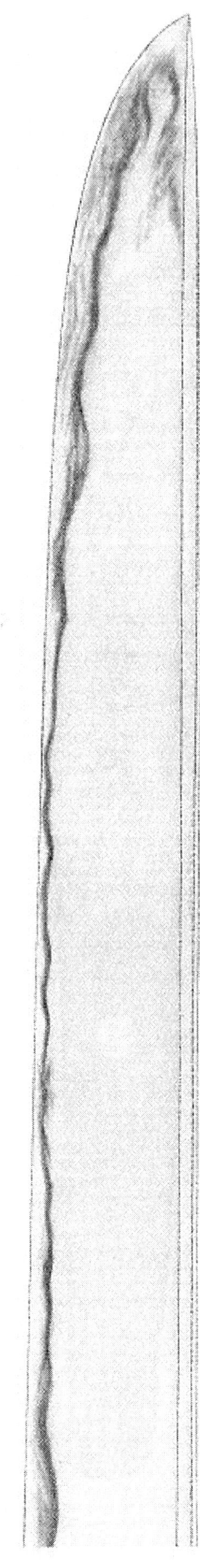

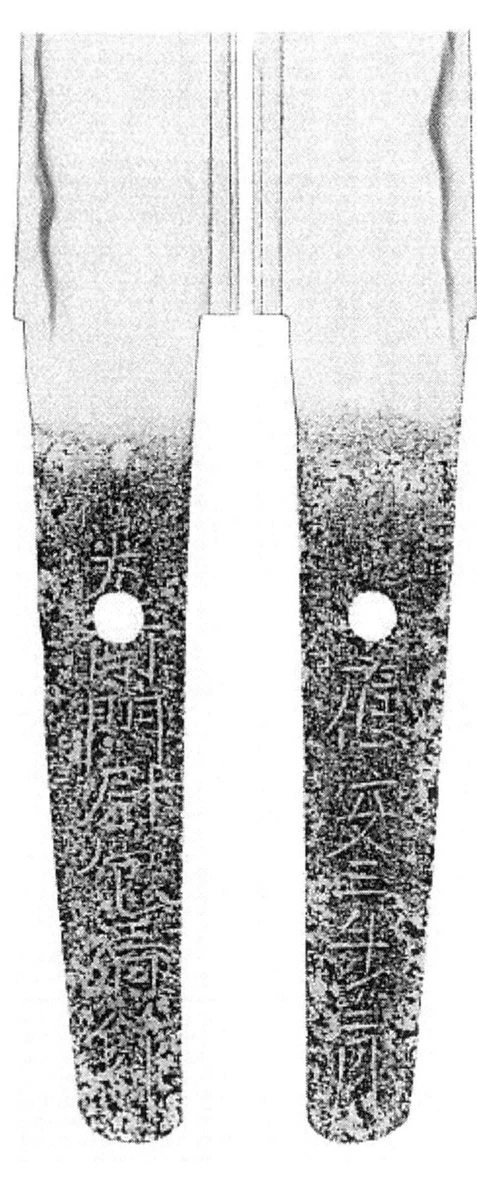

4.652 *tantō*
mei: ?-shū Saemon Kanekiyo saku (○州左衛門包清作)
Ōan sannen nigatsu (応安三年二月, „second month Ōan three [1370]")
nagasa 28,6 cm, *uchizori*, *hira-zukuri*, *mitsu-mune*

ji: relative dense *hada* which tends to *masame*, plentiful of *ji-nie* and *chikei*
hamon: shallow *notare* with *sunagashi* and fine *kinsuji*, the width of the *nioiguchi* is inconsistent, much *ko-nie*
bōshi: a little *midare-komi* with strong *hakikake* and a wide *kaeri*

Generally speaking, there are not many signed blades extant from Yamato smiths and most of them belong to Tegai Kanenaga (手掻包永) or other smiths of the Tegai school. Kanekiyo was the son of Kanenaga but there were several generations active until the late Muromachi period. We know Kanekiyo blades with datings of the fourth year of Karyaku (嘉暦, 1329), the third year of Ōei (応永, 1396) and the second year of Kyōroku (享禄, 1529).

This blade shows much *ji-nie* and *chikei* and also the *notare-hamon* is quite *nie*-loaden. When you take a closer look at the *yakiba* you see fine *hotsure* and *sunagashi* as well as *uchinoke*, *kuichigaiba* and *nijūba* along the *habuchi*. The *yakiba* becomes wider at the *monouchi* and runs into a *bōshi* with *hakikake*. All these are typical features of the Yamato tradition and on the basis of them, we can identify the blade as Yamato work from the Kamakura or Nanbokuchō era. At that time, all of the so-called „Five Yamato Schools" were active, i.e. Senjū´in, Tegai, Shikkake, Taima and Hoshō. There are only very few signed *tantō* extant from the Senjū´in and Taima school whereupon we can practically exclude them from our observations. At the Shikkake school, the *hamon* shows more *gunome* and the *nie* are somewhat more unobtrusive. And at the Hoshō school, we would expect a pure *masame* or at least more *masame* than we see it on the *kantei* blade.

Well, it was rather difficult to nail down the smith at the first round so it was anough to bid on the Tegai school at the second or third round.

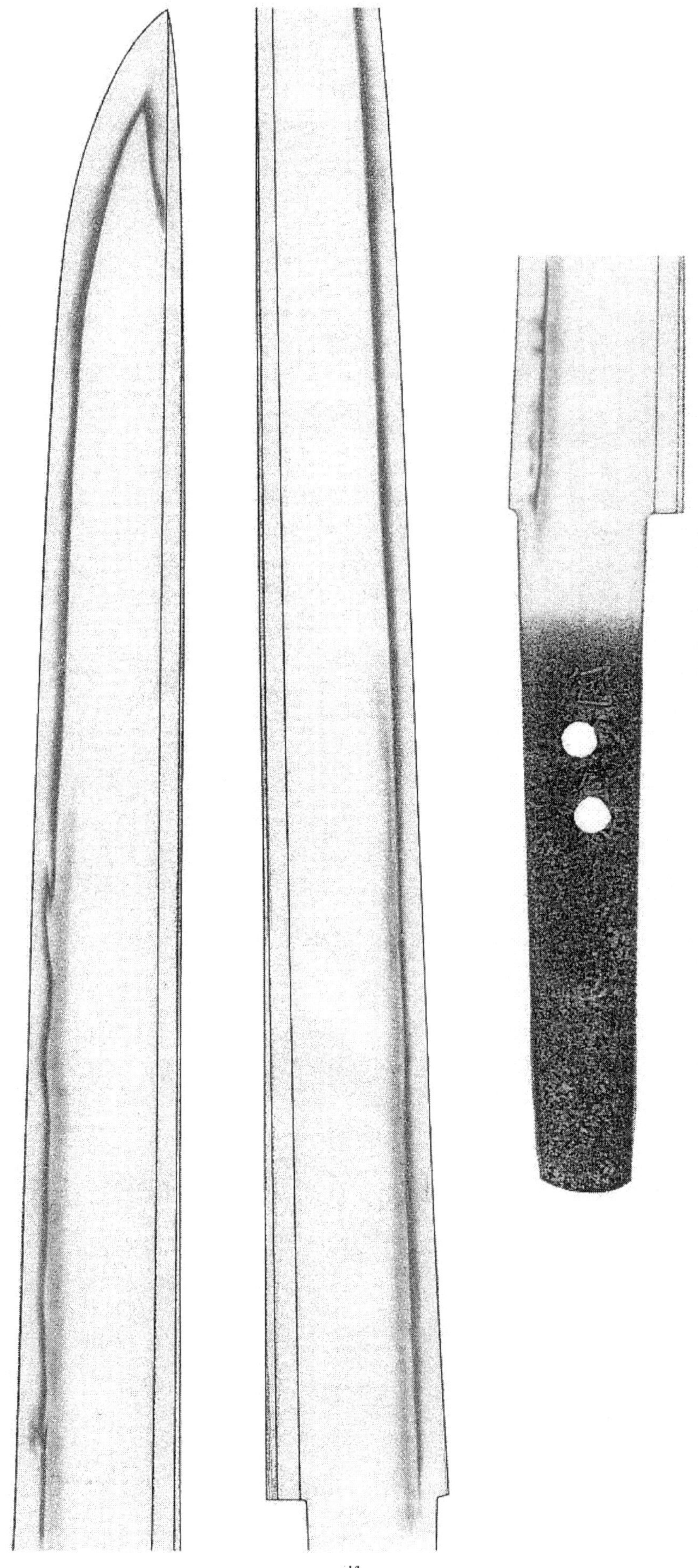

5.643k *tantō*
mei: Kanesada (包貞, Sue-Tegai)
nagasa 26,06 cm , *uchizori*, *moto-haba* 2,3 cm, *moto-kasane* 0,7 cm, *nakago-nagasa* 10,3 cm no *nakago-sori*

hira-zukuri, *mitsu-mune*, normal *mihaba*, the *nagasa* is in proportion to the *mihaba* rather long, thick *kasane*, strong *uchizori*, scarce *fukura*. The *jigane* is an *itame* mixed with *mokume* and *nagare-masame* which stands rather out. In addition plentiful of *ji-nie* and *chikei*. The *hamon* and the *bōshi* can be seen on the *oshigata*. In addition *hotsure*, *nijūba*, *kuichigaiba*, *ko-ashi*, plentiful of *ko-nie* and also some *sunagashi* appear. The tang is *ubu*, has a *kurijiri*, a round back, the typical *yasurime* for the school, two *mekugi-ana*, and bears centrally on the *sashi-omote* side below the *habaki* area a *niji-mei*.

The blade has a normal *mihaba*, is *sunnobi*, has a thick *kasane*, a noticeable *uchizori* and scarce *fukura*. That means we can place it on the basis of the *sugata* into the Muromachi era. The *jigane* is *itame* mixed with *mokume*, *nagare* and *masame* and the *hamon* is a *suguha-chō* with *hotsure*, *nijūba*, *kuichigaiba*, plentiful of *ko-nie* and *sunagashi*. That means we are facing the typical features of the Yamato tradition. The latter spread over several provinces during the *kotō* era and still in the Muromachi period offshoots like Sue-Tegai, Uda, Sue-Mihara, Sue-Niō and Naminohira were quite flourishing. Among these trends, the Sue-Tegai school did not show a locally influenced style, i.e. a blackish *jigane*, but forged a bright *jiba* which testifies a little bit to the continuation of the refined *deki* of the old Tegai school. Another important characteristic are the long *nijūba*. Like seen on the *kantei* blade, the *hada* of the Sue-Tegai school is a somewhat standing-out but dense *itame* mixed with *nagare* and *masame* whereas also *shirake-utsuri* can appear. The *bōshi* is *sugu* with a standard *ko-maru-kaeri* or *sugu* with a pointed *ko-maru-kaeri*. But mostly *hakikake* appear on any *bōshi* interpretation. From time to time we see Sue-Tegai blades where the *kaeri* runs back quite long on the *mune*.

The tip of the tang of Sue-Tegai-*tantō* is *kurijiri*, the back of the tang is often round and the *yasurime* are *higaki*. So one should pay attention to the tips given in the *kantei* text and read between the lines. The signatures of Sue-Tegai are in the case of *tantō* chiselled above the *mekugi-ana*, that means we have often blades where the uppermost character is almost vanished because of repeated polishing of the *habaki* area and very beginning of the tang.

The most representative Tegai smith of the Kamakura period was of course Kanenaga (包永). He is dated by some to the early and by some to the middle Kamakura period. Well, on the back side of extant documents from the Daigo-ji (醍醐寺) a list of names of smiths was found which worked for the Tōdaiji. The document is dated with Kōchō three (弘長, 1263) and the list divides the smiths into two guilds, namely the „*hon'za*" (本座) and the „*shin'za*" (新座). The *hon'za* guild shows names like Kanenaga (包永) and Heisaburō (平三郎) but does not mention any other smiths of the Tegai school. So it is unclear if „Kanenaga" and „Heisaburō" referred to the same person or if this Kanenaga was Tegai Kanenaga. It is namely possible that the listed smiths just made metal fittings for the Tōdaiji and were responsible for repair and maintenance and had nothing to do with contemporary swordsmiths. In short, this matter needs further study.

The vast majority of all bids was on Kanesada, followed by Kanetoshi (包俊), Kanezane (包真), and other Sue-Tegai smiths. Because all Sue-Tegai smiths displayed more or less the same workmanship and it is hard to nail down a certain smith, all bids on „Sue-Tegai" were counted as *atari*. The famous Kanenaga was, as mentioned, active in the Kamakura period but his name was continuously used over the Nanbokuchō until the Muromachi period. There are some Muromachi-era Kanenaga *tantō* extant but none of the first generation. Also a big gap in quality can be grasped between the early and the Sue-Tegai Kanenaga smiths. So a bid on „Kanenaga" was only *atari* when it came with the note „Sue-Tegai" or „Muromachi". Otherwise a *dōzen* was given. The same applies to „Tegai" bids, i.e. without the supplement „Sue".

Besides of these *atari* and *dōzen* bids, relative many reckoned the blade as a work of No-Sada (兼定). He too forged a *kitae* which is mixed with *nagare* and applied a *hamon* in *suguha-chō* and *higaki-yasurime*, so a bid on him is understandable. But Kanesada´s *tantō* in *suguha* are mostly copies of Rai Kunitoshi (来国俊). That means there are in *nioi-deki* with a dense *nioiguchi* and don´t show *hotsure*, *nijūba* or *kuichigaiba* along the *habuchi*. Also it should not be forgotten that Kanesada didn´t sign his *tantō* above the *mekugi-ana*.

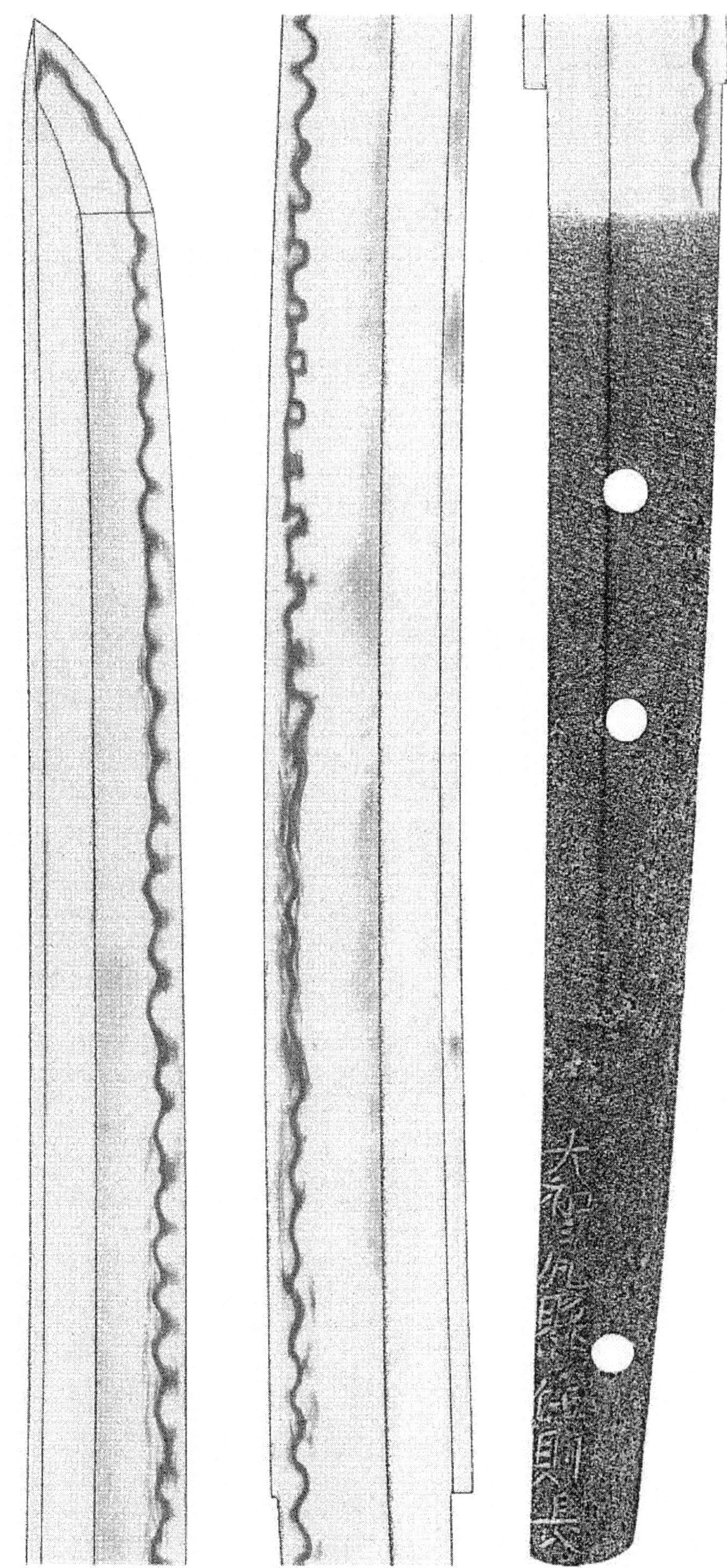

6.667 *tachi*
mei: Yamato Shikkake-jū Norinaga (大和尻懸住則長)
nagasa 71,2 cm, *sori* 1,8 cm, *shinogi-zukuri*, *iori-mune*

ji: rather standing-out *itame* with much *nagare* and partial *mokume*, plentiful of fine *ji-nie*, faint *nie-utsuri* towards the *shinogi*
hamon: *midareba* consisting of connected *ko-gunome* which runs partially as *suguha* in betweem, also some angular elements at the lower half, in addition many *ashi* and *yō*, some *yubashiri*, scarce *muneyaki*, *hotsure* and *sunagashi*, the *nioiuchi* is relative wide and bright and the *nie* appear as *mura-nie* in places
bōshi: shallow *midare-komi* with a *ko-maru-kaeri* which runs back shorty, also *hakikake*

The blade has a normal *mihaba*, tapers, has a relative deep *koshizori* which increases towards the tip and shows a *chū-kissaki*. As there is no *funbari* present we can assume that the blade is shortened. That means it had once a rather long *nagasa* and can therefore be identified as *tachi* of the late Kamakura period. In addition, the *shinogi-ji* is rather wide and the *shinogi* is high, that means we have here typical Yamato characteristics. The *kitae* is a somewhat standing-out *itame* with much *nagare*. There is a *nie-utsuri* and the *hamon* shows *yubashiri*, *hotsure* and *sunagashi*. The *nioiguchi* is bright and the *bōshi* has a short *kaeri* with *hakikake*. Thus Yamato characteristics can also be seen in the *jiba*.

Regarding Yamato works of that time, we find a *midareba* mixed with connected *ko-gunome* first and foremost at Shikkake Norinaga, and his *nie* are rather unobtrusive compared to other contemporary Yamato smiths. Interesting on this *tachi* is that the *hamon* appears – besides of the middle part – entirely as *ko-gunome*, that means not as *suguha-chō* which is partially mixed with *ko-gunome* as we know it from most of Norinaga´s works. So when other Yamato smiths sticked to the old traditions, Norinaga adopted more than his contemporaries the up and coming Osafune style, which means a connected *ko-gunome*.

Because of this peculiarity, some thought the blade is a work of the Yoshii school (吉井). But at the latter, the *utsuri* appears as negative shadow of the *gunome-midare hamon*. Also the *jigane* is not that strong as those of Yamato works, i.e. the *ji-nie* are weaker and the *itame* is more dense. Some Yoshii blades show also an *utsuri* which runs parallel to a mixed-in *ayasugi-hada* but besides of the similar *hamon*, considerably different characteristics can be made out between this blade and the usual Yoshii workmanship.

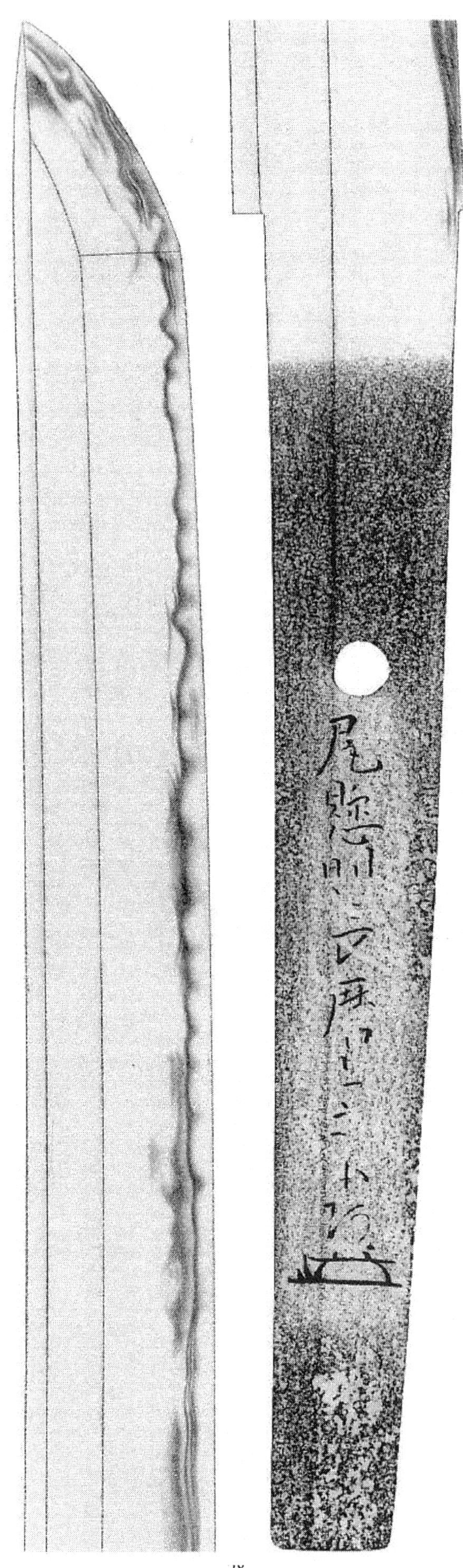

7.653 *katana*
kinzōgan-mei: Shikkake Norinaga suriage kore (尻懸則長磨上之, „shortened Shikkake Norinaga")
Hon´a + *kaō* (本阿) [Kōshitsu, 光室]
nagasa 70,3 cm, *sori* 2,7 cm, *shinogi-zukuri*, *iori-mune*

ji: partially standing-out *itame* mixed with some *nagare*, plentiful of *ji-nie*, much *chikei*
hamon: *chū-suguha-chō* mixed with *ko-gunome* and *ko-notare*, many *ashi* and *yō*, thick *nioi* and much thick *nie*, *kinsuji*, *nie-suji*, *sunagashi*, partially *hotsure* along the *habuchi*, also *yubashiri* and *nijūba*
bōshi: *yakitsume* with *nie-kuzure* and *hakikake*

The participants were informed at this *kantei* that this is an *ō-suriage* blade. So nobody went for *shintō* or *shinshintō* of course. Important features of the work are the broad *shinogi-ji*, the high *shinogi*, the thick *kasane* and the resulting robust and heavy *sugata*. The partially mixed-in *nagare* areas, *hataraki* like *hotsure* and *nijūba*, and the *yakitsume-bōshi* speak clearly for Yamato and so almost all focused on this tradition.

Let us turn our attention to the five Yamato schools. At Hoshō we would expect a *masame* all over the blade and a Senjū´in work would be older and more classically interpreted. At the Tegai school – at least regarding unsigned works attributed to this school – the *ha-nie* would be more emphasized and the *jigane* would be somewhat finer. Also the steel of Tegai-*mono* has the brightest shine among all Yamato works.

This *katana* was attributed by Hon´ami Kōshitsu to Shikkake Norinaga but on the basis of its rough and thick *ha-nie*, also an attribution to Taima would be possible. Well, the connected *ko-gunome* and the overall composition of the *hamon* as well as the *nie*-loaden hardening are very similar to an extant signed blade by Norinaga (*jūyō-bunkazai*, *tachi*, signed „Yamato Norinaga saku", preserved in the Kurokawa Institute of Ancient Cultures). So all in all the attribution of Kōshitsu is remarkable and very sensitive.

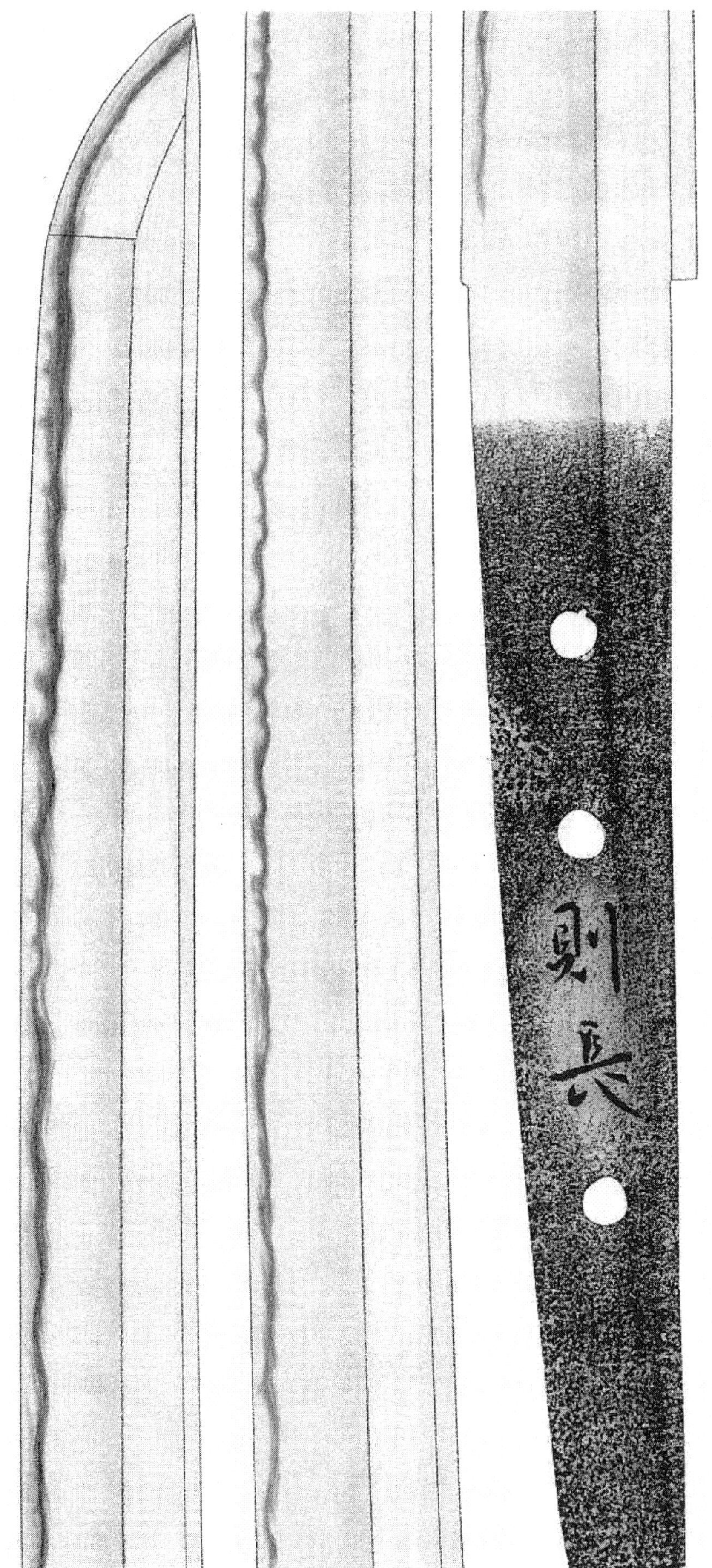
則長

8.651 *katana*
kinzōgan-mei: Norinaga (則長)
Hon´a + *kaō* (本阿, Hon´ami Kōson 本阿弥光遜)
nagasa 70,9 cm, *sori* 1,7 cm, *shinogi-zukuri*, *iori-mune*

ji: rather standing-out *itame-hada*, partial strong *nagare*, plentiful of *ji-nie*, fine *chikei*, faint *nie-utsuri*
hamon: *chū-suguha-chō* mixed with *ko-gunome* and *gunome*, some connected *midare* elements in places, much *ashi*, *yō*, broad *nioiguchi* with plentiful of *ko-nie*, in addition *hotsure*, *uchinoke*, *sunagashi* and *kinsuji*
bōshi: *sugu* with much *hakikake* which ends in *yakitsume*

The blade has a classical *jiba*, a broad *mihaba*, a wide *shinogi-ji*, a thick *kasane*, a quite high *shinogi* and a *chū-kissaki*. That means the shape is overall rather robust. The *kitae* shows much *nagare* and a faint *nie-utsuri* and the *hamon* is a *nie*-loaden *suguha-chō* with plentiful of *hotsure*, *uchinoke*, *kinsuji* and *sunagashi*. The *yakihaba* becomes wider at the *monouchi* area. The *bōshi* is *yakitsume* with much *hakikake*. All these are typical features of the late Kamakura period Yamato tradition and so the bids focused on the three smiths Shikkake Norinaga (尻懸則長), Tegai Kanenaga (手掻包永) and Taima Kuniyuki (当麻国行).

Some also went for Hoshō or Senjū´in but at the former, we would expect *masame* over the entire blade and at the latter, the *jiba* as well as the *sugata* would be even more classical and antique-looking. In addition, the vivid *midareba* of the Senjū´in differs from the other four Yamato schools and does not correspond to the *hamon* of the *kantei* blade.

At Tegai Kanenaga, the *kitae* would be more dense and he displayes the fewest *nagare* amount of all Yamato-*mono*. On the other hand, the *ha-nie* are stronger and we see *ara-nie* and brightly sparkling *nie* in the *ha*. That means among all Yamato works, those of Kanenaga show the most excellent *nie* and his *hamon* is different in width.

At signed blades of Taima Kuniyuki, the *nie* of *ji* and *ha* are finer and more unobtrusive but at unsigned blades attributed to him, it is the other way round, namely strong and rough *nie* and *nie*-based *hataraki* like *kinsuji* and *sunagashi* as well as plentiful of *chikei* in the *ji* appear. So his workmanship of the latter category has something of Sōshū and the former is too quiet for the *kantei* blade.

The point of this attribution to Norinaga is the *midareba* which consists of connected *ko-gunome* and *gunome* elements. Or in the case of *suguha*, the latter is mixed at regular intervals with *gunome-ashi* which suggest a „*gunome*-like“ appearance of the *hamon*. And among all the Yamato-*mono*, Norinaga´s show a rather standing-out *hada* and more calm *nie*. This is exactly the case at the *kantei* blade and so the attribution is spot-on.

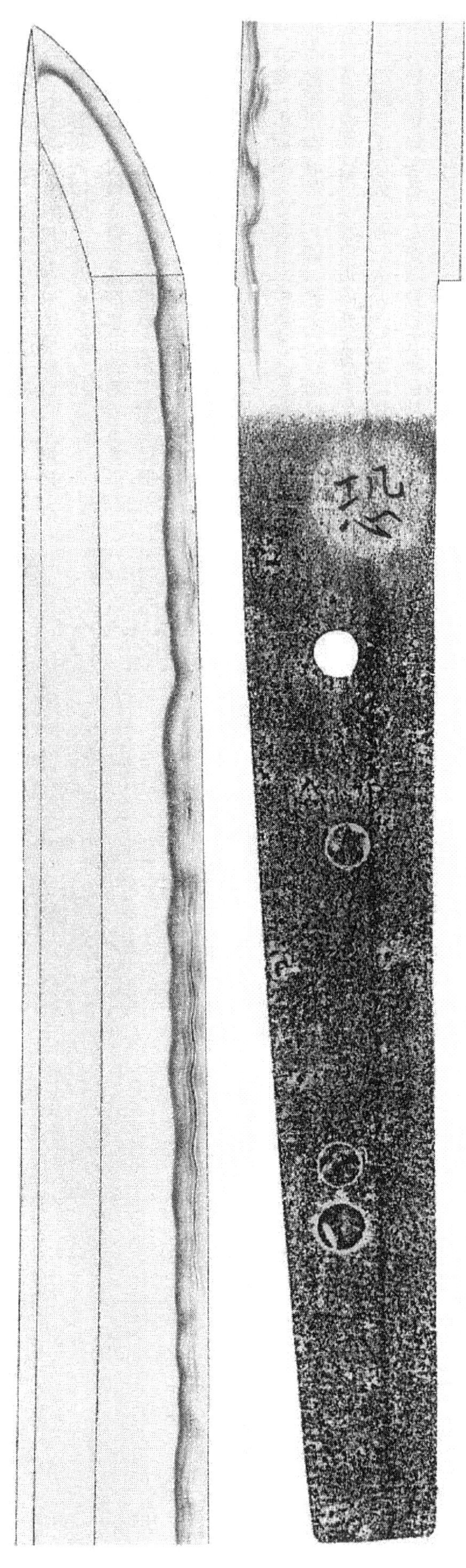

9.611 *katana*
mumei: Taima (当麻), with a *kin-zōgan-mei* „Kyō“ (恐, „dreadful, aweful, terrible“)
nagasa 75,74 cm, *sori* 1,55 cm, *shinogi-zukuri, iori-mune*

ji: *itame* mixed with *mokume* and *nagare*, the *nagare* is more prominent on the *sashi-ura* side and the *shinogi-ji* tends almost entirely to *masame*, plentiful of *ji-nie*, much *chikei*, the *hada* tends somewhat to stand out
hamon: based on *chū-suguha* mixed with *ko-gunome* and *ko-notare*, *ashi*, and much, also somewhat rougher-*nie*, in addition *sunagashi*, *kinsuji* and some *hotsure*
bōshi: *sugu* in *ko-maru* and a quite short *kaeri*

This is a *tokubetsu-jūyō katana* attributed to the Taima school. When you take first a look at the *jiba*, the plentiful of *ji-nie* and the conspicious *chikei* are immediately visible. That means the blade has a strong *jigane*. This concerns especially the area of the base and the tip where the *ji* and the *ha* become more *nie*-loaden. Also we have very prominent *kinsuji*, *sunagashi* and *nie-suji* which show Sōshū characteristics but the *kitae* on the *sashi-ura* tends at almost the entire length to *masame-nagare* and also *hotsure* appear along the *habuchi*. This and the broad *shinogi-ji* and high *shinogi* make it easy to stay within the Yamato tradition.

But on the other hand, blades which look like Sōshū with Yamato characteristics at a glance or Yamato interpretations with a strong Sōshū influence are the main point to come to Taima. So most of the participants focused either directly on Taima or on Tegai and Shikkake, but some left Yamato and bade on Yukimitsu (行光). Already in olden times there was the saying: „*Yukimitsu de iya-nara, Taima e*“ (行光でイヤなら当麻へ, „when it is not a Yukimitsu, go for Taima“). That means it is well known that their styles are very close. In short, when your bid on Yukimitsu is not correct after the first round, go the next time for Taima.

There are two signed blades extant by Kuniyuki (国行), the founder of the Taima school. Both show fine *nie* within the *ha* which remind of the calm style of Kyō-*mono*. But at the *ō-suriage-mumei* works attributed to Kuniyuki, it is exactly the other way round because they are highly *nie*-loaden. At Tegai, the *nie* within the *ha* are not that strong as on the unsigned Kuniyuki works. And from a work of the Shikkake school, we would expect some connected *gunome* elements.

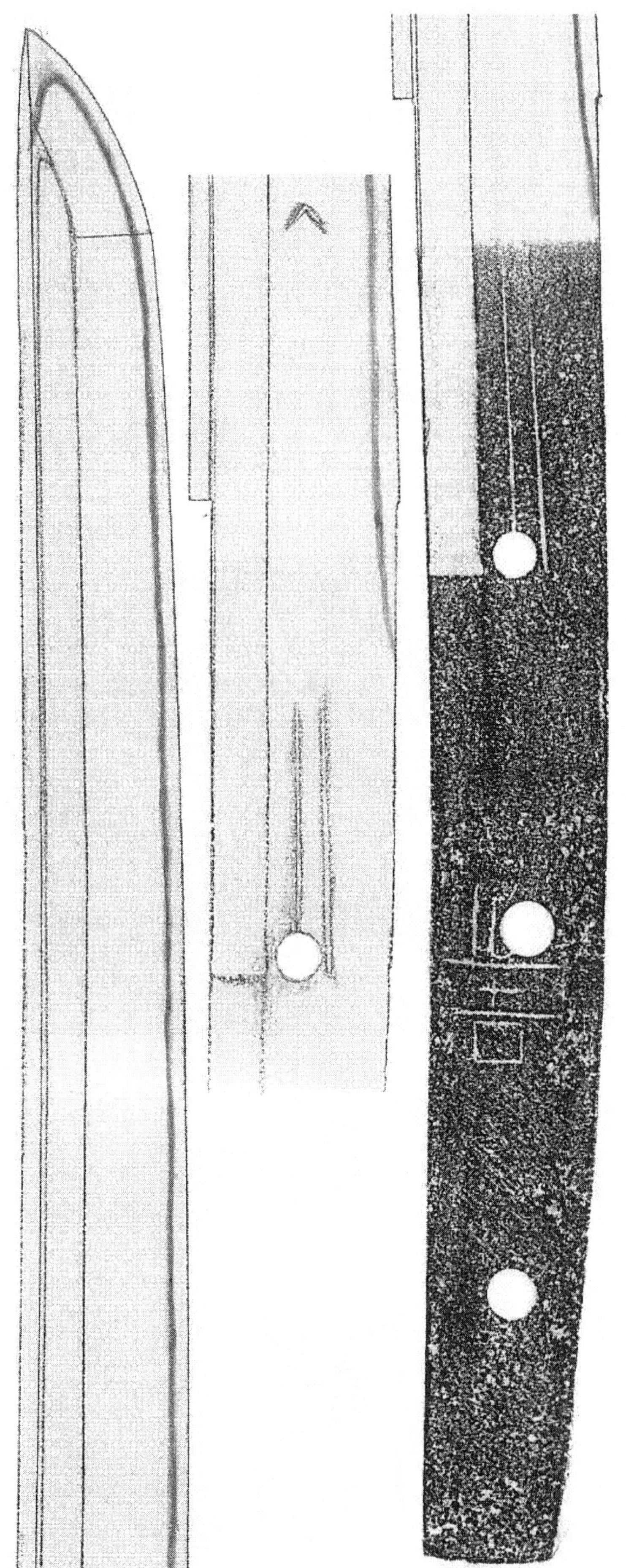

10.666 *tachi*
mei: Nobuyoshi (延吉)
nagasa 64,8 cm, *sori* 2,3 cm, *shinogi-zukuri*, *iori-mune*

ji: *itame* mixed with *mokume* and *nagare* which tends to *masame* in the *monouchi* area, the *hada* stands out, *ji-nie*, fine *chikei*, *jifu* and and a faint *nie-utsuri* appear
hamon: *suguha* with a very compact *nioiguchi* in *ko-nie-deki*
bōshi: *sugu* with a *ko-maru-kaeri*
horimono: on both sides a *bōhi* with *kaku-dome* is engraved and on the *haki-omote* side towards the base of the blade and in the tang we see traces of a *suken*

Nobuyoshi was a later smith of the Senjū´in school who worked in the Ryūmon manor (龍門) of Yamato´s Yoshino district (吉野郡). Therefore he is called „Ryūmon Nobuyoshi". His works show basically two kinds of interpretations: The one are in *suguha* without *utsuri* and are rather calm, that means they tend towards Yamato. The other show a vivid *midareba* or a *suguha-chō* mixed with *chōji-ashi* and *utsuri* appears. That means they have Bizen characteristics. Also when it comes to the signature we can make out two groups of *mei*. At one group, the right radical (正) of the character for "Nobu" (延) is chiselled in a simplified manner which reminds of the latin character "G". At the other group, this radical is chiselled in a way which is similar to the grass-script variant of the character (氏). Due to that, several theories exist since oldest times if there were one or more Ryūmon Nobuyoshi active. Ogasawara Nobuo (小笠原信夫) did some comparative studies in issue 478 of the magazine "*Museum*", namely of extant blades and illustrations in old documents. He found out that works of both signature groups have their roots in the Yamato tradition. And Tanobe Michihiro (田野辺道宏) wrote in the December issue 2009 of the magazine "*Menome*" that there is an intermediate group of signatures. So it is quite possible that the differences in signature go back to the transition of the artistic period of one smith.

This blade bears a *mei* which lies somewhere between the grass-script variant (氏) and the interpretation presented by Tanobe-*sensei*. From the point of view of workmanship, it displays a Yamato-Bizen mix and looks at a glance like Aoe or Mihara. As a consequence, many bade on one of these schools, but the blade is closer to Ko-Mihara than to Aoe. However, we would expect at Ko-Mihara more *mokume* in addition to the *nagare* and a *bōshi* with a more acute-angled *kaeri*. At the Aoe school, the *bōshi* would be more pointed, the *mokume* finer, and the *utsuri* would appear as *dan-utsuri*. Some reckoned the blade as Rai Kunitoshi (来国俊) or work of the Enju school (延寿). This is understandable too but at Kunitoshi, more *hataraki* would appear along the *habuchi* and for Enju, we would expect an *ō-maru-bōshi*.

By the way, there are not often works of Ryūmon Nobuyoshi on display at a *kantei*. Judging from the few extant signed works of the Yamato school, Nobuyoshi was always on a rather high quality level and there are basically no "outliers" found. The best example of him is the *kokuhō-tachi* which is owned by the NBTHK.

Yamashiro

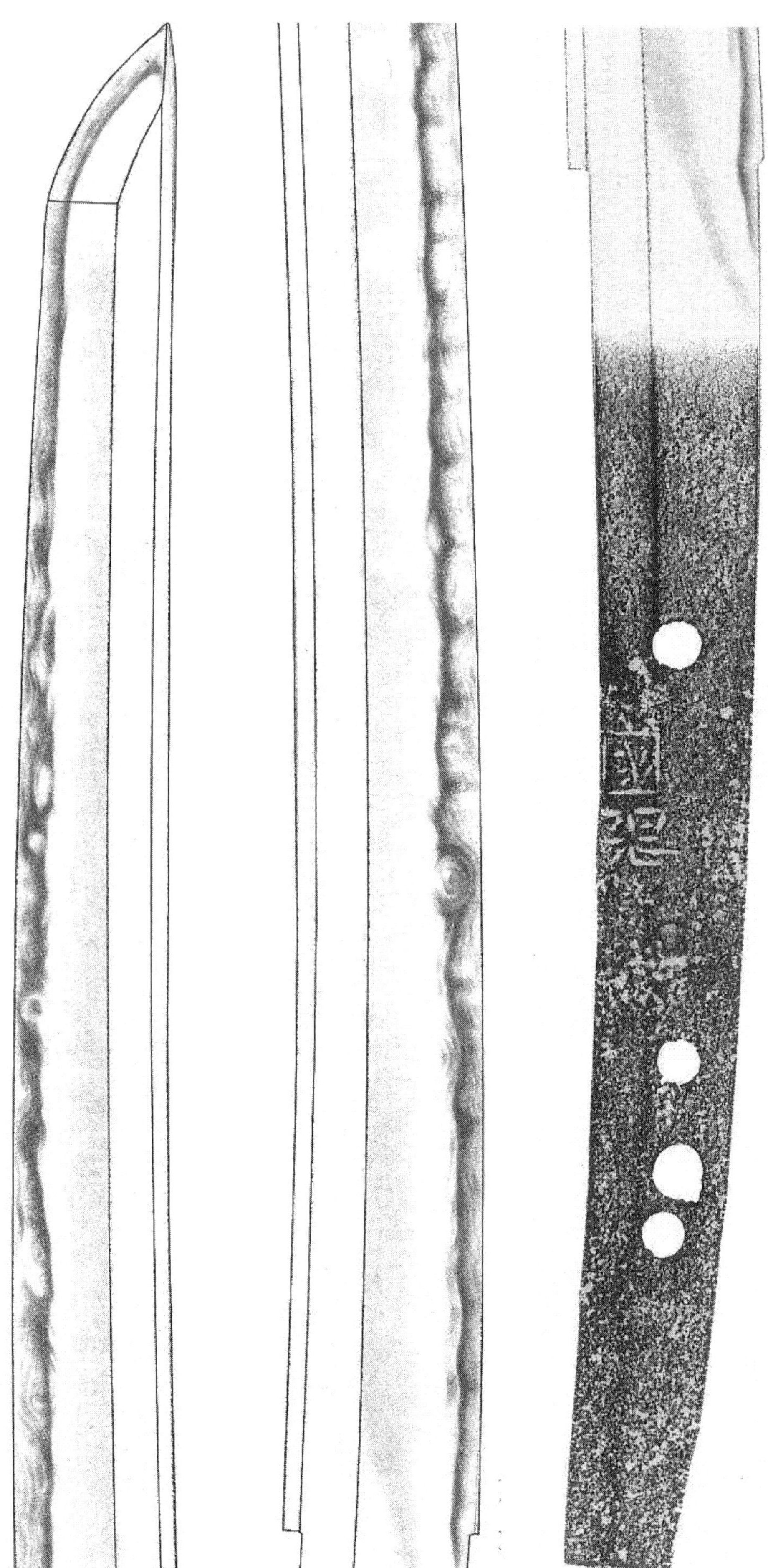

11.619k *tachi*
mei: Kunitsuna (国綱)

nagasa 67,27 cm *sori* 2,5 cm
moto-haba 2,5 cm *saki-haba* 1,6 cm
moto-kasane 0,6 cm *saki-kasane* 0,4 cm
kissaki-nagasa 2,6 cm *nakago-nagasa* 20,3 cm
nakago-sori 0,4 cm

shinogi-zukuri, *iori-mune*, slender *mihaba*, noticeable tapering, deep *koshizori*, a little *funbari*, the *sori* increases towards the tip, *ko-kissaki*. The *jigane* is an *itame* mixed with *mokume*, *ō-itame* and *nagare* and stands out. There is plentiful of *ji-nie* and *chikei*, and towards the base of the blade, a *mizukage*-like *utsuri* appears. The latter turns then to a connected *jifu-utsuri*. The steel is bright. The *hamon* and *bōshi* can be seen on the *oshigata*. There are *hotsure*, *uchinoke*, *yubashiri*, plentiful of *ashi* and *yō*, highly sparkling *nie*, *kinsuji* and *sunagashi* along the wide *nioiguchi*. The *nakago* is a little *suriage* and has a *kirijiri* (originally a *kurijiri*). The *yasurime* are indistinguishable but were once *katte-sagari*. There are five *mekugi-ana* of which one is plugged. A *niji-mei* is chiselled on the *haki-omote* side above the second, the *ubu-mekugi-ana*, somewhat towards the *nakago-mune*. (The school to which this smith belonged forged mostly a very dense *ko-itame* with plentiful of *ji-nie* and fine *chikei* which results in a peculiar *hada* appearance. But he forged a comparatively coarse mix of *itame* and *mokume* and applied a broad *yakihaba* with strong *nie* within the *ha*. But only very few of his works are extant.)

The *kantei* blade is a *tachi* of Awataguchi Kunitsuna. It has a slender *mihaba*, tapers, has a deep *koshizori*, a little *funbari* and ends in a compact *ko-kissaki*, that means we can date it into the early Kamakura period. However, the fact that the *sori* does not bend down towards the tip but increases again is not common for a *sugata* of that time.

Only very few works of Kunitsuna are extant today and we don´t know any date signatures. Some Kunitsuna blades are even hard to attribute and/or date. But we can say that he was active during the early Kamakura period and that he was the youngest of the so-called „six Awataguchi brothers". It is said that he followed the call of the Hōjō regents and moved to Kamakura to forge swords in the new warrior capital. Old sword texts put this moving into the Kenchō era (建長, 1249-1256), which means that his artistic period was not only the early but also the mid Kamakura era. Kunitsuna did not only make *tachi* with a deep *koshizori* but also some where the *sori* increases again towards the tip. This might be related to the somewhat later artistic period in his career. But we also know blades with a broader *mihaba* and a more elongated *chū-kissaki* than seen on the *kantei* blade, which are similar in *sugata* to the *gyobutsu* Onimaru-Kunitsuna (鬼丸国綱).

The *jigane* of the Awataguchi school is a dense *ko-itame* and the steel is deep blue. Much *ji-nie*, fine *chikei* and the well-known *nashiji-hada* appear. Kunitsuna in turn forged a comparatively coarse and strong *jigane* in the form of a large standing-out *itame* and *mokume* with plentiful of *ji-nie*. This peculiarity is also seen on the *kantei* blade and was mentioned in the description too.

The *hamon* of the Awataguchi school bases on *suguha* but shows mostly mixed-in *ko-chōji-midare* and/or *ko-midare* elements. Kunitsuna´s *hamon* has a broader *yakihaba* and shows some variety, that means some ups and downs. In addition we can see a trend to more stronger *ha-nie*. Kunitsuna´s *bōshi* is *sugu* with a *ko-maru-kaeri* or sometimes also *midare-komi* with a larger *kaeri*.

Along the *ha-machi* often a *mizukage*-like *utsuri* appears which connects to the „regular“ *utsuri*. This is also one of Kunitsuna´s typical features. (This is especially noticeable at the *gyobutsu* Onimaru-Kunitsuna and is sometimes called „*koshiba*“ but this is in a strict sense incorrect. Incidentally, the *Kokon-mei-zukushi*“ [古今銘尽] writes on Kunitsuna: „A *koshiba* appears about 1 *sun* [~ 3 cm] above the *habaki*. The *ha* is narrow before this *koshiba* [i.e. right at the *ha-machi*]. In addition, the *jiba* appears somewhat smoky in this area.“ It is assumed that this entry refers just to the Onimaru but when we reconstruct the *kantei* blade to its original condition, it might had shown the very same characteristics.)

As mentioned, the *kantei* blade has not only a deep *koshizori* but a *sori* which increases again towards the tip. This is usually not seen at Awataguchi works. The *hada* is a rather coarse mix of *itame* and *mokume* and stands out and the *yakiba* shows some ups and downs in its course. That means when someone is a little bit familiar with Awataguchi blades and takes a look at this one, it might appear uncommon or off, which might also be connected with the *mizukage*-like *koshiba*. Some also say that the Onimaru is an old *saiha* and that all these pecularities go back to a new hardening.

Kunitsuna´s *nakago-jiri* is a *kurijiri*, the *yasurime* are *katte-sagari* and the *niji-mei* is chiselled on the *haki-omote* side above the *ubu-mekugi-ana* and towards the *nakago-mune*.

The vast majority bade *atari* on Kunitsuna but there were also some *dōzen* on Hisakuni (久国), Kuniyasu (国安) and other smiths of the Awataguchi school. Besides of that, some reckoned the blade as a Ko-Bizen or Ko-Hōki work.

Like Kunitsuna, Hisakuni and Kuniyasu belonged also to the six Awataguchi brothers (they were sons number two and three). Hisakuni is regarded as the most skillful of all Awataguchi smiths and his *kitae* appears as the classical *nashiji-hada*. His *hamon* bases on *suguha* and is mixed with *ko-chōji-midare* and *ko-midare*. Also *ko-ashi*, *yō* and rather large and highly sparkling *ha-nie* appear. Such a coarse mix of *itame* and *mokume* like it is seen on the *kantei* blade is uncommon for Hisakuni and also his *yakiba* does not show these ups and downs. So all in all his workmanship is more calm and unobtrusive.

Kuniyasu did work in a large *itame-mokume* which might also stand out in places but his *hamon* is almost always narrow and mixed with densely arranged *ko-chōji* and *ko-midare*. And along the *yakigashira*, small and interrupted *yubashiri* appear and his *nioiguchi* is a little bit more cloudy.

A large *itame-mokume* mix with *jifu-utsuri* is also seen on Ko-Bizen-*mono*, so from that point of view such a bid was understandable. But their *nioiguchi* is brighter and such highly sparkling and thick *nie* within the *ha* like here are not seen at Ko-Bizen. But first and foremost the hint given in brackets at the end of the description about the school the smith belonged to had to be taken into consideration.

The mentioned large *itame-mokume* mix, prominent *ha-nie*, *hotsure* and *yubashiri* along the *habuchi* and a *mizukage*-like appearence at the base can be seen on Ko-Hōki works. But the steel of Ko-Hōki-*mono* is blackish, the *hada* stands more out and the *hamon* has a dull *nioiguchi* and shows plentiful of *ha-hada*. So all in all, the workmanship of the latter school is more rustic.

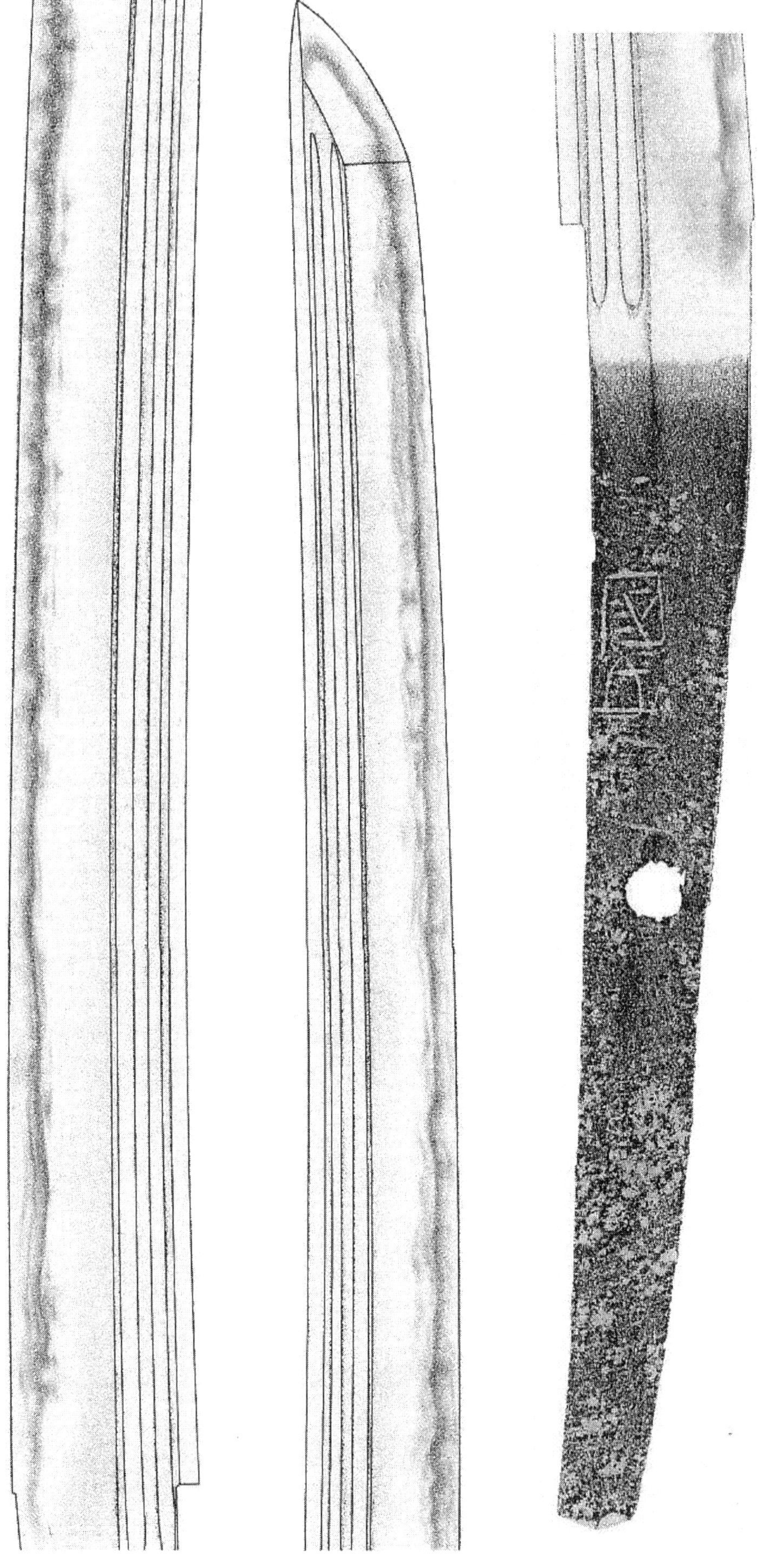

12.641k *tachi*
mei: Kuniyasu (国安) [Awataguchi]
nagasa 71,36 cm *sori* 2,73 cm
moto-haba 2,5 cm *saki-haba* 1,6 cm
moto-kasane 0,65 cm *saki-kasane* 0,4 cm
kissaki-nagasa 2,5 cm *nakago-nagasa* 19,39 cm
nakago-sori 0,3 cm

shinogi-zukuri, *iori-mune*, slender *mihaba*, noticeable taper, deep *koshizori* with *funbari*, the *sori* increases again towards the tip, *ko-kissaki*. The *jigane* is an *itame* mixed with *mokume* and *nagare* which stands out over the entire blade. There is fine *ji-nie*, *chikei* and a faint *nie-utsuri*. The *hamon* and the *bōshi* can be seen on the *oshigata*. *Ko-ashi*, *yō*, fine *nie*, *kinsuji* and *sunagashi* appear. The *nioiguchi* is subdued in placed. On both sides a *futasuji-ji* with *marudome* is engraved. The tang is *ubu* (with a little *machi-okuri*), has a *kijimomo-gata*, a *kurijiri*, *katte-sagari* and two *mekugi-ana* (one of them is plugged and there is also a *yahazu-ana* on the tip of the tang). There is a *niji-mei* chiselled on the *haki-omote* side above the *ubu-mekugi-ana* and towards the *nakago-mune*. Especially the second character is executed in the peculiar manner of that smith. (The *jigane* of this smith can be either a very fine and beautifully forged *ko-itame* with much *ji-nie* or an interpretation like it is seen on the *kantei* blade).

The blade has a slender *mihaba*, tapers, shows *funbari*, a deep *koshizori* which increases again towards the tip and ends in a *ko-kissaki*. That means the *sugata* brings us into the end of the Heian or early Kamakura period.

The *jigane* of the Awataguchi school is mostly a very fine and densely forged *ko-itame* with plentiful of *ji-nie* and fine *chikei*, that means it appears altogether as so-called „*nashiji-hada*". In addition, the *jigane* is bright and clear. But there are also some works with a large-dimensioned, standing-out *hada* mix of *itame* with *mokume* and *nagare* with quite prominent *chikei*. This was given as hint at the end of the *kantei* description. Anyway, the faint but visible *nie-utsuri* speaks for Kyō-*mono*. We see discontinuous *yubashiri* and *nijūba* along the *yakigashira* and a lot of *ashi*, *yō*, *ko-nie*, *kinsuji* and *sunagashi* which is also typical for Yamashiro. Also important are the densely arranged *midare* elements and the hardly noticeable ups and downs of the *yakiba*. Due to these characteristics and the subdued *nioiguchi* only Awataguchi Kuniyasu and Ayanokōji Sadatoshi (綾小路定利) are left.

Kuniyasu signed in general with a *niji-mei* although his writing style is not uniform. He also signed the character for „yasu" (安) in a peculiar cursive manner. This can be seen on the *oshigata* of the tang and was mentioned in the *kantei* descriptions. So when we combine this with all the points we have determined so far it should be possible to nail the blade down to Kuniyasu. Well, Kuniyasu´s and Sadatoshi´s workmanship is quite close. Sadatoshi´s *bōshi* is *sugu* with a *ko-maru-kaeri* or appears as *midare-komi* but always with a lot of *hakikake*. That means his *bōshi* tends to *kaen* and his *ha* is by trend a little more *nie*-loaden. Kuniyasu´s *bōshi* is in comparison *sugu* oder a slightly undulating *notare-komi* with a *ko-maru-kaeri* in both cases. So his *bōshi* and *ha* is more calm.

Kuniyasu´s tip of the tang is a *kurijiri* and the *yasurime* are *katte-sagari*. The signature is chiselled on the *haki-omote* side above the *mekugi-ana* and towards the *nakago-mune* when there is no *hi* with *kake-nagashi*. In the case of a *hi* with *kake-nagashi*, the signature evades to the center of the tang but is still chiselled above the *mekugi-ana*. But sometimes he placed the *mei* also at the very end of the *hi*, i.e. below the *mekugi-ana* and again towards the *nakago-mune*.

Awataguchi-*tachi* of Kunitomo (国友), Hisakuni (久国), Kuniyasu and the like from the early Kamakura period (of which only very few are extant) show a *suguha-chō* mixed with *ko-chōji-midare* or *ko-midare*, many *ashi* and *yō*. That means they show a classical interpretation. *Tachi* of Awatagtuchi Kunimitsu (国光) and Kuniyoshi (国吉) from the middle Kamakura period show in the case of Kunimitsu a *suguha* with a compact *nioiguchi* and in the case of Kuniyoshi a *suguha* mixed with *ko-gunome* and *ko-midare* and with discontinuous *nijūba* elements along the *habuchi*. So both of them display a somewhat different workmanship than other Awataguchi smiths.

Most of the bids were *atari* on Kuniyasu but some also went *dōzen* for Ayanokōji Sadatoshi and even some for Hōki Yasutsuna (伯耆安綱). As mentioned, Sadatoshi´s and Kuniyasu´s workmanship is quite close and so a bid on him is quite understandable. But one had to read the *kantei* description carefully because Sadatoshi executed <u>both</u> characters in a peculiar manner, i.e. the first one in grass script and the second one smaller and in a cursive script.

Well, because of the rather coarse *jigane* in standing-out *itame-mokume* the blade might look like a Yasutsuna at a glance but his works have a more narrow *shinogi-ji*, another steel colour, and not a *nie-utsuri* but a *jifū-utsuri* with *antai*. Also his *ha-nie* and *hotsure* would be woven into a noticeable *ha-hada* and the entire workmanship is therefore a bit more rustic.

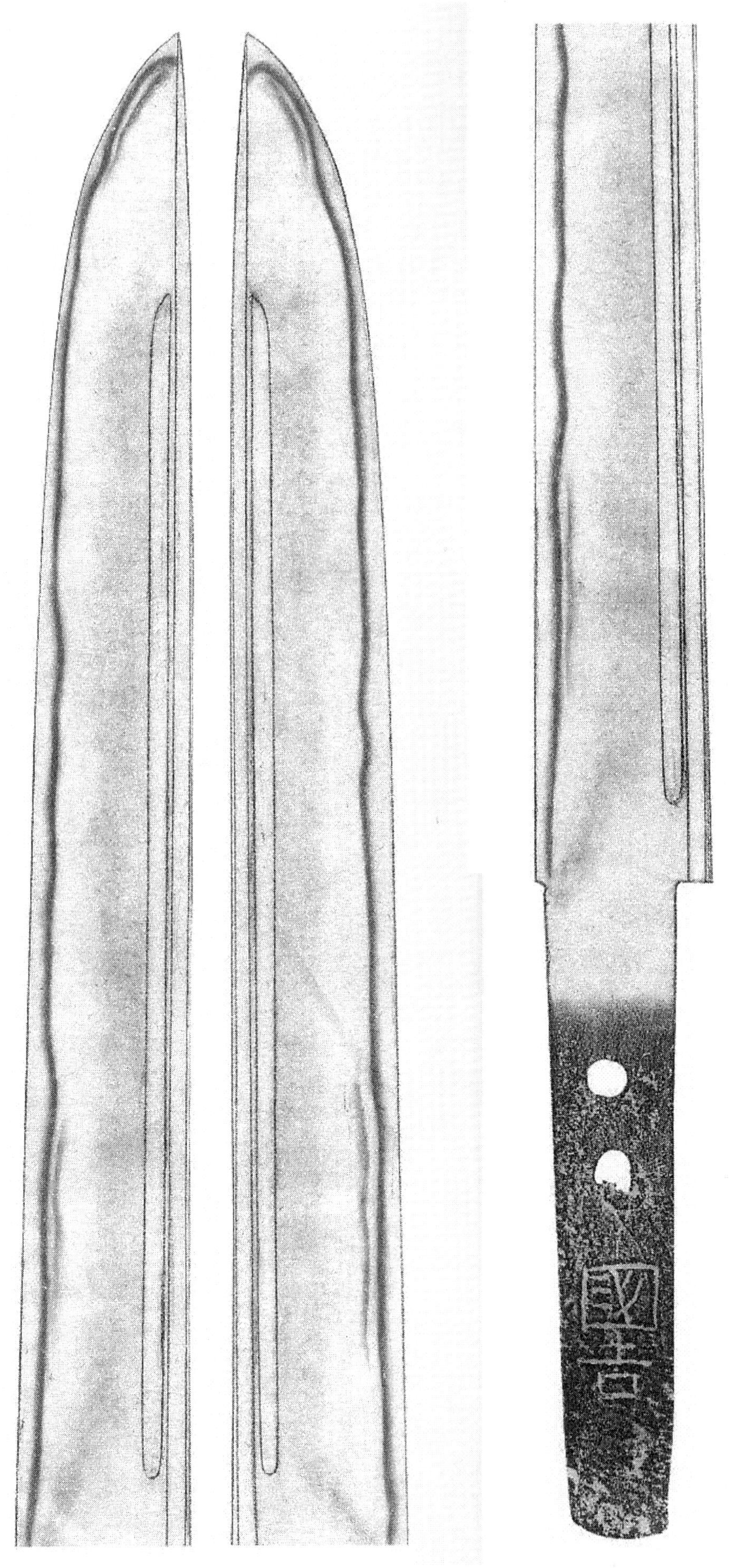
國吉

13.613 *tantō*
mei: Kuniyoshi (国吉)
nagasa 22,1 cm, a little *uchizori*, *hira-zukuri*, *mitsu-mune*

ji: fine and dense *ko-itame-hada*, plentiful of *ji-nie*, many fine *chikei* and a clearly visible *nie-utsuri*, the *jigane* is clear too
hamon: based on *suguha* mixed with *ko-notare*, in addition *ko-ashi*, thick *nioi*, much *ko-nie* and *yubashiri*-like *nijūba* elements as well as *kinsuji*, the *nioiguchi* is bright and clear
bōshi: *ō-maru* with *nijū-ba*
horimono: on both sides a *katana-hi* with *marudome*

Kyōto´s Rai Kunitoshi (来国俊) and Sōshū´s Shintōgo Kunimitsu (新藤五国光) made during the middle and late Kamakura period *tantō* with a blade length of about 8 *sun* (~ 24,25 cm), a narrow *mihaba*, a matching *kasane* and *uchizori*. In contrast, the Awataguchi school made at the same time considerably more compact and broad *tantō* as well as slender and broad *sunnobi* blades.

This *tantō* is a work of Awataguchi Kuniyoshi and has a rather broad *mihaba* for the Kamakura period, so finding out the production time is a bit difficult in this case. But the *deki* of the *jiba* shows a very fine and densely forged *ko-itame*, plentiful of *ji-nie* and many fine *chikei* which results in the Awataguchi-typical *nashiji-hada*. In addition, the *hamon* in elegant *suguha* in *ko-nie-deki* represents with its bright *nioiguchi* the refined and highly noble style of this school. Also the *horimono* are engraved quite close to the *mune* which is another important feature of the Awataguchi school, and many Awataguchi smiths applied such a long *katana-hi* which reaches „almost" the tip.

All these characteristics were grasped and most bids were on Awataguchi Kuniyoshi or Yoshimitsu (吉光). But at Yoshimitsu, the *kitae* would show more larger, standing-out *hada* areas. At the *kantei* blade, the entire *jigane* is fine and dense. Also typical for Yoshimitsu would be a *yakidashi* consisting of uniform *ko-gunome* elements. Besides of that, a *nijūba* is more often seen at Kuniyoshi.

There were also some bids on Rai Kunimitsu (来国光) or the Enju school (延寿). Rai Kunimitsu also made *tantō* with wide *mihaba* but there are usually not that short. His *kitae* is similar but the *ji-nie* and *chikei* are more calm and the *jigane* has a somewhat softer appearance. And some *suguha* of the Enju school do show mixed-in *nijūba* areas but the *jiba* does not have the brilliance and clarity of the Awataguchi school and would appear with more *nagare* and whitish.

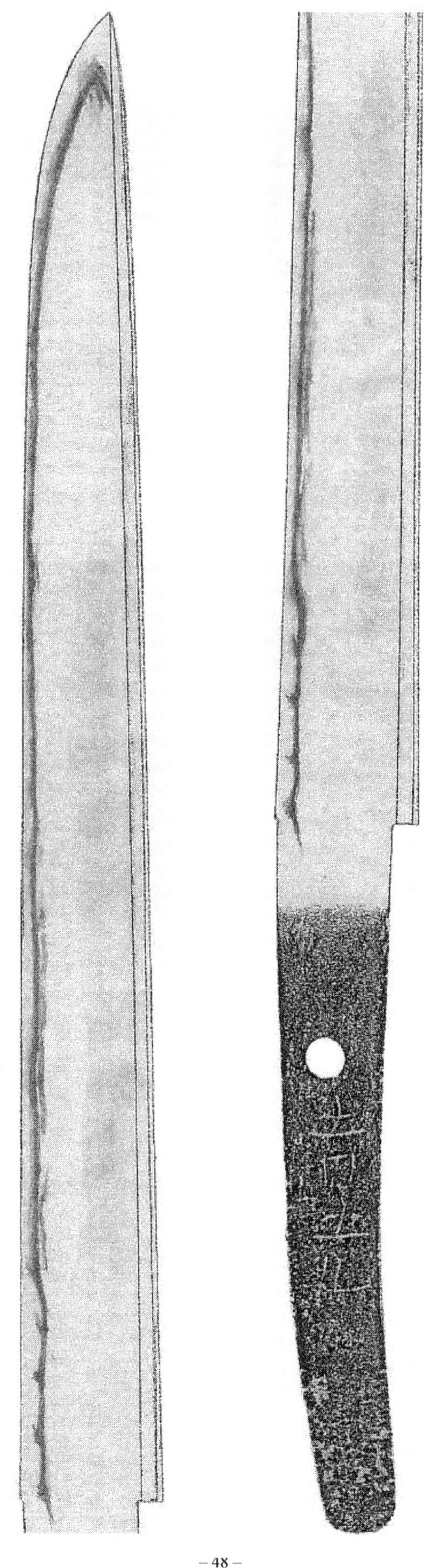

14.650 *tantō*
mei: Yoshimitsu (吉光)
nagasa 21,8 cm, *uchizori*, *hira-zukuri*, *mitsu-mune*

ji: dense *ko-itame* mixed with *itame* and *mokume*, plentiful *ji-nie*, many *chikei*, *nie-utsuri*
hamon: *hoso-suguha-chō* mixed with *ko-gunome* and *ko-notare* and which narrows down at the *monouchi*, much *ko-nie*, *hotsure* and *yubashiri*, fine *kinsuji* and *sunagashi*
bōshi: *sugu* with a *ko-maru-kaeri*, fine *hakikake* and *nie-suji*

This is a small-dimensioned *tantō* which measures around 7 *sun* (~ 21,2 cm). The *mihaba* is in hamony with the *kasane* and an *uchizori* appears, that means the *tantō* has altogether an elegant *sugata* which brings us to the late Kamakura period. In combination with the *hamon* in a regular and beautiful *suguha*, the bids were accordingly on the great *tantō* masters of that time, i.e. Yoshimitsu, Rai Kunitoshi (来国俊) and Shintōgo Kunimitsu (新藤五国光). The *jigane* is a dense *ko-itame* but which is a little coarser than the usual *nashiji-hada* of the Awataguchi school. It shows also some *mokume*. Yoshimitsu worked namely in both styles, a classical *nashiji-hada* of the Awataguchi school and a *hada* like here. But more works in the latter interpretations are extant. In any case we see plentiful of *ji-nie*, fine *chikei* and a *nie-utsuri*.

Let us compare the strength and intensity of the *nie* in the *jiba*. At Rai Kunitoshi they are a little more calm compared to Yoshimitsu or Shintōgo Kunimitsu whereas Kunimitsu applied stronger *nie* than Yoshimitsu. Kunimitsu also added more *chikei* and sparkling *kinsuji* within the *ha*. In short, his *nie* are stronger than those of Yoshimitsu. The *jigane* of this blade is quite close to Kunimitsu but as mentioned, the *kinsuji* are not that prominent and small connected *gunome* elements appear at the base of the blade. (Incidentally, there are also some interpretations of Yoshimitsu where these *gunome* are found all over the *hamon*.) Also we see a narrowing *yakiba* along the *fukura*, strong *nie* in the *bōshi* and *nie-suji* in *kuichigai* manner, which look like as if they would „fume" into the *ji*. These features are very typical for Yoshimitsu and once you have internalized them you will always be able to spot a Yoshimitsu at a *kantei*.

There were also some few bids on his father Kuniyoshi (国吉) which were counted as *dōzen*. By the way, some transmissions say he was „only" his master. But at Kuniyoshi, the *ko-itame* would be especially dense and beautiful.

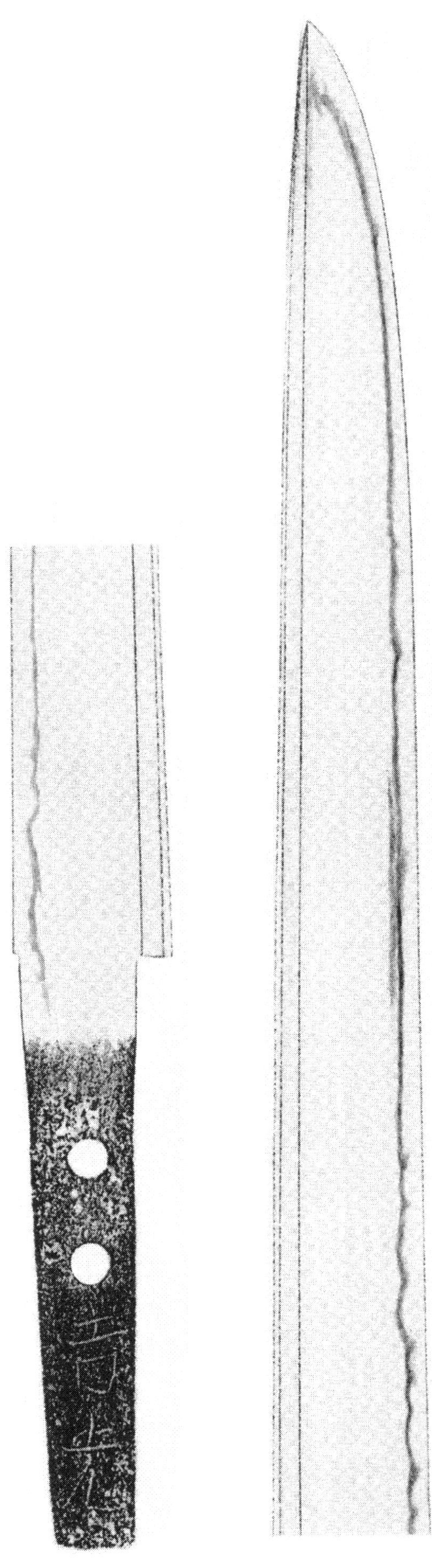

15.671 *tantō*
mei: Yoshimitsu (吉光)
nagasa 23,3 cm cm, *uchizori*, *hira-zukuri*, *mitsu-mune*

ji: *ko-itame*, partially mixed with *ō-hada*, in addition plentiful of *ji-nie*, much *chikei* and a *nie-utsuri*, the steel is clear
hamon: *suguha* with some *ko-gunome* at the base, much *ko-nie*, fine *hotsure* and *uchinoke* which also appear as a kind of *nijūba*, the *niogiuchi* is bright and clear
bōshi: quite *nie*-loaden *sugu-bōshi* with a *ko-maru-kaeri*

The length looks somewhat elongated compared to the *mihaba*, the *kasane* is normal and we see an *uchizori*, that means we have here a typical *tantō-sugata* of the late Kamakura period. Compared to the previous period, there were quite many *tantō* produced during the middle and late Kamakura period and from this time we know great masterworks from Kyōto from smiths like Awataguchi Tōshirō Yoshimitsu (粟田口藤四郎吉光) and Rai Kunitoshi (来国俊) or from Sagami from Shintōgo Kunimitsu (新藤五国光). This blade is a work of Tōshirō Yoshimitsu, the last great Awataguchi master. During the Edo period he was classified with Masamune (正宗) and Gō Yoshihiro (郷義弘) as one of the „three great masters“ (*tenka-sansaku*, 天下三作), that means he even headed this list. Accordingly, every *daimyō* tried to own works of Yoshimitsu.

The *kitae* of this blade shows a partially mixed-in *ō-hada* but is apart from that fine and densely forged and appears as *ko-itame*. And with the plentiful of *ji-nie* and the abundance of *chikei*, we see the Awataguchi-typical *nashiji-hada*. Also a *nie-utsuri* appears. The *hamon* is full of beautifully sparkling *nie*, is hardened in *ko-nie-deki* and appears as elegant *suguha* with a bright *nioiguchi*. Very typical for Yoshimitsu are the small *ko-gunome* elements towards the base, the narrowing *yakiba* at the *fukura* and the „intensifying“ *nie* in the *bōshi* which spill back into the *ji* in a linear manner.

All these characteristics were correctly recognized and the vast majority bade on Yoshimitsu. But some went also for his contemporaries Rai Kunitoshi and Shintōgo Kunimitsu. Well, at Rai Kunitoshi we do not see the above mentioned characteristics of the *hamon* and the *bōshi* and the *nie* of his *jiba* as well as the *chikei* are a bit more unobtrusive compared to Awataguchi-*mono*. At Shintōgo Kunimitsu in turn we would see a more standing-out *itame-mokume* and more *hataraki* like *chikei* and *kinsuji*.

Some few bade on Yoshimitsu´s predecessor Awataguchi Kuniyoshi (国吉). But he applied a much more conspicious *nijūba*. Well, the *kantei* blade does show some *nijūba* areas and so a bid on him is understandable. But hardly we see at Kuniyoshi the mentioned characteristics, like a *hamon* which narrows at the *fukura*, *ko-gunome* at the base and emphasized *nie* in the *bōshi*.

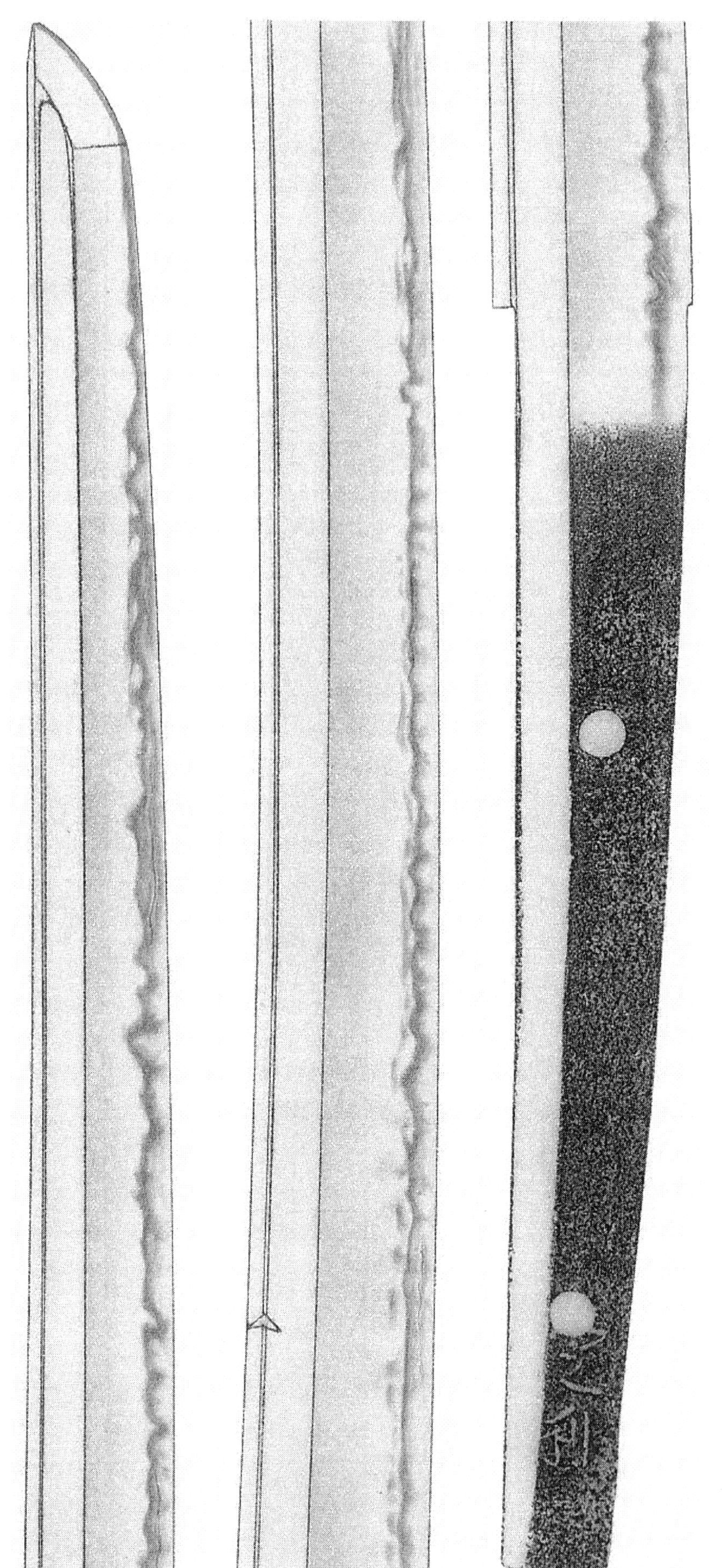

16.589 *tachi*
mei: Sadatoshi (定利) [Ayanokōji]
nagasa 73,8 cm, *sori* 2,4 cm, *shinogi-zukuri*, *iori-mune*

ji: dense *ko-itame* with plentiful of *ji-nie*, fine *chikei* and a *nie-utsuri*
hamon: *suguha-chō* mixed with *ko-midare*, *ko-gunome*, *ko-chōji* and *ko-notare*, the *midare* elements are rather densely arranged and small dimensioned, partially also some connected *gunome* appear, in addition *ashi*, *yō*, much *ko-nie*, *kinsuji*, *sunagashi*, small *tobiyaki* and discontinuous *yubashiri* can be seen, the latter tend towards *nijūba* in places, the *nioiguchi* is wide and subdued
bōshi: *suguha-chō* and *yakitsume*
horimono: on both sides a *bōhi* is engraved with runs as *kake-nagashi* into the tang

Old sword documents date Ayanokōji Sadatoshi to the Bun'ei era (文永, 1264-1275). A theory says that he had friendly relations with Rai Kuniyuki (来国行) and that both made *daisaku* works for each other depending on the order situation. Sadatoshi's workmanship can be clearly seen on the *kantei* blade. He made blades with an elegant shape, a noticeable taper, a deep *koshizori* which bends down towards the tip and a *ko-kissaki*. The *kitae* is a fine and densely forged *ko-itame* and the *hamon* a rather shallow *suguha-chō* mixed with *ko-midare*, *ko-gunome* and *ko-chōji* with not that many ups and downs. The *midare* elements are rather densely arranged and small and also a connected *gunome* can appear. In addition, *ashi*, *yō*, much *ko-nie*, small *tobiyaki* and *yubashiri* appear, whereas the latter might tend to *nijūba* in places. The *nioiguchi* is subdued. In short, his workmanship is a little more classical than those of Rai Kuniyuki and so he is dated today earlier than to the handed-down era, i.e. to the early and not the middle Kamakura period.

Many bids were on Rai Kuniyuki but his *mihaba* does not taper that much, the *sori* is a Rai-typical *toriizori* and at slender interpretations, his *ko-kissaki* tends to *ikubi*. His *hamon* is broad and the *nioiguchi* bright and not subdued. In addition, also *muneyaki* appear and his *sugu-bōshi* has a calm and round *kaeri* and does not appear as *midare-komi* with *hakikake* like on the *kantei* blade.

Because of the *sugata* and the *hamon*, some went also for Awataguchi Kuniyasu (粟田口国安). This was counted as „*jun-dōzen*" (準同然, „almost correct"). But Kuniyasu's *jigane* has a more „sticky" appearance and his interpretations in densely forged *ko-itame* are noticeably more bright than Sadatoshi's. Some also reckoned it as a Ko-Bizen work but there we would expect an *utsuri* with dark *antai* areas and not a clear *nie-utsuri*.

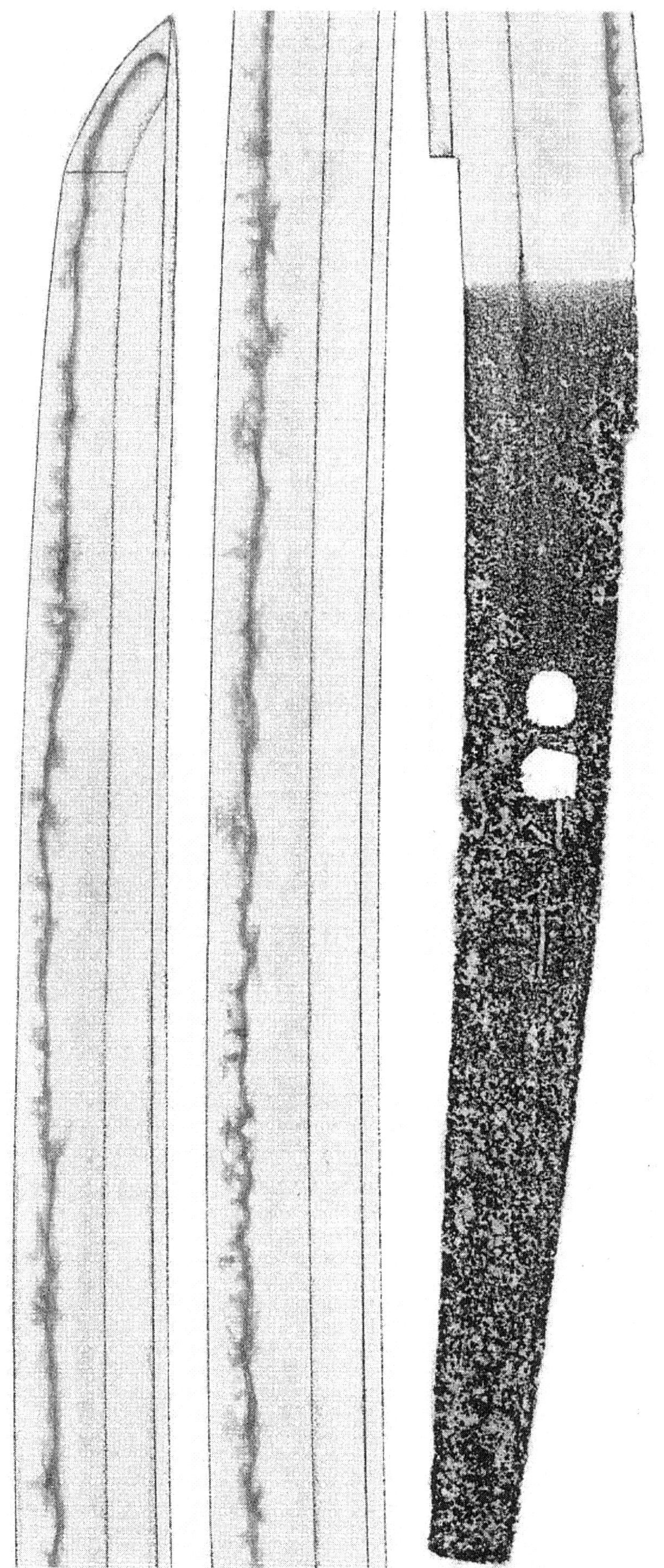

17.666 *tachi*
mei: Kuniyuki (国行) [Rai]
nagasa 82,7 cm, *sori* 3,0 cm, *shinogi-zukuri*, *iori-mune*

ji: *ko-itame* mixed with *mokume* and *nagare*, much fine *ji-nie* and many *chikei*, mixed-in *jifu*-like areas and a *nie-utsuri*
hamon: *chū-suguha-chō* mixed with *ko-midare*, *ko-chōji*, angular elements, *ashi*, *yō*, *uchinoke*, fine *hotsure*, *kinsuji* and *sunagashi*, the *nioiguchi* is broad and shows much *ko-nie*
bōshi: on both sides a shallow *notare-komi* with fine *hakikake* along the *ko-maru-kaeri*

This is an *ubu-tachi* with the signature of Rai Kuniyuki. There are unfortunately no datings extant by Kuniyuki but some from his supposed son Niji-Kunitoshi (国俊), namely from the first year of Kōan (弘安, 1278). Because of this, old sword documents have dated Kuniyuki around Shōgen (正元, 1259-1260) and Bun'ō (文応, 1260-1261). We know *tachi* with a slender and elegant and a broader and more magnificent *sugata*. This blade is quite long, slender and has truly a highly elegant and classical appearance. But you should not miss the *ikubi-kissaki* and the Rai-typical *toriizori*, that means we are no more in the early Kamakura period as the shape might suggest at a glance. When you combine this with the fine and beautiful *jiba*, then it is not that hard to arrive at the Rai school.

Within the Rai school, such a shape is first and foremost seen at Kuniyuki and Rai Kunitoshi. They combine it with a *chū-suguha-chō* which is vividly mixed with *ko-midare*, *ko-chōji* and angular elements. Fine and splendid *hataraki* appear along the *habuchi* and the *ashi* are full and soft. Niji Kunitoshi's works might still have a hint of this classic interpretation but his *midare* is already a little bigger, the *bōshi* appears as *midare-komi*, and the *sugata* is a little more powerful. At Rai Kunimitsu (来国光) and Kunitsugu (来国次), elegant *tachi-sugata* are even more scarce and the *hamon* gets a noticeable amount of *gunome*. Also the *nie* increase at later Rai smiths.

Some bade also on Ayanokōji Sadatoshi (綾小路定利). This was a very sensitive *kantei* but at Sadatoshi, the *yakiba* would be a little narrower and the *hamon* would show more ups and downs. In addition, small *tobiyaki* would appear above the *yakigashira*, the *hamon* would show more *ko-gunome* and the *bōshi* plentiful of *hakikake*. Others went for Awataguchi-*mono* of the early Kamakura period. Here the shape would be different, i.e. even more classical and the *sori* would appear as deep *koshizori* which bends down towards the tip.

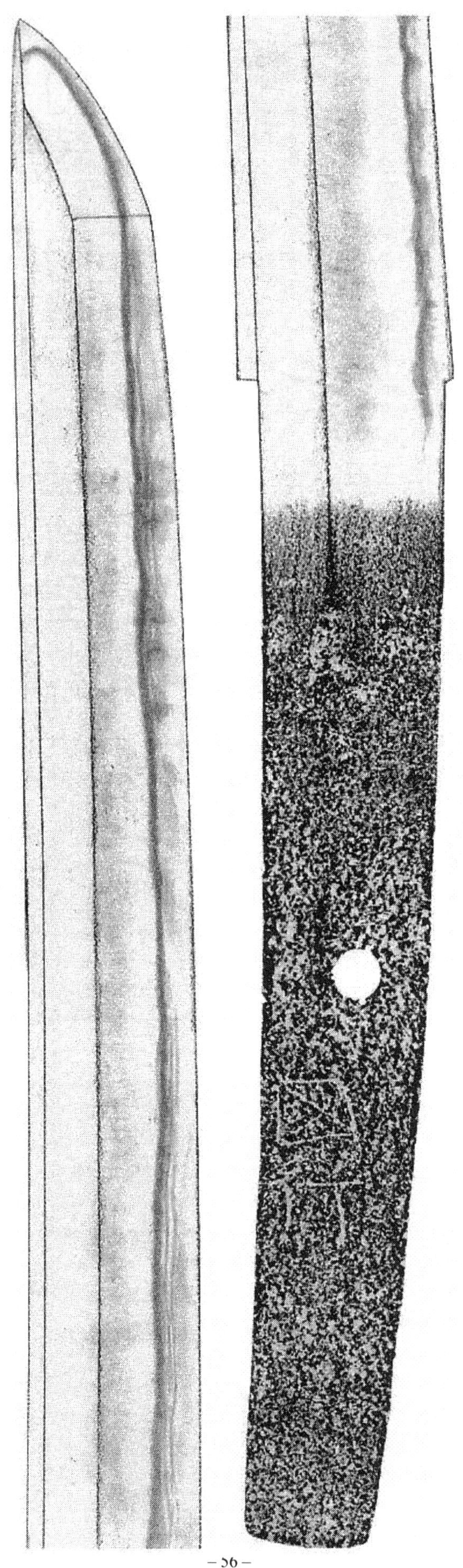

18.629 *tachi*
mei: Kuniyuki (国行) [Rai]
nagasa 74,5 cm, *sori* 2,7 cm, *shinogi-zukuri*, *iori-mune*

ji: dense *ko-itame-hada*, partially mixed with *itame* and *mokume*, plentiful of *ji-nie*, many *chikei* and a *nie-utsuri*
hamon: at the *monouchi* a *suguha*, below a *suguha-chō* mixed with *ko-chōji*, *ko-midare* and *ko-gunome*, in addition many *ashi* and *yō*, thick *nioi*, plentiful of *nie*, *tobiyaki*-like *yubashiri* appear towards the base
bōshi: *sugu* with a *ko-maru-kaeri*

This blade has a *sugata* with a deep *toriizori*, a *kitae* in a very dense and fine *itame* which is partially mixed with *ō-hada*, it shows a *nie-utsuri*, a *suguha-chō*-based *hamon* with *ko-gunome* and *ko-chōji* elements, plentiful of *ko-nie*, and a *sugu-bōshi* with a calm *ko-maru-kaeri*. All these are very typical characteristics of the Kamakura-period Rai school.

The *hamon* appears as pure *suguha* in the upper area but below, it is mixed with *ko-chōji*, *ko-midare* and *ko-gunome*, that means it is as mentioned a *suguha-chō*. Above the *yakigashira* small punctual, *uchinoke*- or *tobiyaki*-like hardened spots appear which are called „*karimata*" (雁股, lit. „geese thighs"). All these features speak for a classical and not a late Rai workmanship.

Most were spot-on and went for Rai, with a focus on Kuniyuki, followed by Niji Kunitoshi (国俊), Rai Kunitoshi, Rai Kunimitsu (来国光) and others. Niji Kunitoshi too applied like Kuniyuki a *midareba* consisting of a mix of *chōji* and *gunome* but his interpretations are by trend larger dimensioned and more flamboyant. At Rai Kunitoshi, the *sugata* wold be more slender and elegant than the *kantei* blade and the *hamon* would not show that noticeable amount of *chōji* and *gunome*. That means his *suguha* or *suguha-chō* is a little bit more calm. At Rai Kunimitsu, we would expect more and larger *gunome* within the *midareba* sections and mixed-in *chōji* like here are rather rare for Kunimitsu when he worked in *midare*.

Incidentally, the mentioned *karimata* are hardly seen at any other Rai smith and can be regarded as one of the most representative peculiarities of Kuniyuki. But as the blade does not show the Rai-typical *bōhi* and *muneyaki* and because the *utsuri* tends somewhat to *midare*, some reckoned it as a Ko-Bizen work. But here the *sugata* and *kitae* would be considerably different, i.e. such a bid could be dismissed after a second thought.

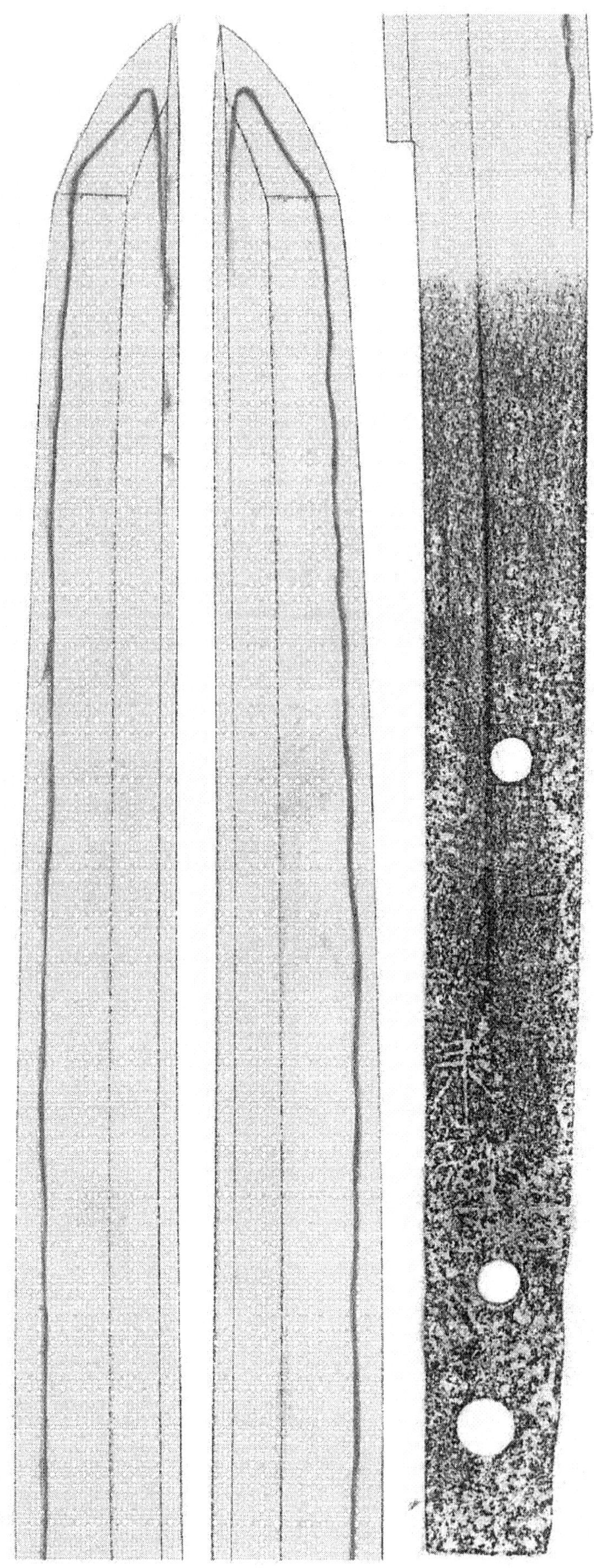

19.661 *tachi*
mei: Rai Kuni-? [Kunitoshi] (来国○[俊])
nagasa 69,4 cm, *sori* 1,8 cm, *shinogi-zukuri*, *iori-mune*

ji: rather dense *itame* with partial *ō-hada*, fine *ji-nie*, faint *nie-utsuri*
hamon: *suguha-chō* which appears as slightly undulating *notare* in places, in addition partially mixed-in *ko-ashi*, the *nioiguchi* is rather compact and shows much *ko-nie*
bōshi: slightly undulating *sugu-bōshi* with a *ko-maru-kaeri* which runs back relative wide along the *mune*

Because there is no *funbari* we can assume that this is a shortened blade. The *tachi-sugata* has a deep *toriizori*, a slender *mihaba* and a high *shinogi*, that means it is on the elegant side. The *kitae* is a densely forged *ko-itame* with *nie-utsuri*, plentiful of fine *ji-nie*, the *hamon* is a *suguha* with some *ko-ashi*, much *ko-nie*, and the *bōshi* appears slightly undulating end ends with a long *ko-maru-kaeri*. If you combine all these characteristics, you will ineviteably arrive at the Yamashiro tradition and therein at the Rai school.

Let´s take a closer look at the *ha*. The few *ko-ashi* require a special attention because they do not point towards the tip like at Bizen or Bitchū but towards the base. This peculiarity is called „*Kyō-saka-ashi*" because it appears mostly on works of Kyōto-based smiths. Such a slender *tachi-sugata* is found within the Rai school – besides of Kunitoshi – also at Rai Kunimitsu (来国光) and Ryōkai (了戒). But at a work of Ryōkai, we would expect some *masame*, a *jigane* which tends to *shirake* and a more subdued *nioiguchi*. Also Ryōkai´s *jiba* would make a more soft or weaker impression. Early works of Rai Kunimitsu are hard to differentiate from Rai Kunitoshi and so bids on him were counted as *atari* too.

Some went also for Osafune but here, the *jiba* would generally not show *nie*. The *bōshi* would not be that wide and the *kaeri* would not run back that long. In addition, a *muneyaki* starting from or right after the *kaeri* which appears just at one side of the *iori* of the *mune* is a typical characteristic of Rai Kunitoshi.

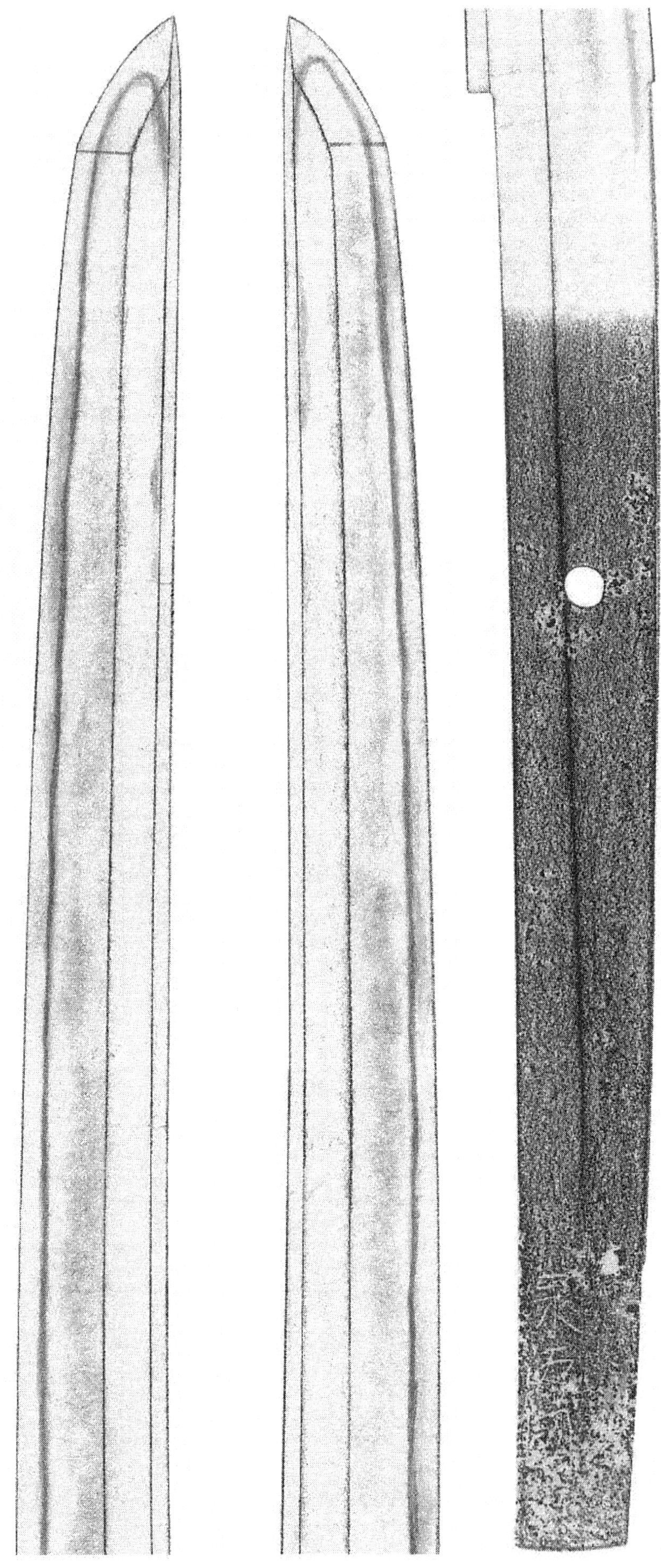

20.621 *tachi*
mei: Rai Minamoto Kunitoshi (来源国俊)
nagasa 63,9 cm, *sori* 1,9 cm, *shinogi-zukuri*, *iori-mune*

ji: dense *ko-itame-hada* partially mixed with *ō-hada*, plentiful of *ji-nie* and a *nie-utsuri*
hamon: *chū-suguha* with much *nioi* but a rather compact *habuchi*, in addition *ko-nie* and some *ko-ashi* appear
bōshi: *sugu* with a *ko-maru-kaeri*

No *funbari* can be seen at the base of the blade and so we can assume that it is shortened. The *sori* is a clear *toriizori*, the *kitae* appears all over as dense *ko-itame* and shows a *nie-utsuri*. The *hamon* is a pure *chū-suguha* with *muneyaki* along the upper area. This and the calm *bōshi* with its *ko-maru-kaeri* are typical features of the Rai school and so almost all bids were on this school, beginning with Rai Kunitoshi over Rai Kuniyuki (来国行), Niji Kunitoshi, Ryōkai (了戒) and others. But some went also for the Rai-offshoot Enju (延寿). A reason for this was that the *nie-utsuri* looks like *shirake* in places, that means some *hada* areas appear a little weak. But this goes back to a repeated polishing and the *jigane* was originally not that whitish.

The blade has a slender and elegant *tachi-sugata* which is, within the Rai school and except Ryōkai, usually seen at Kunitoshi and early works of Kunimitsu. A *deki* in calm *suguha* was applied by both smiths and so it is rather hard at works like this to draw a clear line between the two. Blades of Kuniyuki in turn are even more slender and his *yakiba* shows mixed-in *ko-chōji*, *ko-midare* and *ko-ashi*. That means a pure and perfect *suguha* is hardly found at Kuniyuki.

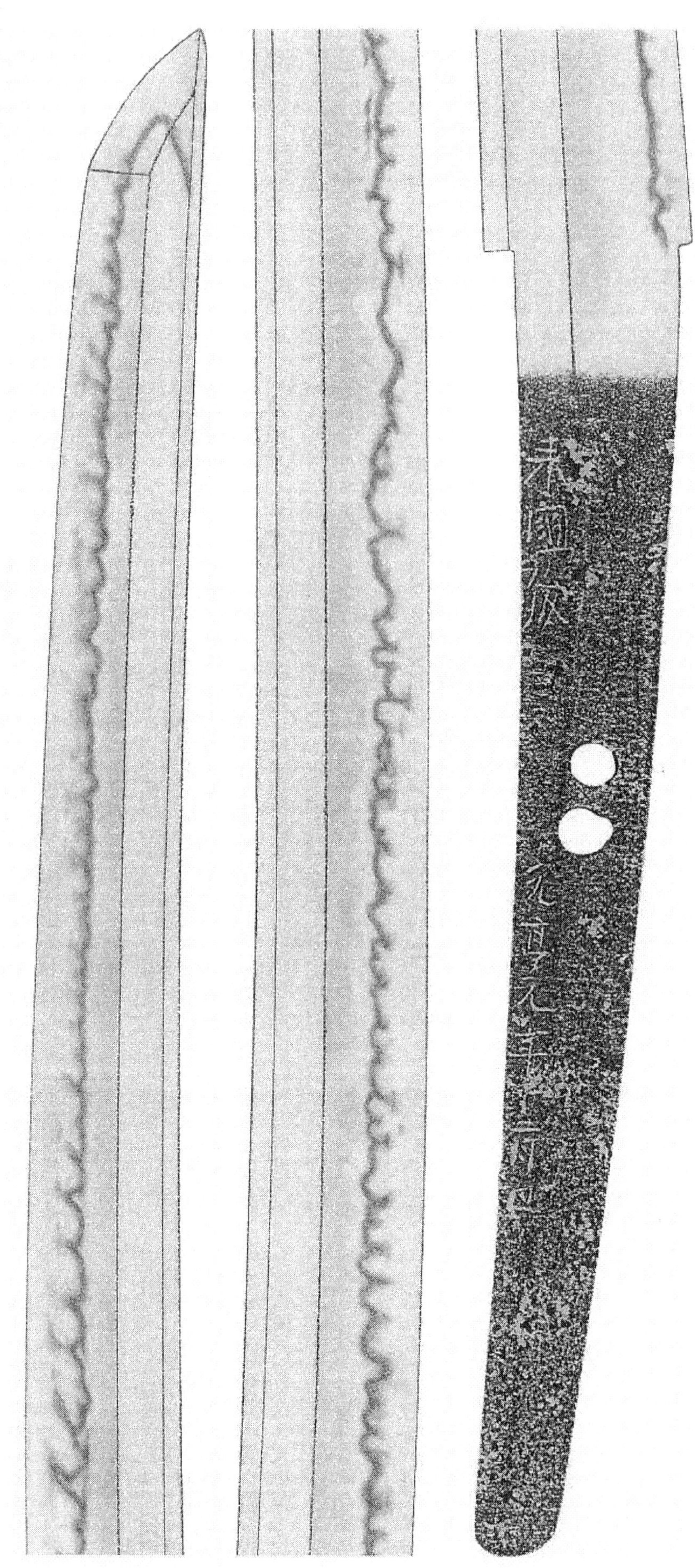

21.599 *tachi*
mei: Rai Kunitoshi (来国俊)
Genkō gannen jūnigatsu-hi (元亨元年十二月日, „a day in the twelfth month of Genkō one [= 1321]")
nagasa 74,25 cm, *sori* 2,45 cm, *shinogi-zukuri, iori-mune*

ji: very fine *ko-itame-hada*, *ji-nie*, fine *chikei*, some *jifu*-like areas are mixed into the *hada*, clear *midare-utsuri*.
hamon: broad *suguha*-based *hamon* mixed with *chōji*, *ko-chōji* and *ko-gunome*, whereas the elements appear also slanted in places, in addition long and densely arranged *ashi* and *yō* and some *saka-ashi*, plentiful of *nie* and fine *kinsuji* and *sunagashi*, the *nioiguchi* is bright
bōshi: *sugu* with a *ko-maru kaeri*.

The slender blade with the *ko-kissaki* and the deep, elegantly curved *sori* represents truly a noble *tachi-sugata* and so many went in the first round to the late Heian and early Kamakura period and bade on Ko-Bizen smiths like Masatsune (正恒) and Tomonari (友成). But the *sori* does not bend down towards the tip. That means one had to pay special attention to the appearance of the curvature which speaks in the end for late Kamakura.

The *kitae* is all over the blade uniformly fine and densely forged and shows *jifu*-like elements in places. The *hamon* bases on a rather regular *suguha* without any major ups and downs. So-called „*Kyō-saka-ashi*" are mixed-in all over the *hamon*. There is plentiful of *nie* in *ji* and *ha* and the *nioiguchi* is bright. In addition, the *bōshi* is *sugu* and has a *ko-maru-kaeri*. All these are typical characteristics of the Rai school.

The *kantei* blade has a somewhat broader *hamon* and noticeably more *chōji* and *midare* then usually expected for Rai Kunitoshi. Because of this many reckoned it as a work of Kuniyuki (国行). Also Kuniyuki made swords with such a slender *tachi-sugata* but his tip would tend towards a compact *ikubi-kissaki* because he was primarily active in the middle Kamakura period. His *hamon* would show more complexely arranged *ko-chōji* and *ko-midare* and would appear overall more classic. Also so-called „*karimata*" would be seen in places.

So it was a bit difficult this time and the keypoint was the *jigane* and the *sugata*. Another hint was the *utsuri*. It is a rather dark *midare-utsuri* and might look therefore like *nie-utsuri* at a glance, but it isn´t. Such an *utsuri* is peculiar to Rai Kunitoshi and Ryōkai (了戒).

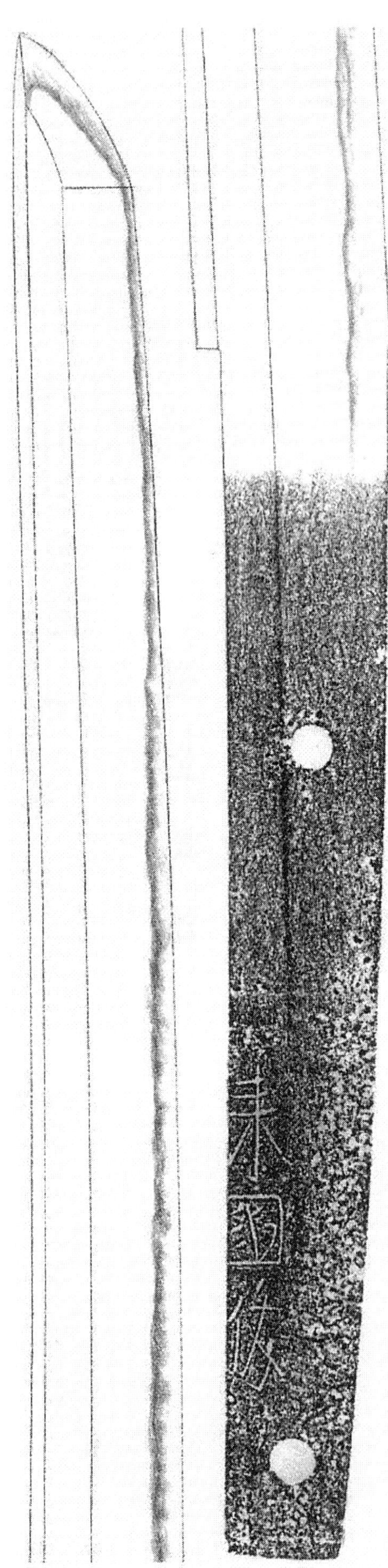
来国俊

22.601 *tachi*
mei: Rai Kunitoshi (来国俊)
nagasa 69,39 cm, *sori* 1,80 cm, *shinogi-zukuri*, *iori-mune*

ji: somewhat standing-out *itame-hada* mixed with some *ō-hada*, plentiful of *ji-nie*, *chikei*, and a clearly visible *nie-utsuri*
hamon: based on *suguha*, mixed with *ko-gunome*, *kinsuji* and a few *sunagashi*, *nie-ashi*, and much *ko-nie*
bōshi: *sugu* with a *ko-maru kaeri*

The blade doesn´t show *funbari* at the base and so we can assume that it is shortened. Nevertheless it shows a deep and even *toriizori*. The narrow *mihaba* with the *ko-kissaki* and the relative high *shinogi* speaks for a classical and elegant *tachi-sugata*. The *kitae* is a very dense *ko-itame* with a clearly visible *nie-utsuri*. The *hamon* is very *ko-nie*-loaden and bases on *suguha*. It is mixed with *ko-gunome* and *ashi*. These characteristics and the *sugu-bōshi* with its *ko-maru-kaeri* lead one inevitably to Yamashiro and in a narrower sense to Rai. Also we see *Kyō-saka-ashi* on the *haki-omote* side. This dinstinguishes the blade from works of the Bizen or Bitchū schools. Especially Rai Kunitoshi is known for his good use of such *Kyō-saka-ashi*.

Due to the slender *tachi-sugata* some also bade on Ryōkai (了戒) or Rai Kunimitsu (来国光). At Ryōkai, we would expect some *masame*, a whitish *jigane* and a more subdued *nioiguchi*. Also the *jiba* would make all in all a more weark appearance. The differentiation between Rai Kunitoshi and Rai Kunimitsu is a bit more difficult because both displayed such a workmanship. This is particularly true for Kunimitsu´s early artistic period.

Incidentally, the blade can be dated on the basis of the signature style around Shōō (1288-1293) and Einin (1293-1299).

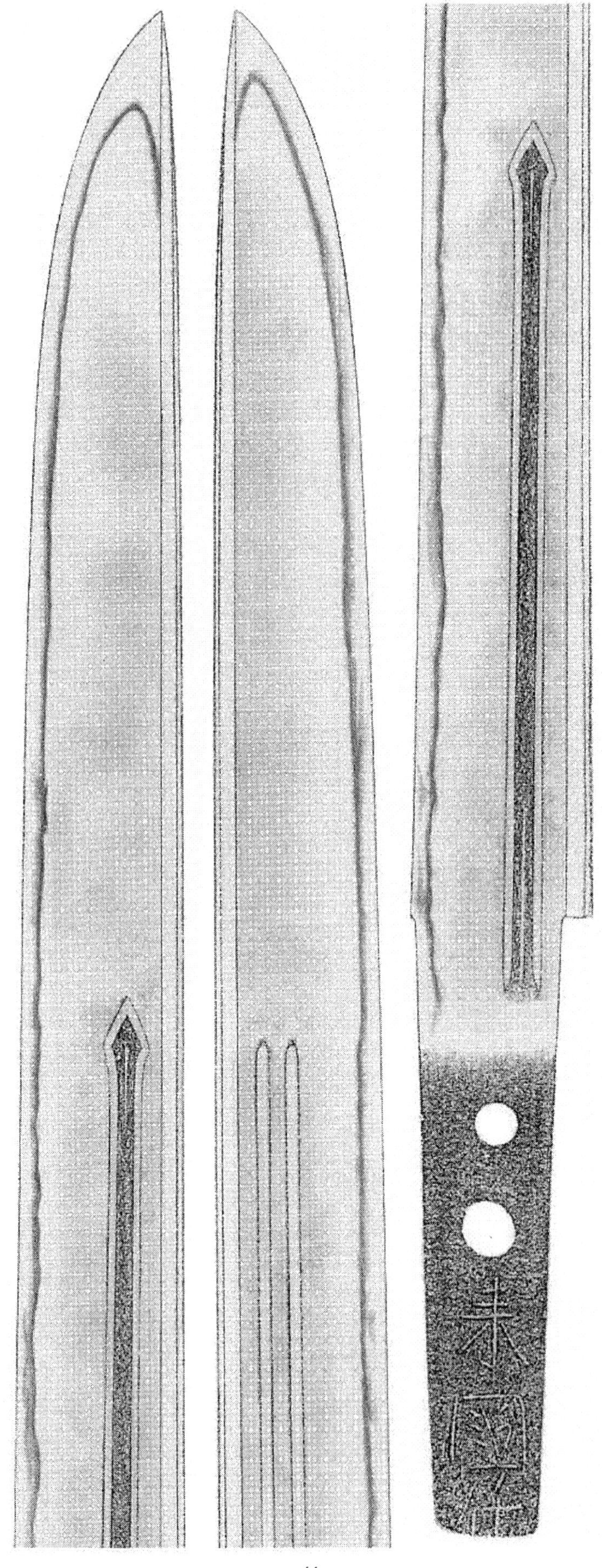

23.659 *tantō*
mei: Rai Kunitoshi (来国俊)
nagasa 25,7 cm, some *uchizori*, *hira-zukuri*, *mitsu-mune*

ji: dense *ko-itame*, partially also mixed with larger *hada* areas, plentiful of *ji-nie*, *nie-utsuri*
hamon: *chū-suguha* with fine *sunagashi* and a relative wide *nioiguchi* with mich *ko-nie*
bōshi: *sugu* with a *ko-maru-kaeri*
horimono: a *suken* on the *omote* side and *gomabashi* on the *ura*, both run with *kake-nagashi* into the tang

This *tantō* has a normal *mihaba* and *nagasa* (and is besides of the slightly cut-off *nakago-jiri* and the *machi-okuri* almost *ubu*). The *kasane* is also in harmony with the *mihaba* and *nagasa*, there is an *uchizori* and the middle surface of the *mitsu-mune* is broad. All these features speak clearly for the late Kamakura period. The *jigane* is a dense, „wet" looking *ko-itame* which is partially weak. These weak areas are called „Rai-*hada*". In addition, a *nie-utsuri* appears. The *hamon* is an elegant *suguha* with a wide *nioiguchi* and beautiful *ko-nie*. There are fine *hataraki* and the *bōshi* is *sugu* with a *ko-maru-kaeri*. When you take a closer look at the *bōshi*, you will see that the *kaeri* leans somewhat towards the *ha*. This so-called „Fuji-*bōshi*" (富士帽子) – it resembles a little the two symmetrical flanks of Mt. Fuji – is typical for Rai Kunitoshi and therefore most of the bids focused on him. The signature is somewhat roundish and the three small strokes on the left inner side of the character for „Kuni" (國) point from the bottom right to the top left. On the basis of this, we can date the blade around the Shōwa era (正和, 1312-1317).

Some went for Rai Kunimitsu (来国光). This is understandable because the blade is from the late artistic period of Kunitoshi, like for example the *jūyō-bunkazai tachi* dated Shōwa four (1315) which mentions his age of 75. That means this already overlaps with the early artistic period of his successor Kunimitsu. The latest extant dating of Rai Kunitoshi is from the Genkō era (元享, 1321-1324) and the earliest of Kunimitsu from Karyaku (嘉暦, 1326-1329). But most of Kunimitsu´s works reflect in general his later artistic period, that means his *tantō* become *sunnobi*, have a wider *mihaba*, almost no *sori* and a thicker *kasane* like it is typical for the late Kamakura and early Nanbokuchō period and a precursor for the heyays of the latter era. A proverb says: „Rai Kunitoshi is superior to Kunimitsu in terms of elegance, but Kunimitsu is superior when it comes to vitality and ambition." In short, the *kantei* blade is rather on the elegant side and when there are no other hints for Kunimitsu, one should go directly for Rai Kunitoshi and not speculate about the early artistic period of Kunimitsu.

Well, there were also some bids on Awataguchi Yoshimitsu (粟田口吉光). But we would expect a regular *ko-gunome* around the base and a narrowing *yakiba* along the *fukura*. Also his *horimono* would be engraved noticeably closer to the *mune* and would show the same design on each side.

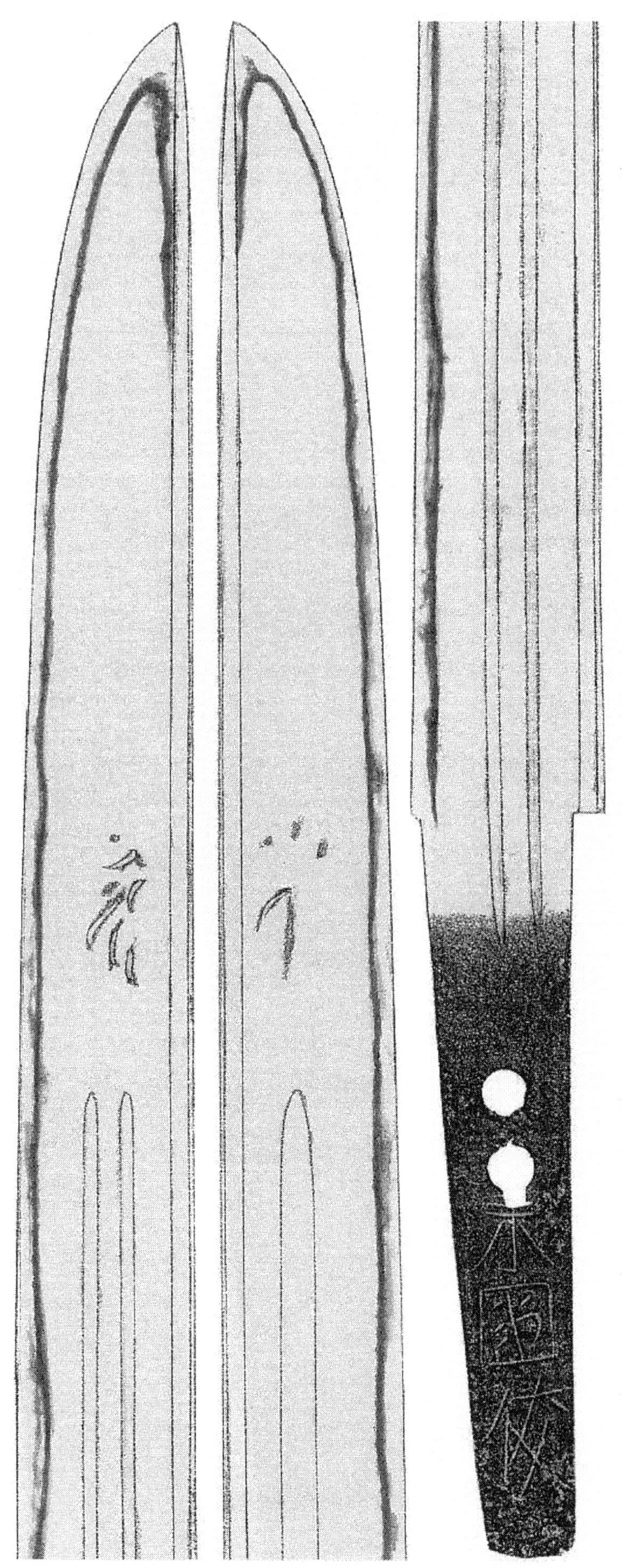

24.650 *tantō*
mei: Rai Kunitoshi (来国俊)
nagasa 27,6 cm, no *sori*, *hira-zukuri*, *mitsu-mune*

ji: *ko-itame* mixed with *mokume* and some areas which tend to *nagare*, plentiful of *ji-nie*, fine *chikei*, faint *utsuri*
hamon: *chū-suguha-chō* with some shallow *notare* sections, wide *nioiuchi*, many *ko-nie*, fine *sunagashi* and *kinsuji*
bōshi: *sugu* with a *ko-maru-kaeri*, there are some *hakikake* on the *omote* side but on both sides the *kaeri* runs back long
hoirmono: on both sides a *bonji* is engraved whereas the *omote* side shows below a *futasuji-hi* and the *ura* side a *katana-hi*, both *hi* run with *kake-nagashi* into the tang

This is a *tantō* of Rai Kunitoshi which is compared to works of Awataguchi Yoshimitsu (吉光) with its 9 *sun* relative large. The *mihaba* is broad and the *kasane* thick, that means the blade gives all over a somewhat robust impression. *Tantō* of the Awataguchi school – especially from Kuniyoshi (国吉) and Yoshimitsu – can have a broad *mihaba* in combination with *sunnobi* or a broad *mihaba* with a shorter *nagasa*. That means there is no general rule here. Even the *sori* varies. But at the Rai school, the *tantō* always corresponded to the time. This was grasped by the most participants but because of the broad *mihaba*, some went for the later Rai Kunimitsu (来国光) or even to Enju (延寿). And because of the *kasanebori* (重ね彫, several kinds of *horimono* on one blade), it was also reckoned as a somewhat later work of another Yamashiro smith, namely Nobukuni (信国).

Let´s start with Nobukuni. The 1st gen. was active in the heyday of the Nanbokuchō era, that means his *tantō* have a broad *mihaba*, a shallow but noticeable *sori*, and a thin *kasane*. So he can be ruled out on the basis of the shape. But Rai Kunimitsu and Enju are very sensitive bids, also in respect of the *jiba*. But the *bōshi* is typical for Rai Kunitoshi, that means it runs parallel to the *fukura* as *sugu* and turns back shortly in a *ko-maru-kaeri*. This interpretation is also called „Rai Kunitoshi´s Fuji-shaped *bōshi*“ because with the *kaeri*, it resembles a bit the flanks of Mt. Fuji. However, the Fuji-shaped *bōshi* is not that pronounced here so the length of the *kaeri* was the key issue to come to Kunitoshi.

Incidentally, on the basis of the signature we can date the blade around Shōō (正応, 1288-1293) and Einin (永仁, 1293-1299). That means we are in the early artistic period of Rai Kunitoshi.

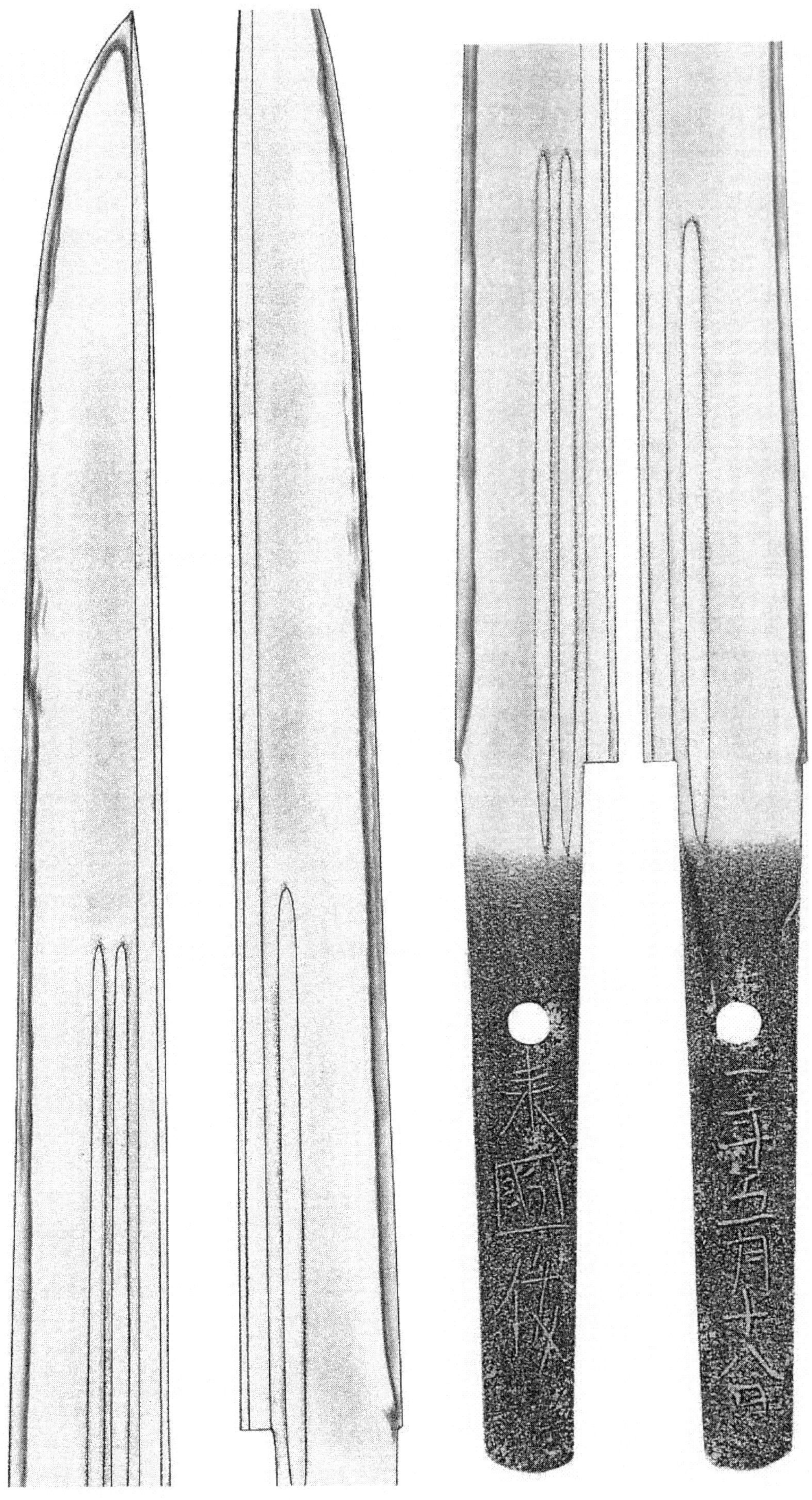

25.593k *tantō*

mei: Rai Kunitoshi (来国俊)

Shōō ninen gogatsu jūhachinichi (正応二年五月十八日, „18th day of the fifth month Shōō two [1289]")

nagasa 23,94 cm	*uchizori*
motohaba 2,1 cm	*moto-kasane* 0,75 cm
nakago-nagasa 11,21 cm	no *nakago-sori*

hira-zukuri, *mitsu-mune*, well-balanced *mihaba* and *nagasa*, relative thick *kasane*, *uchizori*, altogether a highly elegant *tantō-sugata*. The *kitae* is a very densely forged *ko-itame* with plentiful of *ji-nie*, many *chikei* and a clearly visible *nie-utsuri*, and also some characteristical forging structures appear in places. The *hamon* and the *bōshi* can be seen on the *oshigata*. In addition, much *hotsure*, *kuichigai-ba*, plentiful of *ko-nie* as well as fine *kinsuji* and *sunagashi* appear. The *nioiguchi* is rather wide, bright and clear. There are *gomabashi* engraved on the *omote* side and a *koshi-bi* on the *ura* side. Both run with *kake-nagashi* in the tang. The latter is *ubu*, has a *kurijiri*, shallow *katte-sagari yasurime* and one *mekugi-ana*. Centrally under the *mekugi-ana*, a *sanji-mei* is chiselled on the *sashi-omote* side. A date signature is found on the *ura* side which runs over the *mekugi-ana*.

The *tantō* has a normal *mihaba/nagasa* ratio, that means it is neither noticeably broad nor too long, and with the slight *uchizori* towards the tip, a elegant *sugata* is the result which puts it straightforward to the middle or late Kamakura period. When we now bring Kyō-*mono* into play we remember that *tantō* of the Awataguchi school (粟田口) are rather varied in size and shape. Also their *sori* is more or less varied. In contrast, the *tantō* of the Rai school (especially of Rai Kunitoshi and Ryōkai [了戒]) show a more „standardized" *sugata* in terms of *mihaba/nagasa* ratio and principally *uchizori*. Anyway, this ratio is the most important factor for the balance and evaluation of a *tantō-sugata*.

The *jigane* of Rai Kunitoshi´s *tantō* is a very densely forged *ko-itame* (sometimes also mixed with *nagare*), with plentiful of *ji-nie*, fine *chikei* and a clearly visible *nie-utsuri*. And in placed, a somewhat weaker so-called „Rai-*hada*" (来肌) is mixed in. This peculiarity was mentioned in the description of the *kantei* with „characteristical forging structures".

Tantō from his later artistic period like the *jūyō-bijutsuhin* with a date signature of the Bunpō era (文保, 1317-1319) show a slightly undulating *notare* mixed with *gunome*, whereas the *nie* are stronger than on his early works. The *bōshi* starts late and tapers. This interpretation with *gunome* is considered as a first step towards the *midareba* of his successors Rai Kunimitsu (来国光) and Rai Kunitsugu (来国次). But the majority of his works show a *suguha* or *suguha-chō*. In that case, the *habuchi* does not show many variation and the *suguha* with its compact *nioiguchi* is therefore quite uniform. Another variant is a *suguha-chō* like seen on the *kantei* blade which is loosened with some *kuichigai-ba* and *hotsure*. But the *nioiguchi* is always very *ko-nie*-loaden, bright and clear and fine *kinsuji* and *sunagashi* appear. The *bōshi* of Rai Kunitoshi runs parallel to the *fukura* as perfect *sugu*, whereas the *ko-maru-kaeri* starts as mentioned late, tapers and runs back long. This late start, which makes the *bōshi* appear to lean towards the *ha*, is a very typical feature of Rai Kunitoshi and is compared with the flanks of Mt. Fuji. Already old sword documents like the „*Kokon-mei-zukushi*" (古今名尽) indicate this characteristic when they write: „The *bōshi* tapers and has a long *kaeri*".

Kunitoshi´s *tantō* show *horimono* like *katana-hi*, *suken*, *gomabashi* or *koshibi*, whereas elaborate engravings are usually not seen. Some pieces show a *katana-hi* accompanied by a *suken*. These carvings were applied by all Rai smiths and are more or less always positioned on the same area of the blade.

The tip of the tang of Kunitoshi´s *tantō* is a *kurijiri*, the *yasurime* are shallow *katte-sagari* or *kiri*, and the signature is chiselled centrally on the *sashi-omote* side below the *mekugi-ana* as *sanji-mei* „Rai Kunitoshi". In rare cases he also signed with the prefix „Minamoto" as *yoji-mei* „Minamoto Rai Kunitoshi" (源来国俊). Unfortunately not that many date signatures are extant by him. The date of the second year Shōō seen on the *kantei* blade is by the way the earliest one known.

The vast majority was spot-on and received an *atari* on Rai Kunitoshi but many bade also on Rai Kunimitsu. Also Kunimitsu applied such a *suguha* and in such a case, it is hard to differentiate the two smiths. So bids on him were this time also counted as *atari*. As mentioned before, most works of Rai Kunitoshi are in *suguha* or *suguha-chō* but Kunimitsu worked often also in *midareba*. (Of course there are also some in-between interpretations but when we rule them out and just cound *suguha* and *midareba*, then we arrive at a ratio of 10:6 at Kunimitsu. That means six out of ten blades are in *midareba*.) In addition, *tantō* of Kunimitsu are longer, i.e. *sunnobi*, have a thinner *kasane* and a shallow *sori*. This has to do with his later artistic period and the fashion of the advancing Nanbokuchō era. When we take this into consideration and can´t decide between a bid on Kunitoshi and Kunimitsu at a *suguha* or *suguha-chō* interpretation with a hard-to-place *sugata*, then you should better go for Kunitoshi.

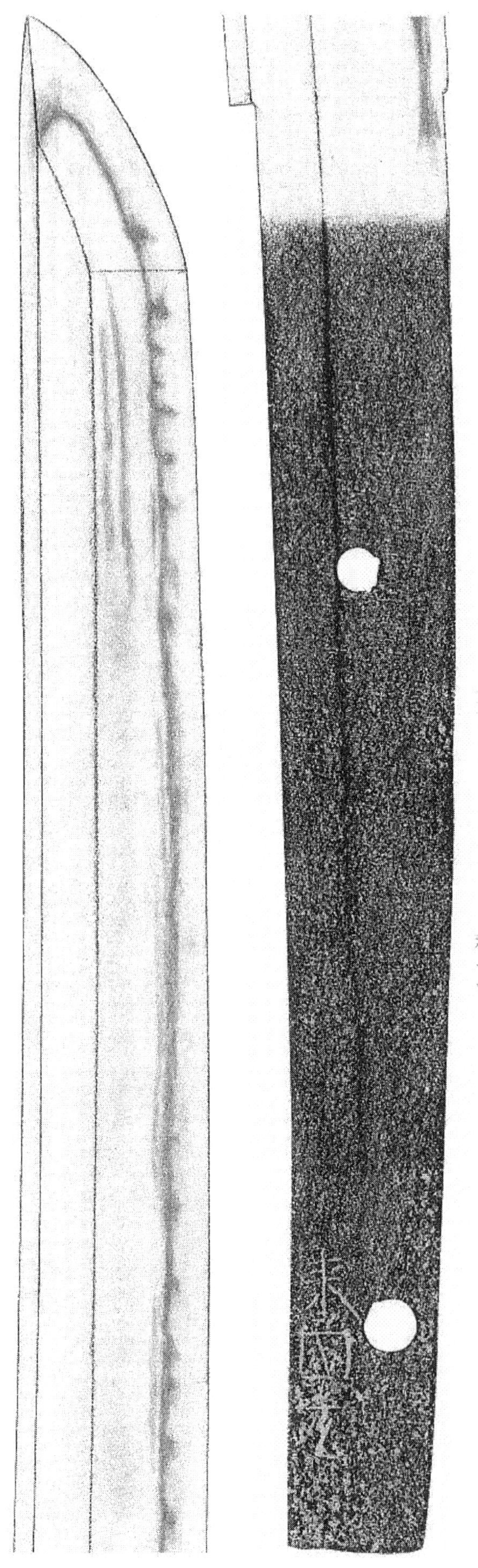

26.640 *tachi*
mei: Rai Kunimitsu (来国光)
nagasa 68,9 cm, *sori* 2,5 cm, *shinogi-zukuri*, *iori-mune*

ji: dense *itame* partially with larger, standing-out *hada* areas, *ji-nie*, fine *chikei*, and a *nie-utsuri*
hamon: *suguha-chō* with *ko-gunome*, *ko-chōji* and *gunome*, in addition many *ashi* and *yō*, plentiful of *nie*, *kinsuji* and *sunagashi*, also *yubashiri*-like punctual *tobiyaki* in places, the *nioiguchi* is bright and clear
bōshi: *sugu* with a *ko-maru-kaeri* on the *haki-omote* and a pointed *kaeri* on the *ura* sides, but on both sides fine *hakikake* are seen

Because there is only a hint of *funbari* at the base, we can assume that the blade is *suriage*. But it keeps a *tachi-sugata* with a deep *toriizori*. Let us turn to the *jigane*. We see large dimensioned *hada* areas mixed into a generally fine *itame* and a conspicious *nie-utsuri* is seen towards the *yakiba*. The latter is a *suguha-chō* with *ko-gunome*, *ko-chōji*, plentiful of *ashi* and *yō* and much *nie*. There are *Kyō-saka-ashi* seen on the *haki-omote* side and the *bōshi* is a calm *suguha* with a *ko-maru-kaeri*.

If you combine all these characteristical features of the *jiba* and the interpretation of the *bōshi*, it shouldn´t be too hard to arrive at the Rai school. And because the blade does not taper that much, shows a *kissaki* which tends to an elongated *chū-kissaki* and has a *hamon* with *ko-gunome* and partial roundish *gunome*, a bid on Rai Kunimitsu is inevitable.

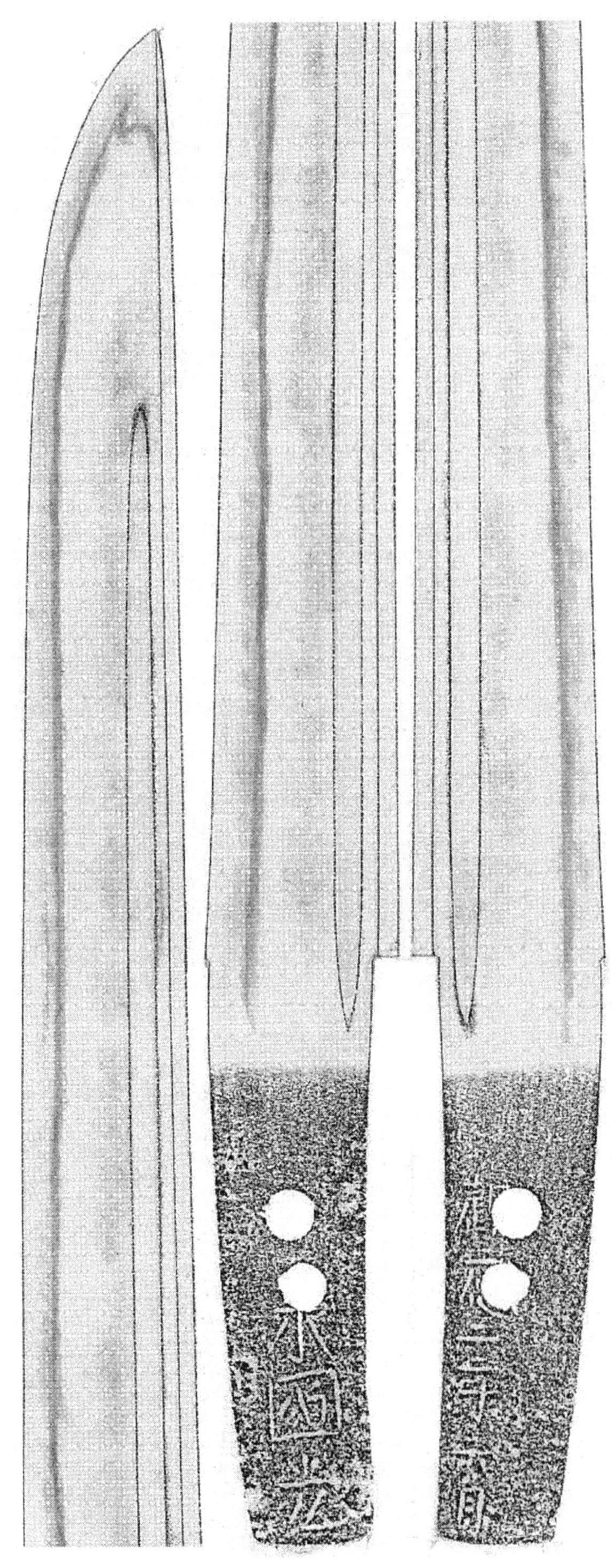

27.654 *tantō*
mei: Rai Kunimitsu (来国光)
Kan´ō ninen rokugatsu (観応二年六月, „sixth month of the second year of Kan´ō [= 1351]“)
nagasa 25,9 cm, only a little *sori*, *hira-zukuri*, *iori-mune*

ji: densely forged *ko-itame*, partially mixed with *itame*, *ji-nie*, fine *chikei* and a faint *nie-utsuri*
hamon: bright and clear *chū-suguha* with a broad *nioiguchi* and *ko-nie*
bōshi: on the *omote* side a little *notare* and a tapering *kaeri*, on the *ura* side *sugu* with a *ko-maru-kaeri*

Here we have a *tantō* of Rai Kunimitsu which is dated with the second year of Kan´ō. According to transmission, Kunimitsu was the son of Rai Kunitoshi (来国俊). He was active from the late Kamakura into the subsequent Nanbokuchō period and we know date signature from the first year of Karyaku (嘉暦, 1326), i.e. late Kamakura, to Kan´ō two (1351), i.e. early Nanbokuchō. So this *tantō* bears the latest known date signature of this smith. It has a broad *mihaba*, a thick *kasane*, is a little longer than earlier *tantō* and has almost no *sori*. That means the *sugata* shows the transitional shape from the slender and rather short *tantō* with *uchizori* from the middle and late Kamakura period to the broader and thinner *sunnobi-tantō* and *ko-wakizashi* with *sakizori* from the Nanbokuchō-period Enbun (延文, 1356-1361) and Jōji eras (貞治, 1362-1368).

Representative for such a shape in combination with a *deki* in dense and fine *ko-itame*, a wide *nioiguchi* and a normal wide *suguha* are Rai Kunimitsu and Rai Kunitsugu (来国次) from Kyōto or the Enju school (延寿) from Higo. And because this *tantō* has an *iori-mune* which is atypical for Rai Kunimitsu (usually he applied a *mitsu-mune*), many went for Enju. This is understandable but at Enju, we would expect a weaker *ji-nie*, *nagare* along the *kitae* and a *shirake-utsuri*. The *nioiguchi* would be more subdued and the *jiba* is not that bright and clear. In addition, the *bōshi* would be an *ō-maru* and also very typical for Enju is a *nijūba* in the vicinity of the *bōshi*.

So we are in the Rai school. When it comes to a traditional *deki* in *suguha* in combination with that shape, Kunimitsu and Kunitsugu are both possible *kantei* but by trend, Kunimitsu applied a little more often *suguha* than Kunitsugu and the *nie* are somewhat stronger too. Thus a *tantō* which shows the transitional *sugata* between late Kamakura and heyday Nanbokuchō in *suguha* with strong *nie* should lead one to a bid on Kunimitsu rather than on Kunitsugu.

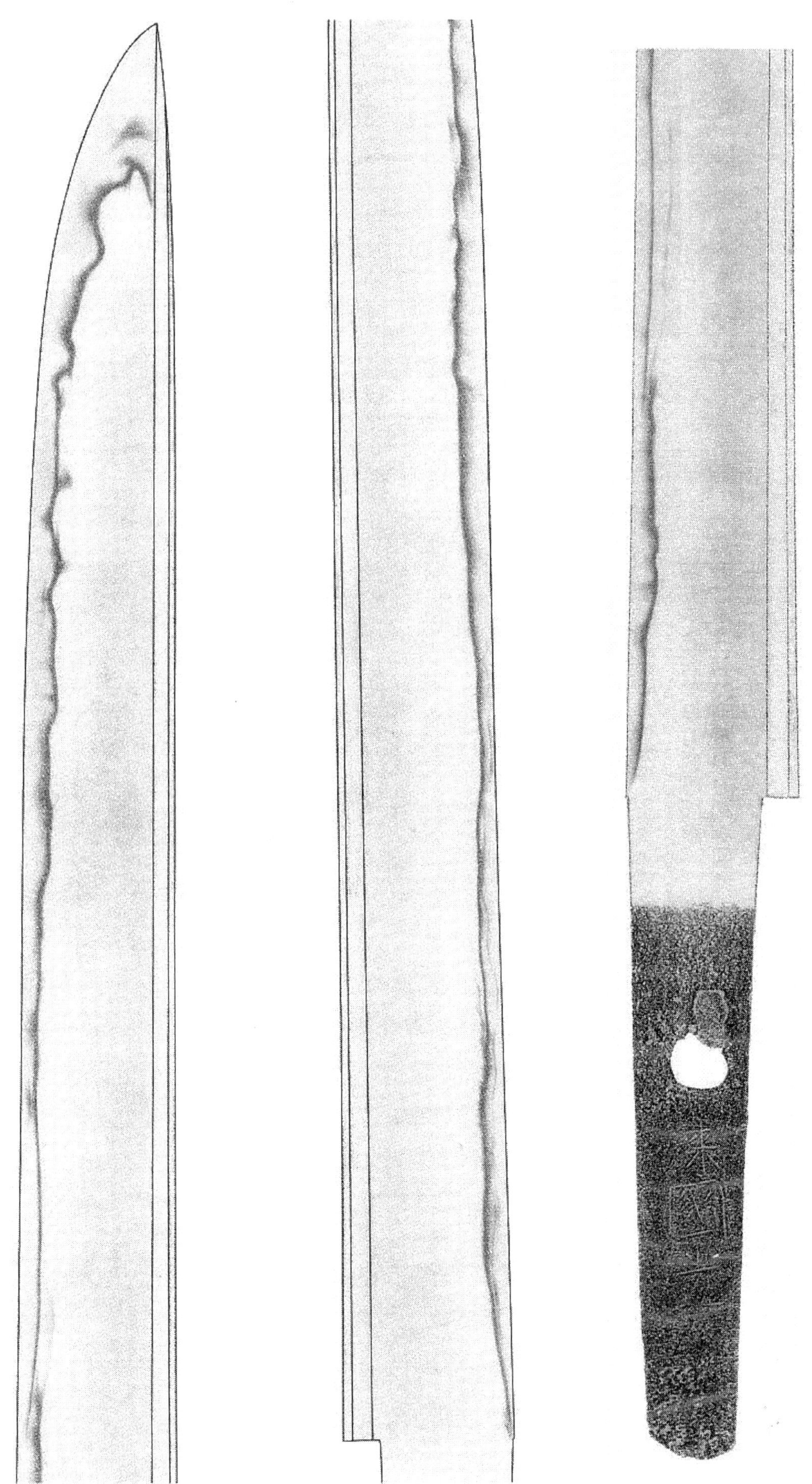

28.646k *tantō*
mei: Rai Kunimitsu (来国光)
nagasa 28,33 cm *uchizori*
moto-haba 2,35 cm *moto-kasane* 0,75 cm
nakago-nagasa 10,45 cm no *nakago-sori*

hira-zukuri, *mitsu-mune*, relative wide *mihaba*, *sunnobi*, thick *kasane*, almost no *sori*, only a slight *uchizori* towards the tip. The *jigane* is a dense and finely forged *ko-itame* with plentiful of *ji-nie* and fine and beautiful *chikei*. *Nie-utsuri* and a characteristical *hada* structure appear. The *hamon* and the *bōshi* can be seen on the *oshigata*. In addition *ashi*, *yō*, much *ko-nie* as well as fine *kinsuji* and *sunagashi* appear. The *hamon* is bright and clear. The tang is *ubu* with a *kurijiri*, shallow *katte-sagari yasurime*, two *mekugi-ana* (one is plugged), and shows centrally on the *sashi-omote* below the *mekugi-ana* a *sanji-mei*.

The blade has a relative wide *mihaba*, is *sunnobi*, has a thick *kasane* and except the slight *uchizori* towards the tip otherwise no *sori*. That means from the point of view of *sugata* we are in the late Kamakura or early Nanbokuchō period.

The *jigane* of Rai Kunimitsu´s *tantō* is a densely forged *ko-itame* with plentiful of *ji-nie*, fine *chikei* and is bright and clear. That means this fineness and beauty is typical for Kyō-*mono*. In addition, a clear and Rai-typical *nie-utsuri* and Rai-*hada* appears. This was mentioned in the description of the *kantei* as „characteristical *hada* structure“. The *hamon* on Kunimitsu´s *tantō* is either a Rai-typical highly elegant *suguha* or like at the case of the *kantei* blade a *nie*-loaden *midareba*. The latter interpretations looks dynamic and indicate a strong Sōshū influence. Blades of that kind can also show a bright and clear *notare-chō* with much *ko-nie* which is mixed with *gunome* (or in some rare cases mixed with a connected *gunome* from base to tip). In addition, repeated *kinsuji* and *sunagashi* appear. The *bōshi* is in *midare-komi* with a *ko-maru-kaeri*, whereas the *midare-komi* shows sometimes a small *togari* element towards the tip (which can be seen on the *kantei* blade too).

Kunimitsu´s *tantō* have a *kurijiri*, shallow *katte-sagari* or *kiri-yasurime*, and the *sanji-mei* „Rai Kunimitsu“ is chiselled centrally below the *mekugi-ana* on the *sashi-omote* side. Only few of the relative many extant signed blades by Kunimitsu bear a date signature.

Within the Rai school, only one *tantō* (or to be more precise a *hira-zukuri wakizashi*) is extant by each Kuniyuki (国行) and Niji-Kunitoshi (国俊). That means we can´t say that much about their *tantō* interpretations. The *hira-zukuri wakizashi* of Kuniyuki has *tokubetsu-jūyō* papers and comes from the former possessions of the Shimazu family (島津). It has a *nagasa* of a little more than one *shaku* (30,3 cm), a broad *mihaba*, is *sunnobi*, and has a *sori*. The *jigane* is a densely forged *itame* mixed with *jifu* and the *hamon* is a *ko-notare* mixed with *gunome*. The *nioiguchi* is wide and full of thick *nie* as well as of *kinsuji* and *sunagashi*. That means we can get a hint of the subsequent *midareba* interpretations of Rai Kunimitsu and Kunitsugu (国次).

The *tantō* of Niji-Kunitoshi is the famous *meibutsu* „Aizen-Kunitoshi“ (愛染国俊). It has a *nagasa* of 28,8 cm, a wide *mihaba*, is *sunnobi* and has a *sori*. The *jigane* is a dense *ko-itame* with *nie-utsuri* and the *hamon* a *notare* mixed with *gunome* and *togariba* which shows plentiful of *nioi* and *nie*. Almost all extant *tantō* of Rai Kunitoshi (whereas it is still not settled if he was the same smith as Niji-Kunitoshi) show a *suguha* or *suguha-chō*. But the *jūyō-bijutsuhin tantō* with the date signature of the Bunpō era (文保, 1317-1319) displays a *deki* in *notare-chō* mixed with *gunome* and shows in addition with the stronger than usual *ha-nie* a more „free“ interpretation.

That means the Rai-predecessors of Kunimitsu do all show more or less a hint of his later *midareba*. That means even Kunimitsu applied often a *suguha*, he also focused on the succession, further development and perfection of a *midareba*. This trend was then adopted and continued by Kunitsugu.

Almost all bids were on Rai Kunimitsu, followed by some on Kunitsugu. Kunitsugu too made such *tantō* with a wide *mihaba* and *sunnobi* in combination with a *nie*-loaden *midareba* which are hard to differentiate from Kunimitsu. So bids on him were counted as *atari* too. But it can be said that Rai Kunitsugu made by trend somewhat larger and wider *tantō* and *wakizashi*. Also his *nie* in *ji* and *ha* as well as the *kinsuji* and *sunagashi* are stronger. That means he displayed more Sōshū influence than Kunimitsu.

Some few bade *dōzen* on Rai Kunitoshi or Kuniyuki. As mentioned, there is one *tantō* of the former in a conservative *midareba* (the one with the date signature of the Bunpō era). But this blade is with 22,6 cm noticeably smaller, has an *uchizori*, and shows more unobtrusive and calm *ha-nie*. Regarding Kuniyuki, it was mentioned before that there is only one *tantō* or *hira-zukuri wakizashi* respectively extant by him. So it would be inadvisable to bid on him at such a blade. In addition, Kuniyuki did not sign with a *sanji-mei*.

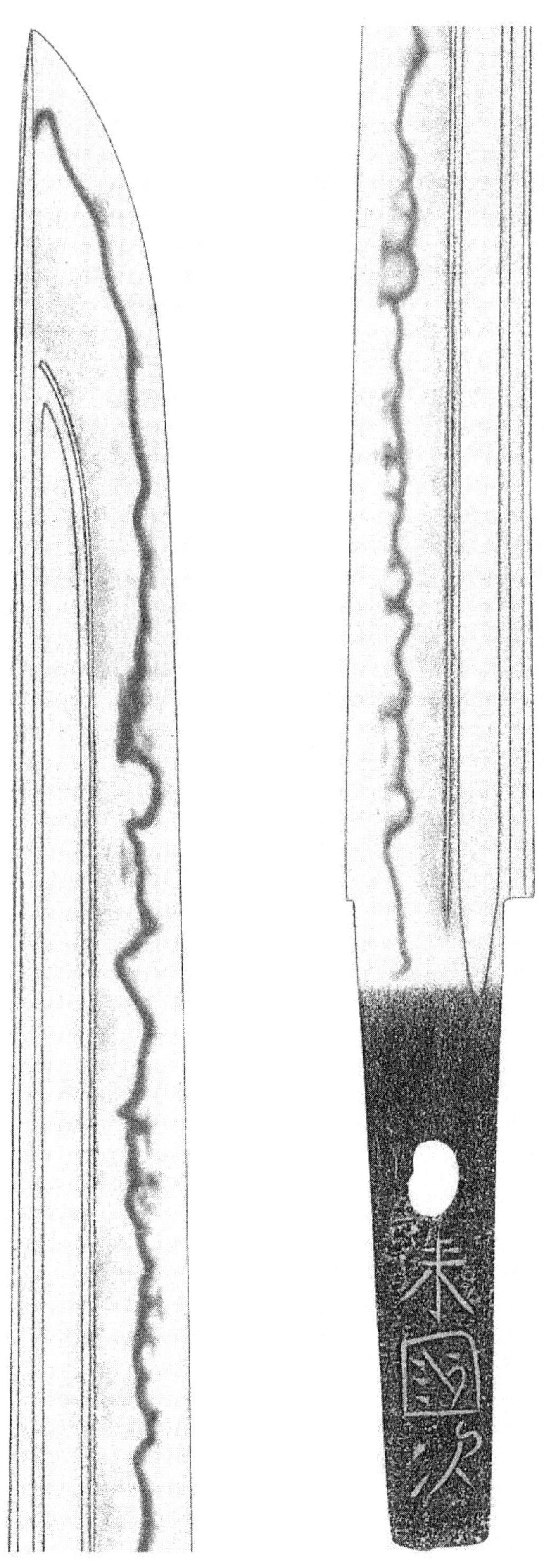
来国次

29.669 *tantō*
mei: Rai Kunitsugu (来国次)
nagasa 22,5 cm, almost *muzori*, *hira-zukuri*, *mitsu-mune*

ji: altogether very densely forged *ko-itame* with *ji-nie* and fine *chikei*, there are also some *ō-hada* areas in places, clearly visible *nie-utsuri*, the *jigane* is clear too
hamon: *ko-notare* mixed with *gunome*, *ko-gunome*, angular *gunome*, *ashi*, *yō*, *yubashiri* as well as *kinsuji* and *sunagashi*, the *nioiguchi* is bright and clear and shows plentiful of *ko-nie*
bōshi: *suguha-chō* to slightly undulating *notare*, thre is a slightly roundish *kaeri* on the *omote* and a pointed, rather „laced-up" *kaeri* on the *ura* side
horimono: on both sides a *katana-hi* with *tsurebi* which runs with *kake-nagashi* into the tang

The blade has a relative wide *mihaba*, a thick *kasane*, is *sunnobi* and has almost no *sori*. That means we have a *tantō-sugata* from the end of the Kamakura and early Nanbokuchō period. The *ko-itame* is dense and beautifully forged and there is plentiful of *ji-nie*, much fine *chikei* and a clearly visible *nie-utsuri*. The steel is clear too. The *hamon* is a quite *nie*-loaden *ko-notare* mixed with *gunome*, *ko-gunome*, *kinsuji* and *sunagashi*. The *nioiguchi* is also bright and clear and so we end up at the Rai school and smiths like Kunimitsu (国光) or Kunitsugu. Both applied such a pointed and somewhat „laced-up" *kaeri*. From Kunimitsu we know date signatures from the first year of Karyaku (嘉暦, 1326) to the second year of Kan´ō (観応, 1351) and from Kunitsugu one from the second year of Karyaku (1327). That means they were basically active at the same time. And because they worked very similar, both bids were counted as *atari*.

Well, the differences. Kunitsugu applied a wider *notareba* and the *nie* and *hataraki* are noticeably stronger and wilder on his works. That means he displayed more Sōshū influence than Kunimitsu. Kunimitsu is by the way listed as one of the „Ten Students of Masamune" and the „*Kokon-mei-zukushi*" has an extra note along his entry which says „went to Kamakura".

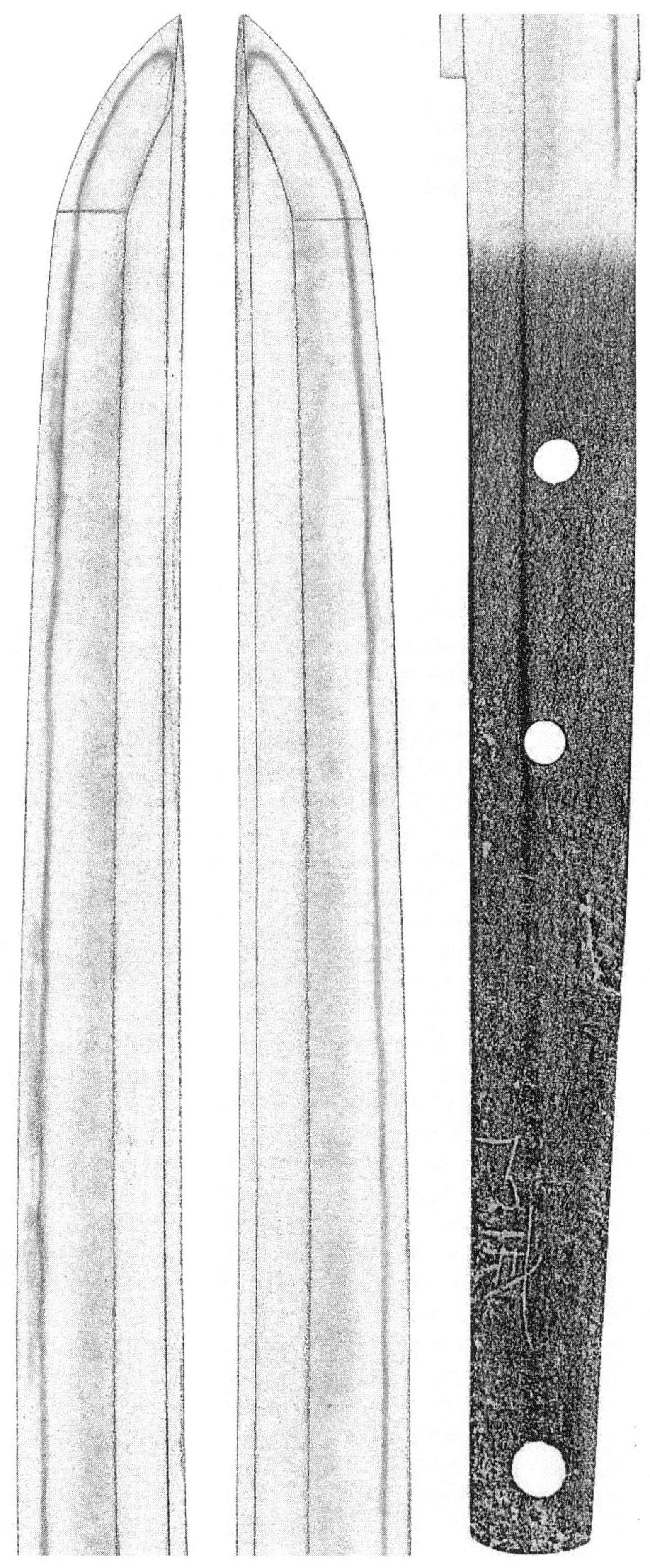

30.638 *tachi*
mei: Ryōkai (了戒)
nagasa 70,3 cm, *sori* 1,5 cm, *shinogi-zukuri*, *iori-mune*

ji: dense *ko-itame* which tends somewhat to *nagare*, fine *ji-nie* and all over the blade an *utsuri* which tends to *shirake*
hamon: *suguha* mixed with *ko-gunome*, in addition *ko-ashi* and *yō*, the *nioiguchi* is partially somewhat dull and some *ko-nie* appear
bōshi: on both sides a shallow *notare-komi* with a *ko-maru-kaeri* which hardly runs back

The blade does not show *funbari* at the base and so we can assume that it is *suriage*. The *toriizori* is rather shallow but gives the slender blade a well-balanced *tachi-sugata*. In combination with the *kitae* in dense and fine *ko-itame* with plentiful of *ji-nie* and a faint *nie-utsuri* and a calm and elegant *suguha* as well as a *sugu-bōshi* with round *kaeri*, inevitably Yamashiro comes to mind and therein especially the Rai school.

But when you take a closer look at the *jiba* you see also some *nagare* areas along the fine and dense *ko-itame* and the *utsuri* tends to *shirake*. In addition, the *nioiguchi* is rather compact and is noticeably subdued and dull in places. In short, the *jiba* is not that bright and clear as we would expect it from a Rai work. So the *tachi* is a work of Ryōkai who was a Yamashiro smith too. As mentioned, the *jiba* of for example Kunitoshi (国俊), Kunimitsu (国光) and other Rai smiths would be clearer and brighter, the *nioiguchi* wider and more *nie* and *hataraki* would appear within the *ha*. Some also went for the Enju school (延寿). This is a sensitive *kantei* because the style is obviously close but the *bōshi* appears as *ō-maru* at the Enju school and mostly a *nijūba* is seen somewhere on the blade.

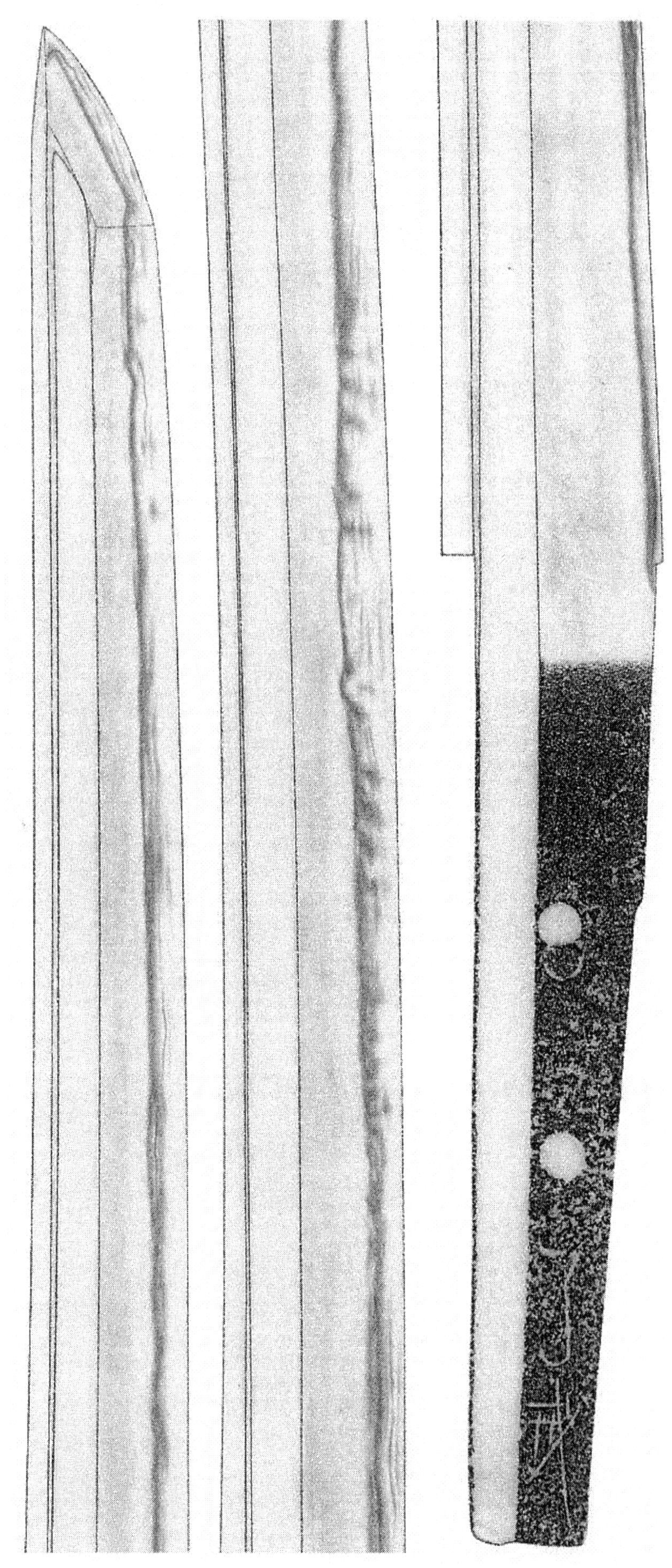

31.590 *tachi*
mei: Ryōkai (了戒)
nagasa 68,0 cm, *sori* 1,7 cm, *shinogi-zukuri*, *iori-mune*

ji: dense *ko-itame*, partially mixed with *masame* and a strong tendency to *nagare*, in addition plentiful of *ji-nie*, fine *chikei* and a *shirake-utsuri*
hamon: *suguha-chō* mixed with *ko-chōji*, *ko-gunome*, *ko-midare*, *ashi*, *yō*, *kinsuji* and *sunagashi*, the *nioiguchi* is clear but subdued in places, it is also full of *ko-nie*
bōshi: *sugu* with a *ko-maru-kaeri* which runs hardly back, also fine *hakikake* and *kinsuji*
horimono: on both sides a *bōhi* which runs with *kake-tōshi* through the tang

There is *funbari* and so we can assume that the blade is in its original length or is only somewhat shortened. The *sori* is deep and appears as *toriizori*. The *jigane* is a dense *ko-itame* and the *hamon* a *suguha* in *ko-nie-deki* with a clear *nioiguchi* which shows *Kyō-saka-ashi* around the middle of the *haki-omote* side. And the *bōshi* is *sugu* with a *ko-maru-kaeri*. Because of these characteristics, one should be able to arrive at the Rai school and because the blade is rather quiet, many went for Rai Kunitoshi (来国俊).

But when you take a closer look you see that the finely forged *jigane* shows also some *masame* and that not a Rai-typical *nie-utsuri* but a faint *shirake-utsuri* appears. The *nioiguchi* is even subdued and dull in places and the entire *jiba* looks weaker than we would expect it at Rai Kunitoshi. Ryōkai was a Rai smith and worked similar to Kunitoshi but because of the mentioned differences, it should be possible to differentiate the two smiths.

There were also some bids on Kunimitsu (来国光), Rai Kunitsugu (来国次) or Enju (延寿). Kunimitsu and Kunitsugu belong of course to the lineage of Kunitoshi but their *jiba* is noticeably more *nie*-loaden and the *jigane* stronger. In contrast, the Enju smiths did work very close to Ryōkai but their *hamon* would show less *hataraki* and the *nioiguchi* would be more compact and not partially but entirely subdued. In addition, the *bōshi* would appear as plain *ō-maru* and a *nijūba* would appear somewhere along the *hamon*.

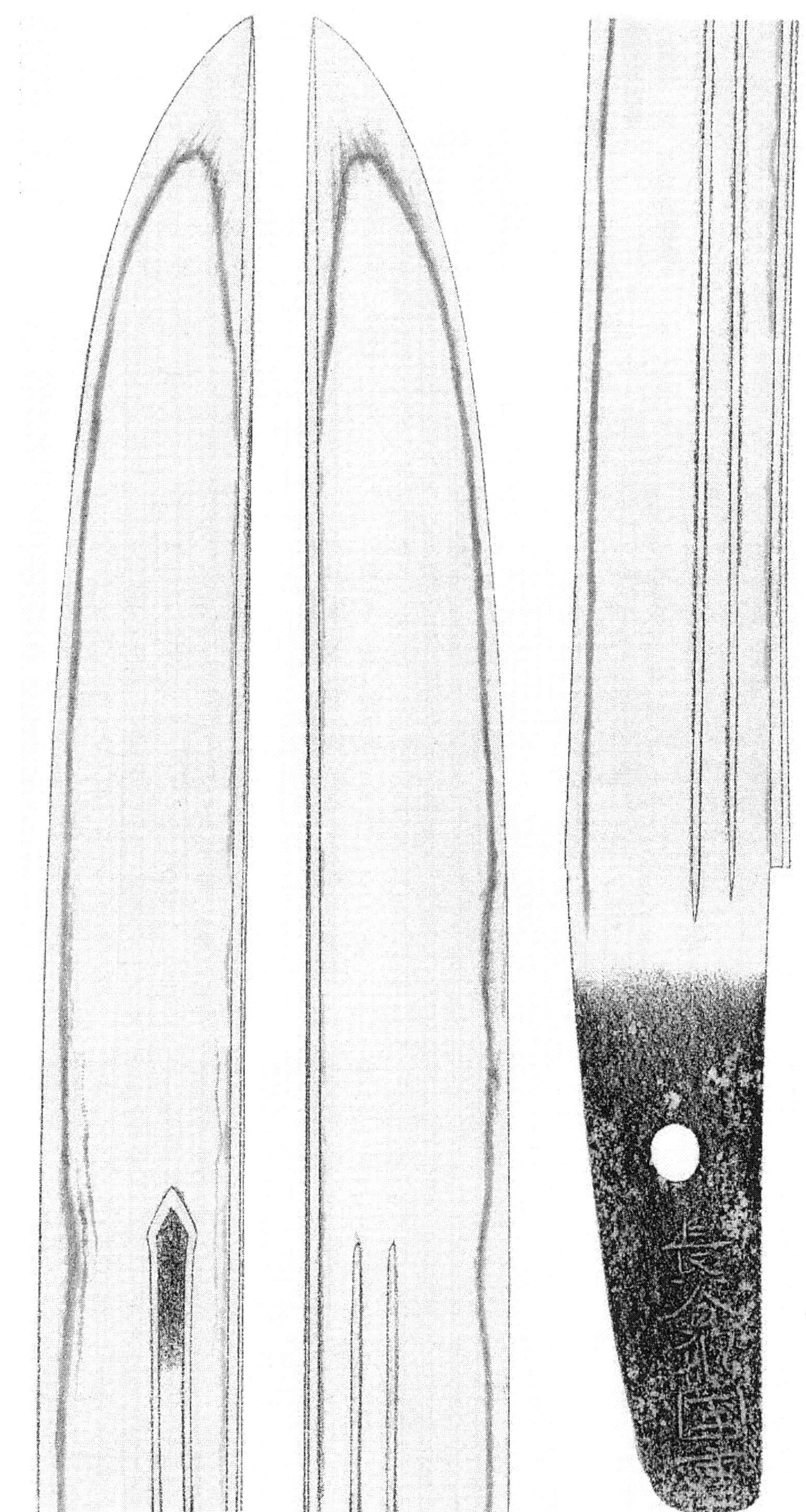

32.630 *wakizashi*
mei: Hasebe Kunishige (長谷部国重)
nagasa 32,4 cm, *sori* 0,3 cm, *hira-zukuri*, *mitsu-mune*

ji: standing-out *itame* mixed with *mokume* which tends to *masame-nagare* towards the *ha* and the *mune*, in addition *ji-nie* and *chikei*
hamon: *hoso-suguha* which tends to *notare*, also *hotsure* all over the blade, *ko-ashi*, plentiful of *nie*, *kinsuji* and *sunagashi*
bōshi: on both sides *sugu* with a round *kaeri*, *kinsuji* and *hakikake*, the *kaeri* runs back long
horimono: a *suken* is engraved on the *omote* side and *gomabashi* on the *ura* side

This is a *wakizashi* of Hasebe Kunishige in *suguha*. There are not many works like that extant by this smith but most of the participants grasped this and were nevertheless spot-on. But some bade also on one of the Nobukuni (信国) smiths. Well, this *hira-zukuri wakizashi* has a typical Enbun-Jōji-*sugata* with wide *mihaba* and thin *kasane* and such a shape is typical for the Hasebe school. The *kitae* is a standing-out mix of *itame* and *mokume* and even if it is not that obvious at the *kantei* blade, there is a tendency to *masame* towards the *ha* and the *mune*.

The *hamon* is *suguha* and due to the *masame* along the *ha*, it is accompanied by fine *hotsure*. The width of the *yakiba* does not increase towards the tip but is uniform all over the blade. The round *kaeri* – even if it is not that big as usually for this smith – runs back long with discontinuous *muneyaki* down to the base. Combining all these characteristics, it should not be too hard to arrive at Hasebe.

Like Nobukuni, also Rai Kunizane (来国真) or Kuninaga (国長, who went later to Settsu) made such Nanbokuchō-era *wakizashi* in the Hasebe-Yamashiro style, showing a standing-out *itame* and *mokume* mix. But Nobukuni´s *jigane* tends only to the *ha* to *masame* and is otherwise a dense, bright and fine *itame*.

But it has to be mentioned that there were hardly any other than the Hasebe smiths making such a thin *kasane* and a *bōshi* in such an elegant *ko-maru* and very long running back *kaeri*.

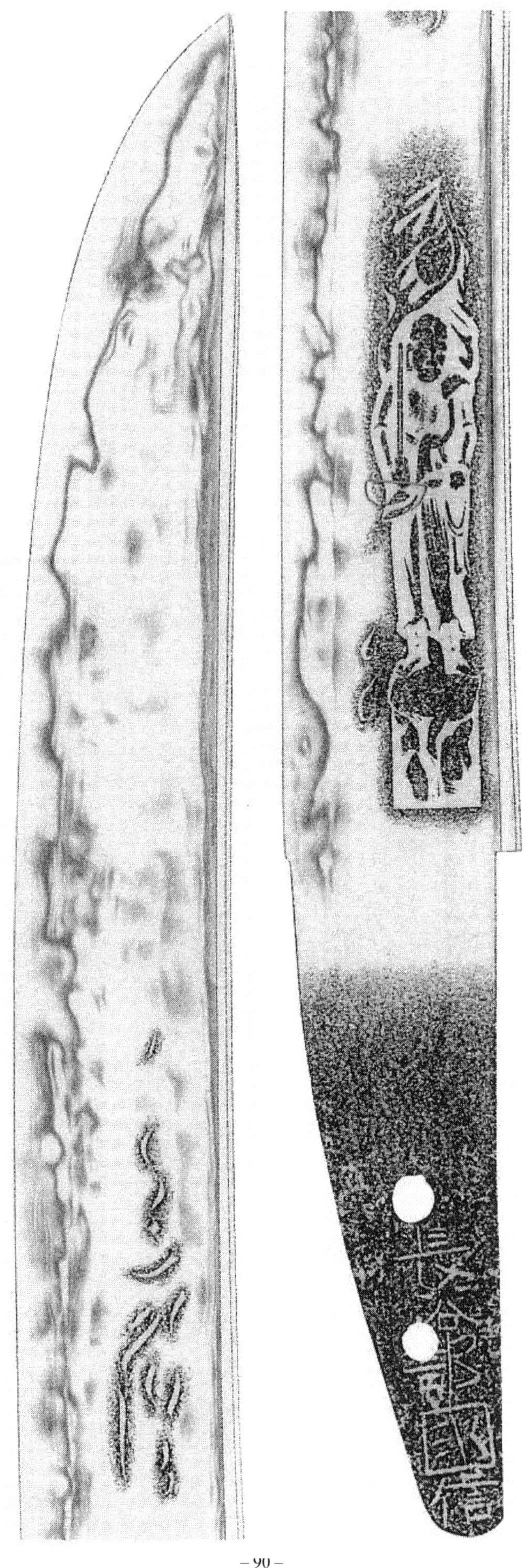

33.653 *wakizashi*
mei: Hasebe Kuninobu (長谷部国信)
nagasa 33,5 cm, *sori* 0,6 cm, *hira-zukuri*, *mitsu-mune*

ji: *itame* mixed with *mokume* which stands out and tends to *nagare* towards the *ha* and the *mune*, in addition *ji-nie* and fine *chikei*
hamon: mix of *ko-gunome*, *ko-notare*, angular elements and *yahazu*, in addition *ashi*, many thick *nie*, *kinsuji*, *sunagashi*, *tobiyaki*, from the base to the tip a continuous *muneyaki*, the *hamon* appears altogether as *hitatsura*
bōshi: *midare-komi* with a pointed *kaeri* on the *omote* side and a *ko-maru-kaeri* on the *ura* side, on both sides the *kaeri* connects with the *muneyaki*
horimono: a *bonji* and underneath a Fudō-Myōō is engraved on the *omote* side and a *gyō no kurikara* on the *ura* side

Because of the noticeably thin *kasane* of this *hira-zukuri wakizashi* (or if your want *sunnobi-tantō*), the *nagare* towards the *ha* and *mune*, the prominent *hitatsura* with *tobiyaki*, *yubashiri* and *muneyaki*, and the characteristical forging of the *hagane* which is probably the reason for the interrupted kind of tempering along the higher elements of the *yakiba*, it is not difficult to recognize that this is a Nanbokuchō-era work of Yamashiro´s Hasebe school.

The most outstanding smiths of that school were Kunishige (国重) and Kuninobu (国信). The majority of Kunishige´s works shows a *hamon* in *notare-gunome* but we also know interpretations consisting of angular and *yahazu*-like elements where the *hamon* runs in between relative low. This workmanship is considered as precursor of the later Ōei-Nobukuni (信国) and is sometimes also seen on works of Kunishige. Usually *horimono* (also simple ones) are rare for Hasebe but elaborate engravings like Fudō-Myōō and a *kurikara* like seen on the *kantei* blade or a *kenzaku* (羂索, the rope of Fudō-Myōō) or a *hata-hoko* (halberd with banner) are well found at Kuninobu, so this can be regarded as a characteristic of that smith.

Some bade on the contemporary Yamashiro smith Nobukuni (信国) or on Sōshū Hiromitsu (広光) who was active around the same time too. At the former, we would see a *hamon* basing on a lower *notare* and at the latter, the *hamon* would get wider towards the tip and show roundish so-called „*dango-chōji*" (団子丁子, lit. „dumpling *chōji*").

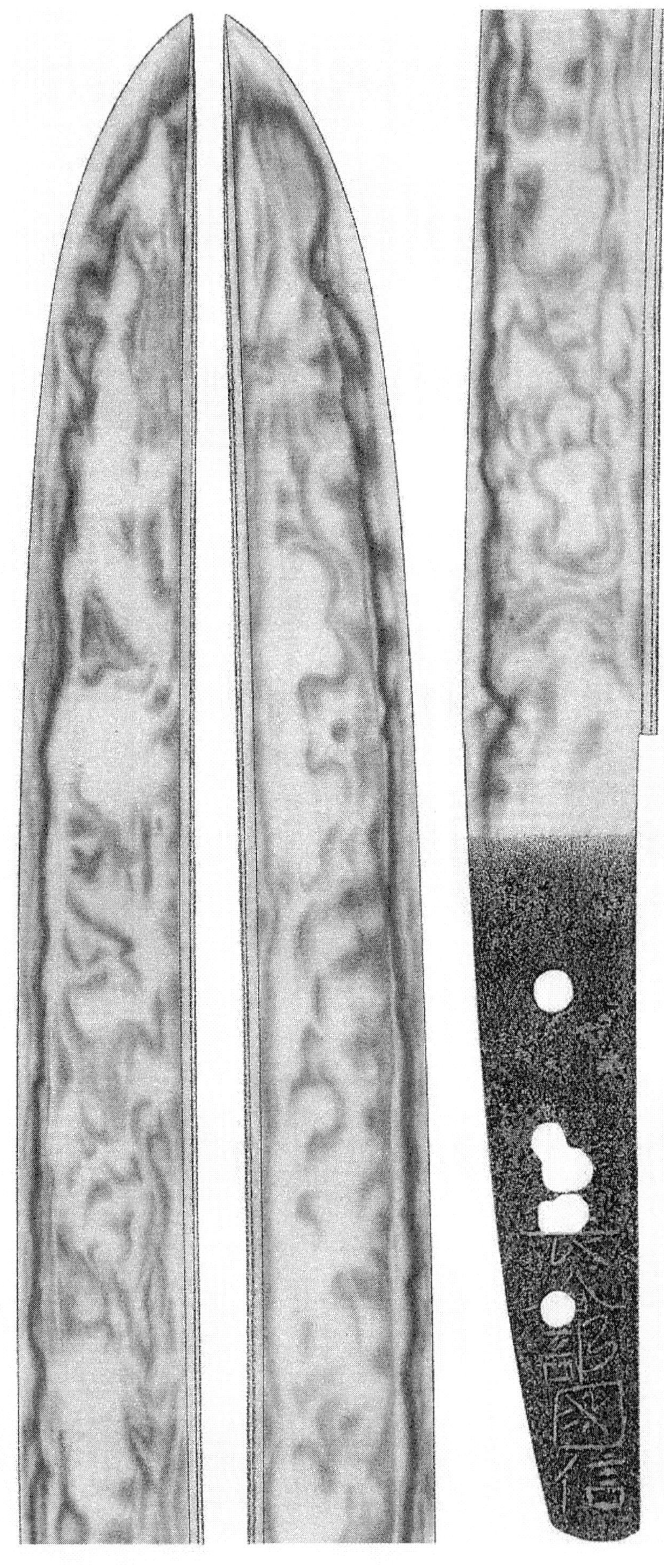

34.607 *wakizashi*
mei: Hasebe Kuninobu (長谷部国信)
nagasa 30,6 cm, *sori* 0,3 cm, *hira-zukuri, mitsu-mune*

ji: standing-out *itame-hada* mixed with *ō-itame* and *mokume*, *masame* towards *ha* and *mune*, in addition plentiful of *ji-nie* and many *chikei*
hamon: basing on a shallow *notare* partially mixed with *ko-notare*, *gunome*, and angular elements, thick *nioi*, many strong *nie*, *kinsuji*, *nie-suji* and *sunagashi*, *yubashiri* and *tobiyaki* all over the blade and *muneyaki*, so the entire *hamon* appears as *hitatsura*
bōshi: *midarekomi* with strong *hakikake*, the *omote* side appears as a kind of *yakitsume* and the *ura* side as *suguha-chō* with an *ō-maru* whose long *kaeri* connects with the *muneyaki*

The Hasebe school was active during the Nanbokuchō period, forged mostly a larger dimensioned *hada* with many *chikei*, and applied a vivid *hamon* which tends to *hitatsura*. Besides of Sōshū Hiromitsu (広光) and Akihiro (秋広), this was the typical style of the Hasebe school. Also the slightly elongated *sunnobi-tantō* or *hira-zukuri wakizashi* with broad *mihaba*, think *kasane* and shallow *sori*, i.e. a so-called „Enbun-Jōji-*sugata*" is typical for this school. But within this trend, the *kasane* of the Hasebe blades is even a bit thinner than usual, similar than works of contemporary Aoe and Hokke smiths. Hiromitsu and his colleagues on the other hand added more *chōji* and their *hamon* gets wider towards the tip. Their *bōshi* appears also in a pointed manner. At the Hasebe school, usually a *notare* or *ko-notare* mixed with *gunome-midare* is seen which has an evenly wide *yakiba* from top to bottom.

When you take a closer look you will find more or less strong *masame* towards the *ha* and the *mune*, especially towards the *ha*. This linear forging structure makes visible the connection of the *hagane* and *kawagane* and as a result, long and conspicuous *kinsuji* and *nie-suji* appear.

There are also small blades with a *nagasa* of around 7 *sun* (~ 21,2 cm) extant by Kuninobu but also noticeably larger pieces which measure around 1 *shaku* and 3 or 4 *sun* (39,4 ~ 42,4 cm). His *midare* is a *gunome* with a flat *notare* in between and angular as well as *yahazu* elements. The *kantei* blade doesn´t show this feature very clearly and so also bids on Kunishige were counted as *atari* this time.

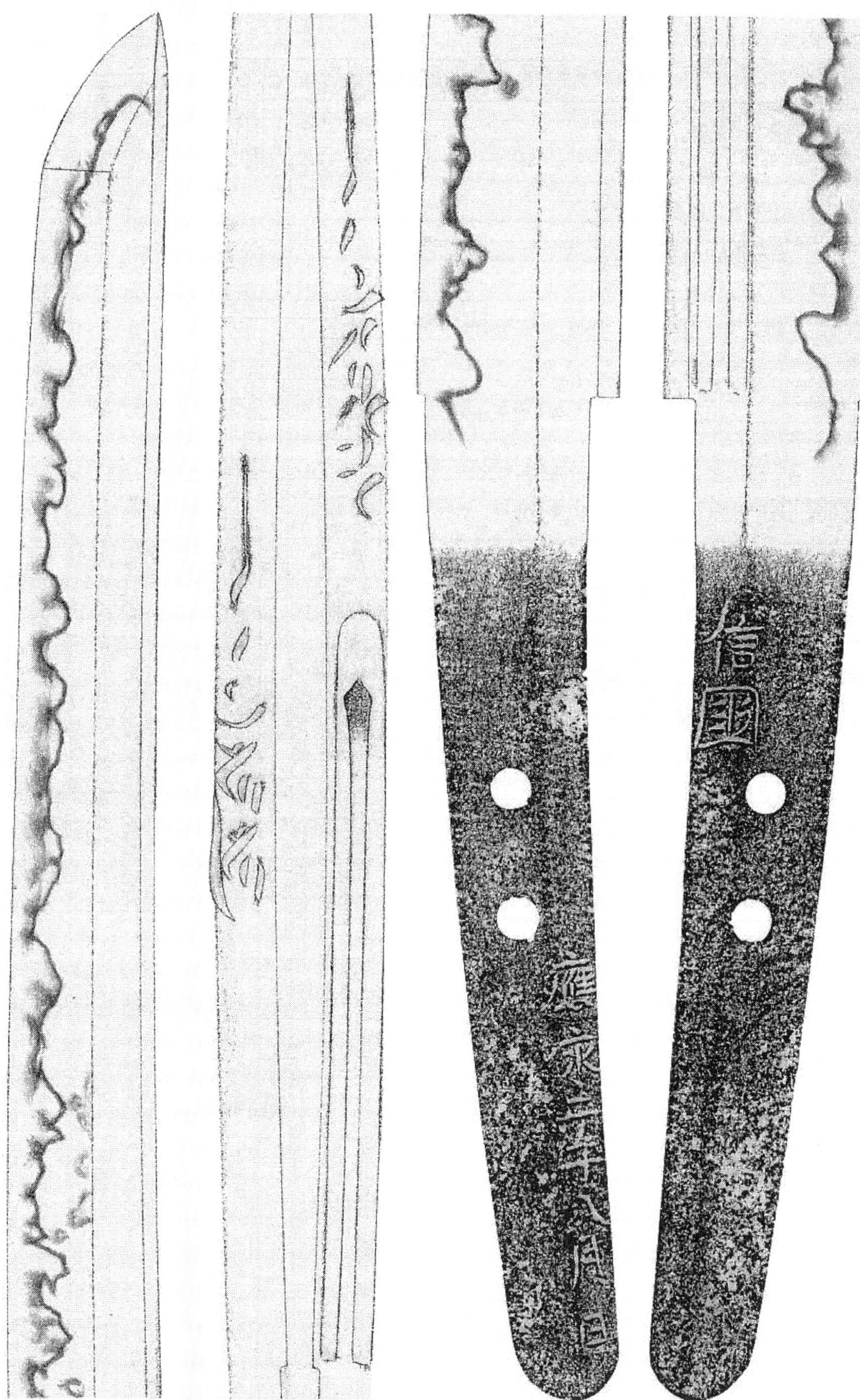
信国

35.635 *tachi*
mei: Nobukuni (信国)
Ōei ninen hachigatsu-hi (応永二年八月日, „a day in the eighth month Ōei two [= 1395]")
nagasa 68,2 cm, *sori* 2,4 cm, *shinogi-zukuri*, *iori-mune*

ji: standing-out *itame-hada* with partial *nagare*, *ji-nie*, also some *tobiyaki*
hamon: *notare-gunome* with *yahazu-ba* and pairs of *gunome*, in addition *ashi*, *yō*, plentiful of *ko-nie* and some *sunagashi*
bōshi: *midare-komi* which tends to *ō-maru* on the *haki-omote* and to *hakikake* with a short *kaeri* on the *ura*
horimono: a long *bonji* and a *suken* as relief in a *koshibi* is engraved on the *omote* side, the *ura* side shows just a long *bonji*

This blade has a normal *mihaba* and *kissaki* but the *kasane* is relative thick, and when we combine this with the *sakizori* then we are in the early Muromachi period, i.e. around Ōei (応永, 1394-1428). Dated works of the 1st gen. Nobukuni go back to the middle Nanbokuchō period, or to be more precise to the Enbun (延文, 1356-1361) and Jōji eras (貞治, 1362-1368). Somewhat later, between Shitoku (至徳, 1384-1387), Kakyō (嘉慶, 1387-1389) and Ōei, there was a shift in generations whereas the later smith who worked mostly around Ōei is commonly called „Ōei-Nobukuni".

Regarding the workmanship, Ōei-Nobukuni continued the style of the 1st gen., which means a *suguha* with compact *nioiguchi*, or worked like seen at the *kantei* blade in a *gunome-midare*-based *hamon* with some peculiarities. The latter are for example *gunome* elements arranged to pairs, whereas the pair stands out in a *yahazu*-like manner. And the *midare* areas between these elements tend to a shallow *ko-notare* or sometimes also to a plain *gunome*. Such an interpretation can already be seen on dated works from the Eitoku (永徳, 1381-1384) and Meitoku era (明徳, 1390-1394). This style was then succeeded by the Ōei-period Nobukuni smiths Genzaemon no Jō Nobukuni (源左衛門尉信国) and Shikibu no Jō Nobukuni (式部丞信国). Basically, this style was either applied in a regular, repeated manner all over the blade or freely and just in places. And in general we can say that interpretations in *midare* show more *ko-nie* and more conspicious *hataraki* like *kinsuji* and *sunagashi* than works in *suguha*. When you see the *nagare* areas on this *tachi* you will be able to trace back the origins of the school, namely the 1st gen. Nobukuni was according to transmission the grandson of Hisanobu (久信), who in turn was the son of Ryōkai (了戒).

Some just bade on „Nobukuni" but as such a workmanship is not seen at the 1st gen. and so the participants were asked to substantiate their bid at the next round, for example by „late Nanbokuchō to Ōei" or just by „Ōei". Some few went also for the contemporary Bizen smiths Morimitsu (盛光) and Yasumitsu (康光). The *sugata* is matching for Ōei-Bizen of course but we would expect more *mokume* and a *midare-utsuri* and the *bōshi* would appear as *midare-komi* with a small and pointed *kaeri* which doesn´t run back very long. Also the *hamon* would tend more clearly to *nioi-deki* and there wouldn´t appear that strong *nie* along the *jiba*.

Incidentally, each generation Nobukuni added peculiar but always skillfully engraved *horimono*. They can also be used to nail down a specific generation.

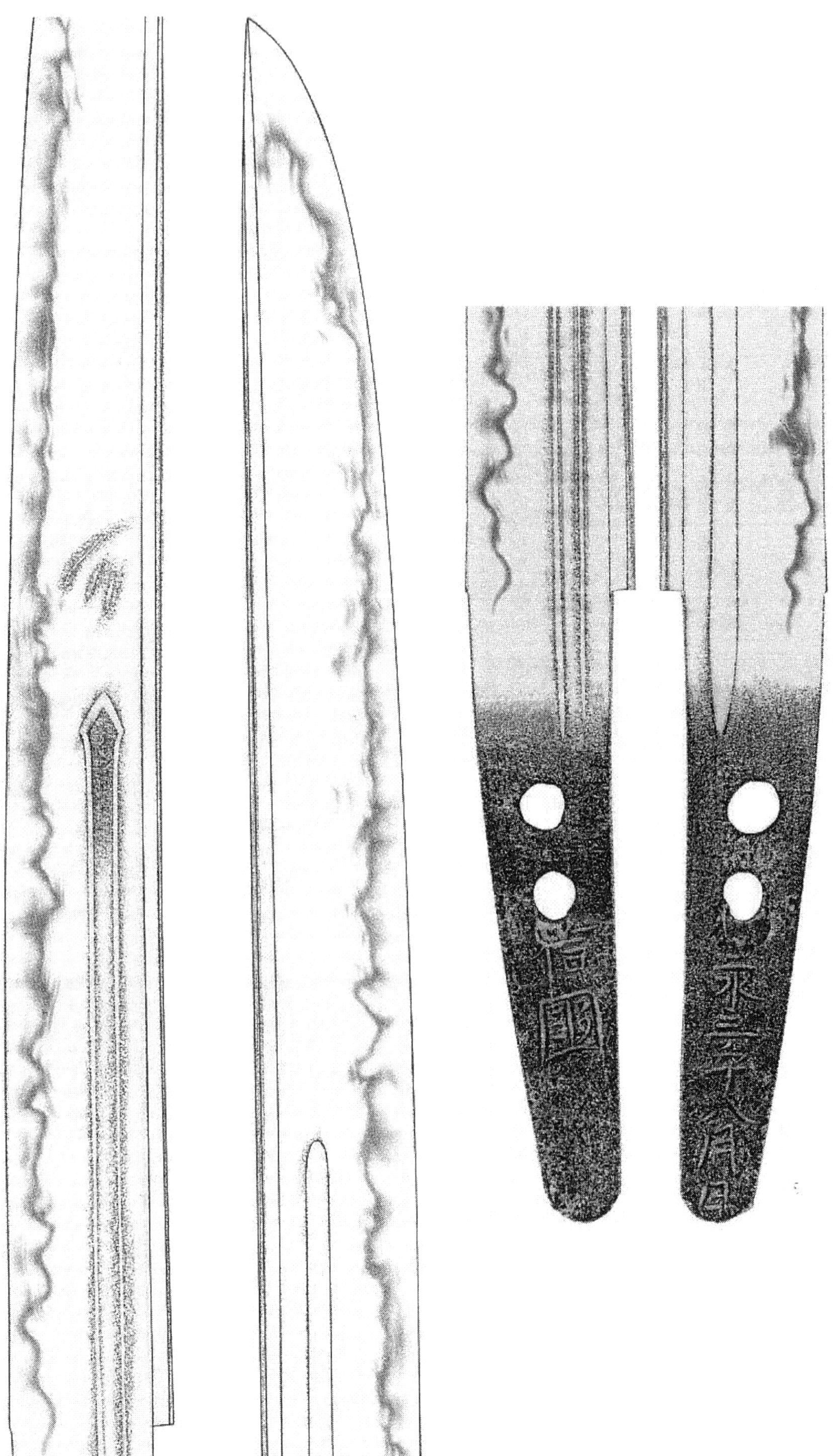

36.648k *tantō*
mei: Nobukuni (信国) – Ōei sannen hachigatsu-hi (応永三年八月日, „a day in the eighth month Ōei three [= 1396]")
nagasa 28,33 cm *sori* 0,21 cm *moto-haba* 2,4 cm *moto-kasane* 0,65 cm
nakago-nagasa 10,0 cm only very shallow *nakago-sori*

hira-zukuri, *mitsu-mune*, normal *mihaba*, the blade appears as *sunnobi* and shows a *sakizori*. The *jigane* is a altogether densely forged *itame* mixed with *mokume*. *Ji-nie* and *chikei* appear. The *hamon* and the *bōshi* can be seen on the *oshigata*. In addition *hotsure*, *yubashiri*, *ashi* and *yō*. The *nioiguchi* is tight and shows plentiful of *nie*, *kinsuji* and *sunagashi*. There are *gomabashi* and a *suken* engraved on the *omote* and a *koshibi* with *kake-nagashi* on the *ura* side. The tang is *ubu*, has a roundish *kurijiri*, shallow *katte-sagari yasurime* and two *mekugi-ana*. There is a *niji-mei* chislled on the *sashi-omote* side centrally below the *mekugi-ana* [Translators note: It is not mentioned which *mekugi-ana*.] The date signature on the *ura* side is chiselled on the same position.

This *tantō* has a normal *mihaba*, is *sunnobi* and shows a *sakizori* along the upper area, so we can place it to the early Muromachi period, i.e. Ōei (応永, 1394-1428). The *jigane* of Ōei-Nobukuni is a dense *itame* with fine *ji-nie* and *chikei* which shows the typical characteristic of Yamashiro-*mono* but he combines it also with some *nagare*. The workmanship of the 1st gen. Nobukuni which was active around Enbun (延文, 1356-1361) and Jōji (貞治, 1362-1368) orientates even more towards Yamashiro, that means *suguha*, but he also applied some Sōshū-like *notare* in the style of Sadamune (貞宗). So Ōei-Nobukuni continued these approaches and enlarged them by a *midareba* in *gunome-chō*. The latter consists of a pair of *yahazu*-like *gunome* whereas the areas between these elements lower noticeably. That means the *yahazu*-like *gunome* pairs are connected by a *ko-notare*. This can continue all over the blade or appear more freely just in places.

In the case of Ōei-Nobukuni´s *suguha*, he tempered a rather compact *nioiguchi* with *ko-nie* and at an interpretation like here in *midareba*, considerably more *ha-nie* appear than at a *suguha*. Also *hataraki* like *kinsuji* and *sunagashi* occur more frequently on a *midareba*. In conclusion we can say that the precursors of such a *midareba* can already be seen on late Nanbokuchō-period Nobukuni works with datings of the Eitoku (永徳, 1381-1384) and Meitoku eras (明徳, 1390-1394) but were later perfected by Ōei-Nobukuni. The *bōshi* of Ōei-Nobukuni is in the case of *suguha* also *sugu* with a *ko-maru-kaeri* and at a *midareba* a *midare-komi* with a *ko-midare-kaeri* or with a pointed *kaeri*.

Each generation Nobukuni was a skillful engraver and so also Ōei-Nobukuni added various *horimono*, from a simple *bonji* and *suken* to more complex motifs like the *shiketsu* (四橛, see page 239) or the *kurikara*. His tip of the tang is a shallow *kurijiri* and the *yasurime* are shallow *katte-sagari*. The *niji-mei* „Nobukuni" is chiselled on *tantō* and *hira-zukuri wakizashi* centrally and below the *mekugi-ana* on the *sashi-omote* side. Often a date signature is found in the *ura* side.

The vast majority bade *atari* on Ōei-Nobukuni but some also went particularily for Saemon no Jō Nobukuni (左衛門尉信国) and Shikibu no Jō Nobukuni (式部丞信国). Well, the *jiba* shows all the characteristics of Ōei-period Nobukuni smiths but the signature does not match with the two smiths. As the workmanship is quite close, a bid on „Ōei-period Nobukuni" was enough this time.

Some also bade on the 1st gen. Nobukuni which was counted as *dōzen*. As mentioned, he was active earlier and applied either a Yamashiro-typical *suguha* or a *notare* in the style of the Sōshū tradition but not a *midareba*. And due to his eralier artistic period, we would expect a typical Enbun-Jōji-*sugata*.

Besides of *atari* and *dōzen* there were also some who reckoned it as a work of Kashū Sanekage (加州真景). We know a date signature of the sixth year of Jōji (1367) from him, that means from the heyday of the Nanbokuchō period. Many of his *tantō* and *hira-zukui wakizashi* are *sunnobi* over a length of 9 *sun* (~ 27,3 cm) with a broad *mihaba*, a relative thin *kasane* and a shallow *sori*. His *jigane* is a large *itame-mokume* mixed with *nagare* which stands-out all over the blade. In addition, his steel is mostly blackish. The *hamon* is a *notare-chō* mixed with *gunome* or consists of narrow and connected *gunome*. *Ha-nie* and conspicious *sunagashi* appear and a *midare* like it is seen on the *kantei* blade is not found at Kashū Sanekage. Also the mentioned signature had to be beared in mind because he never signed with a *niji-mei* but always either with „Kashū-jū Sanekage" or „Fujiwara Sanekage".

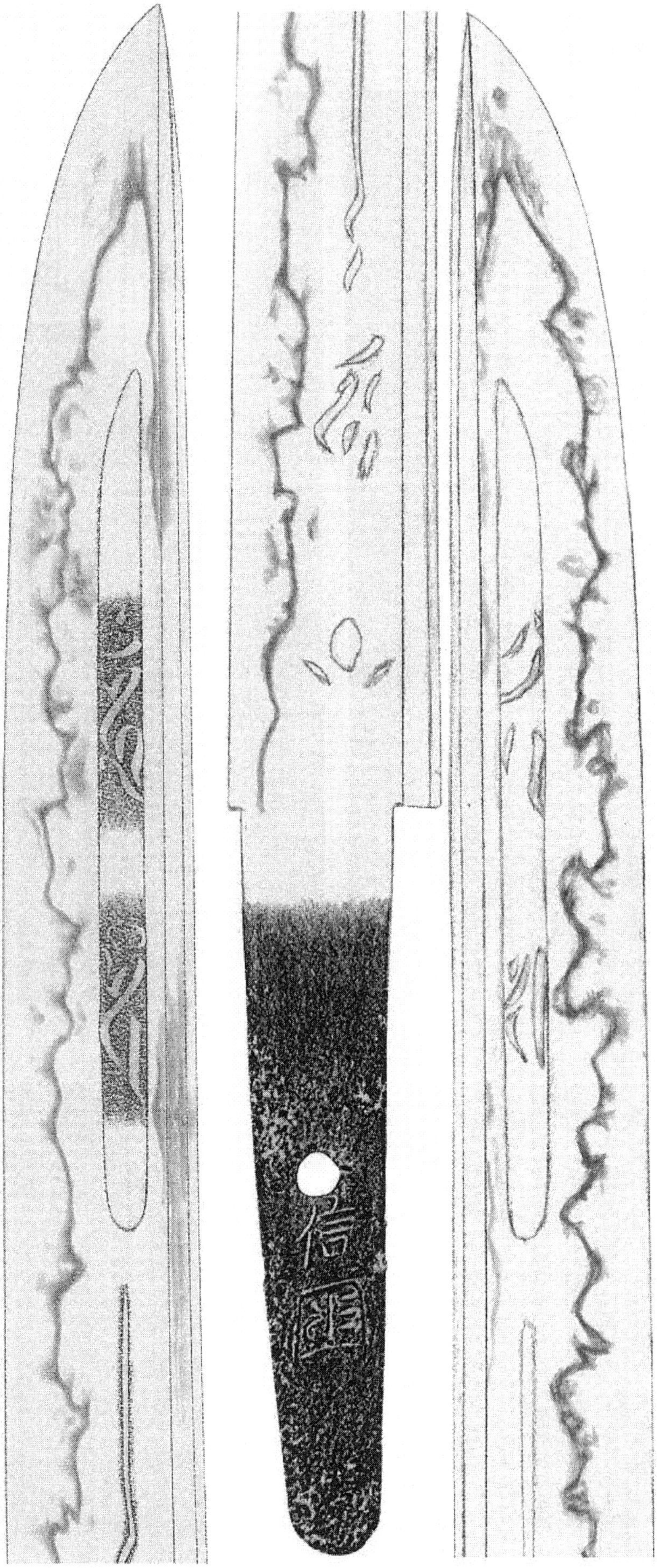

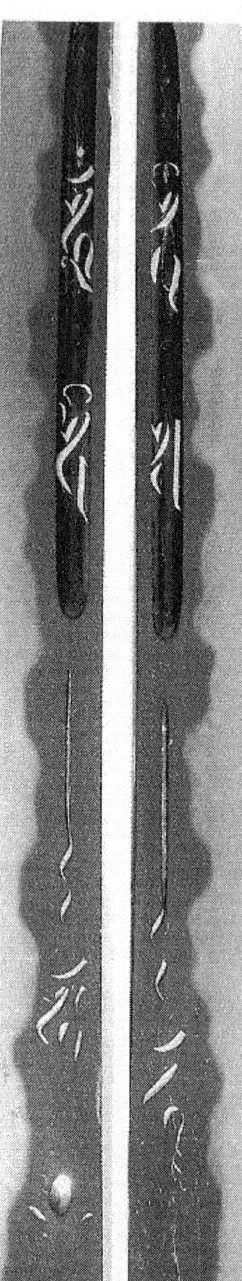

37.633 *wakizashi*
mei: Nobukuni (信国)
nagasa 30,6 cm, only a little *sori*, *hira-zukuri*, *mitsu-mune*

ji: *ko-itame* mixed with *mokume* which tends to *nagare* towards the *ha*, plentiful of *ji-nie* and *chikei*

hamon: based on *gunome-midare* and mixed with *ko-gunome*, *ko-notare* and *togari*, also *yahazu*-like *midare* of a pair of connected *gunome* elements can be seen, in addition *ashi*, *yō*, much *nie*, fine *sunagashi*, *yubashiri* and many *muneyaki*, the *nioiguchi* is bright

bōshi: on the *omote* a shallow *notare*, the *ura* side begins with a *suguha*, but both sides rund back long with *hakikake* and a pointed *kaeri* and connect with the discontinuous *muneyaki*

horimono: on both sides a *katana-hi* with *maru-dome*, in this *hi* two negative *bonji* are engraved as relief and below the *hi*, a long *bonji* is added which shows an additional *rendai* base on the *ura* side

The Nobukuni smith which is counted as 1st gen. was active in the heyday of the Nanbokuchō period, namely between Enbun (延文, 1356-1361) and Jōji (貞治, 1362-1368), but there were until the early Muromachi period successively several Nobukuni generations and smiths active. The character for „Kuni" on this blade has a peculiarity because the inner part is chiselled in mirror writing. Because of this, we can attribute the work to the Ōei-era Saemon no Jō Nobukuni (左衛門尉信国).

The blade has an elongated *nagasa* in proportion to the *mihaba*, a thick *kasane* and a shallow *sori*. This thick *kasane* combined with a *hira-zukuri wakizashi-sugata* is the first hint for an Ōei-era Nobukuni. Ōei-Nobukuni´s *hamon* is a compact *nioiguchi* and can either appear as *suguha* or as *gunome*-based *midareba*. At these later Nobukuni smiths, the *gunome* were arranged as pairs to *yahazu*-like elements leaving some shallow valleys in between. This characteristic can be seen to a certain extent on the *kantei* blade too. Interpretations in *midareba* show more and stronger *nie* than *suguha* works and also the *hataraki* within the *ha* are more conspicious. The *jigane* is a *ko-itame* with *ji-nie* and *chikei* and even there is a fine Yamashiro-like *jigane*, there are also some mixed-in *nagare* towards the *ha*. This leads you to the Ryōkai lineage (了戒) of the Yamashiro tradition.

Then we have the *kasane-bori* (重ね彫, several different *horimono* on one blade). Each generation Nobukuni was known for excellent engravings and this is of course valid for Ōei-Nobukuni too. We know several blads which show different, sometimes elaborate *horimono* combined with *bonji*.

It seems that all these characteristics were grasped because most of the participants got an *atari* at the first round. During the Ōei era, „Saemon no Jō" and „Shikibu no Jō Nobukuni" (式部丞) were famous but a differentiation on the basis of the workmanship and signature of just „Nobukuni" is hard. So it was enough to bid on „Ōei-Nobukuni". But some also went for the earlier 1st gen. Nobukuni. But here the *kasane* would be thinner and the blade would show either a *suguha* in Yamashiro tradition or a *notare* in the Sōshū tradition, but not such a *gunome-midare*.

38.593 *tantō*
mei: Nobukuni (信国)
nagasa 28,8 cm, only a little *sori*, *hira-zukuri*, *mitsu-mune*

ji: dense *itame* with *nagare* towards the *ha*, plentiful of *ji-nie*, fine *chikei*, *nie-utsuri*, the steel is clear
hamon: *chū-suguha* with some *notare*, rather compact and clear *nioiguchi* with much *ko-nie*, partially the *nie* are quite strong, in addition *hotsure*, *kuichigaiba*, fine *kinsuji* and *sunagashi*
bōshi: *sugu* with a rather long *ko-maru-kaeri* and some *hakikake*
horimono: a *shin no kurikara* as relief in a *hitsu* on the *omote* and a *suken* with *kake-nagashi* on the *ura*

The blade has a wide *mihaba*, is *sunnobi*, has a little *sori* and a thin *kasane*, that means it can be placed into the Nanbokuchō period. Some also reckoned it as a Keichō-*shintō* work and went for Horikawa Kunihiro (堀川国広), the 1st gen. Yasutsugu (康継) or the 1st gen. Hizen Tadayoshi (忠吉) at the first round. From the point of view of shape this is quite understandable, but at Keichō-*shintō*, the *kasane* would be noticeably thicker.

The workmanship of the Nanbokuchō-era Nobukuni, who was active around Enbun (延文, 1356-1361) and Jōji (貞治, 1362-1368), can be basically divided into two groups. The first adapts the interpretations of Sadamune (貞宗), that means we find a *notare-chō* with plentiful of *nie* in *ji* and *ha* and conspicious *hataraki* like *chikei* and *kinsuji*. The other orientates towards the Kyōto roots, that means we find an interpretation in *suguha* in *ko-nie-deki* with a more compact *nioiguchi*. So the latter works are more calm and classical. A typical characteristic of Nobukuni is the *nagare*, especially towards the *ha*. This feature shows that he came from Yamashiro´s Ryōkai lineage (了戒).

Nobukuni focused rather on traditional *horimono*. There are simple but also elaborate engravings but almost any blade shows some kind of *horimono*. Anyway, each generation Nobukuni was a skillful engraver.

The *meikan* lists the 1st gen. Nobukuni around Kenmu (建武, 1334-1338) but there are no works extant which could be dated back that far. The oldest extant date signature is by the way from the third year of Enbun (1358) and it is nowadays assumed that these Enbun and similar works go back to the actual 1st gen. Nobukuni, i.e. there was no generation before him and the Kenmu era is just a too early assumption. Furthermore, blades with date signatures of the Kōan (康安, 1361-1362) and Jōji era (貞治, 1362-1368) show still the same signature style (which is by the way the style seen on the *kantei* blade). In short, this *tantō* is probably a work of the 1st gen. Nobukuni. But at the *kantei*, the generation question was put aside and it was enough to bid on „Nobukuni“ and „Nanbokuchō“. Or in other words, most did recognize the somewhat earlier production time but bade just on Nobukuni but as the lineage was active until the Muromachi period, this was insufficient and a narrowing-down of the time was necessary.

Some went also for Rai Kunitoshi (来国俊), Rai Kunimitsu (来国光) or Rai Kunitsugu (来国次). These bids might go back to the *suguha* in *ko-nie-deki* and the *nie-utsuri* but at Kunitoshi, we wouldn´t expect an Enbun-Jōji-*sugata* at *tantō* and at Kunimitsu or Kunitsugu – who did make such larger dimensioned blades – an *uchizori* or no *sori* at all. In addition, Rai Kunitsugu applied a wide *midareba* to his larger *tantō* and a *suguha* is only found on his smaller *tantō*.

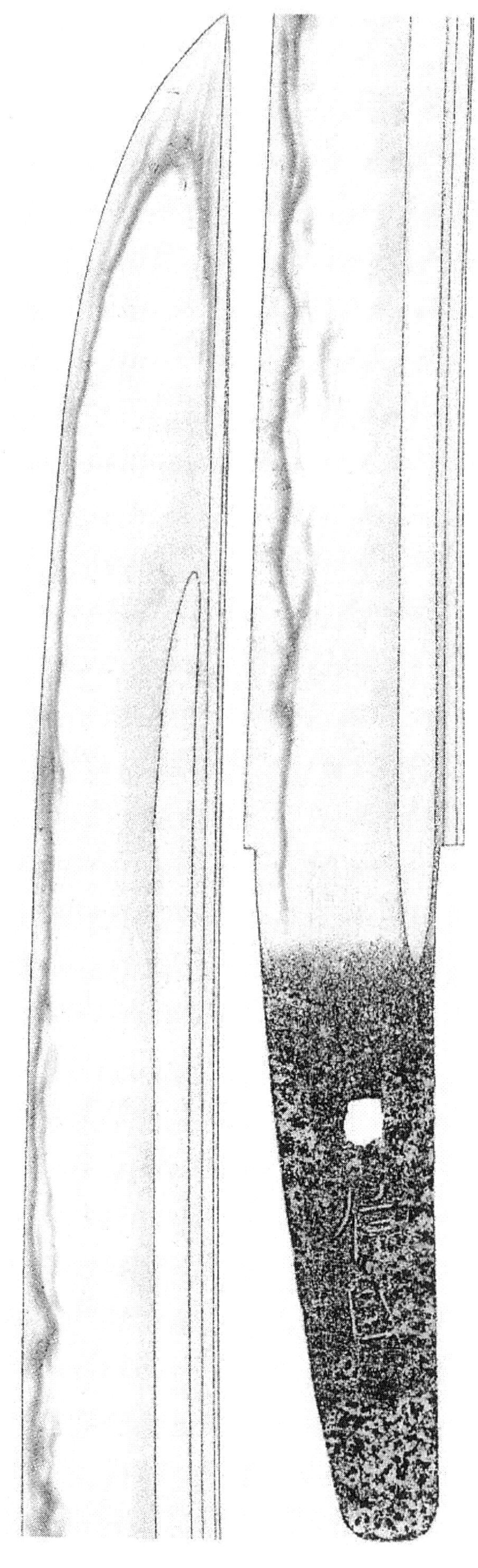

39.628 *wakizashi*
mei: Nobukuni (信国)
nagasa 34,3 cm, *sori* 0,3 cm, *hira-zukuri*, *mitsu-mune*

ji: somewhat standing-out *itame* mixed with *mokume* and *nagare*, in addition plentiful of fine *ji-nie*, much *chikei*, and a *nie-utsuri*
hamon: the lower half bases on a *notare* mixed with *gunome* which turns towards the tip to a *hoso-suguha-chō* with some *ko-notare*, in addition many *ko-nie*, *kinsuji* and *sunagashi*, also some *yubashiri* appear on the lower half
bōshi: almost *suguha-chō* on the *omote* side, the *ura* tends somewhat to *midare-komi*, both sides end in a *ko-maru-kaeri* with *hakikake* which runs back
horimono: on both sides a *katana-hi* which runs with *kake-nagashi* into the tang, there are traces of a *soebi* on the base of the *ura* side

It is said that the 1st gen. Nobukuni was either the son or grandson of Ryō Hisanobu (了久信). Ryō Hisanobu in turn was the son of Ryōkai (了解). So Nobukuni continued at one hand the traditional *suguha* of the Rai school but as he was together with Osafune Motoshige (元重) and Hōjōji Kunimitsu (法成寺国光) one of the „Three Students of Sadamune", he was also strongly Sōshū influenced.

The *kantei* blade has a wide *mihaba*, is elongated and has a thin *kasane*, all characteristical features of the middle Nanbokuchō period. The *itame* comes with plentiful of *ji-nie*, much *chikei* and a *nie-utsuri*. The *notare*-like *hamon* shows strong *ha-nie*, *kinsuji*, *sunagashi*, and *yubashiri*. The *bōshi* has a *ko-maru-kaeri* with *hakikake*. That means we see at a glance all typical characteristics of this smith as well as a conspicious *nagare* towards the *ha* on the *sashi-ura*. Because of the thinner *kasane*, a result of repeated polishing, one might think that this is a work of the Hasebe school and also from the point of quality there would not be a big difference. But at Hasebe, we would expect *nagare* also towards the *mune* and some *mokume* in between the two *nagare* areas. Also conspicious *tobiyaki* and *yubashiri* would appear. The *bōshi* would be more roundish and the *kaeri* would continue with the *muneyaki* and go down until the base of the blade.

Incidentally, the 1st gen. Nobukuni was a skillful *horimono* artist who learned this art from Daishinbō (大進房), a famous *horimono* carver himself and student of Shintōgo Kunimitsu (a theory says that „Daishinbō" was the Buddhist name of Kunimitsu´s son Kuniyasu [国泰]). There are hardly any Nobukuni blades extant without *horimono* wereas most show a *katana-hi*, *futasuji-ji* or rather simple carvings like a *suken* for example. But this Nobukuni added sometimes also a *kurikara* or *hatahoko* (halberd with banner) in the *hitsu*.

Bizen

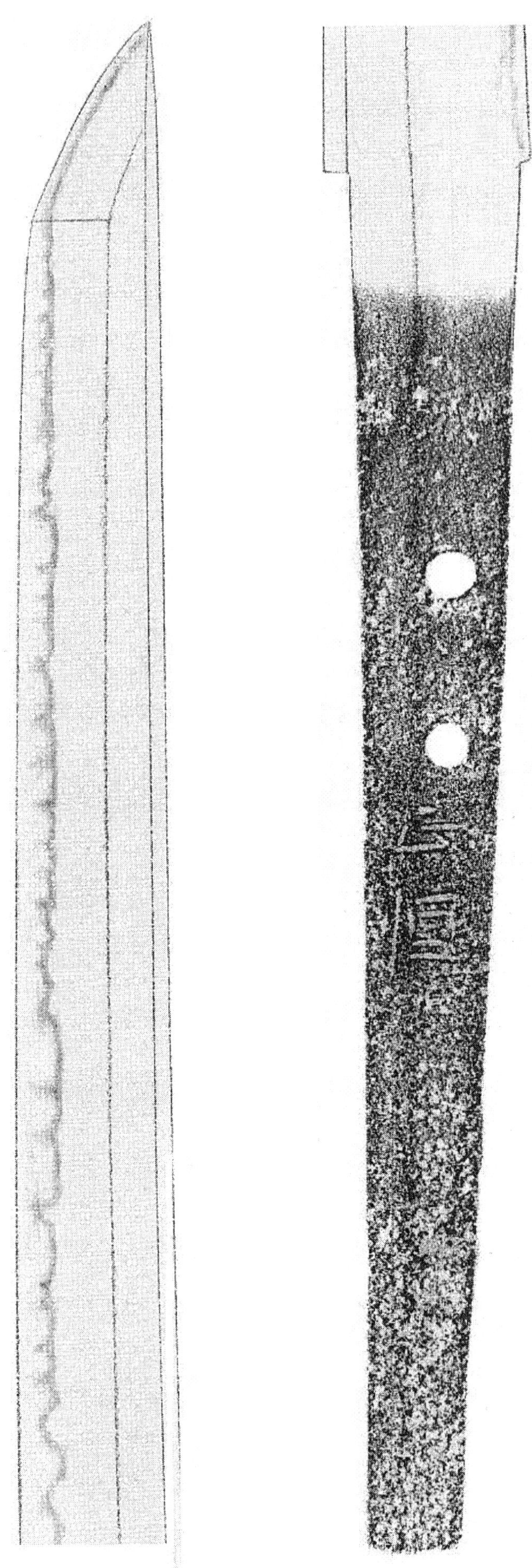

40.664 *tachi*
mei: Masatsune (正恒)
nagasa 71,9 cm, *sori* 1,3 cm, *shinogi-zukuri*, *iori-mune*

ji: dense *ko-itame* mixed with some *ō-hada*, *ji-nie*, *chikei* and *jifu-utsuri*
hamon: *ko-chōji-midare* in *nie-deki* based on *suguha*, mixed with *ko-midare* and partially with *chōji* with larger heads and also some angular *gunome*, in addition, *ashi*, *yō*, *kinsuji* and *sunagashi*
bōshi: *notare-komi* which runs out as *yakitsume*

This is a *jūyō-bijutsuhin-tachi* by Ko-Bizen Masatsune. It shows a dense and finely forged *ko-itame* and a *ko-chōji hamon* typical for Masatsune which is rather „modern" for Ko-Bizen. The heads of the *chōji* are noticeably larger on the upper half of the *haki-ura* side and the *chōji* are mixed with broader and angular *gunome* elements. That means all in all we have a rather flamboyant interpretation for Ko-Bizen and so some went for Nagamitsu (長光) or Motoshige (元重). Well, the blade has a relative shallow *sori*, is slender and ends in a small *ko-kissaki*, that means it could pass for a late Kamakura work. But the *sori* bends down towards the tip and there is *jifu-utsuri* with dark *antei* which goes beyond the *shinogi* and appears even along the *mune* in places. This makes it clear that we are not later than in the early Kamakura period. In addition, the *hamon* is considerably more narrow along the first 10 cm and is full of *nie* and *kinsuji*. These are typical characteristics for Ko-Bizen, Ko-Hōki and Ko-Aoe and are another hint that we are in the late Heian or early Kamakura period.

In the case of a late Kamakura-period Bizen work we would expect a *sori* which increases again towards the tip and a *midare-utsuri*. And in the case of a *jifu-utsuri*, the dark *antai* areas would always stay below of the *shinogi*. And at a flamboyant *chōji*, there would be some *gunome* with round and not angular *yakigashira*.

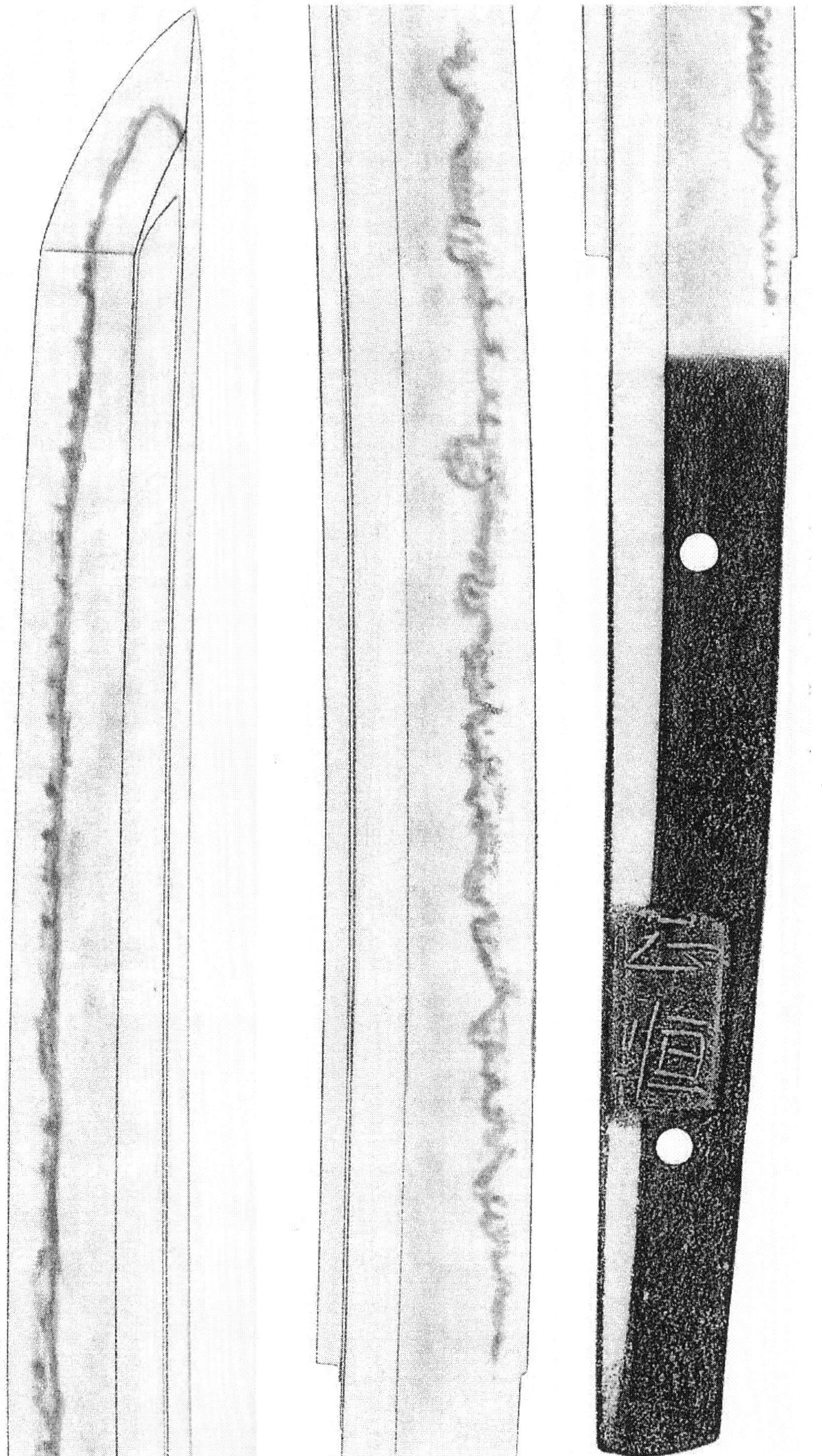

41.631 *katana*
gaku-mei: Masatsune (正恒)
nagasa 68,2 cm, *sori* 2,4 cm, *shinogi-zukuri*, *iori-mune*

ji: dense *itame* with *ji-nie*, fine *chikei* and *jifu-utsuri*
hamon: a kind of *chōji* towards the base which is mixed with *ko-gunome* and on the *ura* side with large-headed *chōji*, the *yakiba* shows also noticeable ups and downs in this area, the upper half appears as *suguha* with *ko-midare* and *ko-chōji* which is rather wide and mixed with plentiful of *ashi*, *yō* and *nie*
bōshi: *sugu* with a *ko-maru-kaeri*
horimono: on both sides a *bōhi* which runs with *kake-nagashi* into the tang

This is a *katana* with a *gaku-mei* of the Ko-Bizen smith Masatsune. The style of the Ko-Bizen school varies according to the production time and so the workmanship of the numerous smiths is quite diversified. Most assume that Ko-Bizen stands for a narrow *yakihaba* based on *ko-midare* but there are also some Ko-Bizen works with a broad, flamboyant *hamon* and it might be said that this variety is a characteristic of this group of smiths. So one should see the *kantei* blade with this in mind.

The blade has a wide *mihaba*, not much tapering, the *sori* increases towards the tip and the *kissaki* tends to an *ikubi-kissaki*. The *jigane* is fine and clear and shows *jifu-utsuri* with dark *antai*. The latter characteristics speak for Bizen and if you take a look at the *hamon*, you will see that the upper half in classical *ko-midare* shows the Ko-Bizen, and the lower half with the larger-headed *chōji* the Fukuoka-Ichimonji style. Towards the base and tip also homogenous *ha-nie* appear and the *hamon* is generally rather *nie*-loaden.

The lower half leaded some astray and they thought it is a later work but the *ko-nie* all over the blade were the keypoint and with them in mind, it shouldn´t be too hard to arrive at Masatsune.

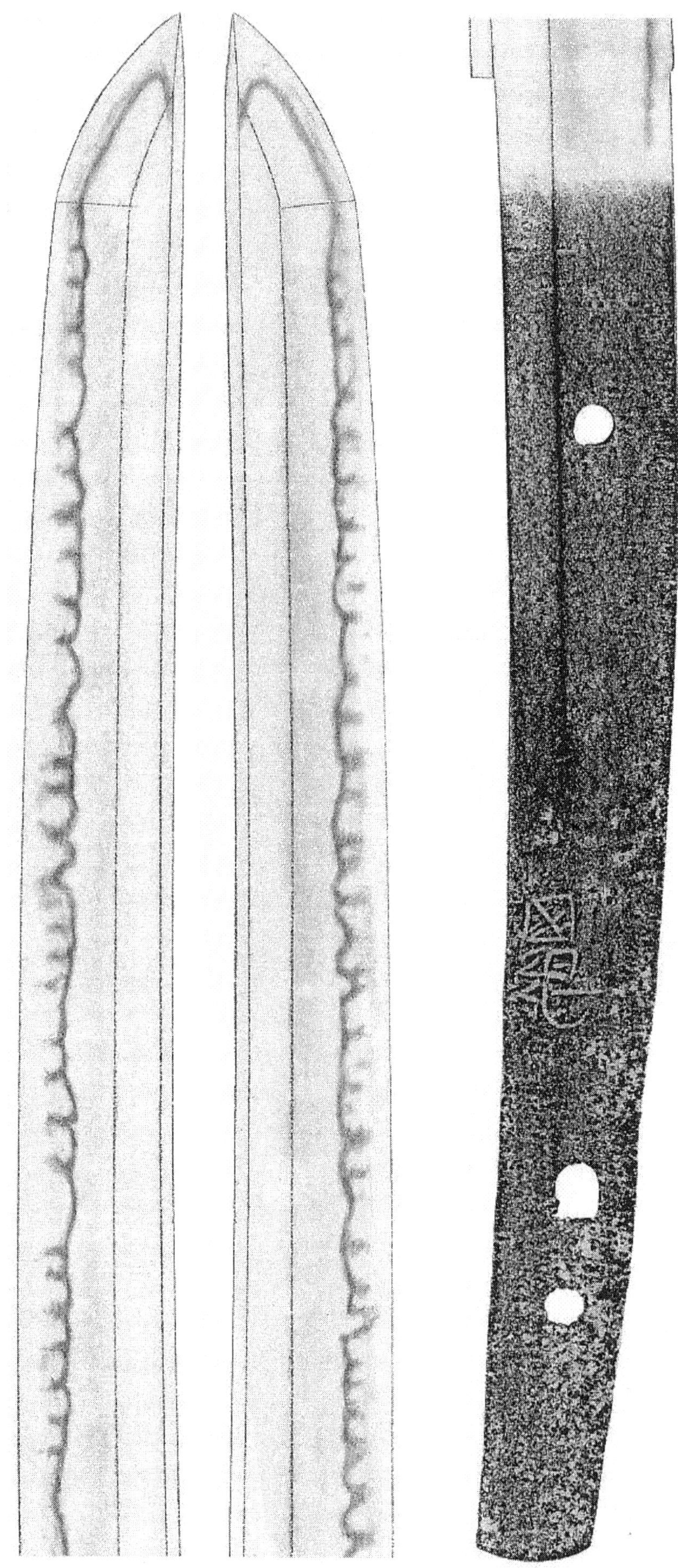

42.639 *tachi*
mei: Kunitsuna (国綱) [Ko-Bizen]
nagasa 70,3 cm, *sori* 1,8 cm, *shinogi-zukuri*, *mitsu-mune*

ji: standing-out *itame* mixed with *mokume*, in addition *ji-nie*, *chikei* and a *midare-utsuri*
hamon: wide *suguha* with *ko-chōji-midare* whereas the upper half shows larger-headed *chōji* and the lower half more smaller dimensioned *chōji*, in addition many *ashi* and *yō*, plentiful of *nie* (which are more prominent in the lower half) as well as *kinsuji* and *sunagashi*
bōshi: on both sides *sugu* with a *ko-maru-kaeri*

This is a *jūyō-bijutsuhin-tachi* by the Ko-Bizen smith Kunitsuna. According to the *meikan* records, Kunitsuna is dated around Tenpuku (天福, 1233-1234) and the blade shows contrary to earlier Ko-Bizen works the transitional style from the early to the middle Kamakura period, that means *chōji* with larger heads arranged in a wide *mihaba*. This *deki* is in turn a precursor to the later Fukuoka-Ichimonji style of the middle Kamakura period but if you are not aware of that context, you might think that this is a later work of Yoshifusa (吉房), Norifusa (則房), Kunimune (国宗) or Nagamitsu (長光). Accordingly, many bids were found on these smiths.

It is not easy to differentiate mid-Kamakura period Ko-Bizen and Ko-Ichimonji works and also senior experts and appraisers have sometimes difficulties with an attribution. When we take a look at the shape we see that there is hardly any *funbari* left and so we can assume that the blade is shortened. It tapers noticeably, has a deep *koshizori*, a small and compact *kissaki* and the curvature bends down towards the tip. These are important characteristics to tell that the blade does not date later than the middle Kamakura period. This observation has to be combined with the *midare-utsuri* which shows dark *antai* areas along the upper half and turns into a clearly visible *jifu-utsuri*. In addition, the *antai* is rather high and goes over the *shinogi*. In combination with the *hamon* with its frequent *nie* we are in the end able to narrow this blade down to a Ko-Bizen work not later than mid-Kamakura.

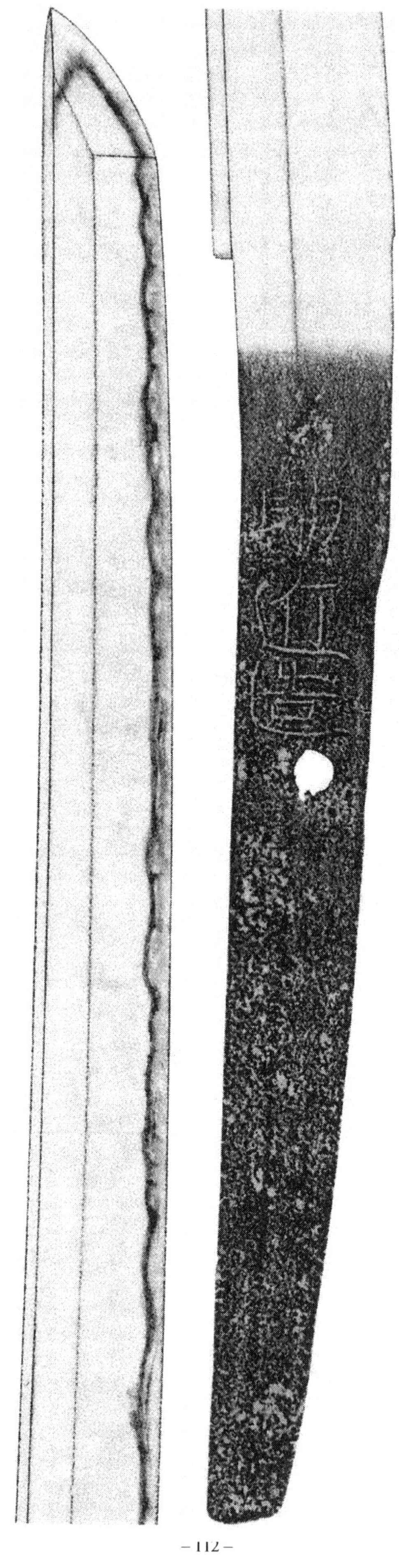

43.641 *tachi*
mei: Sukechika tsukuru (助近造) [Ko-Bizen]
nagasa 69,7 cm, *sori* 2,5 cm, *shinogi-zukuri*, *iori-mune*

ji: *itame* mixed with *mokume* which is somewhat larger dimensioned and stands out, in addition plentiful of *ji-nie*, thick and repeated *chikei* and also some *jifu*-like elements in places
hamon: pronounced *yaki-otoshi* which turns into a *suguha-chō* mixed with *ko-notare*, *ko-gunome*, *ko-ashi*, plentiful of *nie* and many *kinsuji* and *sunagashi*, the *nioiguchi* is relative wide and partially subdued
bōshi: on the *haki-omote suguha-chō* and on the *ura* some *midare-komi*, but on both sides with a *ko-maru-kaeri* which doesn´t run back very long

The blade has an *ubu-nakago*, is slender, has a deep *koshizori* and ends in a *ko-kissaki*, that means it shows the noble, highly elegant *sugata* of the late Heian or early Kamakura period. The *meikan* records list one Ko-Bizen and one Fukuoka-Ichimonji Sukechika but the *kantei* blade can be attributed to the former.

The blade has a rather large dimensioned, standing-out *hada* for Ko-Bizen and because of the *suguha* with its *nie*, *kinsuji* and *sunagashi* which is subdued and dull in places, but especially because of the *yaki-otoshi*, some bade on Ko-Hōki Yasutsuna or the Ko-Naminohira school. Well, the *yaki-otoshi* is actually rare for Ko-Bizen but at Ko-Hōki, we would expect a pronounced *hira-niku* and a *sori* which does not bend down towards the tip. Also the *jigane* would be blackish. The *kantei* blade has a *hamon* which is based on *suguha-chō* mixed with *ko-notare* and *ko-gunome* whereas the *hamon* of the Ko-Hōki school is a *ko-midare* which is only partially mixed with *ko-notare* and *ko-gunome*. The distance in between these *ko-gunome* elements is especially large at Yasutsuna and Ko-Hōki-*mono* and they show a clearly standing-out *ha-hada* and *kinsuji* and *sunagashi* which are interwoven with the *hada* of the *ji*.

At a work of Kyūshū´s Ko-Naminohira school, the *jigane* would tend to *nagare* and would show the characteristical „stickiness".

Bids on Ko-Bizen were all counted as *atari*, whereas most participants focused on Masatsune (正恒). Masatsune too worked sometimes in such a *jifu*-like *hada* but his *kitae* is generally rather fine, dense and beautifully forged. At Tomonari (友成) on the other hand, the *utsuri* would not be that pronounced and there are only rarely and blades found with a standing-out *hada*.

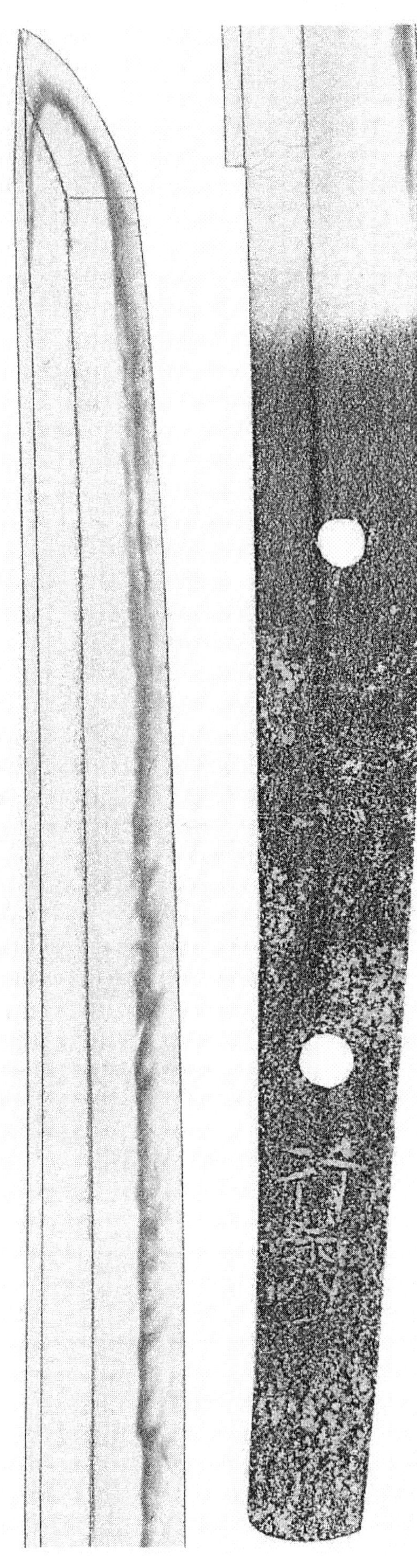

44.594 *tachi*
mei: Yukihide (行秀) [Ko-Bizen]
nagasa 69,7 cm, *sori* 1,7 cm, *shinogi-zukuri*, *iori-mune*

ji: *itame* with plentiful of *ji-nie*, *chikei* and a *midare-utsuri*
hamon: *ko-midare* mixed with *ko-chōji*, partially conspicious *saka-ashi*, in addition *ko-ashi*, *yō*, fine *kinsuji* and *sunagashi*, the *nioiguchi* is rather broad and very *nie*-loaden
bōshi: tends to *sugu* with a *ko-maru-kaeri* and *hakikake*

There is no *funbari* visible at the base so we can assume that the blade is shortened. The *sori* is nevertheless a deep *koshizori* which bends down towards the tip. The blade itself is slender and ends in a compact *ko-kissaki*, that means we are from the point of view of *sugata* in the early Kamakura period. And when we combine this with the visible *midare-utsuri*, we arrive at Bizen.

At that time, the Ko-Bizen and Ko-Ichimonji schools were flourishing. Both applied a rather calm *hamon* which is based on *ko-midare* or *ko-chōji*. This blade shows conspicious *saka-ashi* and among all Ko-Bizen smiths, such *saka-ashi* are characteristical for Yukihide. Without them and on the basis of the mixed-in *ko-chōji*, one could also go easily for Ko-Ichimonji. However, the *saka-ashi* made some to bid on Ko-Aoe (古青江) or Chikakage (近景). But at a Ko-Aoe work, one would expect *jifu* along the *hada* and not a linear *utsuri* but a *dan-utsuri*. Chikakage´s interpretations in turn are not that *nie*-loaden and the *bōshi* would appear as *sansaku-bōshi*. Also the *sugata* would be different at Chikakage because he was active later.

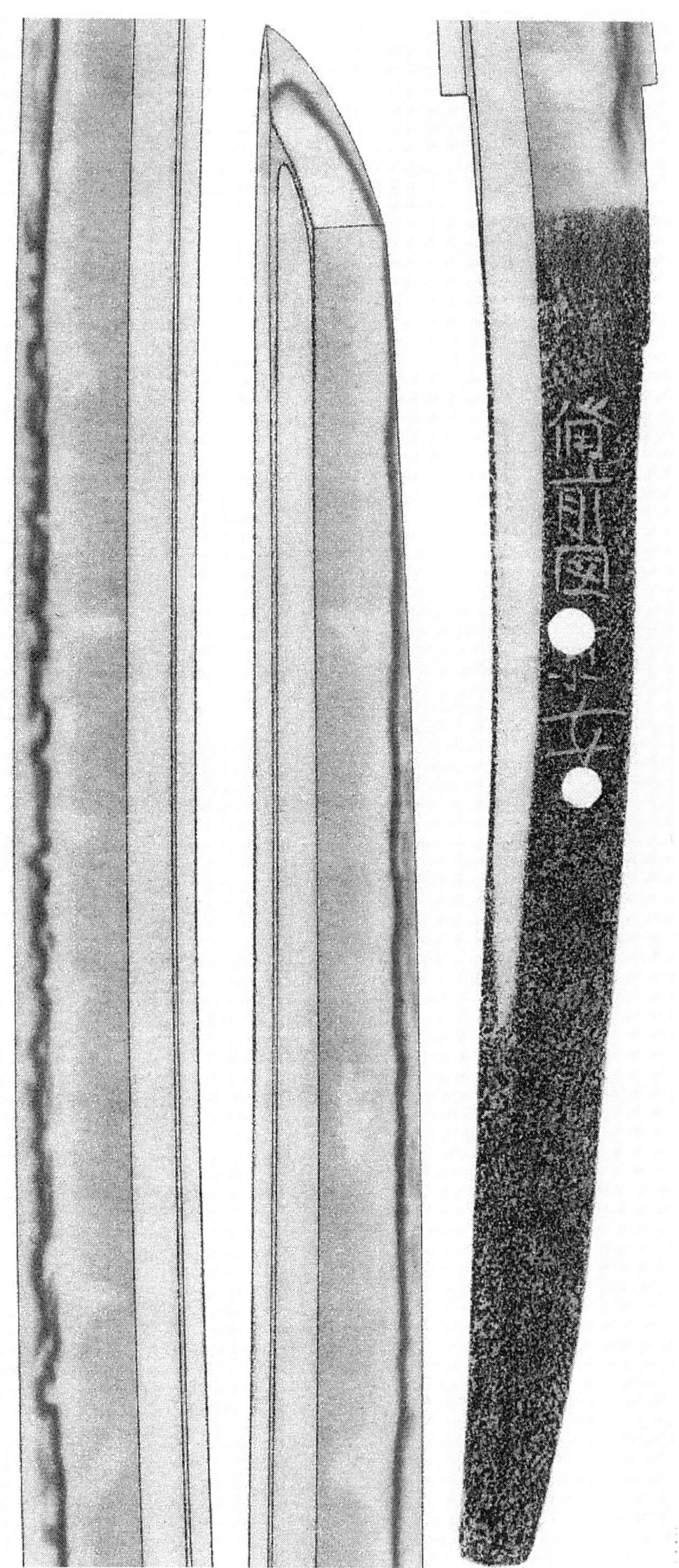

45.628 *tachi*
mei: Bizen no Kuni Kageyasu (備前国景安)
nagasa 80,6 cm, *sori* 2,3 cm, *shinogi-zukuri*, *iori-mune*

ji: rather standing-out *itame* mixed with *mokume* and *nagare*, also fine *ji-nie*, much *chikei*, and along the lower half a faint *jifu-utsuri*
hamon: basing on *chū-suguha* with angular *gunome*, *gunome*, and *ko-midare* in the lower half, in addition plentiful of *ashi* and *yō*, there are some rough and large *nie* scattered over the *nioi* and also *kinsuji* and *sunagashi* appear in places
bōshi: *sugu* with a *maru-kaeri* which does not run back very long
horimono: on both sides a *bōhi* which runs with *kake-nagashi* into the tang

First the *sugata*. We see a deep *koshizori* which bends down towards the tip, a *funbari*, and altogether a slender and elegant shape which brings us to early Kamakura. The *jigane* is an excellently forged *itame* mixed with *mokume* which shows *ji-nie*, fine *chikei* and an irregular and faint *jifu-utsuri* along the lower half of the blade. The *nie*-loaden *hamon* bases on *suguha* and is mixed with *ko-midare*. So all in all one should be able to arrive at Ko-Bizen.

Most of the bids were spot-on but many focused on Tomonari (友成) and Masatsune (正恒). Of course these are excellent bids too but when you take a closer look than you can see peculiar angular *gunome* on the lower half of the *haki-ura* side. This is a characteristical feature of Kageyasu and the keypoint to nail down the smith.

Relative many went also for Ko-Aoe. This would fit from the point of view of time and quality and because the *kantei* blade shows a kind of similar workmanship, bids on Ko-Aoe were counted as „*jun-dōzen*" (準同然, „almost correct"). Well, Ko-Bizen and Ko-Aoe have a lot in common and an exact differentiation is sometimes difficult but at Ko-Aoe, the *itame-mokume* would stand out as *chirimen* and *sumigane* would appear somewhere along the *hada*. Also the *nioiguchi* would be a little more subdued in comparison to the *kantei* blade.

Incidentally, there are relative many blades extant by Kageyasu and besides of a *niji-mei* he signed also with a *goji-mei* „Bizen no Kuni Kageyasu". But the latter works seem to be older then the *niji-mei* blades and show a more classical but not so refined workmanship.

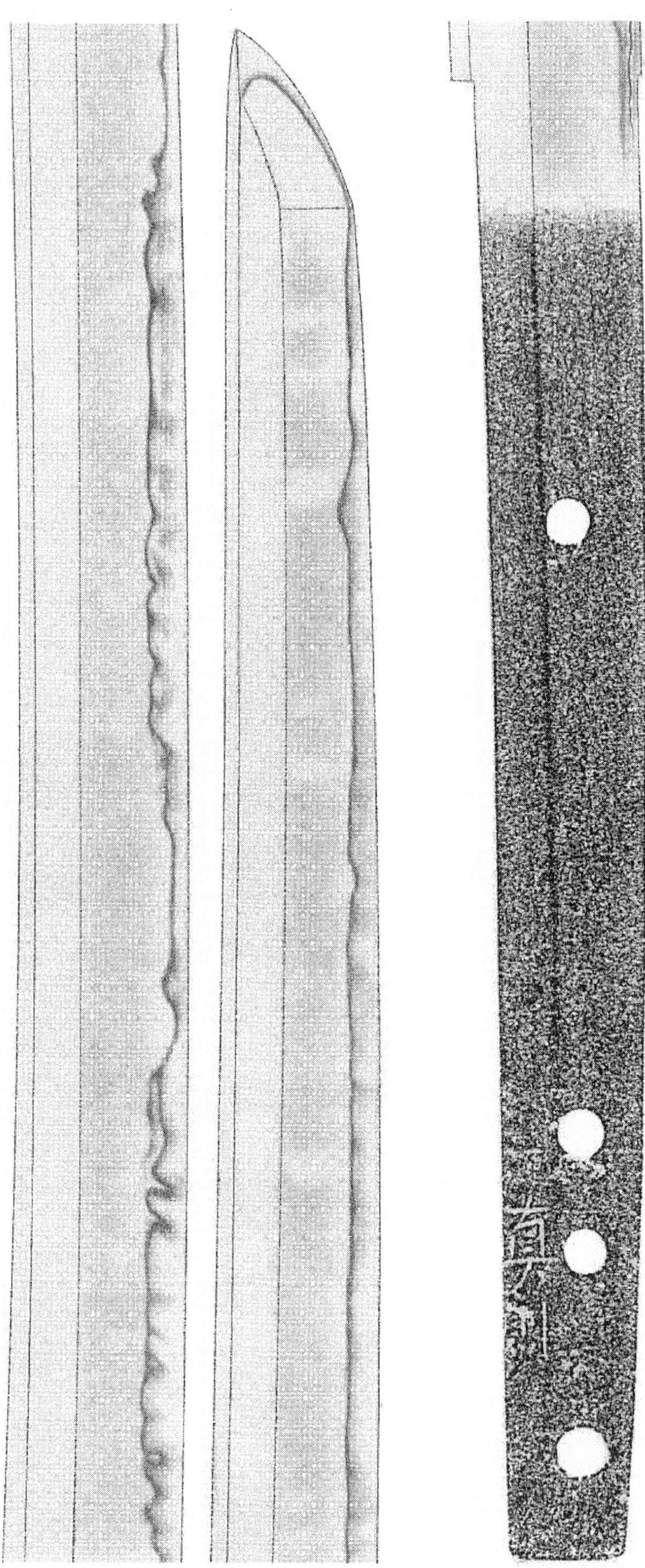

46.662 *tachi*
mei: Sanenori (真則) [Ko-Ichimonji (*jūyō-bijutsuhin*)]
nagasa 66,2 cm, *sori* 1,5 cm, *shinogi-zukuri*, *iori-mune*

ji: *ko-itame* mixed with *masame* and *mokume*, also a *jifu-utsuri*
hamon: *chū-suguha-chō* mixed with *ko-chōji*, *ko-gunome*, many *ashi* and *yō*, and some *kinsuji* in places, the hardening is in *nioi-deki* with a tendency to (partially accumulating) *ko-nie*
bōshi: *sugu* with a *maru-kaeri*

First we see that there is no *funbari* which let us assume that the blade is *suriage* or *ō-suriage*. The *sori* bends down towards the tip and in some areas we see an irregular *jifu-utsuri* with dark *antai* spots which also goes over the *shinogi*. So we can safely assume that this is a work from the early Kamakura period. The *jigane* is fine and well forged and relative bright which brings us to one of the main schools (i.e. no *wakimono* from northern or southern provinces) and in a more narrow sense to Bizen. For the time we spotted before, Ko-Bizen and Ko-Ichimonji come into question. Well, the *hamon* consists of *ko-chōji* mixed with *ko-gunome* and shows some ups and downs. These characteristics does rather not speak for Ko-Bizen but for Ko-Ichimonji.

Most bids were *atari* on Ko-Ichimonji but because of the *jifu-utsuri*, some bids were also in the vicinity of Nagamitsu (長光) and of the Un group (雲). But at the second round, the *sori* and the *utsuri* were examined closer and so most participants were able to arrive at Ko-Ichimonji.

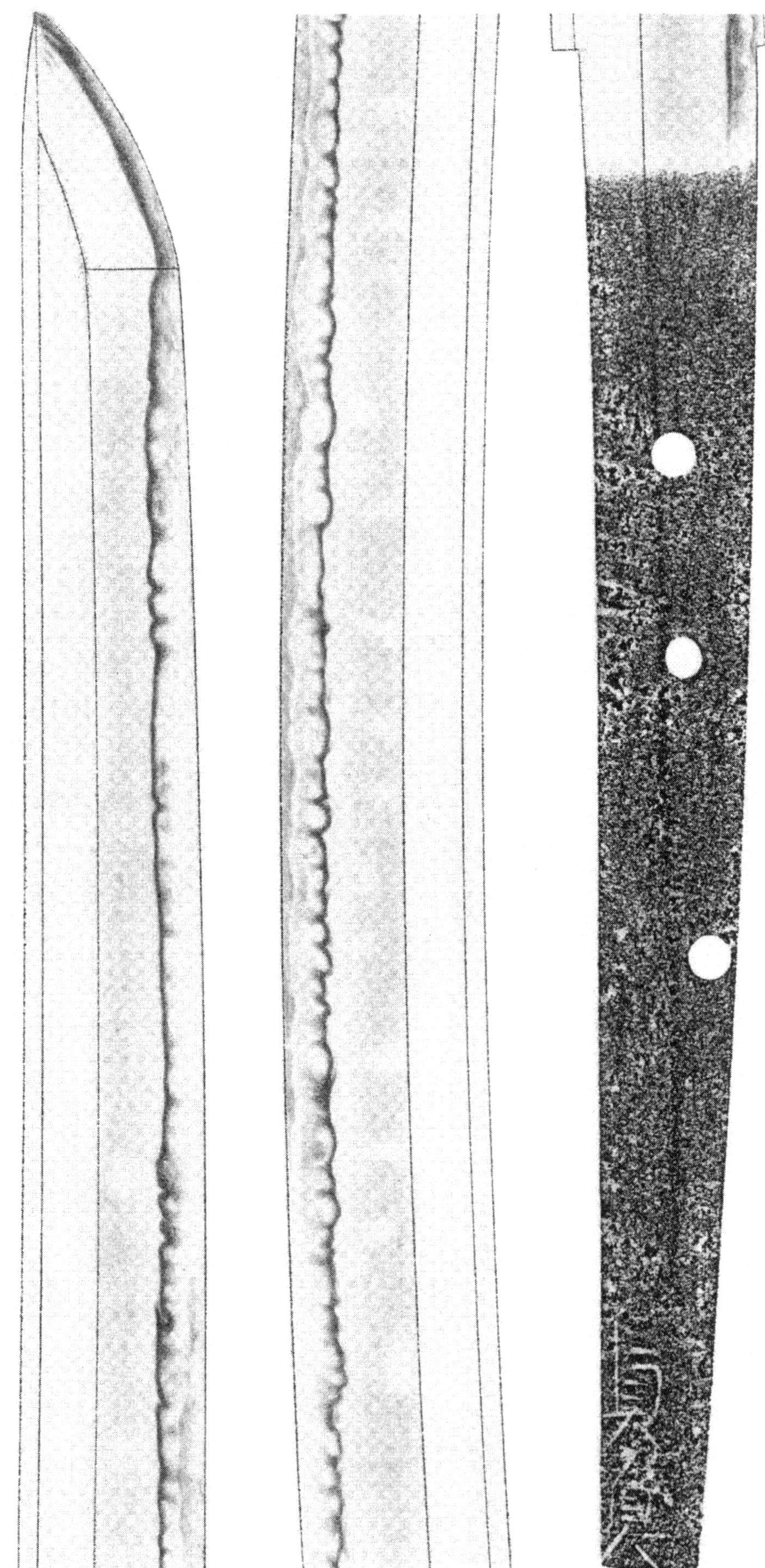

47.670 *tachi*
mei: Sadazane (貞真) [Note: The signature shows the old character for „zane" (眞).]
nagasa 71,5 cm, *sori* 2,1 cm, *shinogi-zukuri*, *iori-mune*

ji: densely forged *ko-itame* with *ji-nie* and a *jifu-utsuri*
hamon: based on *ko-chōji* and mixed with *ko-gunome* and *ko-midare*, in addition plentiful of *ashi* and *yō*, the hardening is in *nioi-deki* with *ko-nie*, faint *nie-suji* and *kinsuji*-like elements appear
bōshi: *sugu* with *yakitsume* and some *kuzure* on the *omote* side and a some *kaeri* on the *ura* side

This is a *tachi* of Ko-Ichimonji Sadazane but relative many bade on the middle or late Kamakura-period Bizen or Rai school. But when we take a closer look at the *ji* we see a conspicious *jifu-utsuri* with dark *antai* areas which go over the *shinogi* in places (especially on the *haki-ura* side). As mentioned repeatedly in the course of *kantei* explanations, such an *utsuri* is characteristic for the late Heian and early Kamakura period. So this blade is rather an early example for such an *antai*-loaden *utsuri* and we are surely not later than the beginning Kamakura period. The *hamon* has no noticeable ups and downs, bases on a *ko-chōji* and is mixed with *ko-gunome* and *ko-midare*. The hardening is in *nioi-deki* and the *nioiguchi* is relative bright. So the blade is generally rather refined.

From the point of view of arrangement of the *hamon* and brightness and clarity of the *jiba*, we are obviously not at Ko-Aoe, Ko-Hōki or Ko-Kyūshū, so Ko-Bizen remains. But the *utsuri* is too clear, the *nioiguchi* too *nioi*-based, and the *hamon* too refined for Ko-Bizen, and this leads us eventually to Ko-Ichimonji.

Well, Sadazane is widely known but not many signed blades are extant from him. In this sense it is understandable that hardly anyone bade directly on him and it was by the way anough to go for Ko-Ichimonji to get an *atari*. Incidentally, all the extant *zaimei* works of Sadazane are rather *nie*-loaden and so older sword documents classify him as Ko-Bizen smith. Therefore this blade with its refined *deki* is an important reference for the assumption that he belonged rather to the Ko-Ichimonji group.

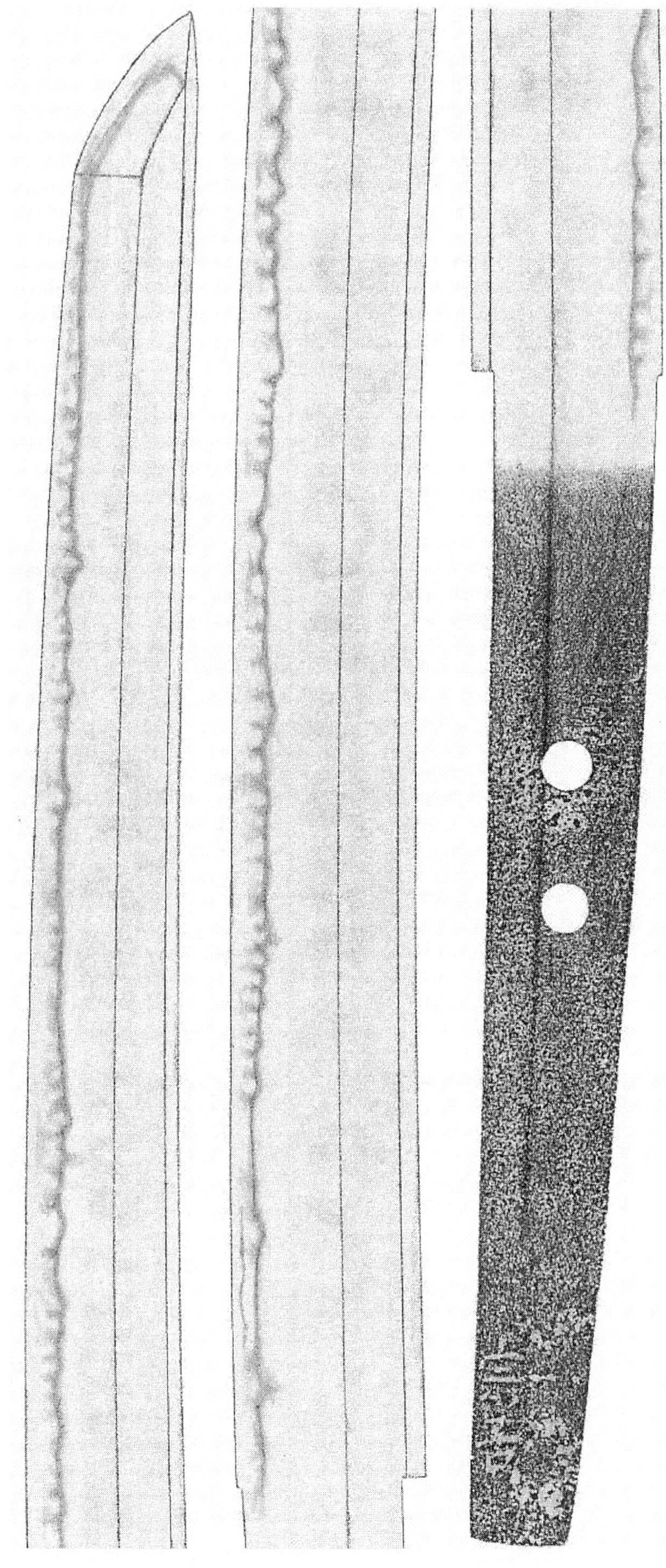

48.597 *tachi*
mei: Muneyoshi (宗吉)
nagasa 69,54 cm, *sori,* 2,58 cm, *shinogi-zukuri, iori-mune*

ji: *ko-itame-hada* mixed with *ko-mokume*, plentiful of *ji-nie* and fine *chikei*, the *hada* stands out slightly and a clear *jifu-utsuri* is visible
ha: *ko-chōji* and *ko-gunome* which base on *suguha* in a rich *ko-nie-deki* with *ashi, yō, kinsuji* and fine *sunagashi*
bōshi: *sugu* with a short *ko-maru*-*kaeri*

Muneyoshi belonged to the early Fukuoka-Ichimonji school, i.e. the Ko-Ichimonji school. Old sword documents list him as Gotoba´s *goban-kaji* for the seventh month. The blade has a slender *mihaba*, a *ko-kissaki* and a *sori* which bends down towards the tip, thus the typical elegant shape of the late Heian and early Kamakura period. And there is also the clear *jifu-utsuri* in the *hira-ji* and *shinogi-ji* which is not seen after the early Kamakura period.

There are relative many *zaimei* blades extant by this smith which are signed with „Muneyoshi" or „Muneyoshi saku" in more or less large characters. The workmanship resembles in general Ko-Bizen but we can also see already a newer, more flamboyant approach.

The *hamon* bases on *suguha* and is mixed with *ko-chōji* and *ko-gunome* and is hardened in *ko-nie-deki*. This *deki* is similar to Ko-Bizen too and so many bade on Ko-Bizen at the *kantei*. This was also counted as *atari* because the blade is interpreted rather in the classical than the newer style of Muneyoshi. Some went also for Nagamitsu (長光) and other Ko-Osafune smiths from the late Kamakura period. Bids like that go probably back to the hardly visible *funbari*. But smiths like Nagamitsu applied a clear *midare-utsuri* which does not go over the *shinogi*. And their *suguha*-based *hamon* with *ko-chōji* and *ko-gunome* elements would be hardened in *nioi-deki*.

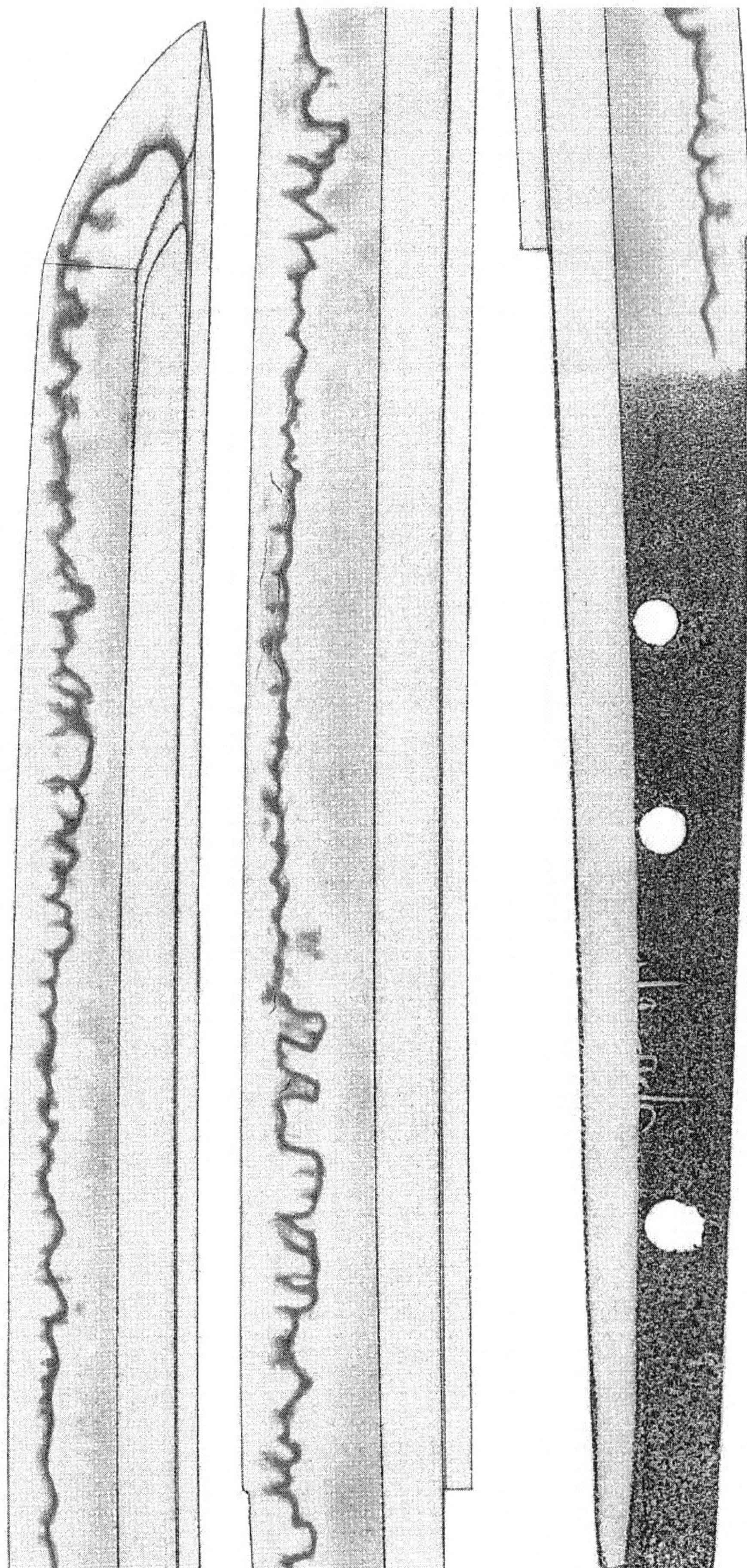

49.665 *tachi*
mei: Yoshifusa (吉房)
nagasa 70,45 cm, *sori* 1,8 cm, *shinogi-zukuri*, *iori-mune*

ji: somewhat standing-out *itame* with *ji-nie*, fine *chikei* and a *midare-utsuri*
hamon: *chōji-midare* mixed with *ō-chōji*, *ko-gunome* and *togariba* with conspicuous ups and downs, also some *fukuro-chōji* are seen in places as well as long *ashi*, *kinsuji* and *sunagashi*, the *nioiguchi* looks soft and the hardening is in *nioi-deki*
bōshi: *midare-komi* with *hakikake* and a somewhat pointed *ko-maru-kaeri*
horimono: on both sides a *bōhi* which runs through as *kake-tōshi* on the *haki-omote* side and which ends with *kake-nagashi* on the *haki-ura* side

The blade has a wide *mihaba*, does not show a noticeable taper, has a thick *kasane* and plentiful of *niku* which appears as *hamaguri-ba*, and even it is shortened, it remains some *funbari*. The *sori* appears as *toriizori* and the tip tends a little to *ikubi*. So we have here a typical *tachi-sugata* of the middle Kamakura period. And because of the flamboyant *chōji-midare* in *nioi-deki*, the ups and downs of the *yakiba* and the clearly visible *midare-utsuri*, most participants were spot-on at Fukuoka-Ichimonji. Also many were able to recognize the high quality and the *fukuro-chōji* which are typical for Yoshifusa and went straightforward for that smith.

But some bade within the Ichimonji school on Sukezane (助真) or Norifusa (則房). At Sukezane, the *nioiguchi* would be a bit wider and would show more and stronger *nie*. Also the *kitae* would show more *chikei* and so his blades are noticeably „wilder" and „intensive" than Yoshifusas´s. At Norifusa, the steel is very densely forged and the *jiba* is bright and clear. His *midareba* tends to slant a bit and the heads of the *chōji* would be smaller. In addition, Norifusa´s works have a higher amount of *ashi* and *yō*.

Besides of Ichimonji, some went also for Hatakeda Moriie (畠田守家) or early Osafune smiths like Mitsutada (光忠), Kagehide (景秀) and Nagamitsus (長光). At Moriie and Mitsutada, the blade would show a considerable amount of *kawazu-no-ko chōji*. Kagehide´s most famous work, the „Kuronbo-giri", displays a workmanship similar to Ichimonji so with that in mind, a bid on him is understandable. But usually he added more *togariba* and *sunagashi* and the hardening is in *ko-nie-deki*. And like at early works of Nagamitsu, Kagehide mixed conspicious *gunome* into his flamboyant *midareba* even the *yakiba* does not vary so much in height. In addition, his *gunome* and *chōji* are a bit more densely arranged.

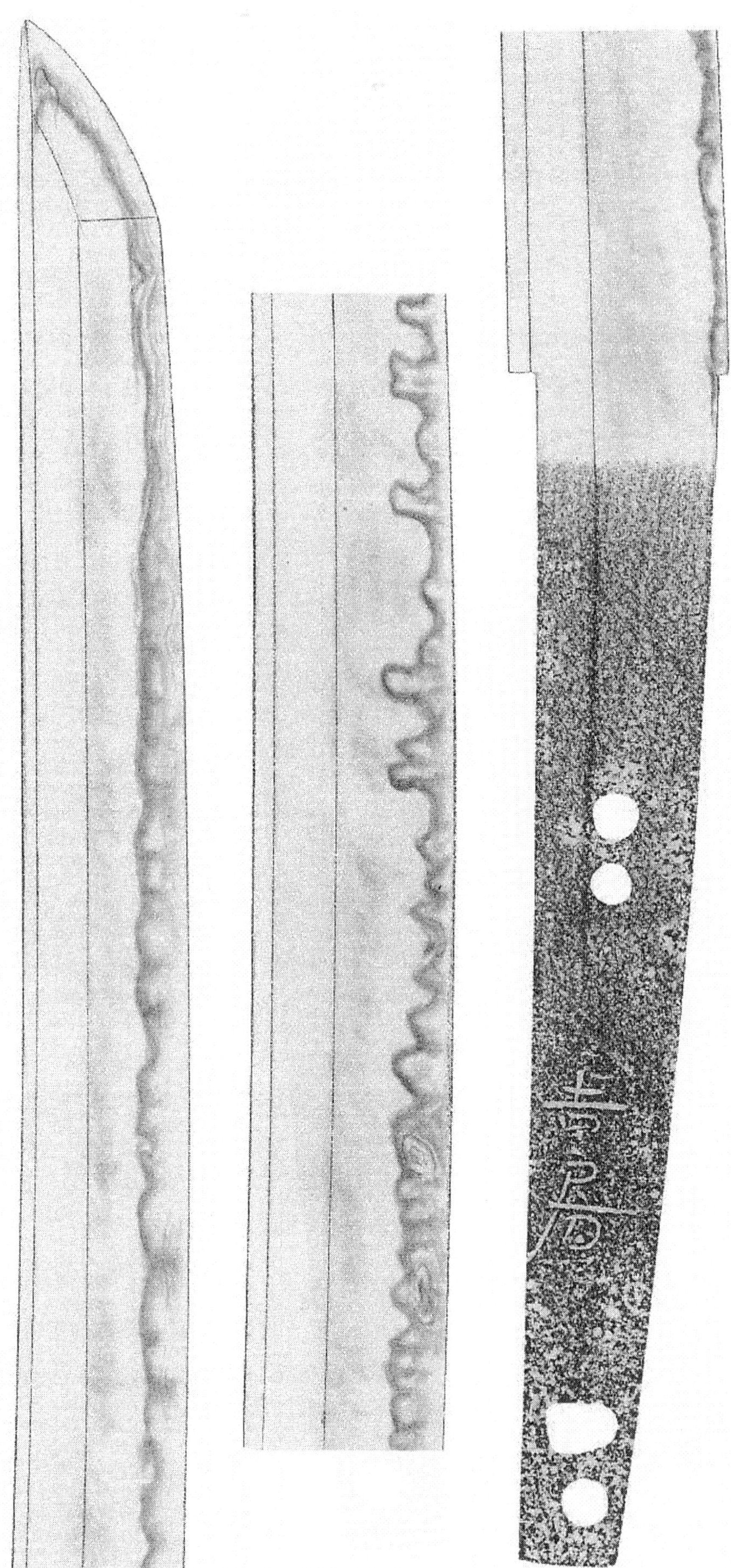

50.591 *tachi*
mei: Yoshifusa (吉房)
nagasa 67,6 cm, *sori* 2,4 cm, *shinogi-zukuri*, *iori-mune*

ji: rather standing-out *itame* mixed with *mokume*, plentiful of *ji-nie*, *chikei*, clear *midare-utsuri*
hamon: *chōji* in *ko-nie-deki* mixed with *ko-chōji*, *ko-gunome*, *ashi*, *sunagashi* and *kinsuji*, the *midare* elements are rather small dimensioned
bōshi: *suguha-chō* with some *notare* and a *ko-maru-kaeri*

The blade has a normal *mihaba* and *kasane*, a shallow *koshizori* which increases again towards the tip and a rather compact *chū-kissaki*, that means we can place it in the middle to late Kamakura period. The *jigane* shows a clearly visible *midare-utsuri* and the *hamon* consists of a *chōji-midare* which brings us to Bizen. Also we see some *funbari* whereas we can assume that the blade is not or only a little shortened.

The *deki* of this Yoshifusa is somewhat different from his other known works. The *chōji-midare* is not that flamboyant and the blade looks with its *nioiguchi* in *ko-nie-deki* more classical and older, and so some bade on Ko-Bizen and smiths like Tomonari (友成) and Masatsune (正恒) or on Ko-Ichimonji. But with bids like that we would be in the late Heian or early Kamakura period and the *koshizori* would bend down towards the tip. At some areas, the *midareba* shows some conspicious ups and downs and the *gunome* is not very obvious. So we do have in the end a work of the Fukuoka-Ichimonji school from the middle Kamakura period.

Generally, Yoshifusa′s blades have a somewhat broader *mihaba* and a *kissaki* which tends to *ikubi*, that means he demonstrates a magnificent and robust *sugata*. Furthermore his *nioiguchi* is usually wider and the *midareba* shows some *fukuro-chōji* which makes it look more flamboyant. Therefore it was a bit difficult to arrive at Yoshifusa and all bids on Fukuoka-Ichimonji smiths were counted as *atari*.

Incidentally, we must not forget that there were many other smiths who still made slender blades in the middle Kamakura period, for example Sukezane (助真), Saburō Kunimune (三郎国宗), Norifusa (則房) or Rai Kuniyuki (来国行) from Yamashiro. Also it has to be mentioned that we know several different signature variants of Yoshifusa. Namely large dimensioned *mei* (on a *kokuhō* from the former possessions of the Shimazu family, 島津), a medium-size *mei* (on the *kokuhō* Okada-giri, 岡田切り), a *mei* like here on the *kantei* blade in combination with a rather *nie*-loaden *chōji* (another blade in this interpretation is preserved in the Ise Shrine Museum), and a smaller dimensioned *mei* in combination with a calm *suguha-chō* (51st *jūyō-tōken-shinsa*, from the former possessions of the Honma family, 本間).

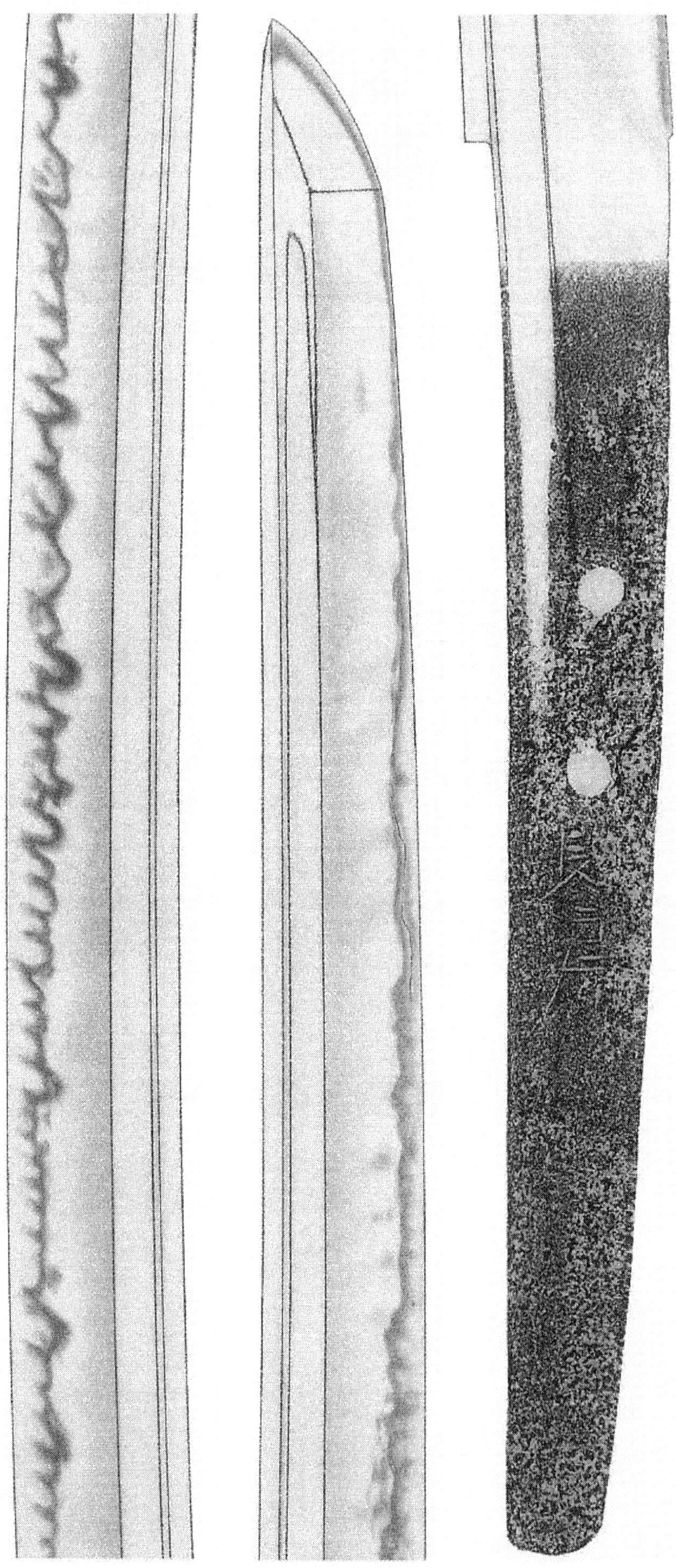

51.589 *tachi*
mei: Norifusa (則房)
nagasa 74,5 cm, *sori* 2,7 cm, *shinogi-zukuri*, *iori-mune*

ji: dense *ko-itame* with plentiful of *ji-nie*, fine *chikei*, and a *midare-utsuri*
hamon: *chōji-midare* which tends to slant, in addition *ashi*, *yō*, *nie*, *kinsuji* and *sunagashi*, the *nioiguchi* is wide, bright and clear
bōshi: *sugu* which appears almost as *yakitsume* and which shows *hakikake*
horimono: on both sides a *bōhi* which runs with *kake-nagashi* into the tang

The blade is relative slender, has a thick *kasane*, plentiful of *hira-niku* (= *hamaguri-ba*), a deep *koshizori* which increases again towards the tip, and ends in a *chū-kissaki*. That means we can place it in the middle or late Kamakura period. Because of the slender *sugata* some also reckoned it as Ko-Ichimonji work but in that case, the *sori* would bend down towards the tip. Also the *chōji-hamon* with its ups and downs is too flamboyant for Ko-Ichimonji because from the latter smiths, we would expect a *suguha-chō* mixed with *ko-midare* and/or *ko-chōji*. In short, the Ko-Ichimonji style is a bit more classical and shows some remnants from the somewhat earlier Ko-Bizen workmanship.

Well, the flamboyant *chōji* and the *sugata* brought most spot-on to mid-Kamakura-period Fukuoka-Ichimonji and to bids on Norifusa, Sukezane (助真) or Yoshifusa (吉房). The very dense *kitae*, the bright and clear *jiba* and the somewhat smaller dimensioned, slanting *midare* elements are very typical for Norifusa and this was recognized by many participants. But some were lead astray by the *nie* and went for Sukezane. He made blades with a magnificent *sugata* with a wide *mihaba* and applied the most flamboyant *hamon* of the three mentioned smiths. That means his *yakiba* has the most ups and downs and also his *nioiguchi* is a bit wider and even more *nie*-loaden. And at Yoshifusa, we would expect some *fukuro-chōji* within the *ha*.

Some bade also on Nagamitsu (長光), but his flamboyant interpretations have a noticeable amount of *gunome* and the *yakiba* has not that many ups and downs.

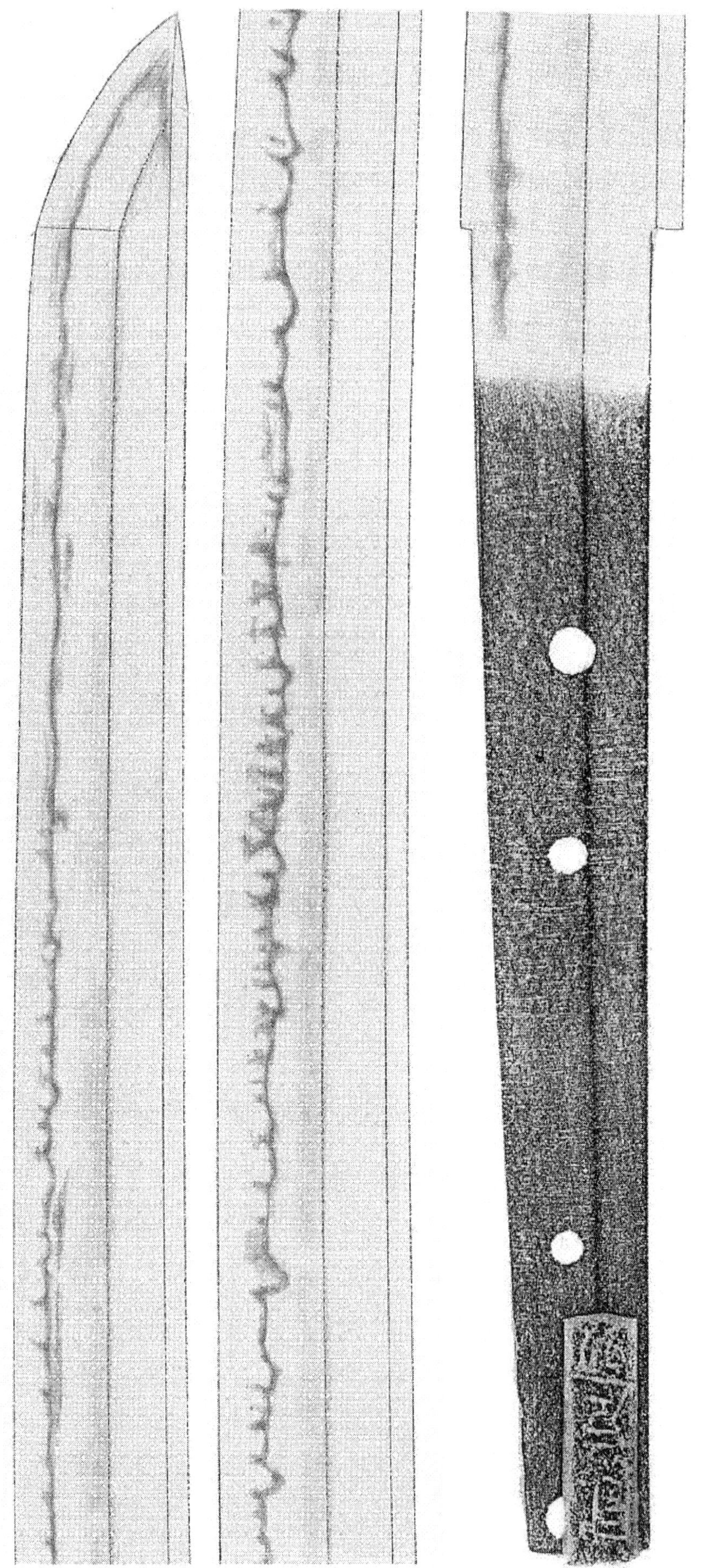

52.655 *katana*
orikaeshi-mei: Norifusa (則房)
nagasa 68,9 cm, *sori* 1,5 cm, *shinogi-zukuri*, *iori-mune*

ji: dense *ko-itame* with plentiful of *ji-nie*, fine *chikei* and a faint *midare-utsuri*
hamon: rather narrow *chōji-midare* which tends to *suguha-chō* along the *monouchi* area, in addition partially slanting elements and *yō*, *nie* appear and the *ha* is bright and clear
bōshi: on both sides somewhat *midare-komi* and a *ko-maru-kaeri* with *hakikake*

When the majority hears the name „Katayama-Ichimonji Norifusa", they think immediately of the *kokuhō-tachi* from the former possessions of the Tokugawa family. This blade has a wide *mihaba*, tapers not that much and ends in an *ikubi-kissaki*, that means the *sugata* is magnificent and imposing. The *hamon* of that blade is an *ō-chōji* mixed with *jūka-chōji*, *kawazu-no-ko chōji* and *fukuro-chōji*, whereas the *yakiba* shows many ups and downs and some elements of the *hamon* tend to slant.

This blade is designated as *jūyō-bijutsuhin* and has a rather slender *mihaba* and a smaller dimensioned *chōji* which tends even to a calm *suguha-chō* along the *monouchi* area. And so it is no surprise that many bids were rather at late than early Kamakura. [Translators note: Norifusa is dated around Kenchō (建長, 1249-1256).] Let us address the *hamon*. We don´t see the typical *gunome* amount of a Bizen-*chōji* from the late Kamakura period. The *chōji* are densely arranged and don´t show much ups and downs which brings us back to a middle Kamakura-period Ichimonji work. In addition, the little tapering and the *ikubi*-like *kissaki* let us definitely stay at this attribution. Regarding Norifusa´s workmanship, his *jigane* shows plentiful of *ji-nie* and many *chikei*, that means it is strong. His *chōji* tend to slant in places and there are fine *ashi* and *yō*. Also the *ha* is bright and clear.

Incidentally, all the famous Fukuoka-Ichimonji smiths like Yoshifusa (吉房), Norifusa (則房) and Sukezane (助真) (of which some say that several generations existed) signed in a varied manner and when it comes to their workmanship, we find broad blades with an *ikubi-kissaki* in combination with the Fukuoka-Ichimonji-typical flamboyant *ō-chōji* as well as relative slender blades with a rather small dimensioned *hamon*. So it is assumed that these changes go back to the transition of their artistic periods, i.e. there was anyway an univeral trend from the middle to the late Kamakura period from broader and more flamboyant to narrower and more quiet blades. However, old sword documents say that there are even some blades in Nanbokuchō shape extant by these smiths which resemble an Enbun-Jōji-*sugata*.

Let us briefly address the changes in shape during the Kamakura period. During the middle Kamakura period, a magnificent shape with wide *mihaba* and an *ikubi-kissaki* was in fashion. But this peculiar *sugata* was only made at a certain time of the middle Kamakura period. Therefore I think that we have a lot of intermediate shapes, i.e. from the slender *sugata* from the early Kamakura period to the *ikubi-kissaki tachi* which gradually grew thicker and larger and eventually became shorter and narrower again towards the end of the Kamakura period.

As we know hardly any date signatures of these smiths some questions concerning one or several generations remain unsolved. Maybe we will be able in the future to grasp the changes in workmanship of smiths like Norifusa or Yoshifusa better and then we can nail down the production time of blades like this more precisely.

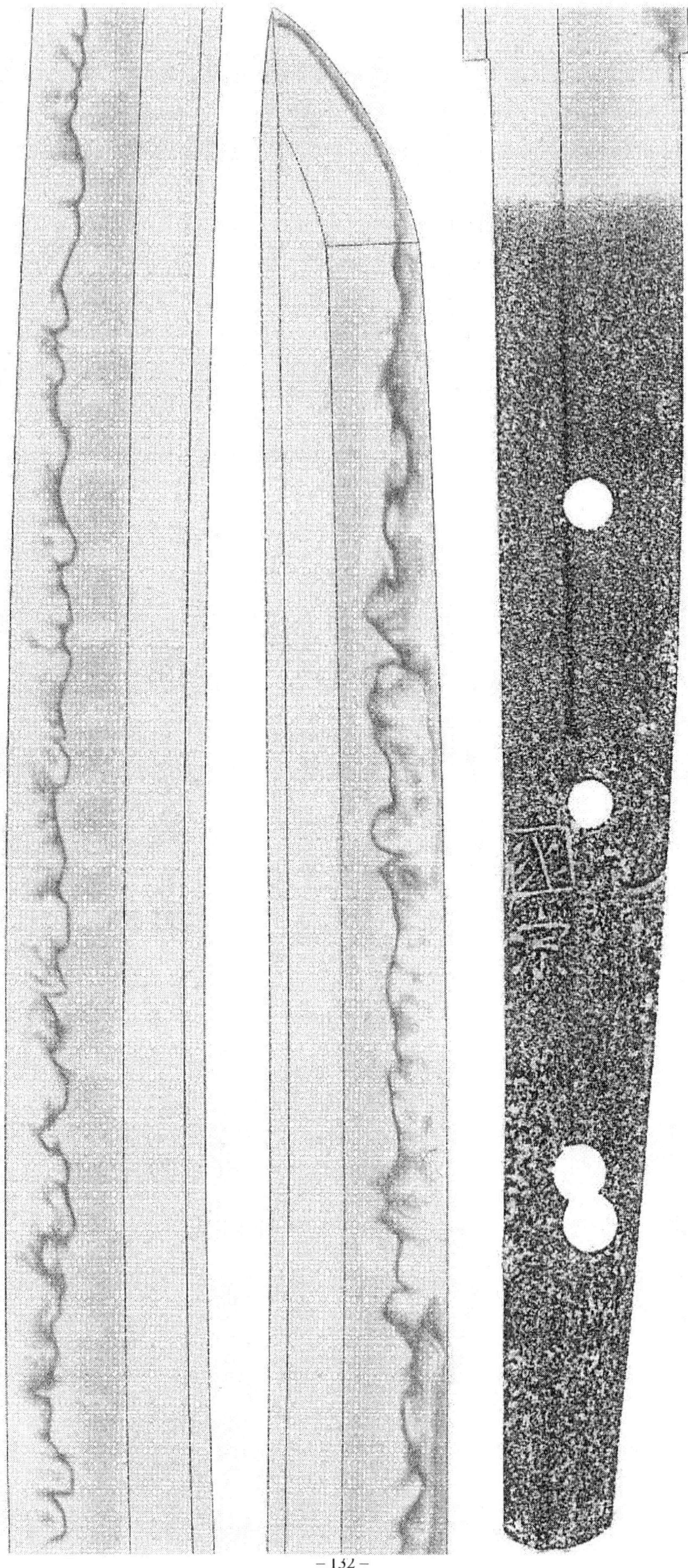

53.662 *tachi*
mei: Kunimune (国宗) [Bizen-Saburō]
nagasa 73,2 cm, *sori* 2,5 cm, *shinogi-zukuri*, *iori-mune*

ji: partially standing-out *itame* mixed with *mokume*, in addition *ji-nie*, some *chikei* and a clearly visible *midare-utsuri*
hamon: the *hamon* bases on a kind of *chōji* and is mixed with *ko-gunome* and angular elements, the *yakiba* is relative wide and vivid but also smaller dimensioned in places, in addition we find many *ashi* and *yō*, the *hamon* appears on the *haki-omote* side from the middle section upwards whitish (*hajimi*)
bōshi: on the *omote* side almost *sugu* with *yakitsume*, on the *ura* side *midare-komi* with a *ko-maru-kaeri*

This blade has almost no *funbari* and therefore we can assume that it is *suriage* or *ō-suriage*. The *mihaba* is relative wide, the *sori* does not bend down towards the tip and the latter is a *chū-kissaki*. That means the *sugata* is altogether quite strong and magnificent. When we bring this in combination with the clearly visible *midare-utsuri* and the flamboyant *chōji*-based *hamon*, we arrive inevitably at a mid-Kamakura period Bizen work. At a closer inspection, the *jihada* turns out to stand out in places, that means it is not all over densely forged. And the *chōji* are not that differently sized and do not have these ups and downs like we would expect it for a work from the heyday of the Ichimonji school. This lead some to Mitsutada (光忠) or the early Nagamitsu (長光) or even to Hatakeda Moriie (畠田守家), but there are no *kawazu-no-ko-chōji*.

This blade is a work of Bizen Saburō Kunimune who was a contemporary of Mitsutada and Moriie. He often forged a stout *tachi-sugata* with wide *mihaba* in combination with a flamboyant *chōji*-based *midareba*. So the *kantei* blade is a perfect example for such a *deki*. But he also made slender and more elegant blades with a calm *suguha*-based *hamon*. At a *midareba*, the *yakiba* is rather wide and is sometimes also mixed with smaller, more angular elements in places. This peculiarity can be seen on this blade too. Furthermore, there are the typical *hajimi* in the upper half of the *haki-omote* side. So when you combine all these characteristics, you should be able to arrive at Bizen Saburō Kunimune.

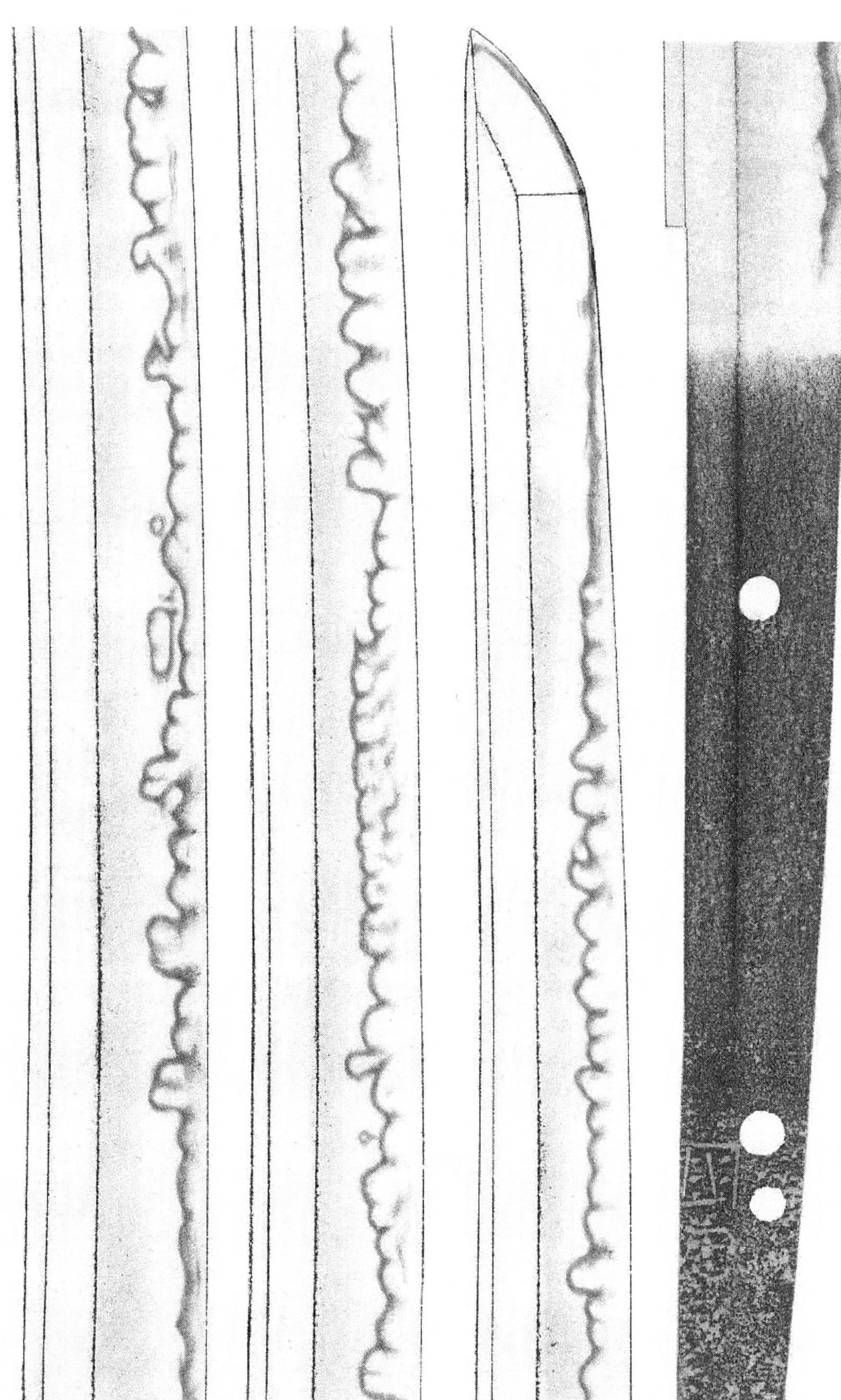

54.600k *tachi*
mei: Kunimune (国宗) [Bizen Saburō]
nagasa 69,7 cm *sori* 2,3 cm
moto-haba 2,8 cm *saki-haba* 1,8 cm
moto-kasane 0,7 cm *saki-kasane* 0,4 cm
kissaki-nagasa 2,6 cm *nakago-nagasa* 19,24 cm
only a little *nakago-sori*

shinogi-zukuri, iori-mune, normal *mihaba*, little tapering, despite the *suriage* a deep *koshizori* which increases again towards the tip, compact *chū-kissaki* which tends somewhat to *ikubi*. The *jigane* is a standing-out *itame* mixed with *mokume* and shows a fine *ji-nie*, *chikei* and a clearly visible *midare-utsuri*. The *hamon* and the *bōshi* can be seen on the *oshigata*. The *midare* is partially angular and there are many *ashi* and *yō* which appear also in a slanting manner all over the blade. The *nioi*-loaden *habuchi* shows *ko-nie*, *kinsuji* and *sunagashi* and the *hada* is clearly visible in the partially characteristically white *yakiba*. The *nakago* is *suriage* and had originally a *kurijiri*. The *yasurime* are *katte-sagari*. There are three *mekugi-ana* and a *niji-mei* is chiselled on the *haki-omote* side on the end of the tang towards the *mune* (Note: The smith worked besides of that flamboyant also in a more calm style on *suguha* basis.)

This blade has a normal *mihaba*, doesn´t taper that much and keeps despite of the *suriage* a deep *koshizori* which increases again towards the *ikubi*-like *chū-kissaki*. This speaks for a typical *sugata* of the middle Kamakura period.

Saburō Kunimune demonstrated a quite varied workmanship but mostly he made a strong *sugata* with a somewhat wider *mihaba*, little tapering and an *ikubi*-like *chū-kissaki*. Blades in that style show an *itame* which stands out, a clearly visible *midare-utsuri*, and a *hamon* in a flamboyant *chōji-midare*. In the case of a more slender *tachi-sugata*, he applied a finely forged *itame* and a more calm *suguha*-based *hamon* mixed with *ko-gunome* and *ko-chōji*. (Due to this two different styles some think that there was a second generation, whereas the first worked in the flamboyant and the second in the calm style. Those who follow the one-generation theory say that these different styles go back to the changes in the life of a single smith.)

So this blade shows the more flamboyant style in *chōji*. However, the peculiarities of the latter are somewhat hard to grasp. In comparison with flamboyant *chōji* interpretations of other Bizen smiths like for example of the Fukuoka-Ichimonji school, his *ōbusa-yakigashira* of the *chōji* are not that high and individual *chōji* elements do not overlap to *jūka-chōji*. Also their shape does not change towards the base of the blade but the *ha* shows on the other hand more ups and downs. But compared to the roundish *chōji* and *gunome* of Osafune Nagamitsu (長光, like on the more calm *meibutsu* „Tsuda Tōtomi Nagamitsu"), the *gunome* of this blade are a bit more pronounced and the *chōji* tend more to *ōbusa*.

In conclusion we can say that the flamboyant style of Kunimune can be dated somewhat later then the heyday of the Fukuoka-Ichimonji school, that means around the Bun´ei era (文永, 1264-1275) when already Osafune Mitsutada (光忠), Hatakeda Moriie (畠田守家) or the young Nagamitsu were active. Old sword documents date Kunimune in the early Kamakura period but according to the current state of studies, this dating is no longer tenable. But when we follow the one-generation theory, then we have to assume that he enjoyed a very long life because there is a *tachi* preserved the Tōkyō National Museum which is dated with the Shōwa era (正和, 1312-1317, this is probably the only existing dated work of Kunimune anyway).

There are relative many blades extant by him and when we count all from *jūyō* papers up to the signed *kokuhō*, then we arrive at about 60 pieces. Incidentally, because of the standing-out *hada* and the *ha-hada* combined with the flamboyant *chōji*, Kunimune is put together with Hatakeda Moriie into a Bizen sideline.

Often we see peculiar linear *hajimi* (whitish spots within the *ha*) at blades of Kunimune. Because they are so typical they are just called „Bizen Saburō´s *hajimi*". This was mentioned with „partially characteristically white *yakiba*" in the description of the *kantei*. The „*Kokon mei-zukushi*" (古今名尽) describes this characteristic as „the area above the *ha* looks like *sashimi*". [Translators note: This might go back to the colour of *sashimi* because they appear pale and white when they are cut very thinly.]

In the case of the flamboyant interpretation in *chōji*, the *bōshi* is a *midare-komi* and at a *suguha*, the *bōshi* continues as *suguha* and ends in a round *kaeri*. The tang has a *kurijiri* and *katte-sagari yasurime*. Without a *bōhi*, the *niji-mei* is mostly chiselled above the *ubu-ana* and somewhat towards the *nakago-mune*. As mentioned, there is probably only one date signature extant.

The majority got all these characteristics and went *atari* for Kunimune. Besides of that, many bade on Osafune Nagamitsu. As mentioned, both were active at about the same time and so it is only natural that they show some similarities as they were both Bizen smiths too. Nagamitsu succeeded Mitsutada as head of the Osafune school and so his workmanship demonstrates generally the style of the Osafune mainline. That means a fine and densely forged *itame*, a clear and bright *jigane*, a clearly visible *midare-utsuri* and a *chōji-hamon* with bright *nioiguchi*. Although Nagamitsu´s *hada* can stand out like here, he usually does not show such a pronounced *ha-hada*. It has also to be mentioned that Nagamitsu´s *ashi* point right-angled to the *ha* and are usually not slanting. And conspicious *hajimi* are totally uncommon for Nagamitsu. So at this *kantei*, it was necessary to make out the subtle differences between the *chōji* interpretations of the Bizen main and sidelines.

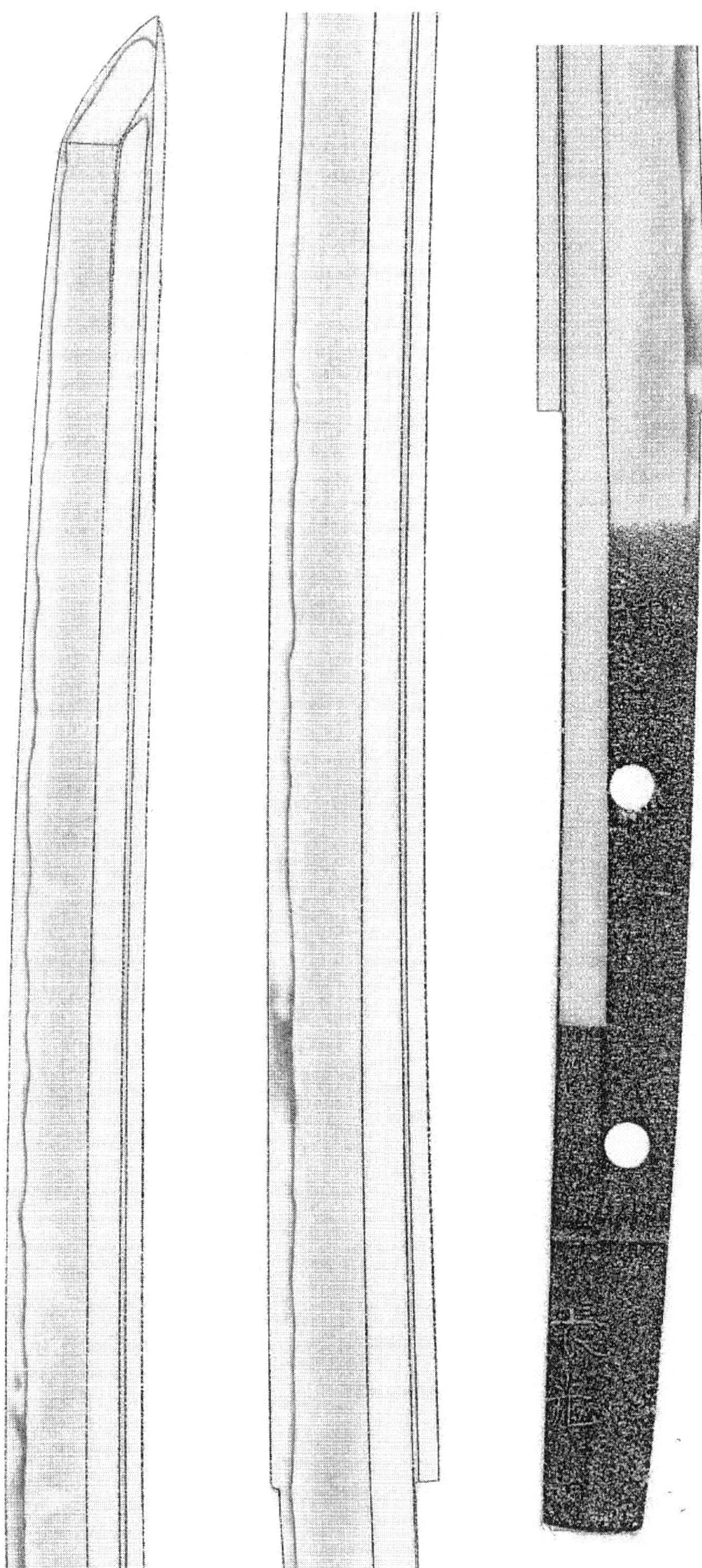

55.661k *tachi*
mei: Nagamitsu (長光)
nagasa 63,48 cm *sori* 2,12 cm
moto-haba 2,2 cm *saki-haba* 1,4 cm
moto-kasane 0,6 cm *saki-kasane* 0,4 cm
kissaki-nagasa 1,8 cm *nakago-nagasa* 16,82 cm
nakago-sori 0,1 cm

shinogi-zukuri, *iori-mune*, quite slender *mihaba*, noticeable taper, despite the *suriage* a deep *koshizori* which bends down towards the tip, the latter is a *chū-kissaki*. The *jigane* is a dense *itame* with fine *ji-nie* and a clearly visible *midare-utsuri*. The *hamon* and the *bōshi* can be seen on the *oshigata*. In addition, *ko-ashi* appear. The *nioiguchi* is bright and rather compact and the hardening is in *nioi-deki* with *ko-nie* (or in *ko-nie-deki* with a tendency towards *nioi-deki* respectively). On both sides a *bōhi* with *kakudome* (inside the tang) is engraved. The tang is *suriage*, has a *kurijiri*, *katte-sagari yasurime* and two *mekugi-ana*. There is a *niji-mei* on the tip of the tang, chiselled somewhat towards the *mune*.

The blade has a rather slender *mihaba*, tapers noticeably and keeps despite the *suriage* a deep *koshizori* which increases again towards the tip. The tip is a compact *ko-kissaki* and so we can say that this is a shape from the late Kamakura period. The *jigane* is a dense, fine and excellently forged *ko-itame* with a clearly visible *midare-utsuri* and speaks truly for the Osafune mainline. The *hamon* is a *suguha-chō* or slightly undulating *notare* with *ko-ashi* and a rather compact *nioiguchi*. The hardening is in *nioi-deki* with *ko-nie*. The *kataochi-gunome* and the *saka-ashi* are not that conspicious and the *bōshi* is a *sansaki-bōshi*. Accordingly, almost all bids were *atari* on Nagamitsu.

Nagamitsu made early in his career blades with a wide *mihaba* and a compact *ikubi*-like *kissaki*. The *hamon* is in such a case like the *meibutsu* Daihannya-Nagamitsu (大般若 長光) or the „Tsuda-Tōtōmi-Nagamitsu" (津田遠江長光) an *ō-chōji* mixed with *kawazu-no-ko chōji*, that means it is quite flamboyant and reminds of his father Mitsutada (光忠).

Later his *hamon* gets more calm and does not show that many ups and downs. The *yakigashira* of the *gunome* and *chōji* are rather roundish and there is also some *togariba*. This is the most characteristical style of Nagamitsu and most of his blades show this *deki*. Later on, his *tachi* become more slender and the *hamon* tends to a *suguha-chō* mixed with *ko-chōji* and *ko-gunome* or shows like the *kantei* blade a *suguha* with compact *nioiguchi*. These are basically the changes in style of Nagamitsu in the course of his artistic period.

The *bōshi* is in the case of a flamboyant *midareba* mostly a *midare-komi* with a pointed *kaeri* (or a *midare-komi* with a *ko-maru-kaeri*). A *sansaku-bōshi* is more often found in combination with a *suguha-chō* or with a pure *suguha*.

The tip of the tang is a *kurijiri*, the *yasurime* are *katte-sagari* and the signature is chiselled in the case of a *niji-mei* on the *sashi-omote* above the *mekugi-ana* and towards the back of the tang.

There were relative many bids on Sanenaga (真長) who also applied a *suguha-chō* similar to the *kantei* blade. So a differentiation is rather difficult and bids on him were counted as *atari* too this time. Incidentally, blades of Sanenaga in such an interpretation have a very compact *nioiguchi* and show also some mixed-in *ko-notare* elements.

There were also *dōzen* bids on Kagemitsu (景光) and Chikakage (近景). These smiths too made many *tachi* in *suguha-chō* with a compact *nioiguchi* but the two were active a little later than Nagamitsu and Sanenaga and so their *suguha-chō* shows also some *ko-gunome* and/or *ko-chōji* elements which tend to slant. Or also a perfect *kataochi-gunome* appears in their work. Also the *ashi* are by trend rather slanting whereas Nagamitsu´s and Sanenaga´s *ashi* run in a right angle towards the *ha*. Chikakage´s *hada* stands more out and shows *ō-hada*. His *utsuri* is a bit weaker and the *hamon* is mostly hardened in *ko-nie-deki*.

Let us briefly address the dated works of these smiths. Works of Nagamitsu with date signatures from the eras Einin (永仁, 1293-1299), Shōan (正安, 1299-1302) and Kagen (嘉元, 1303-1306), and works from Sanenaga with date signatures Shōan (正安, 1299-1302), Kagen (嘉元, 1303-1306) and Tokuji (徳治, 1306-1308) do not show a slanting *hamon*. On the other hand, works of Kagemitsu from the Genkō era (元享, 1321-1324) and of Chikakage from Karyaku (嘉暦, 1326-1329) and Kenmu (建武, 1334-1338) do show slanting *hamon* interpretations. So it is obvious that this trend towards slanting is connected to the later production time and this „phenomenon" can be seen among all late Kamakura-period Bizen schools.

Anyway, there is no single *tachi* extant by Nagamitsu which has a slanting *gunome*. But we know *tantō* and *naginata* which show an angular *gunome* which is regarded as the precursor of the little later *kataochi-gunome*. But there is no angular *gunome* found on later works of Nagamitsu which could directly connect to the interpretations of Kagemitsu or Chikakage. Two early *tantō* of Nagamitsu with datings of the eighth year of Kōan (弘安, 1285) and the third year of Einin (永仁, 1295) show a little angular *gunome*. So we can assume that the foundation stone for *gunome* has already been set back then, even if it took a while to apply it in a more full scale also on longer blades.

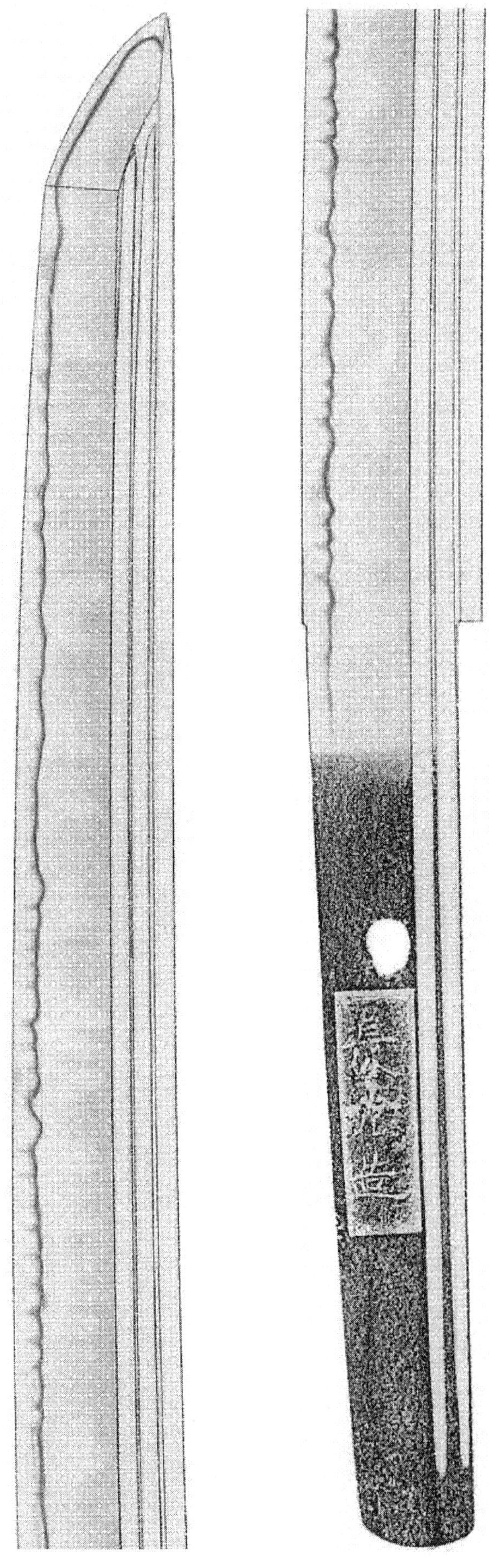

56.659 *wakizashi*
gaku-mei: Nagamitsu tsukuru (長光造)
nagasa 49,0 cm, *sori* 1,2 cm, *shinogi-zukuri*, *iori-mune*

ji: very dense *ko-itame* with plentiful of *ji-nie* and a *midare-utsuri*
hamon: *chū-suguha-chō* mixed with connected *ko-gunome* and some *ko-chōji*, in addition many *ashi*, the *nioiguchi* looks soft and is bright, the hardening is in *ko-nie-deki* but partially the *nioiguchi* tends to *nioi-deki*
bōshi: *sugu-chō* with a short *ko-maru-kaeri*

Many reckoned this blade as a *kodachi* or *uchigatana* but it should not be overseen that there is no *funbari*, that means the blade is shortened. And when you reconstruct the original form then you arrive at a slender *tachi-sugata* of the late Kamakura period with a slightly increasing *sori* towards the tip.

The *kitae* is fine and dense and a clear *midare-utsuri* appears. The *hamon* is a *suguha-chō* mixed with connected *ko-gunome* and *ko-chōji*. There are many *ashi* and the *bōshi* does not run parallel to the *fukura* but as straight *suguha* up to the *ko-maru-kaeri*. This so-called „*sansaku-bōshi*" is a typical characteristic of Nagamitsu. All in all we can place the blade to the late artistic period of this smith where he signed often with „Sakon Shōgen" (左近将監).

Most of the bids were in the vicinity of Nagamitsu, for example on Sanenaga (真長) or Kagemitsu (景光). Maybe the fine and beautiful *hada* leaded some to the former but at Sanenaga, we would expect a more conspicious *ko-notare* within the *hamon* and a more compact *nioiguchi*. And at Kagemitsu, who worked of course in a fine and beautiful *hada* too, we would see more slanting *midare* and *ashi*.

However, some focused on the *ko-nie* and went for Chikakage (近景). But at Chikakage, the *hada* would stand out more, the *midare* and *ashi* would slant and the individual elements of the *hamon* would be more densely arranged. In addition, his *nioiguchi* is rather subdued. By the way, his *ha-nie* are noticeably stronger and the *sansaku-bōshi* starts a little later after the *yokote* and appears more as *notare-komi*.

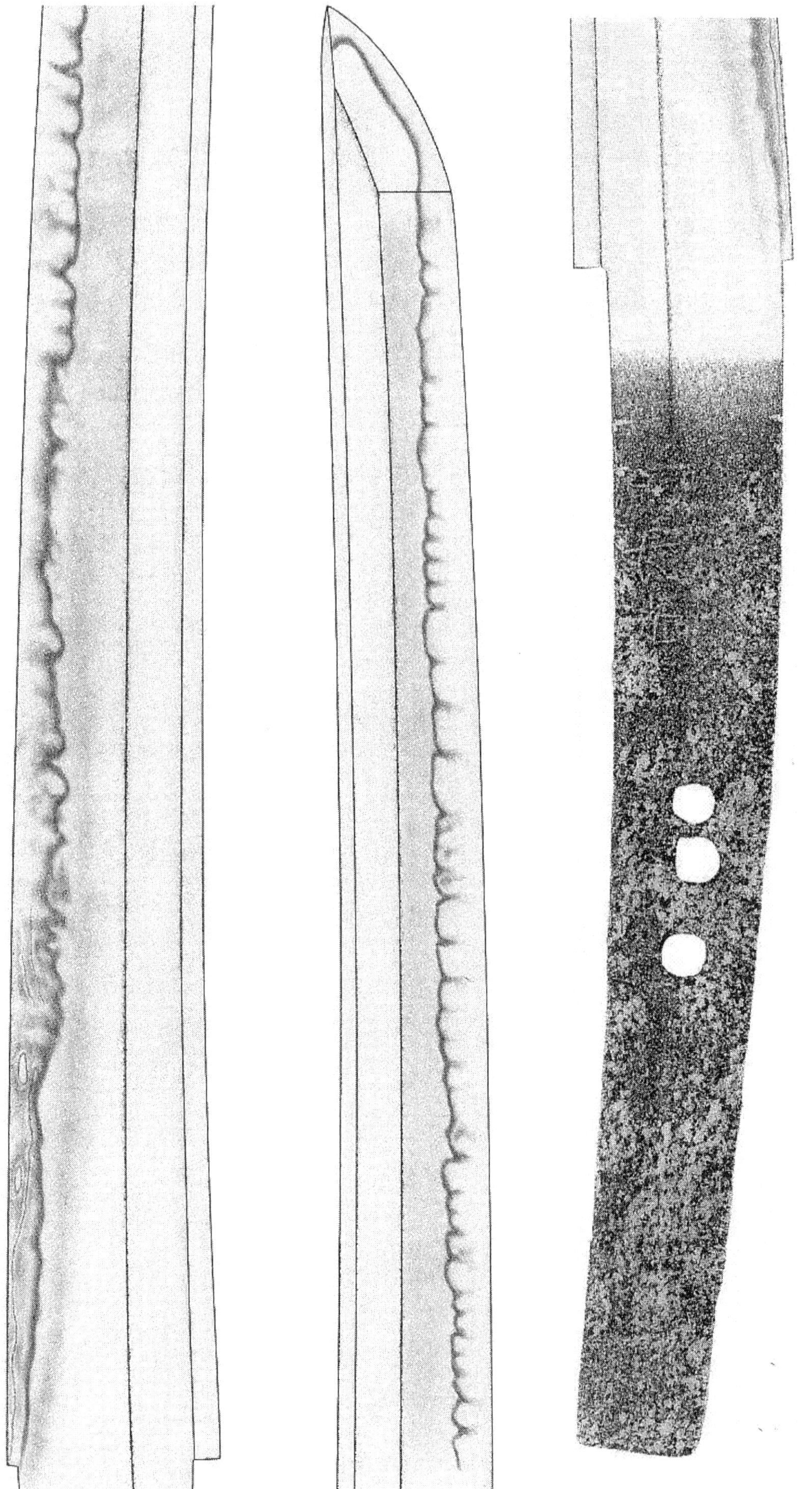

57.646 *tachi*
mumei: Nagamitsu (長光)
nagasa 72,1 cm, *sori* 2,4 cm, *shinogi-zukuri*, *iori-mune*

ji: rather dense *itame* with plentiful of *ji-nie* and *chikei* and a *midare-utsuri*
hamon: *chōji* mixed with *gunome* and *togariba*-like elements, in addition many *ashi* and *yō*, relative wide *nioiguchi*, *ko-nie*, *kinsuji* and *sunagashi*
bōshi: shallow *notare* with a very short *maru-kaeri*

Due to the *funbari* we can assume that the blade is *ubu* or almost *ubu*. In combination with the normal *mihaba*, the deep *koshizori* which increases again towards the tip, the *chū-kissaki* and the clear *midare-utsuri* we can definitely say that this is a Bizen blade from the middle Kamakura period and not earlier. The relative flamboyant *midareba* which consists mainly of *chōji* mixed with *gunome* and *ko-notare* leads us towards Ichimonji or Hatakeda or to Osafune smiths like Mitsutada (光忠) or Nagamitsu. This *tachi* is a work of the latter, the 2nd gen. Osafune mainline. Nagamitsu applied in his early years a similarily flamboyant *deki* as his father but later also a calm *suguha-chō* with compact *nioiguchi*. That means he showed a very varied range of styles and the *kantei* blade belongs to the former group.

Most bids were on Bizen smiths. In the case of the Fukuoka-Ichimonji school, the *chōji* woud be more conspicious compared to Nagamitsu and the flamboyant *midareba* would show more ups and downs. At the Hatakeda school or at Mitsutada, the *hamon* would be somewhat larger dimensioned and there would he some densely arranged *kawazu-no-ko chōji* towards the base. Ichimonji and Hatakeda works would also show a more standing-out *hada* than this Nagamitsu, whereas the *kitae* of Mitsutada is noticeably finer. One should also pay attention to the *bōshi*. This *sansaku-bōshi* is a typical characteristic of the Osafune smiths of the later Kamakura period, for example of Nagamitsu, Sanenaga (真長) or Kagemitsu (景光). Such a *bōshi* is not seen in the early Kamakura period.

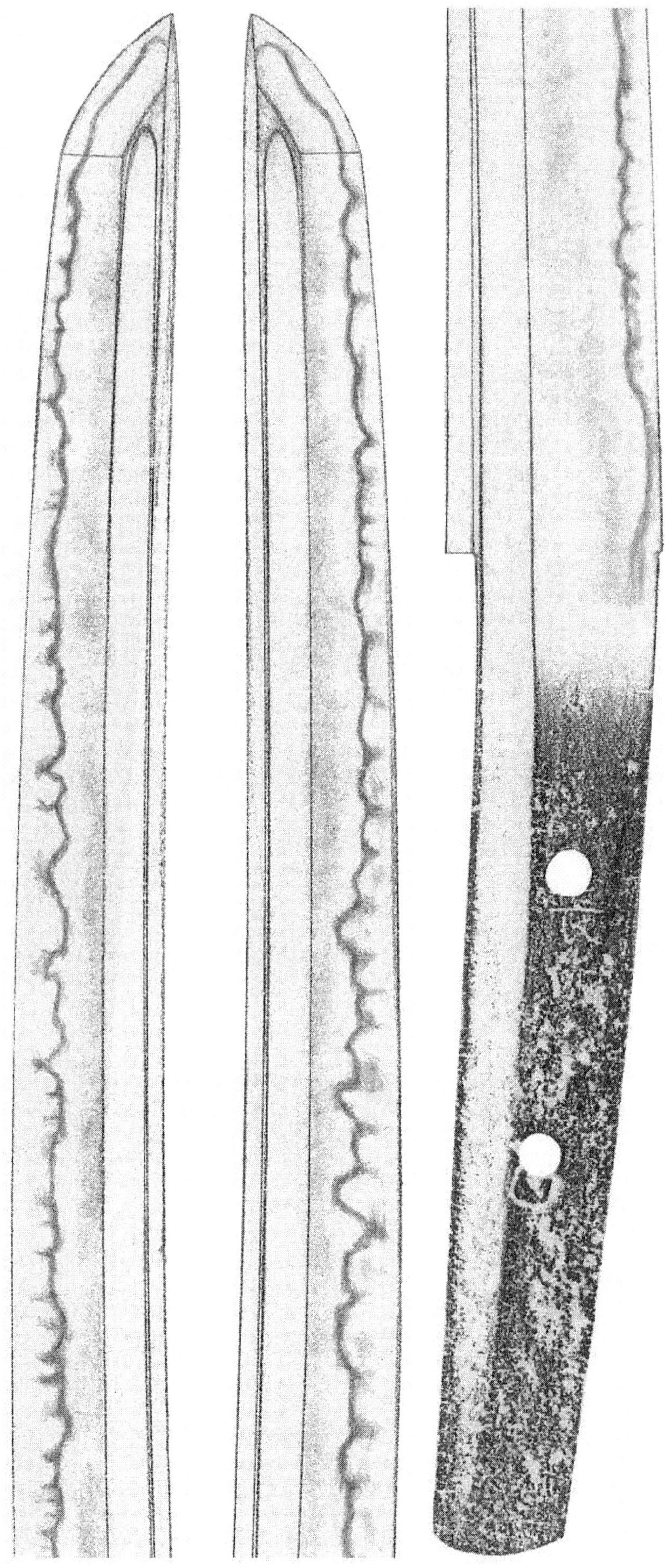

58.621 *tachi*
mei: Nagamitsu (長光)
nagasa 70,9 cm, *sori* 2,8 cm, *shinogi-zukuri*, *iori-mune*

ji: *itame-hada* mixed with *mokume*, in addition plentiful of fine *ji-nie* and a *midare-utsuri* which appears as *sugu* in places
hamon: *chōji* mixed with *gunome* and *ko-notare*, there is a large *koshiba* at the base on the *haki-ura* side, the *hamon* is quite flamboyant and in *nioi-deki* with *ko-nie*
bōshi: shallow *notare-komi* with a *ko-maru-kaeri*
horimono: on both sides a *bō-hi* which runs with *kake-nagashi* into the tang

As there goes a straight *sugu*-like *utsuri* out of the *machi* we can assume that the blade is *ubu* or almost *ubu*. It has a deep *koshizori* which increases again towards the tip and this is typical for the middle and late Kamakura period. The *utsuri* tends to *midare* in places and the flamboyant *hamon* bases on *chōji* and is mixed with *gunome* and *ko-notare*, so we are at Bizen. When we try to narrow the workmanship in combination with the time down, we arrive at the Ichimonji or Hatakeda school or at the earlier Osafune smiths Mitsutada (光忠) and Nagamitsu.

Well, the *kantei* blade is actually a work of Nagamitsu. His varied style ranges from a flamboyant *chōji*-based *hamon* in the *deki* of his father Mitsutada to a calm *suguha* with compact *nioiguchi* in his later years. So this blade dates clearly to his earlier artistic period.

Some bade also on Ichimonji and Hatakeda and this is as mentioned also understandable. But the *hamon* which narrows down and gets more calm towards the *monouchi* is typical for the Osafune school of that time. Also the round and swelling *yakigashira* are typical for Nagamitsu. At Ichimonji or Hatakeda, there wouldn´t be so conspicious *gunome* but contrary mostly *ō-chōji* and/or *kawazu-no-ko chōji*. Also their *hamon* is even a bit more flamboyant than at Nagamitsu. Also the *kitae* would stand more out at Ichimonji and Hatakeda and in the case of Mitsutada, the *hada* would be a little finer.

One should also pay attention to the *bōshi*. This is namely not uniform but appears as *sansaku-bōshi*. This characteristic is not seen at the earlier Ichimonji or Hatakeda smiths and peculiar to Nagamitsu, Sanenaga (真長), Kagemitsu (景光), Chikakage (近景) and other Osafune smiths.

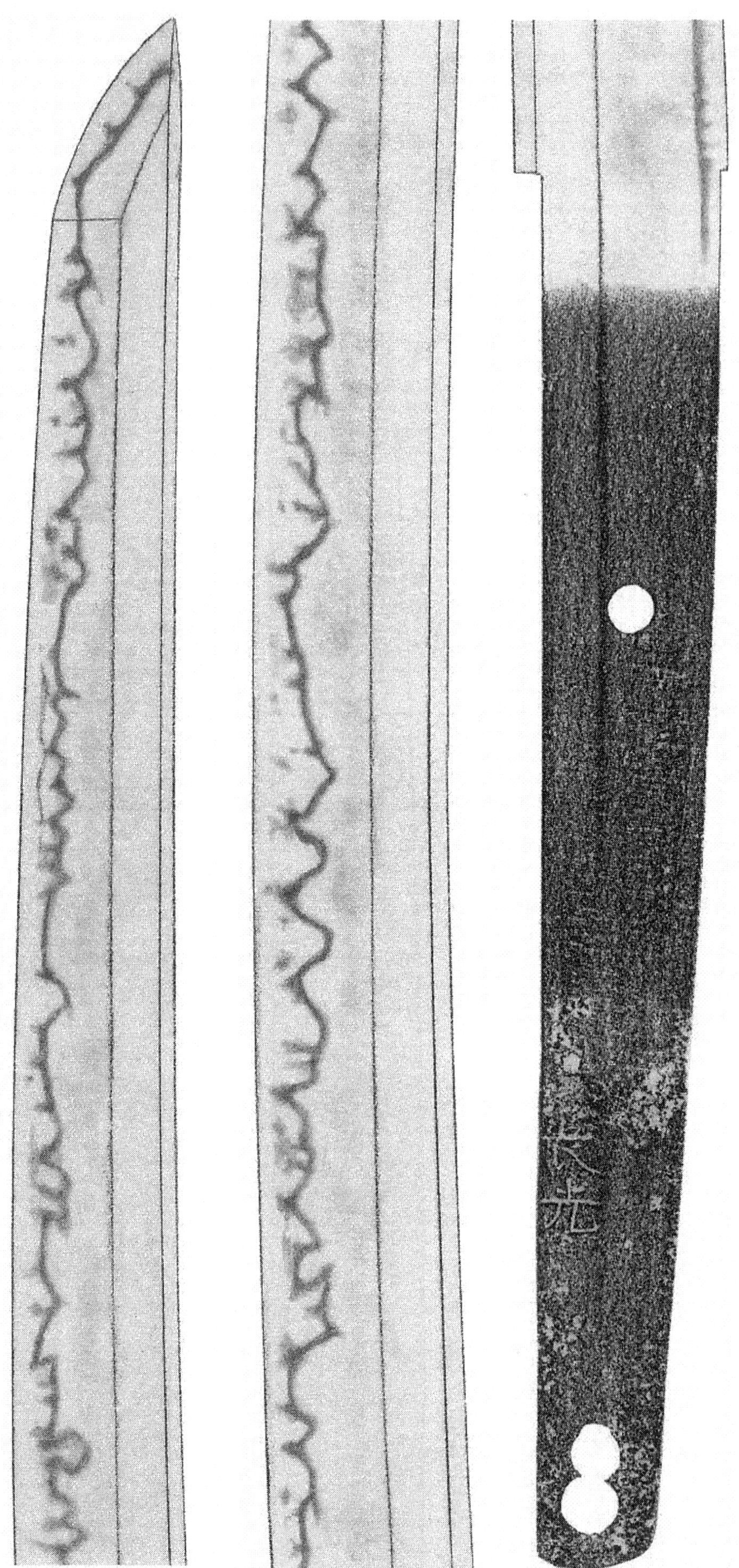

59.606 *tachi*
mei: Nagamitsu (長光)
nagasa 68,7 cm, *sori* 2,7 cm, *shinogi-zukuri, iori-mune*

ji: standing-out *itame-hada* mixed with *mokume* and *nagare*, fine *ji-nie*, many *chikei*, and a clearly visible *midare-utsuri*
hamon: based on *chōji* mixed with *gunome*, *ko-chōji*, and *kawazu*-like *chōji*, these elements are rather densely arranged in places, thick *nioi*, plentiful of *nie*, also *ashi* and connected *yō* and *kinsuji*, *sunagashi* and *yubashiri* in places
bōshi: shallow *midare-komi* with *yakitsume*-like end and almost no *kaeri* at all

Because of the wide *mihaba* and the deep *koshizori* which increases again towards the tip we can attribute this blade on the basis of its *sugata* to the middle Kamakura period. And the *chōji*-based *hamon* with the clear *midare-utsuri* narrows the attribution down to Bizen. As there are some wide and flamboyant *chōji* around the middle section, many went for Fukuoka-Ichimonji, and because of the standing-out *hada*, the plentiful of *nie* in *ji* and *ha*, and the conspicious *nie*-based *hataraki* like *kinsuji* and *sunagashi*, some bade also on Saburō Kunimune (三郎国宗). And the *kawazu-no-ko chōji* in turn leaded sonm to Hatakeda Moriie (畠田守家) and Mitsutada (光忠). All these bids are quite understandable.

But the more shallow *yakiba* at the *monouchi* area and the way the *gunome* are connected, the partially slanting *hamon*, the right-angled *ashi* and the swollen *gunome* around the middle section of the *haki-ura* side and below the *yokote* are typical for Nagamitsu.

There are many different styles and signature variations extant by Nagamitsu. Some blades show a wide *mihaba* and a flamboyant *kawazu-no-ko chōji* or *ō-chōji* and some are slender and show a calm *suguha* with a compact *nioiguchi*. At a *yakiba* with a mix of larger and smaller *gunome* and *chōji*, the latter are mostly arranged to groups of five. He also added much *nie* from time to time and a densely arranged, classical *midareba* reminds of Ko-Bizen or Ichimonji. This style is not limited to Nagamitsu but can also be seen at his father Mitsutada or his student Sanenaga (真長). So the similarities in workmanship of these three smiths should always be kept in mind.

Incidentally, we would generally expect a *suguha*-based *bōshi* in *sansaku* manner. Such an irregular interpretation like seen on the *kantei* blade is rather rare, although a hint of *sansaku* can be nevertheless grasped.

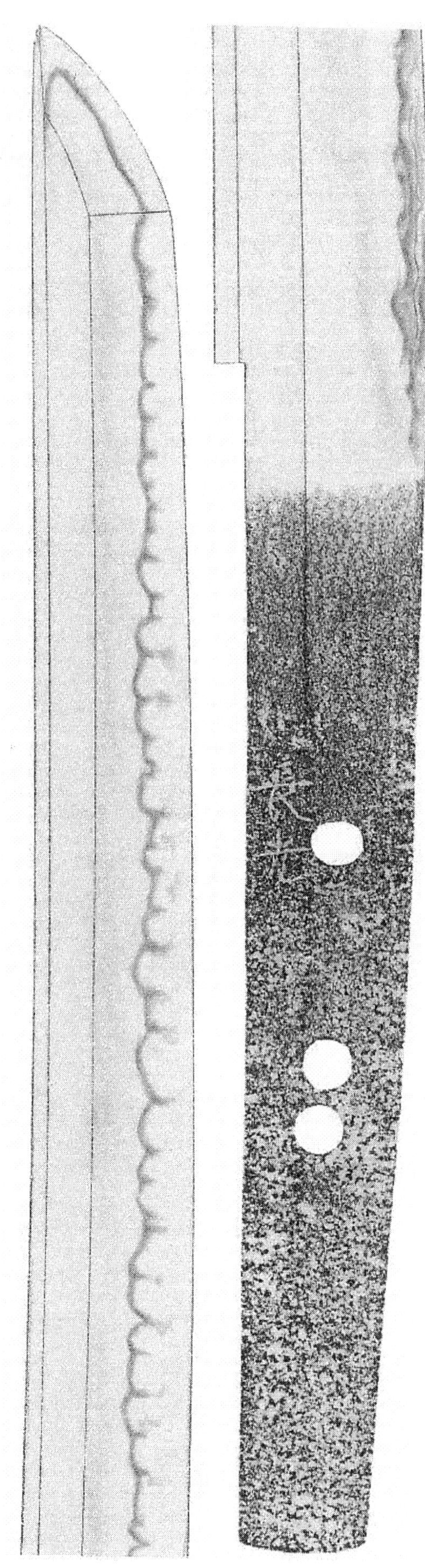

60.591 *tachi*
mei: Nagamitsu (長光)
nagasa 73,0 cm, *sori* 2,6 cm, *shinogi-zukuri, iori-mune*

ji: densely forged *itame* mixed with *ko-mokume*, fine *ji-nie*, an *utsuri* going out from the *machi* which devlops in its course to a clearly visible *midare-utsuri*
hamon: *suguha-chō* mixed with *ko-gunome*, the upper half of the blade shows a noticeable trend towards *gunome*, also *chōji*, *ashi* and *yō* are seen, the hardening is in *nioi-deki* but the compact *nioiguchi* shows also *ko-nie*
bōshi: slightly irregular *suguha-chō* with a *ko-maru-kaeri* (= *sansaku-bōshi*)

On the basis of the *koshizori* which increases again towards the tip, we can place this elegant *tachi* into the middle Kamakura period. There is *funbari* and an *utsuri* goes out from the *machi*, so it is safe to assume that the blade is *ubu* or almost *ubu*. The clearly visible *midare-utsuri* leads us to Bizen and with the *suguha-chō* in *nioi-deki* mixed with *gunome* and the *sansaki-bōshi*, we arrive at Nagamitsu, Sanenaga (真長), Kagemitsu (景光) or Chikakaga (近景), thus at earlier Osafune-*mono*.

A *yakiba* with not that obvious slanting elements, *ashi* pointing right-angled to the *ha* and a rather densely arranged *gunome* with roundish *yakigashira* is among the mentioned smiths first and foremost typical for Nagamitsu and Sanenaga. But as we have a *deki* with a compact *nioiguchi* which was often applied in a very similar manner by Sanenaga too, also bids on him were counted as *atari*. But at Sanenaga, we would generally expect some mixed-in *ko-notare* and a *bō-utsuri* which appears slightly narrower towards the *ha*.

At Kagemitsu and Chikakage on the other hand, angular *gunome* and/or *kataochi-gunome* would appear which tend to slant. And we would also expect conspicious *saka-ashi*. Kagemitsu in turn forged a finer *ko-itame* of a slightly higher qualty which shows also a finer *ji-nie*. At Chikakage on the other hand, the *hada* would stand out and his *ha* is quite *nie*-loaden for such early Osafune-*mono*.

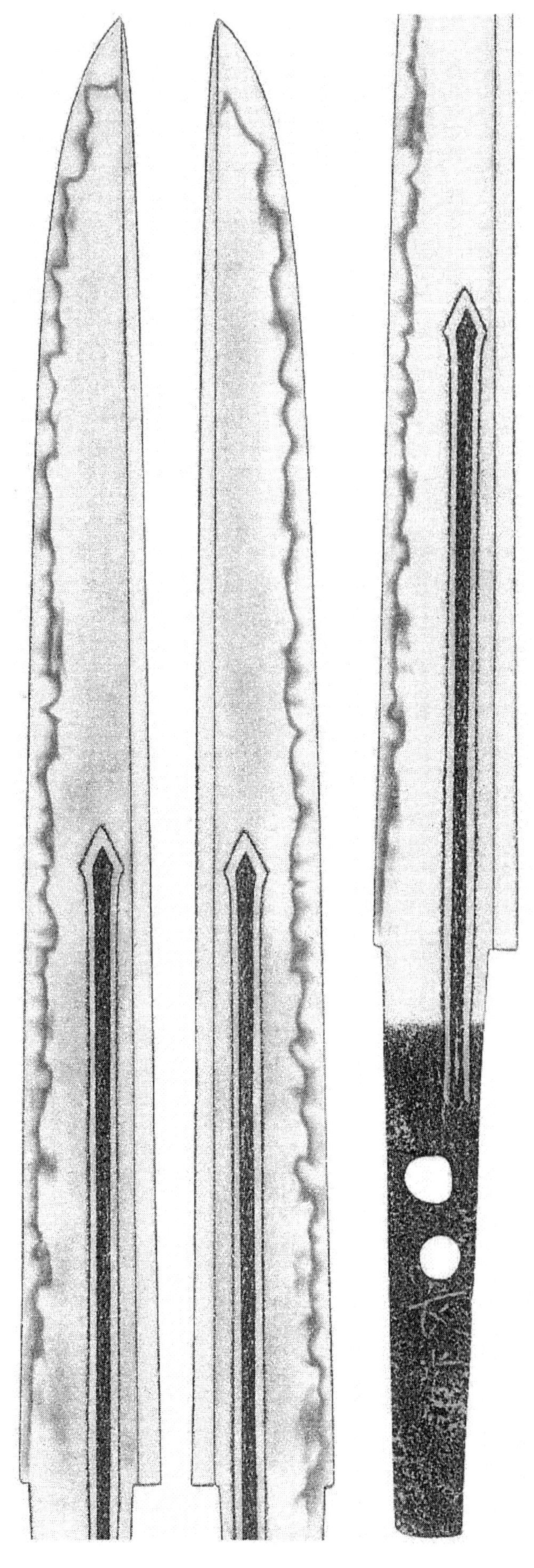

61.613 *tantō*
mei: Nagamitsu (長光)
nagasa 21,2 cm, some *uchizori*, *hira-zukuri*, *iori-mune*

ji: rather dense *itame* with *ji-nie* and a clearly visible *utsuri*
hamon: *ko-gunome-chō* mixed with *ko-chōji* and *togari*, *nioi-deki* with some *ko-nie*
bōshi: *midare-komi* with a *ko-maru-kaeri*
horimono: on both sides towards the base a *suken* which runs with *kake-nagashi* into the tang

This *tantō* has with its *uchizori* the highly elegant *sugata* typical for the Kamakura period, although the *nagasa* looks a little long in comparison with the *mihaba*. As there is an *utsuri* and a *ko-gunome*-based *midareba*, many went for Bizen smiths of the Kamakura period, especially for Kagemitsu (景光) and Motoshige (元重).

Of course, there are pieces of both of them with a typical Kamakura-period *tantō-sugata* extant and the strong point of them was a *ko-gunome*-based *midareba* too. But Kagemitsu´s *gunome* shows mostly slanting *yakigashira* which result in a so-called „*kataochi-gunome*". Well, the *gunome* elements of this blade show a slight tendency to *kataochi* too so a bid on Kagemitsu is quite understandable. But when we compare the full *kataochi-gunome* of Kagemitsu-*tantō* with this *hamon*, we see here plentiful of *ko-chōji* and *togariba* and the interpretation lacks the „orderliness" of Kagemitsu. Motoshige too applied a *gunome* similar to Kagemitsu but his *yakigashira* are horizontally stretched and form over the entire blade an uniform straight top line, i.e. there are no major ups and downs or breaking-out *yakigashira*.

There are extremely few *tantō* extant by Nagamitsu. Analogous to his son Kagemitsu, we know some few *tantō* with a *ko-gunome*-based *midareba* like here. But Nagamitsu´s *tantō* tend towards a *yoroidōshi*-like shape with a thicker *kasane*. And also this blade has a relative thick *kasane*. This might be the keypoint to come to Nagamitsu. But the rarity of his *tantō* was taken into account at the *kantei* so more hints than usual were given to the participants.

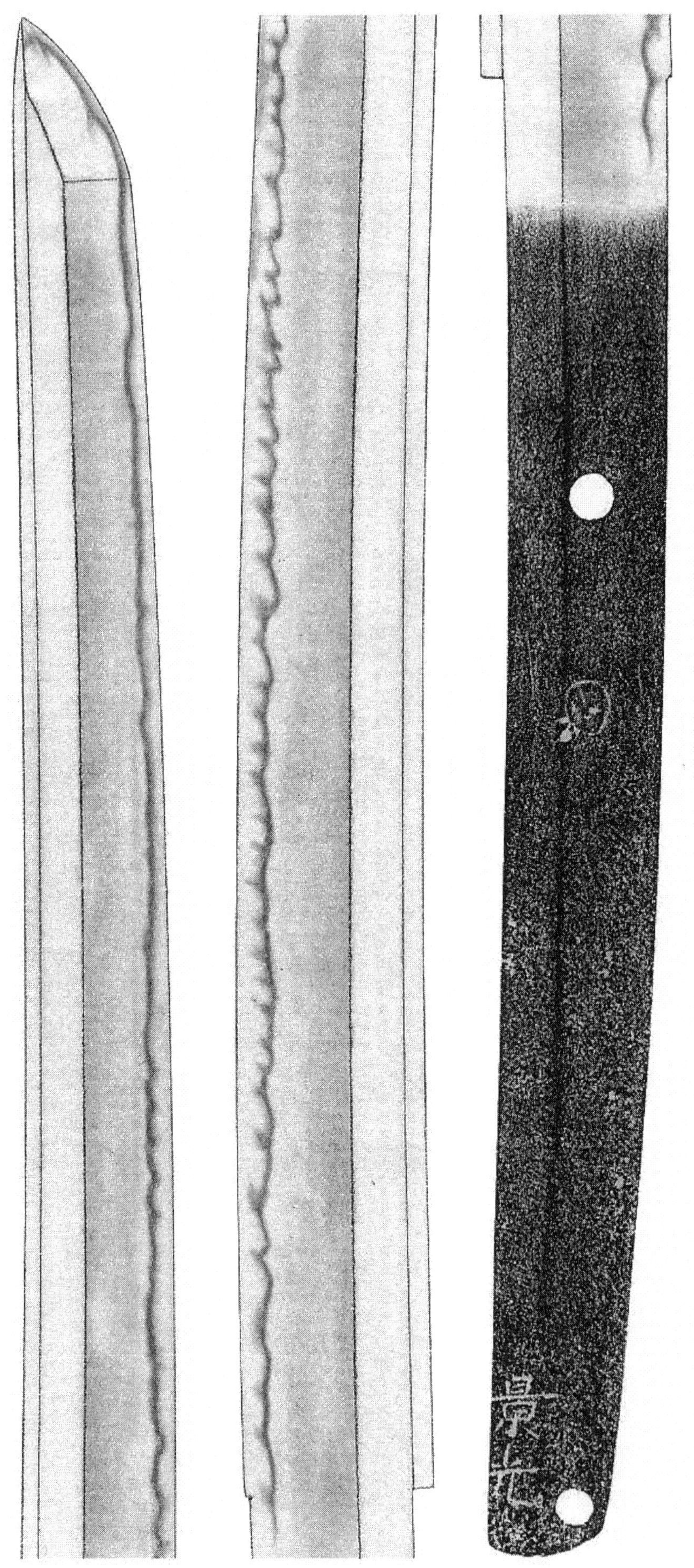

62.626 *tachi*
mei: Kagemitsu (景光)
nagasa 67,9 cm, *sori* 2,1 cm, *shinogi-zukuri*, *iori-mune*

ji: very dense *ko-itame-hada* with plentiful of *ji-nie* and *utsuri*, the steel is bright and clear
hamon: based on *suguha* and mixed with *ko-gunome* and *ko-chōji*, the *midareba* tends to slant along the lower half of the blade, in addition *ashi* and *saka-ashi* are seen, the hardening is in *nioi-deki*
bōshi: a little *midare-komi* with a *ko-maru-kaeri*

Despite the *suriage* the blade keeps a deep *koshizori* and when we combine this with the slender, tapering shape and the small *kissaki*, we would arrive inevitably at a *tachi-sugata* which does not date later than early Kamakura. But the *sori* increases again towards the tip and does not bend down as we would expect it for that time. So we are actually in the late Kamakura period and Kagemitsu is well known for making such a *tachi-sugata*.

The *kitae* is a truly beautiful, very dense *ko-itame* with plentiful of *ji-nie* and a clearly visible *utsuri*. The *hamon* bases on *suguha* and is mixed with *ko-gunome* and *chōji* which appear somewhat slanted in the lower half of the blade. The hardening is in *nioi-deki* and we see *saka-ashi*. So all in all we have the typical characteristics of Kagemitsu in the *ji* as well as in the *ha*.

There were many *dōzen* bids on Nagamitsu (長光) and Chikakage (近景). They too made slender blades but no conspiciously slanting *hamon* with *saka-ashi* is known from Nagamitsu. And at Chikakage, the *hada* would stand out and the *ha* would show more *nie*. There were also some bids on Sanenaga (真長). He too made many slender blades with a finely forged *kitae* but from him we would expect more mixed-in *midare* and *notare* and a more compact *nioiguchi*. In addition, he applied almost always a classical *sansaku-bōshi*.

Besides of *dōzen*, some went also for Ko-Aoe or Aoe. But when this is an Aoe blade from the Kamakura period, then *chirimen* would appear and the *hamon* would be very *nie*-loaden. At Osafune Motoshige (元重) – some reckoned the blade as his work – the *kitae* would tend to *masame* and the *hamon* would consist of an angular *midare* or *kataochi-gunome*. And his *bōshi* would be pointed.

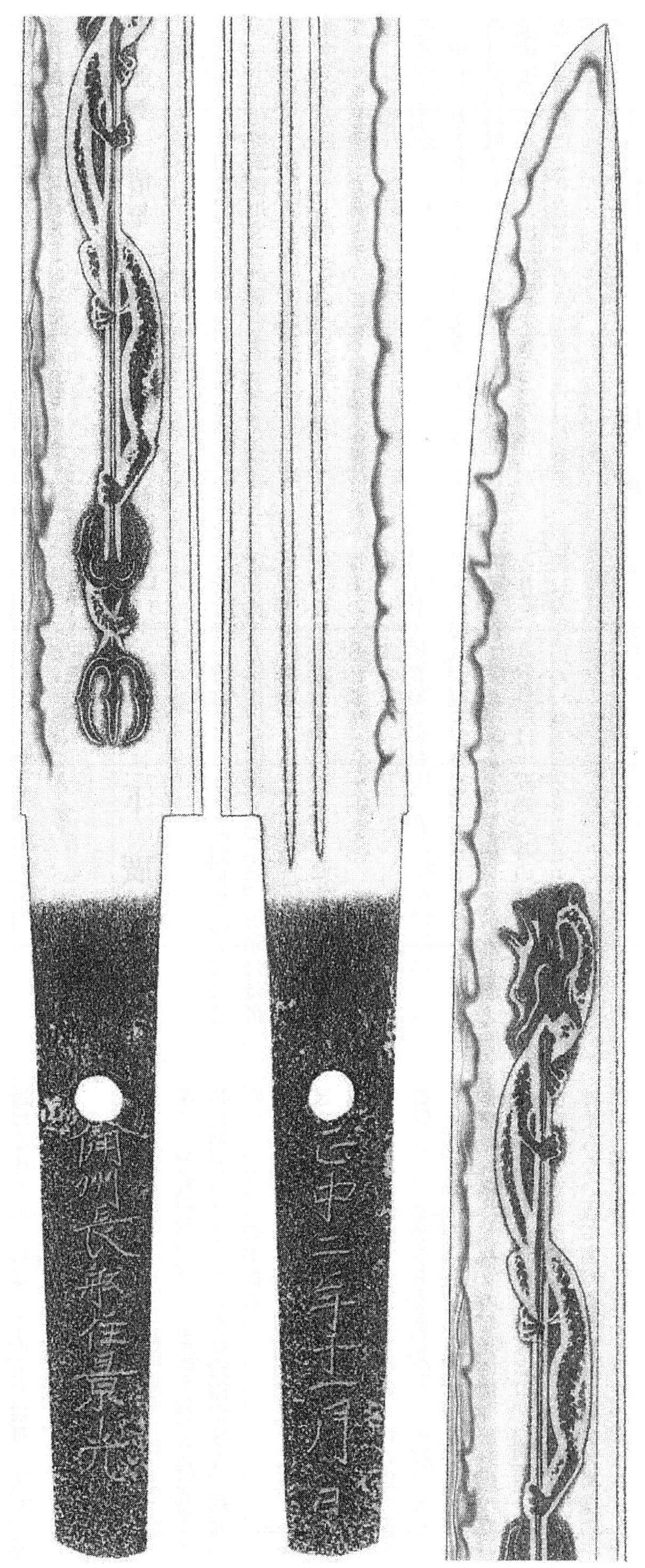

63.615 *tantō*
mei: Bishū Osafune-jū Kagemitsu (備州長船住景光)
Shōchū ni-nen jūichi-gatsu-hi (正中二年十一月日, „a day in the eleventh month Shōchū two [= 1325]")
nagasa 25,91 cm, only very little *uchizori*, *hira-zukuri*, *mitsu-mune*

ji: dense *itame* with *ji-nie* and fine *chikei* and a *bō-utsuri*
hamon: *kataochi-gunome* mixed with angular and other *gunome* elements, in addition *ashi*, *kinsuji* and *sunagashi*, the hardening is in *nioi-deki* with *ko-nie* and the *nioiguchi* is bright
bōshi: on the *omote* a shallow *notare* and on the *ura* side *sugu*, on both sides with a *ko-maru-kaeri*
horimono: there is a *kurikara* engraved on the *omote* and *gomabashi* with *kake-nagashi* on the *ura* side

The blade shown here is a *tantō* of Osafune Kagemitsu dated Shōchū two (1325). We know date signatures of that smith from the Kagen (嘉元, 1303-1306) to the Kenmu era (建武, 1334-1338). Later works, that means *tantō* from the late Kamakura period, are wider, more elongated, have a thicker *kasane* and no *sori*. This *tantō* dates somewhat earlier and shows the transitional shape to that interpretation.

The *jigane* is a dense and very fine *itame* with a *bō-utsuri*. The *hamon* is a pure Kagemitsu *kataochi-gunome* and accordingly, most were spot-on at the very first round. But some bade also on other smiths which worked in *kataochi-gunome*. His son Kanemitsu (兼光) for example continued his style in his early years, although his *ha* is more regular and the individual elements are somewhat smaller dimensioned.

A similar workmanship is also seen at Motoshige (元重) from the same province. He too applied sometimes a pure *kataochi-gunome* but his individual angular *gunome* elements are wider apart and the *yakigashira* form allover an uniform line. In addition, his *bōshi* is mostly pointed and the *jigane* shows *nagare*, what distinguishes him from the Osafune mainline.

If you take a closer look at the course of the *hamon* of the *kantei* blade, you see that the *kataochi* elements are slanting and that there are almost always two angular *gunome* arranged to one pair of *kataochi-gunome*. This is very typical for Kagemitsu.

The body of the dragon on this *kurikara-horimono* is engraved somewhat apart from the *suken*. This posture is also called „pregnant dragon" (*harami-ryū*, 孕龍) because the leg makes this area look like a pregnant belly. Such a *horimono* is often seen at Nagamitsu (長光) and later successors of the Osafune mainline.

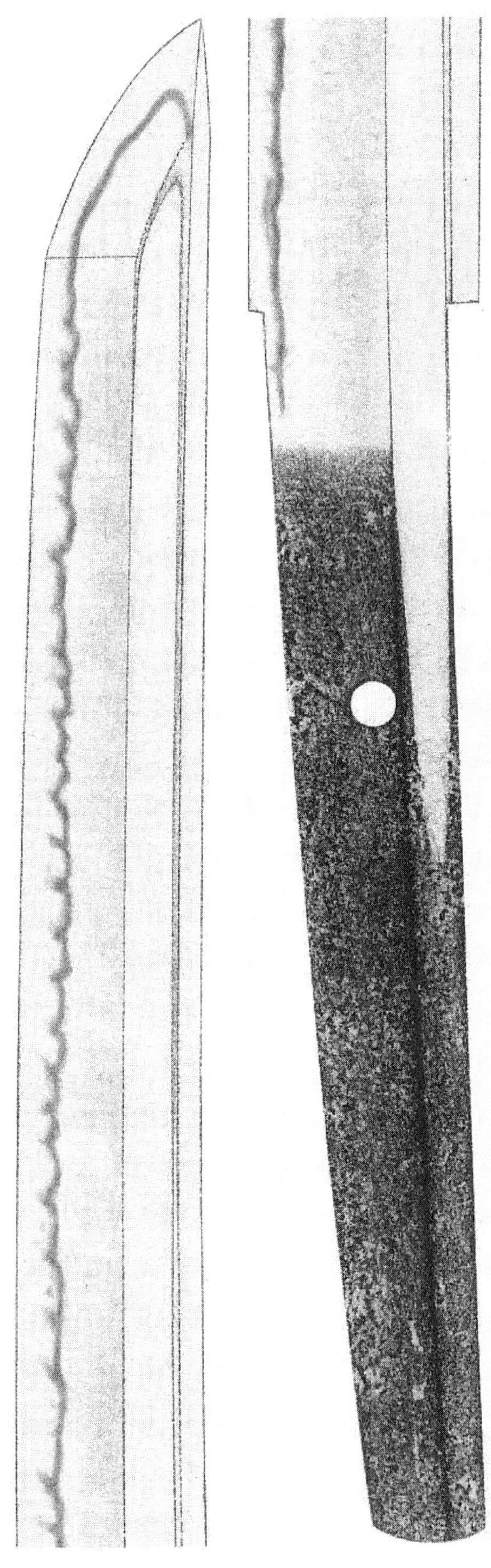

64.614 *katana*
mumei: Kagemitsu (景光)
nagasa 71,8 cm, *sori* 2,2 cm, *shinogi-zukuri*, *iori-mune*

ji: very dense and clear *ko-itame* with plentiful of *ji-nie*, fine *chikei* and a *midare-utsuri*
hamon: *suguha-chō* with *ko-chōji*, *ko-gunome* and angular *gunome*, in addition many *ashi* and *yō* which are slanting all over the blade, the *nioiguchi* in *nioi-deki* with *ko-nie* is bright and clear, there are also some few *kinsuji* and *sunagashi*
bōshi: on both sides *midare-komi* with a *ko-maru* on the *omote* and a pointed *kaeri* on the *ura* side
horimono: on both sides a *bōhi* is added, on the *omote* side it runs with *kake-nagashi* into the tang and on the *ura* it ends in *maru-dome* and shows below an additional *bonji*

This is an *ō-suriage-mumei* blade of Kagemitsu with *jūyō* papers. The *kitae* is a very dense and finely forged *ko-itame* which stands out all over the blade and shows plentiful of *ji-nie*. The steel has a deep blue shimmering. So this blade has amongst all Osafune-*mono* the utmost fine and beautiful *jigane* which is so typical for Kagemitsu.

Kagemitsu´s father Nagamitsu (長光) applied on some few *tantō* and *naginata* a slightly angular *gunome* but it was Kagemitsu who perfected it to the well-known *kataochi-gunome*. But a *deki* with a continuous, regular *kataochi-gunome* from tip to base is only seen on *tantō* and *ko-wakizashi*. At *tachi*, like the *kantei* blade, the *hamon* bases on *suguha* and shows angular *gunome*, *ko-chōji*, *ko-gunome* and of course *kataochi-gunome*. There appear *ashi* and *yō* which usuall slant throughout the blade. However, an uniform *kataochi-gunome* on *tachi* can be seen at his son Kanemitsu (兼光).

There were some bids on the Un group (雲). The blade shows a *midare-utsuri* with some *antai* areas so it could be mistaken as *jifu-utsuri*. But such a *midare-utsuri* with partial *antai* or a slanting *utsuri* is often seen at Kagemitsu, Chikakage (近景) an other Osafune mainline smiths of the late Kamakura period. In the case of the Un group, the *sori* would appear as *toriizori* and the *bōshi* would be usually a large *ō-maru*. But the beautiful *kitae* leads one right away to Kagemitsu anyway.

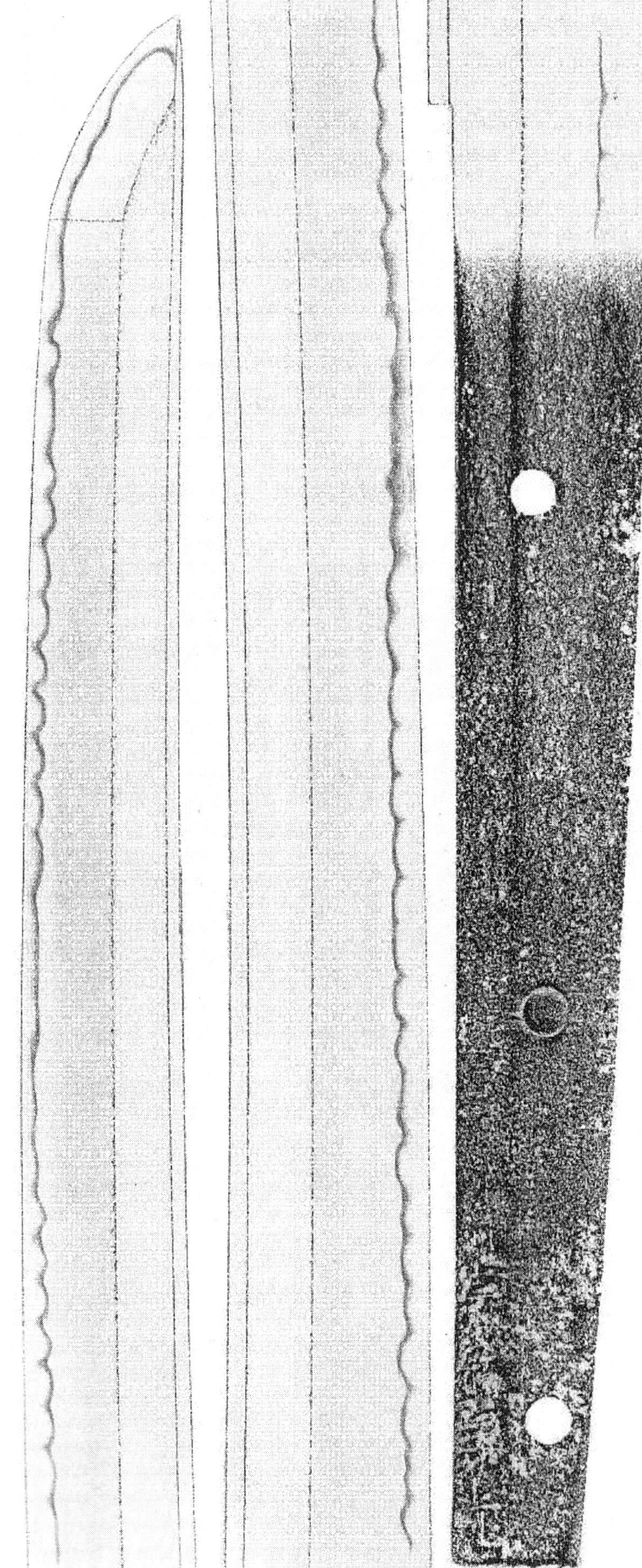

65.664 *tachi*
mei: ?-shū Osafune Kanemitsu (◯州長船兼光)
nagasa 72,7 cm, *sori* 2,1 cm, *shinogi-zukuri*, *iori-mune*

ji: rather densely forged *itame* mixed with *mokume*, *ji-nie*, *chikei* and a clear *midare-utsuri*
hamon: angular *gunome* based on *kataochi* which is mixed with *ko-gunome*, *ashi* and *yō*, all elements tend to slant and the *kataochi-gunome* elements are noticeably apart, the hardening is in *nioi-deki*
bōshi: *midare-komi* with a *ko-maru-kaeri*

The blade has almost no *funbari* and therefore we can assume that it is shortened. When we reconstruct the original shape then we have a *sugata* with a normal *mihaba* with a noticeable taper and a *koshizori* which increases again towards the tip. On the basis of that we can date the blade into the late Kamakura period. And in combination with the *midare-utsuri* and the *kataochi*-based *gunome* we come inevitably to an early work of Kanemitsu.

Regarding the Osafune smiths, it was Nagamitsu (長光) who applied the first prototype of a more angular, i.e. a *kataochi-gunome*. We know such a *deki* from two *tantō* dated Kōan eight (弘安, 1285) and Einin three (永仁, 1295). That means he applied such a *hamon* only on *tantō* and *naginata* and there are no *tachi* of Nagamitsu with a *kataochi-gunome*. But his son Kagemitsu (景光) did so, even not in a pure form on long swords. He hardened namely a mix of angular *ko-gunome*, *ko-chōji* and *kataochi-gunome*. An uniform *kataochi-gunome* which runs continuously from tip to base is restricted to *tantō*. On long swords, an uniform *kataochi-gunome* is then found by Kagemitsu′s son Kanemitsu but the latter applied also a *midareba* which is mixed with longer uniform *kataochi-gunome* sections like we can see it on the *kantei* blade. Works in such a *deki* do not show a *sansaku-bōshi* but a *midare-komi* with a round *kaeri*. This peculiarity applies to the *kantei* blade too and is a hint to recognize works of this smith.

Some also went for the Yoshii school (吉井). This might go back to the fact that the blade suffered many polishes and so the quality of the original *jigane* is no longer present. Also the *hamon* is somewhat smaller dimensioned as usually seen at Kanemitsu and so the blade leaves at a glance a rather unspectacular impression. But in the case of a Yoshii work, the *utsuri* would follow closely the course of the connected *ko-gunome*. Well, there are some Yoshii blades in *ko-gunome* with roundish and angular *yakigashira*, but principally none with a slanting *kataochi-gunome*.

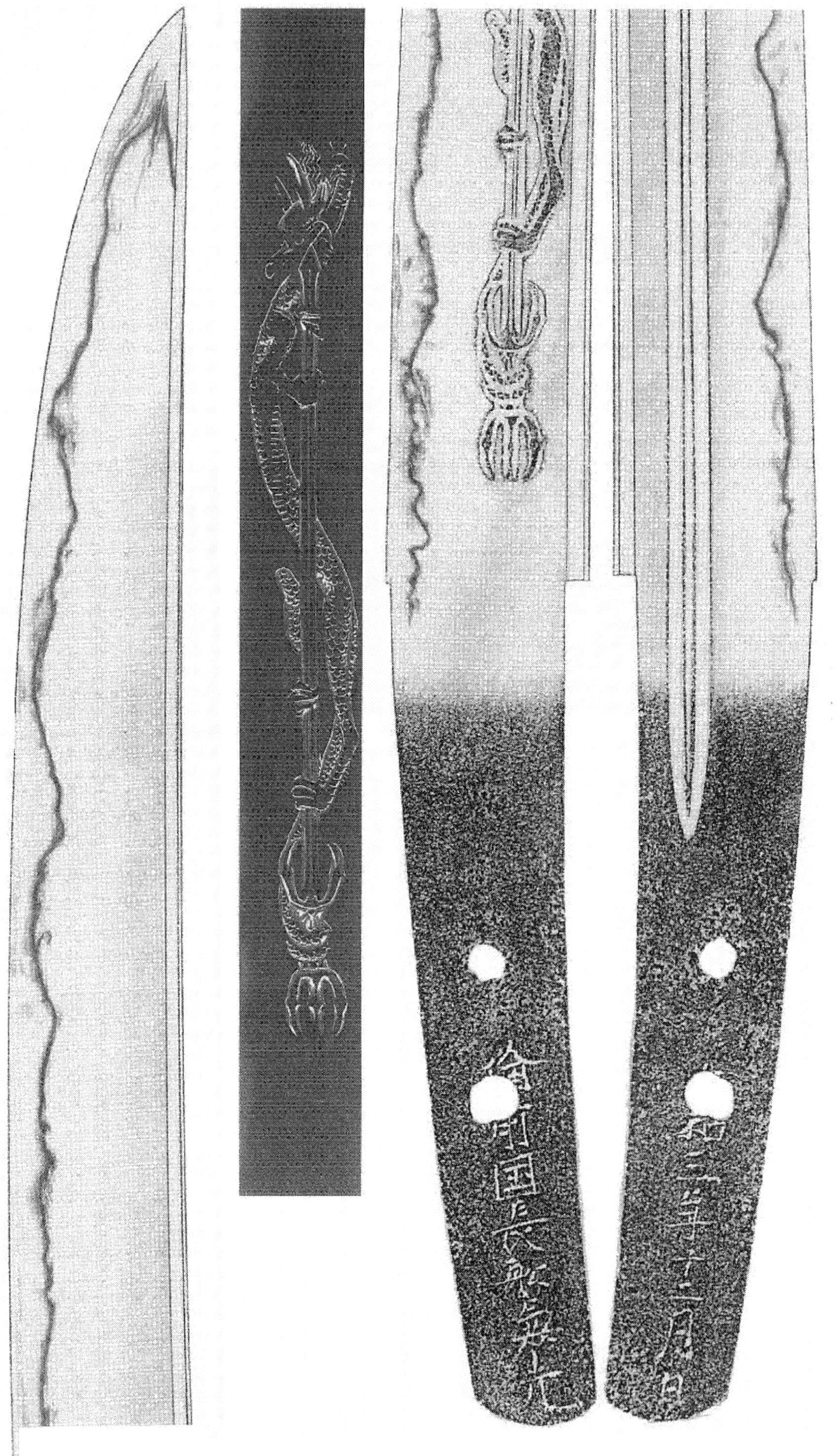

66.659 *wakizashi*
mei: Bizen no Kuni Osafune Kanemitsu (備前国長船兼光)
Jōwa sannen jūnigatsu-hi" (貞和三年十二月日, „a day in the twelfth month Jōwa three [1347]")
nagasa 53,0 cm, *sori* 1,2 cm, *hira-zukuri*, *mitsu-mune*

ji: slightly standing-out *itame* mixed with *mokume*, some *nagare*, *ji-nie*, *chikei*, *utsuri* appears towards the *mune*
hamon: *notare-chō* mixed with *ko-gunome* and *ko-chōji*, in addition some *ashi* and *yō*, much *nie*, *yubashiri*, small *tobiyaki*, *kinsuji* and *sunagashi*
bōshi: *notare-komi* with *hakikake*, it ends in a pointed manner on the *omote* side and in *ō-maru* on the *ura* side
horimono: a *naga-bonji* and a „pregnant" *kurikara-ryū* is engraved on the *omote* side and a *naga-bonji*, *bonji*, and a *suken* with *kake-nagashi* on the *ura* side

Hira-zukuri long swords were introduced to Japan at a very early age so they can look back to a long history of usage and change. To achieve a better stability at a constant cutting ability, they went over the intermediate step *kiriba-zukuri* to a *shinogi-zukuri*. The most famous longer swords in *hira-zukuri* are the Nakigitsune (鳴狐) of Awataguchi Kuniyoshi (粟田口国吉) and the Suijin-giri (水神切) of Osafune Kanemitsu. Although longer *hira-zukuri* were made continuously in every epoch, relative few of them are extant today and those we have are mostly superior works of higher ranking persons made on order.

The characteristical features of the *sugata*, the typical *horimono* and the *notare-midare* were spotted by the most and so many bids were *atari* on Kanemitsu at the first round. Besides of the *hira-zukuri* shape, many other characteristics of that smith are present: A *sunnobi* with a wide *mihaba* in combination with a thin *kasane* – i.e. a typical Nanbokuchō shape – an *itame* with *chikei* and a *nie*-loaden *notare* which shows Sōshū influence, and a clearly visible *utsuri* which shows the Bizen origins. Within the so-called „Sōden-Bizen-*mono*", such a „pregnant" *kurikara-ryū* in combination with a rather calm *hamon* is mostly seen at Kanemitsu.

Well, there are also works of Morikage (盛景) which resemble closely the style of Kanemitsu. But they have a wider *notare* which tends to be angular in places and the end of the hilt of the *sankozuka-ken* is noticeably rounder. In addition, the inner linear relief element of the *suken* is shorter than the right and left outlines at Morikage.

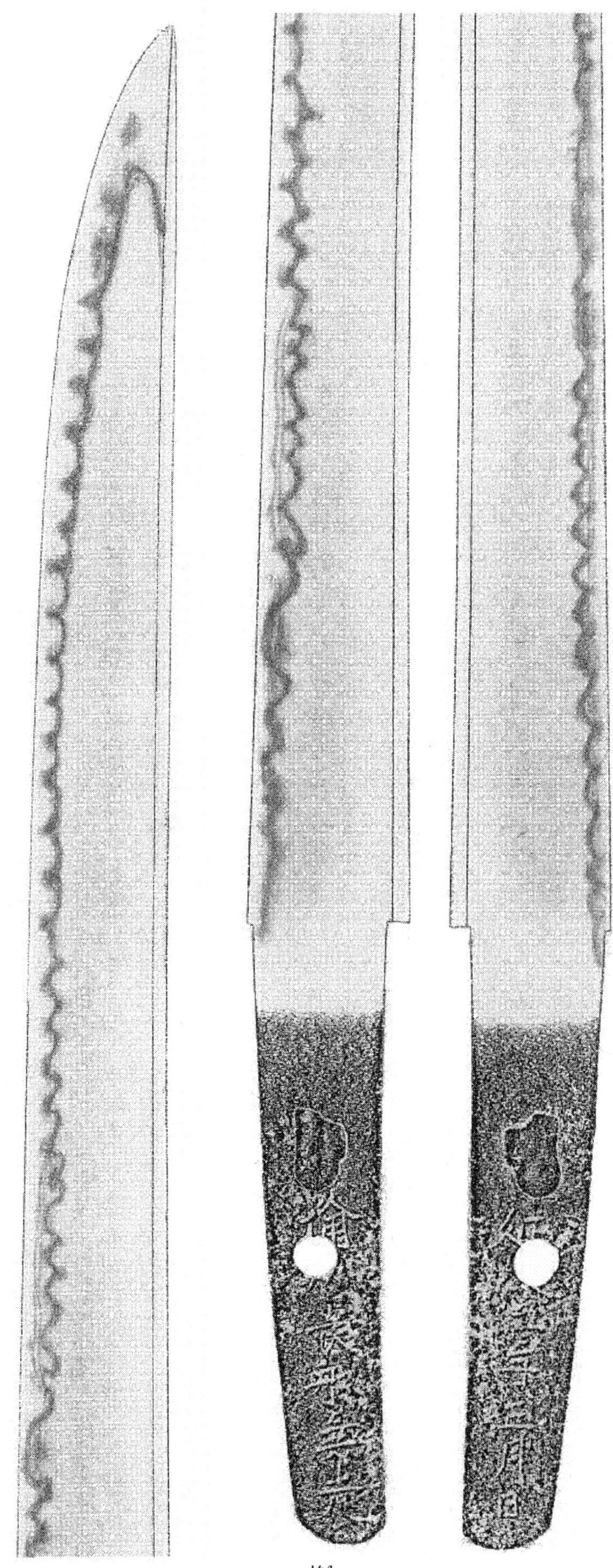

67.665 *tantō*
mei: Bishū Osafune Kanemitsu (備州長船兼光)
Enbun gonen sangatsu-hi (延文五年三月日, „a day in the third month of Enbun five [= 1360]")
nagasa 25,0 cm, *sori* 0,3 cm, *hira-zukuri*, *iori-mune*

ji: dense *itame* with plentiful of *ji-nie*, *chikei* and a faint *bō-utsuri*
hamon: *suguha-chō* mixed with angular *gunome*, *kataochi*-like *gunome* and *ko-gunome*, the *hamon* gets wider in the upper area and tends a little to slant there, the hardening is in *nioi-deki* and there are *kinsuji* and *sunagashi*, the *nioiguchi* is bright and clear
bōshi: on the *omote* side *midare-komi* with a *ko-maru-kaeri* and on the *ura* side *notare-komi* with a pointed, rather late turning-back *kaeri*

At this *tantō* you have to examine the shape carefully. At a glance, it doesn´t look very large but it has a little *sori* and a thin *kasane*, that means we are despite the normal long *nagasa* nevertheless in the Nanbokuchō period. Regarding the *jiba*, the *jigane* is bright and clear and appears as dense and finely forged *itame*. The *hamon* is a somewhat slanting angular *gunome* or *kataochi*-like *gunome*. And so many participants went for Kagemitsu (景光) or Kanemitsu. But when you once got the time, then it was easy to decide for Kanemitsu instead of the earlier Kagemitsu.

Also some bade on Sa (左). The time would be basically correct but the *jigane* would be even brighter at Sa and a *nie-utsuri* would appear. Also his *hamon* wouldn´t show any *kataochi-gunome* but would base on *notare* and show a plentiful of *nie*. In addition, the *kaeri* of his *bōshi* starts considerably later.

This *tantō* was also provided for *kantei* to demonstrate the differences between the Osafune mainline and the sideline of Motoshige for example. It is namely first and foremost the *jiba* which differs. Kanemitsu´s *jigane* is fine and dense and those of Motoshige stands out. At Kanemitsu, a *kataochi*-like *gunome* appears whereas Motoshige shows angular *gunome* elements but which are horizontally elongated and form an uniform line.

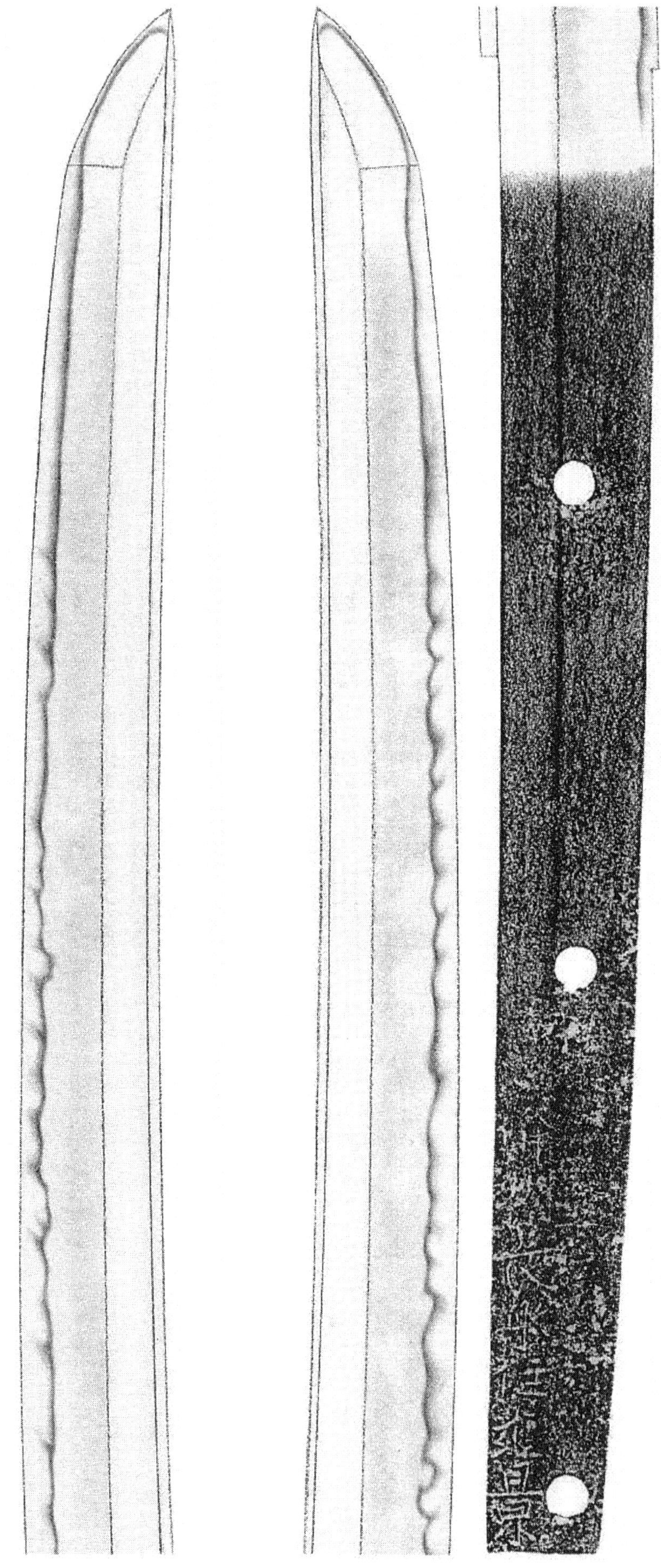

68.625 *tachi*
mei: Bishū Osafune-jū Chikakage (備州長船住近景)
nagasa 65,0 cm, *sori* 2,1 cm, *shinogi-zukuri*, *iori-mune*

ji: *itame* mixed with *mokume* and *nagare* which stands somewhat out, also plentiful of *ji-nie*, fine *chikei* and a *midare-utsuri*
hamon: *suguha-chō* mixed with *ko-gunome*, angular *gunome*, and *ko-chōji*, partially slanting, *nioi-deki* with *ko-nie*, in addition *ashi*, *yō* and fine *sunagashi*
bōshi: on both sides a little *notare* and a *ko-maru-kaeri*

The blade is slender and has a *ko-kissaki* and with the *midare-utsuri*, many went at the first round for Ko-Bizen. But at Ko-Bizen, the *sori* would bend down towards the tip, the *hamon* would base on a *ko-midare* and the *utsuri* would show dark *antai* areas and appear in an irregular manner. But Bizen is definitely correct. When we take into consideration that the *sori* increases again towards the tip and that the blade has a somewhat thicker *kasane*, we end up in the late Kamakura period. And on the basis of the *suguha-chō* mixed with *ko-gunome*, *ko-chōji* and the partially also slanting angular *gunome*, we are in the vicinity of Kagemitsu (景光) and Chikakage.

According to transmission, Chikakage was a student of Nagamitsu (長光) but was slightly later active than Nagamitsu´s son Kagemitsu. Some also say that some works of Kagemitsu are actually *daimei* of Chikakage. Anyway, both show a very similar workmanship but we are nevertheless able to see some subtle differences in the *jigane*, the form of the *ha-nie* and the *bōshi*. First of all, Kagemitsu forged in a very fine and a clear *jigane*, the finest *hada* within the Osafune school by the way. Chikakage on the other hand applied a rather standing-out *hada* and shows more *ha-nie*. Also Chikakage´s *bōshi* is somewhat inferior to the *sansaku-bōshi* of Nagamitsu, Sanenaga (真長) and Kagemitsu. So when we bear this in mind, it should be possible to nail this blade down to Chikakage.

There were also some bids on Nagamitsu and Sanenaga but as mentioned in previous explanations, they did not apply an angular or slanting *gunome* on *tachi*. Also their *ashi* show in a right-angled manner towards the *ha* and Sanenaga applied a thighter *nioiguchi*.

Besides of that *dōzen* bids some went also for Unshō (雲生) because of the *utsuri*. But at works from the Un group, we would expect a more irregular *utsuri* with dark *antai* areas which tend to a *jifu-utsuri*. Also the *kaeri* of the *bōshi* would be noticably larger and rounder and at a *midareba*, the *hamon* would be more calm in the upper half of the blade.

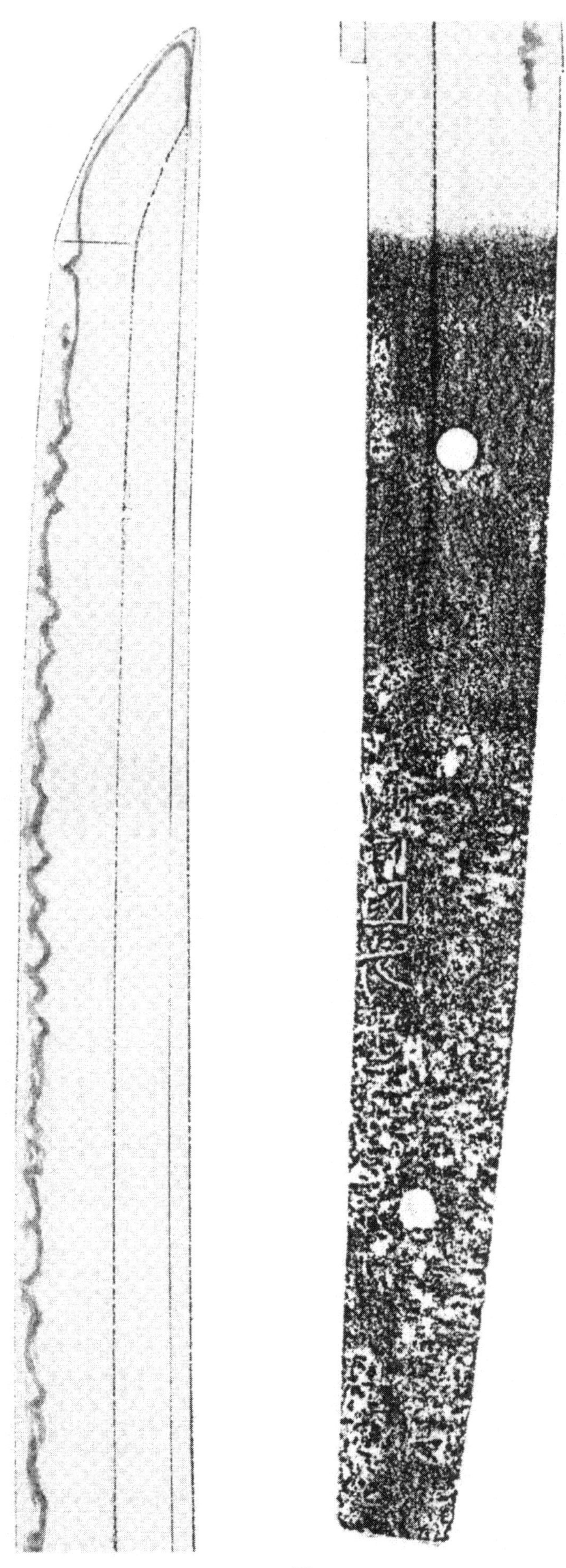

69.671 *tachi*
mei: Bizen no Kuni Osafune-jū Chikakage (備前国長船住近景)
nagasa 75,7 cm, *sori* 2,1 cm, *shinogi-zukuri*, *iori-mune*

ji: rather standing-out *itame* mixed with *mokume* and *jifu*, in addition *ji-nie*, much *chikei* and a *midare-utsuri*
hamon: *suguha-chō* mixed with *ko-gunome*, *ko-chōji*, angular *gunome*, *ko-ashi*, some *saka-ashi*, *ko-nie*, *kinsuji* and *sunagashi*
bōshi: shallow *notare-komi* with a rather pointed *ko-maru-kaeri*

We see no *funbari* and so we can assume that the blade is *ō-suriage* or at least *suriage*. The blade has a *chū-kissaki*, a relative wide *mihaba*, a noticeable taper, a deep *koshizori* which increases again towards the tip and a clearly visible *midare-utsuri*, and so it is not difficult to see that we are facing a Bizen-*mono* from the Kamakura period. The *yakiba* bases on *suguha* and is mixed with *ko-gunome*, angular *gunome* and *saka-ashi*. The *bōshi* appears as shallow *notare-komi* with a *ko-maru-kaeri*, i.e. altogether as so-called „*sansaku-bōshi*“. And so we finally arrive at the late Kamakura-era Osafune school and most of the bids focused accordingly on Kagemitsu (景光) and Chikakage.

Well, the *tachi* is a work of Chikakage who was according to transmission a student of Nagamitsu (長光). On the basis of extant date signatures we can date his artistic period from around the late Kamakura to the early Nanbokuchō period. This makes him a contemporary of Kagemitsu or maybe a younger *kōhai* under Nagamitsu. The workmanship of Kagemitsu and Chikakage is similar but we can see a difference in quality. This concerns first and foremist the *jigane* which is very dense and beautifully forged at Kagemitsu. Chikakage in turn forged a rather standing-out *hada* which is mixed with *jifu* and this is considered as a typical feature of this smith. Like Kagemitsu he also added *saka-ashi* but Chikakage´s *ha* is a hint more *nie*-loaden and this too is typical for him. The *bōshi* deserves special attention. It appears as *suguha* which runs over the *yokote* and turns then into a shallow *notare-komi* with a rather pointed *kaeri*. This somewhat „awkward“ interpretation of a *sansaku-bōshi* is very typical for Chikakage and an important *kantei* point. Also the quite high *shinogi* is a hallmark for him.

But relative many bade on Motoshige (元重). He too applied sometimes like Chikakage a „loose“ *jigane* but his *jihada* is mostly mixed with *nagare*. Also his *hamon* bases more on *gunome* with *saka-ashi* and the *bōshi* is conspiciously pointed, that means he did not apply a classical *sansaku-bōshi*. In addition, Motoshige´s *yakigashira* are angular and horizontally stretched.

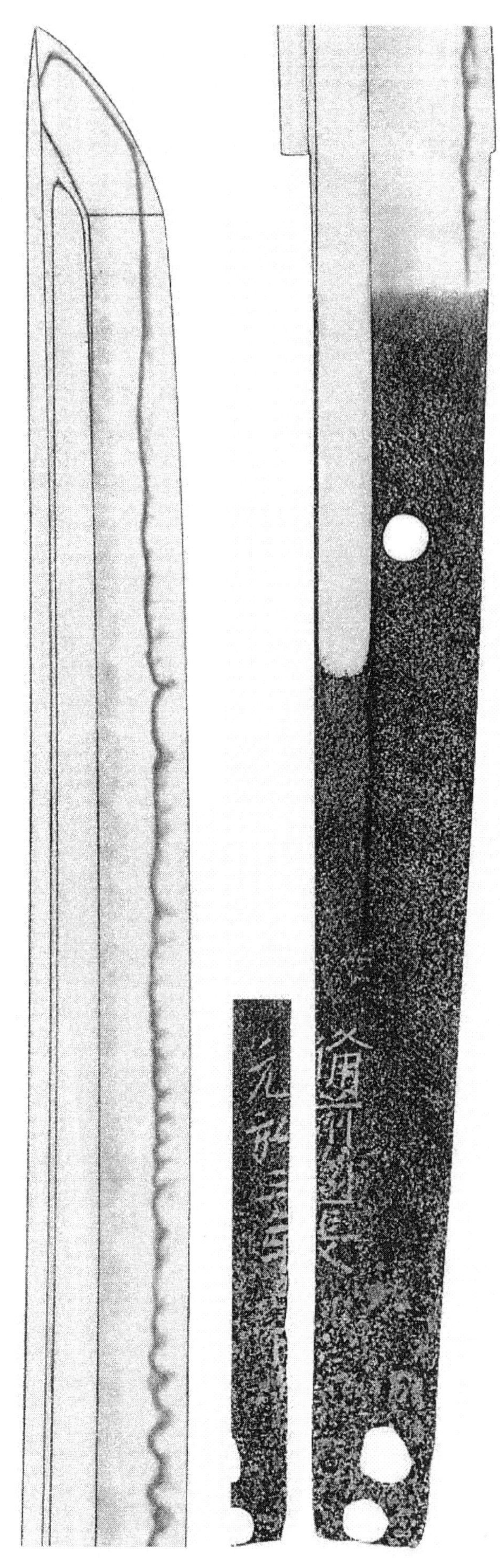

70.651 *tachi*
mei: Bizen no Kuni Osa… (備前国長) (beyond that illegible, „fune Chikakage“, 船近景)
Genkō sannen (元弘三年, 1333) (only the characters „gatsu“ and „hi“ can be seen)
nagasa 71,8 cm, *sori* 2,3 cm, *shinogi-zukuri*, *iori-mune*

ji: *itame-hada*, partially mixed with standing-out *nagare*, *ji-nie*, fine *chikei*, *midare-utsuri*
hamon: *chū-suguha-chō* mixed with *ko-gunome* and angular elements, in addition slanting *midare*, plentiful of *ashi*, *saka-ashi*, *yō*, *ko-nie* as well as some *kinsuji* and *sunagashi*
bōshi: continues as *sugu* over the *yokote* and appears then as *notare* with a *ko-maru-kaeri*
horimono: on both sides a *bōhi* with an end in *maru-dome* (in the tang)

Parts of the signature are illegible but because of the use of *gyaku-tagane* (逆鏨), a chiselling which is contrary to the usual writing direction with the brush, the *sujikai-yasurime* and the workmanship, we can attribute the blade to Chikakage. In addition, Chikakage changed his signature style from his earlier thin and somewhat „hopping“, „skipping“ manner to a orderly block script in later years. Then he signed also with „Bizen no Kuni Osafune-jū“ instead of „Bishū Osafune-jū“ and this matches with the wokmanship of the *kantei* blade too.

The *tachi* has a rather slender *mihaba*, tapers noticably, has a deep *koshizori* which increases again towards the tip and ends in a *chū-kissaki*. Also it shows *funbari* so we can assume that it is *ubu* or only a little shortened, and the shape leads us to the late Kamakura period. The *kitae* shows a *midare-utsuri* and the *hamon* is a *suguha-chō* mixed with *ko-gunome*, *gunome*, angular and slanting elements and *saka-ashi*. The *bōshi* is *notare-komi* and has a *ko-maru-kaeri*, that means from the overall interpretation, it can be identified as *sansaku-bōshi*. And from all these characteristics, the blade can be narrowed down to the vicinity of Kagemitsu (景光).

There is some *nagare* and *masame* seen and the *hada* stands out in places, i.e. it is too irregular for the fine and beautiful *jigane* of Kagemitsu and also the *utsuri* lacks the clarity of the latter smith. In addition, the *hamon* shows *ko-nie* and the *bōshi* runs as *suguha* over the *yokote* before it turns into a *notare-komi*. This „exaggergated“ interpretation of a *sansaku-bōshi* and the other mentioned features are very typical for Chikakage. Thus most went straight to this smith at the first round.

Some bade also on Motoshige (元重). But in his case, the *masame* would be more prominent, the *yakiba* somewhat broader and the angular elements would be horizontally more stretched. Also his *bōshi* is mostly pointed.

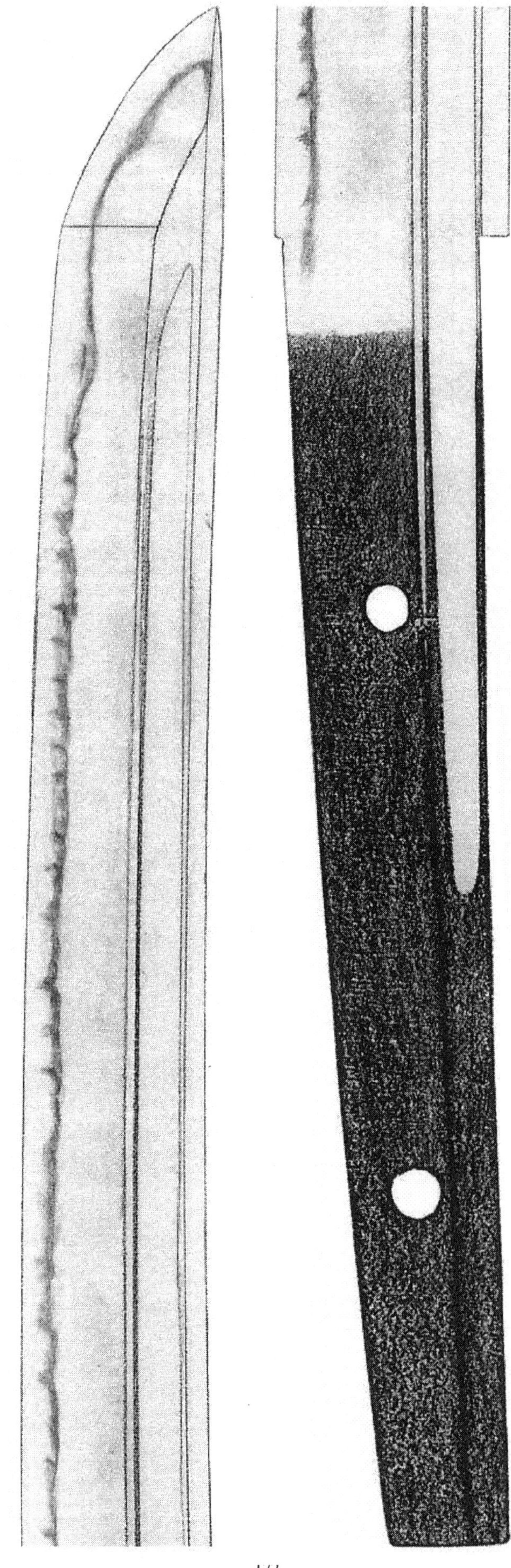

71.631 *katana*
mumei: Chikakage (近景)
nagasa 71,5 cm, *sori* 2,4 cm, *shinogi-zukuri*, *iori-mune*

ji: *itame* mixed with *mokume* which stands out slightly, in addition *ji-nie* and a clear *midare-utsuri*
hamon: basing on *chū-suguha* and mixed with *ko-gunome* and *ko-chōji*, in addition *ashi*, *yō*, *ko-nie*, and *kinsuji*, the hardening is in *nioi-deki*
bōshi: shallow *notare* with a pointed *kaeri*
horimono: on both sides a *bōhi* with *tsurebi* is engraved which stops noticeably before the *ko-shinogi* and which runs with *kake-nagashi* into the tang

This blade is attributed to Chikakage who was active during the turbulent times from the late Kamakura to the subsequent Nanbokuchō period. He belonged to the same school as Kagemitsu (景光) and it is assumed that the latter was in a senior position to him. Some also say that Chikakage made *daimei* blades for Kagemitsu, and because of the very close workmanship it is safe to assume that they worked closely together. But Chikakage did not reach the quality of Kagemitsu or their master Nagamitsu (長光) and this should be beared in mind.

This blade has a wide *mihaba*, tapers noticeably, and keeps despite the *ō-suriage* a deep *koshizori* which increases again towards the tip. So from the shape, we are definitely in the late Kamakura period. Regarding the *kitae*, it shows a clear *midare-utsuri* and the *hamon* bases on a *nioi-deki suguha* which is mixed with *ko-gunome* and *ko-chōji*. The *bōshi* is a so-called „*sansaku-bōshi*". So we have all the characteristics to place the work somewhere in the vicinity of Kagemitsu or Nagamitsu.

Let us now examine the blade a little closer, beginning with the *jigane*. This shows some rough and coarse spots, especially towards the base. Kagemitsu is well known for his fine and perfect *jigane* so he could be rather ruled out. Also the pointed *bōshi* rises more doubts about an attribution to Kagemitsu. But on the other hand, the characteristics of the *kitae* and the *hamon* are definitely typical for the Osafune mainline and as we can rule out Kagemitsu and Nagamitsu from the point of view of quality, the chances are very high that it is a work by Chikakage.

Well, at the *kantei*, many went for Nagamitsu but here we would expect surely a more skillfully applied *bōshi*.

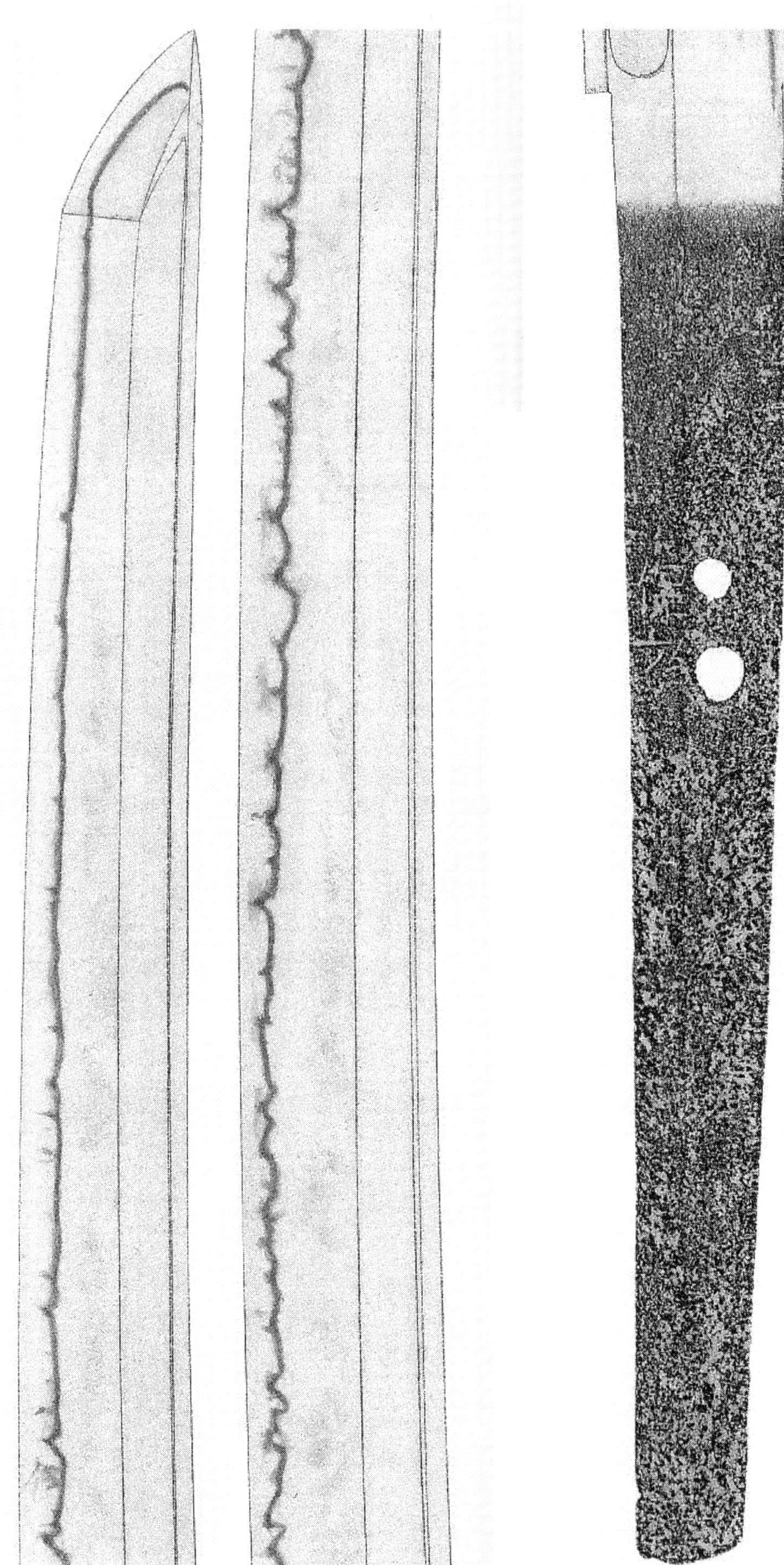

72.641 *tachi*
mei: Yasuhiro (保弘)
nagasa 79,7 cm, *sori* 2,9 cm, *shinogi-zukuri*, *iori-mune*

ji: *itame* mixed with *mokume*, partially *nagare*, fine *ji-nie*, many *chikei*, clear *midare-utsuri*
hamon: basing on *gunome* mixed with *ko-gunome*, *ko-chōji* and *togariba*, the *hamon* appears from the *monouchi* area upwards as *suguha-chō*, in addition plentiful of *ko-ashi*, *yō*, *kinsuji* and *sunagashi*, the hardening is in *nioi-deki*
bōshi: short continuation of the *hamon* over the *yokote* which turns then into a *suguga* which runs parallel to the *fukura* and ends in an *ō-maru* without hardly any *kaeri* at all
horimono: on both sides a *bōhi* with *maru-dome*

There are only very few blades extant by Yasuhiro but on the basis of known *naga-mei* and date signatures from the eras Shōan (正安, 1299-1302) and Tokuji (徳治, 1306-1308) and the supplement „Osafune-jū" in the *mei* we can place him in the late Kamakura period and in the vicinity of the late Nagamitsu (長光) or Kagemitsu (景光) and Sanenaga (真長).

This blade is signed and *ubu*, has a slightly longer *nagasa*, a very deep *koshizori* which does not bend down towards the tip, and a *chū-kissaki*, that means it demonstrates a magnificent but elegant *tachi-sugata*. There is a clearly visible *utsuri* and the *hamon* is a *gunome-chō* in *nioi-deki* which is mixed with *ko-gunome* and *ko-chōji* and which turns into a *suguha-chō* from the *monouchi* upwards. All these are typical characteristics of Osafune-*mono* of that time and so most bids focused on this school.

Well, the *kantei* blade does not have particular features which would attribute it straightforward to Yasuhiro and so all bids on an Osafune smith were counted as *dōzen*, provided that the participant was in the correct period. If we try to differentiate a bit than we have to say that at a Kagemitsu, the *jigane* would be finer and we would see angular elements within the *ha*. The *bōshi* which drops down after the *yokote* leaded some to Chikakage (近景) but his *hada* stands more out and he added a noticeable amount of *ha-nie*.

Probably because of the *ō-maru-kaeri*, some went for the smiths of the Un group (雲). But their blades show a *toriizori* and a *jifu-utsuri* which is accompanied by dark *antai* areas.

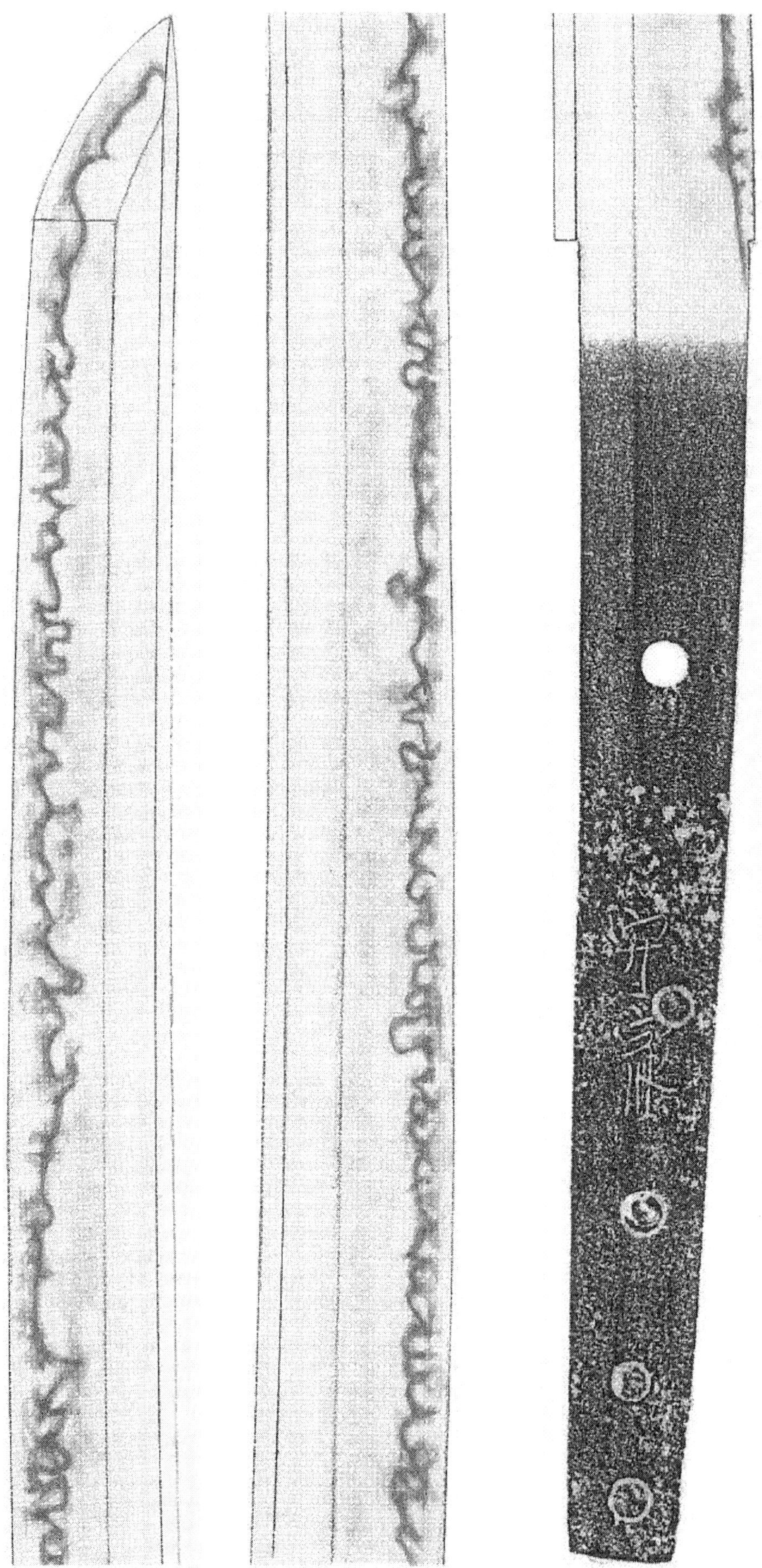

73.666 *tachi*
mei: Moriie (守家)
nagasa 65,0 cm, *sori* 1,5 cm, *shinogi-zukuri*, *iori-mune*

ji: *ko-itame* mixed with *mokume* and *nagare*, plentiful of *ji-nie*, *chikei*, *jifu*-like elements and a *midare-utsuri*
hamon: *ko-chōji* mixed with *ko-gunome*, *kawazu-no-ko chōji*, some *midare*, many *ashi* and *yō* as well as *sunagashi*, the hardening is in *nioi-deki* with *ko-nie*
bōshi: on both sides *midare-komi* with a *ko-maru-kaeri*

There exists a date signature of the Bun´ei era (文永, 1264-1275) from Bizen Hatakeda Moriie (畠田守家) but subsequent smiths with the same name were still active during the Nanbokuchō-period Kentoku era (建徳, 1370-1372). On the basis of the *deki*, this blade can be dated into the middle Kamakura period, that means around the 1st gen. Moriie. It shows a rather slender *mihaba* and so some were too early at the *kantei*. But the *koshizori* which does not bend down but increases again towards the tip had to be grasped. And because of the *chōji-midare* with a broad *nioiguchi* in *nioi-deki* and the *midare-utsuri*, many went for Ichimonji. But when you take a closer look at the *hamon* you will see that some areas tend clearly to *gunome*. In addition, the *yakiba* does not show many ups and dows, despite the partially protruding *chōji* elements. Also the *hamon* gets more calm around the *monouchi* area. Some *chōji* appear as *kawazu-no-ko-chōji* and in places, the round *yakigashi* separate and appear as *tobiyaki*. This peculiarity is first and foremost seen at Osafune Mitsutada (光忠) and at the Hatakeda-smiths Moriie and Sanemori (真守).

Well, the *jihada* does not stand out that much and the *kawazu-no-ko chōji* share is not that obvious, so it would also be possible to place this work in the vicinity of Mitsutada. But at the latter, the *jigane* would be finer and a finer *ji-nie* would appear. In addition, his *bōshi* has a noticeably more pointed *kaeri*. Some bade also on Nagamitsu (長光). He too applied some *kawazu-no-ko chōji*, especially during his early years. But usually his *chōji* do not have such a „laced-up" base and the *yakigashira* are bigger and more roundish. And there would also be more *gunome* and *togariba* within the *hamon*. And others went for Kunimune (国宗). Kunimune´s *kitae* is similar to Moriie but his *hada* stands more out and the *chōji* are more angular.

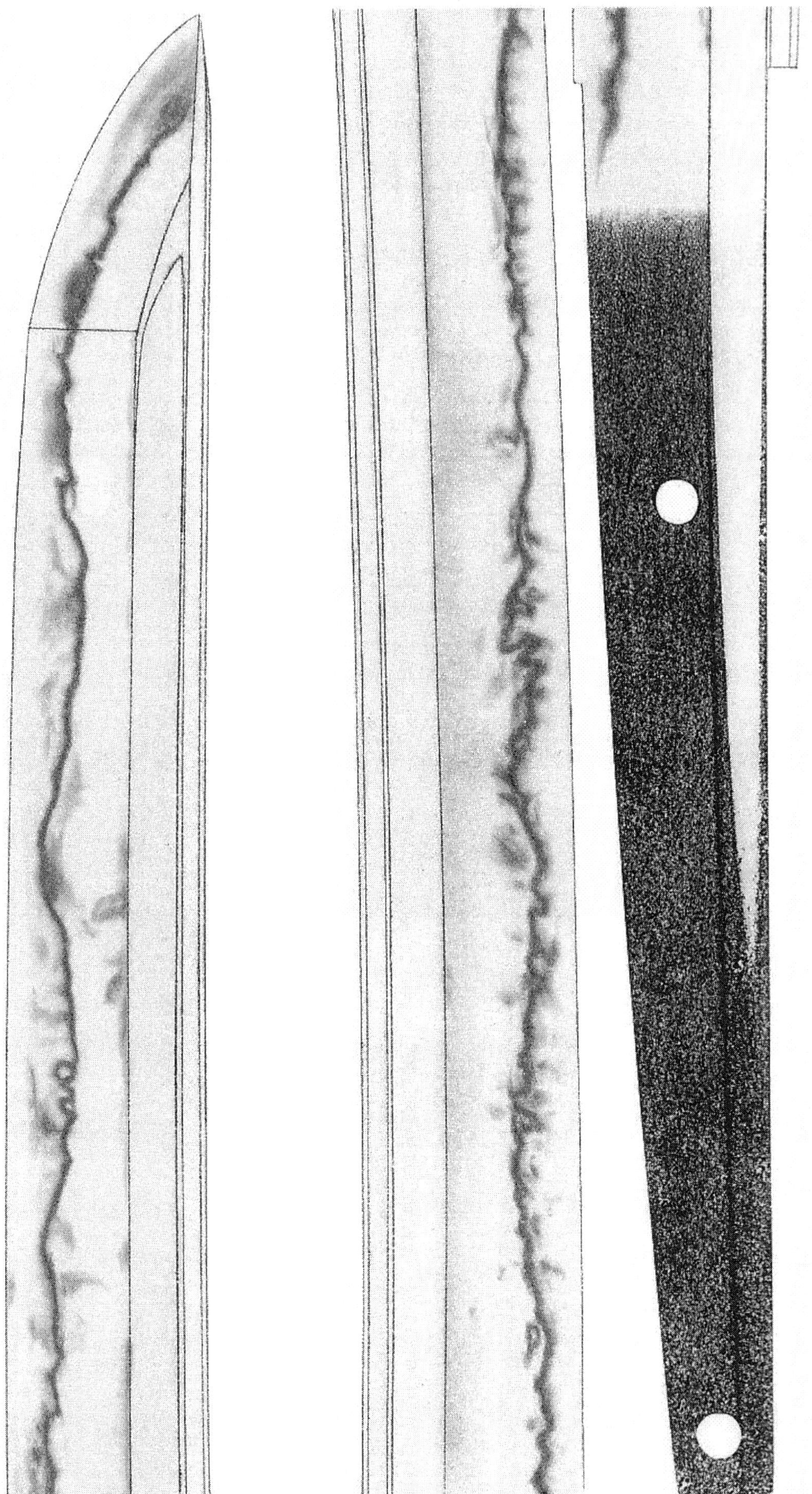

74.642 *katana*
mumei: Chōgi (長義) (*meibutsu* „Hachimonji-Chōgi", 八文字長義)
nagasa 78,5 cm, *sori* 2,1 cm, *shinogi-zukuri*, *mitsu-mune*

ji: standing-out *itame* mixed with *mokume*, plentiful of *ji-nie*, some dull *chikei*, there is a *midare-utsuri* in the middle blade section
hamon: *notare-chō* in large waves mixed with *gunome*, *ko-gunome* and *ko-chōji*, in addition many *ashi* and *yō*, *nie*, *tobiyaki*, *yubashiri*, *kinsuji* and *sunagashi*, the *nioiguchi* is bright
bōshi: *midare-komi* with much *hakikake* which ends as *yakitsume*
horimono: on both sides a *bōhi* which runs with *kake-nagashi* into the tang

This blade with the nickname „Hachimonji-Chōgi" was once a heirloom of the Satake family (佐竹) from Akita. The legend says that once Satake Yoshishige (佐竹義重, 1547-1612) cut with this blade in the tenth year of Eiroku (永禄, 1567) in a battle against the Hōji a mounted enemy into halves. Because the blow went through the helmet down to the saddle, both body halves slided down to the left and right of the horse. This „sliding" resembled the character (*monji*, 文字) for „eight" (*hachi*, 八) and this is why it got its nickname „Hachimonji".

The *katana* has a somewhat wider *mihaba*, does not taper much, has a shallow *sori* and ends in an *ō-kissaki*. In combination with the thick *kasane* it might looks like a *shinshintō* or Keichō-*shintō* blade at a glance. This is correct but then we would see a *funbari* towards the base and as this is not the case here we have to assume that it is shortened and so we are at the original time where such shapes were produced, i.e. in the Nanbokuchō period. So this must have been once a really huge and massive *ō-dachi*. Note: Keichō-*shintō* and *shinshintō* smiths copied exactly such shortened Nanbokuchō forms, that´s why one has to be cautious when checking the *sugata*.

The *jigane* appears as standing-out *itame* with *chikei* and the *hamon* bases on *notare* with much *midare* and plentiful of *nie*. So we can see the characteristics of the Sōshū tradition, but the present *utsuri* leads us to Sōden-Bizen. The two most outstanding Sōden-Bizen smiths were Kanemitsu (兼光) and Chōgi, whereas Kanemitsu tended rather towards more elegant interpretations and Chōgi displayed a more wild and vivid workmaship. The *kantei* blade shows as mentioned a slightly undulating *notare* which is at a glance not so typical for Chōgi. But we can see some mountain- and ear-shaped elements which in turn are typical for Chōgi. But it has to be mentioned that these mountain- and ear-shaped elements are more frequently seen on his *tantō*. This was probably the reason why many went for Kanemitsu. But the *kitae* is a bit too rustic for Kanemitsu and the *gunome*, *ko-gunome*, *ko-chōji* as well as the *ashi* and *yō* would be more unobtrusive at the latter. In addition, the *ha* is full of ambitious *hataraki* like *tobiyaki*, *yubashiri*, *kinsuji* and *sunagashi*, and this ambition is also reflected in the *hakikake* of the *bōshi*. So one should stick at the *kantei* to the following old saying: „When you have a Bizen blade which seems to be farthest away from Bizen, then it is a Chōgi."

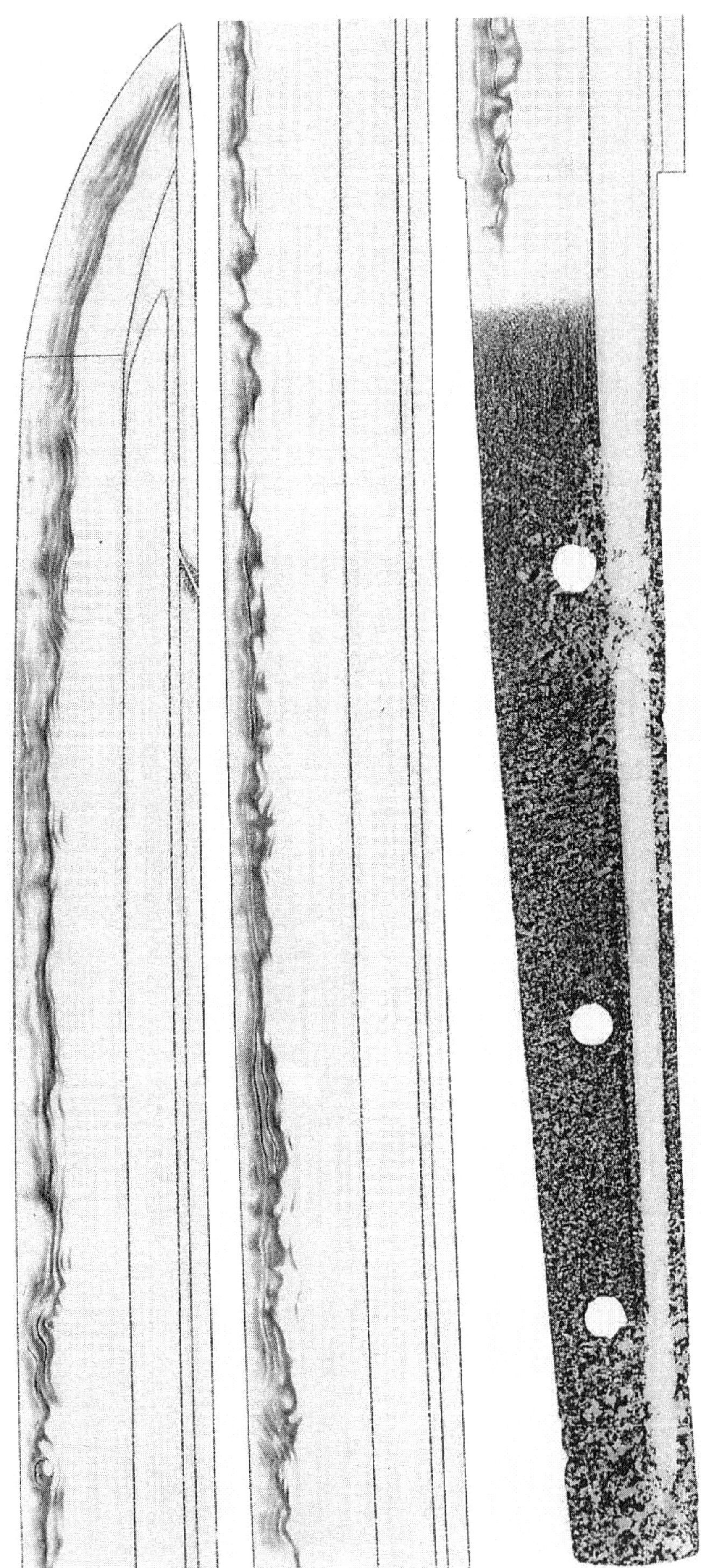

75.637 *katana*
mumei: Den Nagashige (伝長重)
nagasa 71,0 cm, *sori* 1,2 cm, *shinogi-zukuri*, *iori-mune*

ji: *itame* mixed with *mokume*, on the *sashi-omote* a standing-out *nagare* towards the *ha*, plentiful of *ji-nie*, *chikei*, faint *midare-utsuri* at places

hamon: *ko-notare* mixed with *ko-gunome*, *ko-chōji* and *togariba*, the *hamon* is all over rather small dimensioned, in addition *ashi* and *yō*, as well as thick, partially accumulating *nie*, many *kinsuji* and *sunagashi* and small *yubashiri*

bōshi: *sugu-chō* which appears almost as *yakitsume*, also *hakikake* all over the *bōshi*

horimono: on both sides a *bōhi* which runs with *kake-nagashi* into the tang, the tip of the *hi* does not go very far beyond the *yokote*

The Sōshū style introduced by Masamune spread all over Japan during the Nanbokuchō period and even the Bizen smiths which hardened traditionally in *nioi-deki* adopted his approach of forging swords. Thus Bizen smiths like Chōgi (長義), Kanemitsu (兼光) and Morikage (盛景) moved away somewhat from their traditional workmanship and this ended up in a „hybrid tradition", the so-called „Sōden-Bizen" (相伝備前). Especially Chōgi and his lineage stood for that trend, and because of his *nie*-loaden *jiba* there is the saying: „Bizen-*mono* which do not look like Bizen".

This blade is a work of Chōgi´s older brother Nagashige (*jūyō-bijutsuhin*, heirloom of the Shimazu main branch, 島津). Regarding datings, we know the *kokuhō-tantō* of Nagashige from the first year of Kenmu (建武, 1334) and the supplement „*kinoe-inu*" (甲戌, „year of the dog"), a *tachi* and a *tantō* from the second year of Kenmu (1335), and a *tachi* from the first year of Kōei (康永, 1342). Both of the *tachi* show a narrow *suguha* which is mixed with *ko-gunome*. The *tantō* from the second year of Kenmu shows an angular *hamon* in the style of Kanemitsu or Motoshige (元重), and the former *kokuhō tantō* many *nie* and *nie*-based *hataraki* within the *ha*. This blade shows also some „ear-shaped" elements (*mimigata no ha*, 耳形の刃) which are a characteristical element of Chōgi. But in comparison with the latter, this *tantō* comes with a *deki* in a not that wide but rather reserved and controlled *yakiba* without many ups and downs.

In short, Nagashige´s signed blades display a wide range of workmanships. Unsigned blades which are attributed to him are mostly similar to the *kokuhō tantō* from the first year of Kenmu but in general it can be said that he sticks with the workmanship of Chōgi although his style is a little smaller and more unobtrusive. The *kantei* blade too shows a rather small dimensioned *yakiba* but the *nie* visible therein are strong and conspicuous like at Chōgi. However, it is especially because of the partial *mimigata* that the attribution must be to Nagashige.

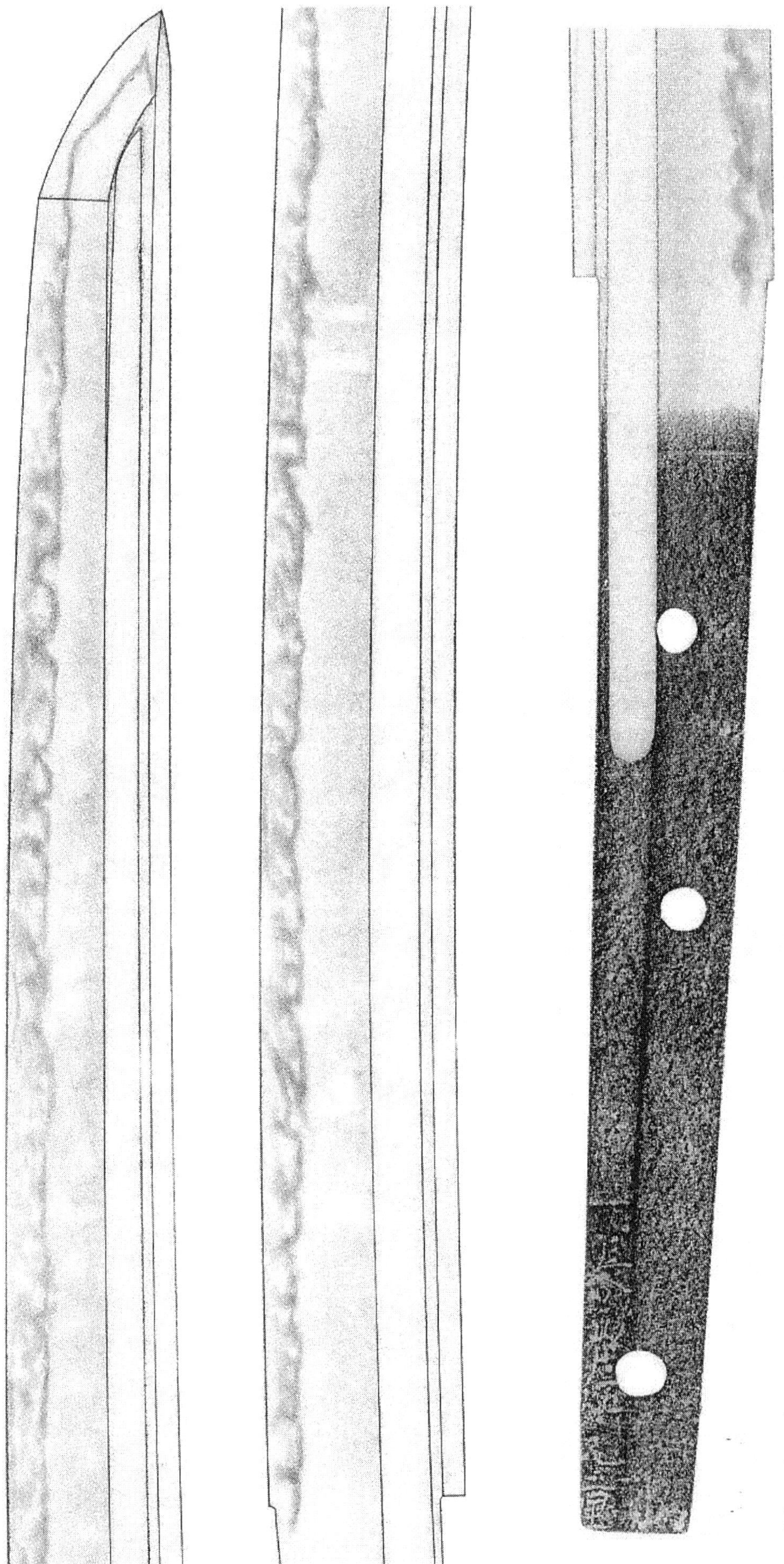

76.651k *tachi*
mei: Osafune-jū Motoshige (長船住元重)
nagasa 70,0 cm *sori* 2,2 cm
moto-haba 2,6 cm *saki-haba* 1,8 cm
moto-kasane 0,65 cm *saki-kasane* 0, 5 cm
kissaki-nagasa 2,7 cm *nakago-nagasa* 18,5 cm
only very little *nakago-sori*

shinogi-zukuri, *iori-mune*, rather slender *mihaba*, noticeable taper, despite the *suriage* a deep *koshizori* which increases again towards the tip, *chū-kissaki*. The *jigane* is an *itame* mixed with *mokume* and *nagare* which stands rather out and shows plentiful of *ji-nie* as well as *chikei*, *jifu* and a *midare-utsuri*. The *hamon* and the *bōshi* can be seen on the *oshigata*. There are conspicious angular elements mixed into the *midare*. In addition many *ashi* and *yō* which appear in a slanting manner all over the blade. Wide *nioiguchi* in thick *nioi* with much *nie* and *kinsuji* and *sunagashi*. On both sides a *bōhi* with *marudome* is engraved. The tang is *suriage*, had originally a *kurijiri*, the old *yasurime* were *katte-sagari* and the new are *kiri*. There are three *mekugi-ana* and there is a *naga-mei* on the *haki-omote* side towards the back of the tang.

The blade has a relative slender *mihaba*, tapers noticeably, keeps despite of the *suriage* a deep *koshizori* which increases again towards the tip and ends in a *chū-kissaki*. That means we can date it on the basis of the *sugata* to the late Kamakura or early Nanbokuchō period.

Motoshige was an Osafune sideline smith. His *jigane* is a standing-out *itame* mixed with *mokume* and *nagare*. We see *jifu* and sometimes also a *midare-utsuri*. His *hamon* shows horizontally stretched angular *gunome* elements and the separation between these *gunome* blocks appear as a kind negative, reverse *togariba*. This peculiarity is sometimes also described as „fangs“. But Motoshige was not the „inventor“ of this *hamon* interpretation. We can see it already on a work of his father Morishige (守重), namely on a *tantō* with the date signature of the fifth year of Shōwa (正和, 1316). And also on a *tantō* of Morishige´s father Hatakeda Moriie (畠田守家, a theory says that there were two generations Moriie but further studies are necessary) some precursors of this *hamon* development can be seen. But at both smiths, i.e. Morishige and Moriie, the *ha* consists of a mix of angular and *kataochi-gunome* rather than of long horizontally stretched *gunome*.

So Motoshige´s *hamon* is either an angular *gunome* which runs more or less uniform from top to bottom, or like seen on the *kantei* blade a variant of this *hamon* which is mixed with *ko-chōji* and/or *ko-gunome*. Motoshige applied more and stronger *ha-nie* as contemporary smiths in his vicinity and conspicious *nie*-based *hataraki* like *kinsuji* and *sunagashi* appear. The best example for this is a *jūyō-bunkazai hira-zukuri wakizashi* from the former possessions of the Shimazu family (島津). The *hamon* is namely a bit different than usual as it appears as *notare-chō* mixed with *ko-gunome*. But the *ha* is full of strong *nie*, *kinsuji* and *sunagashi*, that means the work shows truly a Sōshū influence. Motoshige´s *bōshi* is like the *kantei* blade mostly a *midare-komi* with a pointed *kaeri*.

The majority was spot-on at Motishige but relative many went also for Chikakage (近景). Chikakage´s *hamon* is similar to Motoshige and his *jigane* appears as standing-out *ko-itame* mixed with *ō-hada* and a faint *utsuri*. So a bid on him is quite understandable. But Chikakage´s *bōshi* appears as *sansaku-bōshi*, that means the *hamon* continues for a while after the *yokote* and drops then off to a *notare-komi*. (However, it is unclear if such a *bōshi* is original or goes back to a re-shaping of the *kissaki*.) Some *bōshi* tend a little towards a pointed *kaeri* but a truly pointed one like here on the *kantei* blade is not seen at Chikakage. Another important pecularity of Chikakage is that he chiselled his signature in *gyaku-tagane*. This would have been mentioned in the description of the *kantei*.

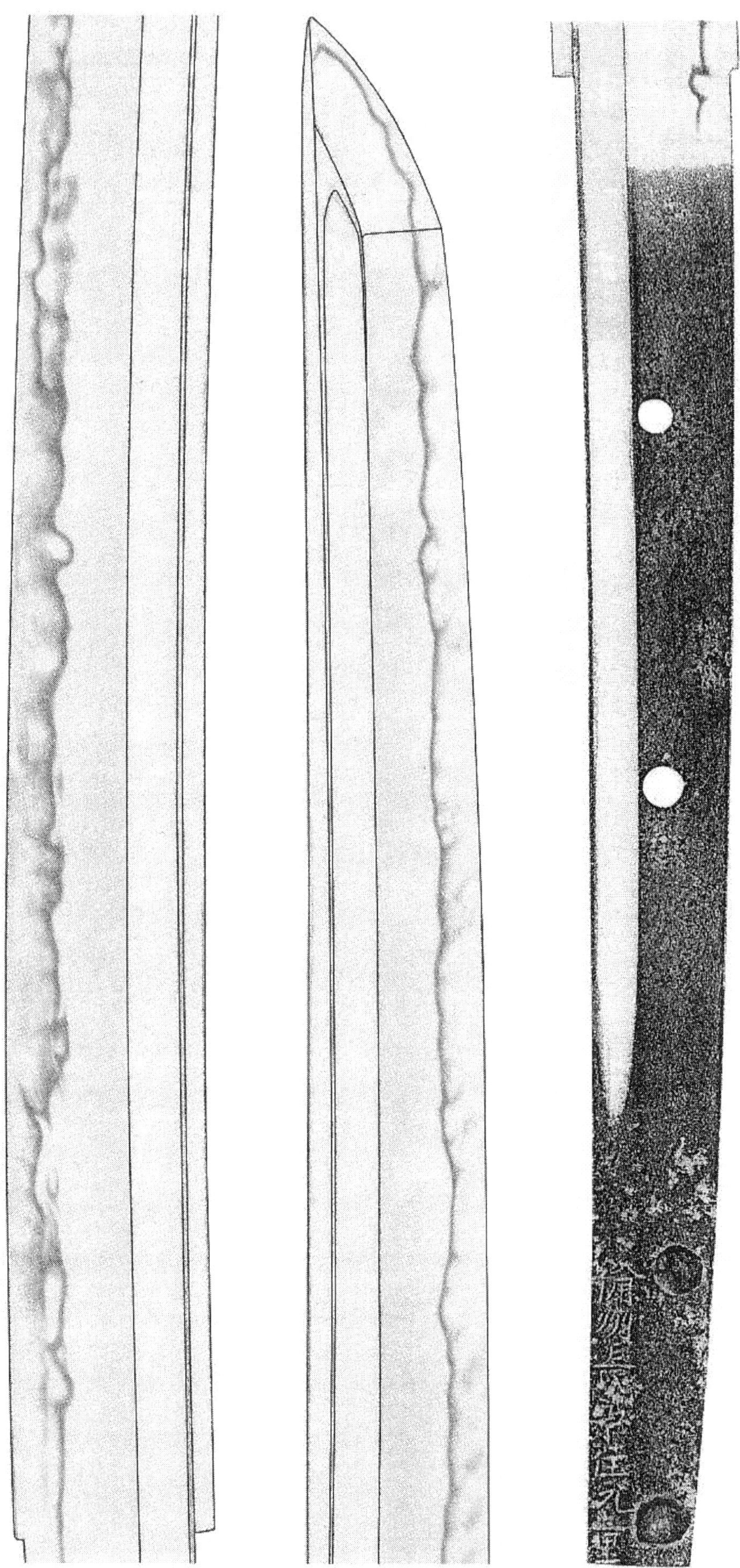

77.621k *tachi*
mei: Bishū Osafune-jū Motoshige (備州長船住元重)
nagasa 71,21 cm *sori* 2,27 cm
moto-haba 2,8 cm *saki-haba* 1,95
moto-kasane 0,7 cm *saki-kasane* 0,4
kissaki-nagasa 3,0 cm *nakago-nagasa* 23,79 cm
nakago-sori 0,3 cm

shinogi-zukuri, *iori-mune*, normal *mihaba*, no noticeable taper, despite the *suriage* a deep *koshizori* which increases again towards the tip, *chū-kissaki*. The *jigane* is an *itame* with *mokume* and partial *nagare*. It stands out all over the blade and shows fine *ji-nie*, *chikei*, *jifu* elements and a *midare-utsuri*. The *hamon* and the *bōshi* can be seen on the *oshigata*. The *hamon* with its *ashi* and *yō* tends allover to slant. The *nioiguchi* is bright and shows *ko-nie*. Also some few *kinsuji* and *sunagashi* appear. On both sides a *bōhi* is engraved which runs with *kake-nagashi* into the tang. The *nakago* is *suriage*, has a *kirijiri* (originally a *kurijiri*), *sujikai-yasurime* and four *mekugi-ana*. There is a *naga-mei* on the *haki-omote* side towards the tip and the back of the tang (the signatures of this smith are not chiselled in *gyaku-tagane*).

The blade has a normal *mihaba*, no noticable taper and keeps despite of the *suriage* a deep *koshizori* which increases again towards the tip. In combination with the *chū-kissaki* we end up in the late Kamakura or early Nanbokuchō period.

Motoshige´s *hamon* consists of an angular *gunome* which has horizontally stretched *yakigashira*. The valleys in between appear as „inverted“ or „negative“ *togari* which are sometimes also described as „fangs“. Besides of these peculiuar characteristics, Motoshige applied like here also a *suguha-chō* which is mixed with *ko-chōji*, *ko-gunome* and angular *ko-gunome*. The *ashi* and *yō* appear all over the blade slanted. The latter *deki* has more of the Osafune mainline than the former with the uniform horizontally stretched *gunome*.

Anyway, Motoshige´s *jigane* is an *itame* mixed with *mokume* and *nagare* which stands out and shows *jifu*. This speaks for an Osafune sideline. Mainline works show namely a finely forged dense *itame* and a bright *jigane*. Motoshige´s *bōshi* is as seen on the *kantei* blade a *midare-komi* with a conspiciously pointed *kaeri*. The tip of the tang is *kurijiri*, the *yasurime* are *sujikai* and the signature is mostly executed as *naga-mei* on the *haki-omote* towards the *nakago-mune*. So the typical finish of his tangs is seen here too. Extant date signatures range from the end of the Kamakura period, i.e. the Shōwa era (正和, 1312-1317), to the middle Nanbokuchō period with the Jōji era (貞治, 1362-1368). On the basis of the signature style, we can date the *kantei* blade somewhere around Kan´ō (観応, 1350-1352). So Motoshige´s artistic period spanned over fifty years and as he signed noticeably smaller from Kan´ō onwards, so there is the theory that a shift in generations took place at that time.

But most swordsmiths tried at *shinogi-zukuri* blades not to sign directly on the *shinogi* ridge of the tang but shifted the *mei* somewhat towards the *nakago-mune*, i.e. on the *shinogi-ji* of the tang. When we now take into consideration that the *shinogi-ji* narrows with the Nanbokuchō period, than also the signature has to become smaller to still fit on the *nakago*´s *shinogi-ji*. This is probably the reason why Motoshige´s signatures did not change on *tantō* or *hira-zukuri* blades and this in turn would speak against a two-generations theory. However, there are nevertheless further studies necessary.

The majority bade *atari* on Motoshie but there were also many who went for Chikakage (近景). Chikakage´s *hamon* is quite similar to the *kantei* blade but his *jigane* is a standing-out *ko-itame* with some *ō-hada* and his *utsuri* is usually faint. Also he applied a typical *sansaku-bōshi* and not such a pointed *kaeri* like here. But another important factor is that Chikakage signed in *gyaku-tagane* and this was given as hint at the end of the description for the *kantei*.

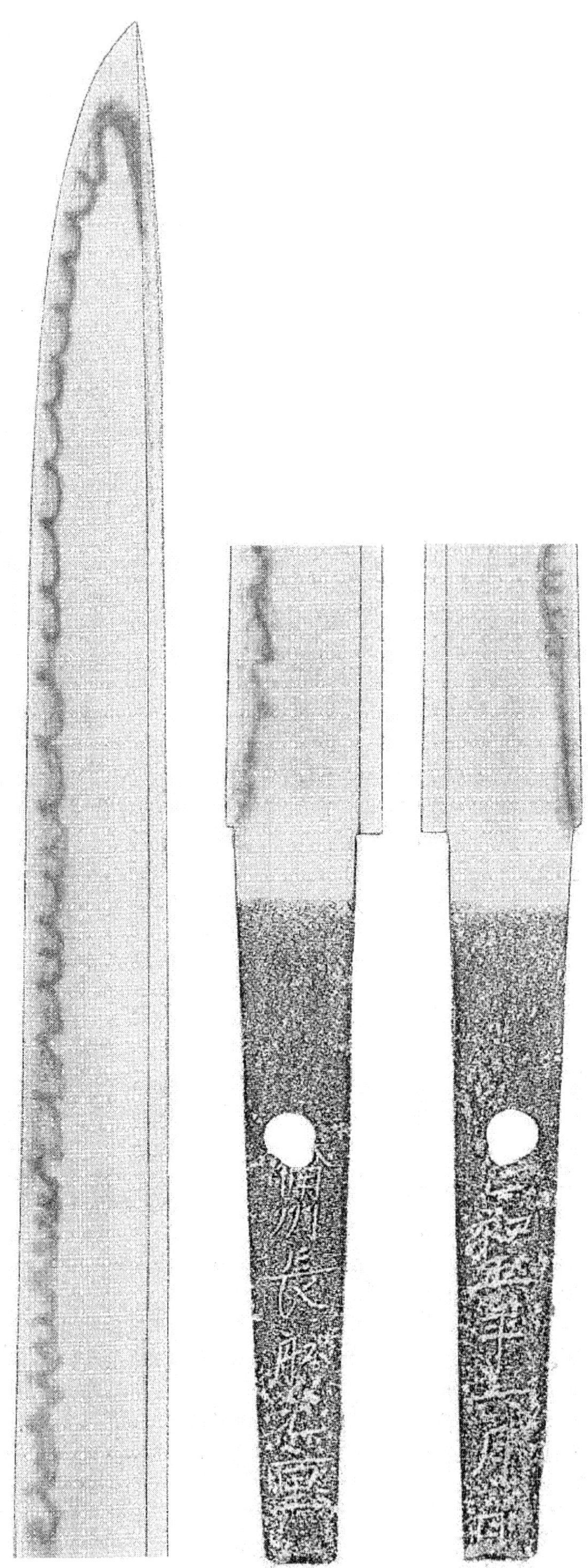

78.665 *tantō*
mei: Bishū Osafune Motoshige (備州長船元重)
Shōwa gonen rokugatsu-hi (正和五年六月日, „a day in the sixth month Shōwa five [1316]")
nagasa 24,8 cm, *uchizori*, *hira-zukuri*, *iori-mune*

ji: standing-out *itame* with much *nagare* and partial *masame*, in addition *ji-nie*, *jifu* and a *midare-utsuri*
hamon: a *gunome* and *kataochi-gunome* mix which bases on an angular *gunome*, the *ashi* are slanting and the hardening is in *nioi-deki* with *ko-nie*
bōshi: *notare-komi* with a rather long *ko-maru-kaeri*

This *tantō* is very typical. The shape with the standard length, the *uchizori* and the thick *kasane* speaks for the late Kamakura period. It is signed with the fifth year of Shōwa, that means less than ten years later – in 1324 – Godaigo´s (後醍醐, 1288-1339) plan to overthrow the Kamakura-*bakufu* was revealed. The latter was namely one step into the subsequent Nanbokuchō period. Let us address the *jigane*. Motoshige´s *jigane* is a standing-out *itame* mixed with *nagare* and shows also differently coloured *jifu* areas. This feature can be seen on this *tantō* too. The *yakigashira* of the *hamon* are angular and horizontally stretched and are separated by „negative" *togari*. Also the heads lie on an uniform line without noticeable ups and downs. And because this blade is so typical, it shouldn´t be that hard to arrive at Motoshige.

There were also some bids on Kanemitsu (兼光). But at Kanemitsu, the *hamon* would basically consist of *kataochi-gunome* and would not be that horizontally stretched. Also the *jigane* would be finer and would not show *masame*. This is by the way the oldest dated work of Motoshige extant. The latest known date signature is from the Jōji era (貞治, 1362-1368).

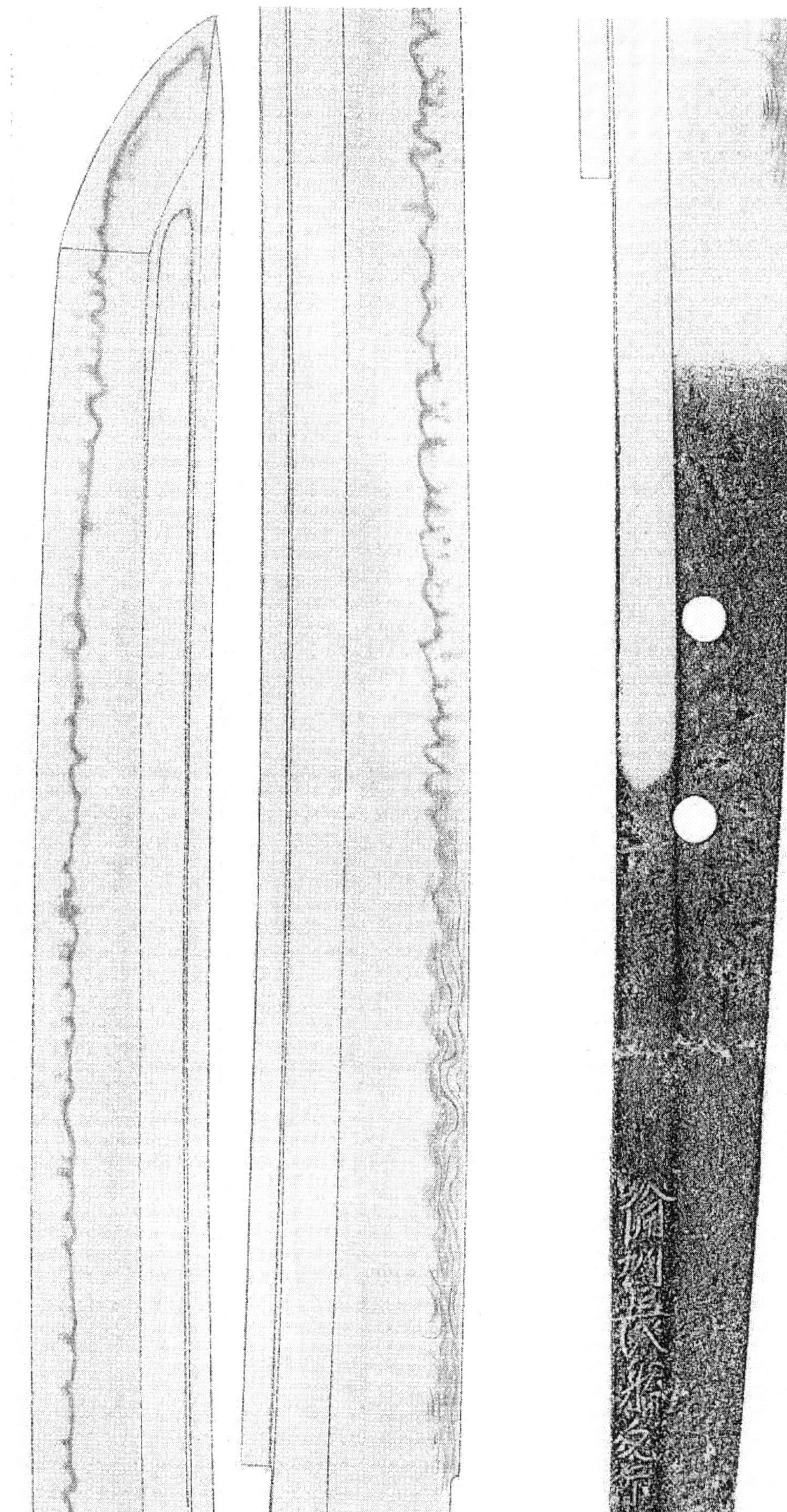

79.664 *tachi*
mei: Bishū Osafune Tsuguyuki (備州長船次行)
nagasa 68,5 cm, *sori* 2,1 cm, *shinogi-zukuri*, *iori-mune*

ji: rather standing-out *itame* mixed with *mokume*, *nagare* and *masame*, in addition *ji-nie*, thick *chikei*-like structures of steel with a different carbon content, *jifu* and a faint *midare-utsuri*
hamon: mix of angular *gunome*, *ko-gunome*, *ko-chōji*, *ko-togariba* and *kataochi-gunome*, the ndividual elements are slanting and closely arranged to each other, also *ashi*, *yō*, *kinsuji* and *sunagashi* appear
bōshi: *midare-komi* with a pointed *kaeri*
horimono: on both sides a *bōhi* which ends with a *maru-dome* on the *omote* side and which runs into the tang with *kake-nagashi* on the *ura* side

This is a *tachi* of the Kozori smith Tsuguyuki who was active towards the end of the Nanbokuchō period. The base shows only a little *funbari* and so we can assume that the blade is shortened. When we reconstruct the original shape then we arrive at a *sugata* with normal *mihaba*, not much tapering and a deep *koshizori* which increases again towards the tip. Many Kozori blades of the late Nanbokuchō period tend namely towards a noticeable *sakizori*. The *mihaba* of this *tachi* measures 2,8 cm and the *kasane* 8,5 mm which is quite thick for that width. So all in all the shape is quite typical for the time between the end of the Nanbokuchō and the beginning of the Muromachi period.

The *jigane* of Kozori works is like the *kantei* blade an *itame* mixed with *mokume* and *masame-nagare*. The *hada* stands rather out and there are thick inhomogenous *chikei* which consist of steel with a different carbon content. Also *jifu* appears in places and so the *jigane* has altogether a somewhat irregular, disharmonious appearance. In addition, a faint *utsuri* appears. The *hamon* bases on a mix of *ko-gunome* and *ko-gunome* or shows a connected *ko-gunome* with round *yakigashira* like seen at the Yoshii school (吉井). This blade shows a varied, irregular and somewhat smaller *hamon* which consists of densely arranged and smaller dimensioned elements. At the later active Ōei-Bizen smiths, the *yakiba* becomes wider and the *hamon* tends towards a *koshi-no-hiraita gunome* with or without *chōji*. As we see also some slanting angular *gunome*, some went also for Motoshige (元重).

At this *kantei*, several blades were put on display after the tangs were revealed. For example a *tachi* of Nagamitsu (長光), a *tachi* of Izumo-Dōei Masanori (出雲道永正則), a *wakizashi* of Kanemitsu (兼光) and a *tachi* of Motoshige. As mentioned, because of the slanting elements and the different appearance of the *jigane*, a bid on a Bizen sideline like Motoshige is quite understandable. But at Motoshige, the *yakigashira* are horizontally noticeably more stretched and the interruptions in between look like „negative“ *togari*. These two characteristics are found on almost every Motoshige work, regardless if the slanting *kataochi-gunome* appears uniformly all over the blade or just in places. Incidentally, a *ko-chōji* or *ko-gunome* based *hamon* with some angular *gunome* are also typical for Osafune-*mono* of the late Kamakura period, but the density and the smaller size of the individual elements as well as the *sugata* does not comply with that production time.

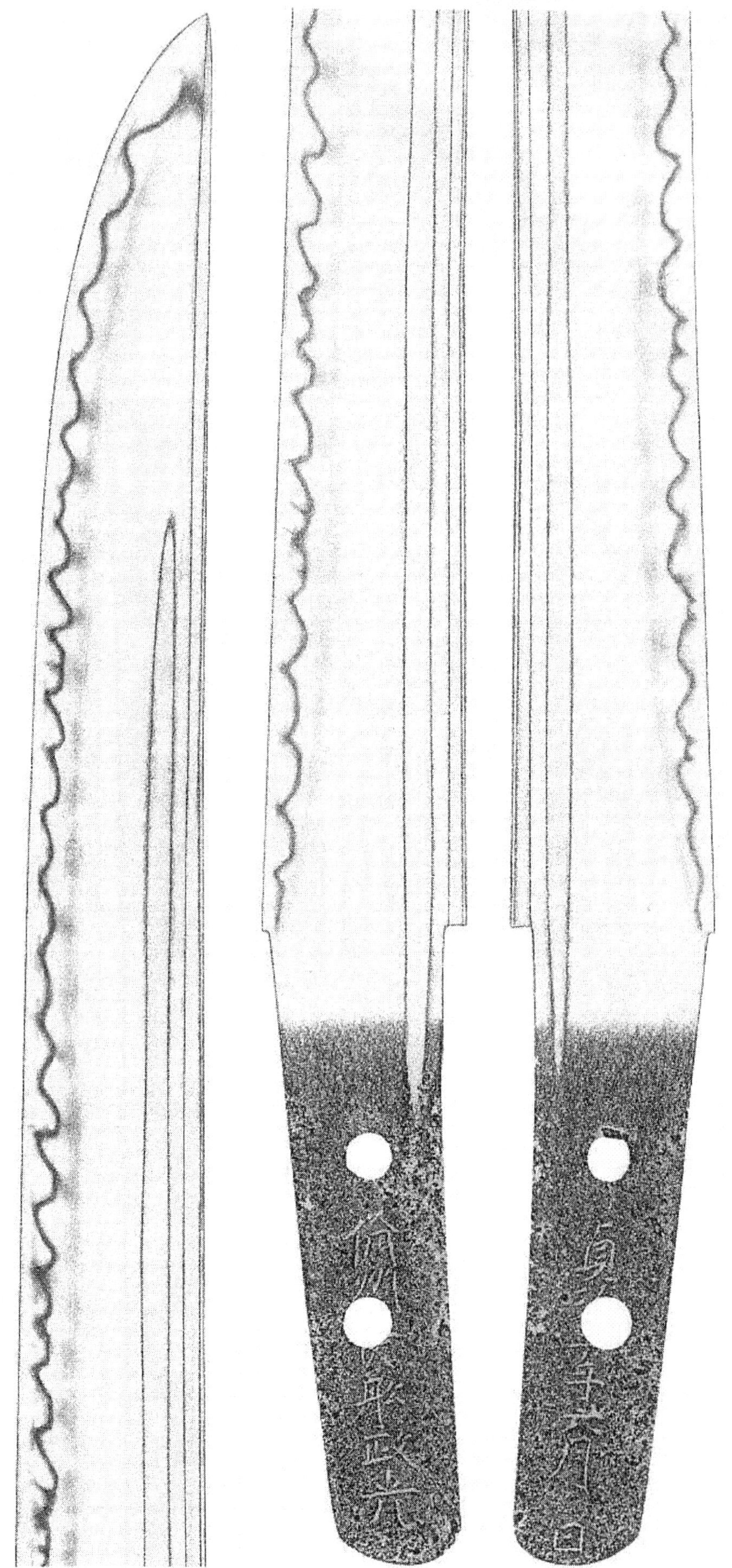

80.657 *tantō*
mei: Bishū Osafune Masamitsu (備州長船政光)
Jō(ji) ?-nen rokugatsu-hi (貞治〇年六月日, „a day in the sixth month of the ? year of Jōji [1362-1368]“)
nagasa 27,2 cm, *sori* 0,3 cm, *hira-zukuri*, *mitsu-mune*

ji: *ko-itame* mixed with *mokume*, *ji-nie*, clear and bright *bō-utsuri*
hamon: mix of connected *gunome*, angular *gunome* and *kataochi-gunome*, there are also some smaller dimensioned elements seen and *ashi* and *ko-nie* appear
bōshi: *midare-komi* with only a little *kaeri*
horimono: on both sides a *katana-hi* which runs with *kake-nagashi* into the tang

The heyday of the Nanbokuchō period gave rise for two *tantō* shapes: Once the wide *mihaba* with a *sunnobi-nagasa*, a thin *kasane* and a little *sori*, i.e. the so-called „Enbun-Jōji-*sugata*“, and second, this Enbun-Jōji-*sugata* „shrinked“ to a rather standard *tantō* length but keeping all the proportions of the Enbun-Jōji-*sugata*. This blade belongs to the latter category and was made during the time of Ashikaga Yoshiakira (足利義詮, 1330-1367, r. 1358-1367).

We have now found out the time and continue with the other characteristics. When we take a look at the *jiba* we see a clear *bō-utsuri* and a *hamon* of connected angular *gunome* and *kataochi-gunome* which is very typical for Kanemitsu (兼光) and his school. Masamitsu was active from the heyday of the Nanbokuchō period, that means from about Jōji, into the early Muromachi period around Ōei (応永, 1394-1427). There are many blades extant by him which are quite similar in *deki* to contemporary Kozori smiths (小反). But early works from around Jōji show like here the typical Nanbokuchō shape in combination with a *kataochi-gunome* or *notare* and are closer to the style of Kanemitsu than the later works.

Also the very dense and beautifully forged *ko-itame* reminds at a glance of Kanemitsu but when you take a closer look at the *hamon*, you can see also a noticeable amount of *gunome* with round *yakigashira* within the *kataochi-gunome*. Also the *hamon* is rather densely arranged and does not reach the quality of Kanemitsu. This is the first approach to recognize that this is an early work of one of his students (some transmissions also say Masamitsu was his son). This *tantō* was put out on display exactly because of this, namely to study the early workmanship of Masamitsu which orientates towards his master or father Kanemitsu.

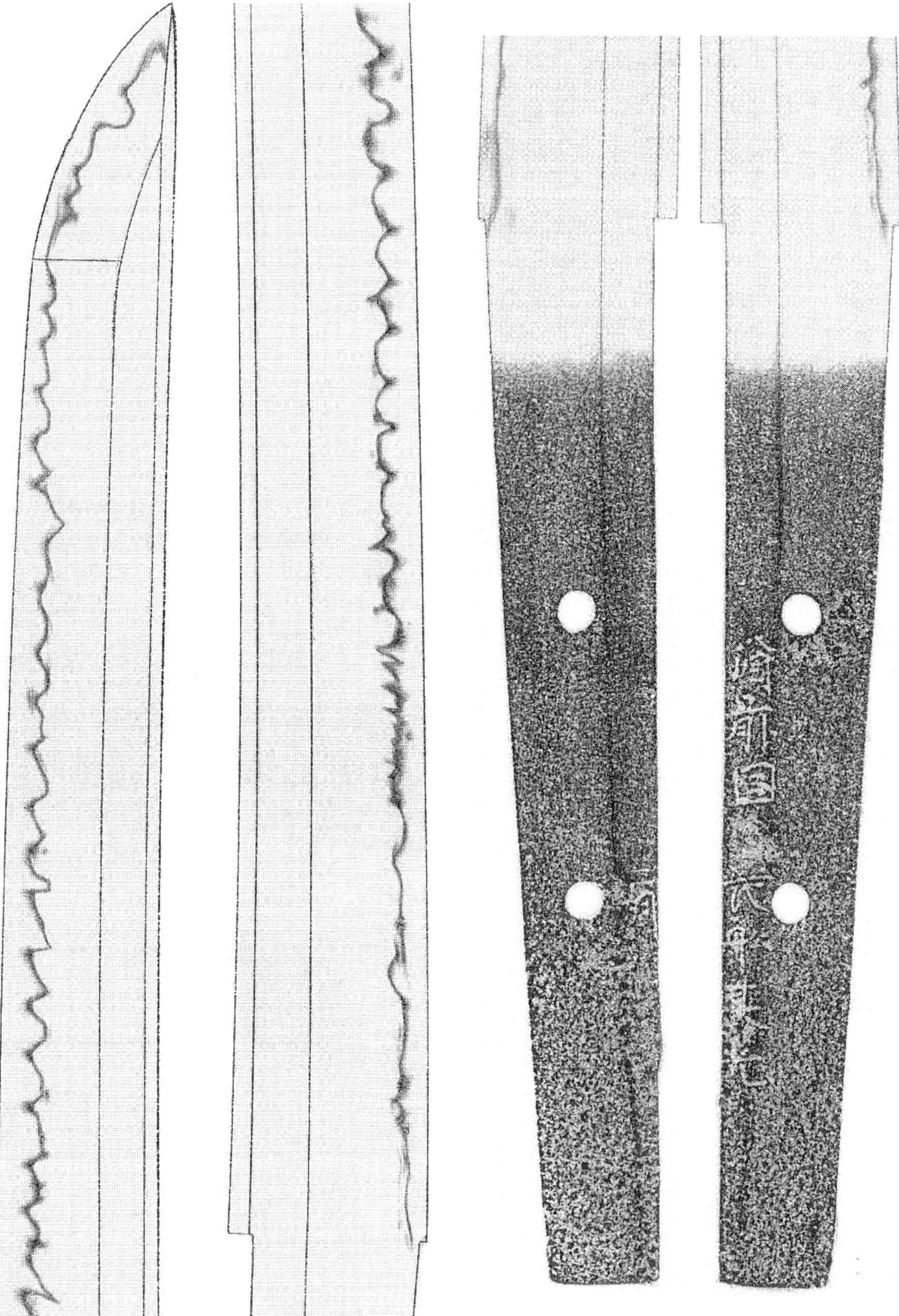
備前国

81.662k *tachi*
mei: Bizen no Kuni-jū Osafune Motomitsu (備前国住長船基光)
nagasa 71,2 cm *sori* 1,8 cm
moto-haba 3,2 cm *saki-haba* 2,3 cm
moto-kasane 0,75 cm *saki-kasane* 0,45 cm
kissaki-nagasa 4,8 cm *nakago-nagasa* 18,94 cm
only a little *nakago-sori*

shinogi-zukuri, *iori-mune*, wide *mihaba*, no noticeable taper, *koshizori* which increases again towards the tip, *ō-kissaki*. The *jigane* is an *itame* mixed with *mokume* which stands out all over the blade. In addition plentiful of *ji-nie*, fine *chikei* and a faint *midare-utsuri*. The *hamon* and the *bōshi* can be seen on the *oshigata*. In addition, *ashi*, *kinsuji* and *sunagashi* appear. The *nioiguchi* is bright and is full of *ko-nie*. The tang is slightly *suriage* and had originally a *kurijiri* which tended somewhat to *ha-agari*. The *yasurime* are *katte-sagari* and the blade has two *mekugi-ana*. The *naga-mei* is chiselled on the *haki-omote* side towards the back of the tang. On the *ura* side we can see some illegible remnants of a date signature.

The blade has a wide *mihaba*, does not taper that much, has a deep *koshizori* which increases again towards the tip and ends in an *ō-kissaki*. That means we can date it into the heyday of the Nanbokuchō period. The *ji* shows a faint *midare-utsuri* and so it is very likely that this is a Bizen work. When we take into consideration the *kataochi* and angular *gunome* and the *bōshi* in *midare-komi* with the pointed *kaeri*, then you will inevitably arrive at Kanemitsu (兼光) and his school.

Motomitsu was a student of Kanemitsu and showed within his school the most standing-out *jihada* which in turn can be considered as one of his characteristics. We know basically three kinds of *hamon* by Kanemitsu: A *suguha-chō*, a *kataochi-gunome* and a *notare-chō*. The interpretations in *notare* were especially continued by Tomomitsu (倫光) and Motomitsu focused on the *kataochi-gunome*. At his *tantō* and *hira-zukuri wakizashi*, this *kataochi-gunome* appears sometimes also in a regular manner but mostly it is a varied mix of slanted *gunome*, „normal" *gunome*, angular *gunome* and *notare*. So the *yakiba* shows quite many variation. This applies also to his extant *zaimei-tachi* which show besides of the *kataochi-gunome*, angular *gunome* and *ko-gunome* also some *togariba*. And at some blades the upper area is of *kataochi-gunome* mixed with angular *gunome*, the middle area of *ko-notare* and the lower area of *koshi-no-hiraita gunome*.

Motomitsu´s tip of the tang is a *kurijiri* which tends to *ha-agari*. The *yasurime* are *katte-sagari* and the signature is in the case of *tachi* mostly executed as *naga-mei* on the *haki-omote* side towards the back of the tang. There are hardly any date signatures on *tachi* extant.

Most of the participants bade on Motomitsu but some also on Kanemitsu, Tomomitsu or Masamitsu (政光). All these smiths belonged to the same school and their workmanship is sometimes hard to differentiate. So all bids on them were counted as *atari* this time. But let us address the differences. At Kanemitsu, the *kataochi-gunome* comes in combination with a dense and finely forged *itame* and a bright *jigane*. Also his *kataochi-gunome* is often very regular. Tomomitsu focused as mentioned rather on a *notare*. Masamitsu on the other hand made more slender *tachi* than Kanemitsu, Tomomitsu or Motomitsu and applied also a *ko-notare* and *ko-gunome* which is vividly mixed with *ko-chōji* and/or *ko-togari*. So his later works – of which more exist today – orientate towards the *deki* of the Kozori group (小反).

Besides of that, many went also for Motoshige (元重). This is understandable because the *hada* stands out and the *yakigashira* are quite pointed for the Kanemitsu school. But the variety of the *hamon* in its entirety is more typical for Motomitsu than for Motoshige. At the latter, the *hada* tends also to *nagare* and shows *jifu*. Also his angular *yakigashira* are horizontally more stretched and are separated by „negative“ *togari* elements. Also Motoshige´s *ha-nie* are stronger and we would expect more *nie*-based *hataraki* like *kinsuji* and *sunagashi*.

By the way, the Nanbokuchō-period overlong *tachi* in Enbun-Jōji-*sugata* were mostly shortened later. But this *tachi* is only a little *suriage* and keeps the signature. This makes it a valuable reference for the original shapes of that time and also that it has a deep *koshizori*. That means there was still a deep *koshizori* applied during the heyday of the Nanbokuchō period. This characteristic can also be seen on the *kokuhō* Kōsetsu-Samonji (江雪左文字), on a *jūyō-bunkazai* of Kanemitsu which is dated Enbun four (延文, 1359), on a *tokubetsu-jūyō* of Kanemitsu which is dated Enbun five (1360), and on a *jūyō* of Unjū (雲重) which is dated Jōji seven (貞治, 1368).

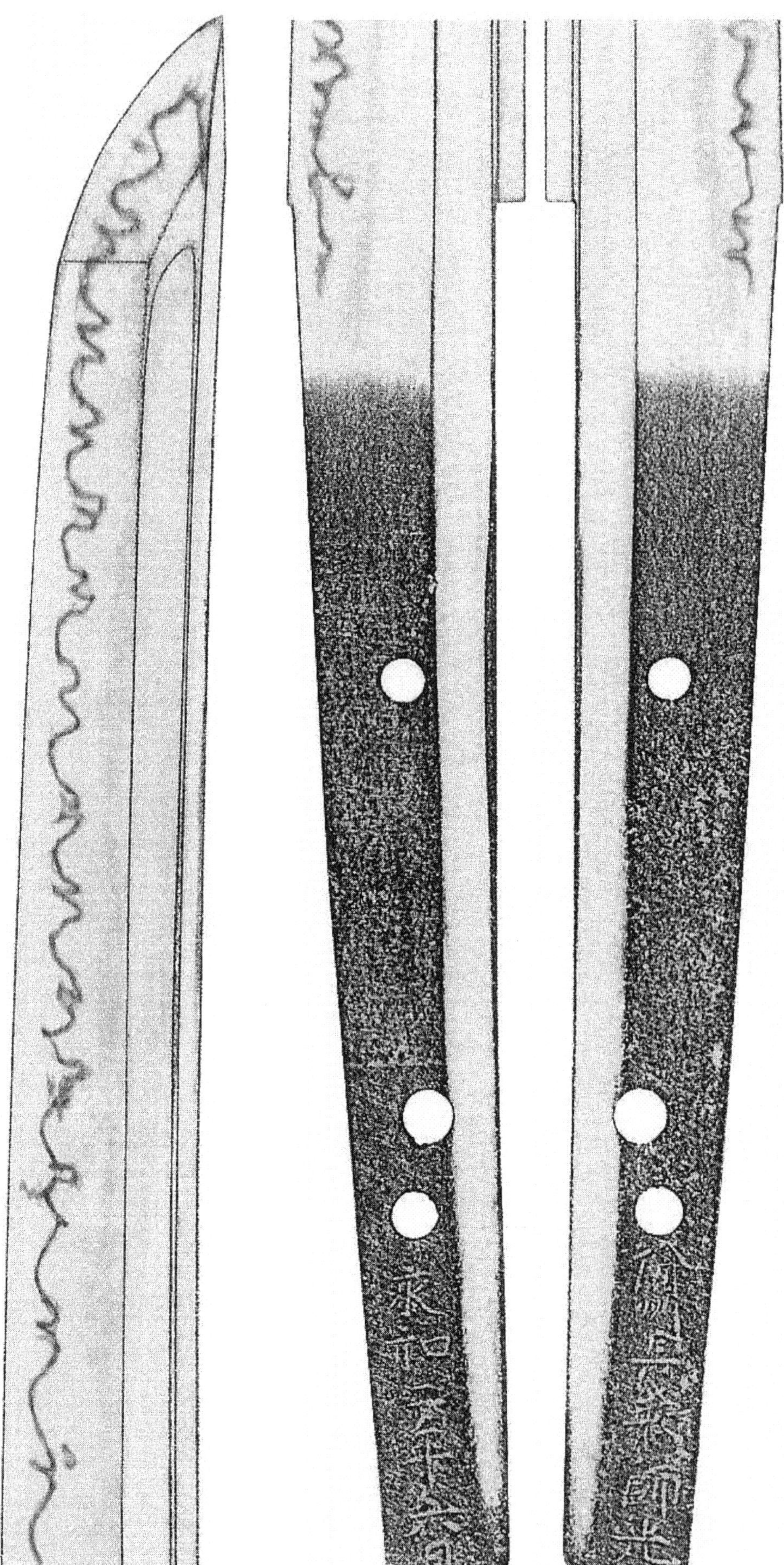

82.646 *tachi*
mei: Bishū Osafune Moromitsu (備州長船師光)
Eiwa ninen rokugatsu (cutted-off below) (永和二年六月, „sixth month Eiwa two [= 1376"])
nagasa 73,0 cm, *sori* 1,9 cm, *shinogi-zukuri*, *iori-mune*

ji: *itame* mixed with *mokume* and *nagare*, in addition *ji-nie*, *jifu*, and a *bō-utsuri* along the lower half and a *midare-utsuri* along the upper half
hamon: *notare* mixed with *gunome*, *chōji* and *togariba* which are all over the blade rather small dimensioned, in addition *ko-ashi*, *yō* and *sunagashi*, the hardening is in *nioi-deki* with *ko-nie*
bōshi: *midare-komi* with a pointed *kaeri* on the *omote* side and a somewhat constricted *maru-kaeri* on the *ura* side
horimono: on both sides a *bōhi* which runs with *kake-nagashi* into the tang

The *ji* shows a conspicious *utsuri* and the *sugata* has a wide *mihaba* and a somewhat elongated *kissaki*, that means we have here obviously a Bizen-*mono* of the Nanbokuchō period. And it is actually a *tachi* of Moromitsu from the late Nanbokuchō period, dated Eiwa two (1376). Motomitsu belonged together with Nariie (成家), Hidemitsu (秀光), Tsunehiro (恒弘), Iemori (家守) and others to the so-called „Kozori group" (小反), a group of Bizen smiths which was active around late Nanbokuchō. Compared to the Osafune mainline around Kanemitsu (兼光) at that time, the Kozori smiths displayed a vivid, standing-out *hada* mix consisting of *itame* mixed with *mokume* and/or *nagare* and also *jifu*, so the *jigane* makes altogether a somewhat loose and weak appearance. The *hamon* is a *ko-gunome* or a varied mix of *togariba*, *ko-notare*, *ko-chōji* and/or angular elements. The individual elements are rather small dimensioned and irregular, when seen over the entirety of the *hamon*. The *kantei* blade has all these characteristics and so the most bids were *atari* on Kozori.

But some went also for the Kanemitsu school or Ōei-Bizen. This might go back to the *sugata* because it is somewhat wider than usual Kozori works and has also an elongated *kissaki*. This speaks namely for the shape of Kanemitsu and his students from around Enbun (延文, 1356-1361) and Jōji (貞治, 1362-1368). Kozori smiths forged namely mostly blades with a slender *mihaba* and a not so magnificent *sugata*. But as mentioned, the *jiba* differs considerably from the Kanemitsu school. At Ōei-Bizen, the blade would show a standard *tachi-sugata* with normal *mihaba* and the *kitae* would be a mix of *itame* and *mokume* which is more uniform than at Kozori. In addition, the *hamon* would appear as a larger dimensioned, somewhat more flamboyant *koshi-no-hiraita gunome* or *chōji*. But the *hamon* does show some similarities to Ōei-Bizen so a bid on that group is not that off.

It must be noted that it was hard to nail the bid down on Moromitsu and so all bids on Kozori were counted as *atari*.

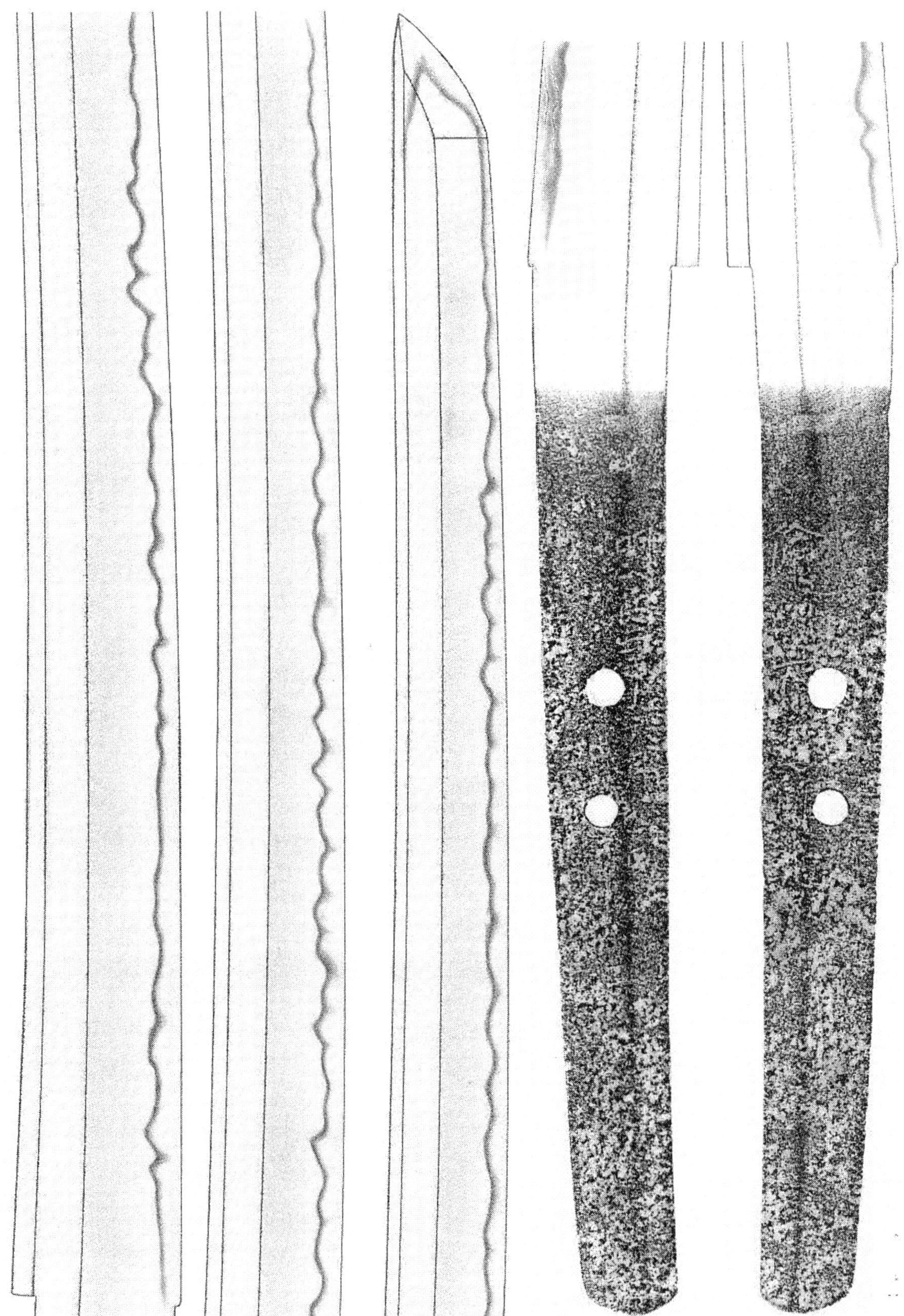

83.599k *tachi*
mei: Bizen Osafune Moromitsu (備前長船師光)
Meitoku san-nen (明德三年六月？？, „third year of Meitoku [= 1392]")
nagasa 65,6 cm *sori* 2,2 cm
moto-haba 2,7 cm *saki-haba* 1,5 cm
moto-kasane 0,75 cm *saki-kasane* 0,4 cm
kissaki-nagasa 2,2 cm *nakago-nagasa* 18,33 cm
nakago-sori 0,15 cm

shinogi-zukuri, iori-mune, mormal *mihaba*, noticeable taper, deep *koshizori* which increases again towards the tip, *chū-kissaki*. The *jigane* is an *itame-hada* mixed with *mokume* and *nagare* and stands rather out. There is *ji-nie* and thick, varied *chikei* and also *jifu* and a faint *midare-utsuri*. The *hamon* and the *bōshi* can be seen on the *oshigata*. *Ko-ashi* and *yō* appear. The *nioiguchi* is basically in *nioi-deki* but *ko-nie* and some *kinsuji* and *sunagashi* appear too. The *nakago* is *ubu* (with a little *machi-okuri*), has a *kurijiri*, *katte-sagari yasurime* and two *mekugi-ana*. There is *naga-mei* on the *haki-omote* which is chiselled towards the *nakago-mune* and which starts above the original *mekugi-ana*. A date signature is added in the same way on the *ura* side. (Note: This smith did not sign in *gyaku-tagane*.)

Moromitsu was active towards the end of the Nanbokuchō period and belonged to the Kozori group. Usually we count today these Nanbokuchō smiths as Kozori which did not belong to the Bizen mainlines at that time which were for example the Kanemitsu, Chōgi, Ōmiya, Motoshige or Yoshii schools. They started to produce from about Eiwa (永和, 1375-1379) onwards, i.e. the end of the Nanbokuchō period, and for about one generation or roughly ten years into the Ōei era (応永, 1394-1428). Although most extant works with date signatures which are classified today as Kozori fit well in that time, there are also some earlier Kozori blades with datings of the Bunna (文和, 1352-1356) and Enbun era (延文, 1356-1361).

However, the *sugata* like the one of the *kantei* blade corresponds to the shape of the late Nanbokuchō period, i.e. a normal wide, tapering shape with a deep *koshizori* which increases again towards the tip in combination with a *chū-kissaki*. But compared to the normal *mihaba*, the *kasane* is rather thick and the *sugata* gets due to the *sakizori* at the beginning of the Muromachi period a noticeably different appearance. There are also some Kozori blades extant by Hidemitsu (秀光) which are dated with the Ōan era (応安, 1368-1375, i.e. his early artistic period) or by Nariie (成家) from the eras Jōji (1362-1368) and Ōan which show the typical *sugata* of the Nanbokuchō period with a wide *mihaba*, almost no tapering, and an *ō-kissaki*.

The *jigane* of the Kozori group is basically a standing-out mix of *itame*, *mokume* and *nagare*. Thick and differently sized *chikei* and a faint *jifu-utsuri* appear. So in terms of quality the *jigane* of the Kozori group is inferior to that of the Osafune Kanemitsu school.

The *hamon* is mostly a *ko-notare* mixed wit *ko-gunome* and *ko-togari* or a *ko-notare* which is more vividly mixed with *ko-gunome*, *ko-chōji*, *ko-togari*, angular *midare* and *kataochi-gunome*. The *midare* elements have either round *yakigashira* like at the Yoshii school or tend to appear as all over the blade slanting *kataochi-gunome*. Another characteristic feature of Kozori-*mono* is that the *yakiba* is rather narrow in comparison to the *mihaba* of the blade.

It has to be said that at the mentioned works from Hidemitsu and Nariie (but also on works from Morisuke [守助] and Morimasa [守正] from the Jōji era), there is a fine and densely forged *itame* on wide *tachi* and *hira-zukuri-wakizashi* in the typical Nanbokuchō shape. They also applied a *notare* or *kataochi-gunome* which reminds of Kanemitsu or an angular *gunome* in the style of Motoshige (元重). That means initially, the smiths we attribute today to the Kozori group were more close to other contemporary Bizen schools than the later representatives.

The *bōshi* of the Kozori group is a tapering *midare-komi* or a *midare-komi* or *sugu-bōshi* with a *ko-maru-kaeri*. The tip of the tang is a *kurijiri* and the *yasurime* are *katte-sagari*. *Tachi* are usually signed with a *naga-mei* on the *haki-omote* side towards the back of the tang. Often also a date signature is added on the *ura* side. An exception was Moromitsu who signed with characteristical small characters.

Well, let´s reveal the result of the *kantei*. Most bids were besides of Moromitsu on Hidemitsu, Iemori (家守), Tsunehiro (恒弘), Shigeyoshi (重吉) and other Kozori smiths. Besides of them some also went for Masamitsu (政光) and because of the later Nanbokuchō or early Ōei era also for Morimitsu (盛光) and Iesuke (家助). As all Kozori smiths (except those from the earlier, the heyday of the Nanbokuchō period) displayed a rather close workmanship and a differentiation is often difficult, all bids on Kozori were counted as *atari*. But also bids on Masamitsu were counted this time as *atari* because he worked in a very close style to Kozori. The same applies to Morimitsu and Iesuke, but an *atari* was only given when „late Nanbokuchō", „end of Nanbokuchō" or „Ōei" was added. So one had to differentiate between them and their earlier generations.

But there were also many bids on Yasumitsu (康光) and Ōei-Bizen. But at Ōei-Bizen, we would expect are more noticeable *sakizori* and a *jigane* of standing-out *itame* and *mokume* with other *chikei*. The *utsuri* would not appear as *jifu* like it is seen on the *kantei* blade but as a clear *midare-* or *bō-utsuri*. Also the Ōei-Bizen smiths applied a wider, irregular and flamboyant *midareba* with *koshi-no-hiraita gunome* or *chōji* and usually not such a narrow *yakiba*.

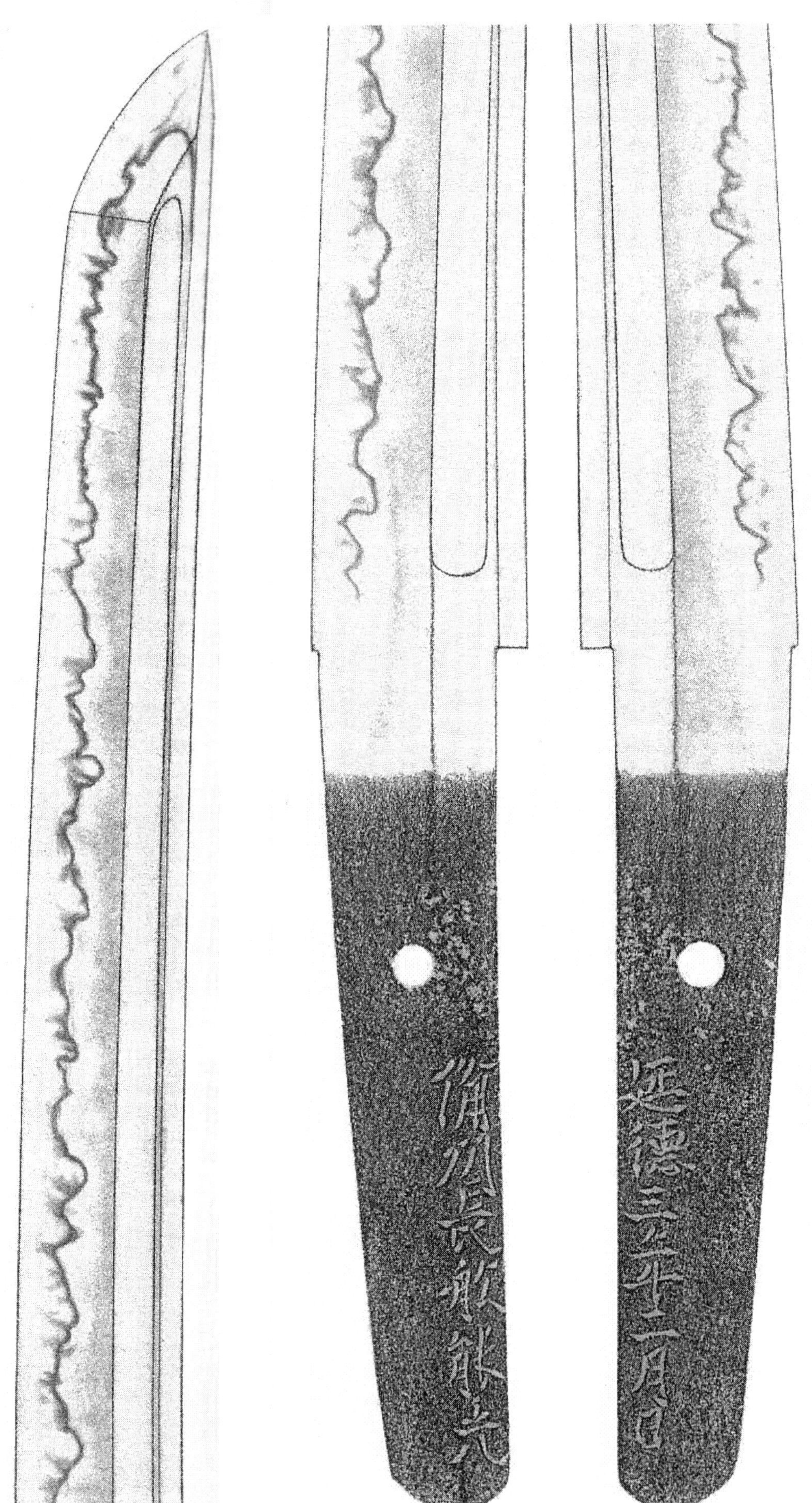
備州長船勝光
延徳三年

84.616 *wakizashi*
mei: Bishū Osafune Yoshimitsu (備州長船能光)
Entoku san-nen ni-gatsu-hi (延徳三年二月日, „a day in the second month Entoku three [= 1491]")
nagasa 55,45 cm, *sori* 1,5 cm, *shinogi-zukuri*, *iori-mune*

ji: dense *ko-itame-hada* with plentiful of *ji-nie* and a *midare-utsuri*
hamon: basing on *ko-chōji* and mixed with *chōji*, *kawazu no ko-chōji*, *gunome*, *koshi no hiraita-gunome* and rather complex *gunome* elements, in addition *ashi* and *yō*, the bright *nioiguchi* is in *nioi-deki* with *ko-nie*, also *kinsuji* and *sunagashi* appear in places
bōshi: *midare-komi* with some *hakikake* and *ko-maru*, the *kaeri* runs back long on the *omote* side
horimono: on both sides a *bōhi* with *marudome*

The *meikan* records list for the Muromachi period three Osafune Yoshimitsu smiths. Extant works of them are very rare and so their excact relationships are somewhat unclear. However, this blade shows a dense and beautifully forged *ko-itame* with a clearly visible *midare-utsuri* and a flamboyant *chōji*-based *midareba*. When we take this blade as basis for his evaluation, than he would be at about the same level as the contemporary Ukyō no Suke Katsumitsu (右京亮勝光), Sakyō no Shin Munemitsu (左京進宗光) or Shirōzaemon no Jō Norimitsu (四郎左衛門尉法光). And we can also assume that all these smiths where somehow closely related.

Because of the excellent *deki* some reckoned the blade as a *kodachi* of the earlier masters Mitsutada (光忠) and Nagamitsu (長光). But if it was a work from that time, then there wouldn´t appear any *koshi-no-hiraita gunome* or such a complex *gunome* mix. Also a *kodachi* of that time would show a conspicious *koshizori*.

Many bids were also on Morimitsu (盛光) and Yasumitsu (康光). These are Ōei-Bizen smiths and so the *jihada* would stand more out and would show mixed-in *mokume* and *nagare*. The valleys of the *midareba* would be a little wider and the *bōshi* would be a *midare* with a pointed, very short *kaeri*.

Incidentally, there were many blades with a relative short *nagasa* of around 2 *shaku* made during the middle Muromachi period, i.e. around Bunmei (文明, 1469-1487), which show a normal or slender *mihaba*, a noticeable taper, a deep *sakizori* and a rather small *kissaki*. Such a *sugata* looks elegant and might resemble a shortened older blade at a glance but one has to check the *kasane* because like the *kantei* blade with 0,9 cm they are rather thick. Some of them tend even to a *yoroidōshi* style. And also in the Ōei era (応永, 1394-1428) there were relative short *shinogi-zukuri* blades with a *nagasa* of aroud 45,45 to 51,5 cm in fashion but in that case, the *sori* is a conspicious *koshizori*.

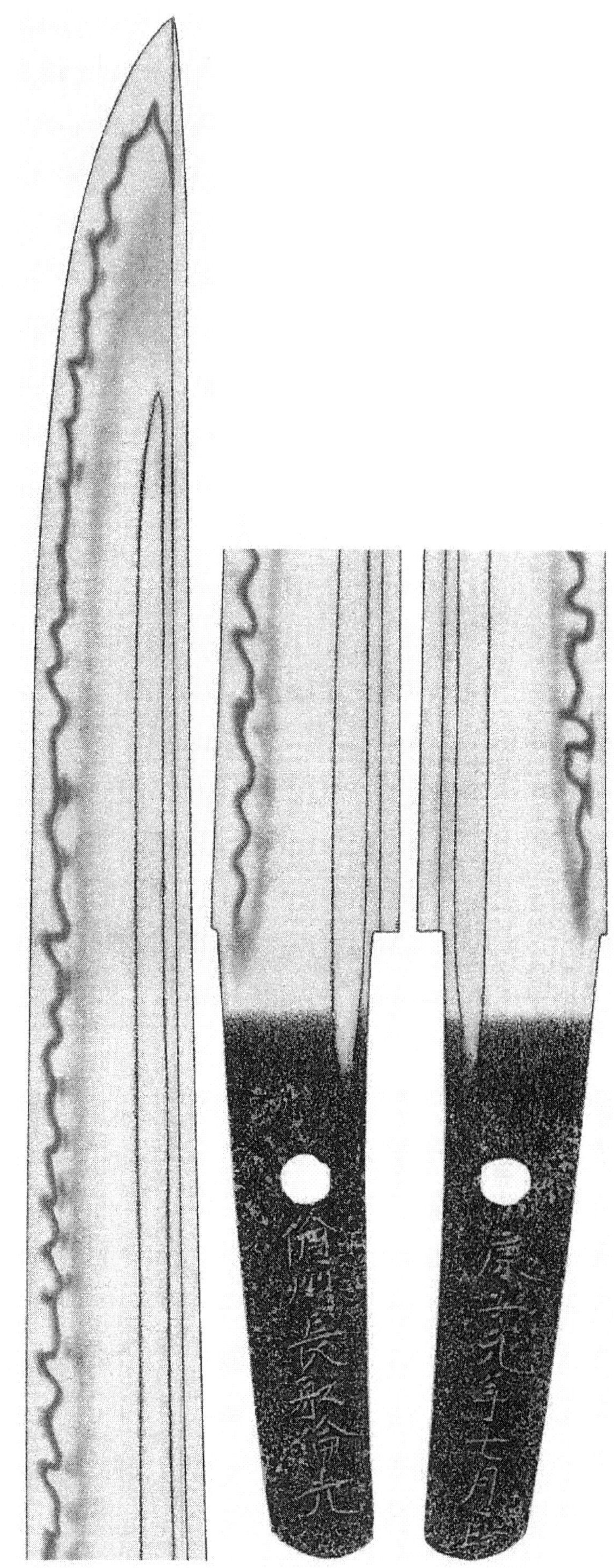
備州長船倫光

85.609 *tantō*
mei: Bishū Osafune Tomomitsu (備州長船倫光)
Kō´an gannen nanagatsu-hi (康安元年七月日, „a day in the seventh month Kōan one [= 1361]")
nagasa 25,1 cm, only very little *sori*, *hira-zukuri*, *iori-mune*

ji: *itame* mixed with *mokume* which rather stands out, *ji-nie*, a *bō-utsuri* starts at the *machi* and runs then parallel to the *yakigashira*
hamon: mix of angular *gunome*, *gunome* and *ko-notare*, partially slanting, also *ashi*, the hardening is in *nioi-deki* with *ko-nie*
bōshi: on the *omote* side a *midare-komi* with pointed *kaeri* and on the *ura* side a *suguha-chō* with some *togari*
horimono: on both sides a *katana-hi* which runs with *kake-nagashi* into the tang

The wide *mihaba* and thin *kasane*, the very shallow *sori* and the not that elongated *nagasa* result in a *tantō-sugata*, which clearly differs from the typical *sunnobi* shape of the Enbun (延文, 1356-1361) and Jōja eras (貞治, 1362-1368. A clear *bō-utsuri* appears and the *hamon* is a (partially slanting) mix of angular *gunome*, *gunome* and *ko-notare*. Together with the hardening in *nioi-deki* with *ko-nie* we are in the vicinity of Kanemitsu (兼光) and so most bids focused on him.

The *tantō* is a work of Tomomitsu and is dated with Kō´an one (1361). As Tomomitsu´s workmanship is principally very similar to Kanemitsu, a bid on the latter is very understandable but we can nevertheless make out some differences. The *kitae* in standing-out *itame* as well as the *ji-nie* and *chikei* do not reach the quality of Kanemitsu. Kanemitsu´s *yakiba* would appear as *kataochi-gunome* which is mixed with some slanting angular *gunome*. But this *yakiba* consists of a mix of angular *gunome*, *gunome*, and *ko-notare* and differs noticeably. If we continue to go into detail then we see that the *yakiba* is smaller dimensioned than at Kanemitsu, that the way the *yakigashira* form an uniform line is different to Kanemitsu too and that the *nioiguchi* is not that clear as we would expect it from a work of Kanemitsu. So there remain his students like Tomomitsu, Motomitsu (元光) or Masamitsu (政光). Among his students, Tomomitsu followed Kanemitsu´s workmanship closely and he is also rather close in terms of skill and quality. Usually he focused on his master´s *notare-chō* but sometimes he also applied like here a *ha* which bases on angular elements. But the latter interpretation was rather the strong point of Motomitsu and the early Masamitsu. So this time it was enough to bid on Kanemitsu and the Kanemitsu school to get an *atari*.

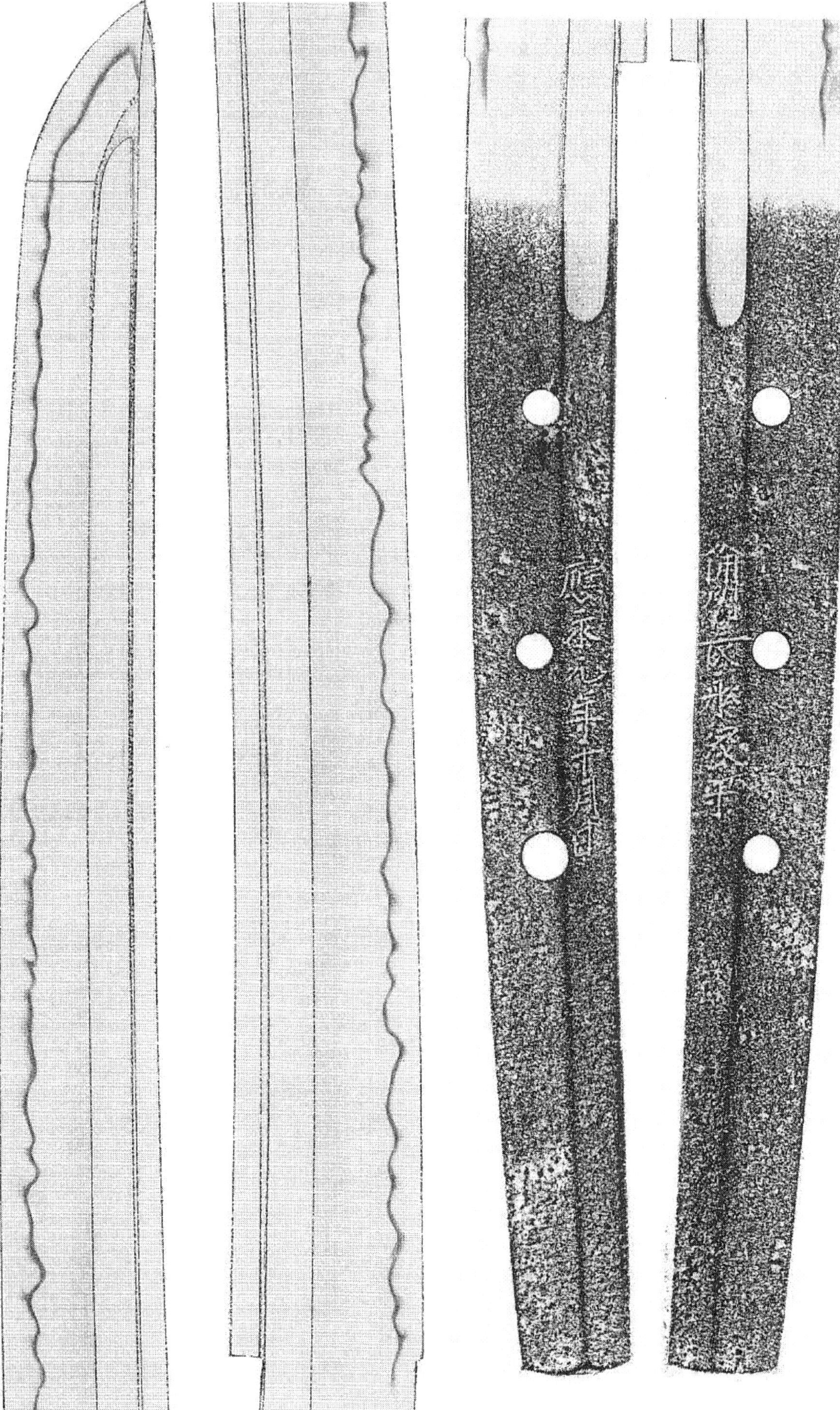
慶長九年十月日

86.656k *tachi*
mei: Bishū Osafune Iemori (備州長船家守)
Ōei gannen jūgatsu-hi (応永元年十月日, „a day in the tenth month of Ōei one [1394]")
nagasa 69,84 cm *sori* 1,97 cm
moto-haba 2,75 cm *saki-haba* 1,8 cm
moto-kasane 0,95 cm *saki-kasane* 0,45
kissaki-nagasa 3,0 cm *nakago-nagasa* 23,18 cm
nakago-sori 0,3 cm

shinogi-zukuri, *iori-mune*, normal *mihaba*, noticeable taper, the blade keeps despite the *suriage* a deep *koshizori* which increases again towards the tip, the *kasane* is quite thick compared to the *mihaba*, the tip is a *chū-kissaki*. The *kitae* is an *itame* mixed with *mokume* which stands out a little. In addition *ji-nie*, thick *chikei* (which consist of inhomogenous steel, i.e. *kawarigane*), some *jifu* and a faint *midare-utsuri*. The *hamon* and the *bōshi* can be seen on the *oshigata*. In addition *ko-ashi*, *yō* and some *sunagashi*. The *yakiba* is rather narrow compared to the *mihaba* and the elements of the *hamon* are small dimensioned and densely arranged. The hardening is in *nioi-deki* with *ko-nie*. On both sides a *bōshi* with *marudome* is engraved. The tang is *suriage*, had originally a *kurijiri*, shows *katte-sagari yasurime* and three *mekugi-ana*. There is a *naga-mei* on the *haki-omote* above the *ubu-mekugi-ana* and towards the back of the tang. Also a date signature is added in the same way on the *ura* side. (Note: This smith did not sign in *gyaku-tagane*.)

The blade has a normal *mihaba*, tapers noticeably, keeps despite the *suriage* a deep *koshizori* which increases again towards the tip, has in proportion to the *mihaba* quite a thick *kasane* and ends in a compact *chū-kissaki*. That means we can date it from the end of the Nanbokuchō to the early Muromachi period.

The *jigane* of Kozori-*mono* is like at the *kantei* blade an *itame* mixed with *mokume* which tends to stand out and show *ji-nie*, characteristical thick *chikei* of inhomogeneous *kawarigane* (steel of different carbon content), and sometimes also *jifu*. So the *jigane* looks a little irregular and coarse and when *utsuri* appears than mostly in a weak manner. The *hamon* is at most Kozori works a *ko-notare* mixed with *ko-gunome* and *ko-togariba* or a *ko-notare* mixed with *ko-gunome*, *ko-chōji*, *ko-togariba*, angular *gunome* and *kataochi-gunome*. That means it is quite varied and appears altogether as irregular *midareba*. But there are also some Kozori works which show a regular *ko-gunome* with round *yakigashira* which remind of the Yoshii school. Other works show an arrangement of connected, pointed *ko-gunome* and some others a *kataochi-gunome* which tends to slant. But in general the *yakiba* is in comparison to the *mihaba* rather narrow and looks often crowded.

Early Kozori smiths like Nariie (成家), from which we know date signatures of the Jōji era (貞治, 1362-1368) or Hidemitsu (秀光) from the Ōei era (応永, 1394-1428) made also blades with a wide *mihaba* and an elongated *kissaki* in the style of an Enbun-Jōji-*sugata*. This shape is combined with a *hamon* which bases on angular *gunome* and which is mixed with *togariba*, *ko-notare* and *kataochi*-like *gunome*. Sometimes they also worked in a *ko-notare* mixed with *ko-gunome*, *togariba* and angular *gunome* which reminds at a glance of Kanemitsu (兼光) and Motoshige (元重). The *bōshi* of Kozori blades is a *midare-komi* with a *ko-maru-kaeri* but sometimes it appears als as *sugu-bōshi* with a *ko-maru-kaeri*.

Most bids were *atari* on Iemori, followed by Moromitsu (師光), Hidemitsu (秀光), Tsunehiro (恒弘) and other Kozori smiths. But some went also for Osafune Masamitsu (政光). Well, all Kozori smiths displayed a very close workmanship and so all such bids were counted as *atari*.

But also Masamitsu worked in a *deki* similar to the Kozori group and therefore an *atari* was given on his bids too. But it has to be mentioned that his *jiba* is usually brighter and that he is in terms of quality superior to his Kozori colleagues. Also Ōei-Bizen Morimitsu (盛光) and Iesuke (家助) worked in the first decade of the Ōei era similar to Kozori and thus bids on them were only counted as *atari* when the participant explicitely mentioned that it is a work of the early Ōei era.

Incidentally, the traditional Bizen style thinned anyway out from the late Nanbokuchō period onwards. This also concerns the lineages of Kanemitsu, Chōgi (長義) and the Ōmiya school (大宮). And with exception of Yoshii, the individual styles of the schools were more and more approaching to each other. So the Kozori group covers basically the smiths of that time whose affiliation is from today´s point of view unclear.

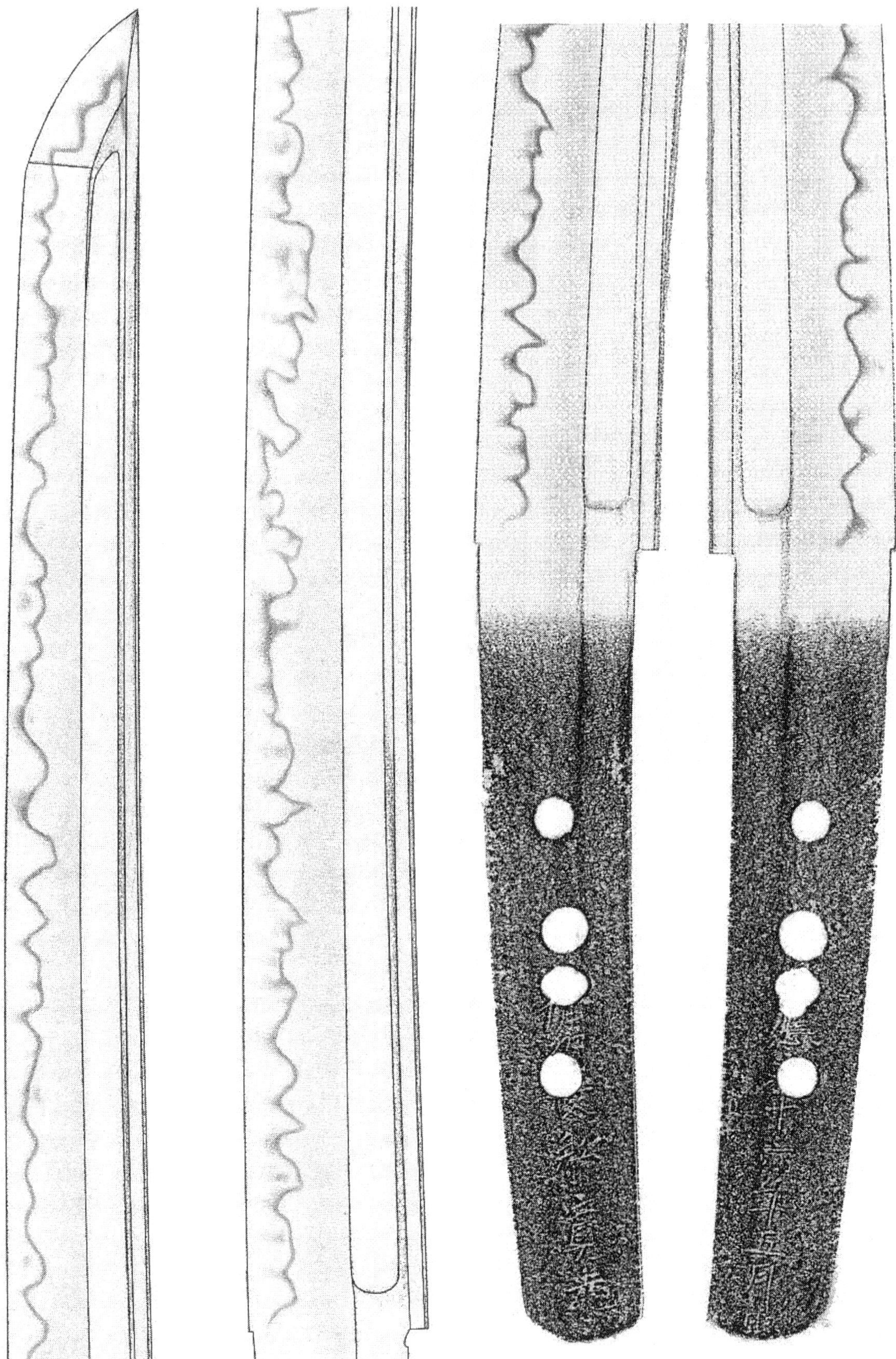

87.653k *wakizashi*
mei: Bishū Osafune Sanemitsu (備州長船実光)
Ōei jūroku-nen gogatsu-hi (応永十六年五月日, „a day in the fifth month Ōei 16 [= 1409]")

nagasa 58,02 cm *sori* 1,36 cm *moto-haba* 2,85 cm *saki-haba* 1,8 cm
moto-kasane 0,7 cm *saki-kasane* 0,4 cm *kissaki-nagasa* 2,6 cm *nakago-nagasa* 13,33 cm
nakago-sori 0,1 cm

shinogi-zukuri, *mitsu-mune*, normal *mihaba*, noticeable taper, *sakizori*, *chū-kissaki*. The *jigane* is an *itame* mixed with *mokume* which stands out all over the blade. In addition, *ji-nie*, plentiful of *chikei* and a *midare-utsuri* appear. The *hamon* and the *bōshi* can be seen on the *oshigata*. There are also *ashi* and *yō* and the *nioiguchi* is bright, in *nioi-deki* with *ko-nie*, and shows also some *sunagashi*. A *bōhi* is engraved on both sides which ends in a *marudome* above the tang. The *nakago* is *ubu*, has a bulbous *kurijiri*, *katte-sagari yasurime*, four *mekugi-ana* and bears centrally on the *sashi-omote* side in the lower half of the tang a *naga-mei*. A date signature is added on the same position on the *ura* side.

There are only few works extant by Sanemitsu but we know a *gassaku* joint work with the two best Ōei-Bizen smiths Morimitsu (盛光) and Yasumitsu (康光). Another *gassaku* work of the three smiths is depicted in the „*Kōzan-oshigata*" (光山押形) and therefore we can assume that he worked closely together with the two great Ōei-Bizen masters.

The blade has a normal *mihaba*, tapers noticeably, has a *sakizori* and ends in a *chū-kissaki*, that means we can date it into the early Muromachi period. The Ōei-Bizen *jigane* is an *itame* mixed with *mokume* which stands out all over the blade. *Ji-nie* and many *chikei*, and either a *midare-utsuri* or a *bō-utsuri* appears. The *hamon* bases in the case of a *midareba* on a *koshi-no-hiraita midare-chōji* mixed with *gunome*, *togari* and other elements. The *yakiba* has conspicious ups and downs and there are *ashi* and *yō* seen. The *nioiguchi* in *nioi-deki* with *ko-nie* is bright. Such a *deki* is usually combined with quite a pointed *bōshi*, the so-called „Ōei-Bizen *rōsoku-bōshi*".

But from time to time this school applied also a *suguha* in *nioi-deki* with *ko-nie* which is mixed with *ko-gunome*, *ashi* and *yō*. Rarely also a slender *tachi-sugata* in combination with a *suguha* with compact *nioiguchi* and *saka-ashi* can be found. Such elegant interpretations remind at a glance of late Kamakura-period Osafune-*mono* like Kagemitsu (景光) or Chikakage (近景).

Many Ōei-Bizen blades bear *horimono* like for example a *bōhi* with *soebi*, *bonji*, *sankozuka-ken*, characters of the deity „Hachiman-Daibosatsu" (八幡大菩薩) or *kurikara* and the like. But a characteristical feature is a *hi* which ends with a *marudome* above the *habaki*. The tang has a bulbous *kurjiri*, *katte-sagari yasurime*, and the signature is in the case of *shinogi-zukuri wakizashi* chiselled on the *sashi-omote* side, namely centrally below the *mekugi-ana* as *naga-mei*. Often a date signature is added on the same position on the *ura* side. From time to time the signature is also chiselled towards the back of the tang.

Most bids were *atari* on Sanemitsu but some went also for Morimitsu, Yasumitsu or other Ōei-Bizen smiths. But others reckoned it also as an Eikyō-Bizen work and bade on smiths like Norimitsu (則光) or Sukemitsu (祐光). As mentioned before, there are only very few works of Sanemitsu going round and because of the very similar *deki* to Morimitsu and Yasumitsu in *koshi-no-hiraita midare-chōji* with round *yakigashira*, bids on them were counted as *atari* too. Also some Eikyō-Bizen smiths like Norimitsu applied a *deki* in flamboyant *koshi-no-hiraita midare-chōji* which reminds of Ōei-Bizen, so this time, he and other smiths from that group were counted as *atari* too.

But the typical workmanship of the Eikyō-Bizen group shows a *midareba* whose elements are smaller dimensioned than at Ōei-Bizen and whose bases start somewhat lower. Also *chōji* are usually rather rare at Eikyō-Bizen and the *hamon* consists mostly of an angular *ko-gunome* or normal *ko-gunome* and is hardened in *nioi-deki*. That means Eikyō-Bizen *hamon* do not have the flamboyance of Ōei-Bizen interpretations and also not the *koshi-no-hiraita midare* consisting of repeated groups of *gunome* which we see at Sue-Bizen. So we have a rather calm, somewhat smaller dimensioned *hamon* which is regarded as a kind of intermediate step between Ōei-Bizen and Sue-Bizen.

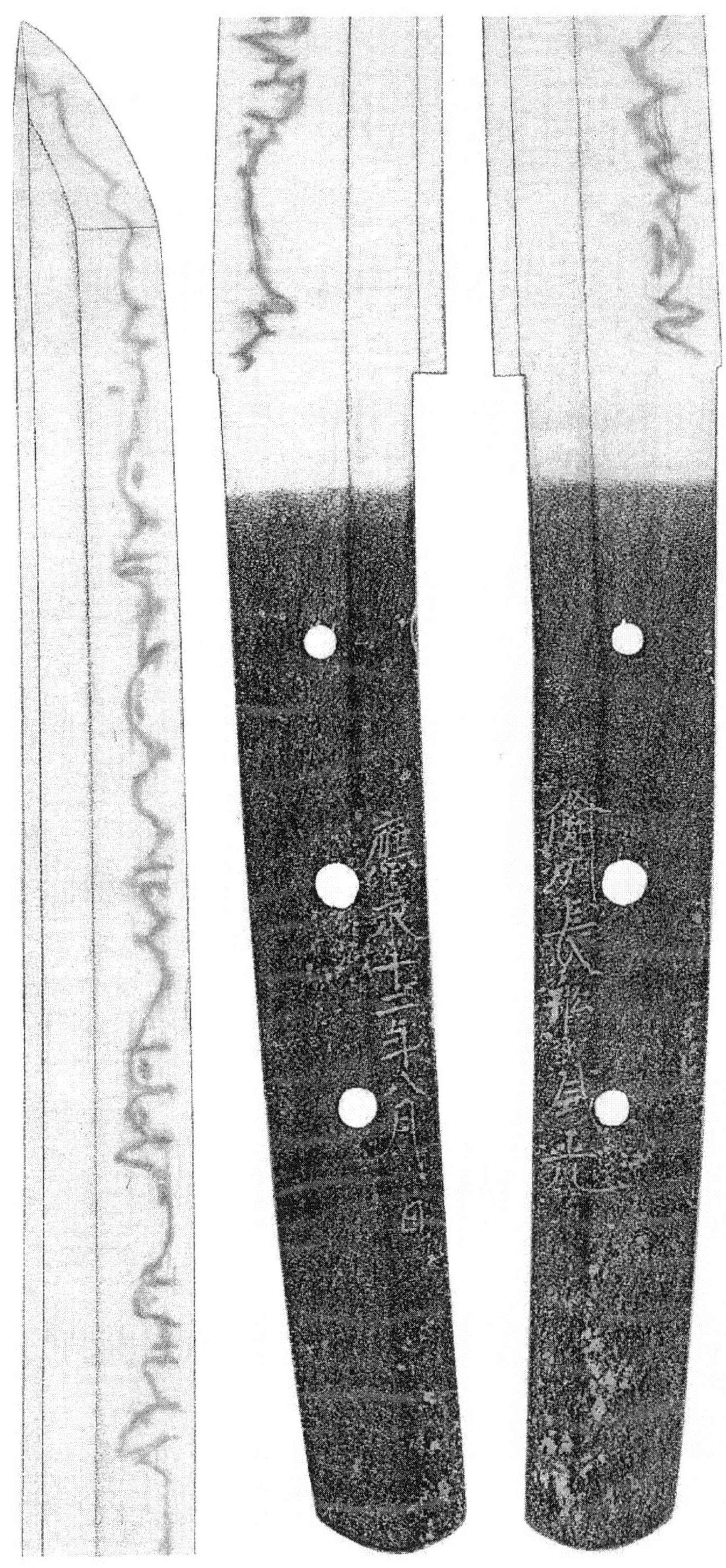

88.649 *tachi*
mei: Bishū Osafune Morimitsu (備州長船盛光)
Ōei jūni-nen hachigatsu-hi (応永十二年八月日, „a day in the eighth month Ōei twelve [1405]“)
nagasa 71,8 cm, *sori* 2,6 cm, *shinogi-zukuri*, *iori-mune*

ji: *itame* mixed with *mokume*, there is a *midare-utsuri* and *ji-nie*
hamon: *koshi-no-hiraita-gunome* in *nioi-deki* with *ko-nie* mixed with *chōji*, the *hamon* appears altogether as flamboyant *midareba*, in addition *ashi*, *yō* and *kinsuji*
bōshi: *midare-komi* with a pointed *kaeri*

The early Muromachi period ushered in a new area of peace after the warring Nanbokuchō period. This peace was initiated by Ashikaga Yoshimitsu (足利義満, 1358-1408). In 1391, the Yamana family (山名) tried to undermine the reign of the new Ashikaha-*shōgun* but was defeated by Yoshimitsu. Their uprising is called „Meitoku Rebellion“ (*Meitoku no ran*, 明徳の乱) because it took place in the Meitoku era (明徳, 1390-1394). And in 1399, Ōuchi Yoshihiro (大内義弘, 1356-1400) tried to overthrow the *shōgun*, a futile attempt known as „Ōei Rebellion“ (*Ōei no ran*, 応永の乱), also named after the Ōei era (応永, 1394-1428).

This time, that means after the establishment of peace during the Ōei era by a stable government, brought also some changes for the Japanese sword. Warriors and smiths remembered the time before the warring Nanbokuchō period and the oversized, massive shapes were given up in favor of a slender *mihaba* with *koshizori* combined – in the case of Bizen – with a *chōji*-loaden *hamon* in the style of Mitsutada (光忠) and Nagamitsu (長光). This *tachi* of Ōei Morimitsu (which comes from the collection of the former NBTHK president Suzuki Kajō) is such a typical revival of the old sword shapes and reminds at a glance of a Kamakura-period *tachi*. But when you take a closer look you can see a slight tendency to *sakizori* and a somewhat thicker *kasane*. In addition, the *gunome* elements get broader towards their base and this is a typical characteristic of the Ōei-Bizen style too.

Many went for Yasumitsu (康光) at the *kantei*. He was also an Ōei-Bizen smith but his *hamon* is generally smaller dimensioned and shows a noticeable amount of *togari* elements. And in a direct comparison, Morimitsu´s *hamon* might look somewhat more graceful. There were also bids on Sue-Bizen Sukesada (祐定). But at Sukesada the shape would be different and the *hamon* would consist of a regular *koshi-no-hiraita gunome* with plentiful of *nie* and would not show much *chōji*.

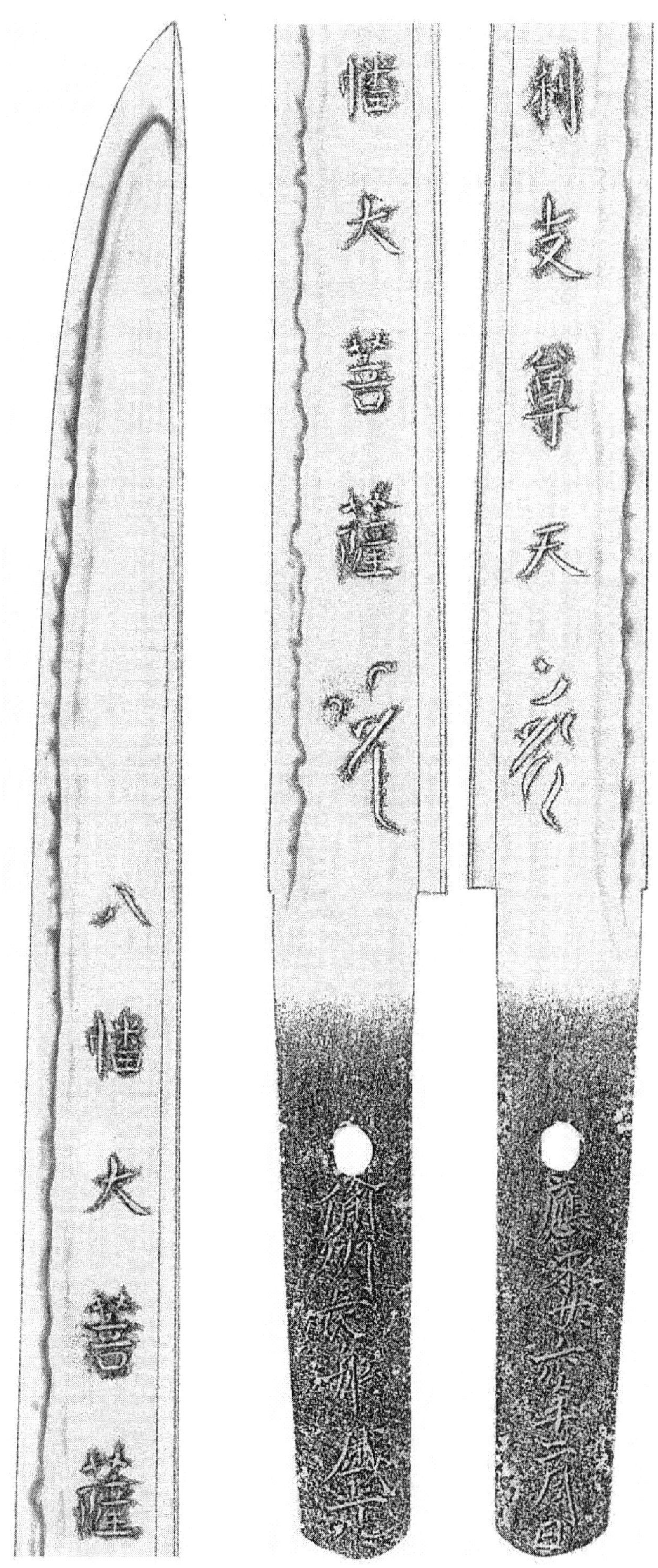

89.618 *tantō*

mei: Bishū Osafune Morimitsu (備州長船盛光)
Ōei nijūroku-nen nigatsu-hi (応永廿六年二月日, „a day in the second month Ōei 26 [1419]")

nagasa 26,3 cm, *uchizori*, *hira-zukuri*, *mitsu-mune*

ji: *ko-itame* mixed with *ko-mokume*, fine *ji-nie* and a clearly visible *bō-utsuri* which is arranged towards the *ha*

hamon: based on *suguha* and mixed with *ko-gunome* and angular elements, in addition *ko-ashi* and *yō*, the hardening is in *nioi-deki* with *ko-nie*

bōshi: *sugu* with a short *ko-maru-kaeri*

horimono: the characters „Hachiman-Daibosatsu" (八幡大菩薩) and a *bonji* are engraved on the *omote* side and the characters „Marishi-sonten" (摩利支尊天) and another *bonji* on the *ura* side [Translators note: Hachiman-Daibosatsu and Marishi-sonten, better known under his abbreviated name „Marishiten", are both gods of war.]

The Bizen warriors and smiths of the early Muromachi period started a backwards trend towards the „good old" Kamakura period. So the so-called „Ōei-Bizen" group introduced *hamon* like *koshi-no-hiraita gunome* with plentiful of *chōji* which remind of the flamboyant Ichimonji style but they also hardened a *suguha*-based *hamon* with *ko-gunome* and *saka-ashi* which followed the style of late Kamakura period Osafune-*mono*.

This *tantō* is an excellent example for the latter trend and so many bids were accordingly on the so-called „Osafune-*sansaku*" (Nagamitsu [長光], Kagemitsu [景光] and Sanenaga [真長]), Motoshige (元重) and the Un group (雲), but also some on the Aoe school (青江). First of all, the blade is modelled on Kagemitsu but there are some differences. One difference can be seen in the *sugata* because *tantō* from the Ōei era show a rather elongated *nagasa* combined with a *mihaba* which is somewhat narrower than in previous times. Also the *bō-utsuri* differs because it is arranged more towards the *ha* and another peculiarity of Ōei-Bizen are engravings of names of deities and *bonji* towards the base of the blade.

As Morimitsu and Yasumitsu (康光) are quite close in terms of workmanship and quality, a differentiation without referring to a signature is mostly very difficult. One hint would be that subjectively, Yasumitsu worked in direct comparison more often in *suguha* than Morimitsu.

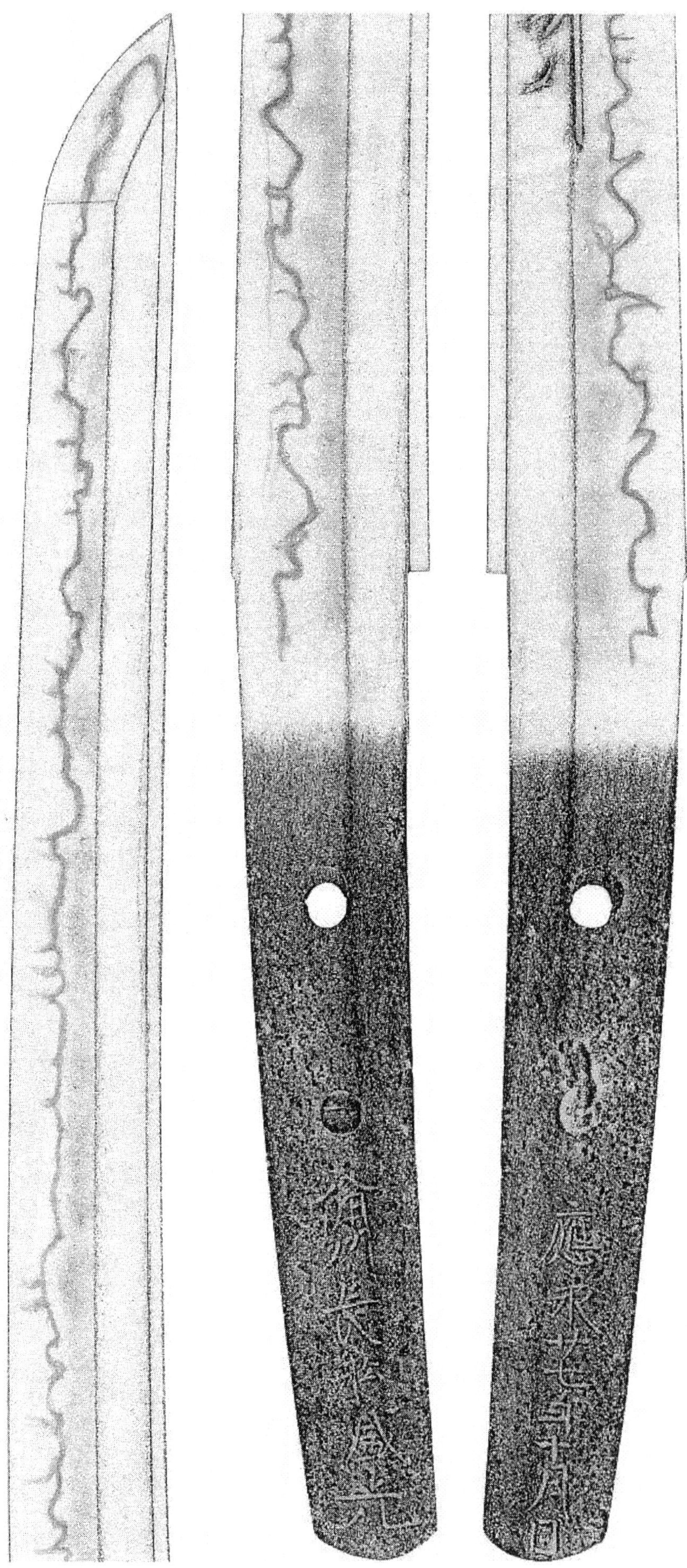

90.638 *wakizashi*
mei: Bishū Osafune Morimitsu (備州長船盛光)
Ōei nijūnana-nen jūgatsu-hi (応永廿七年十月日, „a day in the tenth month Ōei 27 [1420]")
nagasa 48,8 cm, *sori* 1,3 cm, *shinogi-zukuri*, *iori-mune*

ji: *itame* mixed with *mokume*, *ji-nie*, *midare-utsuri*
hamon: *gunome* mixed with *chōji* and *ko-notare*, also *ko-ashi* appear, the *midare* elements show all over the blade a somewhat broad basis (*koshi*), the hardening is in *nioi-deki* with *ko-nie*
bōshi: *midare-komi* with a pointed *ko-maru-kaeri*
horimono: on both sides *bonji* are engraved

This is a *wakizashi* of Morimitsu who belonged together with Yasumitsu (康光) to the most outstanding representatives of the Ōei-Bizen group. Smiths of that group tried to revive the flamboyance of the then lost Kamakura-period *chōji-midare*. The *kantei* blade demonstrates this attempt very obviously because the *hamon* consists of a irregular mix of *gunome* and *chōji* and appears therefore as a vivid *midareba*.

But when you take a closer look than you see that the amount of *mokume* is too obvious compared to the Kamakura period originals and that the *nioiguchi* is too compact. This makes the *habuchi* look somewhat hard. Also different are the elements of the *hamon* which widen towards the base. This feature is called „*koshi-no-hiraita*". Also very typical for Ōei-Bizen is the *sakizori* which is even noticeable at *wakizashi*.

Incidentally, the *bōshi* of the Ōei-Bizen group is also called „*rōsoku no shin*" (ローソクの芯, lit. „candle wick"). It appears as a *midare-komi* which ends in a conspiciously pointed *kaeri*. But such a *bōshi* is not seen on the *kantei* blade. Also typical for Ōei-Bizen is that the *bōhi* ends in *maru-dome* above the *habaki*.

Most bids were on Morimitsu or Yasumitsu. Both show a very close style but we might say that Morimitsu´s *midareba* is a hint larger and more roundish whereas the *ha* of Yasumitsu slants a bit and shows rather mixed-in *togari* elements. The *kantei* blade displays all two styles so it was difficult to nail down the bid either on Morimitsu or Yasumitsu and so it was enough to bid on Ōei-Bizen to get an *atari*.

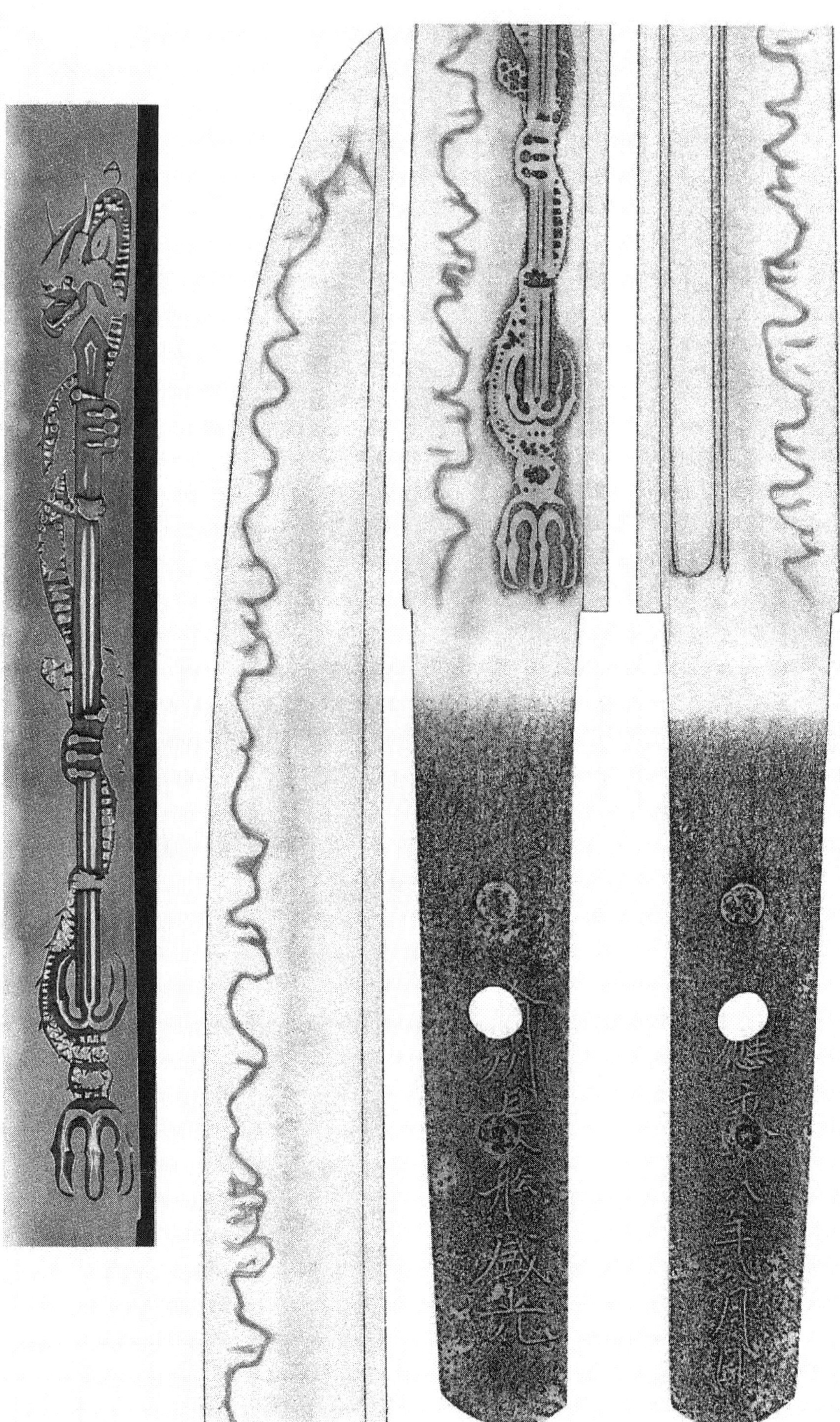

91.603 *wakizashi*
mei: Bishū Osafune Morimitsu (備州長船盛光)
Ōei nijūhachi-nen hachi-gatsu-hi (応永廿八年八月日, „a day in the eighth month Ōei 28 [1421]")
nagasa 47,57 cm, *sori* 0,61 cm, *hira-zukuri*, *iori-mune*

ji: altogether standing-out *itame* with plentiful of *mokume*, in addition *ji-nie*, *chikei*-like areas and a clearly visible *bō-utsuri*
hamon: flamboyant *midareba* in *koshi-no-hiraita gunome* with roundish *gunome* and *chōji* protrusions and „normal" *gunome* and angular *gunome* elements, in addition *ashi* and *yō*, the *nioiguchi* is bright and clear and tends to *nioi-deki*
bōshi: a little *midare*, the *kaeri* of the *omote* side is pointed and the *ura* side shows an *ichimonji*-like *kaeri*, on both sides, the *kaeri* itself does not run back very long
horimono: there is a *kurikara* on the base of the *omote* side and a *katana-hi* with *soebi* on the *ura* side which ends in *maru-dome*

The *nagasa* is elongated in comparison to the *mihaba*. This, the thick *kasane* and the shallow *sori* date this *hira-zukuri wakizashi* to the early Muromachi period, or to be more precise around Ōei (応永, 1394-1428). The blade shows an altogether standing-out *itame* with plentiful of *mokume*. Also a *bō-utsuri* is clearly visible. There are conspicious *koshi-no-hiraita* elements with some *chōji* and *gunome* in between which results in a flamboyant *midareba*. There are also *ashi* and *yō* and the clear and bright *nioiguchi* tends to *nioi-deki*. The *bōshi* in *midare-komi* has a slightly pointed *kaeri*. This characteristic is called „*rōzoku no shin*" (candle wick). Because of all these features, one can narrow down the bid on Morimitsu (盛光), Yasumitsu (康光) and other representative Ōei-Bizen smiths.

At that time, often such *hi* with *soebi* with an end in *maru-dome* above the *habaki* were added. But a *kurikara-horimono* is very rare for Ōei-Bizen. Compared with similar engravings of the Osafune school, the basis of the *sanko* is relative large and rather angular. Also the tines of the hilt are thick and deeply engaved. This interpretation in turn influenced the later Sue-Bizen smiths.

Allmost all bids were on Morimitsu and Yasumitsu, the best smiths of the Ōei-Bizen group. They were equally skilled and do not show any peculiarities at a glance which make a differentiation easy. But we can say that Morimitsu worked more often in a flamboyant *deki* than Yasumitsu. Also his *yakigashira* are more roundish. Yasumitsu's *ha* in turn is a little smaller dimensioned and the mixed-in *togari* elements make a rather stiff impression.

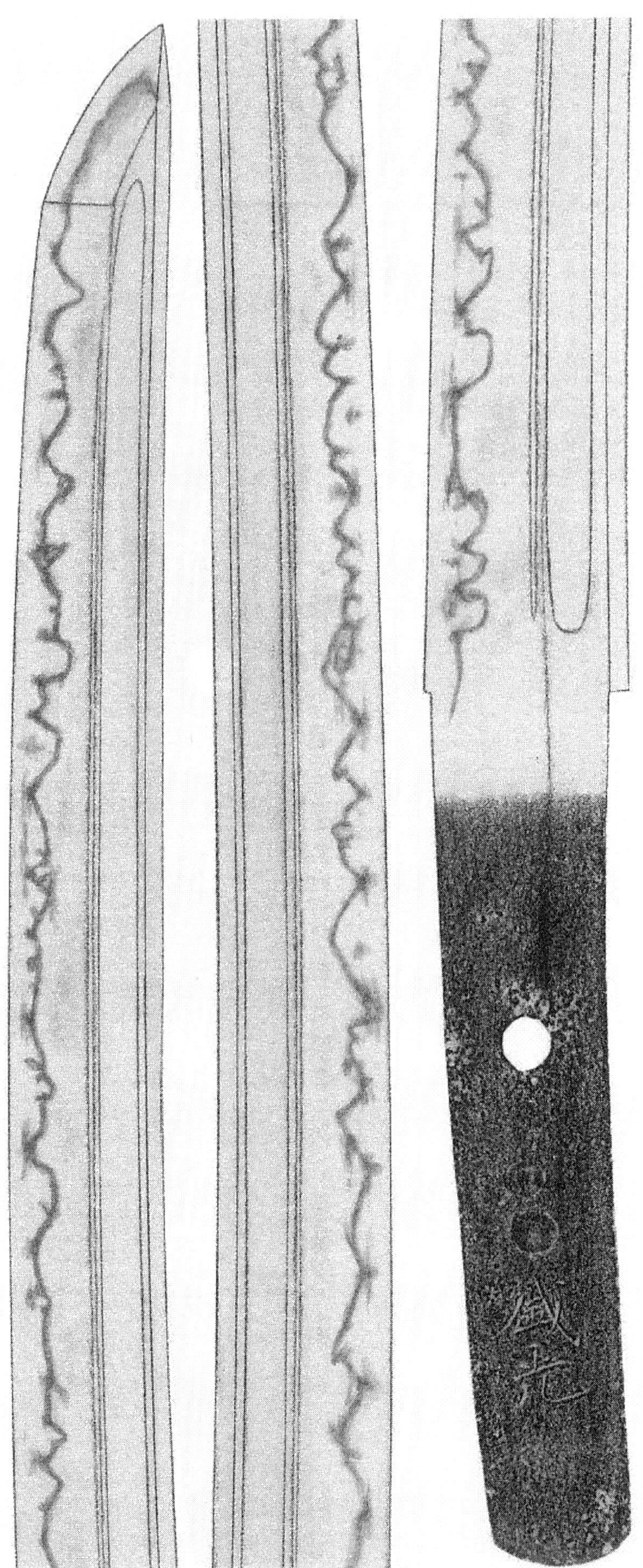

92.606 *wakizashi*
mei: Morimitsu (盛光)
nagasa 53,9 cm, *sori* 1,5 cm, *shinogi-zukuri*, *iori-mune*

ji: *itame-hada* mixed with *mokume*, *ji-nie*, much fine *chikei*, clearly visible *midare-utsuri* (this *utsuri* appears in the middle section of the *sashi-ura* side as a kind of *bō-utsuri*)
hamon: *chōji* mixed with *gunome* and *togariba* with many ups and downs, there appear *koshi-no-hiraita* all over the blade, in addition *ashi*, *yō*, *kinsuji* and *sunagashi* and *ko-nie* in the *nioi*-based *hamon*
bōshi: *notare-komi* with a little pointed *ko-maru* and *hakikake*
horimono: on both sides a *bōhi* with *soebi* which ends in *maru-dome* above the *habaki*

This blade has a *sakizori* and a *chū-kissaki* with rather scarce *fukura*. An *utsuri* is clearly visible and so we can identify it as a Bizen-*mono* of the Muromachi period. In addition, the *mihaba* is rather slender in comparison to the length, or the other way round, the blade looks a little stretched for such a slender *mihaba*. This and the mixed-in *mokume*, the plentiful of fine *chikei* and the *chōji*, *gunome* and *koshi-no-hiraita* elements with many ups and downs lead us to Ōei-Bizen. Also such a *bōhi* with *soebi* which ends in *maru-dome* above the *habaki* is very typical for this group.

The characteristics were well understood and so the vast majority bade on an Ōei-Bizen smith. But some went also for an Osafune-*mono* of the Kamakura period. In that case, we would not expect a partial *bō-utsuri* but just a pure *midare-utsuri*.

Within the Ōei-Bizen group, the workmanship of the *kantei* blade comes closest to Morimitsu (盛光) or Yasumitsu (康光). Both worked in a very similar style but we can say that Morimitsu´s *yakigashira* are by trend a little more roundish and that Yasumitsu added often *togari* elements and applied a somewhat smaller dimensioned *hamon*. If you take these characteristics to heart, you should be able to narrow the bid down on Morimitsu

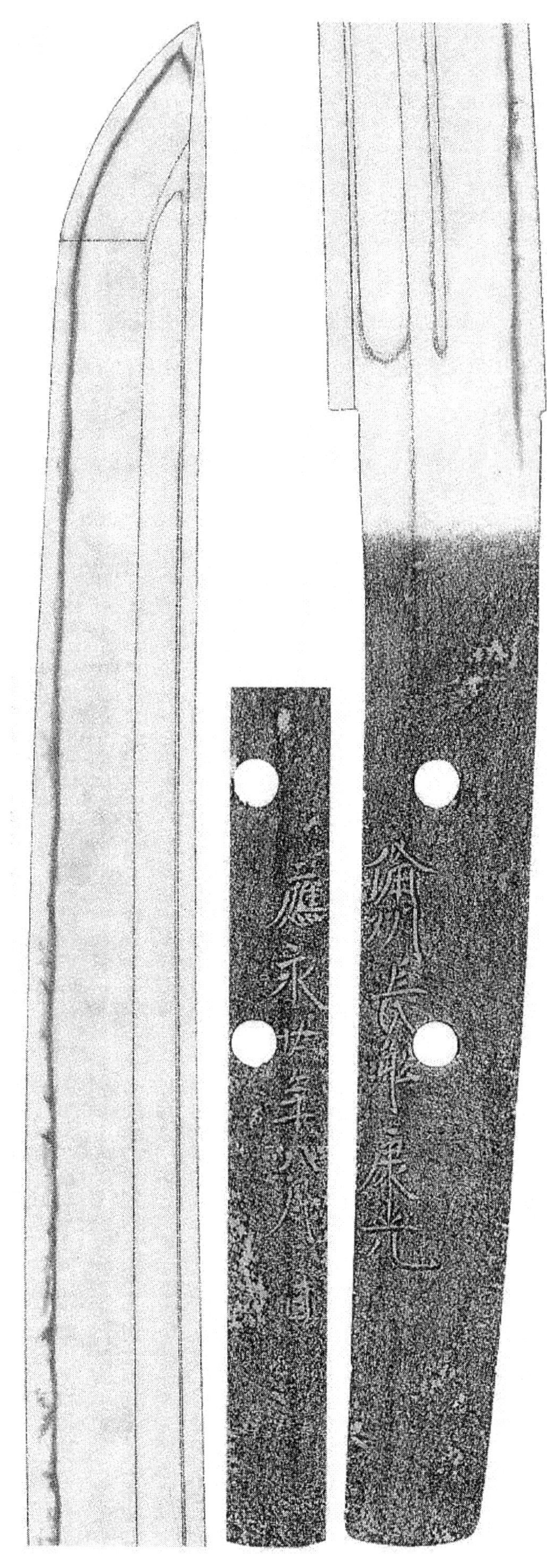
備州長船康光
應永廿年八月日

93.641 *tachi*
mei: Bishū Osafune Yasumitsu (備州長船康光)
Ōei nijū-nen hachigatsu-hi (応永廿年八月日, „a day in the eighth month Ōei 20 [= 1413]")
nagasa 65,9 cm, *sori* 2,1 cm, *shinogi-zukuri*, *iori-mune*

ji: standing-out *itame* mixed with *mokume* and some *nagare*, in addition *ji-nie*, fine *chikei*-like elements and a *midare-utsuri*
hamon: *suguha-chō* mixed with *ko-gunome*, plentiful of *ashi* and *yō*, *saka-ashi*, fine *kinsuji* and *sunagashi*, the compact *nioiguchi* tends to *nioi-deki* but shows also some *ko-nie*
bōshi: *sugu* with a pointed *ko-maru-kaeri*
horimono: on both sides a *bōhi* with *maru-dome* which is accompanied by a *soebi* in the lower half of the blade which ends also in a *maru-dome*

This *tachi* by Yasumitsu shows *funbari*, has a deep *sori*, ends in a *chū-kissaki* and has a *nioi-deki*-based hardening in *suguha*. Some Ōei-Bizen smiths tried to revive the classic Bizen style of the Kamakura period, that means they applied a flamboyant *chōji-midare* in the style of the Ichimonji school but at the same time, some focused also on Osafune-*mono* of the late Kamakura period which means *suguha*. The latter works are often quite difficult at a *kantei*.

Well, and this was the case here too because many bade on Sanenaga (真長) or Kagemitsu (景光), or later Osafune smiths which are famous for their *suguha* like Tadamitsu (忠光) or Kiyomitsu (清光), and some went even for the Un group (雲) and the neighboring Aoe school.

The *hamon* is a *suguha* with *saka-ashi* and a compact *nioiguchi* and the *bōshi* is pointed. This is very typical for the Aoe school and so a bid on the latter is understandable. But at an Aoe work we would expect more *mokume* and a *dan-utsuri* and as the school (not the Ko-Aoe school) was mostly active during the Nanbokuchō period, we would see also noticeable differences in the *sugata*. The *kasane* of the *kantei* blade is namely thick, the *sori* increases towards the *kissaki*, there are fine *chikei*-like elements in the *ji* and we have a *bōhi* with *maru-dome* above the *habaki*. All these characteristics alone speak entirely for Ōei-Bizen, regardless of the hardening in *suguha*.

Some recognized this at the third round and went for a Bizen smith famous for *suguha* at that time and arrived so at Yasumitsu. This rethinking process is a good excercise because you have to reconsider the entire context of the time, the workmanship and the individual characteristics and strong points of smiths. The blade was by the way once a heirloom of the Naitō family (内藤).

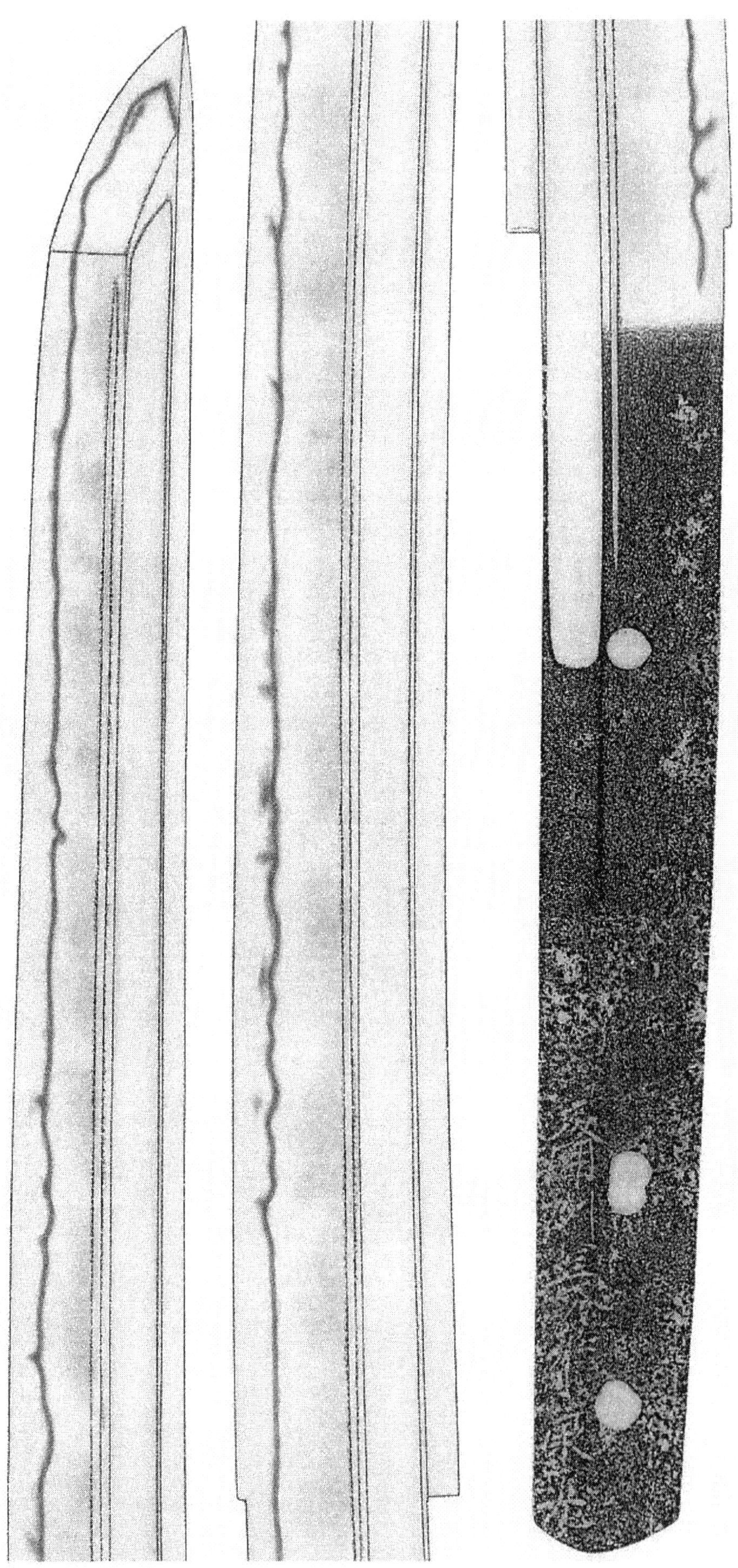

94.590 *tachi*
mei: Bishū Osafune Yasumitsu (備州長船康光)
nagasa 69,4 cm, *sori* 1,5 cm, *shinogi-zukuri*, *iori-mune*

ji: a little standing-out *itame* mixed with *mokume* and some *nagare*, also *ji-nie*, fine *chikei*-like elements and a *midare-utsuri*
hamon: *chū-suguha-chō* which tends somewhat to *notare*, in addition *ko-chōji* and *ko-gunome*, *ashi*, *yō*, *saka-ashi* as well as fine *kinsuji* and *sunagashi*, the *nioiguchi* is rather compact and shows some *ko-nie*
bōshi: slightly undulating *notare* with a *ko-maru-kaeri* on the *omote* side and a pointed *kaeri* on the *ura* side
horimono: on both sides a *bōhi* with *soebi* with *maru-dome* but which runs because of the shortening with *kake-nagashi* into the tang

This *tachi* is a work of the Ōei-Bizen smith Yasumitsu. We can see some *funbari* at the base, the *sori* is relative deep, we have a *midare-utsuri* and a *hamon* in *suguha-chō* in *nioi-deki* with *ko-chōji*, *ko-gunome* and *saka-ashi* in a compact *nioiguchi*. The *bōshi* tends a little to a *sansaku-bōshi* and because of this classical interpretation, many went for Kamakura-period Bizen smiths like Nagamitsu (長光), Sanenaga (真長), Chikakage (近景), Unshō (雲生), Unji (雲次) or Motoshige (元重).

It is well known that the Ōei-Bizen smiths tried to revive the Kamakura style and made again elegant *tachi* in combination with a flamboyant Ichimonji-inspired *hamon*. But besides of that, they also worked in *suguha* which is modelled on Osafune-*mono* from the late Kamakura period. This lead many astray at the *kantei* but when you take a closer look you will be able to see some typical features of Ōei-Bizen. For example the tendency to *sakizori* and the thicker *kasane*, which speak clearly for the beginning Muromachi period. Also the *itame-mokume* with its slight tendency to *nagare* and the fine blackish *chikei*-like elements in the *ji* are very typical for Ōei-Bizen. Another peculiarity of this group are small knobs in the *monouchi* area at a *suguha-hamon* and a pointed *bōshi* (which is better seen on the *ura* side). If you combine all these elements you should be able to recognize that this is an Ōei-Bizen *suguha* interpretation and not an „original“ Kamakura-period Osafune work.

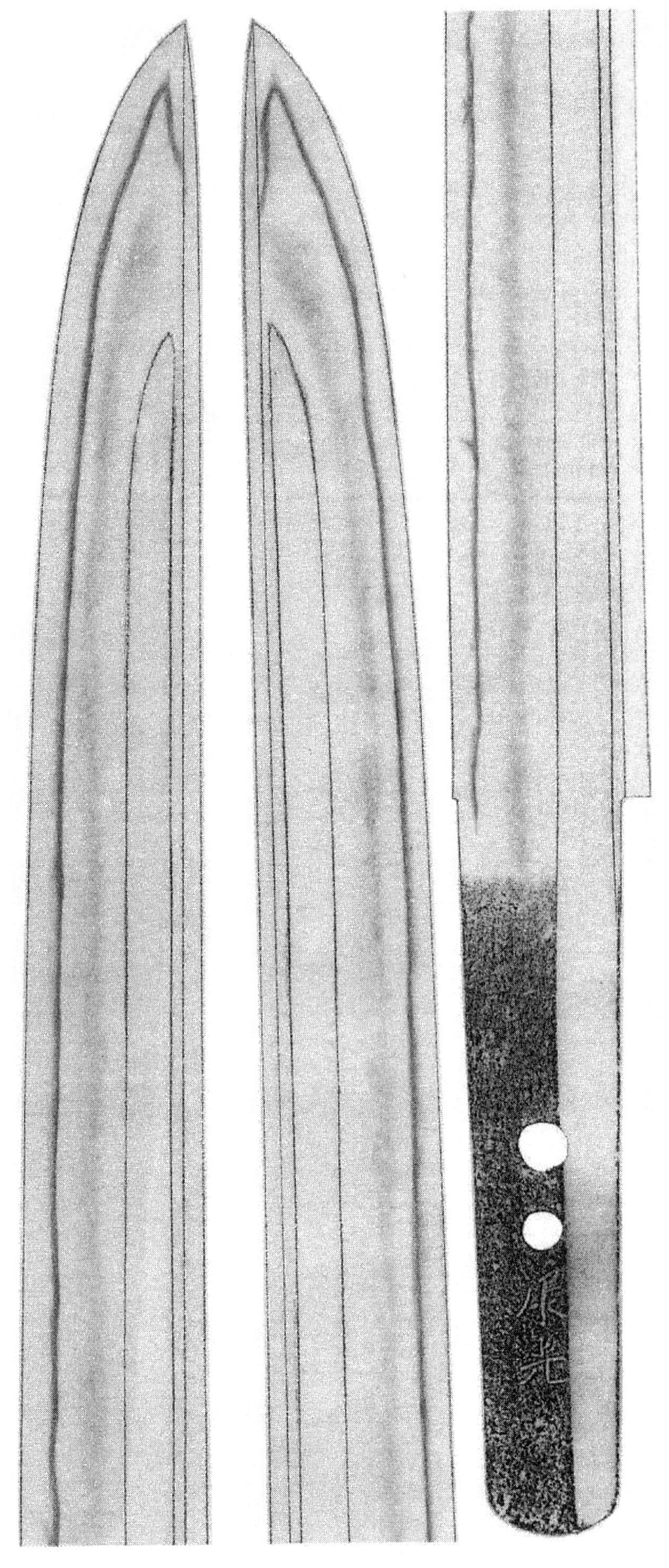

95.610 *tantō*
mei: Yasumitsu (康光)
nagasa 30,6 cm, only a little *sori*, *hira-zukuri*, *iori-mune*

ji: somewhat standing-out *itame* mixed with *mokume* and *nagare*, in addition plentiful of fine *ji-nie*, *chikei* and a clearly visible *bō-utsuri*
hamon: *chū-suguha* with a compact, *nioi-deki*-based *nioiguchi* and some *saka-ashi*
bōshi: slightly undulating *sugu* with a *ko-maru-kaeri*
horimono: on both sides a *katana-hi* which runs with *kake-nagashi* into the tang

The *nagasa* looks a little stretched in comparison to the *mihaba* and there is a shallow *sori*. Such a *sunnobi-sugata* is typical for the Ōei era (応永, 1394-1428). The *kitae* is a somewhat standing-out *ko-itame* which is mixed with *mokume* and which shows fine *ji-nie* and *chikei*.

Due to these characteristics and the clearly visible *bō-utsuri* which is arranged towards the *ha*, it should be possible to identify the blade as an Ōei-Bizen work. This attribution is further supported by the *hamon* in *nioi-deki* with a compact *nioiguchi* and *saka-ashi*.

Accordingly, most bids were on Yasumitsu and Morimitsu (盛光), the two best smiths of that group. They worked in a very close style but there are nevertheless some subtle differences. Yasumitsu for example applied more often such a compact *nioiguchi* and *saka-ashi* which remind at a glance of Aoe.

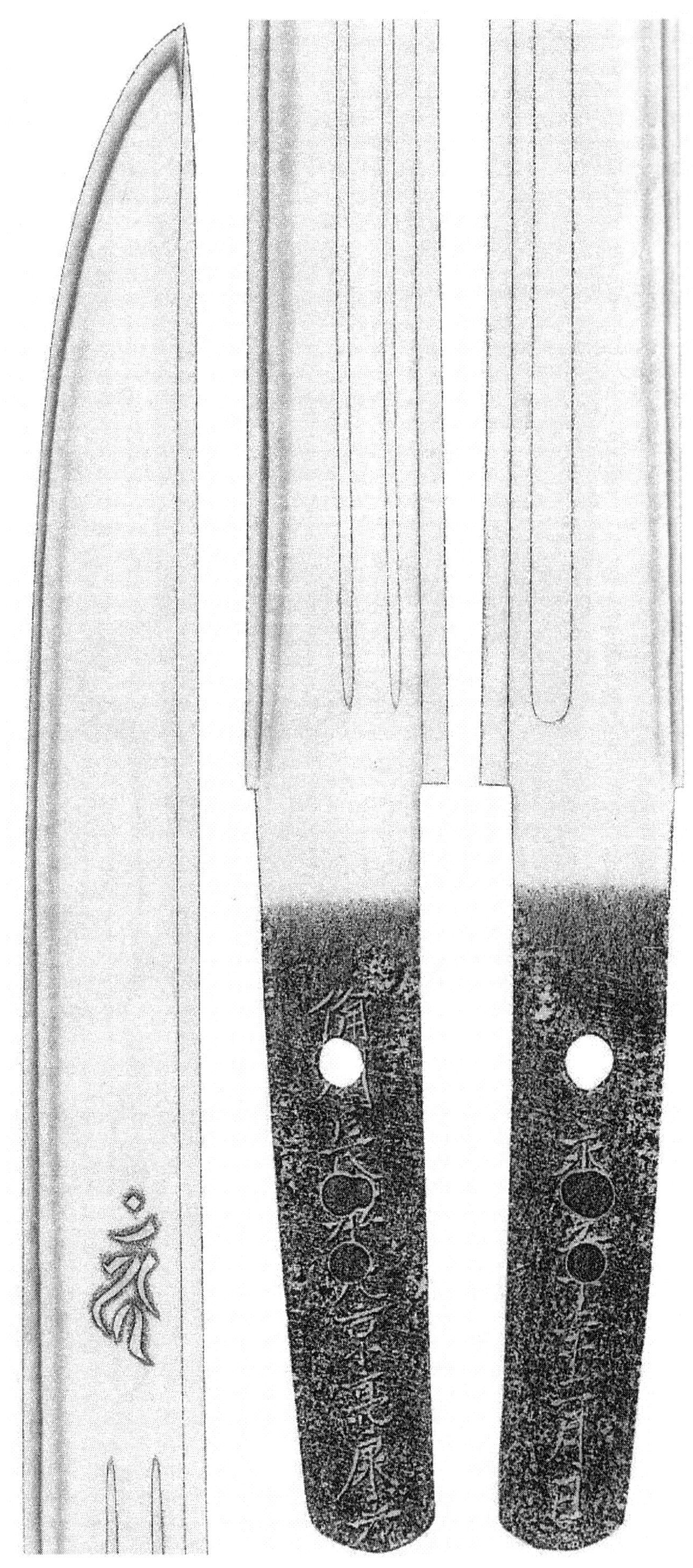

96.611 *wakizashi*
mei: Bishū Osafune Sakyō no Suke Yasumitsu (備州長船左京亮康光)
Eikyō jū-nen ni-gatsu hi (永享十年二月日, „a day in the second month Eikyō ten [= 1438]")
nagasa 35,12 cm, *sori* 0,30 cm, *hira-zukuri, iori-mune*

ji: *itame* mixed with *mokume*, *ji-nie*, *chikei*-like elements in places, in addition a clearly bisible linear *utsuri*
hamon: *hoso-suguha* with some *hotsure* along the *habuchi*, the hardening is in *nioi-deki* with *ko-nie*
bōshi: *sugu* with a *ko-maru-kaeri* which is a little pointed on the *omote* side
horimono: on both sides *bonji* with *gomabashi* below on the *omote* side and a *koshibi* below on the *ura* side, all the *hi* end in a *maru-dome*

At a *kantei* blade like this where just a plain *suguha* is seen, one has to base his attribution on the shape, the *kitae*, the *utsuri* (if present) and the *bōshi*. First of all the shape. This blade has in comparison to the *mihaba* an elongated *nagasa*, that means it is *sunnobi*, has a shallow *sori* and a thick *kasane*, that means we are in the early Muromachi period, or to be more precise around Ōei (応永, 1394-1428). A fine and densely forged *itame* with dark, *chikei*-like structures and a linear *utsuri* are, within the time frame we now have, typical for the Ōei-Bizen group. And if you take a closer look at the *bōshi* of the *sashi-omote* side, you can see a characteristically pointed *kaeri* which is called „candle wick" (*rōsoku no shin*, ローソクの芯 or 蝋燭の芯), another feature of the Ōei-Bizen group.

The Ōei-Bizen workmanship shows mostly a *koshi-no-hiraita gunome* which is mixed with *chōji* and whose ups and downs result in a flamboyant *midareba*. But also a *suguha* was applied which is modelled on Osafune mainline interpretations from the late Kamakura period. It has to be mentioned that such a revival was totally uncommon during the previous Nanbokuchō period and is one of the most typical characteristics for Ōei-Bizen.

The *kantei* blade is dated with Eikyō ten (永享, 1438), that means it is a work of the 2nd gen. Yasumitsu, called „Sakyō no Suke Yasumitsu". The *meikan* records suggest that works from the 30th year of Ōei (1423) can be attributed to the 2nd gen. Yasumitsu and that he started to forge swords under the name of „Yasumitsu" from around Ōei 23 (1416). It is also mentioned that he became a student of the 2nd gen. Morimitsu, i.e. at Shūri no Suke Morimitsu (修理亮盛光) in the 34th year of Ōei (1427). But as Morimitsu and Yasumitsu worked in a very close style, a bid on one of them was enough.

But in a direct comparison it can be said that at Yasumitsu, a subtle tendency towards *suguha* can be seen. This was understood by most of the participants which were spot-on at Yasumitsu. This was very pleasing.

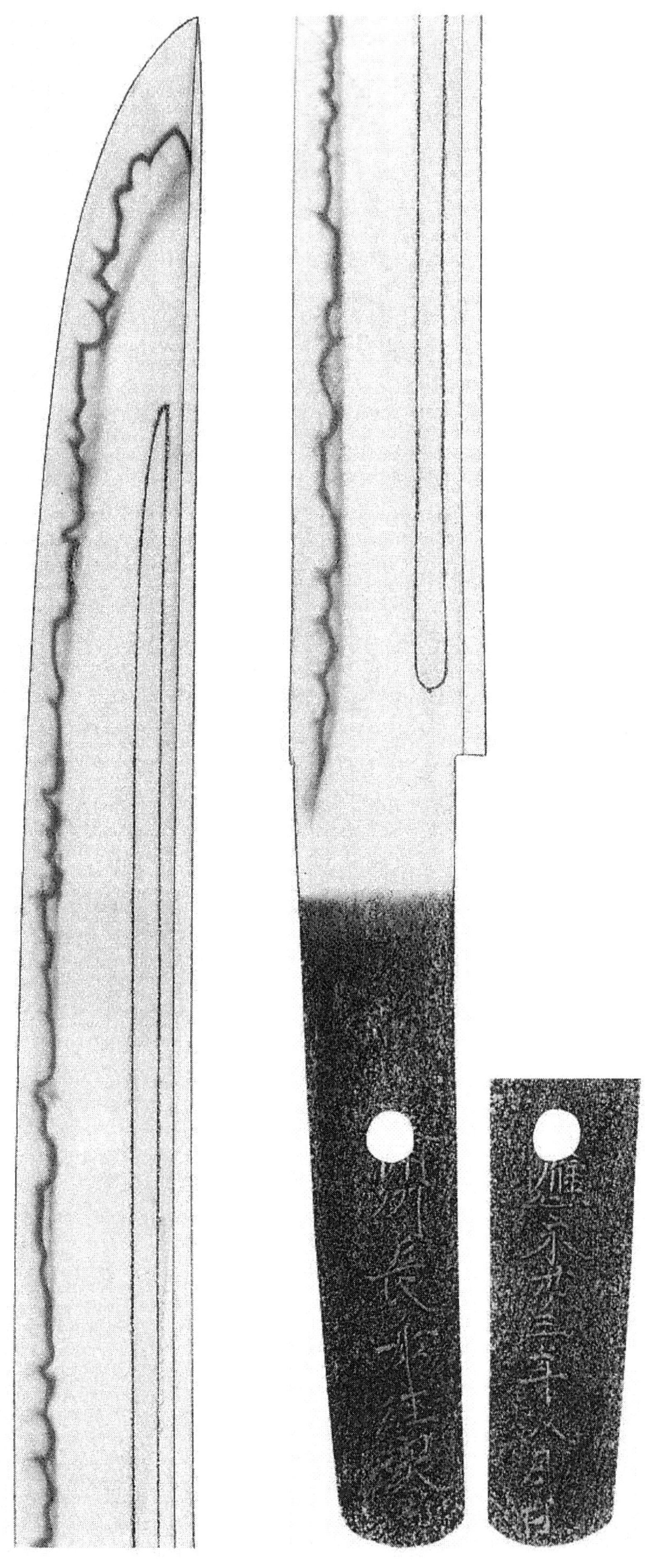

97.642 *wakizashi*
mei: Bishū Osafune Tsuneie (備州長船経家)
Ōei sanjūsan-nen hachigatsu-hi (応永卅三年八月日, „a day in the eighth month Ōei 33 [1426]")
nagasa 37,6 cm, *sori* 0,3 cm, *hira-zukuri*, *iori-mune*

ji: *itame* mixed with *mokume* which tends also a little to *nagare*, in addition *ji-nie*, *chikei* and a *bō-utsuri* which appears right above the *yakigashira*
hamon: narrow, angular, partially slanting and densely arranged *kataochi-gunome* mixed with *ko-gunome* and *notare*, in addition *ko-ashi* and *saka-ashi*, the hardening is in *nioi-deki* with *ko-nie* and the *nioiguchi* is bright
bōshi: *midare-komi* with a somewhat pointed but short *kaeri*
horimono: on both sides a *katana-hi* with *maru-dome*

In the course of the rivalry after the retirement and death of the third Ashikaga-*shōgun* Yoshimitsu (足利義満, 1358-1408, r. 1368-1394), his successor Yoshimochi (義持, 1386-1428, r. 1394-1422) tried to return to a government which bases again more on the values of the warriors. This was willingly accepted by the *bushi* and so it is no surprise that this return to „old values" can also be seen on the then swords. It was a time when the traditional Bizen style was thinning out and a mix like presented by the Kozori smiths was prevailing. But towards the end of the first decade of the Ōei era (1394-1428), the so-called „Ōei-Bizen" group tried to revive the Ichimonji-style and the *suguha-chō* of the late Kamakura-period Osafune mainline. This resulted in the well-known *koshi-no-hiraita gunome* which is mixed with *chōji*. But some of their interpretations in slanting *midare*, angular *gunome* and/or *kataochi-gunome* remind also of Kagemitsu (景光), Motoshige (元重), the Un group (雲) or the Aoe school.

This blade shows a *bō-utsuri* in combination with an angular, partially slanting *hamon* with *kataochi-gunome* elements and so some went for Motoshige, Kagemitsu or Kanemitsu (兼光). But the *sugata* must not be overseen. Another hint for Ōei-Bizen is the *hi* with *maru-dome* above the *habaki*, a typical characteristic of Ōei-Bizen-*mono*. Most of the participants were on the right track, i.e. Ōei-Bizen, but bade on one of the most representative smiths of that group, Yasumitsu (康光). He is well-known for his excellent works in *suguha-chō*, *kataochi-gunome* or somewhat slanting interpretations of the *hamon*. But some did not miss the more densely arranged elements on the *hamon* and the mixed-in *notare* and went spot-on to Tsuneie. Such an *atari* bid was quite impressive.

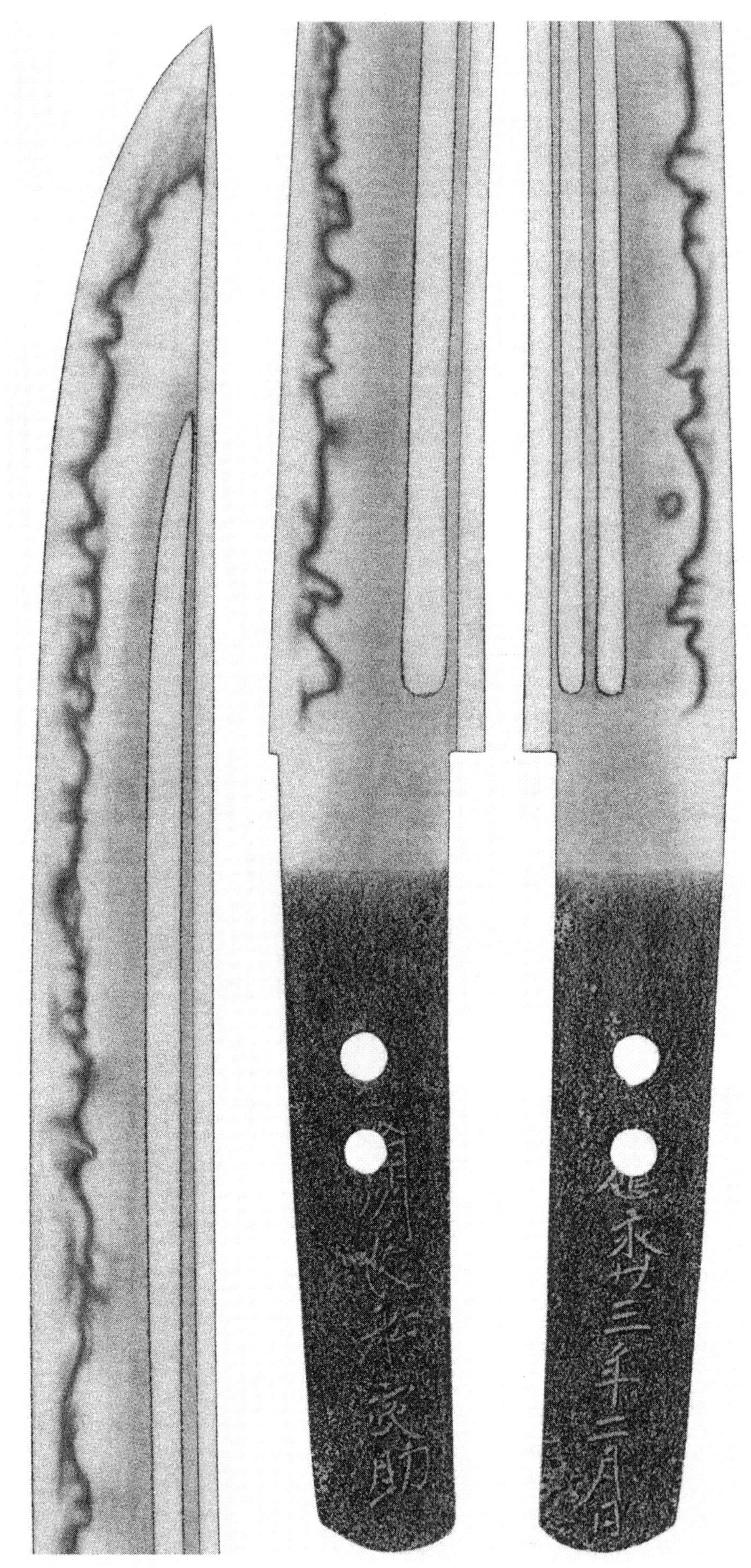

98.657 *wakizashi*
mei: Bishū Osafune Iesuke (備州長船家助)
Ōei nijūsannen nigatsu-hi (応永廿三年二月日, „a day in the second month Ōei 25 [= 1416]")
nagasa 36,4 cm, *sori* 0,6 cm, *hira-zukuri*, *iori-mune*

ji: standing-out *itame* mixed with *mokume*, plentiful of *ji-nie*, *chikei* and a *midare-utsuri*
hamon: *koshi-no-hiraita gunome* mixed with *chōji*, *gunome* and *ko-gunome*, also angular elements in places, as well as *ashi* and *yō*, the lower half appears in *nioi-deki* with *ko-nie* but there appear plentiful of *nie* and some *sunagashi* in the upper half
bōshi: *midare-komi* with a somewhat pointed but short *kaeri*
horimono: a *katana-hi* on the *omote* side and a *futasuji-hi* on the *ura* side, both end in *maru-dome* above the *habaki*

This *wakizashi* dates back to Ōei (1394-1428), an important era for Japan, not only regarding the swords. After a long warring period *shōgun* Ashikaga Yoshimitsu (足利義満, 1358-1408) was able to restore peace. The following longer period of stability is also reflected in the swords.

This blade is in *hira-zukuri*, has a normal *mihaba*, a *sunnobi-nagasa*, a thick *kasane* and a *sakizori*, that means it has all typical features of the Ōei era. Also the *jigane* is an *itame-mokume* mix typical for Ōei-Bizen and so it is quite understandable that many participants thought straightforward of Morimitsu (盛光) and Yasumitsu (康光). But when you take a closer look at the *hamon* you can see that it appears a little „shaky". Also the *midare* bases are a little too deep for Morimitsu and the *hamon* consists rather of smaller dimensioned and densely arranged elements. And when we combine this with the appearance of the *gunome* and *chōji*, the partially somewhat distant *koshi-no-hiraita* and the angular elements, we recognize that this is not a work by the two great masters but of a somewhat inferior smith. And this is the keypoint to arrive at Iesuke.

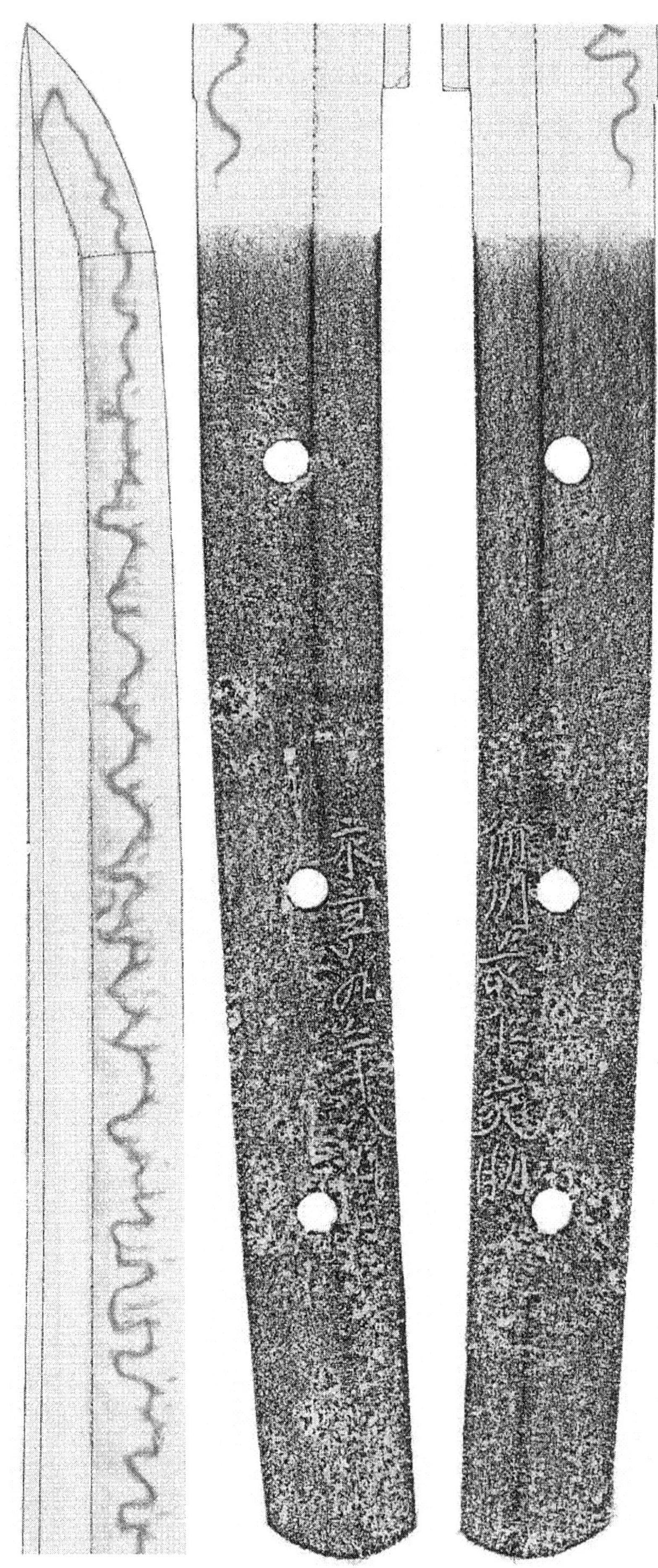

99.655 *tachi*
mei: Bishū Osafune Iesuke (備州長船家助)
Eikyō kyūnen hachigatsu-hi (永享九年八月日, „a day in the eighth month Eikyō nine [1437]")
nagasa 77,7 cm cm, *sori* 2,6 cm, *shinogi-zukuri*, *iori-mune*

ji: standing-out *itame* mixed with *mokume*, also *ji-nie*, *chikei* and a *midare-utsuri*
hamon: *koshi-no-hiraita gunome* mixed with *chōji*, *togariba* and angular *gunome*, in addition *ashi* and *yō*, the hardening is in *nioi-deki* with *ko-nie*
bōshi: *midare-komi* with a somewhat pointed *kaeri*

This is a *tachi* of the Ōei-Bizen smith Iesuke. There is only a little *funbari* and so we can assume that the blade is shortened. When we reconstruct the original shape we recognize a *koshizori* which increases again towards the tip and see a noticeable taper, so we have a typical *tachi-sugata* of the Ōei era (応永, 1394-1428).

The *jihada* is a standing-out *itame* mixed with *mokume* and *chikei*, the *hamon* appears as basically as *koshi-no-hiraita gunome-chōji*, and the *bōshi* is peculiar so-called „*rōsoku-bōshi*" (蝋燭帽子) which reminds of a candle wick. All these are typical characteristics of Ōei-Bizen. Well, in the case of Ōei-Bizen Morimitsu (盛光), we would see more roundish *yakigashira* and a more flamboyant *hamon*. This blade shows some angular *gunome* elements and also *togari* but the entire *yakiba* is rather stiff and smaller dimensioned. Also the *jihada* is not that fine and regular like we would expect it from a work of Morimitsu or Yasumitsu (康光). In addition, the tip of the *rōsoku-bōshi* leans somewhat towards the *ha* and the overall quality does not reach the level of Morimitsu and Yasumitsu. So we are at one of the Ōei-Bizen sideline smiths like Iesuke or Tsuneie (経家). And when we take into consideration the high amount of angular *gunome*, then the bid has to be on Iesuke.

Many went also for Kamakura-period Bizen smiths like Nagamitsu (長光). Well, the blade has surely a longer *tachi-sugata* and shows a flamboyant *midareba* with *chōji* so it might look at a glance like a late Kamakura period *tachi*. But the slight *sakizori* and the *koshi-no-hiraita gunome* differ and a subtle precursor for a *koshi-no-hiraita* interpretation is not seen before the Nanbokuchō period.

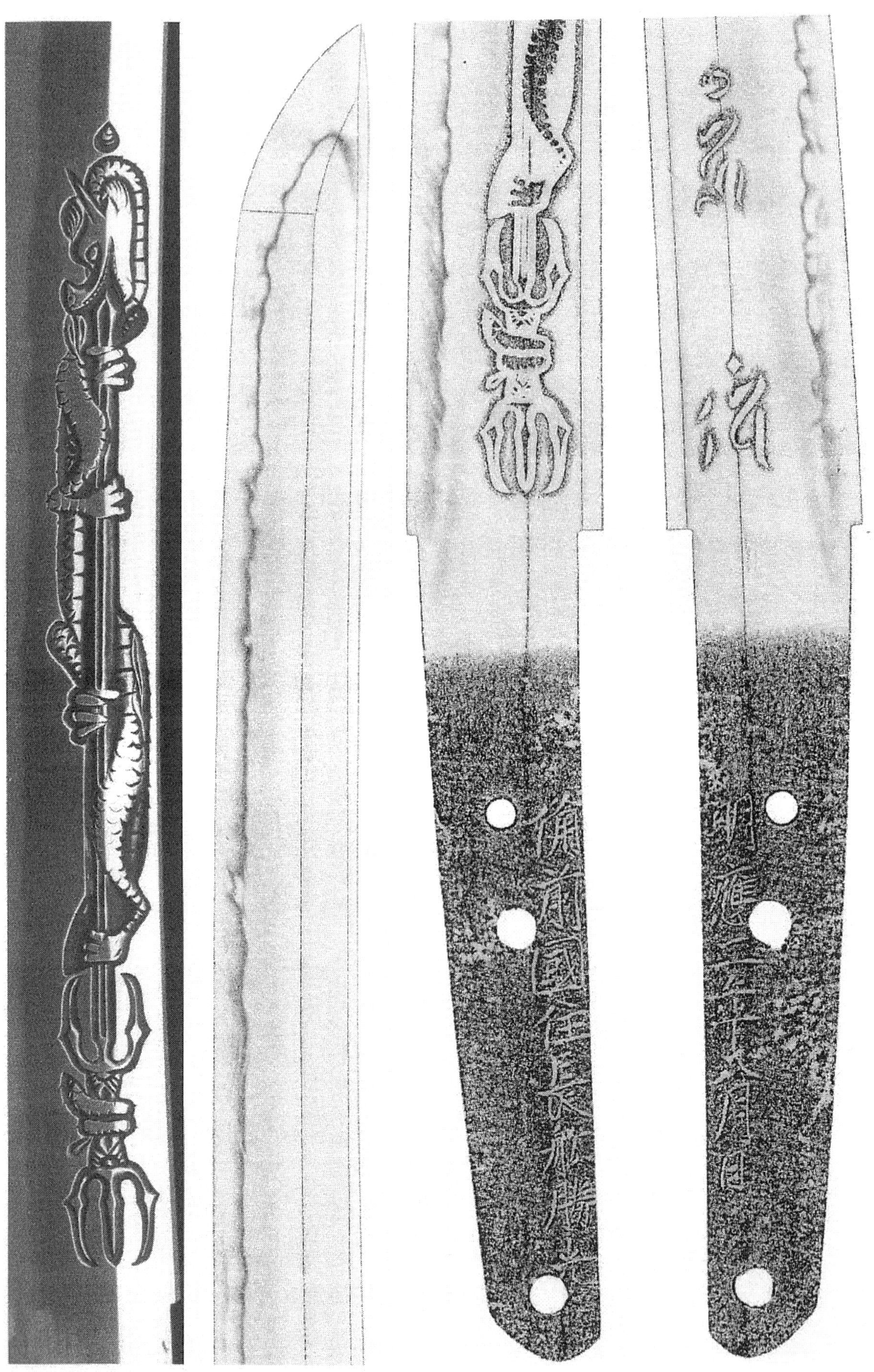

100.603 *katana*
mei: Bizen no Kuni-jū Osafune Katsumitsu (備前国住長船勝光)
Meiō ninen hachigatsu-hi (明応二年八月日, „a day in the eighth month Meiō two [1493]")
nagasa 70,30 cm, *sori* 1,97 cm, *shinogi-zukuri*, *iori-mune*

ji: dense *ko-itame-hada* mixed with *itame* in the upper area, in addition fine *ji-nie*, and a cleary visible linear *utsuri*
hamon: basing on *chū-suguha* and mixed with *ko-gunome* and angular elements, *ashi*, fine *sunagashi* and *kinsuji*, the hardening is in *nioi-deki* but *nie* appear too
bōshi: broad *bōshi* with some *midare* and a round *kaeri*
horimono: a *kurikara* towards the base of the *omote* side and five *bonji* on the *ura* side, also arranged towards the base of the blade

The blade has a length of about two *shaku*, a *sakizori* and does not taper that much. The *shinogi-ji* drops down towards the *mune* because of the high *shinogi* and the *bōshi* shows a relative broad hardening. All these are typical characteristics of an *uchigatana* from the middle Muromachi period.

The *kitae* is a finely forged *ko-itame* and *ji* as *ha* are bright and clear. The excellent quality and the *horimono* lead us to Sue-Bizen but only to the great masters of that group. The semi-cursive interpretation of the *horimono* with the head of the dragon directly over the tip of the *suken* is also important at the attribution of the blade.

Because of the *suguha*, many went for Kiyomitsu (清光), but he forged a not that fine and more standing-out *jihada*. Also we would expect more powerful *nie* and many *yō* along his *suguha*. When we look for exactly such a *kurikara-horimono* interpretation on *jūyō-tōken* and *jūyō-bijutsuhin*, we will arrive at a span of thirty years, i.e. from the tenth year of Bunmei (文明, 1478) to the early Eishō era (永正, 1504-1521) when it was applied. At that time, Katsumitsu (勝光), Munemitsu (宗光), Tadamitsu (忠光), Hikobei no Jō Sukesada (彦兵衛尉祐定) and Yosozaemon no Jō Sukesada (与三左衛門尉祐定) were active. As the aforementioned Kiyomitsu started to work from about Tenbun (1532-1555) onwards, he can be ruled out just on the basis of the *horimono* interpretation. Interestingly, when we compare all these *horimono* we find out that the tail of the dragon winds three times around the *sankozuka* from around Bunki (文亀, 1501-1504) onwards whereas before, he winds only two times around the hilt. The latter feature can also be seen on the *kantei* blade.

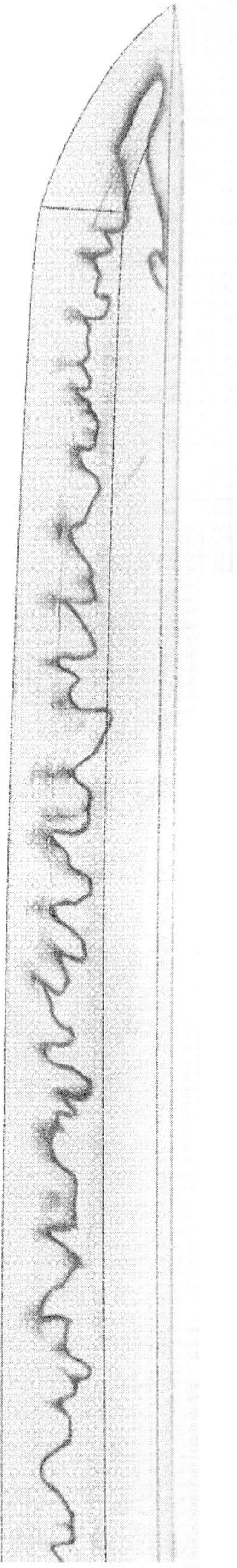

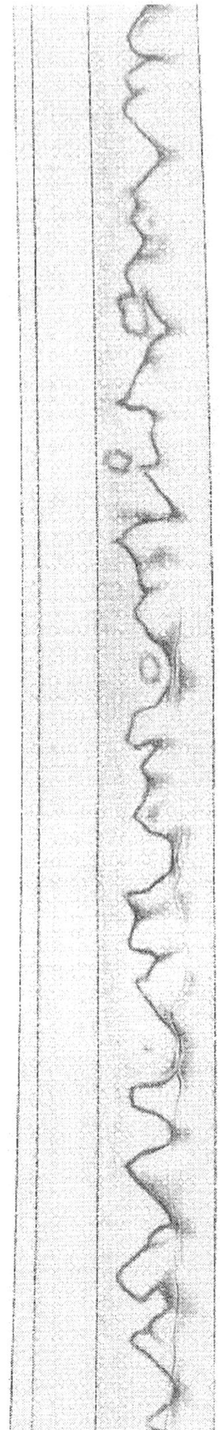

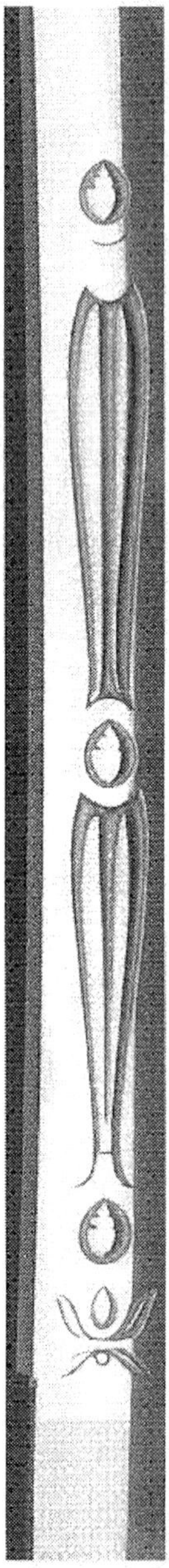

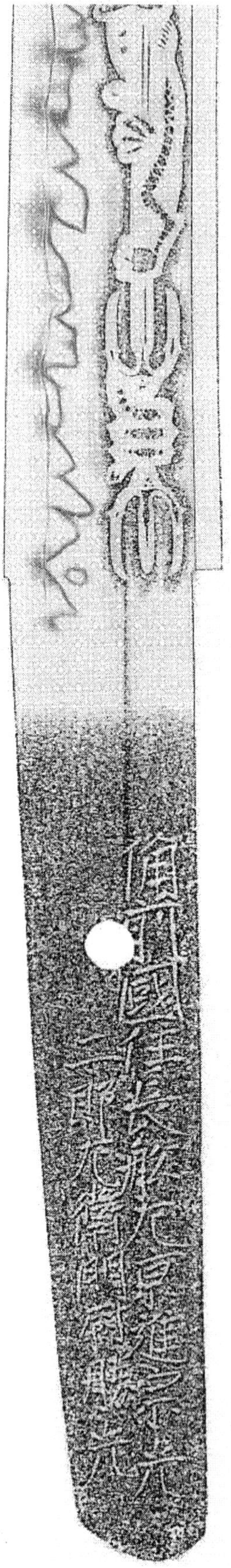

101.662 *wakizashi*

mei: Bizen no Kuni-jū Osafune Sakyō no Shin Munemitsu (備前国住長船左京進宗光)
Jirōzaemon no Jō Katsumitsu (二郎左衛門尉勝光)
Eishō gonen nigatsu kichijitsu (永正五年二月吉日, „a lucky day in the second month Eishō five [= 1508]")

nagasa 53,3 cm, *sori* 1,2 cm, *shinogi-zukuri*, *iori-mune*

ji: very dense *ko-itame* with fine *ji-nie* and a faint *midare*-like *utsuri*

hamon: *gunome* mixed with angular elements, some *togari* and repeated *koshi-no-hiraita* elements in places, the *yakiba* is relative wide and *ashi*, *yō*, as well as partial *kinsuji* appear, there are also some small *tobiyaki* seen on both sides around the middle of the blade, the hardening is in *nioi-deki* with some *ko-nie*

bōshi: there is a conspicuous *yakikomi* at the *yokote*, after that *yakikomi*, the *bōshi* appears as *suguha* on the *omote* and as slightly undulating *notare-komi* on the *ura* side, on both sides a *ko-maru-kaeri* is seen which runs back quite long, the entire *bōshi* itself is rather wide

horimono: a *gyō-no-kurikara* and a so-called „*shiketsu*" (四橛) with *rendai* is engraved on the base of the *omote* side [Translators note: A *shiketsu* is an implement from esoteric Buddhism (*mikkyō*). It is a kind of post – mostly of copper – which symbolically demarcates the four sides of an elevated podestal where religious and/or ascetic practices are performed.]

This is a compact blade measuring under 2 *shaku*. It shows a *sakizori* and a widely hardened *bōshi* with a long *kaeri* which runs back as a pronounced *muneyaki*. So we are clearly facing a *katate-uchi* of the Muromachi period. The *jigane* is a dense and beautifully forged *itame* and the *nioiguchi* as well as the *jiba* are bright and clear. So it must be a work of one of the more well-known masters of that time. When we combine this with the faint *midare-utsuri* we arrive at Sue-Bizen. This assumption is further supported by the interpretation of the *gyō-no-kurikara* where the head of the dragon bites in a linear manner into the tip of the *suken*. (Such a dragon head in profile biting into the tip of the *suken* was also applied by Kamakura-period Bizen smiths like Nagamitsu [長光] and Kagemitsu [景光] or by Nanbokuchō-period masters like Kanemitsu [兼光] and Chōgi [長義] or even by Motoshige [元重]. But at these smiths, the body of the dragon is thinner and the interpretation of the legs and the belly make it look like being pregnant. This feature is called accordingly „*harami-ryū*" [孕み龍], lit. „pregnant dragon" and is clearly different from the *horimono* of this blade.)

The *hamon* is noticeably angular and appears in places as complex *koshi-no-hiraita gunome*. Due to all these characteristics, the vast majority bade on Sue-Bizen, beginning with Katsumitsu (勝光). Jirōzaemon no Jō Katsumitsu (二郎左衛門尉勝光) was the nephew of Sakyō no Shin Munemitsu (左京進宗光). There are quite a lot of *gassaku* works extant by these two smiths whereas mostly Katsumitsu signed first followed by Munemitsu. Interestingly, it is exactly the other way round on this blade. Incidentally, the „*Tsuchiya-oshigata*" (土屋押形) shows a *mei* of Munemitsu with a date signature of the third year of Bunmei (文明, 1471) and the age of 35. So Munemitsu was 72 years old when he made this blade with his nephew Katsumitsu. But there exists another *gassaku* work from the seventh year of Eishō (1510) which is signed with the supplement „otōto Sakyō no Shin Munemitsu" (弟左京進宗光, „younger brother Sakyō no Shin Munemitsu"). So the old handed-down theory about uncle and nephew needs to be rethought.

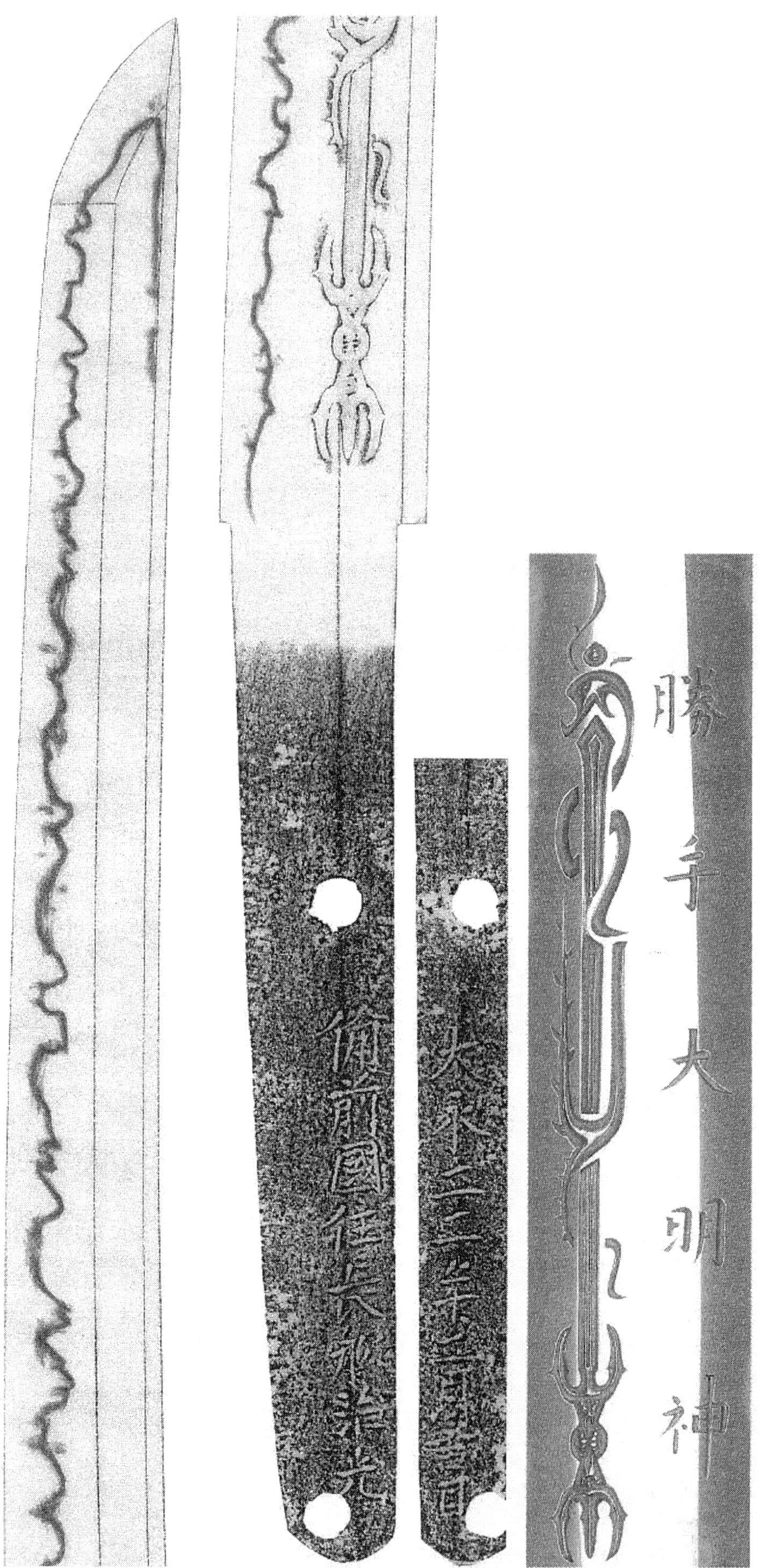
備前國住長船清光
勝手大明神

102.643 *katana*

mei: Bizen no Kuni-jū Osafune Harumitsu (備前国住長船治光)
Daiei yonnen nigatsu-kichijitsu (大永二二年二月吉日, „a lucky day in the second month of Daiei four [1524]")

nagasa 67,3 cm, *sori* 2,7 cm, *shinogi-zukuri*, *iori-mune*

ji: dense *ko-itame* which stands out a little, in addition *ji-nie* and a faint *midare*-like *utsuri*

hamon: *ko-gunome* mixed with *koshi-no-hiraita gunome* and *ko-chōji*, many *ko-ashi* and *yō*, the *nioiguchi* is compact and contains *ko-nie*

bōshi: widely hardened, slightly undulating *notare* with a long *kaeri* which runs back as *muneyaki*

horimono: a *sō-no-kurikara* on the *omote* side and the characters of the deity Katte-Daimyōjin (勝手大明神) on the *ura* side

The blade is with a *nagasa* of not that much over 2 *shaku* rather compact, has a thick *kasane* which makes it appear massive, has a *sakizori* and *horimono* which are arranged towards the base, so we are obviously facing a typical *uchigatana* from the Muromachi period. The *jigane* is bright and appears as dense and beautifully forged *ko-itame* with a faint *midare-utsuri*. Usually late Muromachi-period blades do not show a finely forged *jigane* but custom-made *chūmon-uchi* of the Sue-Bizen smiths are famous for their refined *kitae*. And because the *kantei* blade is of a remarkable quality, it has to be a work of one of the most outstanding Sue-Bizen masters like Yosōzaemon no Jō Sukesada (与三左衛門尉祐定), Jirōzaemon no Jō Katsumitsu (次郎左衛門尉勝光) or Munemitsu (宗光). And most of the bids were on Katsumitsu and Sukesada. On the other hand, many went just for Sue-Bizen which was not counted as *atari* but as *atari-dōzen*.

Jirōbei no Jō Harumitsu (次郎兵衛尉治光) was the son of Jirōzaemon no Jō Katsumitsu and the father of Harumitsu (春光). In terms of quality he was on about the same level as the contemporary Yosōzaemon no Jō Sukesada. Famous is his *jūyō-bunkazai* with the *mei*: Bizen no Kuni-jū Osafune Jirōzaemon no Jō Katsumitsu, shi Jirōbei no Jō Harumitsu – Ichigo-Hitokoshi no saku – Sasaki Iyo no Kami" (備前国住長船次郎左衛門尉勝光・子次郎兵衛尉治光・一期一腰作之・佐々木伊予守). This is namely a *gassaku* of Katsumitsu and his son Harumitsu made for Amago Tsunehisa (尼子経久, 1458-1541) who was once a retainer of the Sasaki family and beared temporarily the title „Iyo no Kami". Later the blade was owned by general Nogi Maresuke (乃木希典, 1849-1912). [Translators note: The Nogi are a branch family of the Amago.]

Attention should also be paid to the hilt of the *sō-no-kurikara horimono* of the *sashi-omote* side. This is interpreted as a kind of two chrysanthemum-like elements to the left and right of the hilt. This peculiarity is typical for Bizen and especially for the Osafune school. We can see it on a *jūyō-bunkazai ken* by Nagamitsu (長光), on a blade by Kagemitsu (景光) from the end of the Kamakura period and on a blade by Kanemitsu (兼光) from the Nanbokuchō period. From that time on, this special interpretation was kept by Bizen smiths until the end of the Muromachi period. Exceptional on this blade is also the other *horimono* because it is the only known blade which bears an engraving of the name of the deity „Katte-Daimyōjin". So it was probably made on custom order for an offering to Nara-Yoshino´s Katte-jinja (勝手神社). The deity worshipped in that shrine is namely Katte-Daimyōjin, also called „Ukenori-kami no mikoto" (愛鬘命) and with its more well-known Buddhist name „Bishamonten" (毘沙門天). But there exists also a legend about Minamoto no Yoshitsune (源義経, 1159-1189) connected to this shrine. Once when Yoshitsune and his men stayed in the region, his concubine Shizuka-gozen (静御前) performed in the shrine a sacred dance at a *shintō* ritual. A messenger sent by the ex-emperor was distracted and so Yoshitsune was able to escape. The remnants of the stage where Shizuka-gozen danced are still extant today.

[Translators note: The deity „Katte-Daimyōjin" is also worshipped as patron saint for a victorious battle („*katte*" means namely „victory"). So it is quite possible that the owner of the sword had engraved the name of the deity out of this context.]

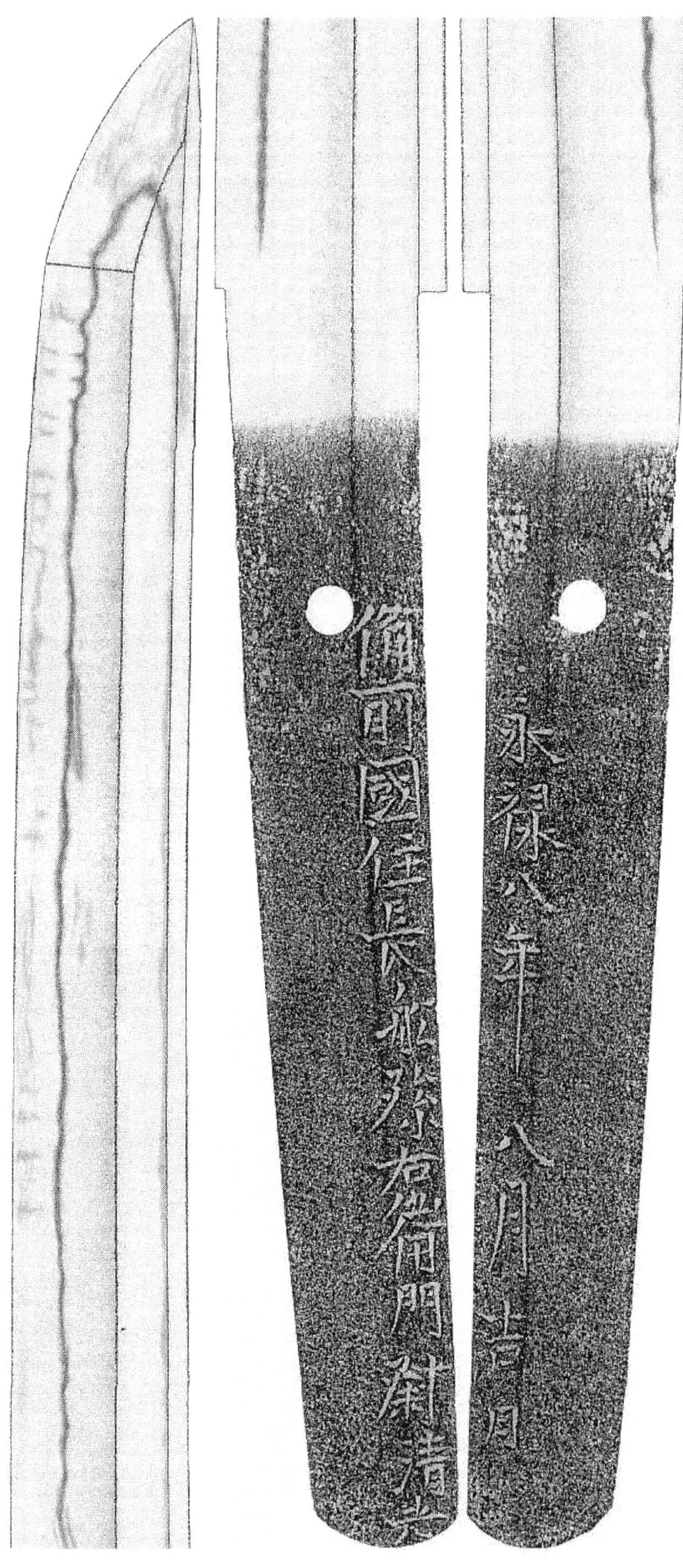
備前國住長舩孫右衛門尉清光
永禄八年八月吉日

103.634 *katana*

mei: Bizen no Kuni-jū Osafune Mago´emon no Jō Kiyomitsu (備前国住長船孫右衛門尉清光)
Eiroku hachinen hachigatsu kichijitsu (永禄八年八月吉日, „on a lucky day in the eighth month Eiroku eight [= 1565]")

nagasa 72,7 cm, *sori* 2,4, *shinogi-zukuri*, *iori-mune*

ji: *itame* mixed with *mokume*, the *jihada* is all over the blade densely forged but stands somewhat out along the lower half, also *ji-nie*, fine *chikei* and a faint *utsuri* appear

hamon: based on *hiro-suguha* and mixed with *ko-gunome* and *notare*, some *ko-ashi*, frequent *yō*, *nie*, some *uchinoke*, *yubashiri*-like elements, and along the upper half several *muneyaki*, the *nioiguchi* is bright

bōshi: widely hardened *suguha* with *hakikake* and a long *ko-maru-kaeri*

This *katana* has a *sakizori* and a widely hardened *bōshi*, both typical characteristics of the late Muromachi period. Furthermore it has a relative wide *mihaba*, does not taper that much, is rather long, has an elongated *kissaki* and a long tang, so it is obviously not a single-handed *katate-uchi* but a two-handed sword, a so-called „*morote-uchi*" (諸手打) or „*ryōte-uchi*" (両手打). And on the basis of that, we can date it somewhere between Eiroku (永禄, 1588-1570) and Tenshō (天正, 1573-1592).

There were many smiths at that time which worked in *suguha* but the dense *kitae*, the *utsuri*, the bright *jiba*, the conspicious *mokume* amount, the repeated *yō* which reach down the *ha* in places (a characteristic which is called „*Kiyomitsu no yodare*" [清光のよだれ], lit. „Kiyomitsu saliva"), and the *hakikake* in the *bōshi* make it relative easy to nail the bid down to Osafune Kiyomitsu.

Well, most got the *sugata* right and some did not went for Kiyomitsu but even straightforward and *atari* on Mago´emon no Jō Kiyomitsu. Such a *kantei* deserves recognition! In the case of his father namely, Gorōzaemon no Jō Kiyomitsu (五郎左衛門尉清光), the *nagasa* and the tang would be shorter because he was mainly active around Tenbun (天文, 1532-1555).

All the numerous bids on Sukesada (祐定) were counted as *dōzen*. Genbei no Jō Sukesada (源兵衛尉祐定) Sukesada was a contemporary of Mago´emo no Jō Kiyomitsu and is also famous for his masterly *suguha*. That means a direct *kantei* on him is very sensitive too. But his *kitae* is a bit more dense and such peculiar *yō* as a *bōshi* which tends to *kuzure* is not seen on his blades.

But there were also some bids on Taira Takada (平高田) or the Kanabō school (金房). We know also Takada blades with a dense *kitae* but not in that high quality. Taira Takada-*hamon* in *suguha* have a hard looking and compact *nioiguchi* and also the *ashi* and *yō* look stiff. Some of them are very fine and conspicious which makes them look as scratched onto the blade with a needle.

In the case of a Kanabō work, we would expect a rather standing-out and whitish *jigane* with a tendency to *nagare*. Also we would find fine *midare*- and *kuzure*-like elements mixed in between the *ashi* and *yō*. These elements are arranged as small islands of unhardened areas (*shimaba*, 島刃). In addition, the *nioiguchi* of the Kanabō school is compart but subdued and the *bōshi* has mostly a pointed *kaeri*.

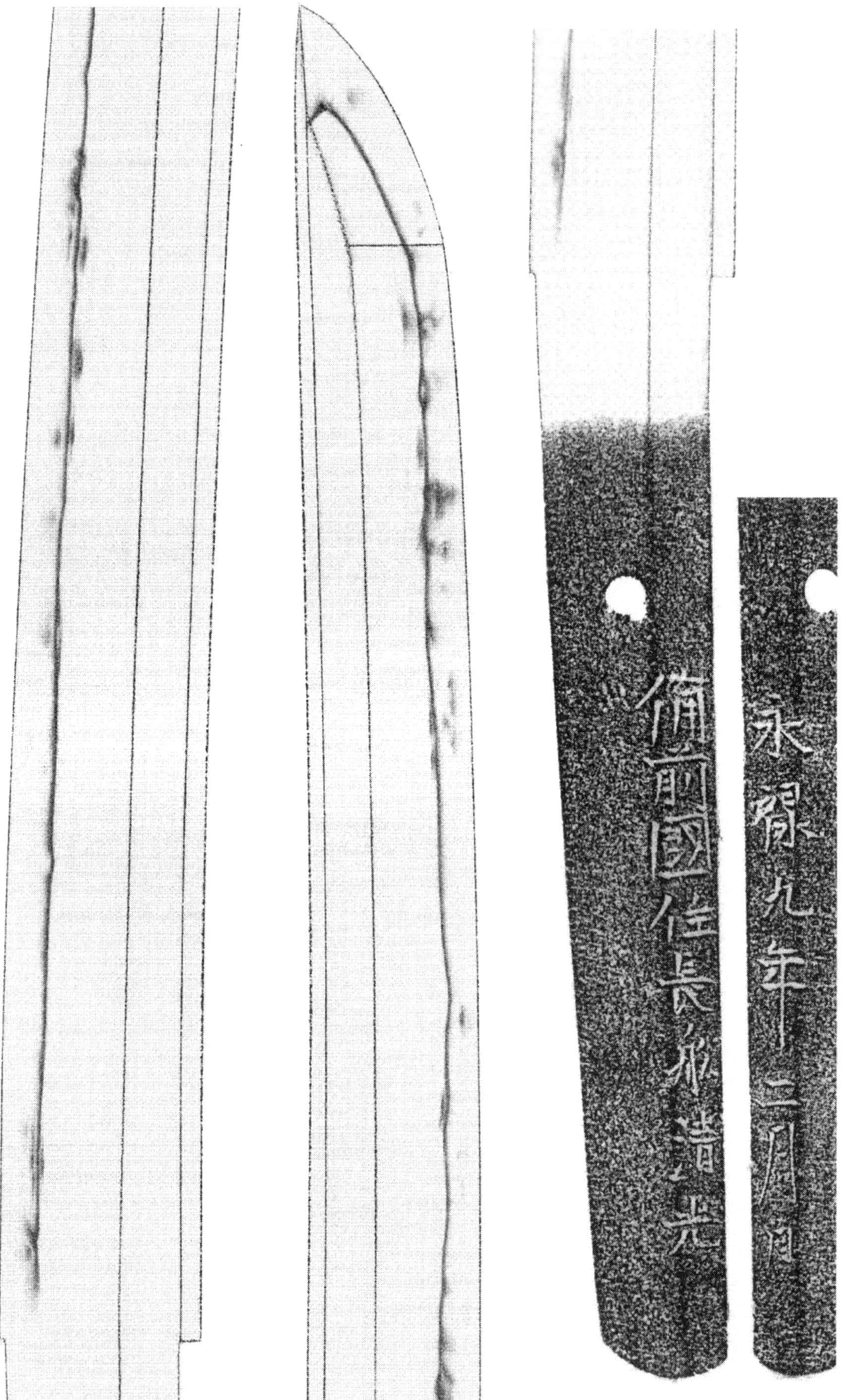

備前國住長舩清光
永禄九年二月日

104.668k *katana*
mei: Bizen no Kuni-jū Osafune Kiyomitsu (備前国住長船清光)
Eiroku kyūnen nigatsu-hi (永禄九年二月日, „a day in the second month Eiroku nine [= 1566]")

nagasa 73,42 cm *sori* 1,97 cm *moto-haba* 3,0 cm *saki-haba* 2,25 cm
moto-kasane 0,85 cm *saki-kasane* 0,45 cm *kissaki-nagasa* 4,0 cm *nakago-nagasa* 17,8 cm
a little *nakago-sori*

shinogi-zukuri, *iori-mune*, wide *mihaba*, no noticeable taper, thick *kasane*, *sakizori*, elongated *chū-kissaki*. The *jigane* is a standing-out *itame* mixed with *mokume*. It shows *ji-nie*, *chikei* and a faint *midare-utsuri*. The *hamon* and the *bōshi* can be seen on the *oshigata*. In addition *ashi*, *yō* and *sunagashi* appear. The *nioiguchi* is bright and shows plentiful of *nie*. The *nakago* is *ubu*, has a bulbous *kurijiri*, *katte-sagari yasurime* and one *mekugi-ana*. There is a *naga-mei* on the *sashi-omote* side below of the *mekugi-ana* and towards the *nakago-mune*. A date signature is added in the same way on the *ura* side.

This is a work of Mago'emon no Jō Kiyomitsu (孫右衛門尉清光). It has a wide *mihaba*, no noticeable taper, a thick *kasane*, a *sakizori* and an elongated *chū-kissaki*. That means together with the longer *nagasa* and robust, magnificent shape we can date it into the late Muromachi period.

The *jigane* shows a faint *midare-utsuri* which brings us right away to Bizen. The *hamon* is a *chū-suguha* with *ko-gunome*, *ashi* and *yō* and has a *nie*-loaden and bright *nioiguchi*. So all in all we arrive eventually at Sue-Bizen. Custom made *chūmon-uchi* of the Sue-Bizen smiths show the finest and most excellent *jigane* of all late Muromachi-period schools. The *kitae* is in that case a very densely forged *itame* and the steel is very bright. Of course also the *hamon* is excellently hardened and the *nioiguchi* is very controlled and does not show *kuzure*. On the other hand, the *jigane* of Kiyomitsu is a somewhat standing-out *itame* mixed with *mokume* and the *hamon* shows *hotsure* and/or *nie-kuzure*. Usually he applied characteristical, soft looking *ashi* and *yō* which go down to the *ha*, but they don't appear that much on the *kantei* blade. His *bōshi* is in the case of a *suguha* also *sugu* with a *ko-maru-kaeri*, but it can also be *sugu* with an *ō-maru-kaeri*, *midare-komi* or almost *ichimai*. Sometimes the *kaeri* runs back quite long. The *kantei* blade is not signed with a first name but on the basis of the signature style we can attribute it nevertheless to Mago'emon no Jō Kiyomitsu. His tip of the tang is a bulbous *kurijiri*, the *yasurime* are *katte-sagari* and the signature is in the case of a *shinogi-zukuri katana* chiselled on the *sashi-omote* side above the *mekugi-ana* and towards the *nakago-mune*. He signed principally with a *naga-mei*. Often an identically interpreted date signature is added on the *ura* side but at a somewhat lower position. However, the *kantei* blade is signed lower than usual.

The majority bade *atari* on Mago'emon no Jō Kiyomitsu, followed by Gorōzaemon no Jō Kiyomitsu (五郎左衛門尉清光), Yosōzaemon no Jō Sukesada (与三左衛門尉祐定), Genbei no Jō Sukesada (源兵衛尉祐定) and other famous Sue-Bizen masters. Also these three late Muromachi-period Sue-Bizen heavyweights applied a *suguha* which is similar to the *kantei* blade and as a differentiation is difficult in such cases, bids on them were this time counted as *atari* too. Well, Mago'emon no Jō Kiyomitsu and Genbei no Jō Sukesada were basically active around Eiroku (永禄, 1558-1570) and Tenshō (天正, 1573-1592). Accordingly, they made somewhat wider blades with an elongated *kissaki*. In turn, Gorōzaemon no Jō Kiyomitsu and Yosōzaemon no Jō Sukesada worked a little earlier and therefore their blades are a hint more slender and the *kissaki* is smaller. There were also some *dōzen* bids on Katsumitsu (勝光) and Tadamitsu (忠光). They too applied a *suguha* with a bright *nioiguchi* but they were even earlier active than Gorōzaemon no Jō Kiyomitsu and Yosōzaemon no Jō Sukesada, namely around Bunmei (文明, 1469-1487) to Daiei (大永, 1521-1528). Therefore their blades are with 2 *shaku* to 2,2 *shaku* (60,6 ~ 66,6 cm) rather compact, have a normal *mihaba* and a *chū-kissaki*. The conspiciously shorter *nagasa* identifies them as single-handed *katate-uchi*. Such a long *nagasa* and wide *mihaba* like here is atypical for their production time and was not in fashion until the end of the Muromachi period.

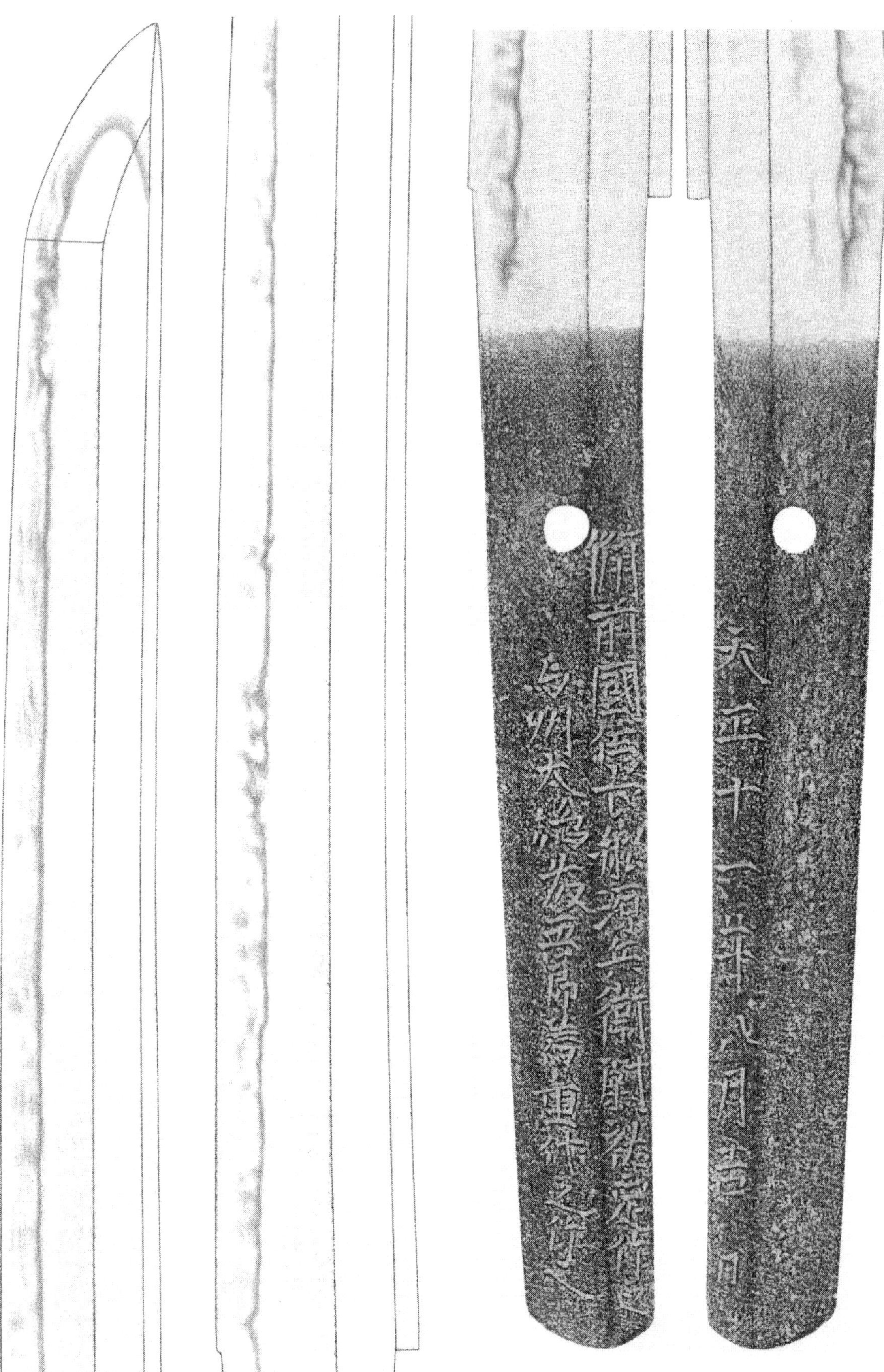

105.597k *katana*

mei: Bizen no Kuni-jū Osafune Genbei no Jō Sukesada kore o saku (備前国住長船源兵衛尉祐定作之)
Tenshō jūichi-nen hachi-gatsu kichijitsu (天正十一年八月吉日, „on a lucky day in the eight month Tenshō eleven [= 1583]“)
Yoshū Ōjima Tomoshirō jūdai no tame ni kore o saku (与州太嶋友四郎為重代之作之, „made for the successive generations of Yoshū Ōjima Tomoshirō“)

nagasa 74,0 cm *sori* 1,67 cm
moto-haba 3,2 cm *saki-haba* 2,0 cm
moto-kasane 0,7 cm *saki-kasane* 0,4 cm
kissaki-nagasa 3,6 cm *nakago-nagasa* 19,54 cm
little *nakago-sori*

shinogi-zukuri, iori-mune, wide *mihaba*, no noticable taper, thick *kasane*, *saki-zori*, elongated *chū-kissaki*, altogether a rather stout and robust *uchigatana-sugata*. The *jigane* is an *itame* mixed with *mokume* and is altogether very fine. There appears a fine and excellently applied *ji-nie* and also *chikei* and a faint *midare-utsuri*. The *hamon* and the *bōshi* can be seen on the *oshigata*. In addition, *ashi*, *yō* and bright sparkling *nie* as well as many *kinsuji* and *sunagashi* appear. The *nakago* is *ubu*, has a *ha-agari kurijiri*, *katte-sagari yasurime* and one *mekugi-ana*. There is a *naga-mei* on the *sashi-omote* below of the *mekugi-ana* and towards the *nakago-mune*. To the left of that *mei*, the name of the customer is engraved and a date signature is added on the *ura* side in the same way as the *naga-mei* but starting somewhat lower.

The blade has a wide *mihaba*, no noticeable taper, a thick *kasane*, a *sakizori* and a slightly elongated *chū-kissaki*. So we have typical characteristics of the late Muromachi period. The faint *midare-utsuri* narrows the bid right down to Bizen, an approach which is further supported by the very dense and fine *itame*. Sue-Bizen was namely the only school which produced such a fine *jigane* at that time, namely for their custom order works (*chūmon-uchi*).

The *hamon* is as so often for Sue-Bizen in *suguha* and the bright and clear *nioiguchi* is well controlled. There are many *ashi*, *yō*, *nie*, *kinsuji* and *sunagashi* seen which are all also typical for a Sue-Bizen *suguha*. Other matching characteristics are the *kurijiri*, the *katte-sagari yasurime*, the *naga-mei* and the date signature.

Well, famous for such an excellently hardened *suguha* within the Sue-Bizen school are for example Yosozaemon no Jō Sukesada, Genbei no Jō Sukesada, Gorōzaemon no Jō Kiyomitsu and Magoemon no Jō Kiyomitsu. Genbei no Jō Sukesada and Magoemon no Jō Kiyomitsu were active around Eiroku (1558-1570) and Tenshō (1573-1592) when exactly such a magnificent *sugata* was in fashion. Yosozaemon no Jō Sukesada and Gorōzaemon no Jō Kiyomitsu in turn were active somewhat earlier and made mostly more compact blades with a narrow *mihaba* and smaller *kissaki*.

It is also known that Genbei no Jō Sukesada´s strong point was a *suguha* and he was the best smith of his time and group when it comes to a high-quality *jigane*. The workmanship of the *kantei* blade testifies to his skill and almost all bids were on him or on the other aforementioned smiths. As their *suguha* is usually hard to differentiate all bids on them were counted equally as *atari*.

Kiyomitsu made the „coarsest“ or most standing-out *jigane* of this group and applied *ashi* and *yō* which reach down to the *ha* in places. There were also some few *dōzen* bids on Hikobei no Jō Sukesada, Katsumitsu or Munemitsu. They too hardened a *suguha* with bright *nioiguchi* but they were active considerably earlier, namely around Bunmei (1469-1487) and Daiei (1521-1528). Accordingly, their blades are with 2 or 2,2 *shaku* (60,6 to 66,6 cm) noticeably shorter and have also a shorter tang because of their single-handed use as *katate-uchi*. So one also had to pay attention to the subtle differences in *sugata* between the late and the end of the Muromachi period.

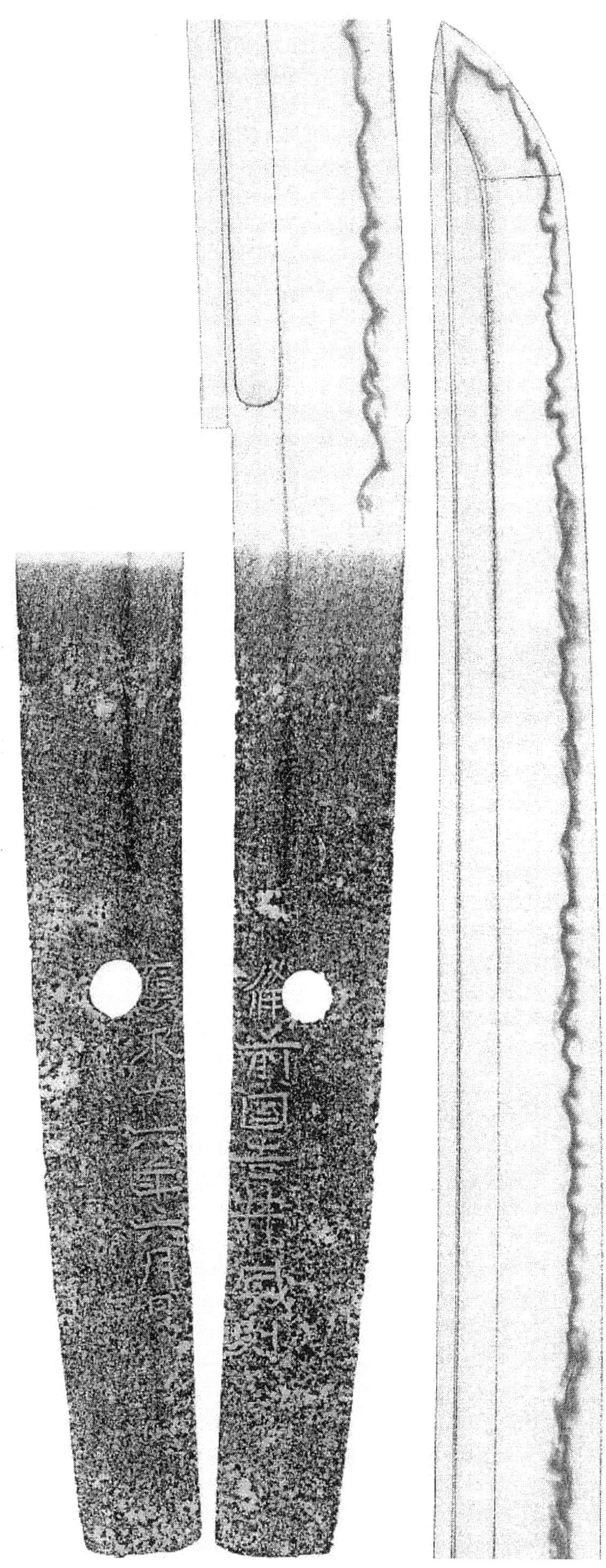

106.643 *tachi*
mei: Bizen no Kuni Yoshii Morinori (備前国吉井盛則)
Ōei nijūrokunen rokugatsu-hi (応永廿六年六月日, „a day in the sixth month Ōei 26 [1419]“)
nagasa 63,6 cm, *sori* 2,1 cm, *shinogi-zukuri*, *iori-mune*

ji: *itame* mixed with *mokume*, in addition *ji-ie*, *chikei* and a faint *midare-utsuri*
hamon: *ko-gunome* mixed with *ko-chōji*, *togari-gunome* and other rather small dimensioned elements, in addition plentiful of *ashi* and much *ko-nie*
bōshi: *midare-komi* with a *ko-maru-kaeri* on the *omote* side and a pointed *kaeri* on the *ura* side, but on both sides the *kaeri* is rather short
horimono: on both sides a *bōhi* with *maru-dome* above the *habaki*

The blade is slender and shows a *sori* around the base and towards the tip. Such a *sugata* is typical for the end of the Nanbokuchō and early Muromachi period, especially for the Ōei era (1394-1428) when the *tachi-sugata* of the middle and late Kamakura period was revived. And if you take a closer look at the *ji* you will see a faint *midare-utsuri* which brings us to Bizen.

According to transmission, the Bizen Yoshii school was founded towards the end of the Kamakura period by Tamenori (為則). Nowadays we differentiate between „Ko-Yoshii“ from the Kamakura and Nanbokuchō periods, and „Yoshii“ from the Muromachi period. And during the Muromachi period, a branch of the Bizen Yoshii school split off and established itself in Izumo province. This branch is called „Unshū-Dōei“ (雲州道永).

Contrary to the uniform *gunome-chō* all over the blade of the Yoshii school, this blade shows only some passages of uniform *ko-gunome* elements and the *hamon* is also somewhat smaller dimensioned and tends to a *nie-deki*. That is also the reason why many went for Kozori from the end of the Nanbokuchō period. Well, this approach is not that wrong because the Muromachi-period Yoshii school worked primarily in *nioi-deki* with only a little *nie*. But at a Kozori work, we would see more varied elements within the *ha* as well as a mixed-in *koshi-no-hiraita gunome*.

Signed and dated blades of Yoshii smiths are quite rare and therefore this *tachi* is a precious reference for this school.

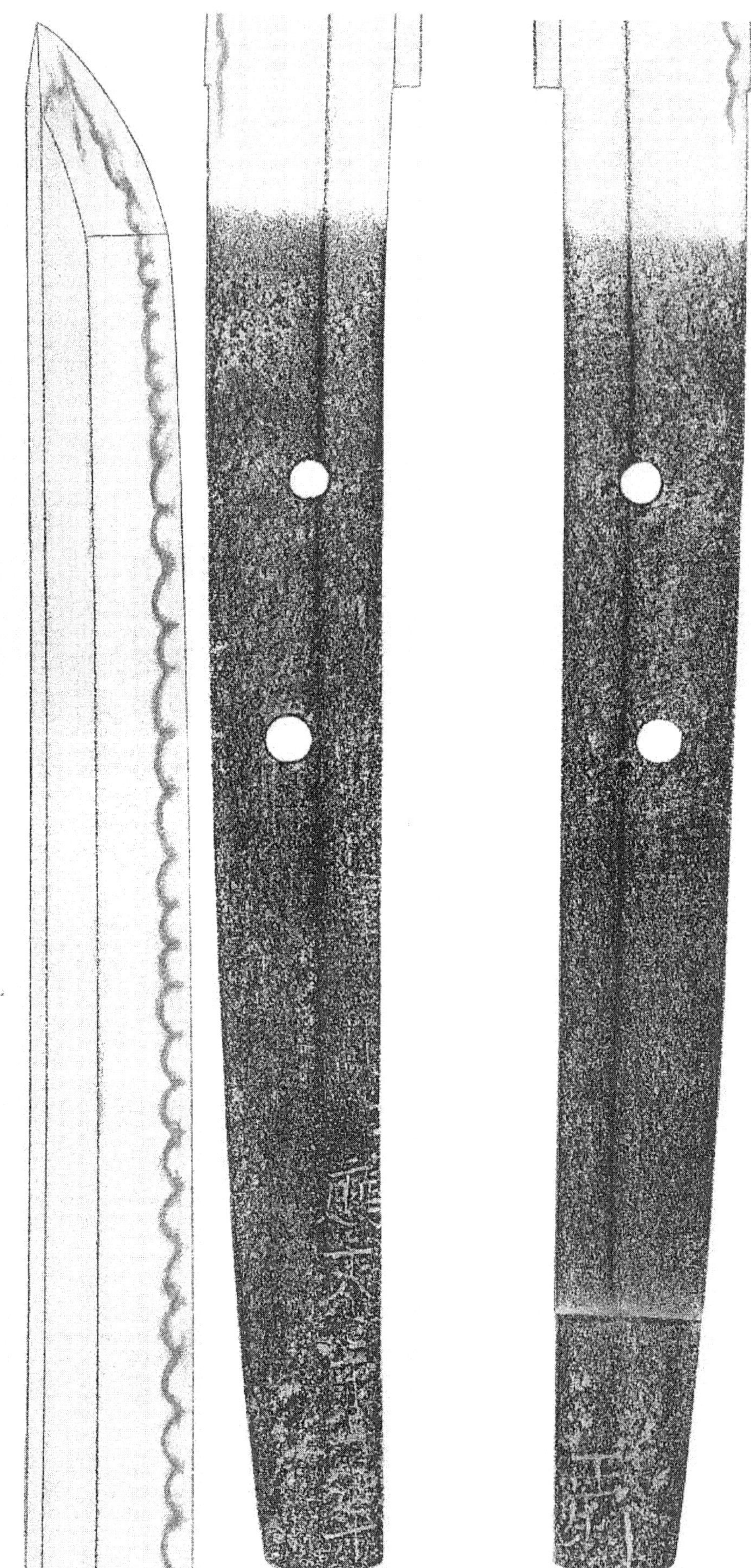

107.622 *tachi*
mei: Masanori (正則) – Ōei sanjū?-nen (応永三十〇年, „Ōei thirty something [= 1423~1428]")
nagasa 71,8 cm, *sori* 1,2 cm, *shinogi-zukuri*, *iori-mune*

ji: dense *ko-itame* partially mixed with *nagare* and *masame*, in addition fine *ji-nie*, *chikei* and a *midare-utsuri*
hamon: uniform *ko-gunome* with *ko-ashi* all over the blade and plentiful of *nie*, the latter appear as *hotsure* in places, in addition *ashi* and *sunagashi*
bōshi: on both sides *midare-komi* with a pointed *kaeri* on the *omote* and a *ko-maru-kaeri* on the *ura* side, also *hakikake* appear on both sides

Some smiths of the Bizen Yoshii school moved to Izumo and founded there their own lineage. This offshoot is called „Unshū-Dōei" school (雲州道永) and Masanori was one of their representative smiths. The fact that the *kantei* blade bears a date signature – which is quite rare for this school – makes it a very precious reference.

The Dōei school kept rather faithfully to the original style of the Yoshii school which is basically a uniform *ko-gumome* and also the *utsuri* follows in the Yoshii-typical manner the course of the *hamon*.

The *kantei* blade dates to the early Muromachi period but shows in comparison with other and later Muromachi-period Yoshii works rather strong *nie* within the *ha*. Also the *hataraki* of the *ha* are quite conspicious and so the *deki* looks somewhat more classic and older than usual Yoshii-*mono*.

But almost all bids were on the Yoshii school. This blade shows despite the *suriage* a noticeable taper, it has a normal *mihaba*, a thick *kasane* and a slight *sakizori*. So it is clearly a work of the early Muromachi period and a bid on „Yoshii" plus „early Muromachi" was especially valued.

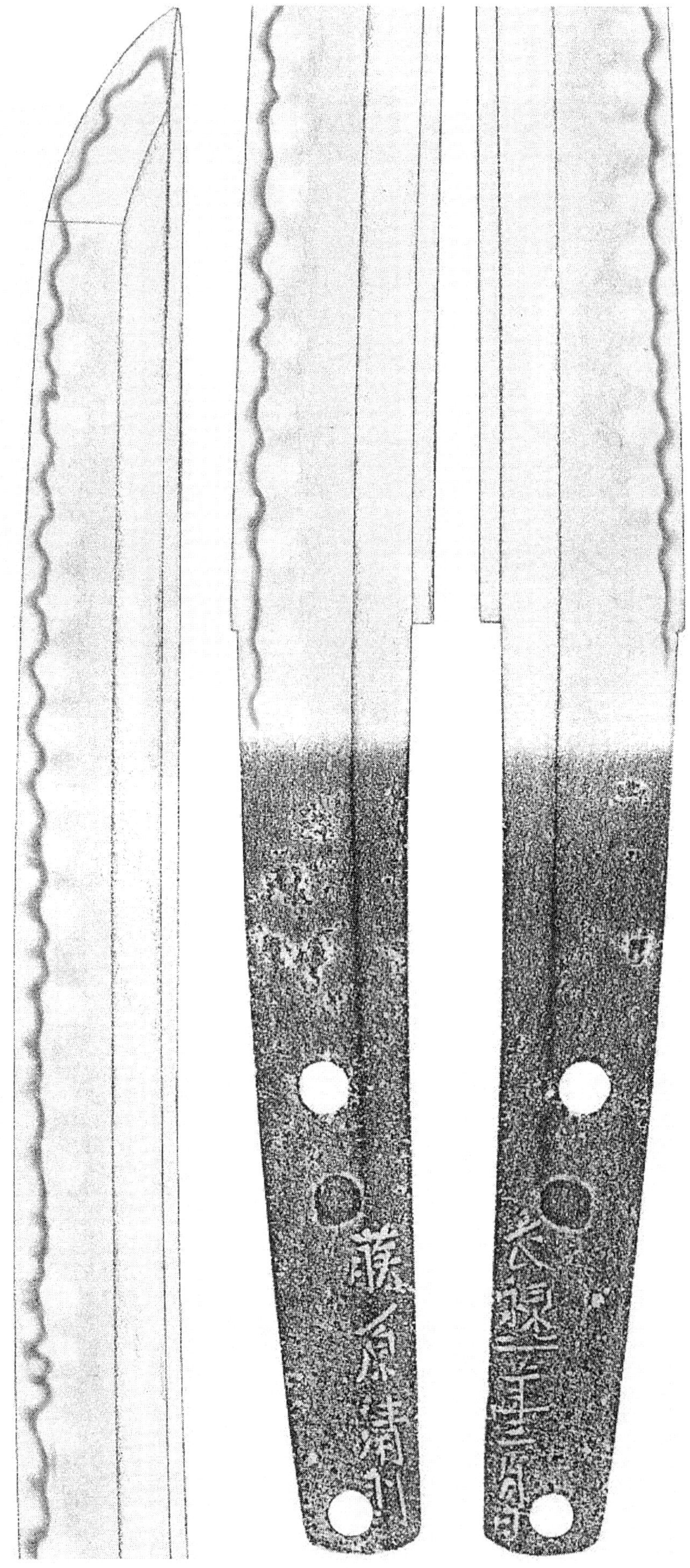

108.594 *wakizashi*
mei: Fujiwara Kiyonori (藤原清則)
Chōroku yonnen sangatsu-hi (長禄二二年三月日, „a day in the third month of Chōroku four [1460]")
nagasa 51,8 cm, *sori* 1,2 cm, *shinogi-zukuri*, *iori-mune*

ji: *itame* mixed with *mokume*, in addition *ji-nie* and a regular *midare-utsuri*
hamon: uniform *ko-gunome* with *sunagashi*, the hardening is in *nioi-deki* with *ko-nie*
bōshi: *midare-komi* with a short *ko-maru*-like *kaeri*

This blade shows a regular *midare-utsuri* along the *ji* and the *hamon* consists of uniform *ko-gunome* elements. This characteristical *deki* leaded most of the participants right at the first round on the right track, namely Yoshii (吉井). But some went also for Kozori (小反), Kanemoto (兼元) or even Sue-Seki (末関). But such an uniform and continuous *gunome* and an *utsuri* which appears as a kind of „parallel shadow" exactly over the *hamon* is very peculiar to the Yoshii school. Well, also Kozori smiths applied a smaller dimensioned *midareba* but in a more irregular, „free" manner with noticeable ups and downs. And at Sue-Seki, we would expect *togari*, *shirake* and *masame*.

The blade is a work of Yoshii Kiyonori and is dated with the fourth year of Chōroku. But it is hard to make out individual characteristics among all the Yoshii smiths and so it was enough to bid straightforward on Yoshii. Incidentally, Yoshii works from the end of the Kamakura or the subsequent Nanbokuchō period show noticably more *nie* than the Muromachi-period works and the *ha* is also richer in *hataraki* like *kinsuji* and *sunagashi*.

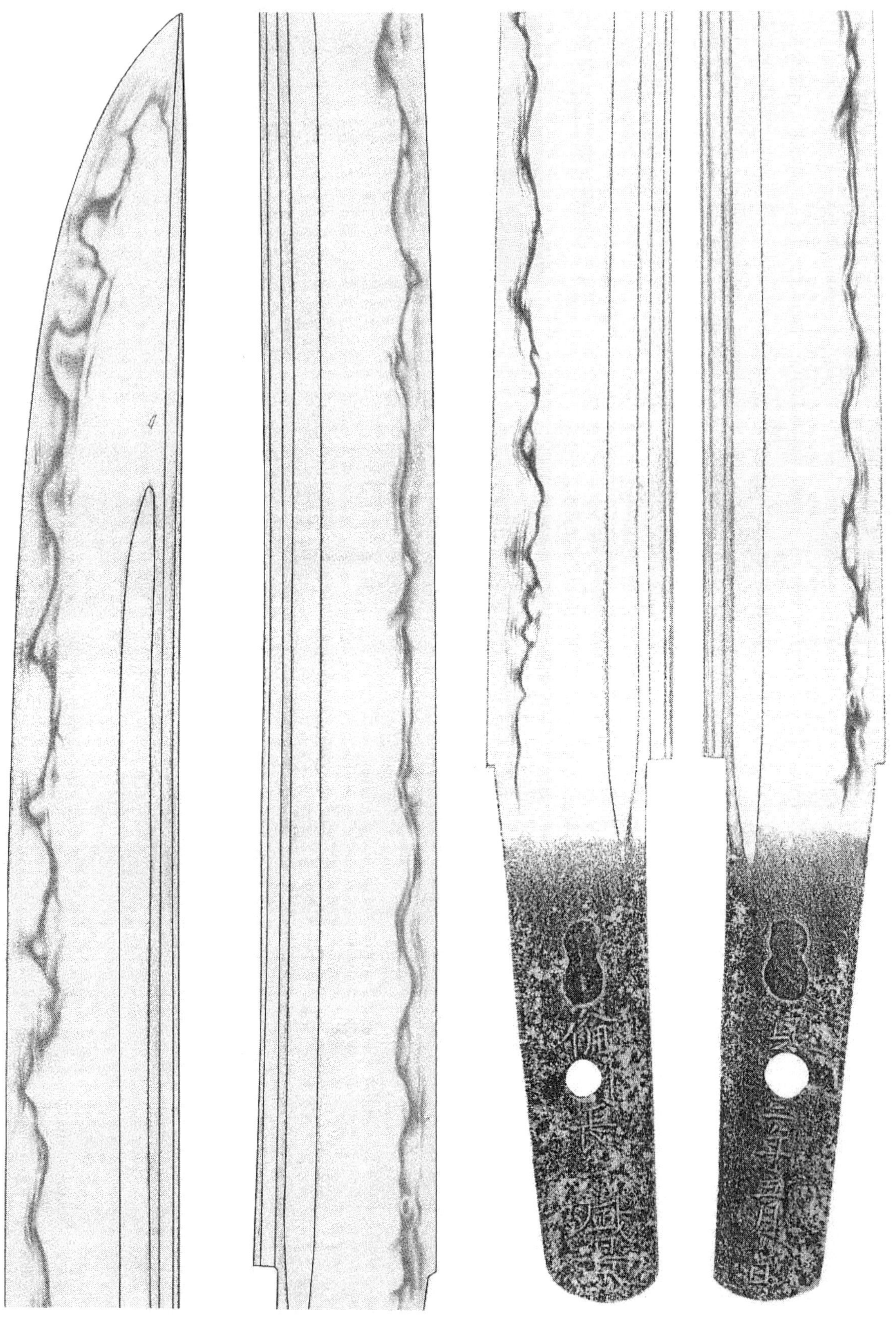

109.620k *wakizashi*

mei: Bishū Osafune Morikage (備州長船盛景)
Jōji sannen gogatsu-hi (貞治三年五月日, „a day in the fifth month Jōji three [= 1364]")

nagasa 30,91 cm *sori* 0,3 cm
moto-haba 2,9 cm *moto-kasane* 0,65 cm
nakago-nagasa 9,39 cm only very little *nakago-sori*

hira-zukuri, mitsu-mune, wide *mihaba, sunnobi*, thin *kasane*, shallow *sori*. The *jigane* is an *itame* mixed with *mokume* and *nagare* which stands out all over the blade. In addition, *ji-nie, chikei*, some *jifu* and a faint *midare-utsuri* appear. The *hamon* and the *bōshi* can be seen on the *oshigata*. The *midareba* tends to be somewhat angular. The *habuchi* shows fine *hotsure* and there are *yubashiri, ko-ashi* and *yō*. The *nioiguchi* is rather subdued and shows *nie, kinsuji* and *sunagashi*. There is a *katana-hi* on both sides which runs with *kake-nagashi* into the tang. Small remnants of a *tsurebi* can be seen at the very end of the *hi*. The *nakago* is *ubu*, has a *kurijiri, katte-sagari yasurime* and two *mekugi-ana* (of which one is plugged). There is a *naga-mei* on the *sashi-omote* centrally under the first, the *ubu-mekugi-ana*. The *mei* shows the typical chiselling style for this smith. A date signature is added in the same way on the *ura* side.

The blade has a wide *mihaba*, is *sunnobi*, has a thin *kasane* and a shallow *sori*, that means we can place it into the heyday of the Nanbokuchō period. Regarding Morikage, we know date signatures from the second year of Kō´an (康安, 1362) to the first year of Ō´ei (応永, 1394). In olden times it was assumed that two generations were active over this time span but today it is more and more accepted that there was just one Morikage whose signature and workmanship changed over these thirty years, which is quite natural and understandable.

So Morikage worked from the heyday of the Nanbokuchō to the beginning of the Muromachi period. That means he made long and broad *tachi* without much taper and an *ō-kissaki* and broad *ko-wakizashi* and *sunnobi-tantō* like the *kantei*-blade. By the way, such shapes are commonly referred to as „Enbun-Jōji-*sugata*". Slightly later and around Eiwa (永和, 1375-1379), i.e. after the peak of oversized blades, his *tachi-sugata* changes towards more slender blades with a noticeable taper and a smaller *kissaki*. These changes can be seen in almost all provinces and schools. Some also speak of an „Eiwa-*sugata*" in that transitional stage. And from the end of the Nanbokuchō period onwards, Morikage shows a normal *mihaba*, a noticeable taper, a *chū-kissaki* and a *koshizori* which increases again towards the tip. Such a *sugata* was also applied by the contemporary Kozori smiths and is a precursor of the Kamakura-revival of the subsequent Ōei-Bizen school.

Morikage did not belong to any of the Bizen mainlines of the Nanbokuchō period. His *jigane* is a standing-out *itame* which is partially mixed with coarse *ō-hada* areas and *jifu* elements of a different colour. His *utsuri* is generally faint. His workmanship is quite varied and ranges from a *deki* in Kanemitsu style (兼光) in a *notare*-based *hamon* like seen on the *kantei* blade, an angular *gunome* in the style of Motoshige (元重), a *suguha* in Aoe-manner to a vivid *midareba* of a mix of *chōji* and *gunome*. (Note: In the case of a Kanemitsu-like interpretation, Morikage´s *hamon* is more angular and not so lenient as the original.)

Works from the end of the Nanbokuchō period in the mentioned *sugata* show a shallow *ko-notare* mixed with *ko-gunome* and *ko-togariba*. The *hamon* is altogether rather narrow and densely arranged and some interpretations are quite close to contemporary Kozori-*mono*. In any case, *ashi* and *yō* appear and the *nioiguchi* shows *mura-nie* and is rather subdued.

The *bōshi* of Morikage is in the case of a *midareba* mostly also a *midare-komi* with a pointed *kaeri* and in the case of a *suguha* a *sugu-bōshi* with a *ko-maru-kaeri*.

As mentioned, Morikage did not belong to any of the Bizen main schools of the Nanbokuchō period and so his *hataraki* of the *jiba* have a more rustic touch. This is a typical characteristic of this smith and seen on any of the previously described workmanships.

There exist blades of Morishige with *horimono* of *bōhi*, *bōhi* with *soebi*, *futasuji-hi*, *bonji*, *sankozuka-ken*, *kurikara* in the „pregnant dragon“ (*harami-ryū*, 孕龍) interpretation and characters of deities like „Hachiman-Daibosatsu“ and the like. His tang has a *kurijiri*, *katte-sagari yasurime*, and the signature is chiselled like on the *kantei* blade at *hira-zukuri wakizashi* and *tantō* on the *sashi-omote* side centrally under the *mekugi-ana*. A *naga-mei* has mostly the syntax „Bishū Osafune Morikage“ or „Bishū Osafune-jū Morikage“. Most of the extant blades bear a date signature on the *ura* side, chiselled in the same style and on the same position as the *naga-mei*. But sometimes he also signed in *gyaku-tagane*, i.e. in the opposite way strokes of a character are written with the brush. This peculiarity can also be seen on the *kantei* blade.

In earlier years it was thought that the signature „Bishū Osafune Morikage“ belonged to a smith who was a successor of father and son Kunimori (国盛) and Sukemori (助盛) respectively, the founders of the Ōmiya school. They once moved from Yamashiro´s Inokuma Ōmiya (猪熊大宮) to Bizen but today it is assumed that „Ōmiya Morikage“ (nicknamed after his original place of residence) and „Osafune Morikage“ were two different smiths, and that the latter came somewhere from the vicinity of Chikakage (近景) and runned like Yoshikage (義景) and Mitsukage (光景) an influental Osafune sideline. This assumption is supported by the signatures in *gyaku-tagane* which was also used by Chikage, Yoshikage and Mitsukage. So for the future, one should also pay attention to hints about the signature in the description of the *kantei*.

The majority bade *atari* on Morikage but there were also relative many who went for Chōgi (長義). Well, although Chōgi belonged to the Osafune school, his *jiba* differs from the then mainline works of Kanemitsu (兼光). That means from this point of view – a different *jiba* – a bid on Chōgi is understandable. But Chōgi forged mostly *tantō* around 7 to 8 *sun* (21,1 ~ 24,2 cm) which seem to have a „shrinked“ Enbun-Jōji-*sugata*, i.e. all proportions like the wide *mihaba*, the thin *kasane* and the shallow *sori* stay the same. However, Chōgi was mainly active from the sixth year of Jōwa (貞和, 1350) to the second year of Kōryaku (康暦, 1380), thus also around Enbun and Jōji. And according to that, he made of course also some larger dimensioned *sunnobi-tantō* and *hira-zukuri wakizashi*. So maybe one thought the *kantei* blade is such a more rare work of Chōgi in the „original“ Enbun-Jōji-*sugata*. However, the *hamon* of these *tantō* and *hira-zukuri wakizashi* bases on *notare* and is mixed with *gunome*. It shows conspicious ups and downs and the *gunome* form groups of two which appear as a kind of „ear shape“. This is one of the most typical characteristics of Chōgi. His *nioiguchi* is somewhat subdued and shows much *nie* and the *bōshi* is a *midare-komi* with a long and pointed *kaeri*. But Chōgi did not sign in a such peculiar manner that it had to be pointed out in the description of the *kantei*.

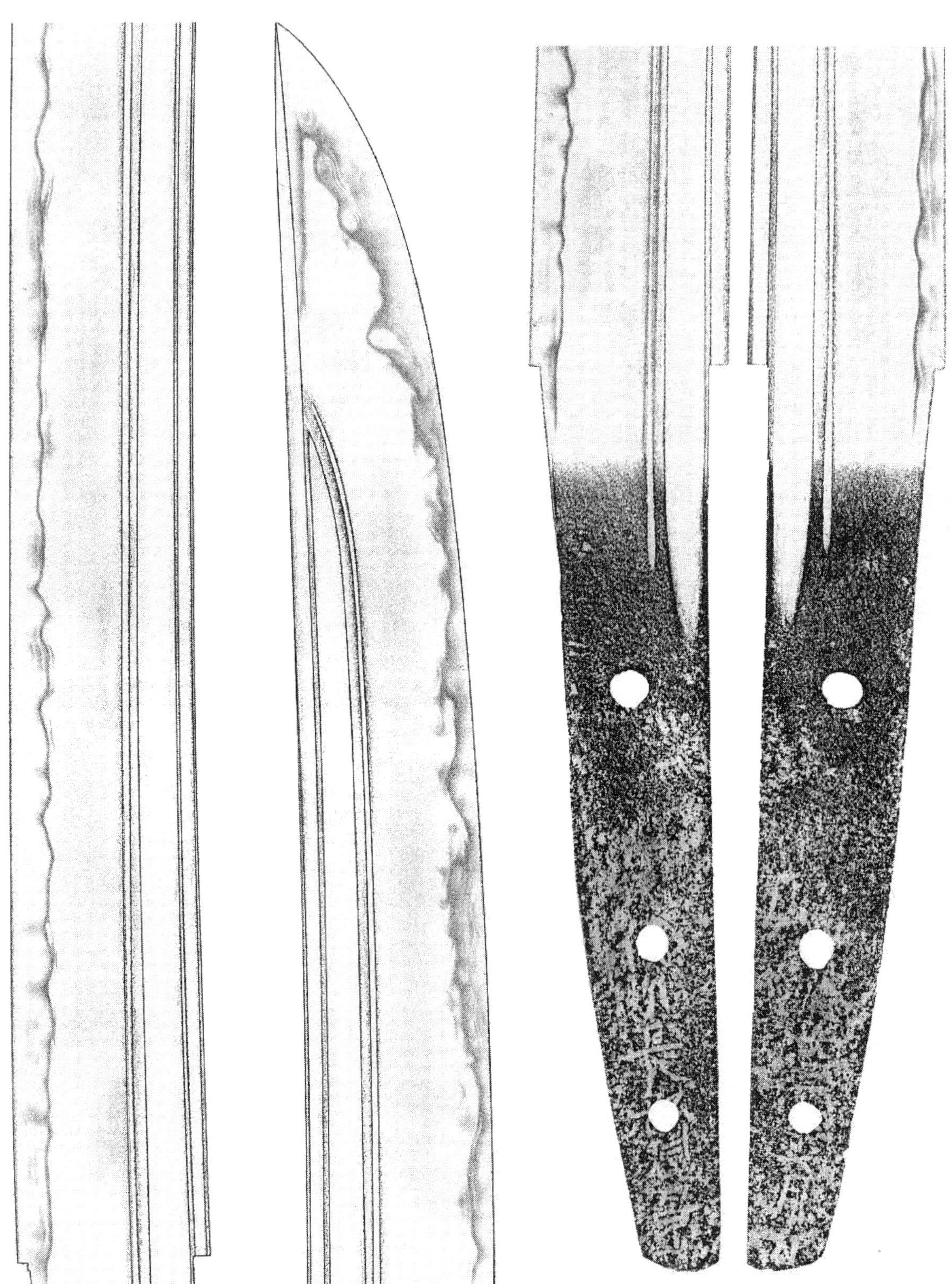

110.633k *wakizashi*

mei: Osafune Morikage (長船盛景) – Ōan sannen (応安三年, „third year of Ōan [= 1370]“)

nagasa 59,84 cm *sori* 1,36 cm *moto-haba* 3,3 cm *moto-kasane* 0,55 cm

nakago-nagasa 16,36 cm no *nakago-sori*

large *hira-zukuri* blade, *mitsu-mune*, *sunnobi*, thin *kasane*, shallow *sori*. The *jigane* is an *itame* mixed with *mokume* and *nagare* which stands out all over the blade. In addition, *ji-nie*, some *jifu* and a faint *midare-utsuri* appear. The *hamon* and the *bōshi* can be seen on the *oshigata*. The *midare* tends to be angular and there are fine *hotsure* along the *habuchi*. Also *yubashiri*, *ko-ashi* and *yō* appear. The *nioiguchi* is rather subdued, shows *ko-nie*, *kinsuji* and *sunagashi*. On both sides a *katana-hi* with *tsurebi* is engraved which runs with *kake-nagashi* into the tang. The *nakago* is *suriage*, has a *kurijiri*, *katte-sagari yasurime* and three *mekugi-ana*. There is a *naga-mei* chiselled in the typical way of that smith centrally on the lower area of the tang´s *sashi-omote* side. The *ura* side bears an identically interpreted date signature. (The *kantei* blade is today classified as *ō-wakizashi* but is actually an *uchigatana* in *hira-zukuri*. Such long *hira-zukuri* blades were rare at the time when this one was made.)

The blade has a wide *mihaba*, looks rather large, is *sunnobi*, has a thin *kasane* and a shallow *sori*, so we can date it into the heyday of the Nanbokuchō period. High-ranking *bushi* wore a *tachi* but not an *uchigatana* from the end of the Heian to the beginning of the Kamakura period. *Uchigatana* were worn by lower ranking warriors who followed the higher-ranking *bushi* into battle as supportive troops. They were in the need for a simple and easy-to-wield sword. Picture scrolls from around that time show us that the then *uchigatana* was smaller than its later counterpart. And we can also assume that most of them were not very sophisticated but produced in masses. Unfortunately, not many examples of that time survived and so the early *uchigatana* form is somewhat obscure.

When higher-ranking *bushi* started to wear an *uchigatana* as their main sword, of course the length had to increase and so did the quality. The commonly accepted theory says that this took place during the early Muromachi period but there are, although very rare, some excellently *uchigatana* extant from the Kamakura and Nanbokuchō period. (Incidentally, we also know some few excellent *uchigatana* from the late Heian and early Kamakura period but it is not clear how or if they were related to the later *uchigatana*.)

Famous are the *jūyō-bunkazai* „Nakigitsune Kuniyoshi“ (鳴狐国吉), a blade by Shizu Saburō Kaneuji (志津三郎兼氏), and the *jūyō-bijutsuhin* „Suijin-giri Kanemitsu“ (水神切兼光). And then there is this blade and another *tokubetsu-jūyō* by Osafune Morikage which is dated Eiwa one (永和, 1375). There are some more blades extant by this smith and most of them are in *hira-zukuri*, although with a considerably shorter *nagasa*. He was a smith from the Nanbokuchō period of one of the Bizen sidelines. His *kitae* is a standing-out *itame* which is in places mixed with a subtle *ō-hada* and *jifū* which results in a varied *jigane*. Also a faint *utsuri* appears. His workmanship is quite varied in general and we know a Kanemitsu-like *notare*-based *hamon* like the one on the *kantei* blade, a *deki* basing on angular *gunome* like of Motoshige (元重), a *suguha* in Aoe-manner, or a vivid *midareba* of *chōji* and *gunome*.

In the case of a *notare*, the mixed-in *midare* elements are angular and in comparison to Kanemitsu, Morikage´s *koshi* start higher but the valleys in between the elements are shorter. This is a typical characteristic of Morikage. In any case, *ashi* and *yō* are found and the *nioiguchi* is rather subdued. Sometimes we also see *mura-nie*. Morikage´s *bōshi* is mostly a *midare-komi* with a pointed *kaeri*.

He engraved *horimono* like *bōhi*, *bōhi* with *soebi*, *futasuji-hi*, *bonji*, *sankozuka-ken*, *kurikata* in the „pregnant dragon“ (*harami-ryū*, 孕龍) interpretation and characters of deities like „Hachiman-Daibosatsu“ and the like. His tang has a *kurijiri*, *katte-sagari yasurime*, and the signature is chiselled like on the *kantei* blade at *hira-zukuri wakizashi* and *tantō* on the *sashi-omote* side centrally under the *mekugi-ana*. A *naga-mei* has mostly the syntax „Bishū Osafune Morikage“ or „Bishū Osafune-jū Morikage“. Most of the extant blades bear a date signature on the *ura* side, chiselled in the same style and on the same position as the *naga-mei*. Morikage signed in *gyaku-tagane*, i.e. in the opposite way the strokes of a character are written with the brush. This peculiarity places him in the vicinity of the Bizen smiths Chikakage (近景) or Yoshikage (義景).

As the blade is very typical, almost all bids were *atari* on Morikage.

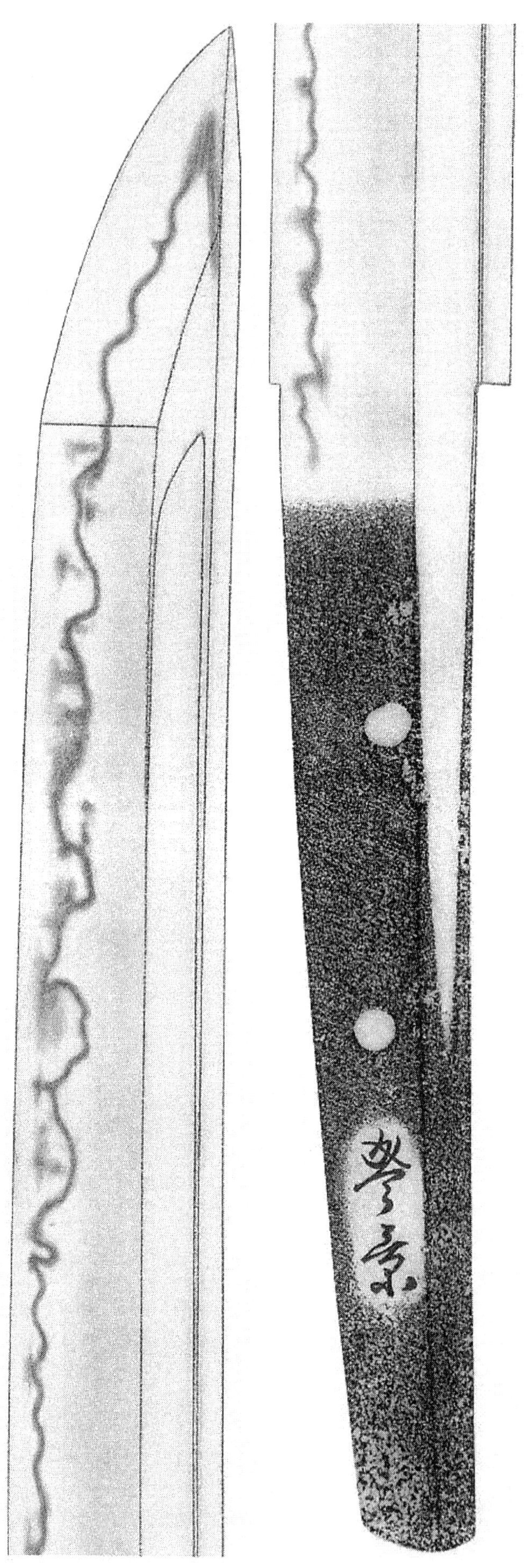

111.664 *katana*
kinzōgan-mei: Morikage (盛景)
nagasa 69,7 cm, *sori* 1,5 cm, *shinogi-zukuri*, *iori-mune*

ji: rather standing-out *itame* mixed with *mokume*, in addition *ji-nie*, *chikei*, *jifu* and a faint *midare-utsuri*
hamon: *ko-notare-chō* mixed with angular *ko-gunome*, *ko-gunome* and *ko-chōji*, the individual elements of the *ha* are rather small dimensioned, the *nioiguchi* in *nioi-deki* with *ko-nie* is rather subdued
bōshi: *midare-komi* with a pointed *kaeri* and fine *hakikake*
horimono: on both sides a *bōhi* which runs with *kake-nagashi* into the tang and which stops noticeably before the *yokote/ko-shinogi*

This blade bears a *kinzōgan* attribution to Ōmiya Morikage. The shape is an *ō-suriage* Enbun-Jōji-*sugata*, there is a faint *utsuri*, the *hamon* is a *notare*-based *midareba* and the *bōshi* is *midare-komi* with a pointed *kaeri*. Thus most did not oversee that this is a Sōden-Bizen work and bade on Morikage, Kanemitsu (兼光), Chōgi (長義) and other smiths known to work in that style.

At Kanemitsu, the *itame* would be more dense and despite it might stand out too, it would be nevertheless finer. Also his *jigane* would be bright and clear. The *kantei* blade shows a standing-out *itame* which is partially mixed with *jifu* of a different colour and some loose *ō-ahada*. This and the faint *utsuri* are typical characteristics of the Ōmiya school.

Compared to Kanemitsu, the valleys of the *notare* start somewhat higher at Morikage but are not as long. The *yakigashira* are more angular and sometimes pointed and the *nioiguchi* is more subdued. As we see all this on the *kantei* blade it should not be too hard to nail the bid down on Morikage.

At Chōgi, the *jigane* is strong and stands out too and he also applied a rather subdued *nioiguchi*, so from this point of view a bid on him is understandable. But his *notare* is larger dimensioned and shows more ups and downs. Also his *ha* is more *nie*-loaden and shows *nie*-based *hataraki* like *kinsuji* and *sunagashi*.

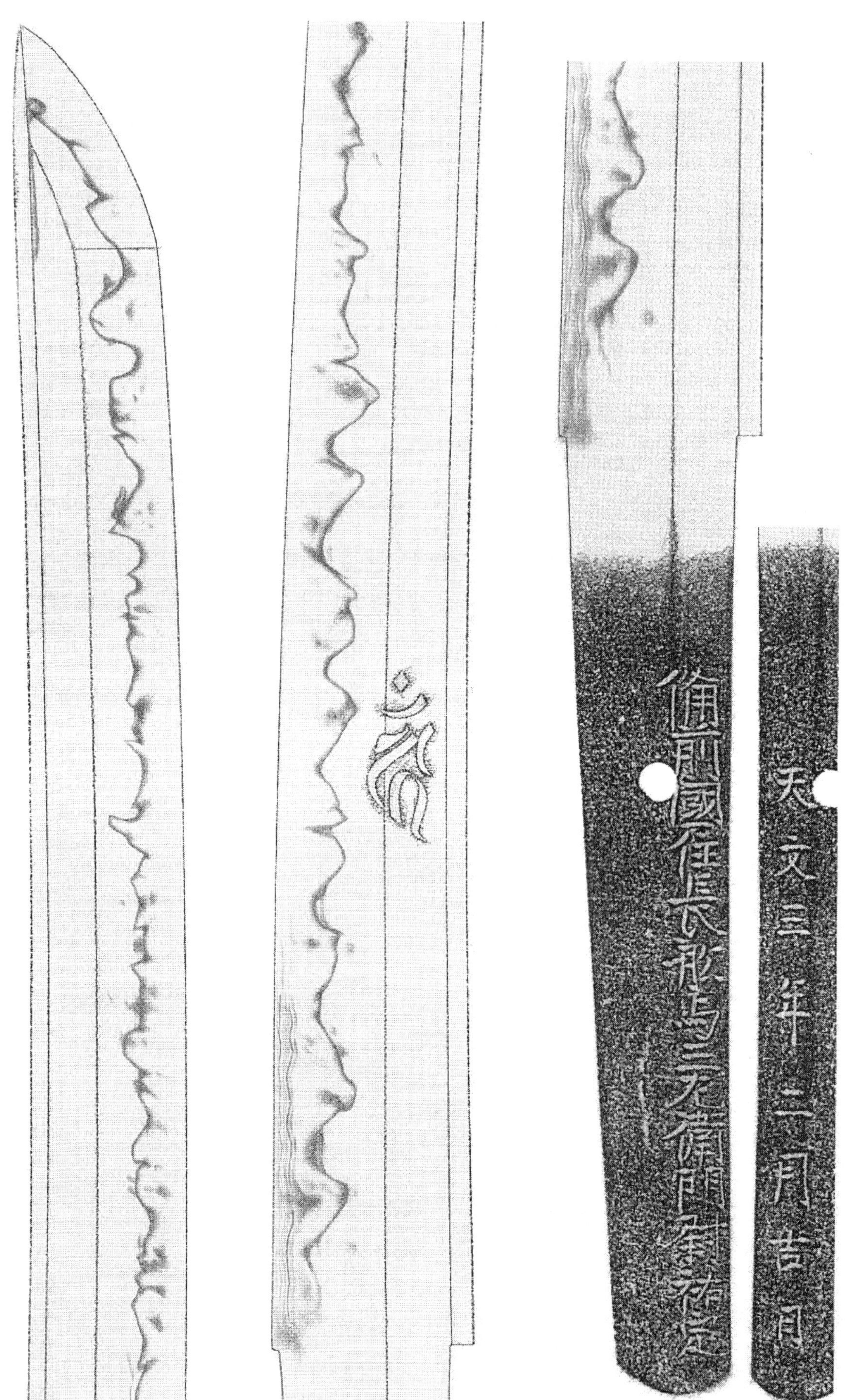
備前國住長船与三左衛門尉祐定
天文三年二月吉日

112.663k *katana*

mei: Bizen no Kuni-jū Osafune Yosōzaemon no Jō Sukesada (備前国住長船与三左衛門尉祐定)
Tenbun sannen nigatsu kichijitsu (天文三年二月吉日, „a lucky day in the second month Tenbun three [= 1534]")

nagasa 64,3 cm	*sori* 2,22 cm	*moto-haba* 3,0 cm	*saki-haba* 2,1 cm
moto-kasane 0,7 cm	*saki-kasane* 0,5 cm	*kissaki-nagasa* 3,7 cm	*nakago-nagasa* 15,9 cm

only very little *nakago-sori*

shinogi-zukuri, *iori-mune*, relative wide *mihaba*, no noticeable taper, the blade feels heavy, *sakizori*, *chū-kissaki*. The *jigane* is a dense *itame* with fine *ji-nie* and a *midare-utsuri*. The *hamon* and the *bōshi* can be seen on the *oshigata*. In addition, many *ashi*, *yō* and *nie* and some *kinsuji* and *sunagashi* appear. On both sides a *bonji* is engraved towards the base. The tang is *ubu*, has a bulbous *kurijiri*, *katte-sagari yasurime* and one *mekugi-ana*. There is a *naga-mei* on the *omote-side* towards the back of the tang and a date signature on the *ura* side which is chiselled in the same way but starts somewhat deeper.

This blade is a work of the 1st gen. Yosōzaemon no Jō Sukesada. It is with its *nagasa* of 64,3 cm rather small dimensioned, has a wide *mihaba*, no noticeable taper, a *sakizori* and ends in a *chū-kissaki*. That means it is a typical *katate-uchi* of the Muromachi-period Eishō (永正, 1504-1521) and Daiei eras (大永, 1521-1528).

Some few custom-order blades (*chūmon-uchi*) of the Sue-Bizen school show a standing-out *itame* but most of them are dense and finely forged and the steel is bright and clear like we know if from the old Osafune mainline. Also a *midare-utsuri* can appear but not necessarily always. The *hamon* of such *chūmon-uchi* is mostly a relative wide *koshi-no-hiraita gunome* mixed with *ko-gunome*, *ko-chōji*, *ko-togari*, *ashi*, *yō* and the typical *gunome* pairs. Other interpretations show a *notare*, *suguha* or sometimes even a *hitatsura*, but the *hamon* is always *nie*-loaden. A characteristic of these Sue-Bizen works is a hardening which ends abruptly after the *ha-machi*. The *bōshi* is in most cases a *midare-komi*.

Sue-Bizen-*mono* can show various *horimono* like *bōhi* with *soebi*, *bōhi* with *tsurebi*, *bonji*, *suken*, *suken* with *tsume* claw, *hōju-bō* (宝珠棒, a Buddhist ornament in the form of a pedestal with a chestnut-shaped ornament on top), *shin no kurikara*, *gyō no kurihara*, or the characters of deities like Hachiman-Daibosatsu or Kasuga-Daimyōjin. The *nakago* has mostly a bulbous *kurijiri* and *katte-sagari yasurime*. *Katana* are principally signed on the *sashi-omote* side towards the *nakago-mune* in a *naga-mei*. Most signed blades are accompanied by a identically chiselled date signature.

Some Sue-Bizen interpretations show a peculiar „double *gunome*" which runs continuous from tip to base and looke like „painted" and the *jiba* is excellent and flawless. Such works are mostly from the Sukesada mainline with its most outstanding master Yosōzaemon no Jō Sukesada. So most of the bids were *atari* on him but some went also for Katsumitsu (勝光), Tadamitsu (忠光) or Harumitsu (春光). All of them worked in a similar *deki* so it is sometimes hard to differentiate them. Accordingly, bids on these three were also counted as *atari*.

But Katsumitsu applied mostly a *koshi-no-hiraita gunome* mixed with *chōji* which is a hint more flamboyant than at Sukesada. He also added more *hataraki* like *ashi* and *yō*. Tadamitsu´s strong point was a *suguha* and Harumitsu forged a more standing-out *hada* and there are often *nie-kuzure* seen along his *habuchi*. And by the way, the average works of Harumitsu does not reach the quality of Sukesada.

Principally the length of a sword followed the needs of its wearer but we can also see several chronological and fashion trends. During the late Muromachi period, as mentioned around Eishō and Daiei, mostly short blades with a *nagasa* of around 60,6 to 63,6 cm with a *chū-kissaki* were in use. These swords were made for a single-handed use (*katate-uchi*). With the eras Kyōroku (享禄, 1528-1532) and Tenbun (天文, 1532-1555), the *nagasa* increased a bit and measures about 66,6 cm. Also the *mihaba* became wider and the *kissaki* somewhat longer. This development was continued throughout the subsequent Genki (元亀, 1570-1573) and Tenshō eras (天正, 1573-1592) and towards the end of the Muromachi period, *katana* blades measured around 69,7 cm, had an even wider *mihaba*, no noticeable taper, a *sakizori* and often an *ō-kissaki*. With the Keichō era (慶長, 1596-1615), the *sakizori* started to disappear again and the so-called „Keichō-*shintō-sugata*" made its arrival which bases basically on shortened Nanbokuchō blades with shallow *sori*.

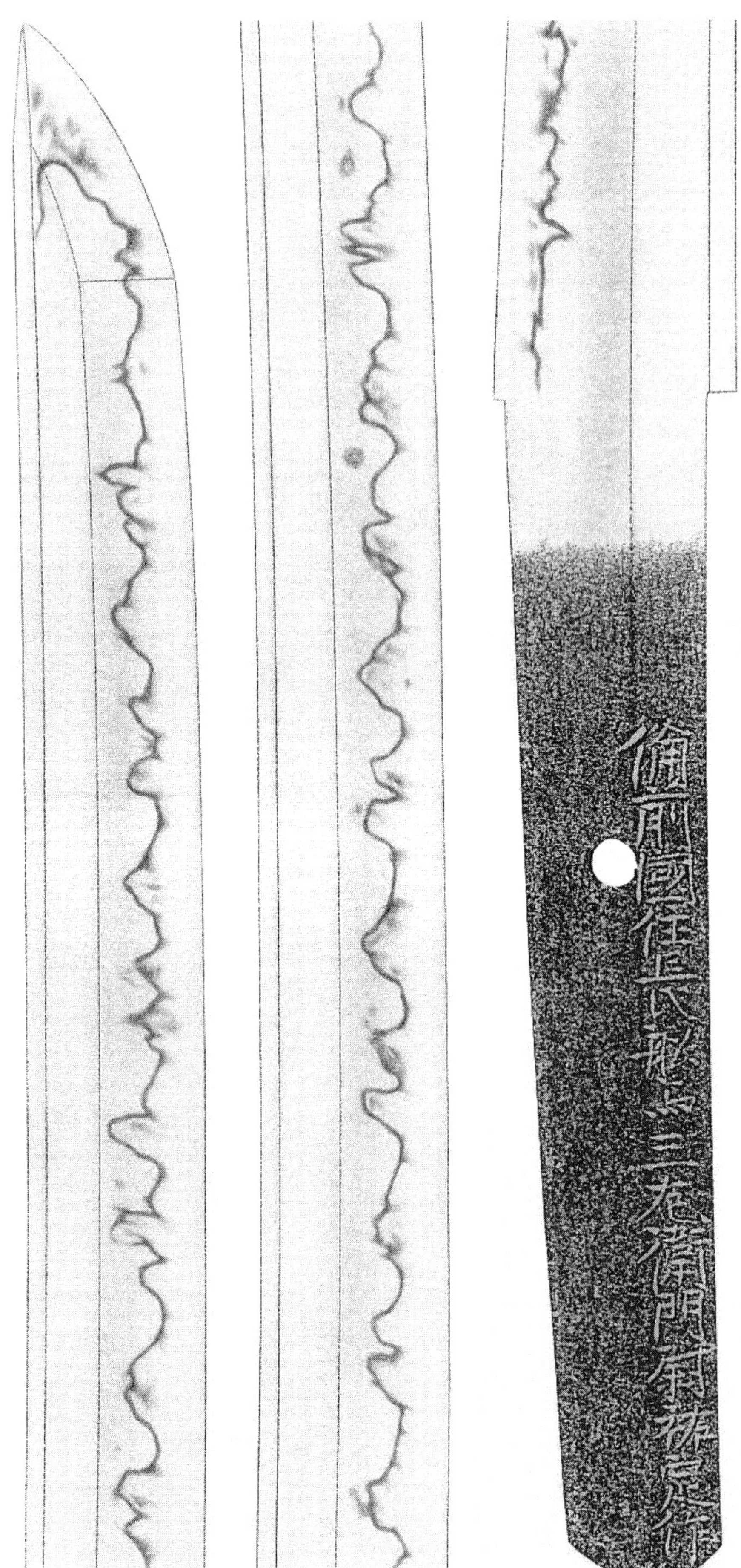
備前國住長船与三左衛門尉祐定作

113.653 *katana*

mei: Bizen no Kuni-jū Osafune Yosōzaemon no Jō Sukesada saku
(備前国住長船与三左衛門尉祐定作)
Tenbun yonnen nigatsu kichijitsu (天文二二年二月吉日, „a lucky day in the second month Tenbun four [= 1535]")

nagasa 70,3 cm, *sori* 2,4 cm, *shinogi-zukuri*, *iori-mune*

ji: very dense *ko-itame* with *ji-nie* and a faint *midare-utsuri*

hamon: *koshi-no-hiraita gunome* mixed with double *togariba* or *ko-gunome* in places, the *hamon* appears altogether as largely undulating *midareba*, in addition *ashi*, *yō*, *ko-nie* and small *tobiyaki* along the upper half appear

bōshi: widely hardened *midare-komi* with an *ō-maru-kaeri*

This is a *jūyō-bijutsuhin katana* by Yosōzaemon no Jō Sukesada. It has a pronounced *sakizori* and can be dated straightforward into the Muromachi period. The very fine and dense *ko-itame* in combination with a *ko-nie*-loaden *hamon* in *koshi-no-hiraita gunome-chō* whose elements are partially arranged to groups of two or three and the relative widely hardened *bōshi* are very typical for Sue-Bizen and so many bade directly on Sukesada. At the time the blade was made, rather shorter *uchigatana* for a single-handed use (*katate-uchi*) were in use but sometimes also noticeably longer pieces were made which are mostly carefully forged and signed with the individual first name of the smith. Because of the length, some went also for the earlier Ōei-Bizen school. Well, also the Ōei-Bizen smiths applied a *koshi-no-hiraita gunome* but in that case, the *nioiguchi* is not that compact but softer and mixed-in *chōji* with roundish *yakigashira* and also more roundish valleys appear. Also the *utsuri* would be clearer visible and darker, *chikei*-like elements would appeart in the *ji*.

Others bade also on the contemporary Katsumitsu (勝光), but at the latter, the *hamon* would tend more towards a densely arranged *chōji*. There were also some bids on the *shintō* smith Tatara Nagayuki (多々良長幸). Nagayuki made during his early years many Sue-Bizen-*utsushi* with a wide *mihaba* and a compact *nioiguchi* like it is seen on the *kantei* blade, but his *bōshi* is usually pointed.

Incidentally, there exists a *tantō* of Yosōzaemon no Jō Sukesada which is dated Tenbun six (1557) and bears the information „made at the age of 71". So he was 69 years old when he forged the *kantei* blade.

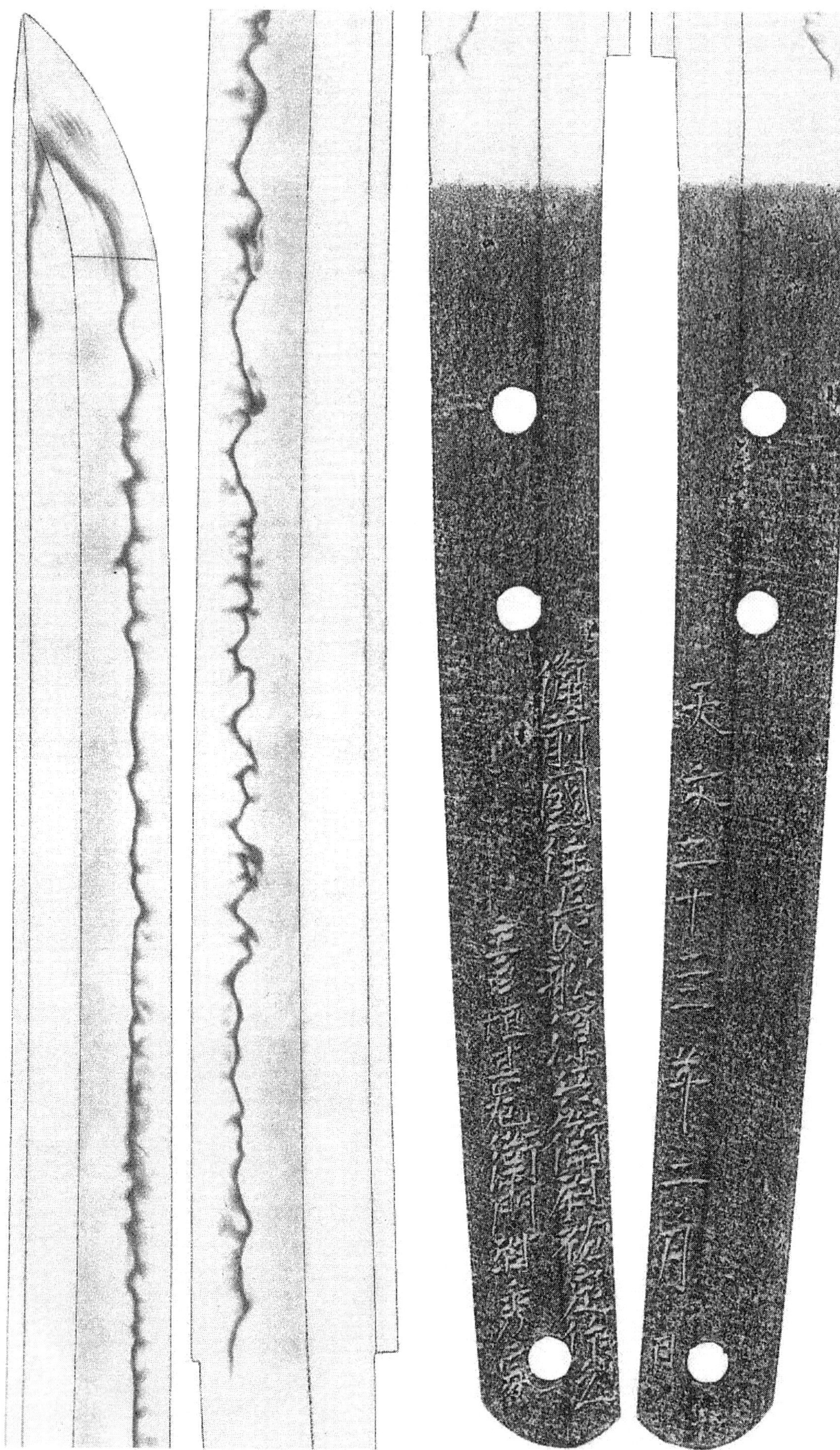

114.611 *katana*
mei: Bizen no Kuni-jū Osafune Genbei no Jō Sukesada kore o saku
(備前国住長船源兵衛尉祐定作之)
Shu Ugaki Jinzaemon no Jō Hideie (主宇垣甚左衛門尉秀家)
Tenbun nijūyonnen nigatsu-hi (天文二十二二年二月日, „a day in the second month of Tenbun 24 [1555]")
nagasa 70,60 cm, *sori* 1,82 cm, *shinogi-zukuri, iori-mune*

ji: very dense *ko-itame-hada*, fine *ji-nie* and a faint *midare-utsuri*
hamon: the lower half bases on *koshi-no-hiraita gunome* and is mixed with angular elements which appear as paired *midare* in places, the upper half bases on *suguha* mixed with *ko-gunome* and pointed *togari*, in addition *ashi*, *yō*, *ko-nie* and fine *sunagashi* appear
bōshi: widely hardened, shallow *notare* with a *ko-maru-kaeri* and *hakikake*, the *kaeri* runs back long

The blade is shortened, has a *sakizori*, a faint *midare-utsuri* and a very dense and finely forged *kitae*. This and the widely hardened *bōshi* with its long *kaeri* and the *nioi*-based *nioiguchi* with *ko-nie* speaks for so-called „*Sue-mono*" (末物), i.e. Sue-*kotō*, and especially for Sue-Bizen.

The blade shows along its lower half a *hamon* which is based on *koshi-no-hiraita*, whereas the *koshi-no-hiraita* elements appear as *midare* pairs in places and result in a *yakiba* with noticeable ups and downs. The upper half shows a *suguha-chō* which is mixed with *ko-gunome* and *togari*, that means both halves are noticeably different. Such a *deki* is sometimes seen on Sue-Bizen works but we also know interpretations from that school which are exactly the other way round, i.e. along the lower half a *suguha-chō* and on the upper half a *midareba*. Furthermore, there are even some blades with a mixed *hamon* interpretation with centrally a *suguha-chō* and towards the tip and base a *midareba*.

The strong point of this smith Genbei no Jō Sukesada (源兵衛尉祐定) is a *hiro-suguha* and he left us many masterworks in that interpretation. This blade is of special interest because with its date of Tenbun 24, it is one of his earlier works. His main artistic period was namely towards the end of the Muromachi period, around Eiroku (永禄, 1558-1570), Genki (元亀, 1570-1573) and Tenshō (天正, 1573-1592). Later, a more stout shape with wide *mihaba* and elongated *chū-kissaki* was in fashion. The *kantei* blade does not show such a *sugata* of course and so there were no *atari* bids on Genbei no Jō Sukesada what is understandable. But most bade as expected and fortunately on Sue-Bizen.

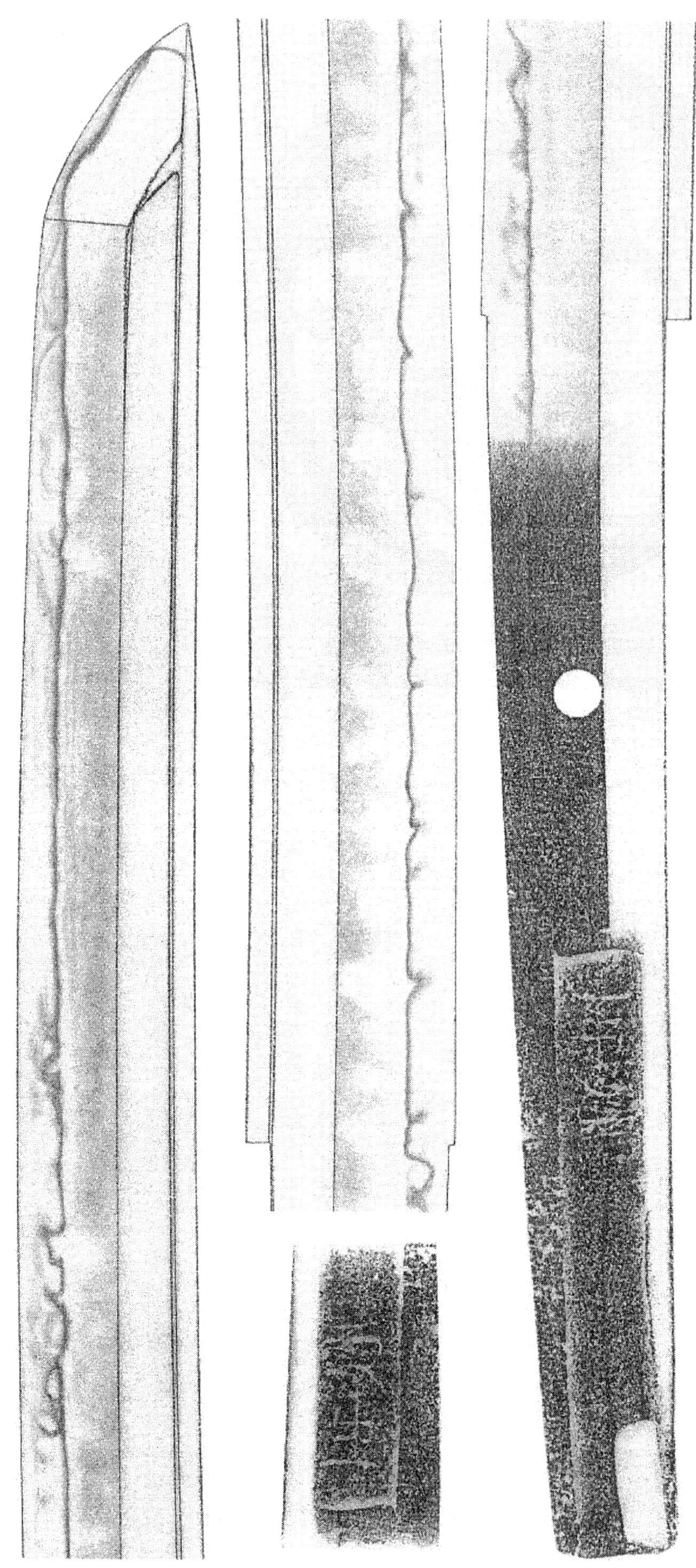

115.616 *katana*
orikaeshi-mei: Unshō (雲生)
nagasa 69,1 cm, *sori* 2,4 cm, *shinogi-zukuri*, *iori-mune*

ji: relative dense *ko-itame-hada* partially mixed with *itame* and *mokume*, in addition plentiful of fine *jinie* and a *jifu-utsuri* wich appears as linear layers in places, the steel is blackish
hamon: based on *hiro-suguha* mixed with angular *gunome* and *ko-gunome*, the *midareba* is a little slanting and shows partial wedge-shaped interruptions (*kage no togariba*, 陰の尖り刃, i.e. „negative *togariba*"), in addition *ashi*, *saka-ashi*, conspicious *yō* and some *kinsuji* and *sunagashi* appear, the *nioiguchi* is compact and rather subdued
bōshi: *notare-komi* with some *hakikake* and a short *ō-maru-kaeri*
horimono: on both sides a *bōhi* which runs with *kake-nagashi* into the tang

This *katana* has a rather uniform *toriizori* but the blade length was originally around 84 cm, what would make it reconstructed to its original form a slender *tachi*, one of Unshō´s characteristics by the way. The *kitae* is relative densely forged and shows a conspicious *utsuri* with dark *antai* areas which look like fingerprints. The steel has a blackish colour. The *hamon* bases on *hiro-suguha* and shows mixed-in angular *gunome* and *ko-gunome* elements. Also wedge-shaped *kage no togariba* interrupt the *suguha* and there are *ashi*, *saka-ashi*, conspicious *yō*, *nie* and *sunagashi*. The *nioiguchi* is rather compact. The *bōshi* is *ō-maru* with a very short *kaeri*. All these characteristics are typical for the so-called „Un group" (雲類).

There exist blades by Unshō which have a narrow *yakiba* and rather unobtrusive *hataraki* but also some like the *kantei* blade which come rather close to the style of Unji (雲次). Accordingly, many bade for Unji but such bids were counted as *atari* too.

But some went also for Ko-Bizen or Osafune. In the case of Ko-Bizen, there would be a *ko-kissaki* and the *sugata* would appear a hint more slender towards the tip. Slanting *hamon* interpretations are known from Yukihide (行秀) but only seen at very vew smiths from this school. Some reckoned the re-shaped *bōshi* as *sansaku-bōshi* and went for Nagamitsu (長光), but the *utsuri* and the *nie* are clearly too different from his workmanship. (Note: A narrow *bōshi* is by no means uncommon among smiths of the Un group.)

Because of the slanting elements there were bids on Chikakage (近景) and Motoshige (元重), but here too, the *utsuri* and the *yō* are too different from their style. Also in the case of Chikakage, the *jihada* would stand out more and the *hamon* would appear as aa slanted *midareba*. In the case of Motoshige, some *masame* and a pointed *bōshi* would be seen.

Some went even for the Rai school because they were leaded astray by the *utsuri* and thought it might be a *nie-utsuri*, but the *jiba* would be much more brighter and clearer at Rai. Well, the *utsuri* appears as parallel lines in some isolated areas and so some thought they were facing a *dan-utsuri* of the late Kamakura-period Aoe school. This is understandable but Aoe works of that time show a bright *nioiguchi*, a pointed *bōshi* and a different *sugata*.

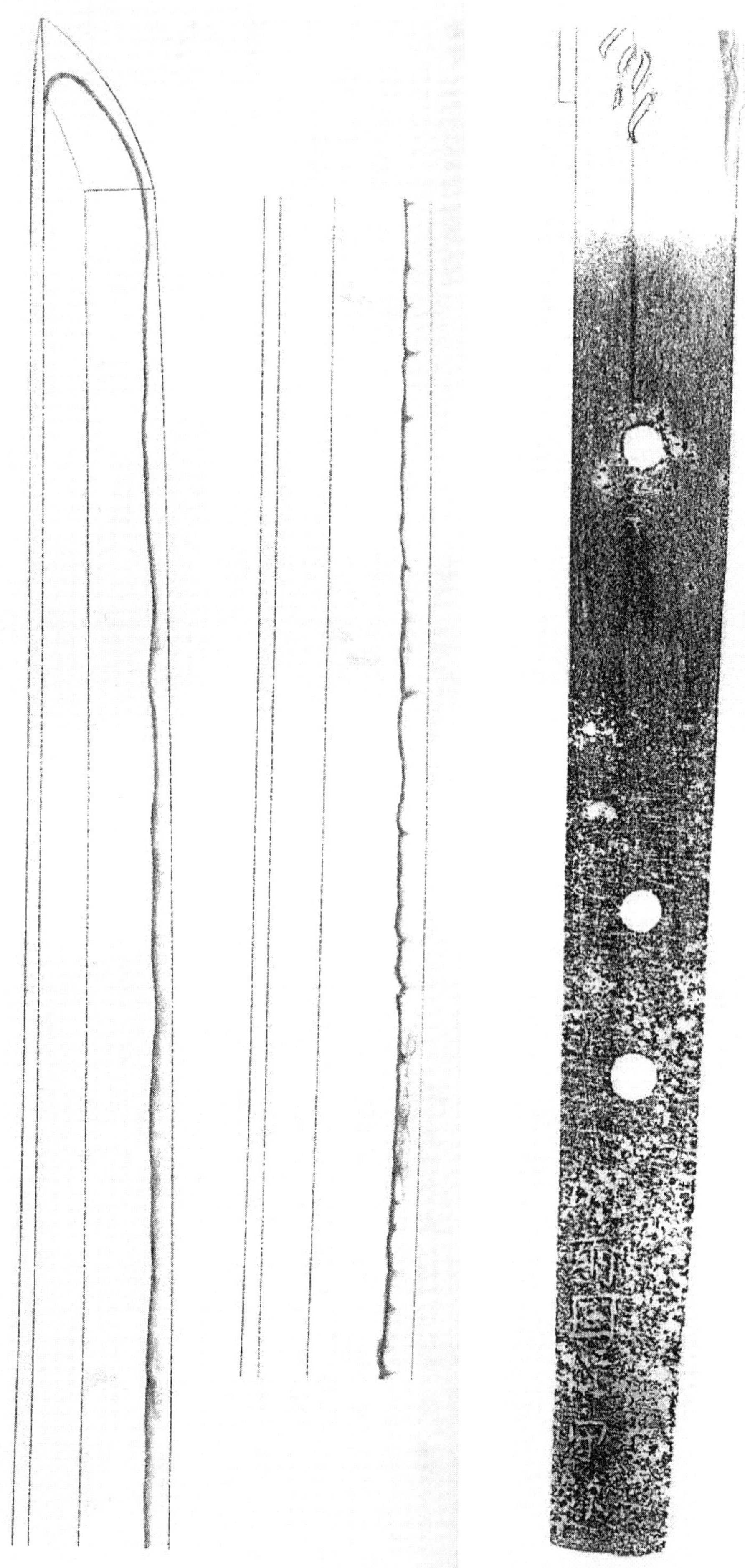

116.601 *tachi*
mei: Bizen no Kuni-jū Moritsugu (備前国住守次)
nagasa 71,45 cm, *sori* 1,21 cm, *shinogi-zukuri, iori-mune*

ji: very dense and slightly standing-out *ko-itame-hada*, fine *ji-nie*, clearly visible *jifu*-like *utsuri*
hamon: based on *suguha* with *ko-ashi*, some *saka-ashi* and a few *Kyō-saka-ashi*, compact *nioiguchi* with *ko-nie* and some *kinsuji*
bōshi: *sugu* with a *maru-kaeri*
horimono: on the *sashi-omote* a *bonji* is engraved towards the base and a *koshi-bi* with *kaku-dome* on the *ura* side

Because of the peculiar chiselling of the signature, especially the surrounding angular radical of the character for „Kuni", Bizen Moritsugu can be attributed to the Un group (雲). There are only three blades extant by Moritsugu: Besides of this *jūyō-tōken* a *tokubetsu-jūyō-tōken* and a *jūyō-bijutsuhin*. Old sword documents date him around Ryakuō (1338-1342) but Honma Junji dates him in his „*Kunzan-hibishō*" (薫山日々抄) somewhat earlier.

This *tachi* has a relative slender *mihaba* and had even before the *suriage* a shallow *sori*. The *kitae* is a well, fine and densely forged *ko-itame*. The *suguha*-based *hamon* in *ko-nie-deki* shows *ko-ashi* and some *Kyō-saka-ashi*. And the roundish *kaeri* of the *bōshi* reminds of Yamashiro and especially of Rai Kunitoshi (来国俊) and Rai Kunimitsu (来国光).

So far, a bid on Rai would be acceptable but when we take a closer look we see some differences in the *ji*. There is namely a dark, *jifu*-like *utsuri* which runs close to the *shinogi*. This brings us namely away from Yamashiro and to Bizen. When we now take into consideration the *ō-maru-kaeri* and *sugu-bōshi* and the arrangement of the *hamon* which tends due to the *ashi* to a *midare* in the lower half and contrary to that to a *suguha-chō* in the upper half, we recognize that there are similar interpretations by Unshō (雲生) and Unji (雲次). As mentioned, the fine and dense *kitae* looks like Yamashiro at a glance but this is a characteristic of Unshō and Unji too. It is namely said that both went to Kyōto for a while and forged there each a blade for emperor Godaigo.

And because of the similar workmanship, also bids on Unji were counted as *atari* because an attribution to a certain smith like Moritsugu is next to impossible here without revealing the signature. But in general there were only very vew bids on Unshō and even fewer on Unji.

Sâshû

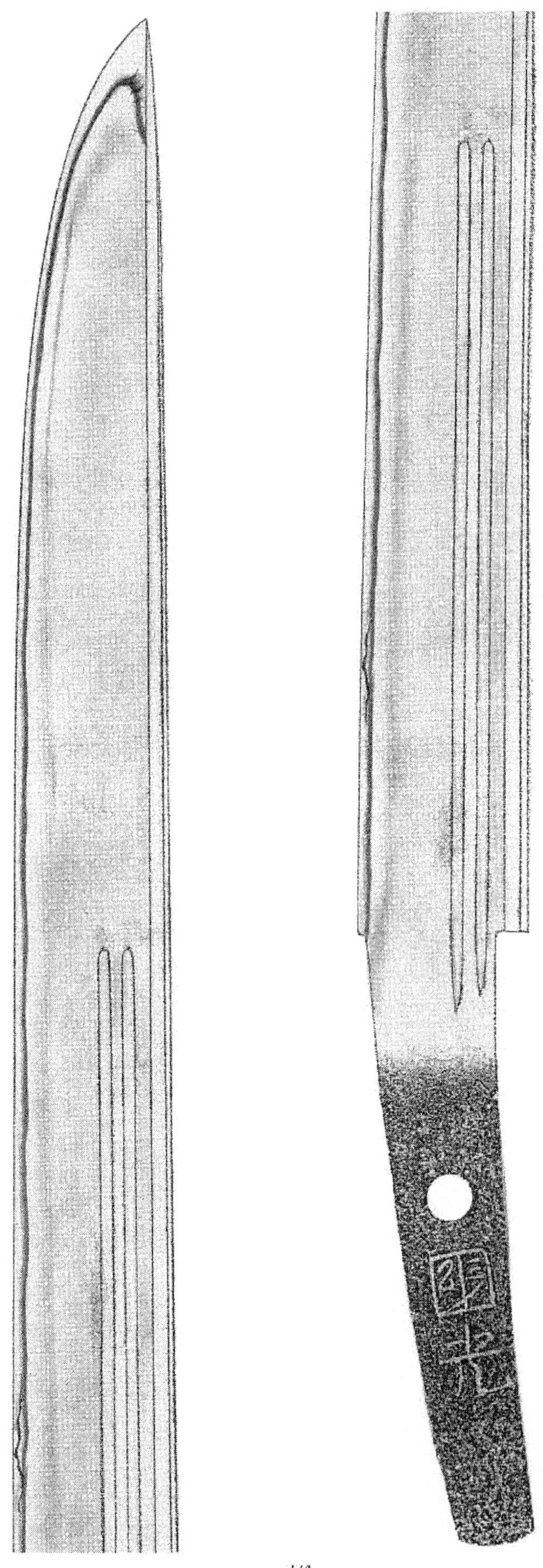

117.667 *tantō*
mei: Kunimitsu (国光) [Shintōgo]
nagasa 24,8 cm, only a little *sori*, *hira-zukuri*, *mitsu-mune*

ji: *itame* mixed with *mokume* which appears also as *ayasugi* towards the *ha*, the *kitae* is densely forged but stands also out, plentiful of *ji-nie*, many *chikei* and a fine *bō-utsuri*, the latter tends to a kind of *nijūba* along the *monouchi*
hamon: *hoso-suguha* with a relative compact and bright *nioiguchi*, much *ko-nie* and some *kinsuji* along the base
bōshi: *sugu* with a *ko-maru-kaeri* and fine *hakikake* towards the tip, there are also small *kinsuji* seen on the *omote* side
horimono: on both sides *gomabashi* which run with *kake-nagashi* into the tang

As Shintōgo Kunimitsu was active during the late Kamakura period, his *tantō* show principally a „standard" *tantō-sugata* with a normal length and *uchizori*, although this blade has a little *sori*. Such a curvature is rare for *tantō* of that time but nevertheless sometimes seen on works of Awataguchi Kuniyoshi (粟田口国吉), Awataguchi Yoshimitsu (粟田口吉光), Rai Kunitoshi (来国俊), Sōshū Yukimitsu (行光) and Shintōgo Kunihiro (新藤五 国広). That means the *kantei* blade is a precious reference for the fact that there were also *tantō* with a slight *sori* made during the late Kamakura period. From the point of view of a sword polisher, it is always tried to save as much of the original *hamon* as possible and therefore material is also removed from the *mune* side when it comes to damages along the *fukura* or *kissaki* respectively. That means an *uchizori* can also emerge from a polishing of that area when a *tantō* hat originally maybe only a little *sori* or no *sori* at all. So this possibility should also always be kept in mind when examining early *tantō*.

Also special on this *tantō* is the narrow *bō-utsuri* arranged towards the *ha* which appears as a kind of *nijūba* at the *monouchi* area. This peculiarity was already mentioned in the „*Kokon-mei-zukushi*" (古今銘尽) as „*utsuri* in the shape of spider threads". That means, it was well-known as characteristic of Shintōgo Kunimitsu in early times. Another representative piece with that characteristic is the *jūyō-bunkazai tantō* from the Municipal Museum Tsuchiura (土浦市).

When you look at the *kantei* blade in total then you see that the *itame* tends a little to *ayasugi*. Also many *chikei* appear and the steel is bright and clear. The *hamon* is a *hoso-suguha* with a bright *nioiguchi*, plentiful of *ko-nie* and some *kinsuji*. The *bōshi* also shows some *kinsuji* and so we have all major characteristics of Shintōgo Kunimitsu present.

Most bids were on Awataguchi-*mono* whereas at Kuniyoshi, the *ko-itame* would be a hint denser and would appear as *nashiji-hada*. At Yoshimitsu, some *ko-gunome* would appear around the *ha-machi* and the *yakiba* narrows down along the *monouchi*.

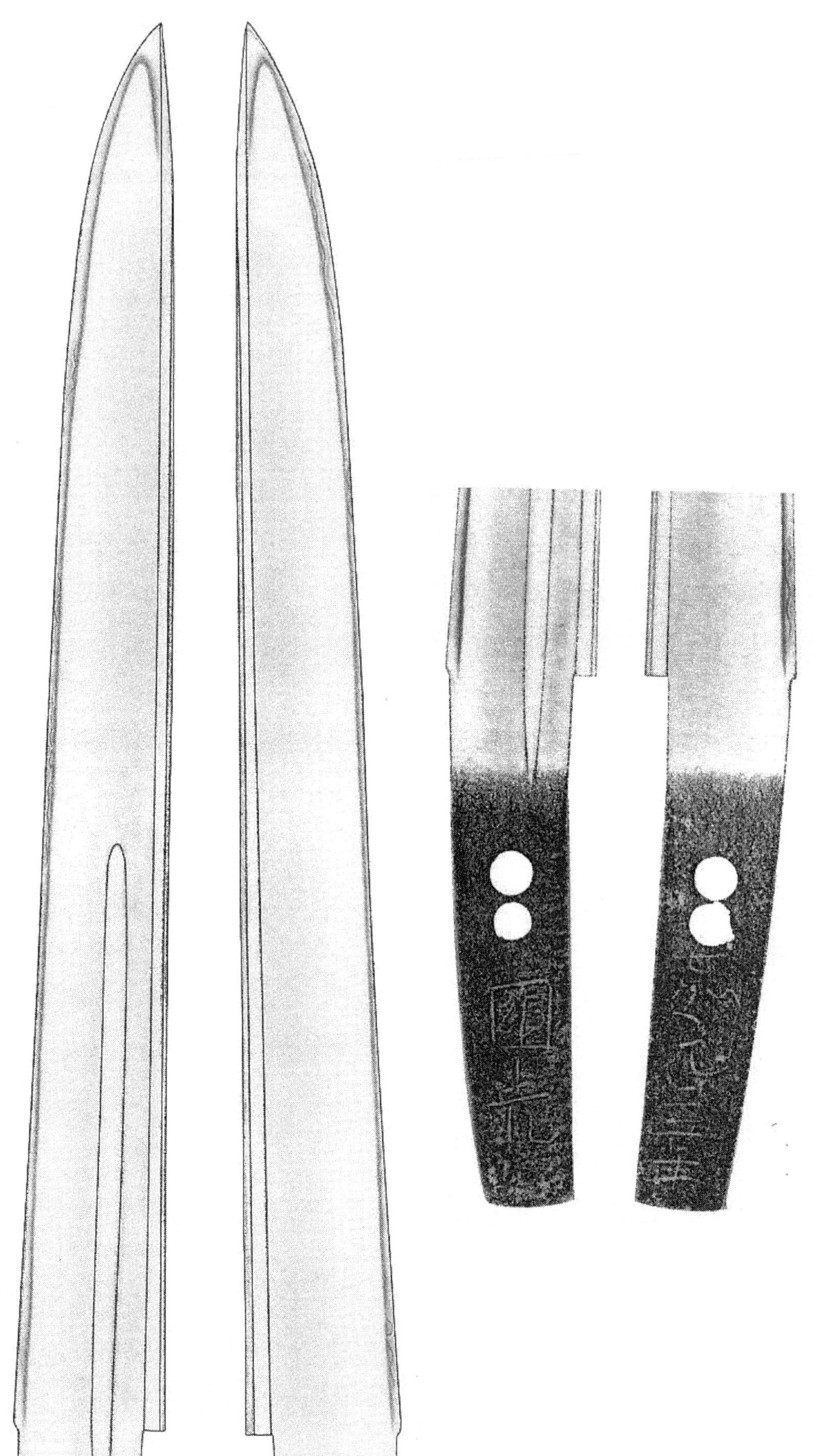

118.606k *tantō*
mei: Kunimitsu (国光) (Shintōgo, 新藤五)
Kagen yonnen (嘉元二二年, 1306)
nagasa 21,4 cm *uchi-zori*
moto-haba 2,1 cm *moto-kasane* 0,6 cm
nakago-nagasa 8,2 cm *nakago-sori* 0,2 cm

hira-zukuri, *mitsu-mune*, relative small blade, normal *mihaba* and *kasane*, *uchizori*, the *mitsu-mune* has a rather wide top surface, so altogether we have an elegant *tantō-sugata*. The *jigane* is a very dense *ko-itame* with plentiful of *ji-nie*, many *chikei* and a clearly visible *nie-utsuri*. The *hamon* and the *bōshi* can be seen on the *oshigata*. The *ha* is full of brightly sparkling *nie* and the *nioiguchi* is bright and clear too and shows all over conspicious *kinsuji* and *sunagashi*. There is a *koshi-bi* on the *omote* side which runs with *kake-nagashi* into the tang. The *nakago* is almost *ubu* (it has only a slightly shortened tip), has a *kurijiri*, *katte-sagari yasurime* and two *mekugi-ana*. The *sashi-omote* side bears centrally below the original *mekugi-ana* a *niji-mei*. A date signature is added on the same position on the *ura* side but datings of that smith are very rare. The characters of the *niji-mei* are chiselled in the peculiar manner of that smith.

The *kantei* blade is rather small but *mihaba* and *kasane* are normal. This and the *uchizori* results in an elegant *sugata* which dates the piece to the late Kamakura period. A *mitsu-mune* of that kind with a wide top surface was mostly applied by Shintōgo Kunimitsu, Masamune (正宗), Sadamune (貞宗), Hiromitsu (広光), Akihiro (秋広) and other Sōshū smiths.

When it comes to the classification of Shintōgo´s workmanship we read comments like „based on the Awataguchi style but more pronounced *jigane* by adding conspiciously interwoven *chikei* and *kinsuji*.“ Well, his *jigane* is a dense *ko-itame* with plentiful of *ji-nie* and many *chikei* and such an appearance can be described as „pronounced“, „strong“ or „powerful“. And such a strong *jigane* is just characteristical for the Sōshū tradition.

Not mentioned in the description was that Shintōgo´s *jigane* shows also large wavy *nagare* within the *ko-itame* which appear as *ayasugi*-like pattern. This characteristical feature is called „*okina no hige*“ (lit. „beard of an old man“). But it has also to be mentioned that there appear especially strong *nie* in the *bōshi* area. They often accumulate to linear elements which reach into the *ji*. In earlier times, this characteristic was just described as „many *kinsuji* in the *ha*“ and so one has to pay attention to the subtleties of descriptions.

There is a *nie-utsuri* on Shintōgo´s *tantō* which appears towards the *mune*. Somewhat below, i.e. towards the *ha*, sometimes also one or two thin linear *utsuri* elements are seen which run almost parallel to the *suguha* and remind of a *dan-utsuri* of the Aoe school.

There is a *jūyō-bijutsuhin tantō* of Shintōgo Kunimitsu, the *meibutsu* „*Midare-Shintōgo*“, which shows as the name suggests a *midareba* which bases on *notare* mixed with *gunome*. This *tantō* is considered as precursor of the *midareba* of subsequent Sōshū smiths like Yukimitsu (行光) and Masamune. Usually he applied a *chū-suguha*, *hoso-suguha* or like here blade an *ito-suguha*. But some *suguha* are wide and even tend a bit towards a *hiro-suguha*. In any case, brightly sparkling and thick *nie* appear within the *ha* and all over the bright and clear *nioiguchi* peculiar *kinsuji* and *sunagashi* are flashing.

The *kantei* blade has no *yakikomi* at the *machi* area but usually we see such a *hamon* protrusion at Shintōgo´s *tantō*. We also know many blades where this characteristic *yakikomi* appears on only one side. The *bōshi* is mostly *sugu* and has a *ko-maru-kaeri*. *Nie*-loaden works show also strong *hakikake* within the *bōshi*.

It has to be mentioned that Shintōgo Kunimitsu´s *tantō* can be dated on the basis of their *sugata* and workmanship clearly into the late Kamakura period. They show mostly the conspicious strong *jiba* of the Sōshū tradition but in some cases, also a more calm and unobtrusive *deki* can be seen. The *kantei* blade is such a case. But this *deki* is original and does not go back to repeated polishing.

On *tantō* of Shintōgo we find *horimono* like *bonji*, *suken*, *gomabashi*, *koshi-bi* and *katana-hi* but they are never elaborate and fancy. The tip of the tang of *tantō* is a *kurijiri* and the *yasurime* are *katte-sagari*. Some rare blades bear a *naga-mei* and a date signature, like for example „Kamakura-jūnin Shintōgo Kunimitsu saku Einin gannen jūgatsu-sannichi" (鎌倉住人新藤五国光・永仁元年十月三日, „third day of the tenth month Einin one [1293]"). But mostly just a *niji-mei* is chiselled on the *sashi-omote* side centrally below the *mekugi-ana*.

Incidentally, Kunimitsu signed the left part of the character for „Kuni" (國) in the form of a „Z" and the upper part of the character for „Mitsu" similar to the grass-script variant (ⅼ"ㇹ) of the character for „north" (北, jap. *kita*). These two peculiarities were summarized in olden times to the saying: „*saiji-kitakanmuri*", which can be translated as „left side [of the character „Kuni"] different and ´north´ as top radical [of the character „Mitsu"]". A hint was given regarding these peculiarities in the description of the *kantei*.

Most participants got all characteristics right and bade *atari* on Shintōgo Kunimitsu.

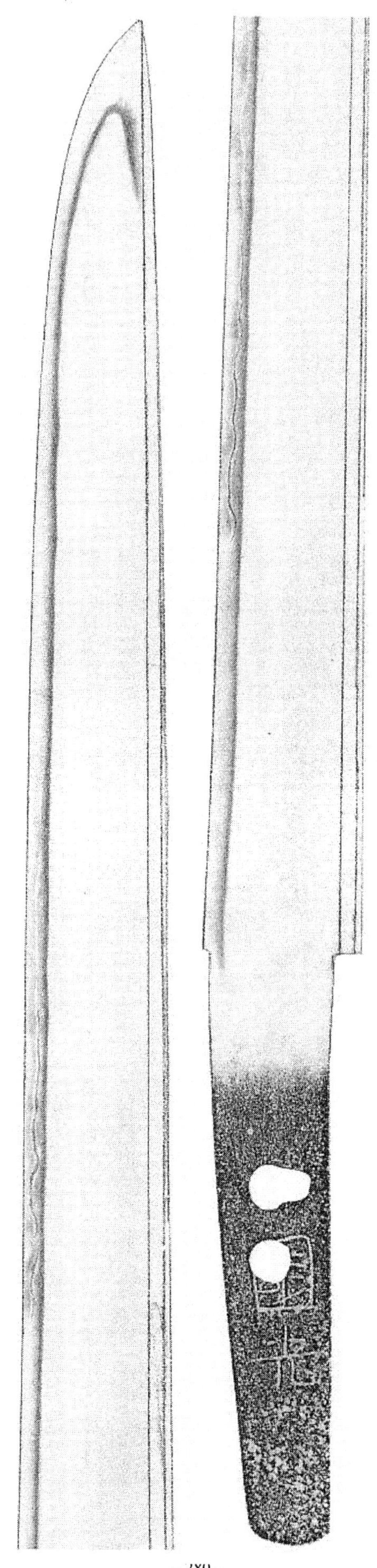

119.594 *tantō*
mei: Kunimitsu (国光) [Shintōgo]
nagasa 23,9 cm, *uchizori*, *hira-zukuri*, *mitsu-mune*

ji: *itame* mixed with *mokume*, partially some *nagare*, *jifu*, plentiful of *ji-nie*, many *chikei* and a *nie-utsuri*
hamon: *suguha* with some *ko-ashi* and *yō*, in addition long *kinsuji*, the *nioiguchi* is rather wide and shows *ko-nie*, the *ha* is very *nie*-loaden in places
bōshi: *sugu* with a *ko-maru-kaeri*

Shintōgo Kunimitsu was with Awataguchi Yoshimitsu (粟田口吉光) and Rai Kunitoshi (来国俊) one of the three great *tantō* masters of the Kamakura period. *Tantō* from that time measure around 24 cm, are slender, have a harmonic *kasane* (that means neither conspiciously thick or thin) and *uchizori*. This *tantō* fits well into this category and most went with their first bid straightforward on one of the mentioned three smiths.

But on this blade, the *ha-nie* are rather unobtrusive in comparison to most of the other Shintōgo-*tantō*. And because also another characteristical feature of that smith does not occur, i.e. the *nie* in the *bōshi* which run into the *ji*, many bids were accordingly on Rai Kunitoshi. But the *kitae* must not be overlooked. The *ji* is full of *ji-nie* and many *chikei* appear which are interwoven with the *itame* structure. The result is a strong *jigane* which is so typical for Shintōgo. Also the partially mixed-in *ayasugi* elements are a peculiarity of that smith. At a work of Yoshimitsu, we would expect the Awataguchi-typical *nashiji-hada* and at Rai, not such a strong *jigane*. Incidentally, the conspicious *kinsuji* on that *tantō* speak also clearly for Shintōgo Kunimitsu.

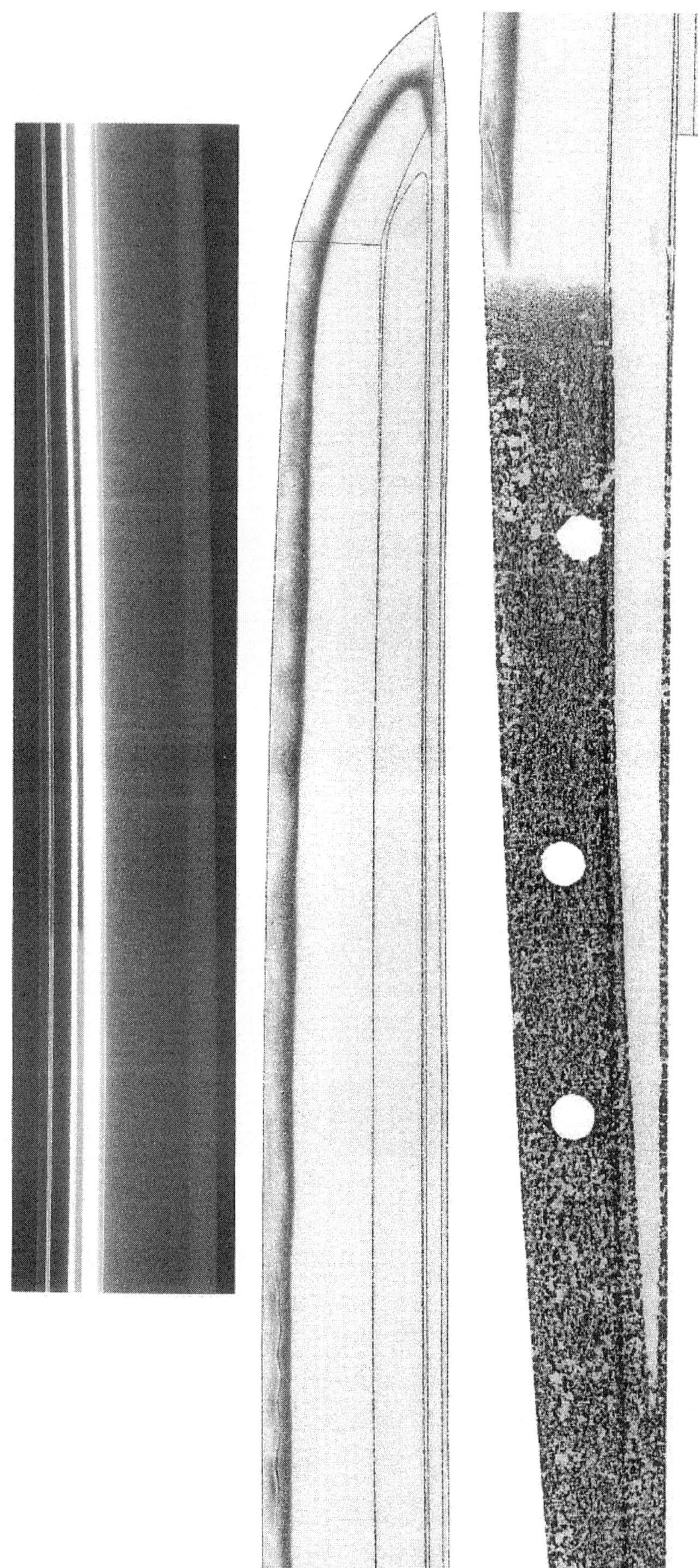

120.645 *katana*
mumei: Yukimitsu (行光)
nagasa 69,5 cm, *sori* 1,5 cm, *shinogi-zukuri*, *mitsu-mune*

ji: *ko-itame* mixed with *itame*, on the *omote* side some *nagare*, in addition plentiful of *ji-nie* and many *chikei*
hamon: *chū-suguha-chō* mixed with *ko-gunome* and *kuichigai-ba*, also many *ashi*, thick *nioi*, many thick *nie* and *kinsuji*, the *nioiguchi* is bright and clear
bōshi: *sugu* with a *ko-maru-kaeri* and some *hakikake*
horimono: on both sides a *bōhi* which runs with *kake-nagashi* into the tang

This is a blade by Sōshū Yukimitsu which got *tokubetsu-jūyō* papers at the first *tokubetsu-jūyō shinsa*. It has no *funbari* at the base and therefore we can assume that it is *ō-suriage*. But when we reconstruct the original shape with the unobtrusive *sori* along the upper area, we arrive at a *tachi-sugata* of the late Kamakura period. When you look at the *jigane* you see plentiful of *ji-nie* and vivid long *chikei* of different size and thickness. Such a *jigane* is circumscribed as „strong", „prominent" or „powerful". The *hamon* looks at a glance like a simple and calm *chū-suguha-chō* which is mixed with some *ko-gunome* and smaller *midare* elements. But when you take a closer look you see many thick *ha-nie*, rougher *nie* which appear as *ara-nie* along the middle section, and *kinsuji*, that means quite a *nie*-loaden *deki*. This rules out contemporary Bizen and Mino works. And as also *shinshintō* and *shintō* can be ruled out because of the *ō-suriage*, there were many bids on Rai or on Tegai, Taima and other Yamato-*mono*.

In the case of the Rai school, the *jigane* would not be that strong but appear as finer *ko-itame*. Also we would expect a clearly visible *nie-utsuri*. At Yamato the *nie* are prominent too but the *shinogi-ji* would be wider, the *shinogi* higher and the *bōshi* different. Also there would be more *nagare* and besides of *sunagashi* and *kinsuji* more horizontal *hataraki* like *hotsure*, *uchinoke* or *nijūba* and the like. So only Sōshū remains. Yukimitsu also applied a *midareba* or *hitatsura* but compared to the other great Sōshū masters like Masamune (正宗), Sadamune (貞宗), Norishige (則重) or the „Ten Students of Masamune", he hardened relative often a calm and slightly undulating *suguha*. So this would be the keypoint to nail down the smith in the end. About half of the participants got that right and bade at least at the third round *atari* on Yukimitsu. That means the *kantei* was a rather difficult one.

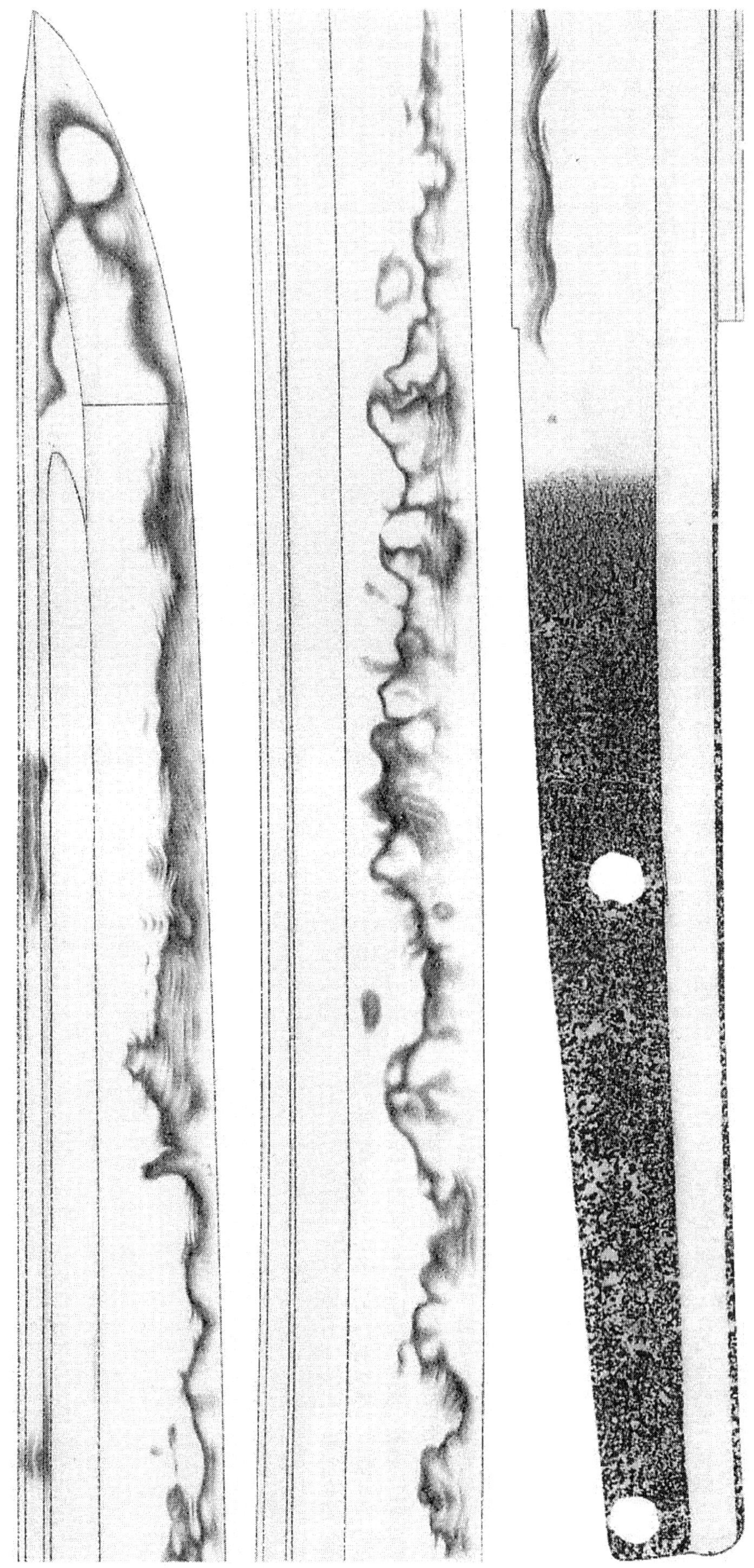

121.637 *katana*
mumei: Den Masamune (伝正宗) (*meibutsu*: Musashi-Masamune, 武蔵正宗)
nagasa 73,9 cm, *sori* 1,2 cm, *shinogi-zukuri*, *mitsu-mune*

ji: *itame* mixed with *mokume* which stands rather out all over the blade, *jifu* in places, plentiful of *ji-nie* and many *chikei*
hamon: *ko-notare* with *gunome*, *togariba*, *yahazu* and angular elements, the *yakiba* goes down deeply, especially on the *sashi-omote* side, but the *ura* side shows a rather large dimensioned and vivid *midareba* with a wider *yakiba*, in addition, *ashi*, *yō*, thick *nie*, *kinsuji*, *sunagashi*, *tobiyaki*, *yubashiri* and some *muneyaki* appear, the *nioiguchi* is wide
bōshi: *midare-komi* with a round *kaeri*, on the *sashi-ura* the *bōshi* and the *kaeri* form a big round isolated area of unhardened *ji* (see *oshigata*)
horimono: on both sides a *bōhi* whose tip ends noticeably before the *yokote*

The „*Kyōhō-meibutsu-chō*" lists this blade under the nickname „Musashi-Masamune". Today it is designated as *jūyō-bijutsuhin*. Many think of Masamune as the greatest swordsmith in Japanese history and his continuation and further development of the workmanship of Kunimitsu (国光) and Yukimitsu (行光) to a *nie-deki*-based *hamon* resulted in the foundation of the Sōshū tradition. He made a huge contribution in the recognition of the Japanese sword as work of art and not only the sword world respected him as great genius. He was primarily active during the late Kamakura period. The blade shown here has a wide *mihaba*, not much taper, an elongated *kissaki*, and a *hi* which ends noticeably before the *yokote*. As a result, many thought this would be a blade of the middle Nanbokuchō period.

Well, Masamune´s style bases in general on a great varity of *hataraki* but not every blade shows all *hataraki* like *sunagashi*, *kinsuji*, *niesuji*, *tobiyaki* or *yubashiri*. Also *nie* and *nioi* can form a harmonious whole or can vary deliberately in size, intensity and accentuation. The same applies to the *nioiguchi*. So studying a Masamune is like looking at an ink painting which shows alternatingly faster and slower, thinner and thicker applied brush strokes. The „*Genki-gannen tōken-mekiki-sho*" (元亀元年刀剣目利書), „*Kokon-mei-zukushi*" (古今銘尽) and other old sword documents describe his *bōshi* as „in conclusion it can be said that there appears a round isolated area in the *yakiba* of the *bōshi*". This peculiarity is well seen on the *kantei* blade.

Masamune´s *tantō* – regardless if they are signed or unsigned – have mostly a normal and onobtrusive *sugata* (also called „*in no tsukuri*", 陰の造り, lit. „introverted shape"). An exception are the three oversized *kokuhō* „Hōchō-Masamune" (包丁正宗). They have a very broad *mihaba*, a feature which is called „*yō no tsukuri*" (陽の造り, lit. „extroverted shape"). But these oversized blades have to be seen as precursor of the following period where noticeably larger shapes become the rule. Incidentally, the *meibutsu* „Ikeda-Masamune" (池田正宗, *jūyō-bunkazai*) has a similar shape like the *kantei* blade.

The „*Kyōhō-meibutsu-chō*" says that the nickname of this blade goes back to the fact that it was once owned by Miyamoto Musashi (宮本武蔵) or that it came once as present from the Kii branch of the Tokugawa into the possession of the main branch of the Tokugawa which was based in Musashi province. However, the exact circumstances for the naming are unclear today. During the *bakumatsu* era, the last Tokugawa-*shōgun* Yoshinobu (慶喜, 1837-1913) presented the sword to the commander of his bodyguards, the famous swordsman Yamaoka Tesshū (山岡鉄舟, 1836-1888). Tesshū also mediated between Saigō Takamori (西郷隆盛, 1828-1877) and Katsu Kaishū (勝海舟, 1823-1899) to arrange a peaceful handing-over of Edo Castle and the surviving of the Tokugawa family. Later Tesshū served emperor Meiji and presented the blade to the aristocrat and Minister of the Right Iwakura Tomomi (岩倉具視, 1825-1883) who contributed greatly to the forming of the new Imperial court.

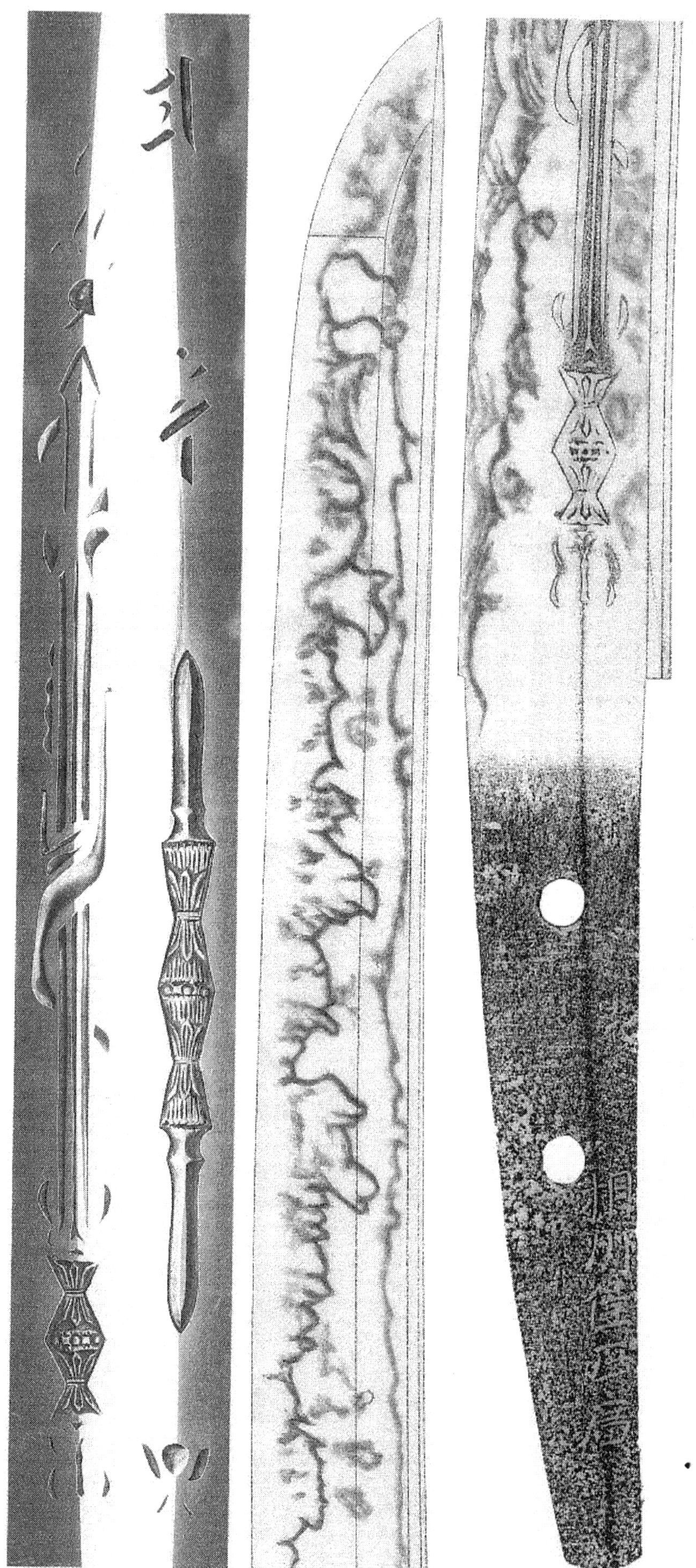

122.643 *wakizashi*
mei: Sōshū-jū Masahiro (相州住正広)
nagasa 58,5 cm, *sori* 2,1 cm, *shinogi-zukuri*, *mitsu-mune*

ji: *itame* mixed with *mokume*, partially also some *nagare*, in addition *ji-nie* and fine *chikei*
hamon: based on a *nie*-loaden *chōji* and mixed with *notare*, *ko-gunome*, *yahazu* and *togari*-like elements, in addition fine *kinsuji* and *sunagashi*, *yubashiri* as well as *tobiyaki* and *muneyaki*, all the elements merge into a *hitatsura*, the *nioiguchi* is rather compact and full of *ko-nie*
bōshi: widely hardened *midare-komi* with *nie-kuzure* and a long *kaeri* which continues as *muneyaki*
horimono: on the *omote* side a *boji* and a *sō-no-kurikata* and on the *ura* side two *bonji* and a *dokken* are engraved

The blade has plentiful of *ji-nie*, fine *chikei* and *yubashiri* and the *hamon* appears with its *tobiyaki* and *muneyaki* as *hitatsura*. In addition, the *jiba* is quite *nie*-loaden and shows *kinsuji* and *sunagashi*, so we have here a typical Sōshū work. And also the deeply and skillfully cut *horimono* speak for Sōshū. The thick *kasane*, the short length and the tendency to *sakizori* bring is to the early Muromachi period.

As we know, a *hitatsura* was the strong point of Muromachi-period Sōshū smiths but we have to be careful. Early Muromachi-period works from around Bun'an (文安, 1444-1449) and Hōtoku (宝徳, 1449-1452) from smiths like Masahiro (正広) and Hiromasa (広正) show a *yakiba* of rather small dimensioned *chōji* whereas later *hamon* cosists more of *gunome* than of *chōji*. Also the interpretation of the middle part of the hilt of a *sō-no-kurikara horimono* shows some characteristics. At the *kantei* blade, this middle part forms a peculiar hexagon. We find it especially on Nanbokuchō-period works from Akihiro (秋広) around Jōji (貞治, 1362-1368) and Shitoku (至徳, 1384-1387) and from Masahiro from around Meitoku (明徳, 1390-1394) and later by Hiromasa and Masahiro from around Bun'an and Hōtoku. But it was kept by later Sōshū smiths until the end of the Muromachi period and is accordingly called „Sōshū-*bori*". That means it is a good hint to recognize a Sōshū work.

Besides of *atari* and *dōzen* there were also some bids on late Muromachi-period smiths like Tsunahiro (綱広), the Odawara-Sōshū smiths Yasuharu (康春) and Fusamune (総宗), Yoshisuke (義助) and other Shimada smiths, and also on Sue-Bizen smiths like Katsumitsu (勝光), Sukesada (祐定) or Kiyomitsu (清光).

But from a late Muromachi-period Sōshū work we would expect a more noticeable *sakizori* and *horimono* which are more closely arranged towards the base. Also the *hitatsura* would show more *gunome* as mentioned before. At Tsunahiro, one of the most representative Sōshū smiths of that time, we would not see such a rather small and compact *hitatsura* but a *gunome-midare* mixed with *ko-notare* with a compact *nie*-loaden *nioiguchi*. At *hitatsura* interpretations of the Shimada school, the *hamon* appears wave-like and shows *togariba* and the latter would connect with some *muneyaki* in places. Also Katsumitsu, Sukesada, Kiyomitsu and other Sue-Bizen smiths applied a *hitatsura* but their blades have a thinner *kasane* and a high *shinogi*, that means their *shinogi-ji* surface drops towards *mune*.

123.626k *katana*
mei: Sōshū-jū Tsunahiro (相州住綱広)
nagasa 74,24 cm *sori* 2,0 cm
moto-haba 2,95 cm *saki-haba* 2,3 cm
moto-kasane 0,95 cm *saki-kasane* 0,6 cm
kissaki-nagasa 4,3 cm *nakago-nagasa* 18,94 cm
only a very little *nakago-sori*

shinogi-zukuri, *mitsu-mune*, wide *mihaba*, no noticeable taper, rather long *nagasa*, thick *kasane*, deep *sakizori*, elongated *chū-kissaki*. The *jigane* is an *itame* mixed with *mokume* which tends to stand out. In addition *ji-nie* and fine *chikei*. The *hamon* and the *bōshi* can be seen on the *oshigata*. There appear *ashi*, *yō*, *tobiyaki* and *muneyaki* which connect to a kind of *hitatsura*. The *nioiguchi* is rather subdued and shows *nie* as well as fine *kinsuji* and *sunagashi*. On both sides a *bōhi* is engraved which runs with *kake-nagashi* into the tang. The *nakago* is *ubu*, tapers noticeably, has *kiri-yasurime* and one *mekugi-ana*. There is a *naga-mei* chiselled centrally below the *mekugi-ana* of the *sashi-omote* side.

The blade has a wide *mihaba*, no noticeable taper, is rather long, has a thick *kasane*, a deep *sakizori* and ends in an elongated *chū-kissaki*. So we can date it into the late Muromachi period. The exact succession of the Tsunahiro generations is not entirely clear and some further studies are necessary but we know at least, that they were active from the late Muromachi to the early Edo period and that their strong point was a *hitatsura-hamon* like seen on the *kantei* blade.

Works in that style show a *jigane* in *itame* which is mixed with *mokume* and which stands out mostly. Also *ji-nie* and fine *chikei* appear. The *hamon* bases on *gunome* and is mixed with *chōji-* and *yahazu*-like elements. In addition, there are frequent *tobiyaki* and *muneyaki* which connect to a peculiar *hitatsura*. The *hamon* gets broader along the upper half and turns into a more complex *midareba* with *nie*, *kinsuji* and *sunagashi*. Although not that prominent at the *kantei* blade, often crescent-shaped *tobiyaki* are seen too. But besides of *hitatsura*, the Tsunahiro smiths also applied a *suguha* which is mixed with *gunome* from time to time and occasionally even a *gunome-chōji* in Seki style. The *bōshi* is either *sugu* with a *ko-maru-kaeri*, a *notare-komi* with a *ko-maru-maeri* or completely *ichimai*.

The *kantei* blade has a *bōhi* but also *sō-no-kurikata*, *sankozuka-ken*, *bonji*, *gomabashi* and *rendai* are seen on Tsunahiro works. At any case, the *horimono* are positioned centrally along the *shinogi-ji* and more towards the base of the blade. The *nakago* tapers and ends usually in a *kurijiri* which tends to *ha-agari*. The *yasurime* are either *kiri* or shallow *katte-sagari*. The signature is chiselled on the *sashi-omote* side, below the *mekugi-ana* and towards the *nakago-mune*. Mostly a *goji-mei* of the type „Sōshū-jū Tsunahiro“ is applied. At the *kantei* blade, the *bōhi* runs almost through the entire tang so the signature – which is still chiselled below the *mekugi-ana* – has to shift towards the center of thc *nakago*.

The majority of the bids was *atari* on Tsunahiro but there were many differentiations between the first, second and third generation. Usually such a differentiation is desired and necessary but as the Tsunahiro generations are as mentioned not entirely clear, each bid on a Tsunahiro smith was counted as *atari*.

Some few went also for Ise no Daijō Tsunahiro (伊勢大掾綱広). According to today´s state of studies, he was the fifth generation of the Tsunahiro family and was active around Kanbun (寛文, 1661-1673) and Enpō (延宝, 1673-1681). So his blades show of course a Kanbun-*shintō-sugata* and a *gunome*-based *midareba* which also tends sometimes to *juzuba*. The *nioiguchi* is thick and shows plentiful of *nie*. That means his interpretations are similar to the Edo-*shintō* style of the Kanbun era. So neither his workmanship nor his *sugata* match with the *kantei* blade.

There were *dōzen* bids on Hiromasa (広正), Yasuharu (康春) and the like. Hiromasa was a Sōshū smith of the early Muromachi period and he made accordingly many smaller dimensioned *tachi* and *katana* with a *nagasa* of around 60,6 to 66,6 cm in combination with a normal *mihaba*. That means his standard *sugata* differs considerably from the *kantei* blade. Also his *hitatsura* is more based on *chōji* and consists of smaller dimensioned elements. Yasuharu, Fusamune (総宗) and the like belonged to the Odawara-Sōshū group which did not apply a *hitatsura* in the classical sense. Their *hamon* is a mix of *gunome* and *notare* mixed with conspicious angular elements and is harded in *nioi-deki* with *nie*.

Besides of *atari* and *dōzen* there were some bids on the Shimada school (島田) of Suruga province. There are many *tantō* and *hira-zukuri wakizashi* extant by this school which are in *hitatsura*. Most of these *hamon* show large *togari* elements and a long *kaeri* as well as conspicious *togari* in the *bōshi*. None of the latter characteristics can be seen on the *kantei* blade.

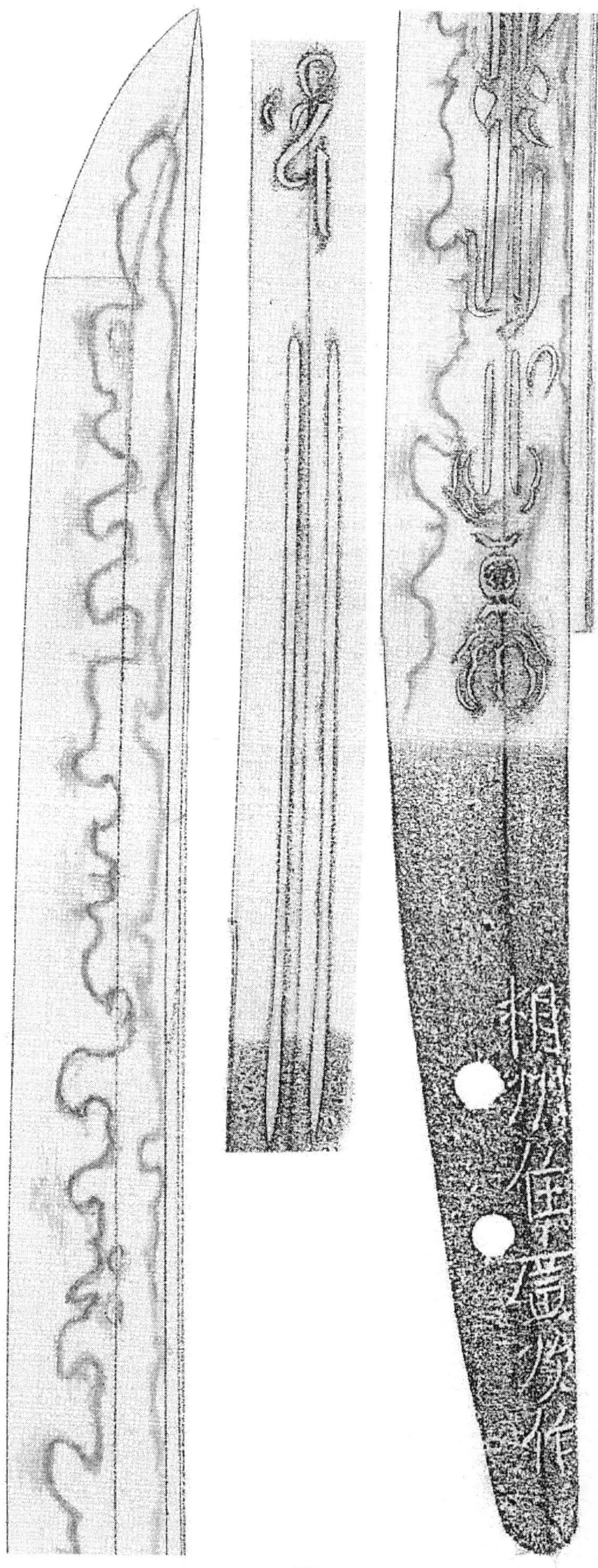

124.654 *wakizashi*
mei: Sōshū-jū Hirotsugu saku (相州住広次作)
nagasa 55,2 cm, *sori* 1,5 cm, *shinogi-zukuri*, *mitsu-mune*

ji: *itame* mixed with *mokume*, many fine *chikei* and plentiful of *ji-nie*
hamon: *gunome* mixed with *chōji*, *tobiyaki* and *muneyaki*, the *hamon* appars altogether as *hitatsura*, in addition *ko-ashi* and *yō*, the hardening is in *nioi-deki* but shows also *nie*
bōshi: *midare-komi* with a round *kaeri* which connects with the *muneyaki*
horimono: there is a *sō-no-kurikara* towards the base of the *omote* side and a *bonji* and *gomabashi* at the same area on the *ura* side

This is a *wakizashi* of Sōshū Hirotsugu. According to the *meikan* records, the 1st gen. Hirotsugu was active around the Nanbokuchō-period Kenmu era (建武, 1334-1338) but extant blades of that lineage do not date earlier than the early or middle Muromachi period, i.e. around Bunmei (文明, 1469-1487). At that time, the Sōshū smiths focused on a flamboyant *hitatsura* like seen on the *kantei* blade and many blades show deeply cut and magnificent *horimono*. This *wakizashi* has plentiful of *ji-nie*, fine *chikei* a wide hardening in *midare* mixed with *gunome*, *chōji*, *tobiyaki* and *muneyaki* which appear altogether as mentioned as *hitatsura*. And with the elaborate *horimono* on both sides engraved towards the base – a *sō-no-kurikara* on the *omote* and a *bonji* with *gomabashi* on the *ura* side – we have a textbook-like *deki* for a Sōshū-*mono* of that time.

Representative smiths of such early Muromachi-period *hitatsura* within the Kamakura-Sōshū group are Masahiro (正広) and Hiromasa (広正) – both active around Bun'an (文安, 1444-1449) and Hōtoku (宝徳, 1449-1452) – followed by Tsunahiro (綱広) who was active later, namely during the late Muromachi period. There are some differences between this Kamakura- and the Odawara-Sōshū group with smiths like Fusamune (総宗) and Yasukuni (康国). The former, earlier group shows conspicious *chōji* in the *ha* and the *hamon* itself is rather small dimensioned. The latter, later group gave up the *chōji* and compose their *hamon* basically just of *gunome*.

Regarding *horimono*, the Odawara-Sōshū smiths added fine and skillfully executed *sō-no-kurikara* and the like as relief in a *hitsu* or *hi*. Kamakura-Sōshū smiths in turn mostly negatively interpreted *sō-no-kurikara*, *bonji* or *gomabashi* direct on the *ji*, i.e. not in a *hitsu* or *hi*. This characteristic can also be seen on the *kantei* blade.

So all these subtle differences had to be beared in mind because many went for the later Sue-Sōshū. But some were too early and reckoned it as a Nanbokuchō-period Sōshū work of Hiromitsu (広光) or Akihiro (秋広). But at their time, such a *shape* with normal *mihaba* in combination with a *sakizori* was not applied. Most of the then *wakizashi* were wide and had a thin *kasane*. In addition, the *nie* of the *ji* and *ha* would be stronger than at the later Muromachi-period Sōshū-*mono* and the *ha* would show more *hataraki*.

Well, some also bade on the Sue-Bizen smith Sukesada (祐定). As we know, also Sue-Bizen smiths applied a *hitatsura* but their *sugata* is noticeably different because the *shinogi* is higher which makes the *kasane* drop towards the *mune*.

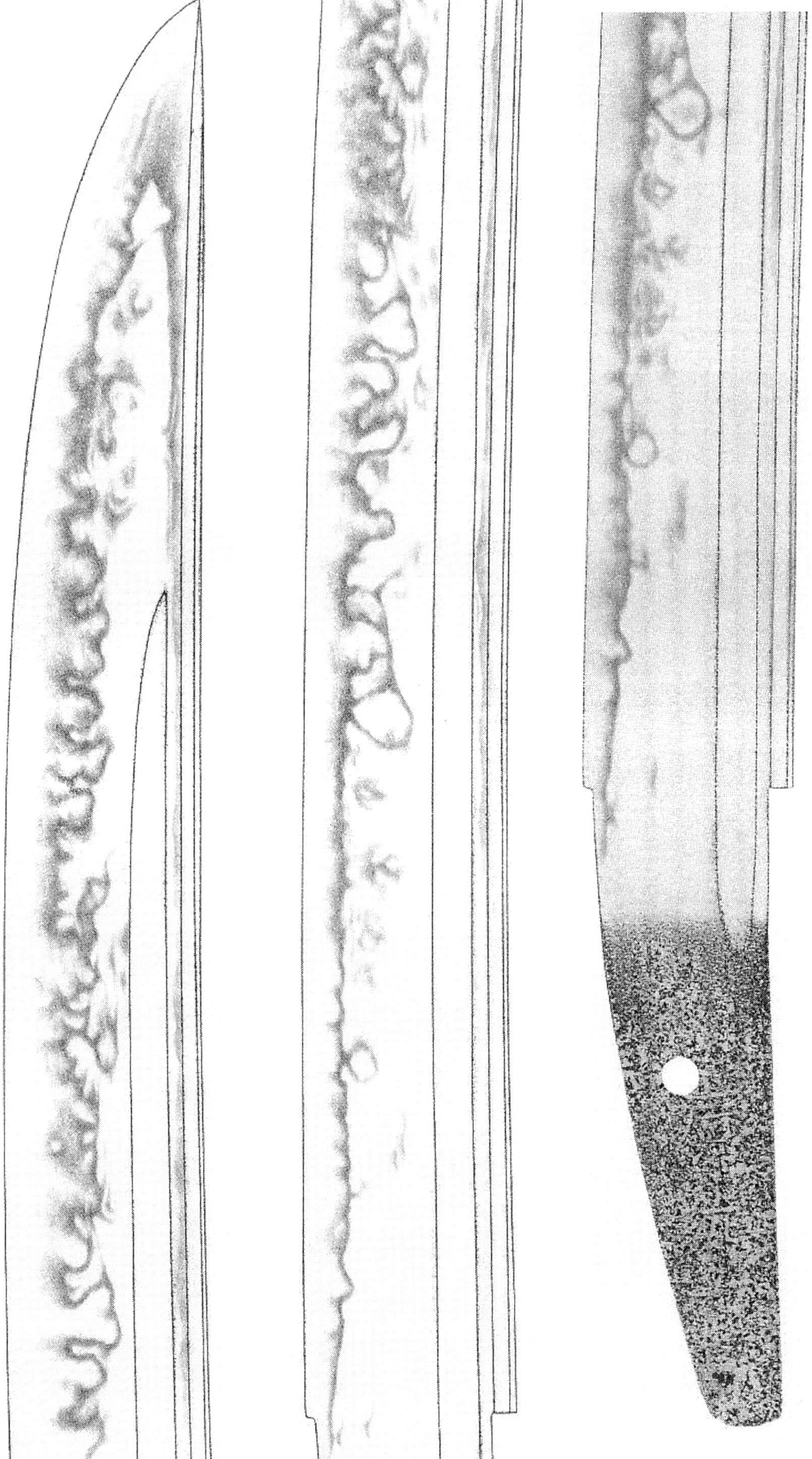

125.594k *wakzashi*
mei: Hiromitsu (広光)

nagasa 37,57 cm *sori* 0,59 cm
motohaba 3,05 cm *moto-kasane* 0,6 cm
nakago-nagasa 10,15 cm no *nakago-sori*

hira-zukuri, *mitsu-mune*, wide *mihaba*, *sunnobi*, very thin *kasane* in proportion to the *mihaba*, shallow *sori*. The *kitae* is an *itame* mixed with *mokume* which stands out all over the blade. In addition plentiful of *ji-nie* and many *chikei* appear. The *hamon* and the *bōshi* can be seen on the *oshigata*. In addition *tobiyaki*, *yubashiri*, *muneyaki*, many *ashi*, *yō*, *nie*, *kinsuji* and *sunagashi*. There is a *katana-hi* engraved on the *omote* side which runs as *kake-nagashi* into the tang. The *nakago* is *ubu*, relative short compared to the *nagasa*, has a *kurijiri*, *katte-sagari yasurime* and one *mekugi-ana*. There is a *niji-mei* chiselled centrally below the *mekugi-ana* on the *sashi-omote* side. (Note: This smith signed rather rarely with a *niji-mei*. Also, relative many large dimensioned blades are known by this smith.)

The blade is *sunnobi*, has a wide *mihaba*, a very thin *kasane* in proportion to the *mihaba* and a shallow *sori*, that means we can date it to the heyday of the Nanbokuchō period. By the way, the tang is relative short when compared to the *nagasa* but this is very typical too for *tantō* and *hira-zukuri wakizashi* of that time. We know date signatures of Hiromitsu from the Kan´ō (観応, 1350-1352) to the Jōji era (貞治, 1362-1368), that means he was exactly active during the mentioned Nanbokuchō heyday which was Enbun (延文, 1356-1361) and Jōji. That is very noticeable because among all the *jūyō-bunkazai* and *jūyō-tōken* of that smith, no single small *tantō* is found, i.e. all blades of that category are *sunnobi-tantō* or *hira-zukuri ko-wakizashi* measuring over one *shaku*. The *jigane* is a rather standing-out *itame* mixed with *mokume*, plentiful of *ji-nie* and many *chikei*.

A *hitatsura-hamon* which is so typical for Sōshū is sometimes seen in a rudimentary way already at Hiromitsu´s predecessor Sadamune (貞宗). But a „full" *hitatsura* was not applied before the time of Hiromitsu. A characteristical feature of him is called „*dango-chōji*" (団子丁子, lit. „dumpling *chōji*"). It describes a peculiar *kawazu-no-ko chōji* interpretation mixed into a *gunome*-based *hamon* and can also be seen on the *kantei* blade in places. Besides of that, the *tobiyaki*, *yubashiri* and *muneyaki* merge into the *hitatsura*. Also plentiful of *ashi*, *yō*, *nie*, *kinsuji* and *sunagashi* are seen. (Note: There are also some works by Hiromitsu in *suguha*.) The *bōshi* gets continuously wider in its course and appears as *midare-komi* with a pointed and long *kaeri*.

The „*Shinkan-hiden-shō*" (新刊秘伝抄) writes about Hiromitsu that „naked, undecorated blades are rare". That means almost every blade shows some kind of *horimono* (for example elaborate interpretations of a *sankozuka-ken* or the like like here just a *katana-ji*). The tip of the tang is a *kurijiri*, the *yasurime* are *katte-sagari* and the signature is in the case of a *niji-mei* mostly chiselled centrally on the *sashi-omote* side below the *mekugi-ana*.

Incidentally, for a long time it was thought that there are no signed *tachi* of Hiromitsu extant. Already before World War II, a *suriage* blade with the *mei* „Sagami no Kuni-jūnin Sae…" (相模国住人左衛) and the date „Bunna ni…" (文和二, 1353) made its round. And after a newer examination in the course of the *tokubetsu-jūyō-shinsa*, it was able to attribute it to Hiromitsu and the blade got *tokubetsu-jūyō* papers. The addition „Sae" (although the „e" is almost illegible) refers namely to his honorary title „Saemon no Jō" (左衛門尉). The *tachi* has a wide *mihaba* and an elongated *chū-kissaki*, that means it shows a classical Enbun-Jōji-*sugata*. But the *hamon* is smaller dimensioned and rather calm. It has a compact *nioiguchi*, much *ko-nie* and neither conspicious *tobiyaki*, *yubashiri* nor *kinsuji* or *sunagashi* like we know them from his *wakizashi*.

He signed only rarely in *niji-mei* and mostly in *naga-mei* of the kind „Sagami no Kuni-jūnin Hiromitsu". Date signatures are only found in combination with a *naga-mei*. As the blades in *niji-mei* show a more classical and calm workmanship, the theory arouse that there were two generations active. Namely a 1st gen. which signed in *niji-mei* and a 2nd gen. which signed accordingly in *naga-mei*. But most experts follow the one-generation theory but further studies are nevertheless necessary.

The majority bade *atari* on Hiromitsu but some also *dōzen* on Akihiro (秋広). Well, we know blades of Akihiro with date signatures of the Enbun and Jōji eras which are also rather close to the *dango-chōji* of Hiromitsu, but generally Akihiro was active somewhat later, namely from Enbun over Jōji, Ōan (応安, 1368-1375), Eiwa (永和, 1375-1379), Kōryaku (康暦, 1379-1381), Eitoku (永徳, 1381-1384) to Shitoku (至徳, 1384-1387). That means he worked more towards the end of the Nanbokuchō period. Accordingly, his blades get smaller. *Tantō* of Akihiro with datings of the Ōan, Eiwa and Shitoku areas are even noticeably smaller and measure around 24,2 to 27,3 cm. In short, his workmanship is noticeaby different from Hiromitsu and by the way, there is only one blade extant of Akihiro which bears a *niji-mei*.

Mino

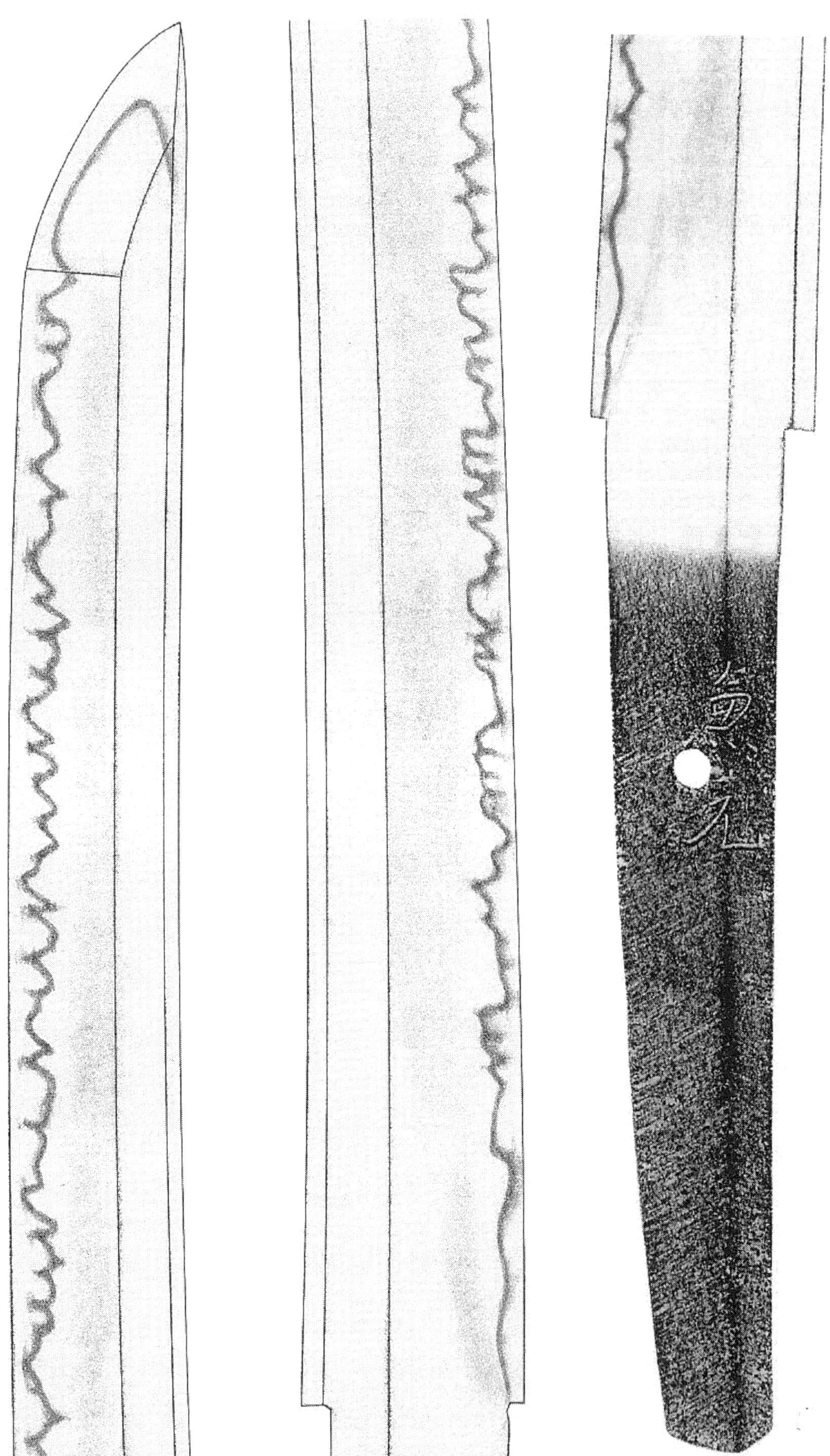

126.635k *katana*
mei: Kanemoto (兼元)

nagasa 68,2 cm — *sori* 1,97 cm
moto-haba 3,25 cm — *saki-haba* 2,25 cm
moto-kasane 0,6 cm — *saki-kasane* 0,4 cm
kissaki-nagasa 4,05 cm — *nakago-nagasa* 16,06
only a little *nakago-sori*

shinogi-zukuri, *iori-mune*, relative wide *mihaba*, no noticeable taper, not much *hira-niku*, *sakizori*, somewhat elongated *chū-kissaki*. The *jigane* is an *itame* mixed with *nagare* and *masame* which tends to stand out a little. In addition, *ji-nie* and a *shirake-utsuri* appear. The *hamon* and the *bōshi* can be seen on the *oshigata*. There are *ashi* which almost reach down to the *ha* in places. The *nioiguchi* is rather compact and shows *ko-nie* whereas the hardening is in *nioi-deki*. The *nakago* is *ubu*, has an *iriyamagata-jiri*, *takanoha-yasurime* and one *mekugi-ana*. There is a *niji-mei* on the *sashi-omote* side between the *mekugi-ana* and the *nakago-mune*. (Note: This smith applied mostly a *midare-komi bōshi*.)

The blade has a relative wide *mihaba*, no noticeable taper, a *sakizori* an a slightly elongated *chū-kissaki*. So we can date it into the late Muromachi period. Magoroku Kanemoto´s artistic period was around Daiei (大永, 1521-1528) and Kyōroku (享禄, 1528-1532). There are some blades extant by him which have an overlong *nagasa* but most *katana* are relative short, just like the *kantei* blade. Also noticeable is the scarce *hira-niku* which is a typical feature of Seki-*mono*.

The *jigane* is a rather standing-out *itame* mixed with *nagare* and *masame* which shows *ji-nie* and a *shirake-utsuri*. Here too, we have typical features of Seki-*mono*. We know signatures of the kind „Nōshū Akasaka-jū Kanemoto“ (濃州赤坂住兼元) which are chiselled in a rather roundish manner. Dated works from the Meiō era (明応, 1492-1501), that means works from the 1st gen. Kanemoto, do not show a clear *sanbonsugi-hamon* but an irregular *midare*-mix of *gunome* and *chōji*. Also fine *uchinoke* and *yubashiri* as well as rough *ha-nie* and *sunagashi* appear along the *habuchi*.

Magoroku Kanemoto was the successor of the 1st gen. Kanemoto and is considered as the „inventor“ of the *sanbonsugi-hamon*, but he too did not apply it in a regular but a rather free course mixed of different elements. So the *yakiba* shows groups of two, three, or sometimes even four or five protruding *togari* elements, whereas in between, the *hamon* drops noticeably off towards the *ha*. Also he applied a *gunome*-based *hamon* with roundish *yakigashira* or a mix of the free *sanbonsugi* and the latter interpretation. The *kantei* blade can rather be classified as a work of the latter group.

Also very typical for Seki-*mono* is an identical *hamon* on both sides and the noticeably dropping valleys which connect the protruding *hamon* elements. Compared to later *sanbonsugi* interpretations, the *yakiba* is here compared to the *mihaba* rather low. Anyway, such an early *sanbonsugi* can´t be mistaken with those of the later generations Magoroku Kanemoto which applied a quite uniform and uncharacteristic *sanbonsugi*.

Magoroku Kanemoto´s *bōshi* is a pointed *midare-komi* in *jizō* manner. A *sugu-bōshi* with a *ko-maru-kaeri* like we can see it on the *kantei* blade is rather rare. But a hint was given regarding this in the description of the *kantei*. The tip of his *katana* is an *iriyamagata-jiri* (or a *kurijiri* which tends somewhat to *ha-agari*), the *yasurime* are *takanoha* and the signature is mostly chiselled as *niji-mei* on the *sashi-omote* side below the *mekugi-ana*.

As this blade is quite typical, the vast majority bade *atari* on Magoroku Kanemoto. But some went also explicitely for Kanemoto (兼基). There are relative few blades extant by this smith and a theory says that he was the same person as Magoroku Kanemoto. Others say he was the father or the younger brother of Magoroku. He too applied a free *sanbonsugi* and an identical *nakago* finish so bids on him were counted as *atari* too.

Some *dōzen* bids were found on the 1st gen. Kanemoto, the 3rd gen. Kanemoto, Kanefusa (兼房), Kanenori (兼則) and other Sue-Seki smiths. As mentioned earlier, the 1st gen. showed a somewhat different workmanship and many of his blades bear a *naga-mei*. Well, the Sue-Seki smiths also applied a *sanbonsugi-hamon* but as described before, this is a more or less uniform and stiff *sanbonsugi* and not so free as at Magoroku Kanemoto.

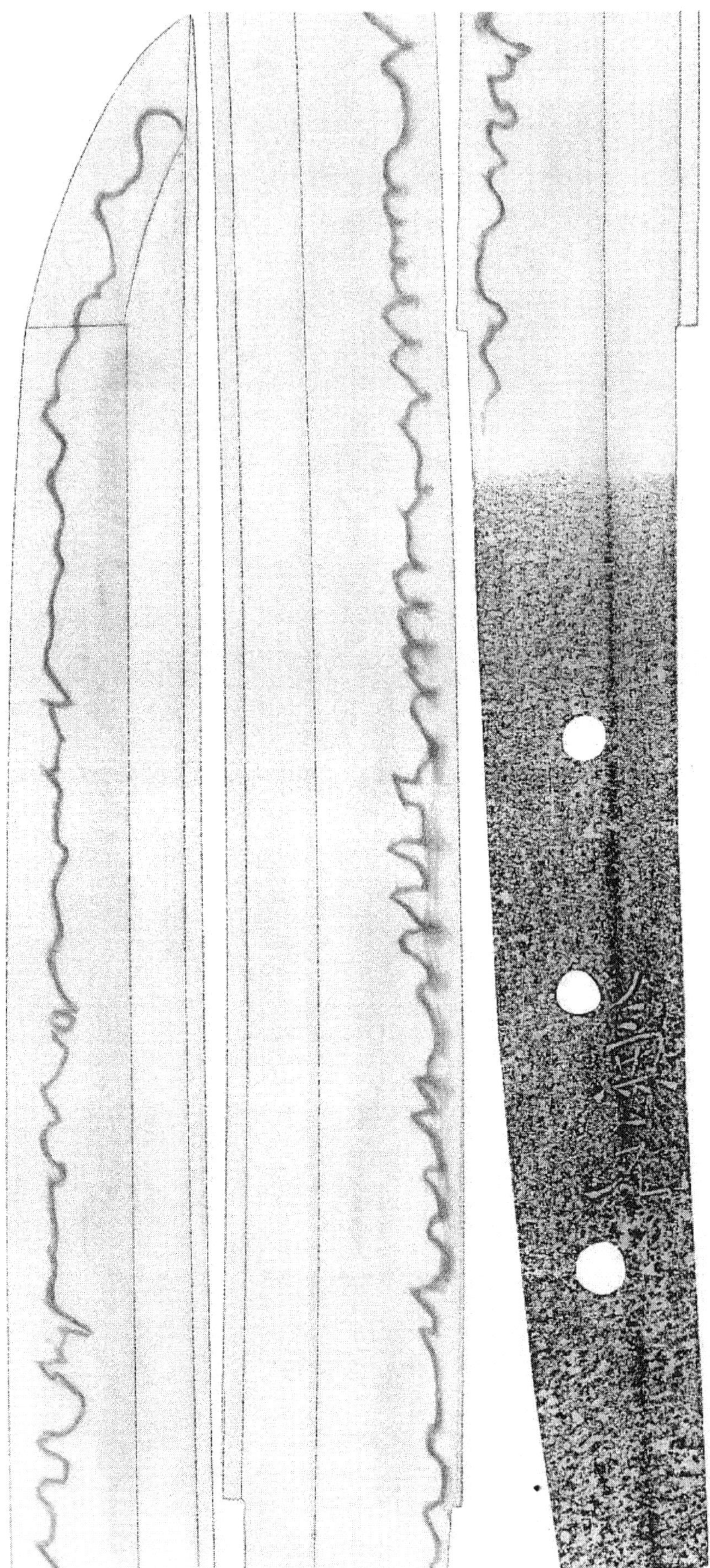

127.652 *katana*
mei: Kanemoto (兼元)
nagasa 71,8 cm, *sori* 1,8 cm, *shinogi-zukuri*, *iori-mune*

ji: *itame* mixed with *nagare*, fine *ji-nie*, some *chikei*, *shirake-utsuri*
hamon: *gunome* with round *yakigashira* and *togariba* which appears as *sanbonsugi* of groups of about five elements, the *yakiba* shows ups and downs, the hardening is in *nioi-deki* but the rather compact *nioiguchi* shows also *ko-nie*
bōshi: on both sides a large *notare-komi* with a round *kaeri* which leans as *jizō-bōshi* towards the *ha*

The blade has only a little *funbari* and so we can assume that it is *suriage*. The *shinogi-ji* drops off towards the *mune*, i.e. the *shinogi* is high. The *kasane* is thin, there is scarce *hira-niku*, the *sori* is a noticable *sakizori* and the tip has scarce *fukura*. So we have the *sugata* of a typical *uchigatana* of the late Muromachi period. The *jigane* is an *itame* mixed with *nagare* which stands out and shows a *shirake-utsuri*. These are characteristics of Sue-Seki works. The *hamon* appears to be a *sanbonsugi*, but a freely interpreted one which consists of differently high, irregular *togari* elements arranged to groups of three, four or five. The valles in between are noticeably deep.

Such a fascinating, lively *sanbonsugi* interpretation in *gunome* with roundish *yakigashira* mixed with *togari* which are freely grouped is typical for the 2nd gen. Kanemoto (Magoroku, 孫六). That means the *hamon* differs greatly from the later *sanbonsugi* interpretations which are rather uniform and stiff. The dynamic course of the *hamon* speaks for Magoroku Kanemoto´s great skill and as the blade is very typical, most were spot-on at the first round and received an *atari*.

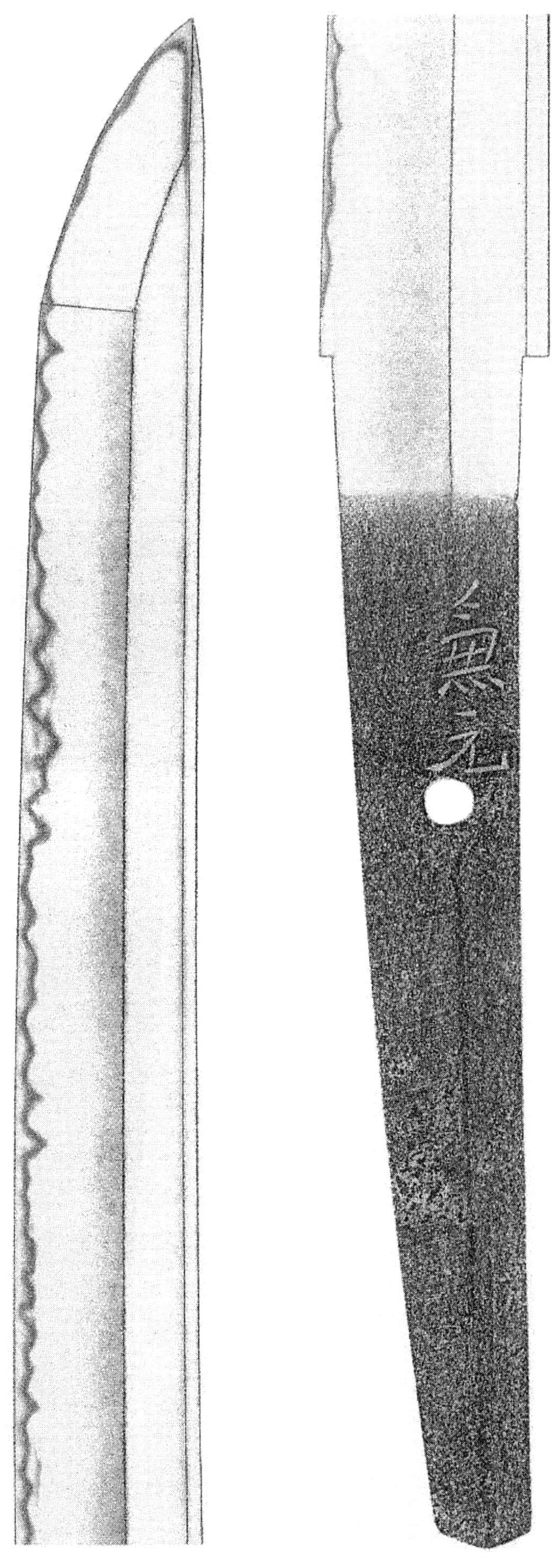

128.616 *katana*
mei: Kanemoto (兼元)
nagasa 67,6 cm, *sori* 2,15 cm, *shinogi-zukuri*, *iori-mune*

ji: standing-out *itame-hada* with partial strong *nagare* areas, in addition *ji-nie* and some *shirake*
hamon: *togari*-like *gunome* with narrow *yakihaba* and mixed with *ko-gunome* and *ko-notare*, the *nioiguchi* is rather soft and there are fine *sunagashi*
bōshi: narrow *bōshi* with a little *midare-komi* and a long and pointed *kaeri*

The 2nd gen. Kanemoto (Magoroku, 孫六) applied mostly a free mix of *togari*-like *gunome* or a *togariba* mixed with *ko-gunome* with a small *yakihaba* whose valleys drop deeply down towards the *ha*. The *nioiguchi* is rather soft and shows *nie* and *sunagashi*. Later generations Kanemoto and *utsushimono* show a regular *togariba* which appears as uniform and stiff *sanbonsugi* and which has a tight *nioiguchi*.

But even the *deki* is quite characteristic, some went also for predecessing Mino smiths like Kaneuji (兼氏) or the Naoe-Shizu school (直江志津). Maybe they were leaded astray by the relative wide *mihaba*, the little tapering and the elongated *kissaki* and landed so in the Nanbokuchō period. But the *nagasa* is too short, the *shinogi* is high and there is only scarce *hira-niku* and a noticeable *sakizori*. These characteristics must not be overlooked because they identify the blade as Sue-*kotō*, especially from around Eishō (永正, 1504-1521). Also the *shirake* and the strongly standing-out *kitae* would rule out a Nanbokuchō-period Mino work.

Others got the *sugata* and time right and were at Sue-Seki but went because of the high quality of the blade for Kanesada (兼定, „No-Sada"). Kanesada applied among all Sue-Seki-*mono* the finest and most excellent *kitae*. His *hamon* does not base on *togariba* elements but is a *notare* mixed with roundish *gunome* which results mostly in a large dimensioned *midareba*. Also we don´t know any works of him with such a narrow *yakihaba* in *midareba*.

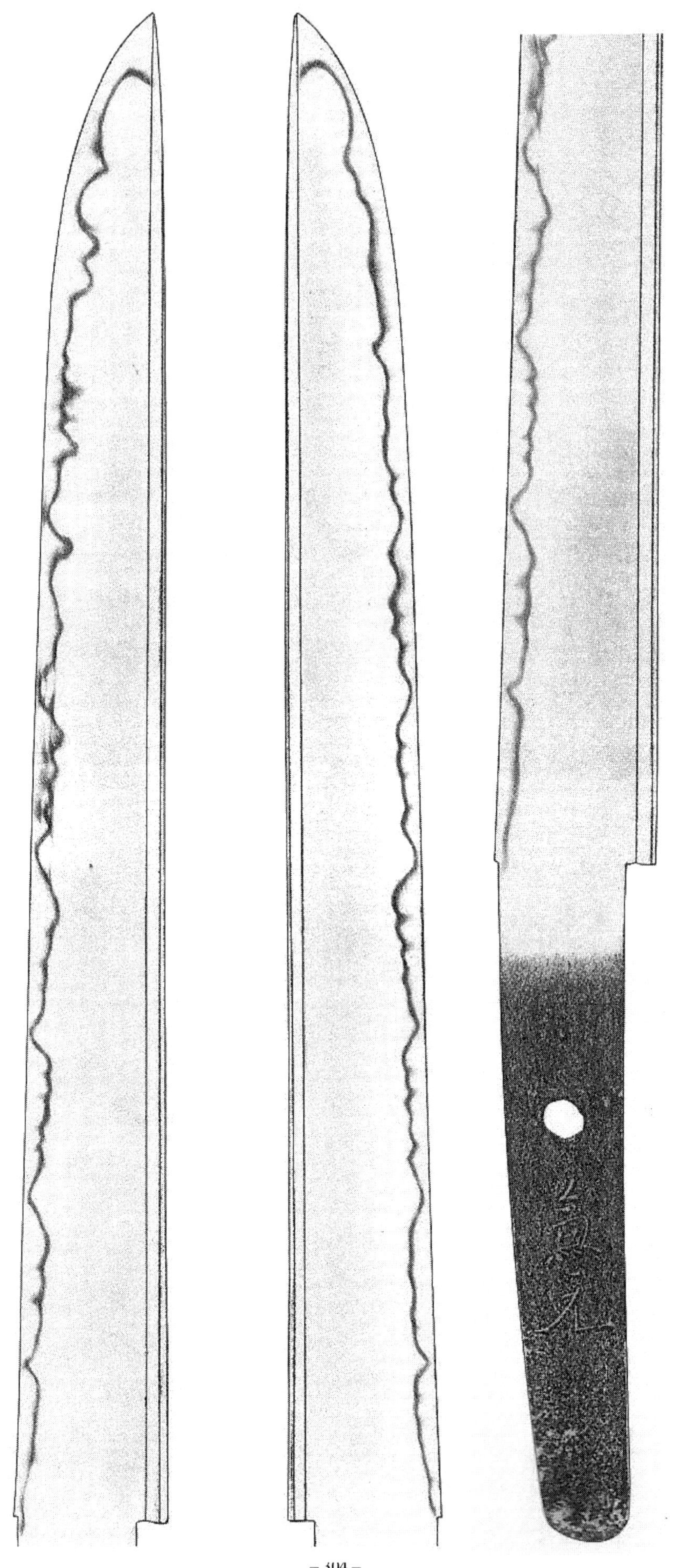

129.602k *tantō*
mei: Kanemoto (兼元)
nagasa 23,4 cm *uchi-zori*
moto-haba 2,2 cm *moto-kasane* 0,5 cm
nakago-nagasa 10,0 cm only a little *nakago-sori*

hira-zukuri, *mitsu-mune*, somewhat narrow *mihaba*, short and compact *nagasa*, strong *uchizori*, scarce *fukura*. The *jigane* is an *itame* mixed with *masame-nagare* and tends to stand out. In addition fine *ji-nie*, *chikei* and a clear *shirake-utsuri* appear. The *hamon* and the *bōshi* can be seen on the *oshigata*. It has to be noted that the *hamon* is quite identical on both sides. In addition, there are *ko-ashi* of which some reach down to the *ha*. The *nioiguchi* is compact and shows *ko-nie*. The *nakago* is *ubu*, has a *kurijiri*, *higaki-yasurime* and one *mekugi-ana*. There is a *niji-mei* chiselled centrally below the *mekugi-ana* on the *sashi-omote* side.

The relative narrow *mihaba* and the short *nagasa*, the strong *uchizori* and the scarce *fukura* date this blade to the late Muromachi period. There are several *tantō-sugata* of Magoroku Kanemoto and other Seki smiths known from that time: A somewhat larger *sugata* (containing *hira-zukuri wakizashi*) with a wide *mihaba* in *sunnobi*-style with a *sakizori*, *tantō* with standard length (*jōsun*) and a normal *mihaba*, or like the *kantei* blade somewhat shorter and relative narrow *tantō* with a strong *uchizori* and scarce *fukura*.

The *jigane* is a standing-out *itame* mixed with *masame-nagare*. Also a fine *ji-nie* and a clearly visible *shirake-utsuri* appear. These are tpical characteristics of Seki-*mono*. The *hamon* of Kanemoto´s *tantō* and *hira-zukuri wakizashi* is mostly a more or less intimidated form of a *sanbonsugi* but sometimes also a *suguha* in the case of a Rai-*utsushi* or in very rare cases also a *notare*. The mentioned *sanbonsugi* by the way is described as „*gyōsō no sanbonsugi*", as „cursive" or „free" *sanbonsugi*. At such a free *sanbonsugi*, individual *togari* elements stand out and form groups of three, four or five whereas the valleys in between drop down noticeably towards the *ha*. These irregularily protruding *togariba* suggest as mention the course of a *sanbonsugi* and the interpretation clearly differs from the later uniform and stiff *sanbonsugi* forms. This free course of the *hamon* is very tasteful and one of the features why Magoroku Kanemoto is held in such a high esteem.

His *midareba* is Seki-typical identical on both sides and some of the valleys touch as mentioned almost the *ha*. The *bōshi* of his *tantō* and *hira-zukuri wakizashi* is in the case of a free *sanbonsugi* a *midare-komi* whose tapering reminds of a *jizō-bōshi*. At a *suguha*, the *bōshi* is *sugu* too and shows a *ko-maru-kaeri* which leans somewhat towards the *ha*.

The two great Seki masters, Magoroku Kanemoto and Kanesada (兼定, No Sada), applied besides of a *midareba* also a *suguha* which is meant to be a Rai-*utsushi*. But it has to be mentioned that Kanemoto´s *tantō* show principally a free *sanbonsugi* and very rarely a *suguha*, whereas Kanesada made a lot of Rai-*utsushi* in *suguha*.

Kanemoto´s *tantō* and *hira-zukuri wakizashi* have a *kurijiri* (which appears sometimes also as *iriyamagata-jiri*), the *yasurime* are *higaki*, and the signature „Noshū Akasaka-jū Kanemoto saku" of the 1st gen. Kanemoto is chiselled on the *sashi-omote* side towards the *nakago-mune*. Rarely also a date signature is added on the *ura* side. But almost all Kanemoto blades are signed with a *niji-mei* below the *mekugi-ana* as it can be seen here.

The vast majority bade *atari* on Magoroku Kanemoto and there were some *dōzen* bids on Izumi no Kami Kanesada, Mutsu no Kami Daidō (陸奥守大道), Kanefusa (兼房), Kanetsune (兼常) and other Seki smiths.

Kanesada´s *hamon* on *tantō* is a *gunome-chōji* with round *yakigashira* and is mixed with *gunome* and *togari* elements. But also a *notare*-based *hamon* mixed with *gunome* or as mentioned a *suguha* in the case of a Rai-*utsushi* is known. Kanefusa also applid a *gunome-chōji* with round *yakigashira* but his peculiar arrangement of the elements is called „Kenbō-*midare*". [Translators note: „Kenbō" is the Sino-japanese reading of „Kanefusa".] At Kanetsune, we find mostly a pure *suguha* or a *suguha* with small protrusions or knobs but not such a *gyōsō no sanbonsugi*. Mutsu no Kami Daidō´s *hamon* bases on *notare* and is mixed with *gunome-midare* or also with *ō-gunome-midare*. He did not apply such a free *sanbonsugi*. In addition, his *yasurime* are not *higaki* but *katte-sagari*.

There were also some bids on Sengo Muramasa (千子村正) which were counted as *dōzen* too because a workmanship from the late Muromachi period which shows an identical *hamon* on both sides and deeply dropping valleys is also typical for Muramasa. Muramasa´s *jigane* is a standing-out *itame* and the steel is somewhat blackish. Also there appears no complete *shirake-utsuri* all over the blade but rather a „*shirake*-like" *utsuri* on places. His *hamon* is mostly a *hako-midare* or bases on *notare-gunome* with protruding *midare* but not with pointed *togari* elements. A *ko-gunome* connected in the way of the *kantei* blade is not seen at Muramasa. Also the tang of Muramasa is a characteristical *tanagobara*, the *yasurime* are *katte-sagari* and the *mei* is chiselled towards the *nakago-mune*. That means at least the peculiar shape of the tang would have been mentioned in the description if it was a blade of Muramasa.

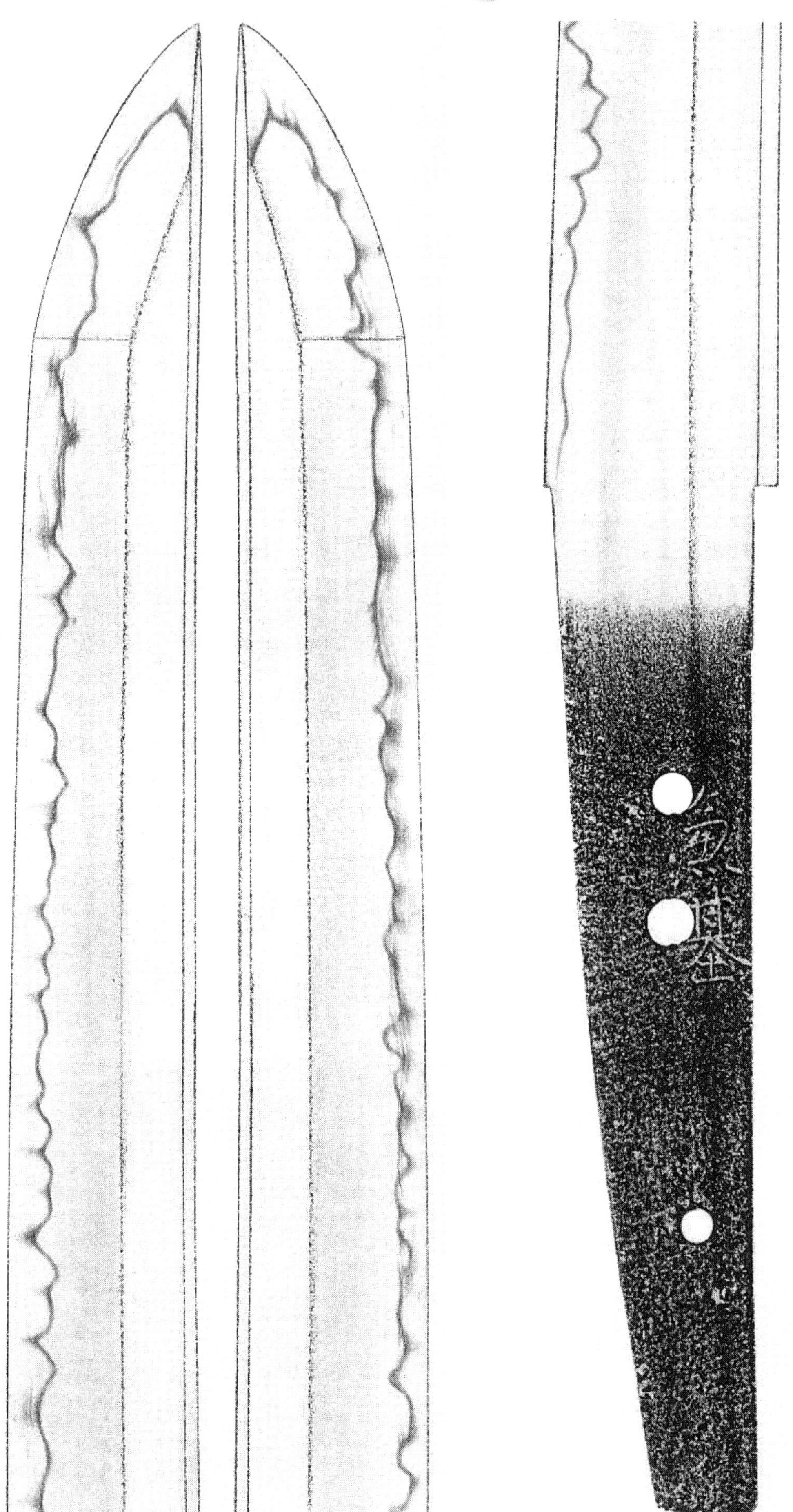

130.627 *katana*
mei: Kanemoto (兼基)
nagasa 66,05 cm, *sori* 0,93 cm, *shinogi-zukuri*, *iori-mune*

ji: standing-out *itame* mixed with *mokume* and partially with *nagare*, in addition *ji-nie* and over the entire blade a *shirake-utsuri*
hamon: small *yakidashi* which turns into a *sanbonsugi*-like mix of *gunome* and pointed *togari-gunome*, also *ashi* appear, the *nioiguchi* is compact and shows plentiful of *ko-nie*
bōshi: on the *omote* side *notare-komi* with a relative large *ō-maru-kaeri* and *hakikake*, on the *ura* side a *midare-komi* with also *hakikake* but with a rather pointed *kaeri*

Because of the relative short length, the *sakizori*, the scarce *fukura* and *hira-niku*, we can date this blade into the late Muromachi period (= Sue-*kotō*). The *hada* stands out and shows a *shirake-utsuri* and the *hamon* is a *gunome* with *sanbonsugi*-like *togari* protrusions, and so we are inevitably at Sue-Seki. All those characteristics were understood and the vast majority went accordingly for Kanemoto (兼元) or Kanesada (兼定, No-Sada).

There are several theories on this Kanemoto (兼基). One say he was the same person as Magoroku Kanemoto, others say he was the father of Akasaka Kanemoto (赤坂兼元), or the older brother of the 1st gen. Kanemoto or that he was „just" a student of Magoroku Kanemoto. However, there are so far no sound references found which allow a final conclusion in this matter. From the point of view of workmanship we can date him around the time of Magoroku Kanemoto, which would be Eishō (永正, 1504-1521), Daiei (大永, 1521-1528) and Tenbun (天文, 1532-1555). And because of the *hamon*, the finishing of the tang and the signature style it is safe to assume that he and Magoroku Kanemoto worked at least closely together. Of course it is difficult to bid on this Kanemoto and so just a bid on Magoroku Kanemoto was enough.

As mentioned, relative many went also for No-Sada. But his workmanship shows a *gunome* with noticeable rounder *yakigashira* and a larger dimensioned *yakiba*. Also his *jihada* differs from other Sue-Seki-*mono* because it is very dense and refined and of an excellent quality. He did not apply a *sanbonsugi* or *sanbonsugi*-like *hamon* but mostly a vivid mix of *togari-gunome* and *gunome-chōji* with *sunagashi*.

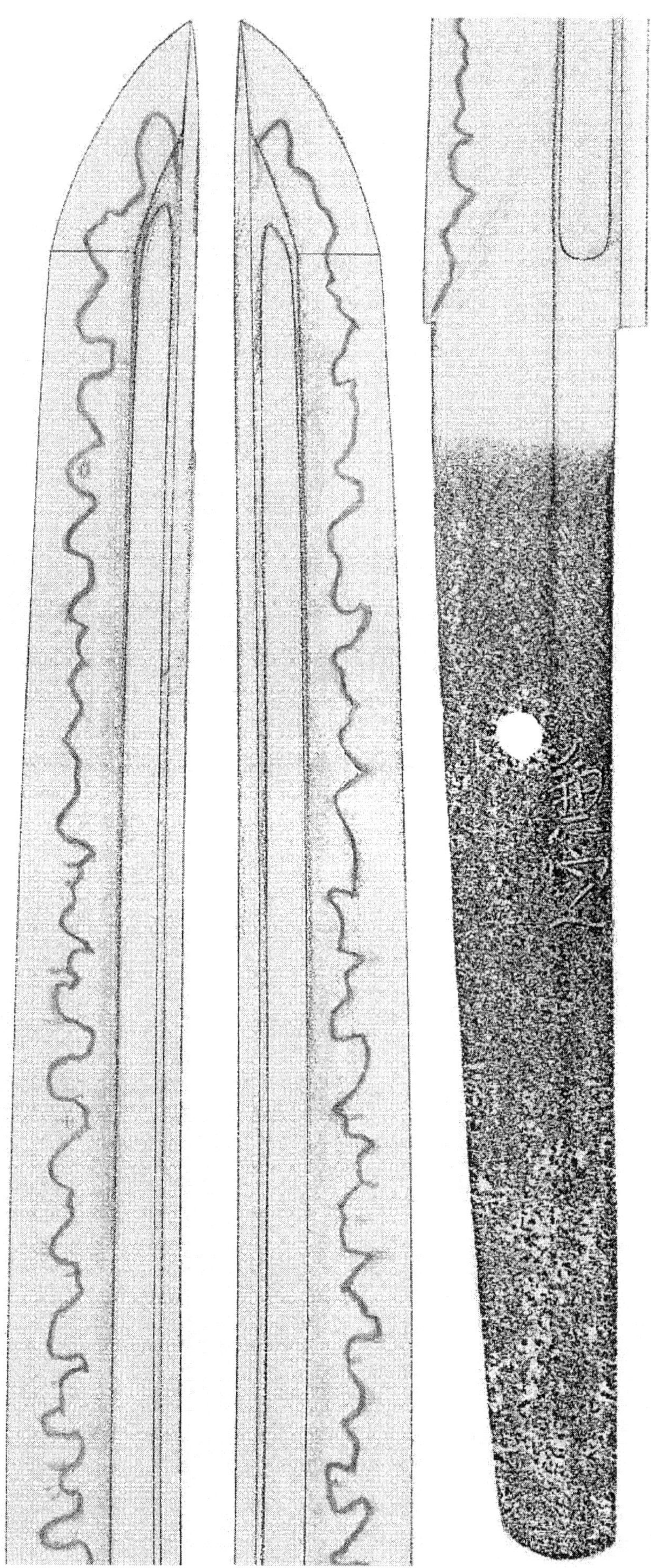

131.663 *katana*
mei: Kanesada (兼定) [No-Sada]
nagasa 69,0 cm, *sori* 1,8 cm, *shinogi-zukuri*, *iori-mune*

ji: *itame* mixed with *mokume* and *nagare*, also *ji-nie*, *chikei* and some *shirake-utsuri*
hamon: *gunome* mixed with *togariba* and *chōji*, in addition *ko-ashi* and small *tobiyaki*, the *nioiguchi* is rather compact
bōshi: *midare-komi* with an irregular *ko-maru-kaeri*
horimono: on both sides a *bōhi* with *maru-dome* above the *habaki*

The *midareba* of this blade bases on a *gunome* and is mixed with *togariba* and *chōji*. The *nioiguchi* is rather compact and the *kitae* is an *itame* with *nagare* and a *shirake-utsuri*. The *bōshi* is *midare-komi* and appears as so-called „*jizō-bōshi*" which looks like as if it would lean towards the *ha*. That means we are obviously facing a Mino work from the late Muromachi period and so most bade from No-Sada over Kanemoto (兼元) to Kanefusa (兼房), Ujifusa (氏房), Daidō (大道) and the like.

No-Sada was with Kanemoto the most representative and outstanding smiths of the Sue-Seki group. Compared to Kanemoto, Kanefusa and other Sue-Seki smiths, his strong point was a vivid *gunome* mixed with *togariba* and *chōji* and this is exactly what we see on the *kantei* blade. He also forged the most beautiful and bright *jigane* of all Sue-Seki smiths.

No-Sada was active around Eishō (永正, 1504-1521) and Daiei (大永, 1521-1528), a time when like here a normal *mihaba*, a *sakizori* and a *chū-kissaki* was common. But Ujifusa and Daidō were active somewhat later, namely around Eiroku (永禄, 1558-1570) and Tenshō (天正, 1573-1592), and so they forged blades with a wider *mihaba* and a *sugata* which starts to tend towards a Keichō-*shintō-sugata* (which bases on shortened oversized Nanbokuchō shapes). Incidentally, such a *mizukage* is often found on works of No-Sada and can be regarded as one of his characteristics.

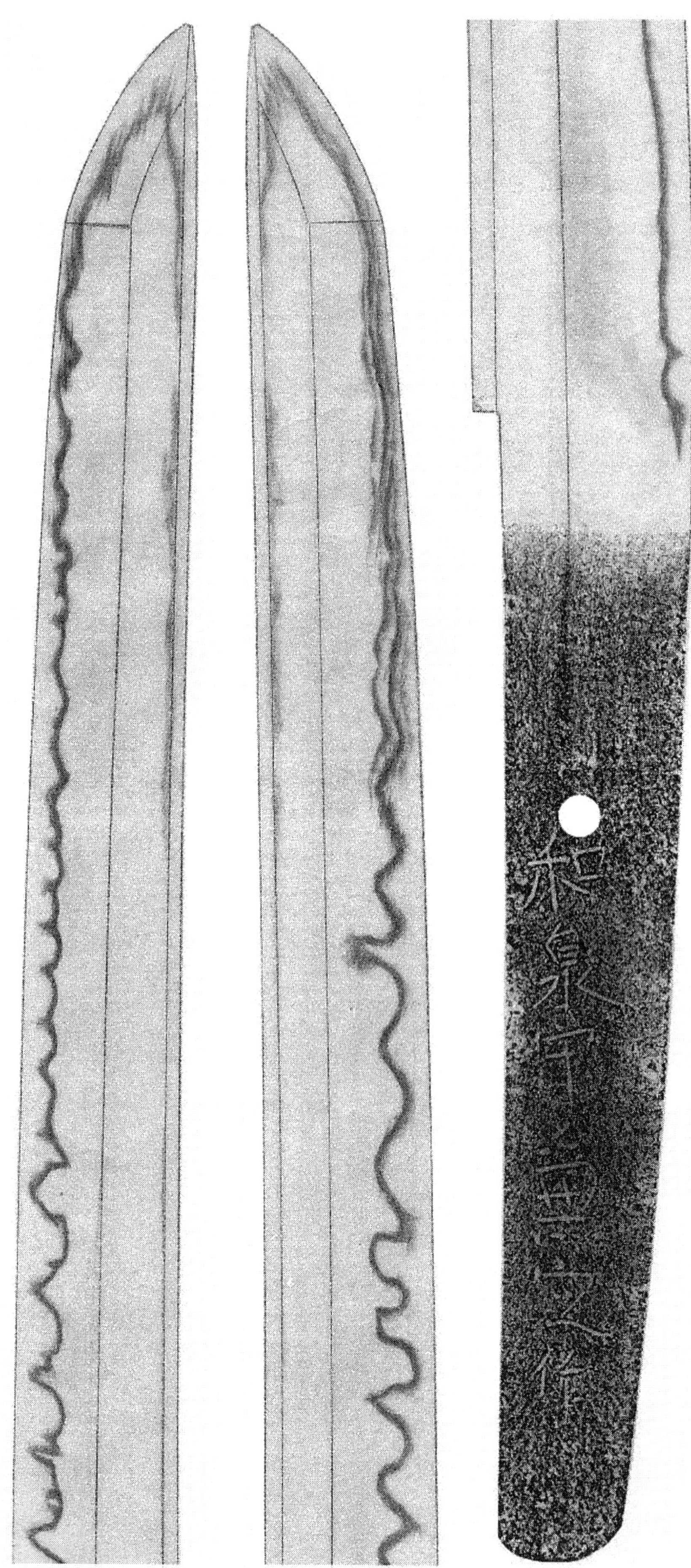

132.610 *tachi*
mei: Izumi no Kami Kanesada (和泉守兼定)
nagasa 75,75 cm, *sori* 1,95 cm, *shinogi-zukuri, iori-mune*

ji: relative dense *itame-hada* partially mixed with *nagare*, in addition *ji-nie* and a faint *shirake-utsuri*
hamon: *gunome* with partial round *yakigashira* and mixed with *gunome-chōji*, compact *nioiguchi* with plentiful of *ko-nie*
bōshi: *notare* with *hakikake* towards the tip and a long *kaeri*

This is a quite long *tachi* by Izumi no Kami Kanesada (No-Sada) which can be dated around Eishō (永正, 1504-1521) and Daiei (大永, 1521-1528). In general, blades of that time had a rather short *nagasa* but the *sugata* and the *sakizori* date this one nevertheless into the late Muromachi period. And with the clearly visible *shirake-utsuri*, we are at Mino.

Most of the Sue-Seki smiths did not show a very characteristic workmanship but this does not apply to Kanesada because he and his successors worked in a very fine and excellently forged *kitae*. His *hamon* consists of *chōji*, *gunome* and *gunome-chōji* but not that much of *togari*. Such a *hamon* composition with a conspicious amount of *chōji* and less *togari* can also be regarded as one of his characteristics.

Besides of Kanesada there were also bids on Kanemoto (兼元), Kanefusa (兼房), Wakasa no Kami Ujifusa (若狭守氏房), Mutsu no Kami Daidō (陸奥守大道) and Izumo no Kami Ujifusa (出雲守氏房). In the case of Kanemoto, the *togari-gunome* would tend to a free but noticeable *sanbonsugi*. Wakasa no Kami Ujifusa, Mutsu no Kami Daidō and Izumo no Kami Ujifusa were also Sue-Seki smiths but active somewhat later than No-Sada, namely around Eiroku (永禄, 1558-1570), Genki (元亀, 1570-1573) and Tenshō (天正, 1573-1592). That means their blades get wider and their *kissaki* larger.

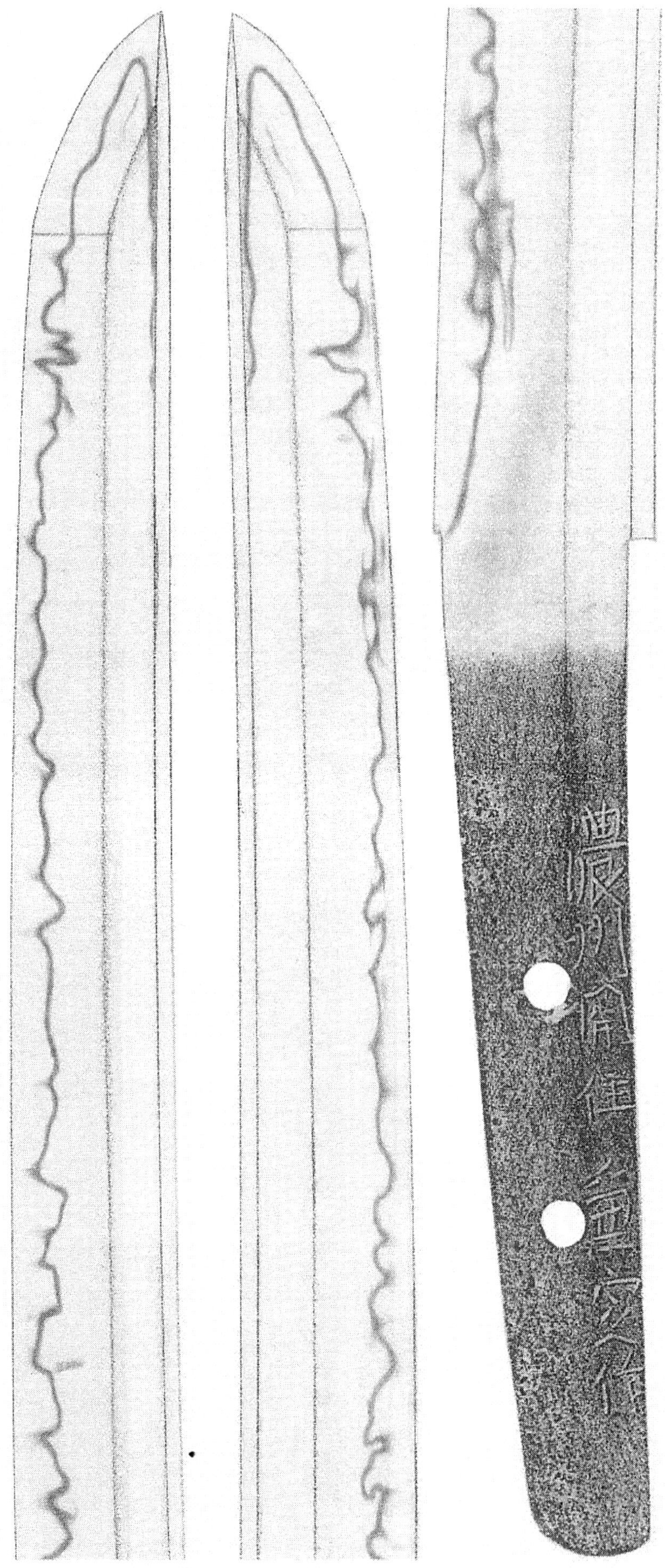

133.604 *katana*
mei: Noshū Seki-jū Kanesada saku (濃州関住兼定作)
nagasa 68,16 cm, *sori* 2,12 cm, *shinogi-zukuri*, *iori-mune*

ji: *itame-hada* mixed with *mokume* and *nagare*, there is *ji-nie* an along the upper half a clearly visible *shirake-utsuri*
hamon: based on *gunome* and mixed with *togari* and *gunome-chōji*, the hardening is in *nioi-deki* with *ko-nie* and some *sunagashi*
bōshi: *midare-komi* with a *ko-maru-kaeri*

The shorter *nagasa* and the *sakizori* identify this blade at a glance as *uchigatana* of the Muromachi period. It shows an *itame* with much *nagare* and a clearly visible *shirake-utsuri*. The *nioiguchi* shows *ko-nie* and the *hamon* is *gunome*-based and is mixed with *togari* and *gunome-chōji* elements, which results in a rather flamboyant *midareba*. The *bōshi* is *midare-komi* and has a *kaeri* which tends to *jizō*.

This is a *katana* of Izumo no Kami Kanesada (No-Sada). He and Kanemoto (兼元) were the most representative and outstanding smiths of the Sue-Seki group and one of his characteristics is a *gunome* with round *yakigashira* which results with the mixed-in *togari* and *gunome-chōji* elements in a vivid *midareba*. This characteristic is well seen on the *kantei* blade. In addition, No-Sada is famous for his excellent *kitae* and his *jigane* is unlike contemporary Sue-Seki-*mono* bright and clear.

All this was perfectly understood and the vast majority bade *atari* on Kanesada. But some reckoned the blade as a work of the Fujishima school (藤島). But in this case, the steel would be more blackish as it is typical for northern *Hokkoku-mono*. Also the *sunagashi* would be more prominent and the tip of the *bōshi* would show *hakikake*.

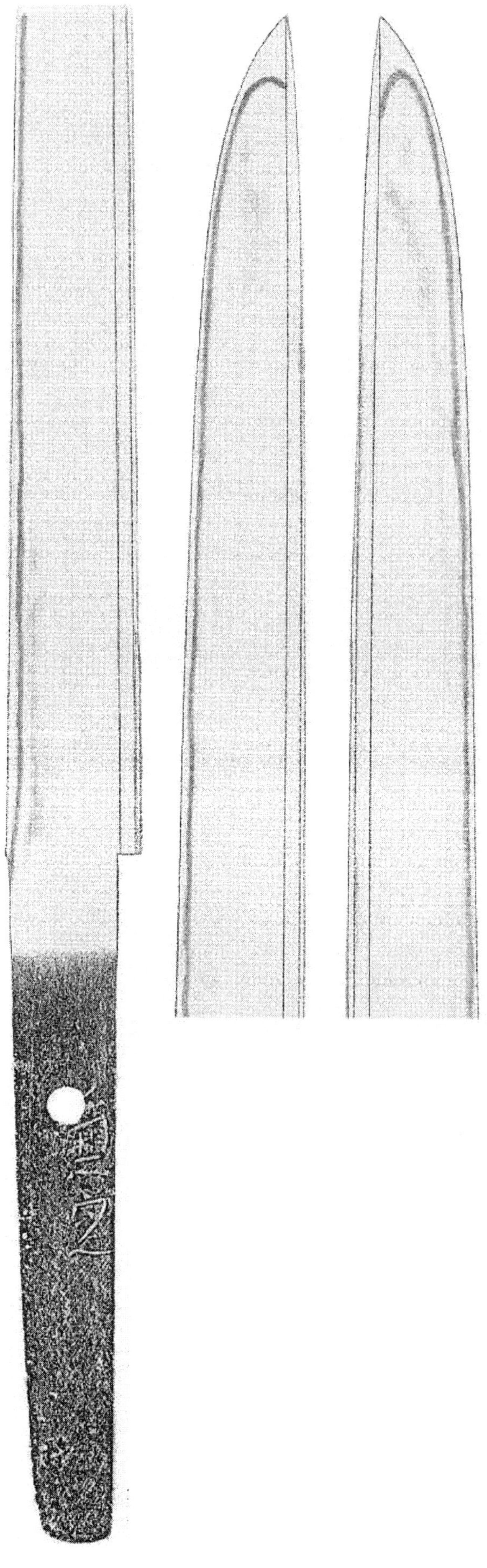

134.658 *tantō*
mei: Kanesada (兼定, No-Sada)
nagasa 19,4 cm, *uchizori*, *hira-zukuri*, *mitsu-mune*

ji: dense *ko-itame* with *ji-nie*, fine *chikei* and *shirake-utsuri* all over the blade
hamon: *hoso-suguha* in *nioi-deki* with *ko-nie*
bōshi: *sugu* with an *ō-maru*-like *kaeri* on the *omote* side and a *ko-maru-kaeri* on the *ura* side, but some subtle *hakikake* appear on both sides

This is a small and elegant *tantō* of No-Sada with a *hoso-suguha*, or to be more precise, it is a Kyō-*utsushi*. Due to the classical shape many bade in the first round on Awataguchi Yoshimitsu (粟田口吉光), Rai Kunitoshi (来国俊) or Shintōgo Kunimitsu (新藤五国光), that means they reckoned it as an original from the Kamakura period. This blade does not show the typical characteristics of other Sue-Seki Kyō-*utsushi*, namely a somewhat thicker *kasane* which gets abruptly thinner towards the tip and a scarce *fukura*. So bids on the great Kamakura-period *tantō* masters are – also in view of the *hoso-suguha* – quite understandable.

The *jigane* is very dense and would speak for Yoshimitsu but at the latter, the *suguha* would not appear as pure *suguha* but show some *ko-gunome* elements (and mostly a *yakikomi* at the *machi*). Also his *yakiba* narrows down along the *fukura*. At Rai Kunitoshi, we would expect some *nagare* and at Shintōgo Kunimitsu, some *mokume* and many *chikei*. At a closer look we also recognize that the *ji-nie* is too weak compared to the originals and that the *hoso-suguha* is „too perfect". Furthermore, the brightness of the *nioiguchi* and the *hataraki* like *kinsuji* and *sunagashi* do not reach the level of the Kamakura masters. In addition, the *kaeri* are different because one ends noticeably shorter at one side. Well, there is an *utsuri* towards the *mune* which runs parallel to the *hamon*, but it is a *shirake-utsuri* and not a *nie-utsuri*. And finally, the top surface of the *mitsu-mune* is rather narrow and with all these hints, one should be able to grasp that this blade is not an original from the Kamakura period.

Most of the participants got that right at least after the third round and went for a Sue-Seki copy. In any other case, a bid on any of the Sue-Seki smiths would be counted as *atari* but because of the utmost quality of this work, only a bid on No-Sada was counted as *atari* this time.

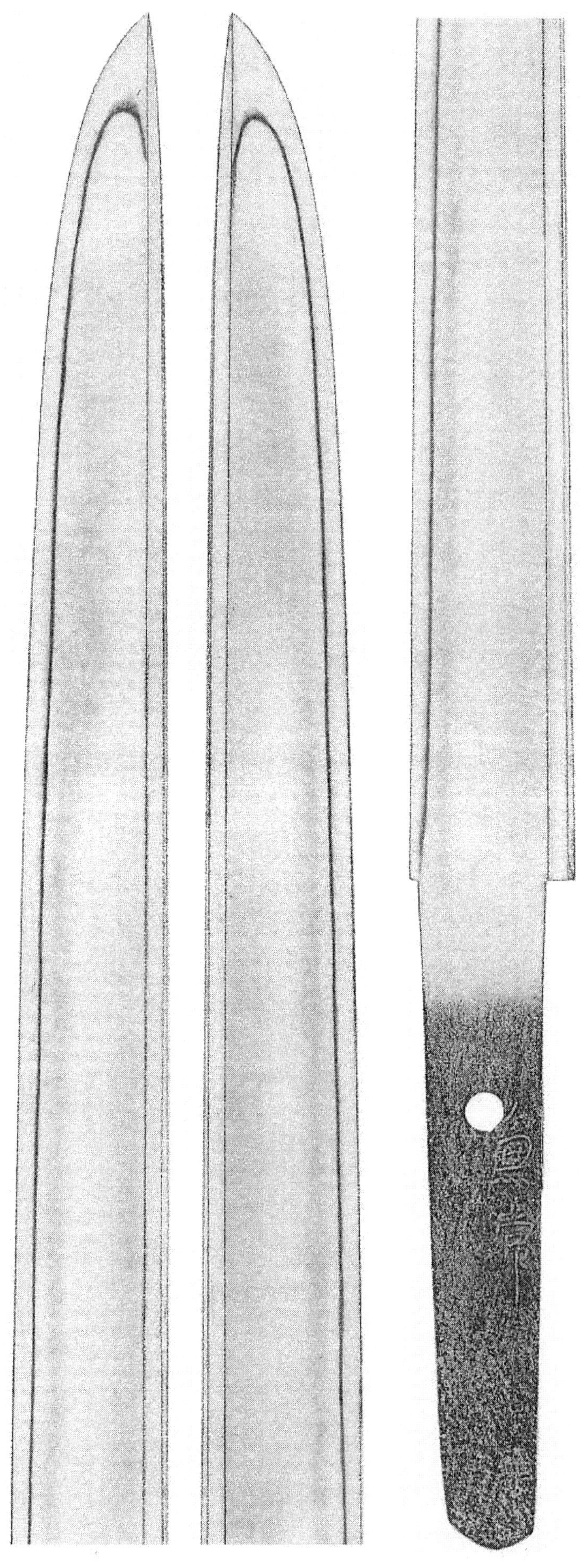

135.604 *tantō*
mei: Kanetsune (兼常)
nagasa 24,54 cm, some *uchizori* towards the tip, *hira-zukuri*, *mitsu-mune*

ji: dense *ko-itame-hada* mixed with *nagare-hada*, also *ji-nie* and a clearly visible *shirake-utsuri*
hamon: *suguha*, relative thick *nioi*, the hardening is in *nioi-deki* but shows some *ko-nie*
bōshi: *sugu* with a *ko-maru-kaeri*

The narrow blade is slightly elongated in comparison to the *mihaba* and has with the elegant *uchizori* a typical and classical *tantō-sugata*. The *kitae* is a fine and densely forged *ko-itame* and shows a clearly visible linear *utsuri* which is rather narrow along the lower half and gets wider towards the upper half of the blade. And because of the bright *nioiguchi* and the *hoso-suguha*, many went for the Rai school of the Kamakura period and especially for Rai Kunitoshi (来国俊).

Indeed, all these characteristics are seen at Rai Kunitoshi too and even the *bōshi* with the standard *ko-maru-kaeri* is applied in the style of this smith. So a bid on him is quite understandable. But important was also the check of the *mitsu-mune* because it has a narrow top surface which is usually not found at Kamakura-period *tantō* whose top face is wide. And although the *jigane* is a fine and dense *ko-itame*, it appears soft and unobtrusive compared to Kunitoshi. Also the *ji-nie* do not reach the quality of the latter and the *utsuri* is not the typical *nie-utsuri* we would expect from a work of this Rai master. As mentioned, the *bōshi* shows a Rai-typical „standard“ *ko-maru-kaeri* but the length of the *kaeri* is different on each side, a feature which is also not seen at Kunitoshi or at Rai in general.

This blade is a work of Sue-Seki Kanetsune. There are several Sue-Seki-*tantō* from the late Muromachi period extant which show similarities to Yamashiro works of the Kamakura period, especially to Rai Kunitoshi, and so it is safe to assume that also the *kantei* blade was meant as so-called „Rai-*utsushi*“. Usually, the *kasane* of such Sue-Seki Rai-*utsushi* gets abruptly thinner towards the tip and the *kaeri* leans in *jizō*-manner somewhat towards the *ha*. Both of these peculiarities – which make a recognition of a copy rather easy – are not found on this blade and so the *kantei* was a bit difficult. Thus one had to focus on the aforementioned differences.

136.669 *tantō*
mei: Kanesaki (兼先)
nagasa 22,1 cm, *uchizori*, *hira-zukuri*, *iori-mune*

ji: very dense and finely forged *ko-itame* mixed with *nagare*, *ji-nie* and *shirake-utsuri*
hamon: *hoso-suguha* in *nioi-deki* with plentiful of *ko-nie*, the *nioiguchi* is rather compact
bōshi: *sugu* with a long *ko-maru-kaeri* which leans somewhat towards the *ha*

This *tantō* is slender, has a normal *kasane*, *uchizori* and shows a *suguha*, that means it looks at a glance like a Rai work from the late Kamakura period. But when you take a closer look you will see that the *nie* are not so strong as expected for Rai, that the *jigane* shows all over *shirake*, that the wide *kaeri* leans towards the *ha*, that the *uchizori* is too noticeable but the *fukura* too scarce, and that the *kasane* thins too abrupt towards the tip. All these are namely typical characteristics for the Muromachi period and especially for Sue-Seki. Smith from that group made namely relative many of such Kyō- or Rai-*utsushi* or Yamashiro-based homages.

The *tantō* seen here of Kanesaki does not show much peculiar features but this is in general the case at Sue-Seki-*mono*. That means it is relative difficult to nail down a certain smith and so all bids on Sue-Seki were counted as *atari*. Well, No-Sada is famous for his Rai-*utsushi* and so many went for him what is quite understandable. Incidentally, these Rai copies focus mostly on works of Rai Kunitoshi (来国俊) and the early Rai Kunimitsu (来国光). Both Rai Kunitoshi and Kunimitsu made a *tantō-sugata* with a well-balanced *mihaba*, *kasane* and *nagasa* in combination with an *uchizori*. Their *jiba* is quite *nie*-loaden and a *nie-utsuri* appears (which is sometimes also called „Rai-*utsuri*" because it is so typical).

But there were also some bids on the Sōshū smith Shintōgo Kunimitsu (新藤五国光). In his case, even more *nie* than at Rai and conspicious *chikei* would appear. In addition, his *ha* would show peculiar *kinsuji*.

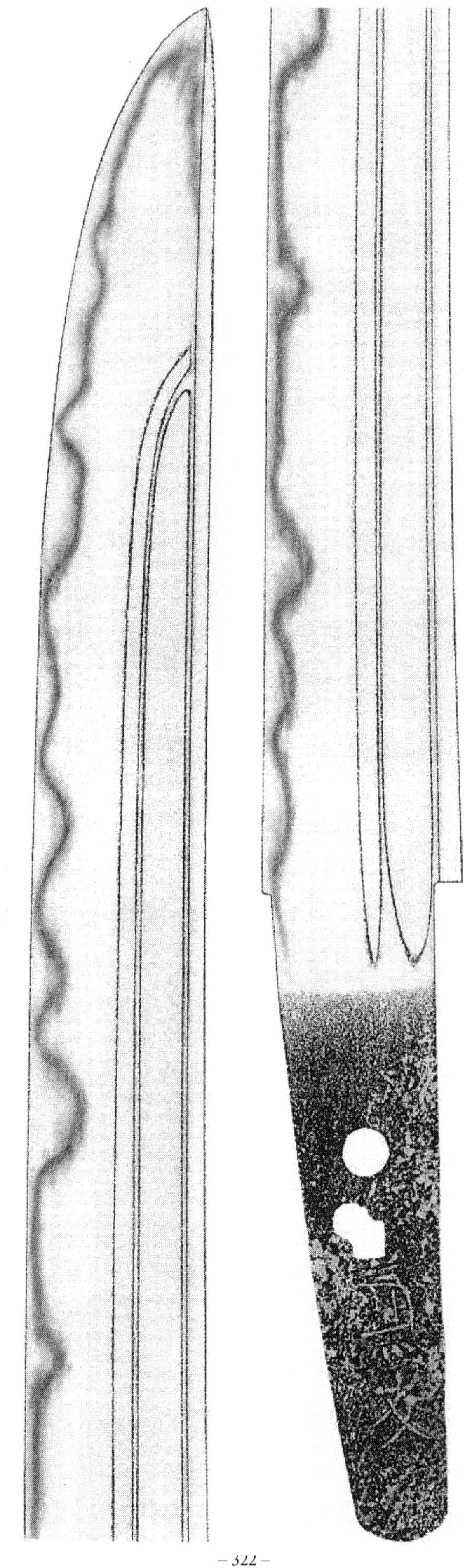

137.626 *tantō*
mei: Kanetomo (兼友)
nagasa 28,1 cm, *sori* 0,3 cm, *hira-zukuri*, *iori-mune*

ji: *itame* with *chikei*, the *hada* stands out and tends strongly to *masame-nagare* towards the *ha*
hamon: *notare* mixed with roundish and some angular *gunome*, the *nioiguchi* is relative wide and there are plentiful of *ko-nie*, all over the blade fine *sunagashi* and some *kinsuji* appear
bōshi: *suguha-chō* with *hakikake* and a pointed *kaeri* on the *omote* and a *nie-kuzure*-like *ko-maru* on the *ura* side, both *kaeri* run back long
horimono: on both sides a *bōhi* with *tsurebi* which runs with *kake-nagashi* into the tang

There exist date signatures of the Kan´ō era (観応, 1350-1352) by Naoe-Shizu Kanetsugu (直江志津兼次) and so Kanetomo from the same school is dated also around that time. This dating is supported by *tantō* like that which show a wide *mihaba*, are *sunnobi*, have a thin *kasane* and a shallow *sori*, that means which have a typical mid-Nanbokuchō-period *sugata*.

The *kitae* is an *itame* which tends strongly to *nagare* and stands out. There are many *chikei* too. The *hamon* is a *notare* which is mixed with roundish *gunome* and shows noticeable ups and downs. And when we combine this with the plentiful of *ko-nie* and repeatedly applied *sunagashi*, we can recognize a Yamato-Sōshū mix which in turn brings us to Mino. The *midare* rises high in places but there are not that many *hataraki* within the *hamon*, like for example *ashi* and *yō*. This however is typical for later Seki smiths like Kanesada (兼定, No-Sada) or Ujifusa (氏房).

Most bids focused on old Mino-*mono*, especially on Kaneuji (兼氏, Shizu) and the Naoe-Shizu school. But Kaneuji´s *tantō* are not that large and show a smaller and more stout *sugata*. Also his *kitae* would not stand out that much but there would be stronger *nie* in the *ha* and much more *kinsuji*. Altogether, Kaneuji is more Sōshū oriented and his *bōshi* would appear as *ō-maru* or shows at least a clearly round and short *kaeri*. A pointed *bōshi* with *hakikake* like it is common for the Naoe-Shizu school is not found at Kaneuji. Well, besides of Kaneuji many went as mentioned also for Naoe-Shizu like Kanetsugu or Kanenobu (兼信). There are relative few blades extant by these smiths and so it is hard to determine individual characteristics. So bids on them were counted as *atari-dōzen*, i.e. „almost correct“.

Some bade also on Sue-Seki or Muramasa (村正), but here, we would see a *tantō-sugata* of the late Muromachi period. That means they might be wide but the *kasane* is thick and a *sakizori* would appear.

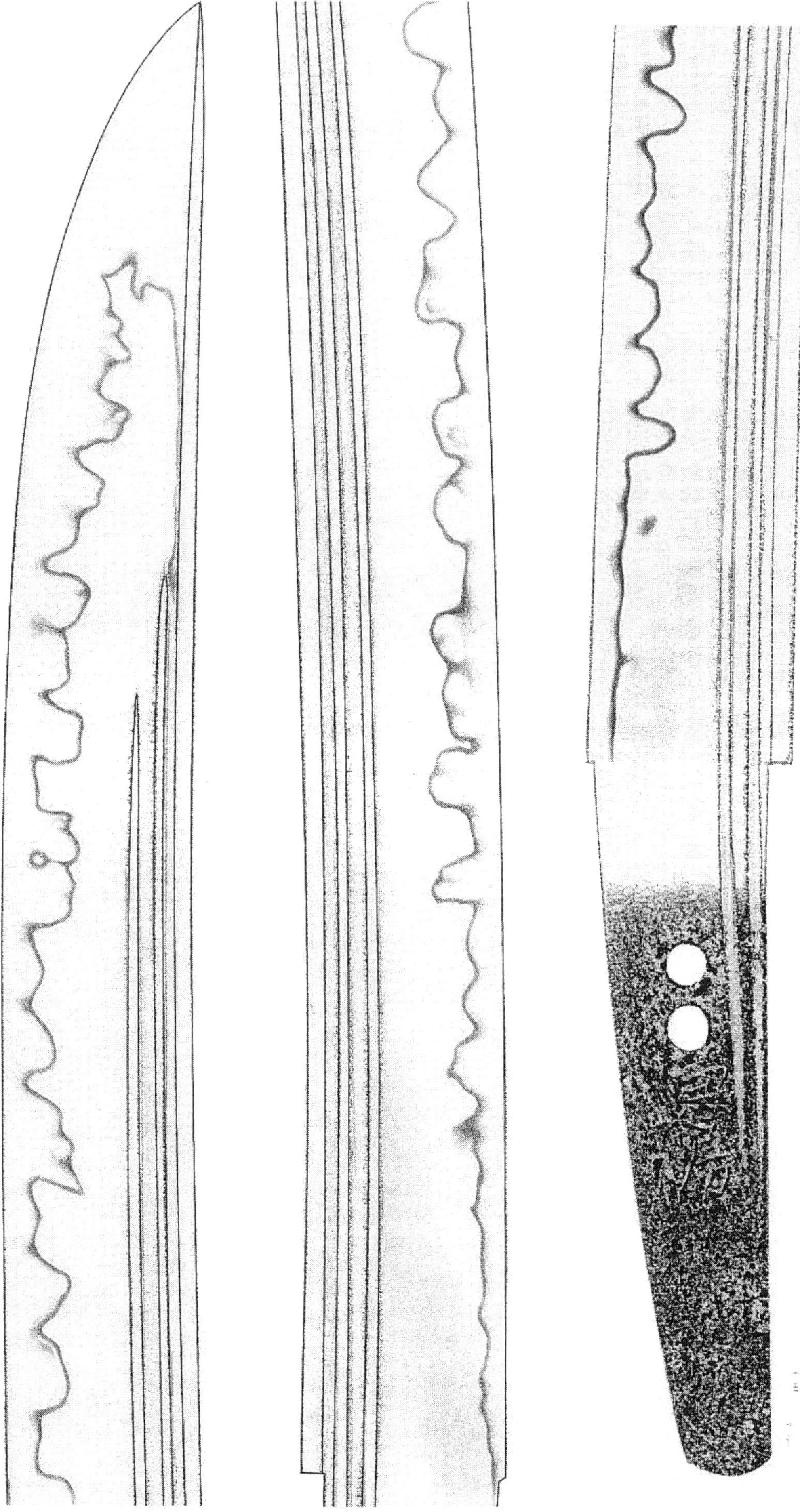

138.644k *wakizashi*
mei: Kanefusa (兼房)

nagasa 36,2 cm | *sori* 0,7 cm
moto-haba 2,9 cm | *moto-kasane* 0,7 cm
nakago-nagasa 11,06 cm | only a little *nakago-sori*

hira-zukuri, iori-mune, wide *mihaba*, conspicious *sunnobi, sakizori*. The *jigane* is an *itame* mixed with *mokume* and *masame-nagare* which stands out all over the blade. In addition, *ji-nie, chikei* and a faint *shirake-utsuri* appears. The *hamon* and the *bōshi* can be seen on the *oshigata. Tobiyaki, ashi, yō* and *sunagashi* can be seen in places. The *nioiguchi* is compact and the hardening is in *nioi-deki* with *ko-nie*. There is a *futasuji-ji* carved on both sides which runs with *kake-nagashi* into the tang. The *nakago* is *ubu*, has a *kurijiri, higaki-yasurime* and two *mekugi-ana*. A *niji-mei* is chiselled centrally on the *sashi-omote* below the *mekugi-ana*.

The blade has a wide *mihaba*, is *sunnobi* and shows a *sakizori*, that means we can date it into the late Muromachi period. The *jigane* of Seki-*mono* is an *itame* mixed with *nagare* which stands usually out all over the blade and shows a *shirake-utsuri*. The *hamon* is a mix of *gunome* with roundish *yakigashira* and *gunome-chōji, togariba* and *yahazu*-like elements, a *sanbonsugi*, or a *notare*. That means this group applied many different *hamon* variants. A connected *gunome-chōji* with roundish *yakigashira* whose bases narrow down is called „Kenbō-*midare*" because it is especially peculiar to works of Kanefusa. [Translators note: „Kenbō" is the Sino-japanese reading of the characters of „Kanefusa".] The latter *hamon* variant can be seen on the *kantei* blade although there exist many blades whose *yakigashira* are even more roundish and the bases more narrow. The *bōshi* of Seki-*mono* is like at the *kantei* blade mostly a *midare-komi* with a *ko-maru-kaeri*. At many works, the *kaeri* leans towards the *ha*. This peculiarity is called *„jizō-bōshi"* and a hint of that can also be seen on the *kantei* blade.

The tip of Kanefusa´s *tantō*- and *hira-zukuri wakizashi-nakago* is *kurijiri*, the *yasurime* are *higaki* or *katte-sagari*, and the signatures can be chiselled in different ways. We know for example a *sanji-mei* „Kanefusa saku" or a *naga-mei* „Nōshū Seki-jū Kanefusa tsukuru" (濃州関住兼房造). Some blades bear also a date signatuee on the *ura* side of the tang.

Well, as mentioned, *tantō* and *hira-zukuri wakizashi* from Seki show mostly *higaki-yasurime*. But also contemporary Sue-Tegai smiths applied such file strokes on *tantō* and *hira-zukuri wakizashi*. At Seki-*mono*, the *higaki* are applied at a more acute angle (they appear as overlapping *ō-sujikai* and *gyaku-ō-sujikai*), whereas at Sue-Tegai tangs, the *higaki* angle is not that acute but more like a *sujikai* crossed with *gyaku-sujikai*.

The majority was spont-on at Kanefusa but there were also many who bade on Kanesada (兼定), Ujifusa (氏房), Daidō (大道) or other Seki smiths. Except the peculiar, free *sanbonsugi* of Magoroku Kanemoto (孫六兼元), many of the Seki smiths worked in a rather uniform style which is similar to the *kantei* blade and so it is difficult to nail down a single smith. So this time, all bids on Seki were counted as *atari*.

Besides of these *atari*, some few went also for Kanetomo (兼友), Kanetsugu (兼次) or other smiths of the Naoe-Shizu school. Sometimes they also applied a *gunome-chō* which reminds of Seki-*hamon*, that means from this point of view a bid on Naoe-Shizu is understandable. But *hira-zukuri wakizashi* have a thin *kasane* and there is no conspicious *sakizori*. Also their *hamon* shows fine *hotsure* along the *habuchi*, their *nioiguchi* is not compact but quite *nie*-loaden, and there are many *sunagashi* and *kinsuji* within the *ha*.

Bitchû

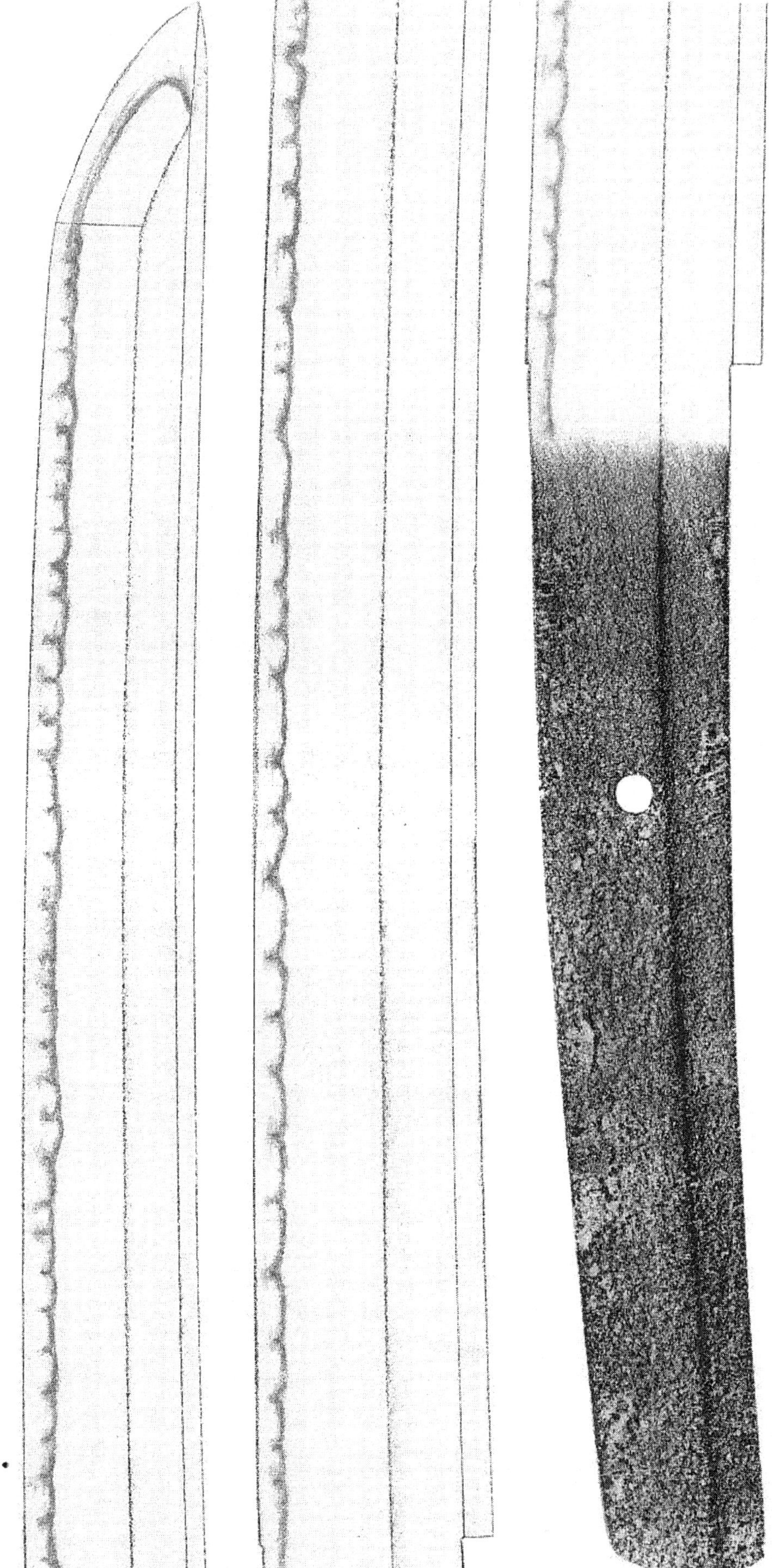

139.622 *katana*
mumei: Ko-Aoe (古青江)
nagasa 76,9 cm, *sori* 3,1 cm, *shinogi-zukuri*, *iori-mune*

ji: *ko-itame* mixed with *mokume* which tends to stand out, in addition *ji-nie*, *chikei* and a *jifu-utsuri*, the steel has a blackish-blue colour
hamon: *suguha-chō* mixed with *ko-chōji-midare* and *ko-midare*, in addition many *ashi* and *yō*, the *nioiguchi* is somewhat subdued and shows *nie* and some few *sunagashi*
bōshi: *suguha* with a *ko-maru*-like *kaeri*

This is an *ō-suriage mumei* blade which is attributed to the Ko-Aoe school and which as *jūyō* papers. The tang has only one *mekugi-ana* which was added after shortening the blade to *uchigatana* length. But when you reconstruct – starting from the remaining *funbari*, the shape of the tang and the *sori* – the original shape, then you arrive at an original length of more than 2 *shaku* 8 *sun* and 5 *bu* (86,4 cm). So this was once an overlong (*chōsun*, 長寸) *tachi*.

From the end of the Heian to the beginning Kamakura period, most schools made a *tachi-sugata* with slender *mihaba*, a noticeable taper and a deep *koshizori* which bends down towards the tip. But the *kantei* blade has a somewhat wider *mihaba* and a *koshizori* which increases again slightly towards the tip. Therefore many went for later Kamakura period Bizen-*mono* and especially for the Un group (Unji [雲次], Unshō [雲生] and the like).

A *tachi-sugata* like seen here is very rare for that early time but we find it not only at the Ko-Aoe but also at the Ko-Bizen school. For example from the Ko-Aoe school, the *tokubetsu-jūyō tachi* by Toshitsugu (俊次) and the *kokuhō* „Kitsunegasaki Tametsugu“ (狐ケ崎為次) have to be mentioned. If you know that these two schools worked also in that *sugata* and when you combine this with the *jigane*, i.e. a rather standing-out *ko-itame* which appears as *chirimen*, and also with the classical *suguha-chō* with *ko-chōji* and *ko-midare*, and when you further realize that such thick *nie* are not common for late Kamakura-period Aoe and Bizen works, then you are able to nail the bid down to Ko-Aoe or Ko-Bizen. After a closer inspection of the *ji*, you will see a *jifu-utsuri* with dark *antai* areas which are different in size and shape. This and the *sumigane* is very typical for Ko-Aoe.

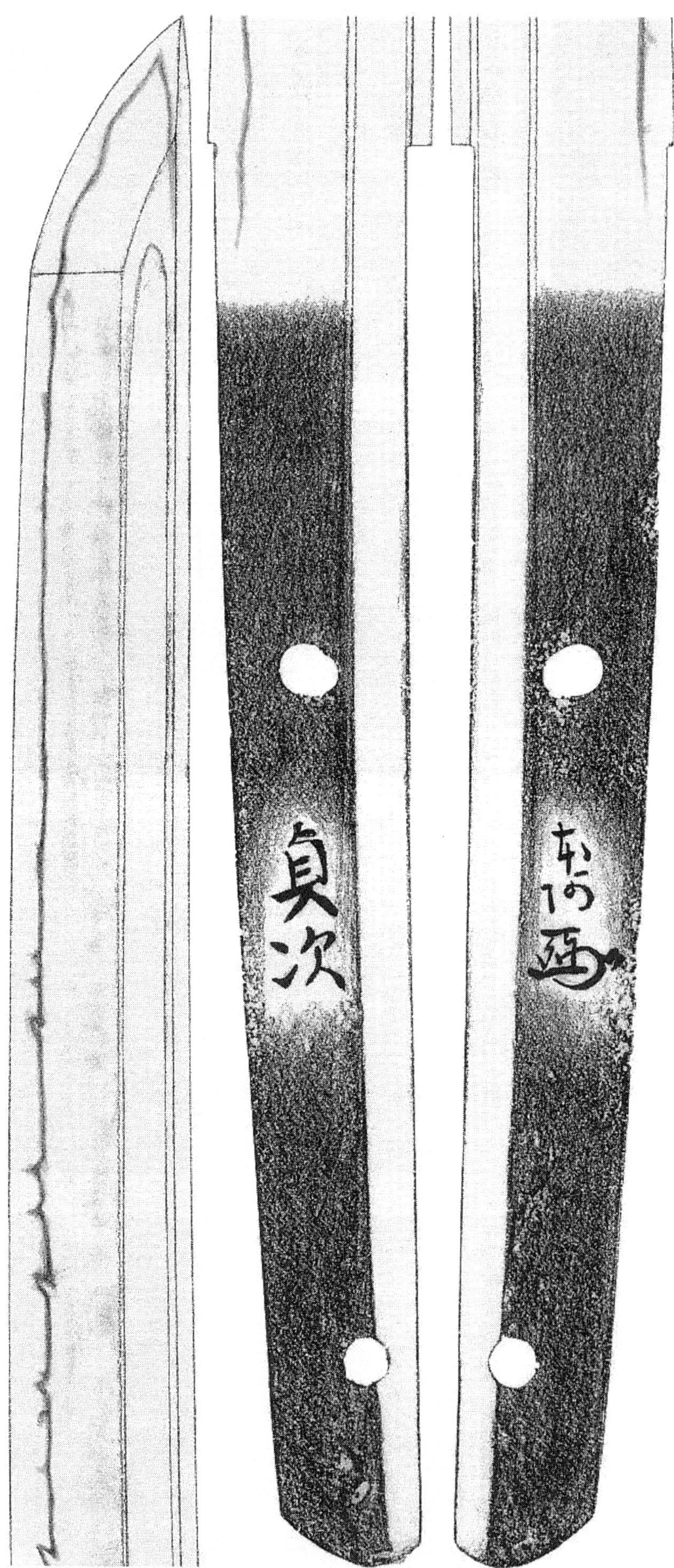
貞次

140.633 *katana*
kinzōgan-mei: Sadatsugu (貞次)
Hon´a [*kaō*] (Ringa, 琳雅)
nagasa 70,0 cm, *sori* 1,8 cm, *shinogi-zukuri*, *iori-mune*

ji: very dense *ko-itame* mixed with *ko-mokume* which stands out finely as *chirimen-hada*, in addition *ji-nie*, fine *chikei* and a *midare-utsuri* which bases on a *jifu-utsuri* towards the *shinogi* and a thin *bō-utsuri* towards the *ha*, the result is a *dan-utsuri*
hamon: based on *suguha* and mixed with *ko-gunome*, angular and partially slanting *gunome*, *ko-ashi*, *yō*, *kinsuji* and *sunagashi*, the *nioiguchi* is bright, rather compact and shows *ko-nie*
bōshi: shallow *notare-komi* with a pointed *kaeri*
horimono: on both sides a *bōhi* which runs with *kake-tōshi* through the tang

There were several Sadatsugu active within the Aoe school, namely from the early Kamakura period (Ko-Aoe) over the late Kamakura period, where find individual names like „Uemon no Jō Sadatsugu" (右衛門尉貞次) who was active around Karyaku (嘉暦, 1326-1329), up to the Nanbokuchō-period „Ōsumi Gonnosuke Sadatsugu" (大隅権介貞次). The *kantei* blade bears „just" the *kinzōgan* attribution to „Sadatsugu" but such a general attribution respectively is common for older appraisals (*ko-kiwame*, 古極め).

The *kantei* blade has a wide *mihaba*, tapers not that much and ends with an elongated *chū-kissaki*. The *kitae* is a *ko-itame* mixed with *ko-mokume* which stands out in a fine manner and appears as *chirimen-hada*. There is a *jifu*-based *midare-utsuri* towards the *shinogi* and a fine *bō-utsuri* towards the *ha*. These peculiarities of the *hada* and the *utsuri* are very typical for Aoe. Also very typical is the *suguha*-based *hamon* with its angular and partially slanting *gunome* elements and the *bōshi* in shallow *notare-komi* with a pointed *kaeri*. So it shouldn´t be too hard to arrive at the Aoe school in this case. Well, the *nioiguchi* is rather compact and shows *ko-nie*, in some places even plentiful of *ko-nie*. When we combine this with the *sugata* then arrive at the late Kamakura period.

Most got that right and went for Aoe, and there were also direct bids on Ko-Aoe or later Aoe smiths like Tsuguyoshi (次吉) and Tsugunao (次直) from the heyday of the Nanbokuchō period. In the case of Ko-Aoe, the *hamon* would also base on *suguha* but would be mixed with a lot of *ko-midare*. There would be more *nie* within the *ha* and the *nioiguchi* would be more subdued. At the latter two mentioned smiths, the *sugata* would be larger and would show an *ō-kissaki*. Also the *hamon* would be in *nioi-deki* and a hint more tight.

Besides of these *dōzen* bids there were also some who went for Motoshige (元重) or Unshō (雲生). Both of them belonged to the Bizen tradition but their works do show Aoe characteristics. The *hamon* here for example is quite close to both of them but in the case of Motoshige, the *hada* would stand out more and show *nagare* and in the case of a work of the Un group, the *sori* would be a *toriizori* and the *bōshi* would show a noticeably round *kaeri*. But it were first and foremost the differences in *utsuri* which should one lead away from Motoshige or the Un group.

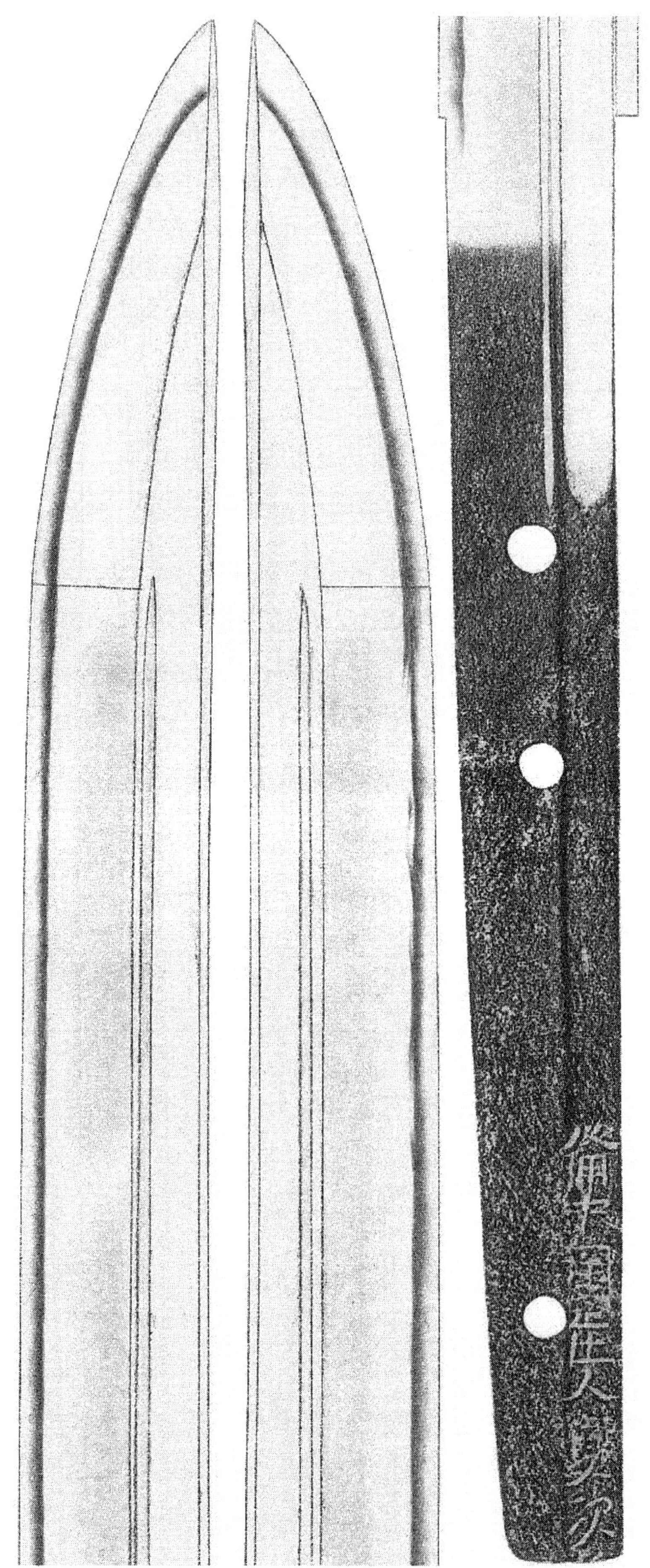

141.615 *naginata-naoshi*
mei: Bitchū no Kuni-jūnin Sadatsugu ? (備中国住人貞次？) [Nanbokuchō period]
nagasa 62,12 cm, *sori* 1,06 cm, *naginata-naoshi-zukuri*, *iori-mune*

ji: all over very densely forged *ko-itame* mixed with *ko-mokume*, in addition *ji-nie*, fine *chikei* and a faint *utsuri*
hamon: based on *hoso-suguha* and with *ko-notare*, *ko-gunome* and *ko-ashi*, the *nioiguchi* is bright and broad and shows plentiful of *ko-nie*, *kinsuji* and *sunagashi*
bōshi: *sugu* with *yakitsume*
horimono: there is a narrow *kuichigai-bi* on the *shinogi* and a *naginata-hi* towards the base on both sides, the latter runs with *kake-nagashi* into the tang

There were several Sadatsugu active within Bitchū´s Aoe school, but the most famous of them was Ko-Aoe Sadatsugu. From around Karyaku (嘉暦, 1326-1329), i.e. the late Kamakura period onwards, we find individual names like „Uemon no Jō" (右衛門尉) and for the Nanbokuchō period names like „Ōsumi Gonnosuke" (大隅権介). From the signature style, the *kantei* blade can be identified as a work of the Nanbokuchō-period Saiga Tarōbei no Jō Sadatsugu (雑賀太郎兵衛尉貞次) of whom a *jūyō-tachi* with the date signature of the Kōryaku era (康暦, 1379-1381) and signed *tantō* from the Shitoku era (至徳, 1384-1387) are extant. The *meikan* records date him between Jōji (貞治, 1362-1368) and Shitoku. The aforementioned Ōsumi Gonnosuke Sadatsugu was active a bit later. As it was common for the Aoe school, Saiga Tarōbei no Jō Sadatsugu too signed with rather small characters and even we don´t have many works from him to compare, it is assumed that he worked mostly in *suguha-chō*.

From the Nanbokuchō period onwards, there was a trend to *nioi-deki* seen among all schools but the Aoe smiths made blades with plentiful of *ko-nie*, *kinsuji* and *sunagashi*. Some show a wide and very bright *nioiguchi* and the *kantei* blade is exactly such a work. Well, just from the *sugata* it was difficult to find out the correct time but on the basis the *ko-itame* mixed with *ko-mokume*, the *ji-nie* and fine *chikei*, and the refined and delicate *jigane*, it should be possible to grasp the Aoe characteristics.

Many bade also on Yamato or the Mihara school because their strong point was also a *suguha*, But in the case of Yamato or Mihara, the *jigane* would show more and conspicious *nagare*.

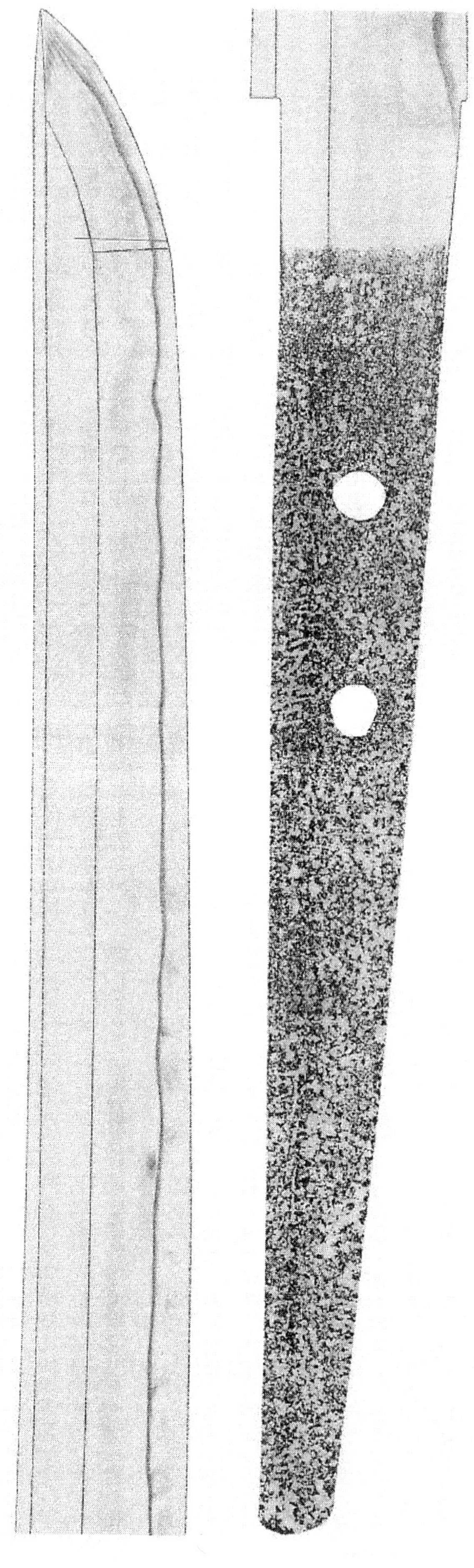

142.591 *tachi*
mei: Bitchū no Kuni-jū Tsuguyoshi (備中国住次吉)
?? [Enbun] ninen jūgatsu-hi (〇〇［延文］二年十月日, „a day in the tenth month of Enbun two [1357]")
nagasa 71,6 cm, *sori* 1,9 cm, *naginata-naoshi-zukuri*, *iori-mune*

ji: dense *ko-itame*, partial *jifu*, the *hada* stands out finely all over the blade, in addition plentiful of *ji-nie* and *chikei*, there appears an *utsuri* at the *machi* which develops into a *bō-utsuri* towards the *ha* and to a *midare-* and *bō-utsuri*-mix towards the *shinogi*, i.e. a *dan-utsuri* can be seen
hamon: towards the base a shallow *notare* which turns into a *suguha-chō*, compact *nioiguchi*, *saka-ashi*, *yō*, *nioi-deki* with *ko-nie*, the *nioiguchi* is bright and clear
bōshi: *sugu* with a pointed *kaeri* with *hakikake*

The date signature is hardly legible but it is definitely the Enbun era. This is a rare *zaimei-tachi* with *ubu-nakago* of Aoe Yoshitsugu. The *mihaba* is not that wide for the production time and the *koshizori* increases again towards the tip, but the slightly elongated *chū-kissaki* speaks eventually for the Nanbokuchō period. There is a *funbari* and an *utsuri* seen which goes out from the *ha-machi*, so we have here an unshortened blade. The *jigane* is a dense *ko-itame* which stands out in a fine manner. A *dan-utsuri* and some *sumigane* appear, the *hamon* is a *suguha-chō* in *nioi-deki* with a compact *niooiguchi* and *saka-ashi*, and the *bōshi* has a pointed *kaeri*. So all in all we have the typical characteristics of the middle Nanbokuchō-period Aoe school. Accordingly the bids focused on Tsugunao (次直), Tsuguyoshi (次吉), Moritsugu (守次), Yoshitsugu (吉次) or Naotsugu (直次).

Well, Tsugunao and Moritsugu worked in exactly the same way as Tsuguyoshi but at Yoshitsugu and Naotsugu, the *kissaki* would not be elongated but smaller and more compact and their *yakiba* would be a hint more *nie*-loaden.

Some got also the province wrong and went for Unji (雲次) or Unjū (雲重). This can be explained by the fact that also the Un group applied a quite peculiar *utsuri* and a somehow similar *hada* structure, but this blade speaks in the end clearly more for Aoe.

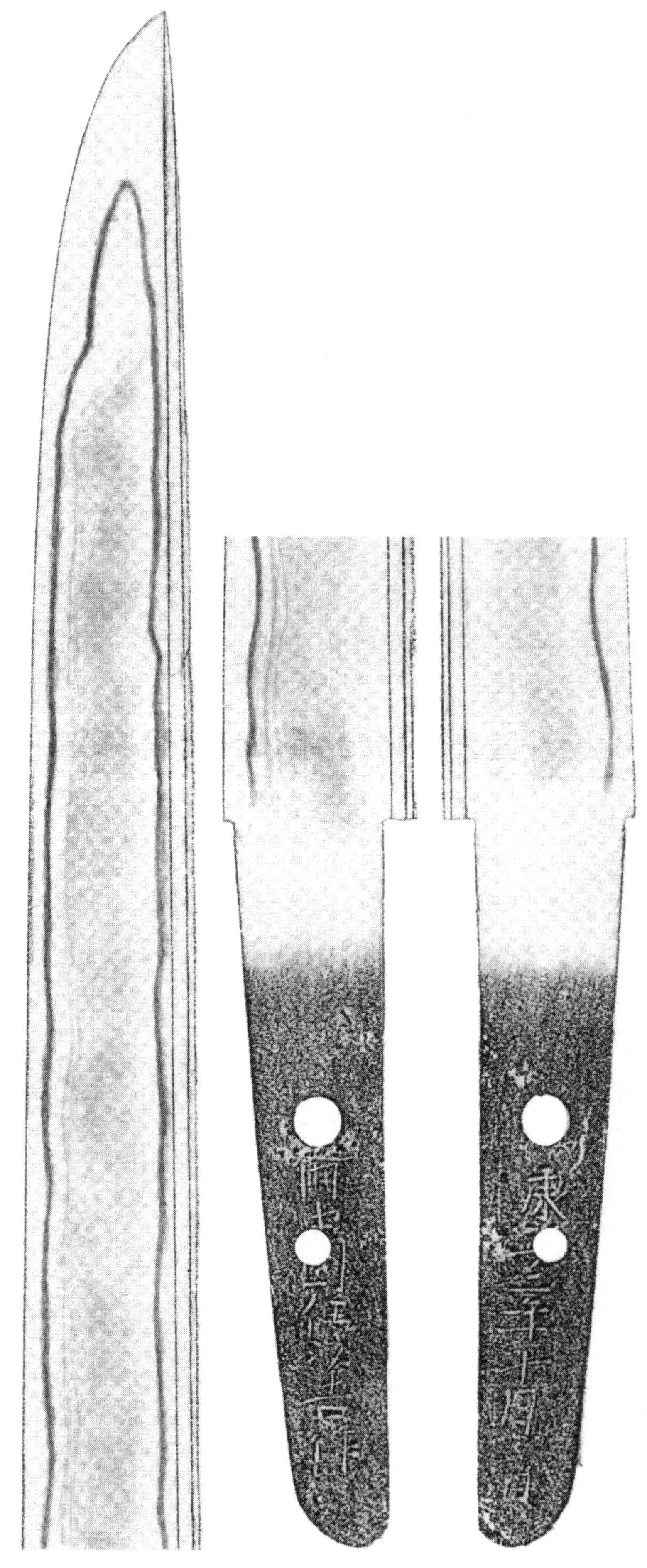

143.671 *tantō*

mei: Bitchū no Kuni-jū Tsuguyoshi saku (備中国住次吉作)
Kōan ninen jūgatsu-hi (康安二年十月日, „a day in the tenth month Kōan two [1362]“)

nagasa 27,5 cm, no *sori*, *hira-zukuri*, *mitsu-mune*

ji: *itame* mixed with *nagare*, *jifu*, *chikei*, *ji-nie*, a *midare-utsuri* and a linear *utsuri*, the linear *utsuri* appears also as *dan-utsuri* in places

hamon: *suguha* mixed with shallow *notare* and some *ko-ashi* and *yō*, the *habuchi* is rather compact, bright and clear, there is a continuous *muneyaki* from the *bōshi* down to the *machi*

bōshi: shallow *notare-komi* with a widely hardened, rather early turning-back *ko-maru-kaeri* which connects with the *muneyaki*

This *hira-zukuri tantō* has a wide *mihaba*, tends to *sunnobi*, has no *sori* and a thin *kasane*, that means it shows the typical characteristics of a *tantō* and *wakizashi* shape of the Nanbokuchō-period Enbun (延文, 1356-1361) and Jōji eras (貞治, 1362-1368). Back then there was a trend to a thin *kasane* and this is particularily true for Kyōto´s Hasebe and Bitchū´s Aoe school.

At the examination of the *kitae*, the *utsuri* deserved special attention. First we see a clearly visible *midare-utsuri* but this turns also into a linear *utsuri* or rather an *utsuri* consisting of parallel linear lines towards the *ha*. Such an *utsuri* where a *midare* and a linear *utsuri* are combined is called „*dan-utsuri*“ and this is a very typical characteristic of the Aoe school. We also see partially some dark *jifu* areas in the *jigane* but this has nothing to do with a tired blade where the *shingane* is exposed. It is namely another feature of this school. In addition, plentiful of *ji-nie* is seen.

The Aoe smiths of the Nanbokuchō period applied basically two different *deki*: The one is a flamboyant *midareba* in a peculiar *saka-chōji* and the other one bases on *suguha*. And as most contemporary smiths focused on a hardening in *nie-deki*, the Aoe school applied – in *suguha* and in *midareba* – a *nioi-deki* at that time. Many of these works show a very tight and quite bright *nioiguchi* and the *bōshi* is mostly a shallow *notare-komi* with an early turning-back and rather pointed *kaeri* or a normal *ko-maru-kaeri*. All these features can be seen on the *kantei* blade too. However, the *kaeri* is especially long and connects with the *muneyaki* which run in a continuous manner down to the *machi*. This is rather rare but a noticeably long *kaeri* is often seen at Nanbokuchō-era Aoe works.

All this was recoginzed at the *kantei* and most of the bids focused on Aoe smiths from the Nanbokuchō period. As mentioned, they applied either a *midareba* or a *suguha* but most of the smiths worked in both ways. However, Tsuguyoshi is famous for his *suguha* because most of the Nanbokuchō-era Aoe works in *suguha* are from him. That means when you see an Aoe blade in *suguha* from that time with all thc mentioned characteristics, than it is safe to go for Tsuguyoshi.

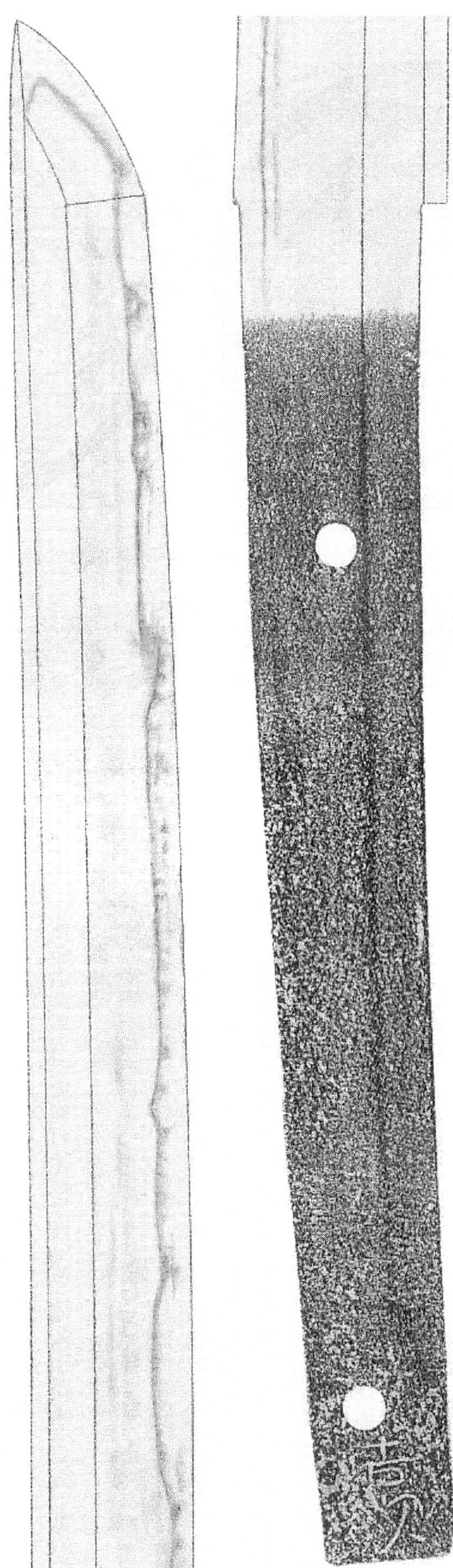

144.597 *tachi*
mei: Yoshitsugu (吉次)
nagasa 73,02 cm, *sori* 2,27 cm, *shinogi-zukuri, iori-mune*

ji: *itame-hada* with *mokume,* in addition plentiful of *ji-nie* and much fine *chikei*, towards the *shinogi* a *midare-utsuri* which turns towards the *ha* into a linear *utsuri*, this characteristic is called „*dan-utsuri*"
hamon: *chū-suguha* with shallow *notare*, some areas on the *sashi-omote* side and the *monouchi* of the *sashi-ura* side are mixed with some *ko-gunome* and *ko-midare*, in addition, *ashi* and *yō* appear, the *nioiguchi* shows *ko-nie* and is bright and clear
bōshi: *sugu* with a pointed and short *kaeri*

Yoshitsugu was one of the leading smiths of the Aoe school from the end of the Kamakura to the early Nanbokuchō period. Other contemporary smiths were for example Suketsugu (助次), Yoritsugu (頼次) and Naotsugu (直次). Despite the *suriage*, this blade keeps a deep *koshizori* which increases again towards the *chū-kissaki*. An important point here was the *utsuri* which appears as *midare* towards the *shinogi* and as discontinuous *bō-utsuri* along the *ha*. This peculiar *utsuri* is called „*dan-utsuri*" and is a typical feature of the Aoe school up to the Nanbokuchō period.

Most participants bade on an Aoe smith but landed in different times. At Ko-Aoe we would see a *jifu-utsuri* with dark *antai* areas, more *nie* within the *ha* and a somewhat more subdued *nioiguchi*. The *hamon* of this blade is namely in *nioi-deki* and has a bright and clear *nioiguchi*.

Tsuguyoshi (次吉) and Tsugunao (次直), active somewhat later than Yoshitsugu namely around Enbun (延文, 1356-1361) and Jōji (貞治, 1362-1382), i.e. at the heyday of the Nanbokuchō period, made *tachi* with a wide *mihaba* and an elongated *kissaki*. Also their *hamon* has a tight *nioiguchi*. Well, it is difficult to nail this *kantei* down to Yoshitsugu and as all Aoe smiths of his time worked in quite a similar style, all such bids were counted as *atari*.

But there were also some who went for Bizen Sanenaga (真長), Yamashiro Ryōkai (了戒) and Rai Kunitoshi (来国俊). But the keypoint was the *dan-utsuri* which is peculiar to Aoe and not seen at any of these smiths.

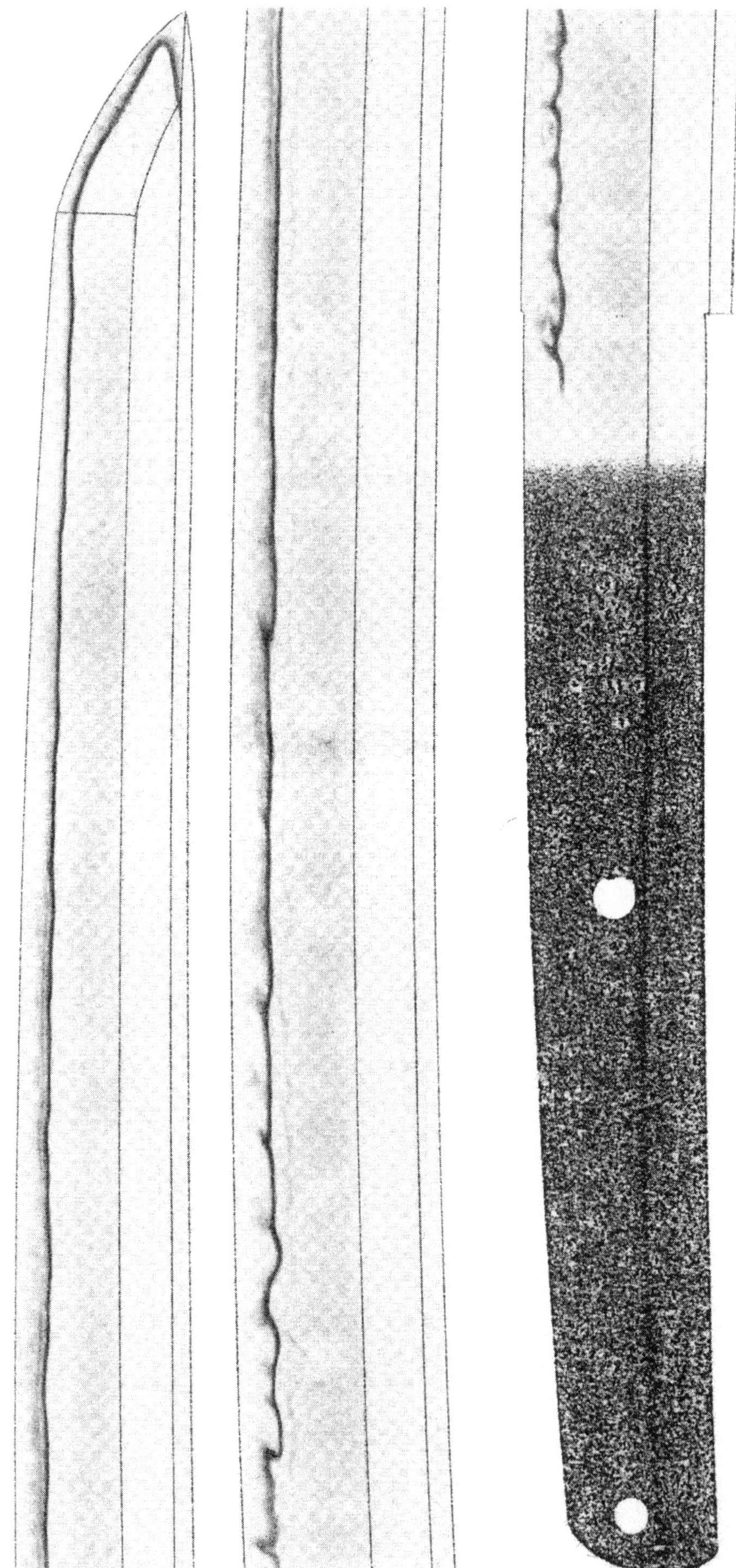

145.670 *katana*
mumei: Den Aoe Tsunetsugu (伝青江恒次)
nagasa 72,7 cm, *sori* 2,1 cm, *shinogi-zukuri*, *iori-mune*

ji: finely standing-out *itame* mixed with *mokume* and partially *jifu*-like areas, in addition *ji-nie*, a *jifu-utsuri* and centrally on the *omote* side a *dan-utsuri*
hamon: *chū-suguha* which is mixed with small *midare* along the lower half, the area of the base on the *omote* side tends to slant, in addition *ashi* and *yō*, the hardening is in *nioi-deki* but there are also *ko-nie* and centrally on the *omote* side some faint *nie-suji* appear
bōshi: shallow *notare-komi* with a *ko-maru-kaeri*

The *jigane* is a finely standing-out *ko-itame* with relative much *mokume*. Also we see *jifu* areas in places which tend to *muji*, a characteristic which is called „*sumigane*" or „*namazu-hada*". And in addition, we have a clearly visible *dan-utsuri* (a faint *bō-utsuri* and on top a *midare-utsuri*). These two characteristics are essential for this *kantei*.

The *hamon* is a *chū-suguha* with *saka-ashi* and some slanting *midare* elements. *Hamon* and *nioiguchi* are bright and clear and when we combine this with the *sugata*, i.e. the *sori* which bends down towards the tip, the noticeable taper and the shape of the *kissaki*, then it is not to difficult to recognize that this is a late Kamakura-period Aoe work.

As the *bōshi* appears as a kind of *sansaku-bōshi*, some went for contemporary Bizen smiths like Osafune Nagamitsu (長光), Sanenana (真長) or Chikakage (近景). But none of them applied a *dan-utsuri*. Their *utsuri* appears as classical *midare-utsuri*. In addition, we don´t know *saka-ashi* but only right-angled *ashi* from the former two and at Chikakage, the *hada* would stand out more and would lack some refinement. Also his *nie* are noticeably stronger.

Due to the *suguha* and the *ko-maru-kaeri*, some few bade also on the Rai school but here too, the *utsuri* is different. That means when there is an *utsuri* at Rai-*mono*, then it is a brightly flashing *nie-utsuri* and not a *dan-utsuri*.

By the way, Satō Kanzan (佐藤寒山) mentions in his *sayagaki* for this blade that it was once a heirloom of the Sakai family (酒井) from Himeji from Harima province.

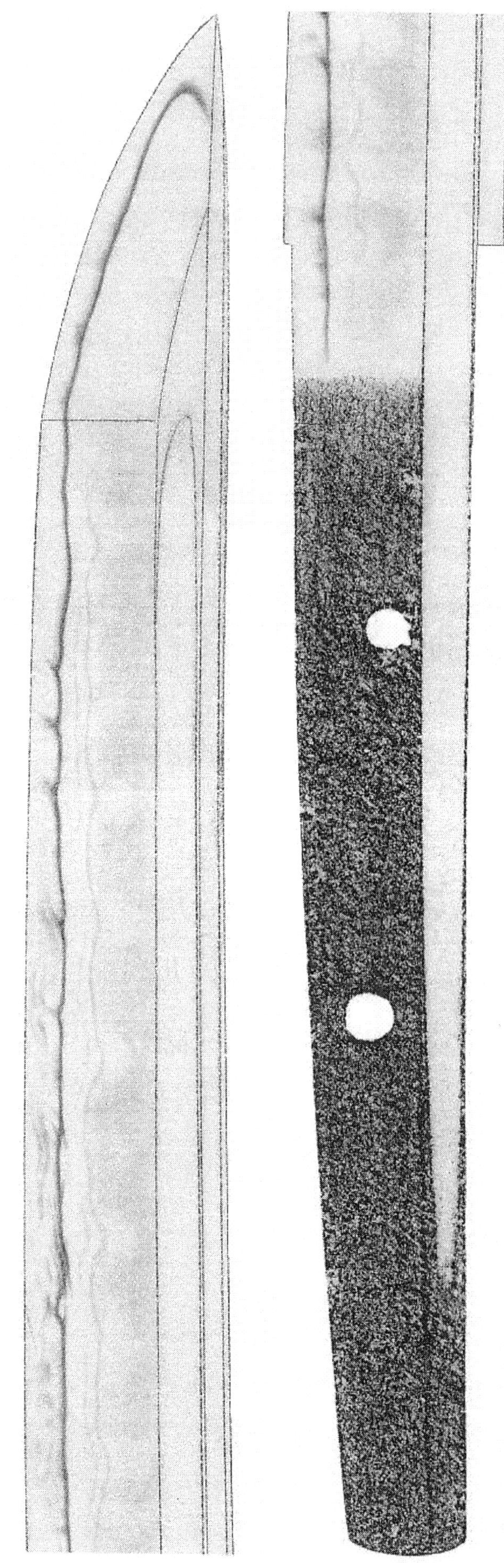

146.602 *katana*
mumei: Aoe (青江)
nagasa 70,00 cm, *sori* 1,97 cm, *shinogi-zukuri, mitsu-mune*

ji: fine and slightly standing-out *itame-hada* mixed with *mokume*, in addition plentiful of *ji-nie* and *chikei*, there is a *midare-utsuri* towards the *shinogi* and a discontinuous, linear and clearly visible *bō-utsuri* along the *ha*
hamon: based on *chū-suguha* and mixed with *ko-gunome*, in addition *ashi*, *yō* and *saka-ashi* in places, *ko-nie*, fine *sunahashi*, *kinsuji* and *nie-suji* appear in the *nioiguchi* which is in *nioi-deki*
bōshi: the *omote* side is almost *sugu* and has a *ko-maru-kaeri*, the *ura* side appears as irregular *midare-komi* and has a round *kaeri*
horimono: on both sides a *bōhi* which runs with *kake-nagashi* into the tang

The wide *mihaba*, the elongated *ō-kissaki* and the *bōhi* which ends noticeably before the *yokote* make it easy to date this blade into the Nanbokuchō period. Important at this *kantei* was to recognize the *utsuri*. That means the *utsuri* appears as a *jifu*-based *midare-utsuri* towards the *shinogi* and a discontinuous *bō-utsuri* along the *ha*. Such an *utsuri* is called „*dan-utsuri*" and seen from the Kamakura period onwards only on Aoe works. During the subsequent Nanbokuchō period, the Aoe school applied generally a *hamon* in slanting *saka-chōji-midare* or in *suguha*, and a *dan-utsuri* appears more with the latter. So alone the shape, the *utsuri* and the *suguha* with its *saka-ashi* in places are enough to attribute this blade to the Nanbokuchō-period Aoe school, even if there are not that many *nie* present here. But in addition, the slightly standing-out *itame* which is mixed with *mokume* appears as *chirimen*, another typical characteristic of the Aoe school. And finally, the clear and bright *jiba* speaks for Nanbokuchō-Aoe too.

Accordingly, the vast majority got Aoe right and went for Tsuguyoshi (次吉), Tsugunao (次直), Moritsugu (守次) and other representative smiths of that school for that time. All of them were counted as *atari* of course because this blade has anyway just an attribution to „Aoe".

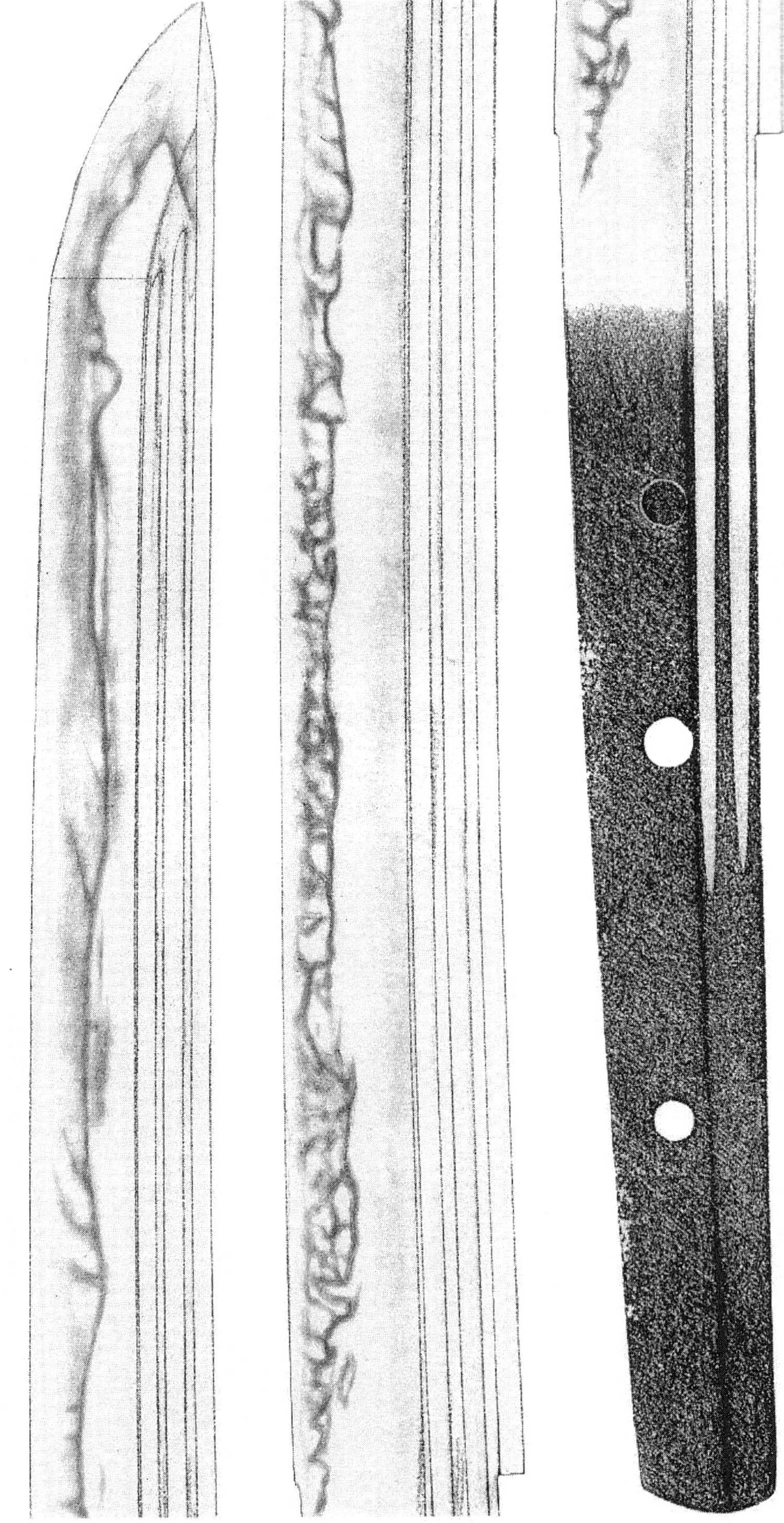

147.630 *katana*
mumei: Aoe (青江)
nagasa 70,6 cm, *sori* 1,8 cm, *shinogi-zukuri*, *iori-mune*

ji: *itame* mixed with *mokume* which stands out all over the blade, in addition *ji-nie* and plentiful of *chikei* as well as a *midare-utsuri*
hamon: *notare-chō* mixed with *saka-chōji*, also many *ashi*, *yō* and *nie*, repated *kinsuji* and *sunagashi*, the *ha* is bright and clear
bōshi: *notare-komi* with a somewhat pointed and long *ko-maru-kaeri* on the *omote* side and a rather angular *bōshi* on the *ura* side, there appear *kinsuji* and *hakikake* on both sides
horimono: on both sides a *futasuji-hi* which runs with *kake-nagashi* into the tang

This is an *ō-suriage-mumei* Aoe *katana* from the early Nanbokuchō period. When you take a look at the *jigane* you will see a mix of *itame* and *mokume* which stands finely out all over the blade, that means it appears as *chirimen*. The steel is blueish black and there are plentiful of *chikei*. All this is very typical for the Aoe school of that time as are the slanting *saka-chōji*. Incidentally, such works show mostly a *midare-utsuri* and not a *dan-utsuri* which is namely usually found at a *suguha*.

The *saka-chōji-hamon* is full of *hataraki* and is whitish and bright. But also *suguha* of the Aoe school are whitish and bright. In the case of an Aoe *saka-chōji-hamon*, the *bōshi* appears mostly pointed and this can also be seen at the *kantei* blade to a certain extant.

Many bids were on Yoshitsugu (吉次) and Naotgsugu (直次) or also on Tsuguyoshi (次吉) and Tsugunao (次直). Well, the blade is *ō-suriage* and *mumei* and so all these heyday Nanbokuchō-period smiths are almost correct (*atari-dōzen*). But if this blade would be a work from that time, than the *sugata* and the *kissaki* would be larger and the *saka-chōji* would be a hint more flamboyant, that means it would show more ups and downs in its course. In comparison, the *kantei* blade has a more elegant *sugata* and not that conspicious *saka-chōji*. Also there are plentiful of *nie* within the *ha* which speaks also for early Nanbokuchō.

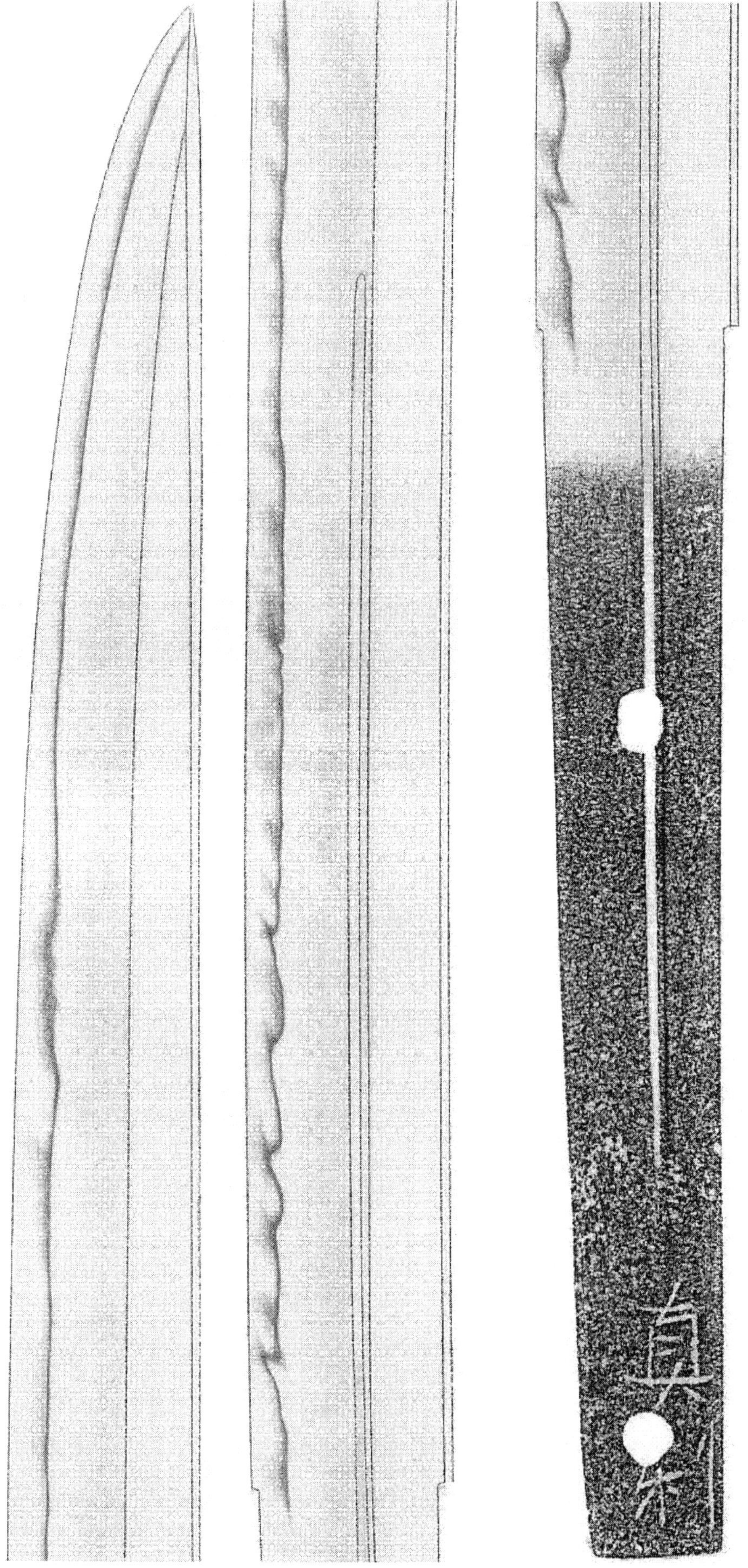

148.662 *naginata-naoshi-wakizashi*
mei: Sanetoshi (真利)
nagasa 60,0 cm, *sori* 0,6 cm, *naginata-naoshi-zukuri*, *iori-mune*

ji: *ko-itame* mixed with *mokume* and *itame* which stands out all over the blade, in addition *ji-nie*, fine *chikei*, partial *jifu*, and a faint *jifu*-like *utsuri*
hamon: *chū-suguha* mixed with *ko-gunome* and *ko-midare* which are partially slanting, there are many *ashi* and *yō* from the middle blade section downwards, the *saka-ashi* are especially noticeably at the *omote* side, the hardening is in *nioi-deki* but there are also *ko-nie*
bōshi: *sugu* with *yakitsume*
horimono: there is a narrow *koshibi* on the *omote* side towards the base in the *hira-ji* and right next to the *shinogi*, this *koshibi* runs with *kake-nagashi* into the tang, on the *ura* side we see also a *koshibi* with *kake-nagashi* but which is on the *shinogi-ji*

This *wakizashi* was once a *naginata* and because there is no *funbari* we can firstly rule out a *shintō* work. The *jigane* is a slightly standing-out *ko-itame* mixed with *mokume* which shows *jifu* in places. The *hamon* bases on *chū-suguha* and shows slanting *midare* elements and *ashi*, whereas the *ashi* appear especially on the *omote* side as *saka-ashi*. Accordingly, most went straightforward for the Aoe school. Regarding the production time, well, there is no *dan-utsuri* but fine *ha-nie* and a not so bright *nioiguchi*, that means we are not later than the late Kamakura period. The Ko-Aoe school was active from the Heian to the early Kamakura period but they did not apply such a conspicious *saka-midare* and so we can nail the time down somewhere between the middle and late Kamakura period.

The *meikan* records list four Sanetoshi (真利) for that time and region. A Ko-Bizen Sanetoshi, a Ko-Ichimonji or Fukuoka-Ichimonji Sanetoshi respectively, an Osafune Sanetoshi and a Bitchū Katayama-Ichimonji Sanetoshi. The transmission says that Ko-Ichimonji Sanetoshi, wo was active around Bun´ei (文永, 1264-1275), moved later to Katayama (片山) to Bitchū province whereupon he is classified as „Katayama-Ichimonji“. Also the „*Nihontō jūyō-bijutsuhin-zenshū*“ (日本刀重要美術品全集) lists this blade as Bitchū-Katayama work. But today it is more and more accepted that the Katayama-Ichimonji school was not active in Bitchū´s Katayama but in the village of the same name in the vicinity of Bizen Fukuoka. The transmission says further that Sanetoshi became eventually the adopted son of Bitchū Aoe Norifusa (則房). Well, in earlier years there was the trend to attribute *naginata-naoshi* in a *deki* like this to the Katayama-Ichimonji school whereas it was assumed that Katayama referred to the place in Bitchū province. However, this blade does not show any Ichimonji characteristics and looks straightforward like an Aoe work. That means the exact connections between Bitchū-Katayama, Katayama-Ichimonji, and the role of the village called „Katayama“ close to Bizen-Fukuoka need further study.

Bingo

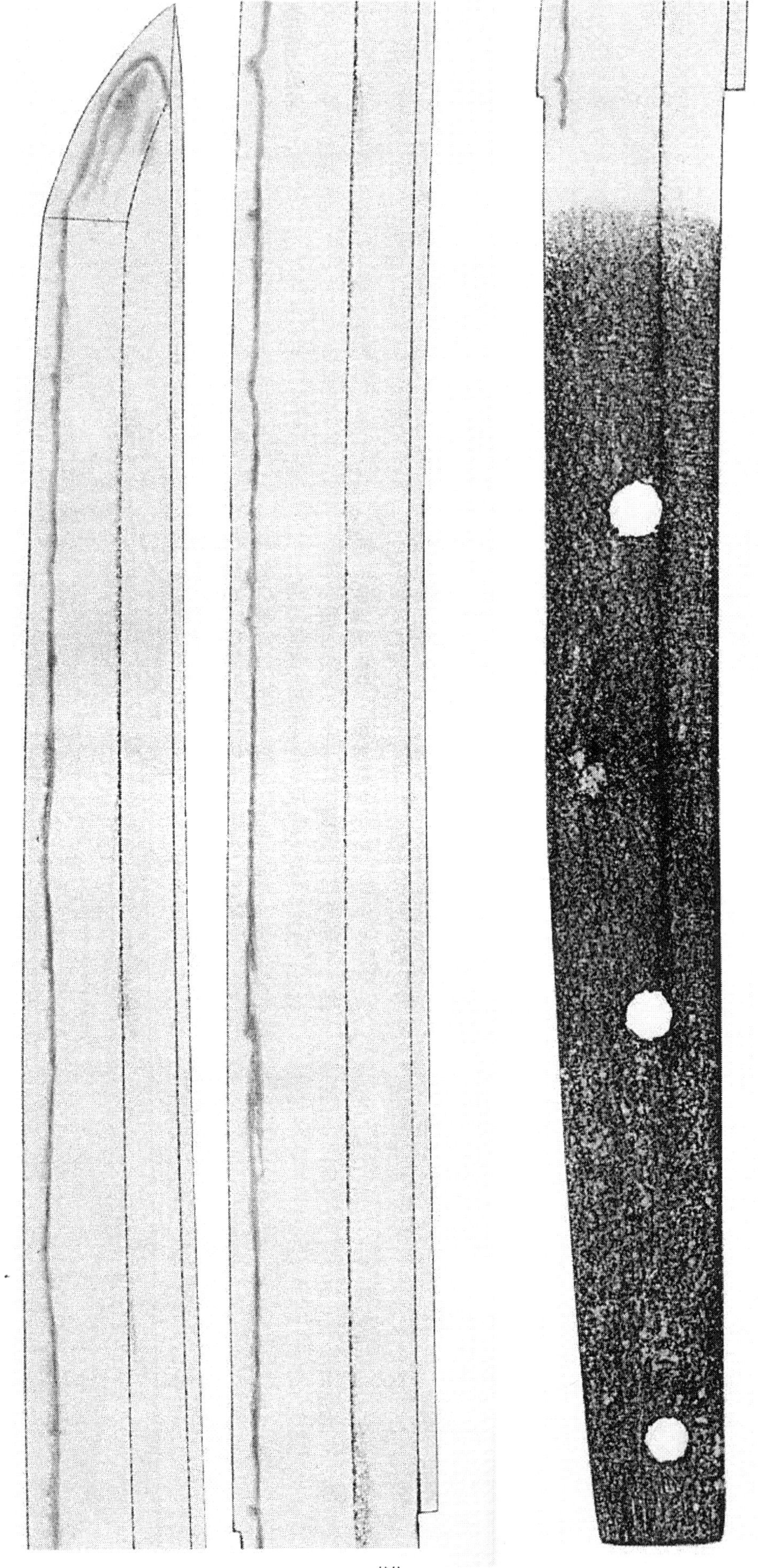

149.605 *katana*
mumei: Ko-Mihara (古三原)
nagasa 71,21 cm, *sori* 1,82 cm, *shinogi-zukuri*, *iori-mune*

ji: standing-out *itame-hada* mixed with *mokume*, in addition *ji-nie* and plentiful of *chikei*
hamon: based on *chū-suguha* mixed with shallow *notare*, in addition *hotsure*, *kuichigaiba*, much *nie*, *kinsuji* and *sunagashi*
bōshi: on the *omote* side a *notare-komi* and on the *ura* side *sugu*, both sides end in a *ko-maru-kaeri* with plentiful of *nie* and a tendency to *nie-kuzure*

This is an *ō-suriage mumei katana* of the Ko-Mihara school which has *jūyō* papers. The *itame* is mixed with *mokume* and stands finely out all over the blade. The *jigane* is dark blue and shows *chikei* and the *suguha* has a bright *nioiguchi* which reminds at a glance of Aoe, whereas many bade on Moritsugu (守次), Naotsugu (直次) and other smiths of that school.

Many Ko-Mihara blades show conspicious Yamato characteristics and old sword documents in turn say: „Look at a glance like *tachi* from Bitchū“. That means the Ko-Mihara school merged the Yamato with the Aoe style and this blade is a good example for that. Truly, at a glance one might think of Aoe but there is no peculiar *dan-utsuri* and with the high *shinogi*, the *hotsure*, the *kuichigaiba* and the *nie*-loaden *nie-kuzure*-like *bōshi*, everything points more towards Yamato. So we can rather exclude a true Aoe work and end up with Ko-Mihara.

All bids on this school were counted as *atari*. The most representative smiths of the Ko-Mihara school were Masaie (正家) and Masahiro (正広). But Masaie was active somewhat later, namely around Enbun (1356-1361) and Jōji (1362-1368) and so he made mostly larger shapes and applied a *suguha*-based *hamon* with a compact *nioiguchi*. Masahiro also made blades with a slightly wider *mihaba* and a noticeably elongated *chū-kissaki*. And in his case, the *habuchi* would show also more *hataraki* than Masaie. So here for this *kantei*, it was better to go for Masahiro instead of Masaie.

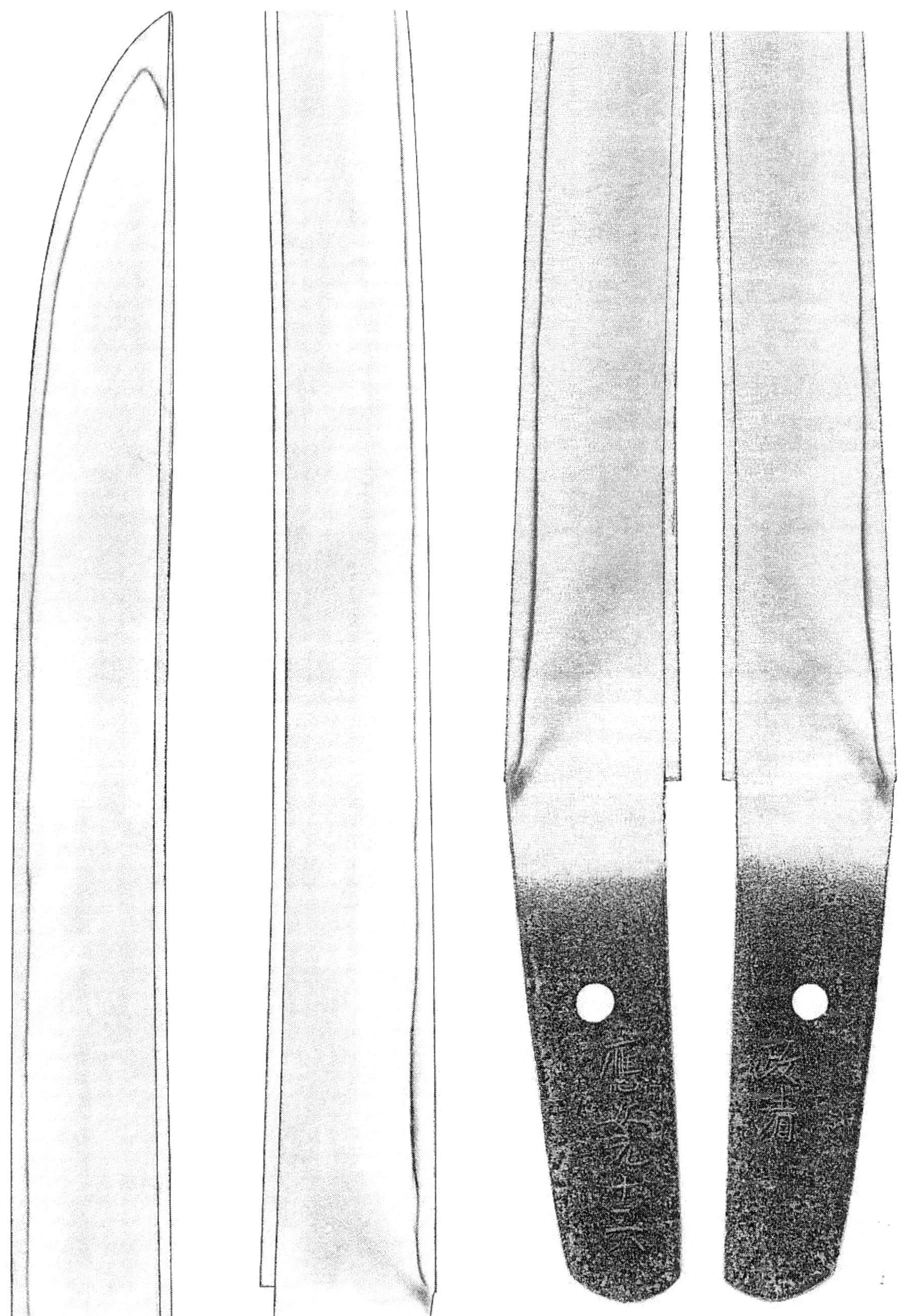

150.663 *tantō*

mei: Masakiyo (正清)

Ōan gan jūni-hachi (応安元十二八, „eighth day of the twelfth month Ōan one [= 1368]")

nagasa 28,6 cm, *sori* 0,45 cm, *hira-zukuri*, *iori-mune*

ji: rather standing-out *itame* mixed with *mokume* and *nagare*, there is *ji-nie* and towards the base a relative wide and linear *shirake-utsuri*

hamon: *suguha* with a hint of slightly undulating *notare*, the *nioiguchi* is rather compact and shows *ko-nie*, some *hotsure* and *kuichigaiba*

bōshi: on the *omote* side *sugu* with a somewhat pointed *ko-maru-kaeri* and on the *ura* side a *ko-maru-kaeri* with *hakikake*

This is a Ko-Mihara-*tantō* with a date signature of the Nanbokuchō-period Ōan era. It is in *hira-zukuri*, has a wide *mihaba*, a relative thin *kasane* and a shallow *sakizori*, that means it matches exactly the typical Enbun-Jōji-*sugata*. Regarding the *deki* of the *jiba*, we see an *itame* mixed with *mokume* and *nagare*, there is an *utsuri*, and the *hamon* is in *suguha* with a compact *nioiguchi*. That means at a glance, it looks like a work from the neighboring Aoe school, or also like Nobukuni (信国) or Rai Kunimitsu (来国光) from Yamashiro province. Let us address the *kitae* first. It shows as mentioned *nagare* and is not that bright and clear. In addition, plentiful of *ji-nie* and *jifu* appear and this is different from the *jigane* of the Aoe school and the finely forged *ko-itame* of Kyō-*mono*. The *utsuri* appears as linear *shirake-utsuri*, that means here too we do not see a characteristic which could come into the category of an Aoe-typical *dan-utsuri* or the *nie-utsuri* of Kyō-*mono*. Also the *nioiguchi* is not that bright like we would expect it from the Aoe or Rai school but rather subdued.

The Ko-Mihara school has its origins in the Yamato tradition and shows accordingly conspicious Yamato characteristics. But also an influence of the neighboring Aoe school can be seen and we know numerous works which display an Aoe-Yamato style mix. The *kantei* blade is such a piece. The *jigane* shows as mentioned *nagare* and there are Yamato-typical fine *hotsure* and *kuichigaiba* along the *ha* and *hakikake* in the *bōshi*. On the other hand, the *ko-nie* of the compact *nioiguchi* and the pointed *bōshi* of the *omote* side are typical for Aoe.

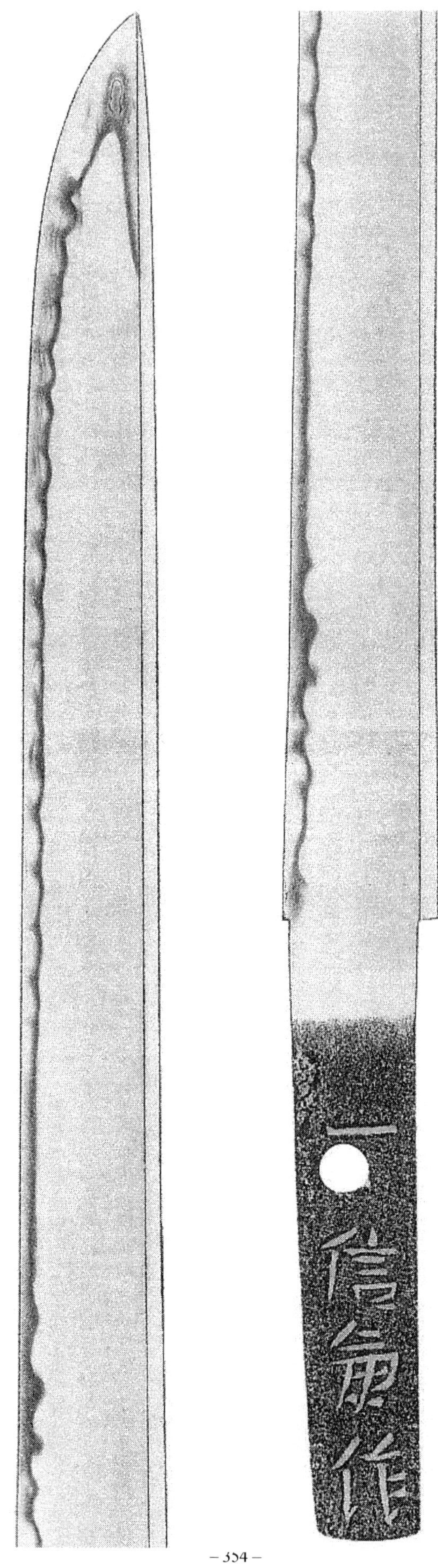
一信兼作

151.623 *tantō*
mei: Ichi Nobukane saku 一信兼作)
nagasa 23,9 cm, only very little *sori*, *hira-zukuri*, *iori-mune*

ji: standing-out *itame* mixed with *mokume* and *nagare*, in addition *chikei*, *ji-nie* and a little *shirake-utsuri*
hamon: a connected *ko-gunome* with plentiful of *nie* which is somewhat dull (*urumi*) along the upper half, also *kinsuji* and *sunagashi* appear
bōshi: *midare-komi* with a *ko-maru-kaeri* on the *omote* side and a pointed *kaeri* on the *ura* side

The blade is slender and has a little *uchizori* and shows so at a glance a *tantō-sugata* of the Kamakura period. But the *nagasa* is somewhat elongated in comparison to the *mihaba* and the *kasane* is rather thick compared to the slender *mihaba*. Such a *tantō-sugata* is typical for the early Muromachi period and so we can date the blade somewhere around Ōei (応永, 1394-1428).

But the *kitae* with its standing-out *hada* mixed with *nagare* and the *shirake-utsuri* make it hard to attribute the piece straightforward to one of the main schools of that time. Actually, it is a work of Hokke Ichijō Nobukane (法華一乗信兼) from the Ōei era. The Hokke-Ichijō school was like the Mihara school active in Bingo province from about the Nanbokuchō to the Muromachi period, but they do not share the same origins. Representative smiths are Ichijō (一乗), Kaneyasu (兼安), Shigeyasu (重安) and Nobukane. They worked in *itame* mixed with *nagare* and the *kitae* stands-out in *zanguri* manner. Also *shirake-utsuri* appears. The *hamon* is a rather narrow and calm *suguha* or a *suguha-chō* mixed with connected *ko-gunome* elements. Both variants remind of the Yamato tradition. All this and a rather rustic overall apprarance are the typical characteristics of the Hokke-Ichijō school.

There were also some bids on Bizen´s Yoshii or on Yamato´s Shikkake school. This is quite understandable but at the Yoshii school, we would see an *utsuri* which runs in a mirrored way exactly over the connected *gunome* and at the Shikkake school, there would be more conspicuous *masame*. In addition, the *bōshi* would show in the latter case more typical Yamato-characteristics like *hakikake*.

Hôki

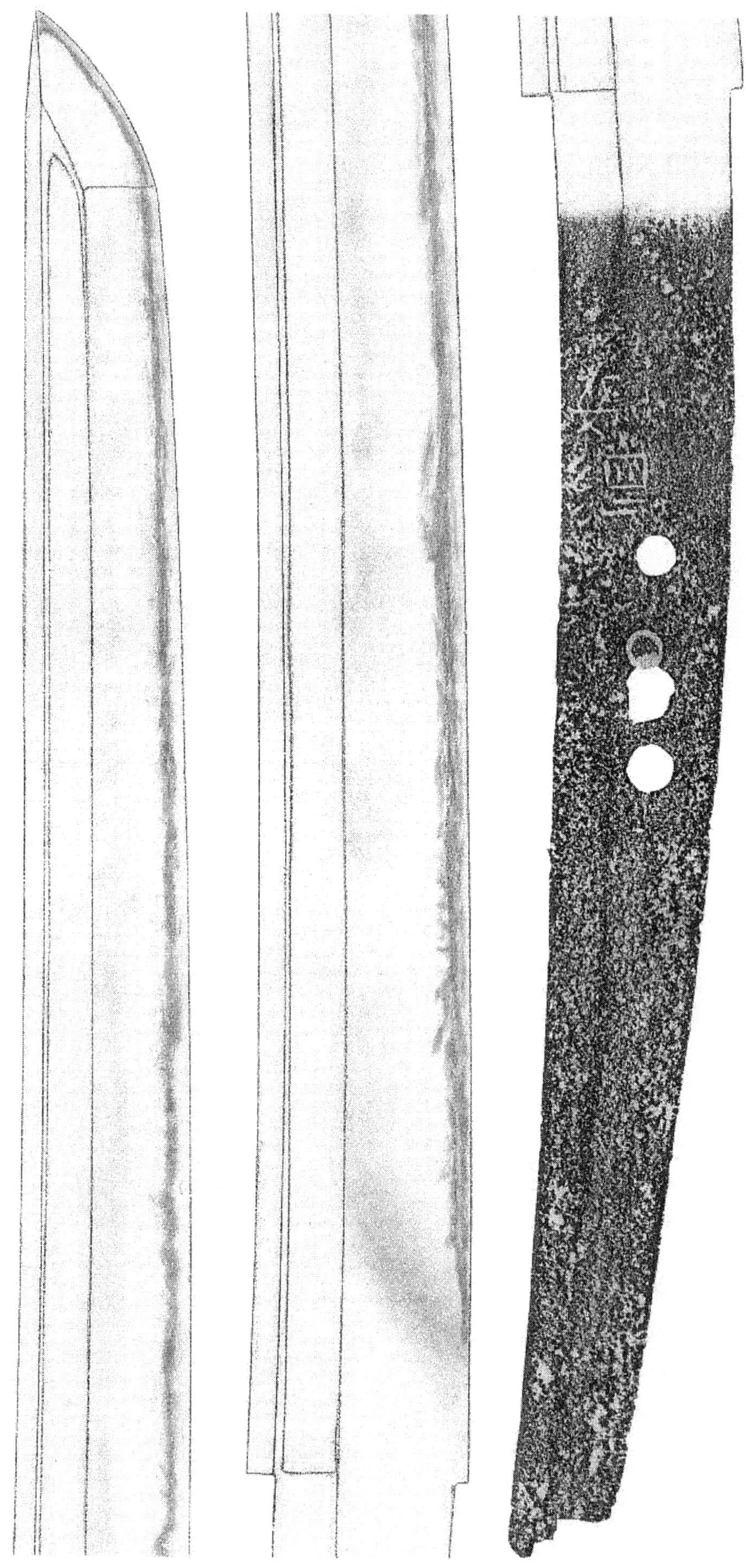

152.640 *tachi*
mei: Yasutsuna (安綱)
nagasa 80,0 cm, *sori* 2,9 cm, *shinogi-zukuri*, *iori-mune*

ji: *itame* mixed with *ō-itame* and *mokume*, the *hada* stands out, in addition plentiful of *jinie*, the *jigane* is blackish and *jifu-utsuri* appears
hamon: the *hamon* starts with a *yaki-otoshi* and turns into a *suguha-chō* which is mixed with *ko-midare*, *ko-gunome* and *ko-chōji*, in addition *nie*, *kinsuji*, *sunaghashi*, *hotsure*, and small *yubashiri* appear, the *nioiguchi* is rather subdued and partially dull (*urumi*)
bōshi: narrow hardening in *notare* and a *ko-maru-kaeri*
horimono: on both sides a *bōhi* with *kaku-dome* at the *habaki*

This is a *tachi* of Ko-Hōki Yasutsuna. It tapers noticeably and ends with a *ko-kissaki*, and the deepest point of the curvature is towards the base whereas the *sori* bends down towards the tip. So we have an early, classical *tachi-sugata* which can be dated to the late Heian or early Kamakura period.

Now we examine the *jigane* and see a standing-out *itame-mokuke* which appears as *ō-itame* in places. An important point is the blackish colour of the steel. The *hamon* is very *nie*-loaden, partially dull (*urumi*) and shows plentiful of *hataraki* like *sunagashi*, *kinsuji* and *hotsure*. In addition, the *hamon* starts with a *yaki-otoshi* and has a subdued *nioiguchi*. Another important factor is the plentiful of *hira-niku* and so it should be possible to arrive at Ko-Hōki and Yasutsuna in particular. In the case of Ko-Bizen namely there wouldn´t be that much *ō-itame*, the steel wouldn´t be blackish and also such a noticeable *yaki-otoshi* is quite uncommon for that school.

In the case of early Kyūshū-*mono*, the *jigane* would have the characteristical „sticky“ appearance and the *hamon* would be more monotonous and not so vivid like on the *kantei* blade.

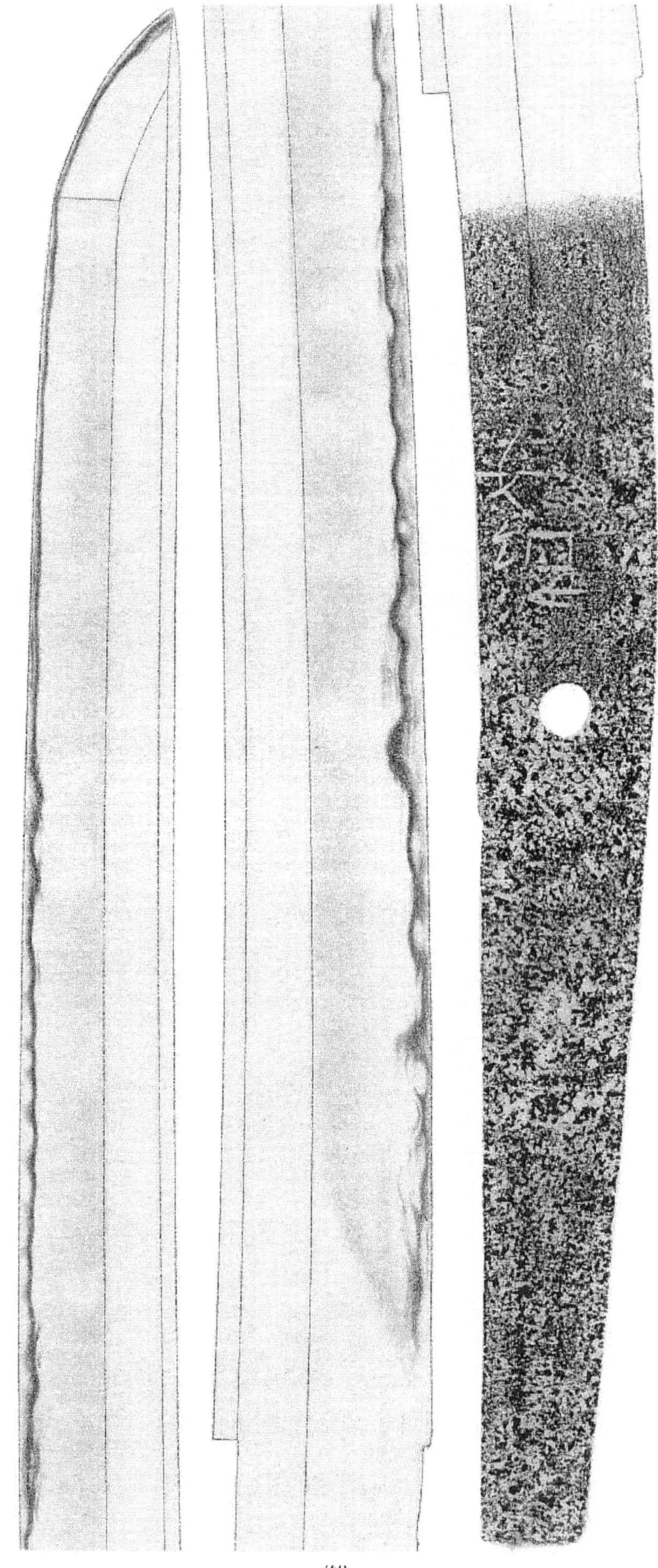

153.619 *tachi*
mei: Yasutsuna (安綱)
nagasa 75,1 cm, *sori* 2,7 cm, *shinogi-zukuri*, *iori-mune*

ji: standing-out *itame* mixed with *ō-itame* and *mokume*, in addition partial *jifu*, also *ji-nie* and a faint *jifu-utsuri*, the *jigane* is blackish
hamon: *yaki-otoshi* which turns into a mix of *ko-gunome* and *ko-notare*, the *monouchi* area bases rather on *ko-midare*, in addition plentiful of *nie*, *sunagashi* and *kinsuji*
bōshi: narrow *sugu* with *yakitsume*

The blade has a deep *koshizori*, *funbari*, tapers noticeably and ends in a *ko-kissaki*, that means it shows an elegant *tachi-sugata*. And because of the faint *jifu-utsuri* with *antai* which partially goes over the *shinogi*, we can date it not later than the late Heian or early Kamakura period.

The *jigane* appears as large-dimensioned *itame* which stands out all over the blade and lacks some refinement. The steel is blackish and the *hamon* is a shallow *ko-gunome* and *ko-notare* with plentiful of *nie*, partial *ha-hada*, *sunagashi* and *kinsuji*. So the entire workmanship is classic but also rustic and with the *yaki-otoshi*, the *sori* which does not bend down towards the tip and the *hira-niku*, it should not be that hard to recognize the typical characteristics o the Ko-Hōki school.

Besides of Yasutsuna there were also some who bade *dōzen* on Ōhara Sanemori (大原真守). But his *yakiba* is generally composed of smaller dimensioned elements and has fewer ups and downs. Also his blades are a little more slender compared to Yasutsuna.

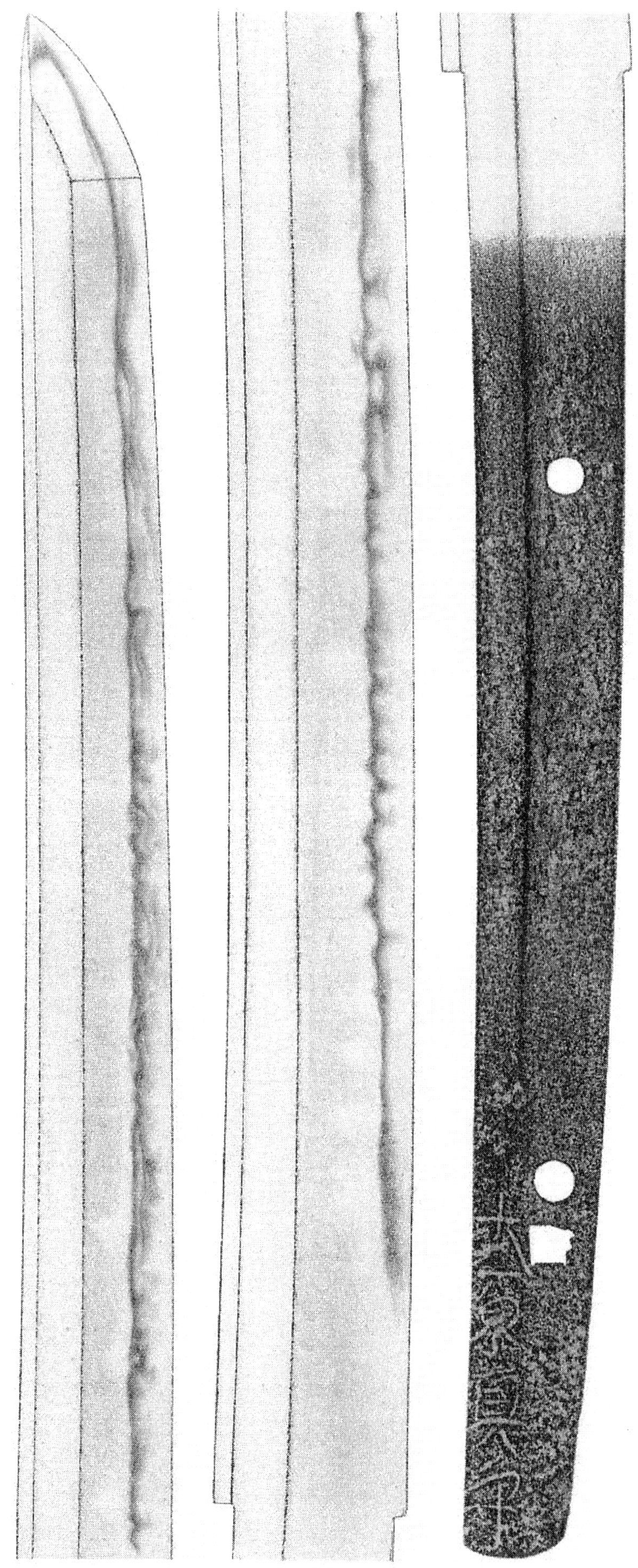

154.647 *tachi*
mei: Ōhara Sanemori (大原真守)
nagasa 70,3 cm, *sori* 2,1 cm, *shinogi-zukuri*, *iori-mune*

ji: standing-out *ō-itame* mixed with *mokume*, in addition plentiful of *ji-nie* and *chikei*, the steel is backish and there is *jifu* and a *jifu-utsuri*
hamon: *suguha-chō* mixed with *ko-chōji-midare*, *ko-midare* and *ko-gunome*, in addition many *ashi* and *yō*, plentiful of *ko-nie*, partial *ha-hada*, *kinsuji* and *sunagashi*
bōshi: on both sides *sugu* with a *ko-maru-kaeri*

This *tachi* of Ōhara Sanemori is designated as *jūyō-bijutsuhin*. It has the typically deep *koshizori* for the late Heian and early Kamakura period, it is slender, and shows a classically interpreted *hamon* in *ko-midare-chō*. The steel is blackish and there is *ha-hada*. All these are typical characteristics of Ko-Hōki-*mono*. But as the blackish colour of the steel and the *ha-hada* are not that conspicious at this blade, some went for Ko-Bizen. Well, there are also Ko-Bizen works with a large dimensioned, standing-out *hada* and from this point of view a bid on this school is understandable. However, the *shinogi-ji* is too narrow for Ko-Bizen but typical for Ko-Hōki. In addition, the *jifu* creates a differently coloured appearance of the *jigane*, a local characteristic which does speak for Hōki and not for Bizen province. Also such a *ko-midare-chō* with clearly pronounced *ko-gunome* elements is not seen at Ko-Bizen. So all in all it should not be too hard to arrive at Ko-Hōki.

According to transmission, Sanemori was the son of Yasutsuna (安綱) but there are fewer signed blades extant by him than by his supposed father. Generally it can be said that Sanemori´s *ko-midare* consists of more densely arranged and smaller dimensioned elements than Yasutsuna´s.

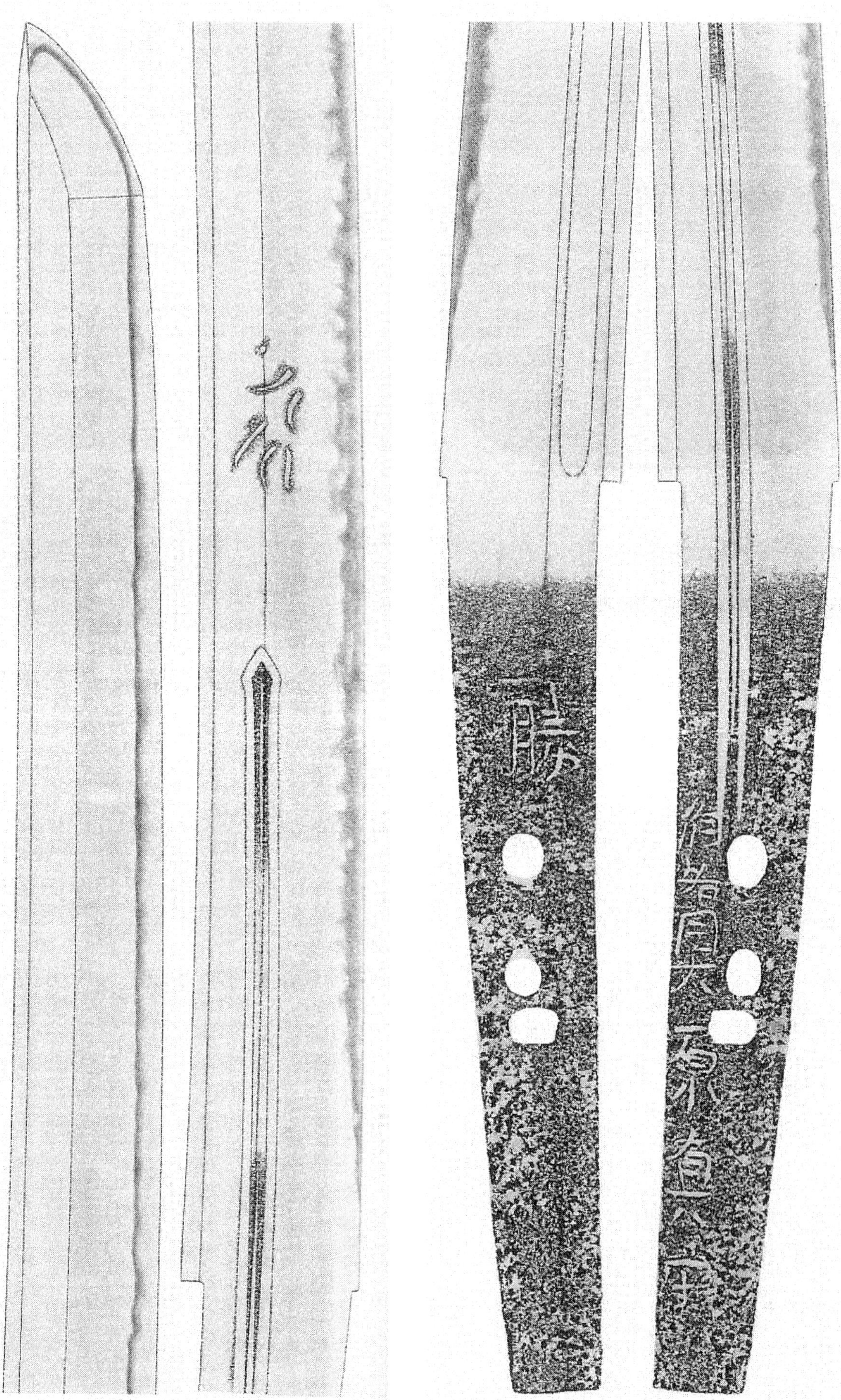

155.593 *kodachi*
mei: Hōki Ōhara Sanemori (伯耆大原真守) – Shō/Kachi (勝, „victory“)
nagasa 61,9 cm, *sori* 1,8 cm, *shinogi-zukuri*, *iori-mune*

ji: standing out *itame* mixed with *mokume*, *ō-itame* and *nagare*, in addition *jifu*, plentiful of *ji-nie*, many *chikei* and a *jifu-utsuri*, the steel is blackish
hamon: *suguha-chō* mit *yaki-otoshi*, there are conspicious *ko-midare*, *ko-gunome* and *ko-chōji* seen in the lower half, also *ko-ashi* and *yō* appear, the *nioiguchi* is wide and dull for about 30 cm from the *machi* and shows *kinsuji* and *sunagashi*, later it gets compact but stays subdued, there are also plentiful of *nie*
bōshi: narrow *suguha* with a *ko-maru-kaeri*
horimono: there is a *bonji* on each side towards the base, on the *omote* side a *suken* with *kake-nagashi* is engraved below of the *bonji* and on the *ura* side a *koshibi* with *maru-dome* above the *habaki*

The blade has a standing-out *itame* with plentiful of *ji-nie* and *jifu-utsuri* and a quite *nie*-loaden *hamon* with a conspicious amount of *ko-midare*. The interpretation looks classical and elegant and reminds at a glance of Ko-Bizen. But the *hada* structure is too large for Ko-Bizen, the *ji-nie* a hint too strong and the *chikei* and *jifu* too prominent. Also the steel is too blackish. And when it comes to the *hataraki* of the *ha*, then we have to say that it is with the *kinsuji* and *hataraki* too *nie*-loaden for Ko-Bizen. Also a *yaki-otoshi* is not common for the latter school. So when we have ruled out Ko-Bizen and take into consideration the subdued *nioiguchi* and the overall rustic impression, than it is easy to arrive at Ko-Hōki.

But let us take a look at the *yakiba* in detail. Conspicious are the small dimensioned *notare* parts which do not occur at Ko-Bizen. And the isolated *ko-gunome* are very typical for Ko-Hōki and especially for Yasutsuna (安綱). Also typical for this school is the plentiful of *hira-niku* and the rather narrow *shinogi-ji*.

Ōhara Sanemori was according to transmission the son of Yasutsuna, but there are less blades extant by him than by his supposed father. This is by the way the only known *kodachi* of this smith. (Note: *Kodachi* are anyway rare for this school. There exists namely just one other Ko-Hōki-*kodachi* which is a work of Sanekage [真景].) Sanemori´s *midare* is by trend a little smaller than Yasutsuna´s but in rare cases he also engraved *bonji*, *suken* or somewhat broader *gomabashi* along the base. So when you have a Ko-Hōki blade with *horimono*, you should rather go for Sanemori.

The additional signature on the *ura* side is interesting. It reads „Shō/Kachi“ (勝, lit. „victory“) but its meaning is unclear (literal meaning, name, nickname?). But the „*Tsuchiya-oshigata*“ (土屋押形) depicts even some more blades of Ōhara Sanemori with that character as additional signature.

Besides of Ko-Hōki there were also relative many bids on Bungo Yukihira (豊後行平). They maybe go back to the *horimono* and the *yaki-otoshi*. But at Yukihira we would see the Ko-Kyūshū-typical soft, „sticky“ looking *jihada* and also *shirake*. The *hamon* would appear as *suguha* with rather few *hataraki*, although his *nioiguchi* is subdued too. Such a complex *yakiba* consisting of *ko-midare-chō* is not found at Yukihira.

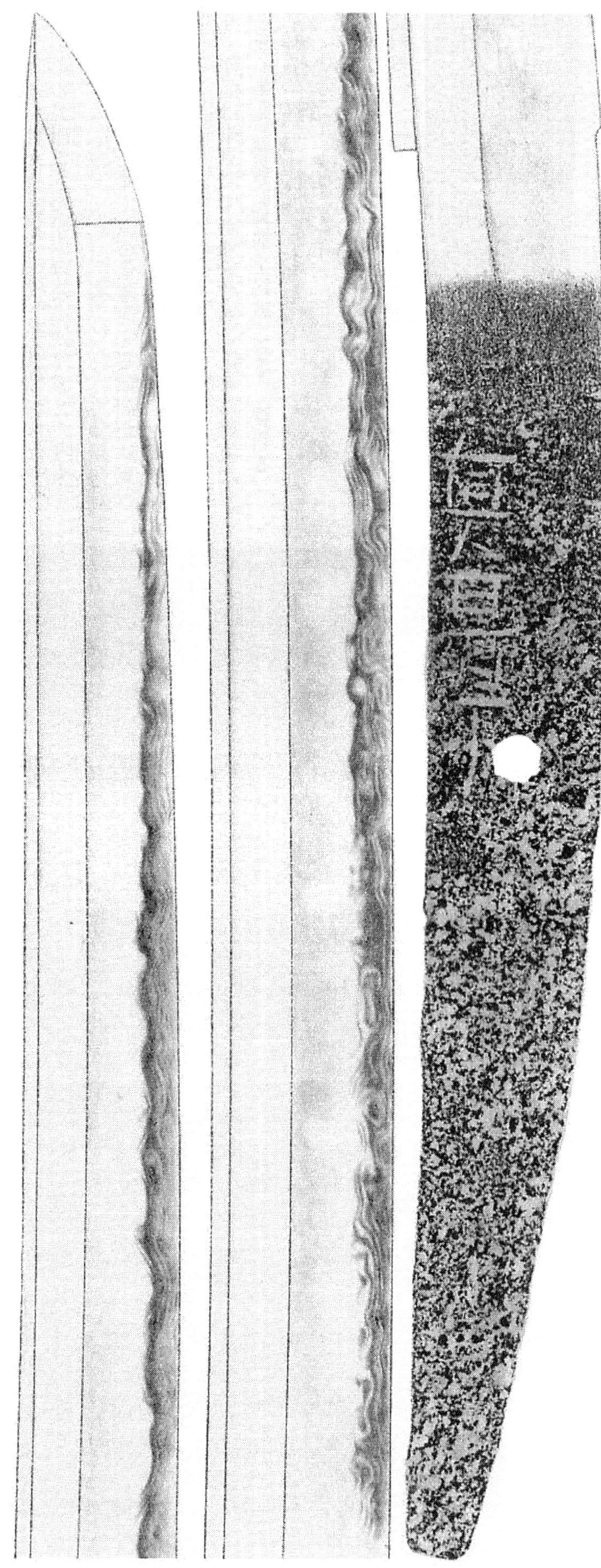

156.637 *tachi*
mei: Sanekage (真景)
nagasa 79,2 cm, *sori* 2,8 cm, *shinogi-zukuri*, *iori-mune*

ji: clearly standing-out *ō-itame* mixed with *mokume*, in addition *jifu*, plentiful of *ji-nie*, much *chikei*, a rather dark (= *antai*) *jifu-utsuri*, the steel is blackish
hamon: there is a *yaki-otoshi*, the *hamon* appears as *ko-midare* and the *haki-omote* side shows along the *monouchi* area some mixed-in *ko-gunome* and *ko-notare*, in addition plentiful of *ashi* and *yō*, many thick *nie*, *ha-hada* and therein interwoven *kinsuji*, *nie-suji* and *sunagashi*, also some *hotsure* along the *habuchi*, the *nioiguchi* is rather subdued at the base
bōshi: unfortunately lost

The blade has a deep *koshizori*, *funbari*, is rather slender, tapers noticeably, and ends in a *ko-kissaki*. That means it has a very elegant *tachi-sugata* and can be dated into the late Heian or early Kamakura period. The *jigane* is a large-structured *itame* which stands clearly out and lacks some refinement. Also *jifu* elements appear and the steel is blackish. The *hamon* starts at the base with a conspicious *yaki-otoshi* and appears later on as *ko-midare-chō* which becomes more varied towards the *monouchi*, i.e. it shows also *ko-gunome* and *ko-notare* in that area. There are many thick *nie* within the *hamon* and in some places the *kitae-hada* is clearly visible in the *yakiba* (= *ha-hada*). Interwoven in this *ha-hada* appear *kinsuji*, *nie-suji*, *sunagashi* and other *hataraki* so that the entire *jiba* makes a very rustic impression. (It is especially the middle area of this blade which served according to Honma-*sensei* as model for Masamune´s copies of Ko-Hōki-*mono*. Please check the *meibutsu* Musashi-Masamune [武蔵正宗] introduced in this volume.) And when we now combine all these characteristics with the production time and the plentiful of *hira-niku*, then we inevitably arrive at Ko-Hōki.

This *tachi* is designated as *jūyō-bijutsuhin* and is a work of Sanekage who came according to transmission from the school of Ōhara Sanemori (大原真守). With this blade, there are only three signed pieces extant by Sanekage and so it is quite difficult to make out individual characteristics for that smith. So a bid on Yasutsuna (安綱) – the most representative Ko-Hōki smith – was counted as *atari* too.

Wakasa

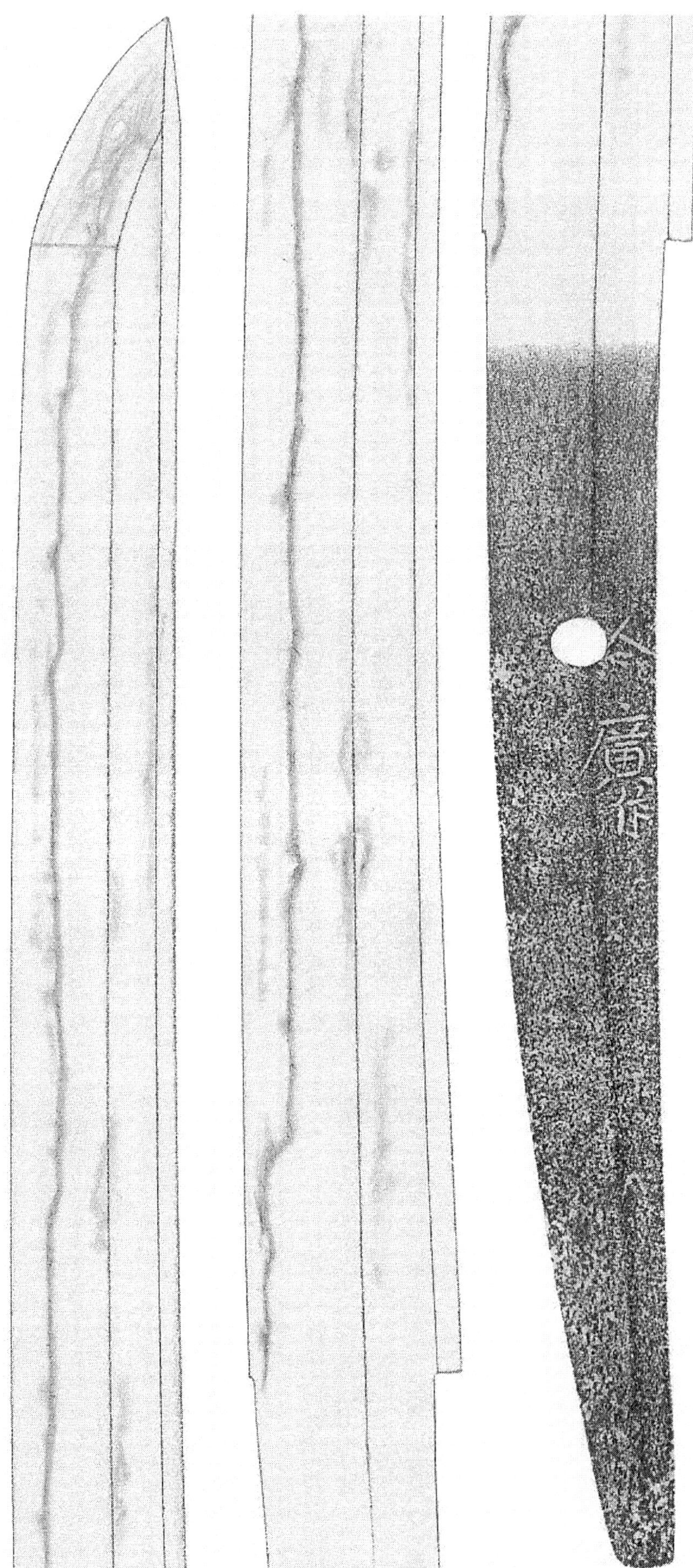

157.597 *katana*
mei: Fuyuhiro saku (冬広作)
nagasa 72,11 cm, *sori* 2,73 cm, *shinogi-zukuri*, *iori-mune*

ji: *itame-hada* mixed with *mokume* and *nagare*, in addition *ji-nie* and *chikei*, the *hada* stands out and is blackish
ha: *hiro-suguha* with a slight tendency to *notare* and mixed with *ko-gunome* in the upper area, in addition, *ko-ashi*, many *yō*, *sunagashi*, *tobiyaki* and *muneyaki*, the hardening is in *nie-deki*
bōshi: wide, almost *ichimai* and plentiful of *hakikake*

The blade has a normal *mihaba* and *kasane*, a deep *sori*, does not taper that much and ends in a *chū-kissaki*. Well, it is in this case rather difficult to determine the time but when we take into consideration the *ichimai*-like *bōshi* and the *sakizori*, we can place it in the late Muromachi period.

As the *bōshi* shows much *hakikake*, the *itame* is mixed with *mokume* and *nagare* and stands out, and the steel is blackish, we can assume that this is a northern *Hokkoku-mono*. It has to be mentioned that the *suguha*-based *hamon* with the numerous *tobiyaki* and *muneyaki* tends to *hitatsura* in places.

Fuyuhiro´s blades show an *ō-midare* mixed with *gunome* and *chōji*, an *ō-notare*, and a *hitatsura* in the Sue-Sōshū style (Fuyuhiro´s origins are namely at Sōshū Hirotsugu [広次]). But he also applied a *suguha* with *ashi* and *yō* like seen at the *kantei* blade. The *hamon* narrows down towards the base and runs almost as *sugu-yakidashi* out. But many of Fuyuhiro´s *hamon* start that way at the base and sometimes we find blades with a similarily deep *sori*. So all these characteristics had to be combined to nail the bid down on this smith.

But there were many bids on Sue-Bizen like Kiyomitsu (清光) and Sukesada (祐定). But they hardened generally a *hamon* with bright *nioiguchi* and forged a bright and clear *jigane*.

Suruga

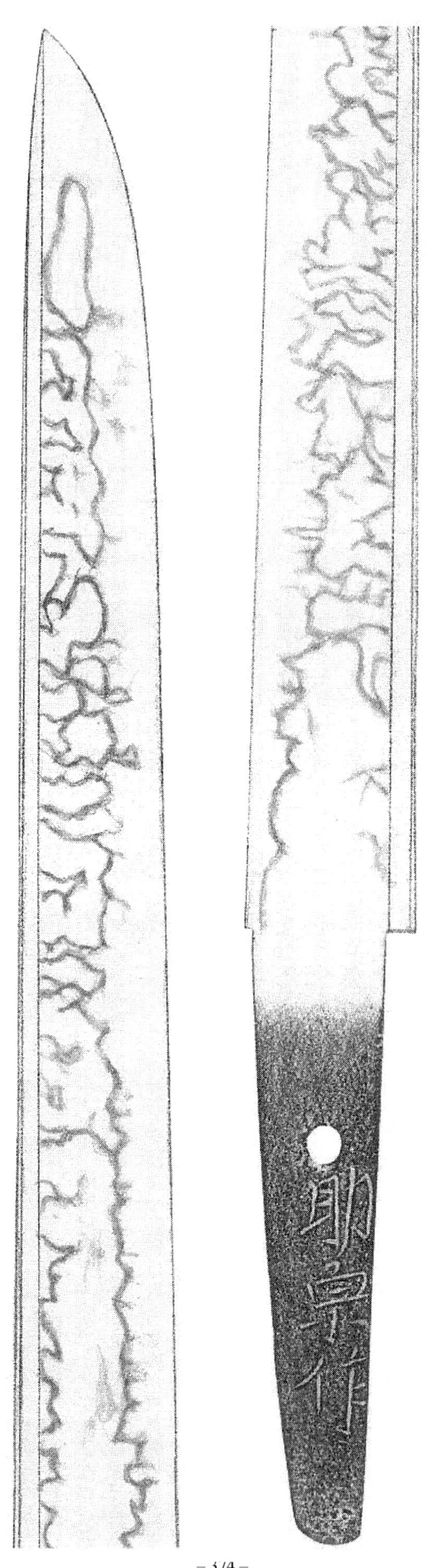

158.621 *tantō*
mei: Sukemune saku (助宗作) (Shimada, 島田)
nagasa 24,5 cm, very small *uchizori*, *hira-zukuri*, *mitsu-mune*

ji: *itame-hada* with *ji-nie*
hamon: *gunome* mixed with *chōji* and *togari*, in addition *muneyaki*, *tobiyaki* and *sunagashi*, the hardening is in *nioi-deki* with *ko-nie*
bōshi: *midare-komi* with a *ko-maru-kaeri* which connects with the *muneyaki* elements

This is a *tantō* in a vivid *hitatsura*. At *hitatsura*, first of all Sōshū Hiromitsu (広光) and Akihiro (秋広), Hasebe Kunishige (長谷部国重) and Kuninobu (国信) from Yamashiro and other Nanbokuchō-period smiths come to mind. But the *sugata* of this *tantō* is slender, *sunnobi*, and the *hitatsura* is in *nioi-deki* with a compact *habuchi*, so it differs clearly from the works of the Nanbokuchō period.

It is a work of Sukemune who belonged to the Shimada school of Suruga province. A *hitatsura* hamon was applied from the Nanbokuchō period onwards and was kept throughout the entire Muromachi period, when it was continued by Sue-Sōshū smiths like the Shimada school, of smiths like Fuyuhiro (冬広) from Wakasa, Hiroyoshi (広賀) from Hōki, or the Sue-Bizen school. From all of them we know flamboyant *hitatsura* interpretations.

A *hitatsura* like here where the tips of the *midare* rise highly and connect with the *muneyaki* and where there is some space in between these elements is typical for the Muromachi period. As mentioned, they are less *nie*-loaden than their Nanbokuchō predecessors and tend towards a pure *nioi-deki*. A *midare* with such peculiar *togari* protrusions is typical for the Shimada school. In addition, the conspiciously leftwards and rightwards bent *togari* elements are also a characteristical feature of this school.

Etchû

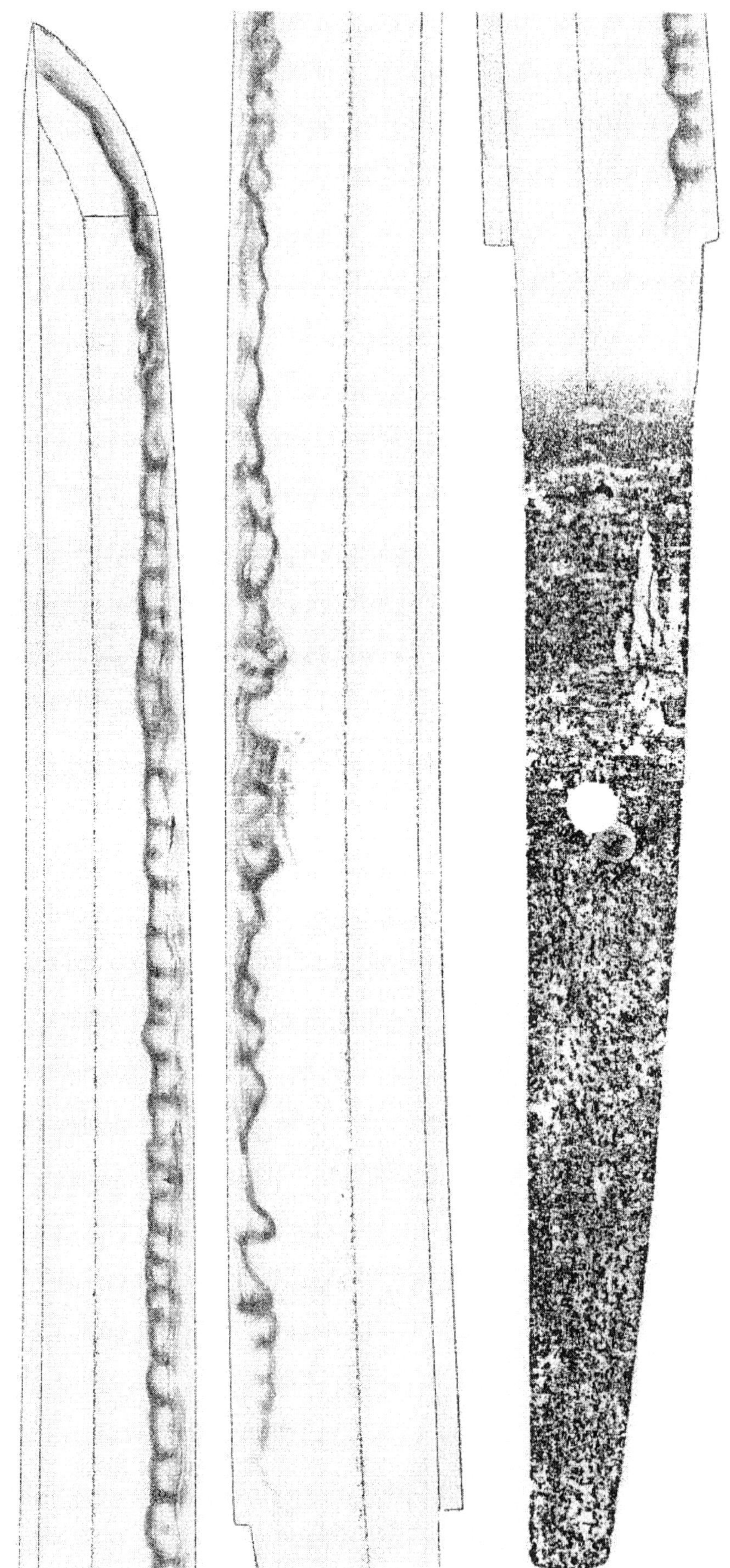

159.669 *tachi*
mumei: Den Norishige (伝則重)
nagasa 79,1 cm, *sori* 2,1 cm, *shinogi-zukuri*, *iori-mune*

ji: *itame* mixed with *mokume* and partially with *ō-hada*, the *hada* is altogether rather densely forged, there is plentiful of *ji-nie*, much *chikei* and the steel is blackish

hamon: *suguha-chō* mixed with *gunome*, *ko-chōji-midare* and *ko-midare*, the *hamon* tends towards the base to a *ko-chōji* with noticeable ups and downs, in addition *ashi*, *yō*, fine *kinsuji* and *sunagashi* appear, the *nioiguchi* is rather wide and shows plentiful of *nie* and also some *ara-nie* in places

bōshi: *sugu* with a *ko-maru-kaeri* and fine *hakikake* towards the tip

The blade has a normal *mihaba*, tapers noticeably and shows a pronounced *funbari*, that means we have to assume that it is *ubu*. The deep *koshizori* increases again towards the tip and so we are in the late Kamakura period. This is a *jūyō-bijutsuhin tachi* which is *mumei* but attributed via „Den“ to Norishige.

Norishige worked principally in an *itame* mixed with *ō-hada* or *mokume* which appears as characteristical *matsukawa-hada*. His steel is blackish and the *hamon* is mostly a *notare-chō* mixed with *gunome*, whereas the *hada* structure is clearly visible within the *ha* and the *habuchi*. Also plentiful of *nie* as well as conspicious *kinsuji* and *sunagashi* appear. Sometimes like seen here he forged also more classical and elegant blades whose *deki* remind of Ko-Hōki or Ko-Bizen. So many were lead astray and went for Ko-Bizen, Ko-Hōki or Ko-Aoe and found themselves in the early Kamakura period.

Well, there is no *matsukawa-hada* and the *ko-gunome-ko-midare* mix is quite classical. But we can see strong and conspicious *nie* within the *ha* which are strongly flashing in places. Also many *kinsuji* and *sunagashi* are found. These characteristics lead us on another track, namely to one of the top Sōshū smiths. When we now combine this with the *sugata*, i.e. the production time, and the blackish *jigane*, we end up with a northern smith from the late Kamakura period who was strongly influenced by the Sōshū tradition, and voila: Norishige!

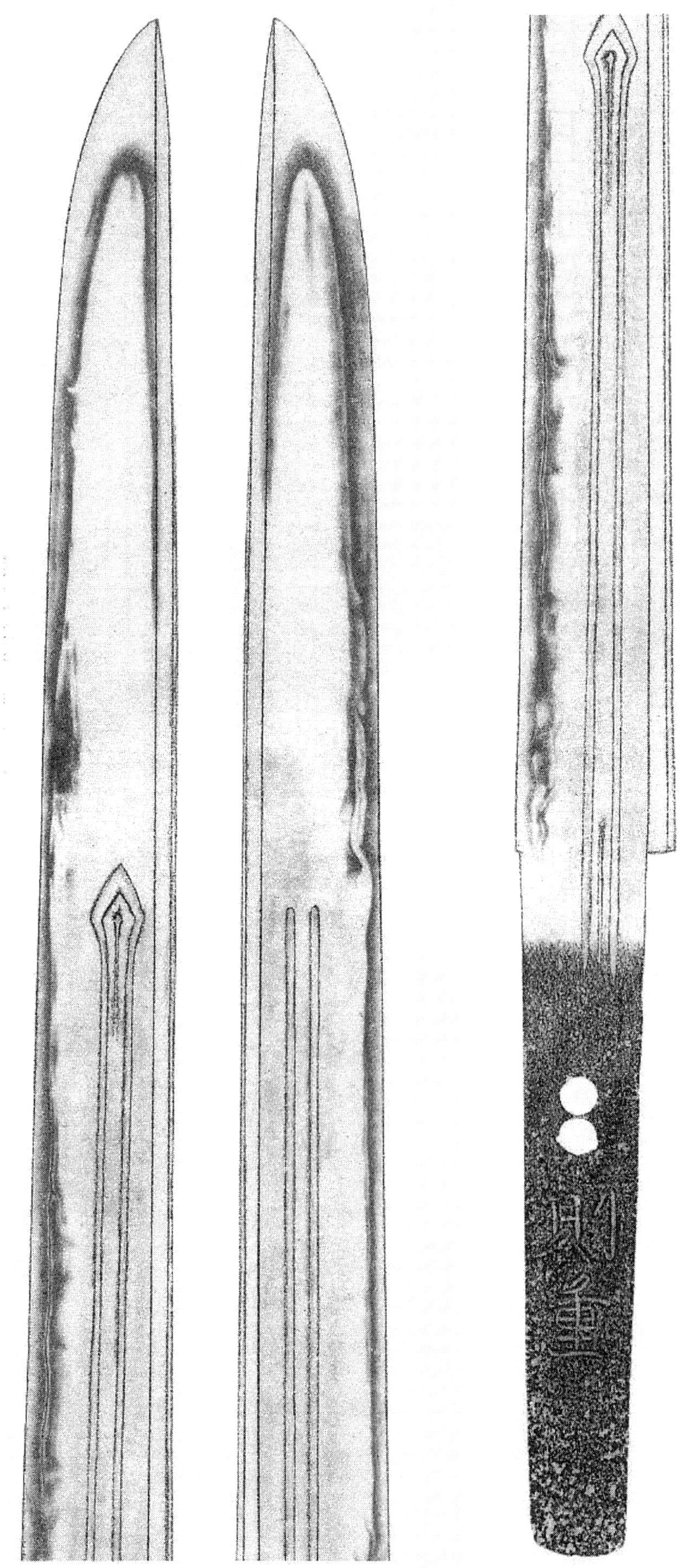
則重

160.613 *tantō*
mei: Norishige (則重)
nagasa 21,2 cm, *uchizori*, *hira-zukuri*, *mitsu-mune*

ji: *itame* mixed with *ō-hada* and *mokume-hada*, large *hada* structure, in addition plentiful of *ji-nie* and all over the blade thick *chikei*, the steel is blackish
hamon: based on *notare* with some *ko-gunome* and *ko-notare*, in addition *ashi*, *yō*, thick *nioi*, many *nie*, *hotsure*, *kuichigai-ba*, *yubashiri*, *tobiyaki*, *muneyaki*, *kinsuji* and *sunagashi*, the *noiguchi* is somewhat subdued
bōshi: *sugu* with a rather early starting *ko-maru-kaeri*
horimono: there is a *suken* on the *omote* side and *gomabashi* on the *ura* side, both *horimono* run with *kake-nagashi* into the tang

On the basis of the shape in *hira-zukuri*, the *mitsu-mune*, the normal length and *kasane* and the *uchizori*, we can date this *tantō* into the Kamakura period. The mix of *itame*, *ō-itame* and *mokume* with its large *hada* structure and the plentiful of *ji-nie* as well as the thick *chikei* result in a very peculiar appearance of the *kitae*. This *kitae* of Norishige goes back to a forging of steels with different carbont content and is called „*matsukawa-hada*" (松皮肌).

Norishige´s *yakiba*, with the thick and strong *nie*, the *kinsuji*, *sunagashi* and other *hataraki*, is strongly Sōshū-influenced. As seen on the *kantei* blade, the *nioiguchi* is mostly subdued and has because of the huge amount of *hotsure*, *kuichigaiba*, *yubashiri*, *tobiyaki* and *nijūba* areas no clear dividing line between *ji* and *ha*.

Norishige´s *tantō* show mostly a strong *uchizori* and scarce *fukura*, a interpretation which is called „*takenoko-sori*" (筍反り). The *kantei* blade does not show this typical characteristic of Norishige but speaks with the acute-angled *mitsu-mune* nevertheless for this smith. Incidentally, a *mitsu-mune* with wide top surface is typical for old Sōshū-*mono*.

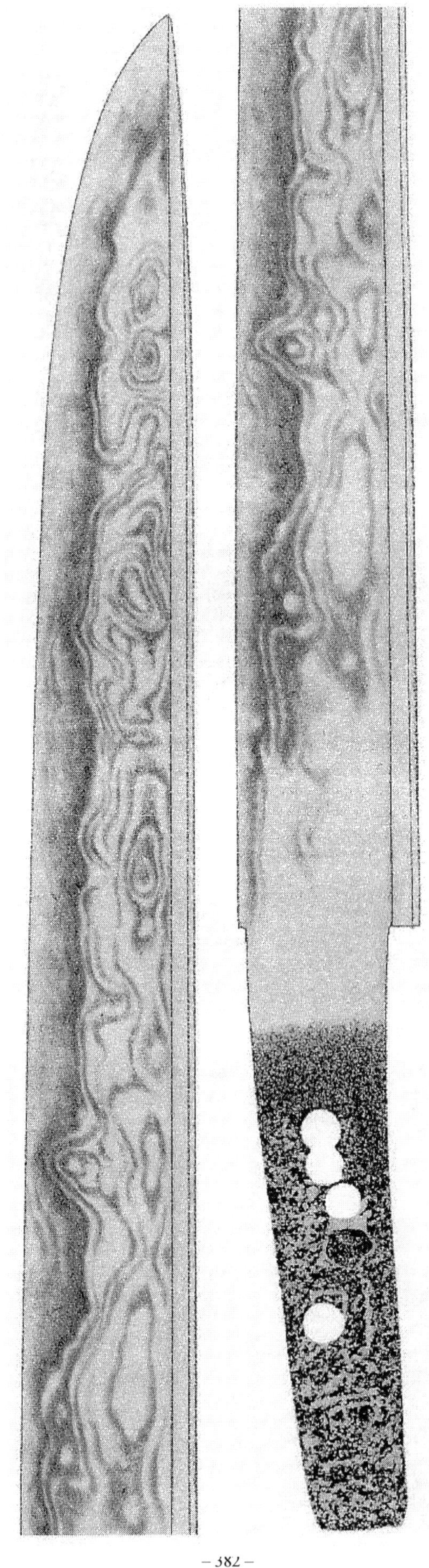

161.592 *tantō*
mei: Norishige (則重)
nagasa 25,4 cm, *uchizori*, *hira-zukuri*, *mitsu-mune*

ji: *ō-itame* mixed with *itame*, *mokume* and whirlpools, the *hada* stands out, in addition *ji-nie* and much *chikei*, the steel is blackish
hamon: *notare* mixed with *gunome*, *ashi*, *yō*, many *kinsuji*, *sunagashi*, *tobiyaki* and *yubashiri*, so altogether the *hamon* tends almost to *hitatsura* and there is plentiful of *nie*
bōshi: *midare-komi* with a pointed *ko-maru-kaeri* and *hakikake*

This *tantō* is „normal" in terms of length, width and thickness, that means it fits most likely into the late Kamakura period. The *hada* is quite peculiar. It consists of an *ō-itame* mixed with *itame*, *mokume* and whirlpools and appears altogether as *matsukawa-hada*. When we combine this with the *nie*-based *hataraki* like *kinsuji* and *sunagashi* which follow the forging structure, only one smith is worth considering, namely Norishige. This *tantō* is a textbook example for the *deki* of this smith and accordingly almost all bids were *atari*.

But some went also for Hankei (繁慶) who is known for trying to emulate Norishige. But in his case, the *mihaba* would be wider compared to the *nagasa* and so the *tantō-sugata* would make a more stubby appearance. Also the *kasane* would be thicker and the overall size rather *sunnobi*. In addition, Hankei´s *mitsu-mune* is even higher and many of his short blades show a *sori*. In short, *tantō* in such a „standard *sugata*" of the Kamakura period are not seen at Hankei.

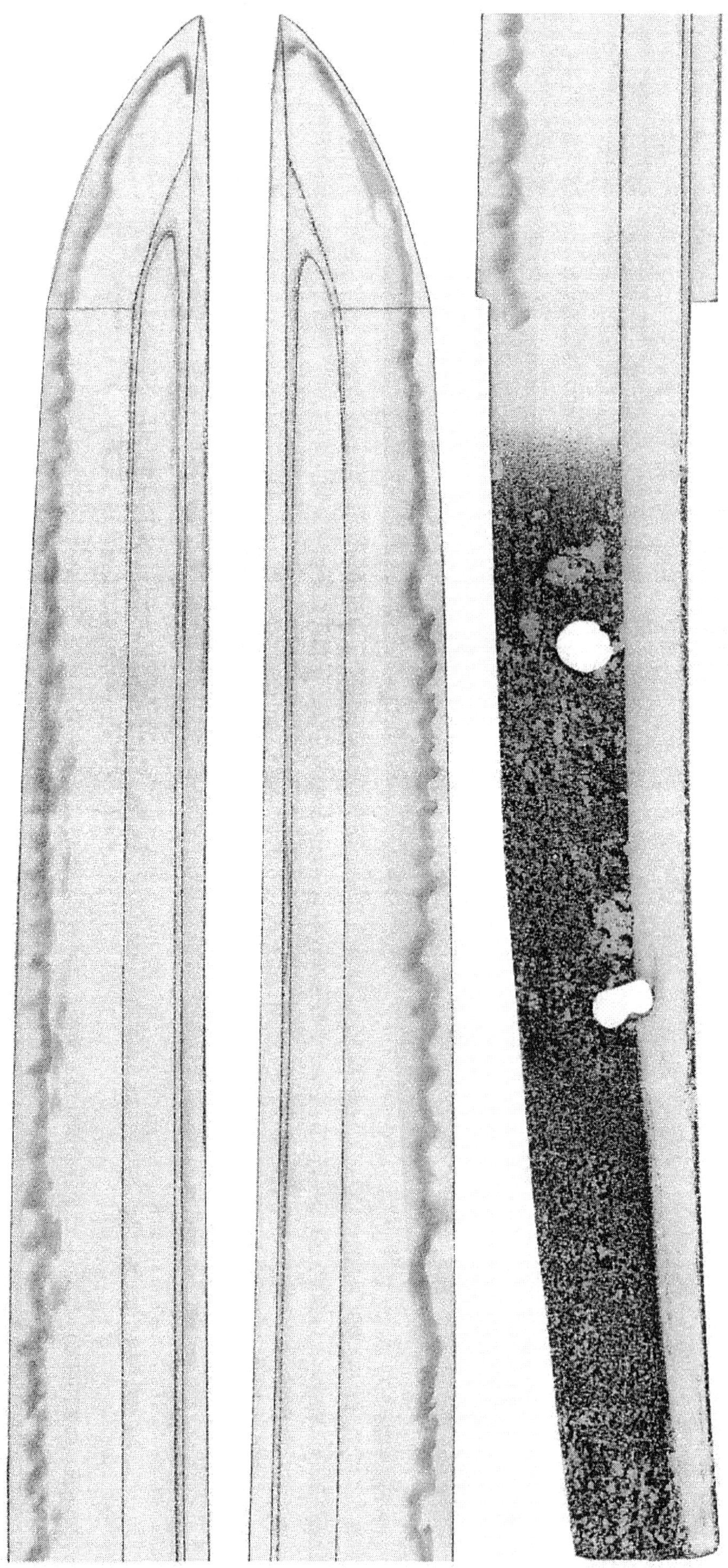

162.647 *katana*
mumei: Ko-Uda (古宇多)
nagasa 72,4 cm, *sori* 1,8 cm, *shinogi-zukuri*, *iori-mune*

ji: standing-out *itame* mixed with *mokume*, in addition *ji-nie* and *chikei*, the steel is blackish and there is *shirake-utsuri*
hamon: *suguha-chō* mixed with *ko-gunome*, also many *hotsure* and *uchinoke* along the *habuchi*, plentiful of *ashi*, *ko-nie*, *kinsuji* and *sunagashi*
bōshi: on both sides a shallow *notare-komi* with a *ko-maru-kaeri*
horimono: on both sides a *bōhi* which runs with *kaki-tōshi* through the tang

This is an *ō-suriage mumei katana* with *jūyō* papers which is attributed to the Ko-Uda school. Many participants reckoned it as a Shikkake work (尻懸) because it shows a Yamato-like *deki* and maybe also the *hamon* with areas of connected *ko-gunome* was a reason for such a bid. Mostly unsigned blades attributed to the Ko-Uda school show a *suguha-chō* with *hotsure* and *habuchi*, that means they have more horizontal *hataraki* and not vertical activities like *ko-gunome*, *ashi* or *yō*. But in the case of a Shikkake work, the steel would be brighter and more finely forged. The *kantei* blade in turn shows a standing-out *hada* mix of *itame-mokume*, a blackish steel and a *shirake-utsuri*. So we are clearly facing a Yamato, but a Yamato sideline work. The *hamon* is as mentioned a *suguha-chō* which is mixed with some *ko-gunome* elements which are more irregular than at the Shikkake school. So this and the very bright *nie* along the *habuchi* – which are very typical for the school – are the keypoint to arrive at Ko-Uda.

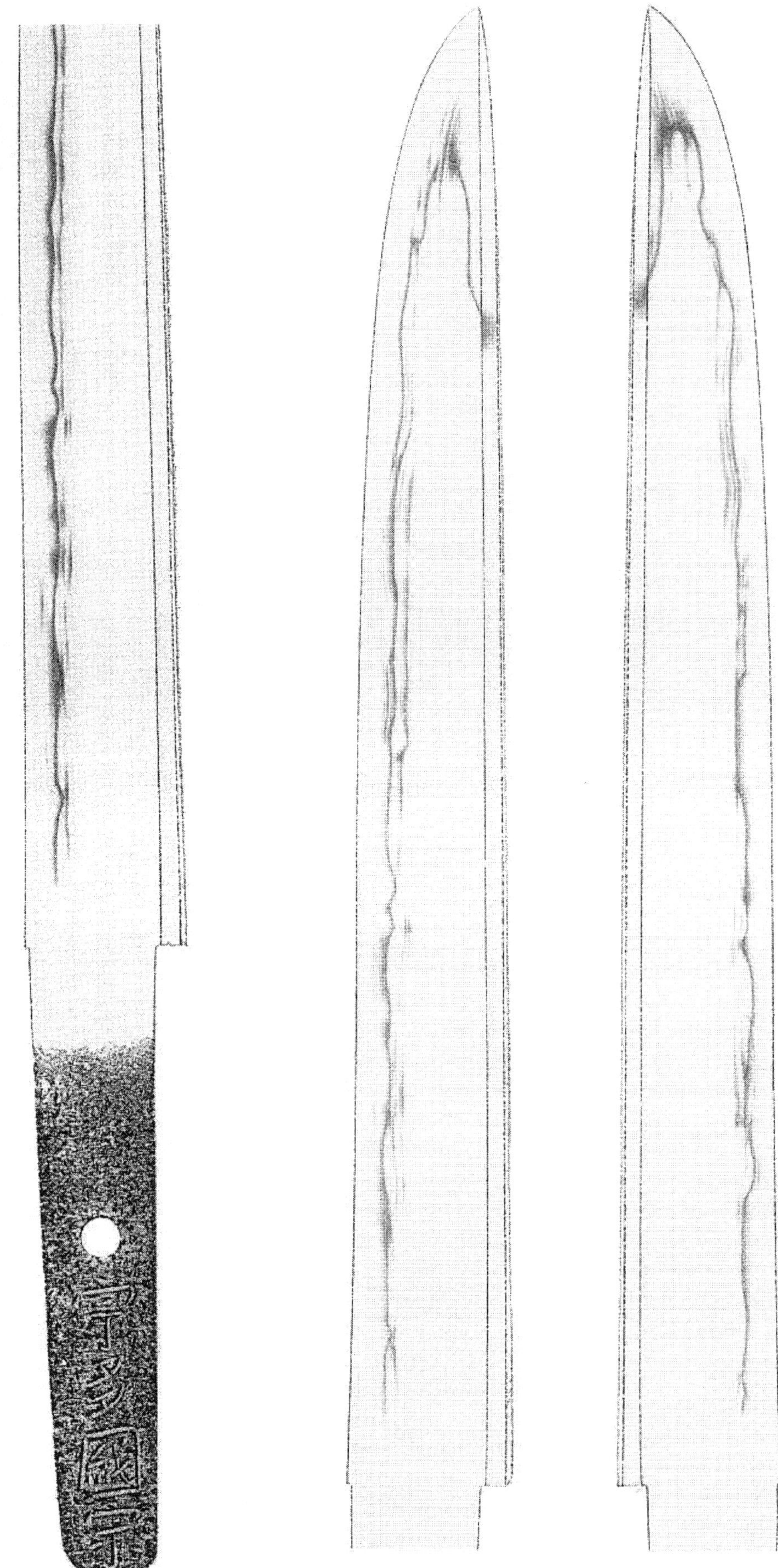

163.666k *tantō*
mei: Uda Kunimune (宇多国宗)
nagasa 21,06 cm *uchizori*
moto-haba 2,0 cm *moto-kasane* 0,65 cm
nakago-nagasa 9,09 cm no *nakago-sori*

hira-zukuri, *mitsu-mune*, rather slender *mihaba*, compact length, conspicious *uchizori*, scarce *fukura*. The *jigane* is an *itame* which tends all over the blade to *nagare* and *masame*. *Ji-nie* and *chikei* appear and the steel is blackish. The *hamon* and the *bōshi* can be seen on the *oshigata*. In addition repeated *hotsure* and *kuichigaiba*, some *yubashiri*, *ko-ashi*, *kinsuji*, *sunagashi* and characteristically round and strongly flashing *nie* appear. The *nakago* is *ubu*, has a bulbous *kurijiri*, a round *mune*, very shallow *katte-sagari* and one *mekugi-ana*. A rather large dimensioned *yoji-mei* is chiselled centrally on the *sashi-omote* side under the *mekugi-ana*.

This blade has a rather slender *mihaba*, a compact length, a conspicious *uchizori* and scarce *fukura*, that means it can be dated into the middle or late Muromachi period. The *jigane* is an *itame* which tends all over the blade to *masame* and *nagare*. The *hamon* is a *suguha-chō* with slightly undulating *notare* which shows *hotsure*, *kuichigaiba*, *kinsuji* and *sunagashi*, that means generally *nie*-based *hataraki*. Thus we can see the typical elements of the Yamato tradition. And because the steel is blackish we are not directly in Yamato but in a more distant province.

Yamato-offshoots of the Muromachi period were for example the Uda school from Etchū, the Mihara school from Bingo, the Niō school from Suō or the Naminohira school from Satsuma. Among those schools, a *suguha-chō* with slightly undulating *notare*, flashing *nie*, and conspiciously granular *ha-nie* speak for the Uda school. The *bōshi* of Uda-*tantō* appears like on the *omote* side of the *kantei* blade somewhat pointed (but can also appear as a *ko-maru*-like *kaeri* as we see it on the *ura* side). The *kaeri* is long and wide and so the Uda-*bōshi* looks at a glance like the *bōshi* of Chikuzen´s Samonji school. This is an important characteristic of that school. The tip of the tang of Uda blades is a bulbous *kurijiri*, the *nakago-mune* is round, the *yasurime* are *katte-sagari* and the signature is in the case of *tantō* chiselled mostly on the *sashi-omote* side centrally under the *mekugi-ana*.

Within the Uda school there were several smith which shared the character for „Kuni“ (国), like for example Kunimune (国宗) or Kunifusa (国房). These smiths signed mostly with a *yoji-mei* like „Uda Kunimune“. But there was another group of Uda smiths which shared the character for „Tomo“ (友), like for example Tomotsugu (友次) or Tomohisa (友久). Smiths of this group signed mostly with a *niji-mei*.

Most of the bids were *atari* on Kunimune, followed by Kunifusa, Kunihisa (国久), Kunitsugu (国次) and other Uda smiths. As the workmanship and the finish of the tang of the Muromachi-period Uda smiths is very close, all bids in that direction were counted as *atari*. But some went also for the 1st gen. Uda Kunimitsu (国光, the so-called „Konyūdō Kunimitsu“, 古入道国光). According to transmission, Kunimitsu moved once during the Kamakura-period Bunpō era (文保, 1317-1319) from Yamato´s Uda district to Etchū province and founded there the Uda school. There exists a *tokubetsu-jūyō tachi* which is attributed to this 1st gen. Uda Kunimitsu. It has a rather slender *tachi-sugata*, a *ko-itame* with *masame-nagare* and a *hamon* in *hoso-suguha* with *ko-ashi*, *hotsure* and plentiful of *nie*. So it differs in terms of production time and workmanship greatly from the *kantei* blade. It is also widely known that there are no signed *tantō* extant by this smith and so bids on the 1st gen. Uda Kunimitsu can´t be counted as *atari*.

Also not counted as *atari* were bids on Fujishima Tomoshige (藤島友重). Well, there exist some Muromachi-period Fujishima works in *suguha* with a similar *jigane* and a *yoji-mei* of the kind „Fujishima Tomoshige“, so from this point of view a bid in that direction is understandable. But most Fujishima works from that time show a *koshi-no-hiraita midare* which is mixed with *togariba*, *yahazuba* and angular elements, a connected *ko-gunome* in the style of the Shikkake school, or a *yahazuba* like we know it from Ōei-Nobukuni (応永信国). Works in *suguha* are rather rare and also the characteristically granular and flashing *ha-nie* are not found at the Fujishima school. But also taken into consideration must be the tip of the tang because Tomoshige did not apply a *kurijiri* but a *ha-agari kurijiri* or a pronounced *katayama-jiri*.

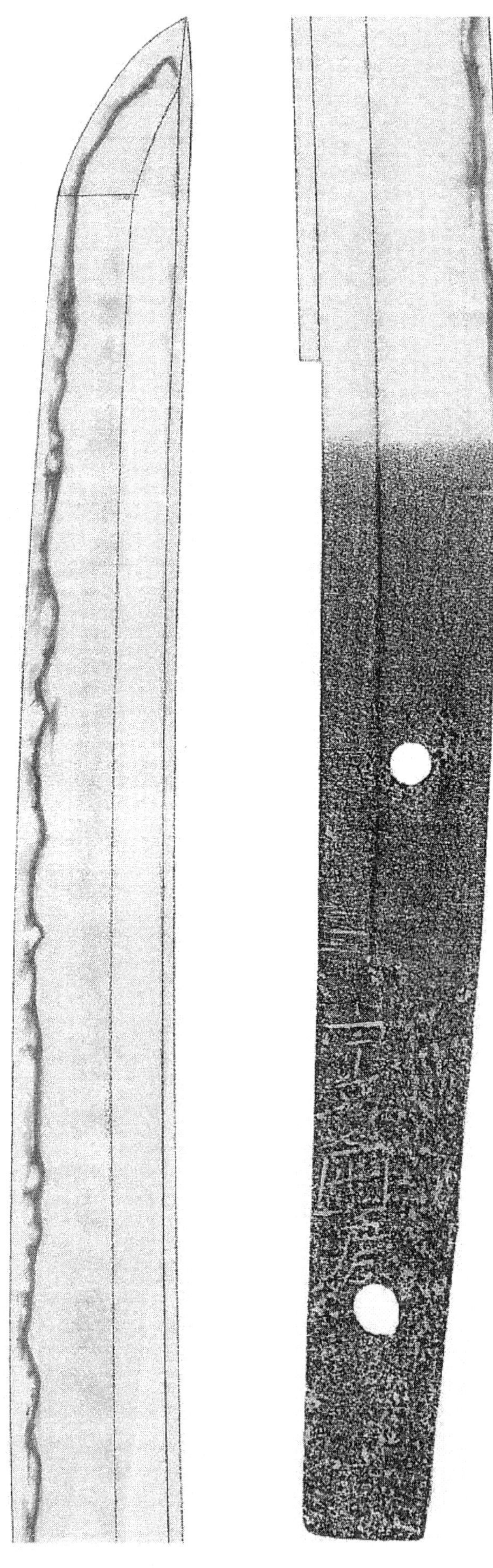

164.650 *tachi*
mei: Uda Kunifusa (宇多国房)
nagasa 70,1 cm, *sori* 2,3 cm, *shinogi-zukuri*, *iori-mune*

ji: *itame* mixed with *mokume*, plentiful of *ji-nie*, *chikei*, the steel is blackish, *jifu* and a *shirake-utsuri* appear
hamon: *suguha-chō* mixed with connected *ko-midare* and *ko-gunome*, in addition *ko-ashi*, the hardening is in *nioi-deki* with *ko-nie*, the *nioiguchi* is rather subdued, larger *nie* appear on the *haki-omote* side along the lower half of the blade, in addition *sunagashi* and *kinsuji* are seen, there are *tobiyaki*-like *yubashiri* on the *omote* side under the *yokote*
bōshi: on the *omote* side *sugu* and on the *ura* side *midare-komi*, both with a short *kaeri*

The blade is relative slender, has a deep *sori* and ends in a compact *ko-kissaki*, that means many were too early with their first bid and went for the early Kamakura period and for Ko-Hōki or Ko-Aoe. Well, also the classical *jiba* supports this approach. But when you take a closer look at the shape you will recognize that the center of the curvature is not towards the base but towards the tip and that the *kasane* is relative thick. Such a *sugata* is namely typical for the late Nanbokuchō and early Muromachi era and was for example applied by Bizen´s Kozori group (小反) or Yamashiro´s Nobukuni (信国).

As the *shinogi* is high, he can lay down the origins of the blade in the Yamato tradition and this was why many went for Shikkake Norinaga (尻懸則長). But here again the *sugata* is not matching because apart from the *sori* the *mihaba* would be wider and the *kissaki* a *chu-kissaki*.

The Uda school came around the Kamakura-period Bunpō era (文保, 1317-1319) from Yamato´s Uda district to Etchū and works until the Nanbokuchō period are classified as „Ko-Uda". The school flourished from the Muromachi period onwards and many smiths shared the character for „Kuni" (国). The most representative of them is Kunifusa. The *kantei* blade shows a similar signature style and workmanship as Kunifusa *tachi* from the Hie-jinja (日枝神社) and the Kurokawa Institute of Ancient Cultures (黒川古文化研究所). Both are designated as *jūyō-bunkazai* and date not later than the late Nanbokuchō period.

As was to be expected, the steel of the *kantei* blade has the typical blackish colour of northern *Hokkoku-mono* but the *kitae* is neither coarse nor rusty but uniform and this is within the Uda school very typical for Kunifusa. The *hamon* in *suguha-chō* is mixed with *ko-midare* and *ko-gunome* and appears as mentioned very classical. However, the quality of the Uda school varies greatly but Kunifusa can be put to the top end. The *ji* shows a *shirake-utsuri*, the *nioiguchi* is subdued and the *bōshi* is lenient and free and so with the *sugata* and the *jigane* we are at the Uda and not at one of the noticeably earlier schools.

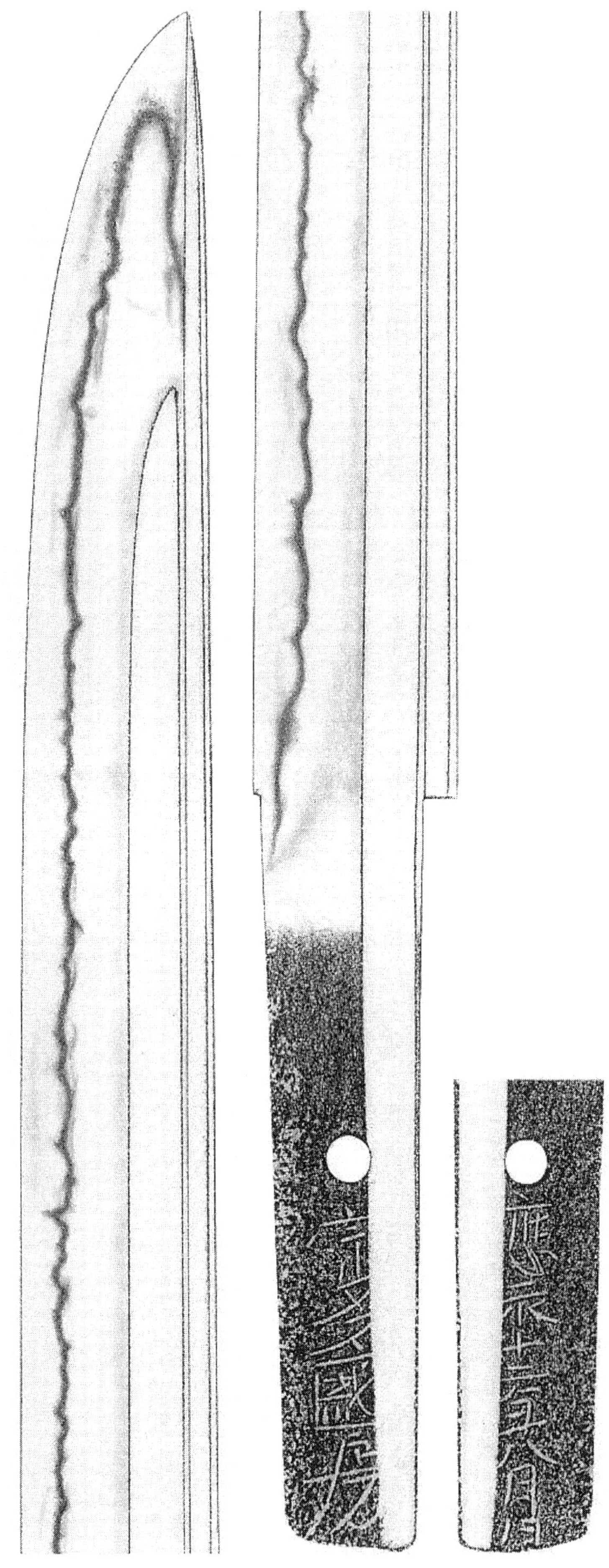

165.642 *tantō*
mei: Uda Kunifusa (宇多国房)
Ōei jūni-nen hachigatsu-hi (応永十二年八月日, „a day in the eighth month Ōei twelve [= 1405]")
nagasa 28,5 cm, no *sori*, *hira-zukuri*, *mitsu-mune*

ji: dense *ko-itame* with plentiful of *ji-nie* and fine *chikei*, a *shirake-utsuri* runs parallel to the *hi*
hamon: *chū-suguha-chō* mixed with *ko-gunome* and *gunome* which are sometimes pointed, in addition *ashi* and many *yō*, the bright *nioiguchi* looks soft and shows *ko-nie*, in addition small *yubashiri*, *sunagashi* and some *kinsuji* appear
bōshi: tends to *midare-komi* with plentiful of *hakikake*, *yubashiri* and small *tobiyaki*, quite *nie*-loaden, the *omote* side shows a *ko-maru-kaeri* and the *ura* side a pointed *kaeri*, both run back in a long fashion
horimono: on both sides a *katana-hi* which runs with *kaki-tōshi* through the tang

Most *tantō* of the Ōei era have a long, elongated *nagasa* (and many have actually an obvious *wakizashi* length). This blade has a rather wide *mihaba*, is only a little *sunnobi*, has a thick *kasane*, no *sori*, is in *hira-zukuri* and shows a *mitsu-mune*. Such a *tantō-sugata* would be typical for the late Kamakura and early Nanbokuchō period but it is dated with Ōei twelve. Well, the Uda school made many of such well-balanced *tantō* during that time (and so did for example also Ōei Nobukuni [応永信国] and the Ōei-Bizen school). Some came on the basis of the pointed *bōshi* (especially noticeable on the *ura* side) with strong *hakikake* and accumulating *nie* and long *kaeri* to the result „Uda" because all these are typical characteristics for a *bōshi* of the Uda school. And when you combine this with the fine and beautifully forged *jigane* it is possible to nail the bid down to Kunifusa. But there were also bids on Kunihisa (国久) which is understandable because of the dense *jigane*. Some went also for Kunimune (国宗). However, there are some Kunimune blades extant which bear date signatures of the Ōei period but the vast majority dates later, somewhere around Bunmei (文明, 1469-1487). Also his *hada* would tend more to *nagare* and would show conspicuous *mokume*. And in addition, the *hada* would stand out more and the steel would be more blackish.

There were also relative many bids on Rai Kunimitsu (来国光) but the *kantei* blade has no *nie-utsuri* but a *shirake-utsuri* which runs along the *hi*. Except the *meibutsu* Shiogawa- (塩川), Uraku- (有楽), and Ikeda-Kunimitsu (池田), his *tantō* with such a *deki* in *midare* show a *bōshi* with normal and short *kaeri* and not such a long running back like seen here.

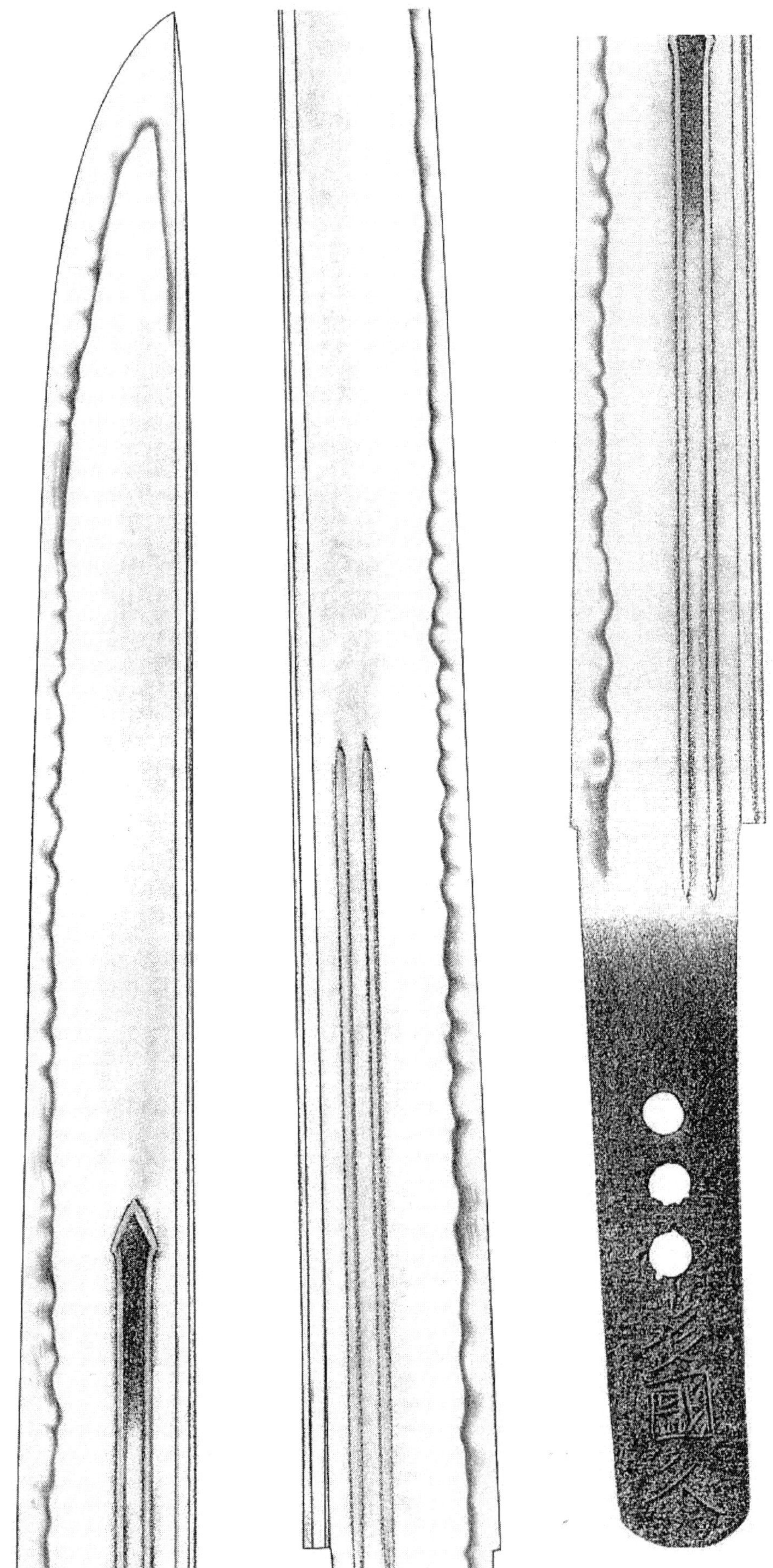

166.634k *tantō*
mei: Uda Kunihisa (宇多国久)
nagasa 29, 64 *uchizori* *moto-haba* 2,55 cm *moto-kasane* 0,65 cm
nakago-nagasa 10,76 almost no *nakago-sori*

hira-zukuri, *mitsu-mune*, normal *mihaba*, *sunnobi*, relative thick *kasane*, a little *uchizori*. The *kitae* is a very densely forged *ko-itame* with plentiful of *ji-nie*, *chikei* and a *shirake-utsuri*. The *hamon* and the *bōshi* can be seen on the *oshigata*. In addition *ko-ashi*, *yō*, strongly flashing fine granular *nie* and *sunagashi*. The *nioiguchi* is bright. There is a *suken* on the *omote* side and *gomabashi* on the *ura* side. The *nakago* is *ubu*, has a bulbous *kurijiri*, a *maru-mune*, *katte-sagari yasurime* and three *mekugi-ana*. The signature is chiselled centrally on the *sashi-omote* below the *ubu-mekugi-ana*.

The *tantō* has a normal *mihaba*, an elongated *sunnobi-nagasa*, a relative thick *kasane* and some *uchizori*. Such a shape is typical for the early Muromachi period. The Uda school is an offshoot of the Yamato tradition, that means their style is of course Yamato-influenced and shows a standing-out *itame* mixed with *nagare*, a blackish steel with *shirake-utsuri*, a *nie*-loaden *suguha* and horizontal *hataraki* like *hotsure*, *kuichigaiba* and *sunagashi*.

But apart from that, the Uda school displayed quite a varied workmanship. So we find blades in *notare-chō* mixed with *gunome*, plentiful of *nie* and conspicious *kinsuji* and *sunagashi* which remind of Gō Yoshihiro (郷義弘) and Norishige (則重). But also *koshi-no-hiraita midare* with *togariba* and *sunagashi* which remind of Fujishima Tomoshige (藤島友重), *suguha* in Nobukuni-manner (信国), or *hitatsura* in the style of the Sue-Sōshū school are known.

Many interpretations are similar to the *kantei* blade. That means they have a dense and beautifully forged *ko-itame*, a *hamon* which bases on a shallow *notare* with bright *nioiguchi* and much *nie* which is mixed with connected *gunome* elements. And because of this rather refined workmanship, maybe Rai Kunimitsu (来国光) or Kunitsugu (国次) from Yamashiro province come to mind.

However, a common characteristic of all Uda-*mono* are the flashing *ha-nie* of which the individual particles can be easily made out with the naked eye. A *deki* in dense and beautifully forged *ko-itame*, a bright *jigane* and a *hamon* with bright *nioiguchi* is mostly found at Uda Kunifusa (宇多国房). In contrary, a blackish *jigane* with standing-out *itame* and plentiful of *sunagashi* is more typical for Uda Kunimune (宇多国宗). Kunihisa is not so well known than these two smiths but his *jiba* is bright and clear too and comes quite close to Kunifusa, and also in terms of quality they are about on the same level.

The *bōshi* of *tantō* and *hira-zukuri wakizashi* of the Uda school is like here often a pointed *midare-komi* with a wide and long *kaeri* (although there are several works where the *bōshi* is even more pointed). So at a glance, the *bōshi* reminds of Chikuzen´s Samonji school (左文字) and this is a typical characteristic of the Uda school.

The tip of the tang of *tantō* and *hira-zukuri wakizashi* is a bulbous *kurijiri*, the tangs have mostly a round back and *katte-sagari yasurime*. The signature is principally chiselled centrally on the *sashi-omote* side below the *mekugi-ana*. Some Uda smiths like Kunifusa, Kunimune, Kunihisa and the like shared the character for „Kuni" (国) and signed mostly in a *yoji-mei* (for example „Uda Kunihisa", 宇多国久). Other smiths shared the character for „Tomo" (友), for example Tomotsugu (友次) and Tomohisa (友久), and this group signed mostly with a *niji-mei*.

Most bids were on any of the known Uda smiths like Kunifusa, Kunihisa or Kunimune. The workmanship of these famous Uda masters is relative close and also the finish of their tangs is the same. Accordingly all bids in that direction were counted as *atari* this time. Incidentally, most of the bids were on Kunifusa. Besides of *atari* there were also some few bids on Rai Kunitoshi (来国俊). We also know some large dimensioned *tantō* with a *nagasa* of around 9 *sun* (~ 27,3 cm) of him but mostly he made *tantō* between 7 and 8 *sun* (21,2 ~ 24,2 cm). In addition, we would expect a *nie-utsuri* but not such conspicious *ha-nie* from Kunitoshi and his tip of the tang is a normal but not a bulbous *kurijiri*.

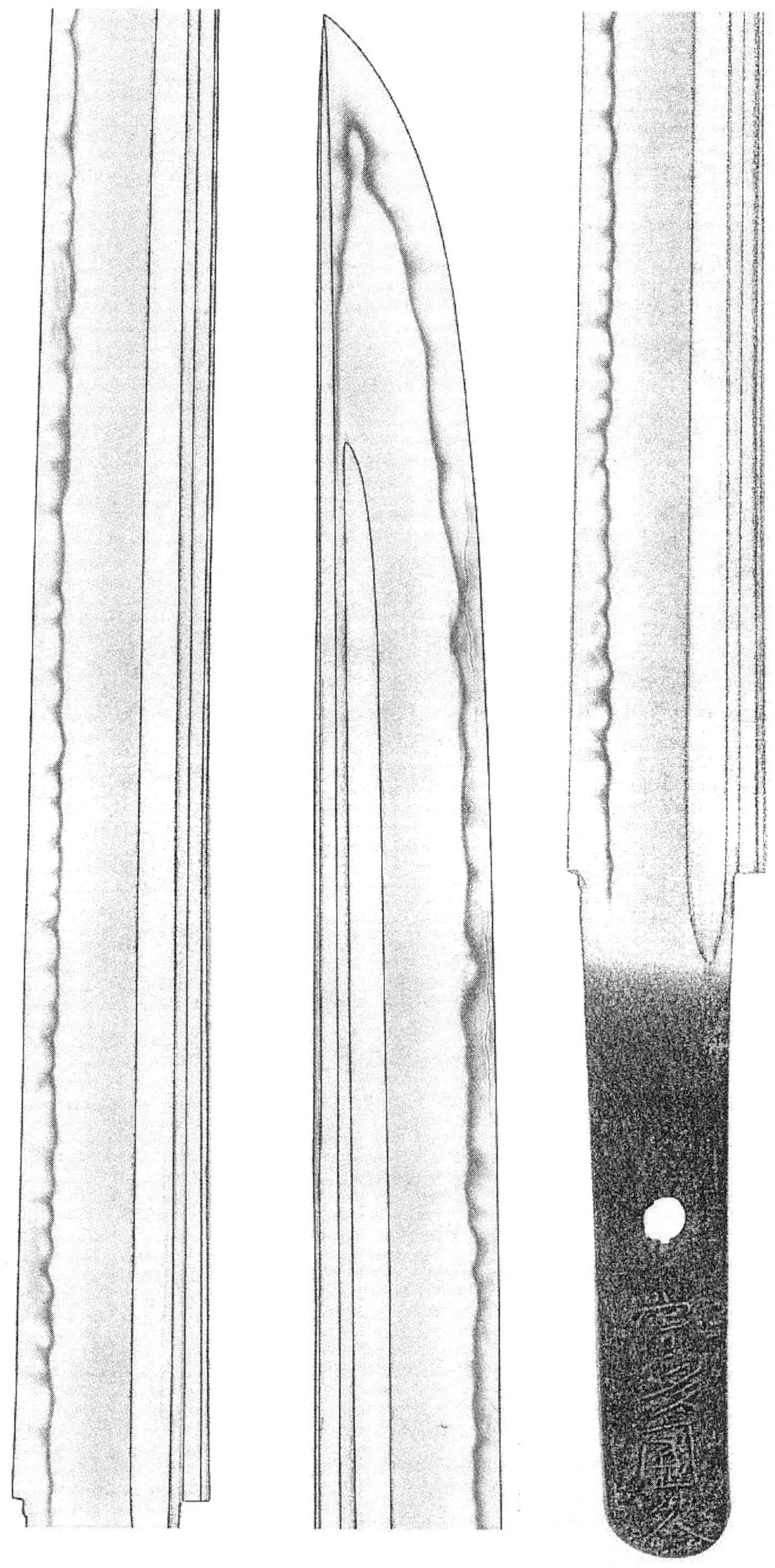

167.609k *wakizashi*
mei: Uda Kunihisa (宇多国久)
nagasa 31,0 cm sori 0,15 cm
moto-haba 2,6 cm *moto-kasane* 0,65 cm
nakago-nagasa 10,0 cm only a little *nakago-sori*

hira-zukuri, *mitsu-mune*, normal *mihaba*, *sunnobi*, relative thick *kasane*, shallow *sori*. The *jigane* is a dense and very fine and excellently forged *ko-itame* with plentiful of *ji-nie*, *chikei* and a clearly visible *shirake-utsuri*. The *hamon* and the *bōshi* can be seen on the *oshigata*. In addition *ko-ashi*, *yō*, *kinsuji*, *sunagashi* and characteristically roundish, strongly flashing *nie*. The *nioiguchi* is bright. There is a *katana-hi* on both sides which runs with *kake-nagashi* into the tang. The *nakago* is *ubu*, has a bulbous *kurijiri*, a round *mune*, *katte-sagari yasurime* and one *mekugi-ana*. The signature is chiselled centrally on the *sashi-omote* side below the *mekugi-ana*.

The *kantei* blade is a work of Uda Kunihisa who was active around Ōei (応永, 1394-1428). It has a normal *mihaba*, is *sunnobi*, has a rather thick *kasane* and a shallow *sori*, which are typical characteristics for *tantō* of the early Muromachi period.

The Uda schools has their origins in the late Kamakura period, or to be more precise around Bunpō (文保, 1317-1319). According to transmission it was founded by Konyūdō Kunimitsu (古入道国光) who moved from Yamato´s Uda district to Etchū province. Their workmanship bases therefore on the Yamato tradition and shows a standing-out *itame* mixed with *nagare*, the steel is blackish, shows a *shirake-utsuri*, and the *hamon* is mostly a *nie*-loaden *suguha* with horizontal *hataraki* like *hotsure*, *kuichigaiba* and *sunagashi*.

But apart from that, the Uda school displayed quite a varied workmanship. So we find blades in *notare-chō* mixed with *gunome*, plentiful of *nie* and conspicious *kinsuji* and *sunagashi* which remind of Gō Yoshihiro (郷義弘) and Norishige (則重). But also *koshi-no-hiraita midare* with *togariba* and *sunagashi* which remind of Fujishima Tomoshige (藤島友重), *suguha* in Nobukuni-manner (信国), or *hitatsura* in the style of the Sue-Sōshū school are known.

Many interpretations are similar to the *kantei* blade. That means they have a dense and beautifully forged *ko-itame*, a *hamon* which bases on a shallow *notare* with bright *nioiguchi* and many *nie* which is mixed with connected *gunome* elements. And because of this rather refined workmanship, maybe Rai Kunimitsu (来国光) or Kunitsugu (国次) from Yamashiro province come to mind. The most representative masterwork of that interpretation is a *jūyō-bijutsuhin tantō* of Uda Kunifusa (宇多国房) which is dated Ōei twelve (1405).

However, a common characteristic of all Uda-*mono* are the flashing *ha-nie* of which the individual particles can be easily made out with the naked eye. Already the *bakumatsu*-era publication „*Kotō mei-zukushi taizen*“ (古刀銘尽大全) writes on the various Uda styles: „*suguha*, *midareba*, many do exist“, „the *deki* is mostly *mokume* with magnificent *sunagashi*, *inazuma* and the like“, „there are also works with an excellent *deki* which are hardly to differentiate from Sōshū-*mono*“, or „also *hoso-suguha* which testifies to the various styles of the Uda school“. And the „*Honchō kaji-kō*“ (本朝鍛冶考) writes: „Works from this group from Etchū´s Ezu (宇津, the place where Kunimitsu had settled) without *nie* all over are doubtful.“ This might refer to the characteristical *ha-nie* of the Uda school.

Most bids were on any of the known Uda smiths like Kunifusa, Kunihisa or Kunimune. The workmanship of these famous Uda masters is relative close and also the finish of their tangs is the same. Accordingly all bids in that direction were counted as *atari* this time. But there were also relative many bids on Rai Kunimitsu, Rai Kunitsugu, Sa Yasuyoshi (左安吉) and Sa Yoshisada (左吉貞). Well, the *kantei* blade does show similarities with Rai Kunimitsu or Kunitsugu but their *hira-zukuri wakizashi* with a *sunnobi-nagasa* have a wider *mihaba* which reflects the style of the Nanbokuchō period. Also the typical Rai-*hada* and not a *shirake-* but a *nie-utsuri* would be seen.

Hira-zukuri wakizashi of Sa Yasuyoshi have a wider *mihaba* and a thinner *kasane*, which is typical for the Enbun (延文, 1356-1361) and Jōji eras (貞治, 1362-1368). The *jigane* would be a standing-out *itame* mixed with *nagare* and would show a *shirake-utsuri* towards the back and a *bō-utsuri* towards the *ha*. Also the *ha-nie* would be more calm and the *nioiguchi* with *ko-nie* would look more like Bizen. Yasuyoshi´s *bōshi* is also a pointed *midare-komi* but which leans somewhat towards the *ha*. (Incidentally, he hardly forged such a dense *itame*.)

At Yoshisada on the other hand we often find such a *sugata* so a bid on him is quite understandable. But like Yasuyoshi he too didn´t forge such a dense and fine *ko-itame*. Also such *ha-nie* like seen on the *kantei* blade are not found at this smith. And Yasuyoshi as Yoshisada applied a tapering tang with a *kurijiri* and *ō-sujikai-yasurime*. This had to be beared in mind too.

Kaga

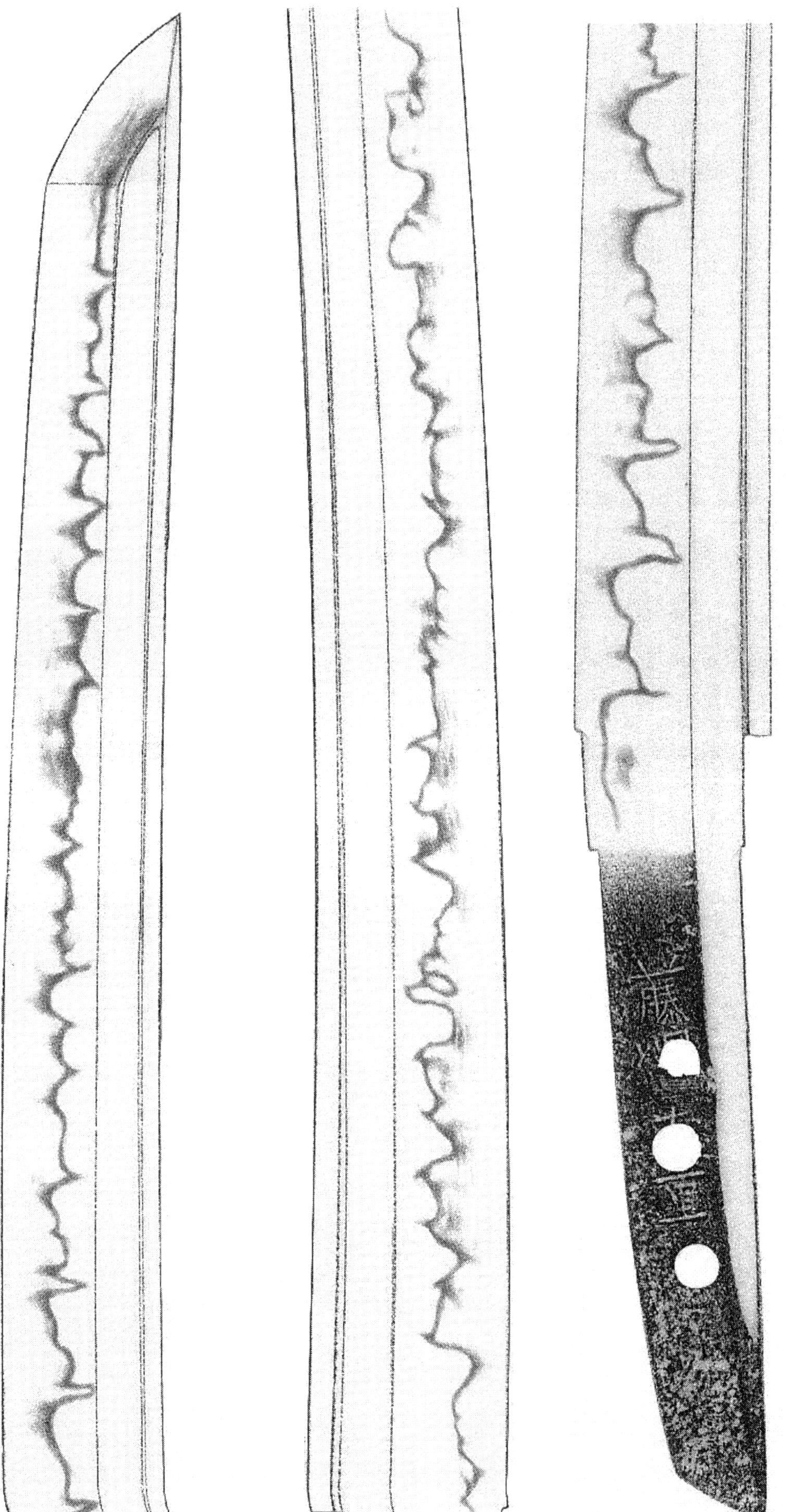

168.601k *wakizashi*
mei: Fujishima Tomoshige (藤嶋友重)
nagasa 50,15 cm *sori* 1,55 cm
moto-haba 2,6 cm *saki-haba* 1,8 cm
moto-kasane 0,75 cm *saki-kasane* 0,35 cm
kissaki-nagasa 2,6 cm *nakago-nagasa* 11,67 cm
onl a little *nakago-sori*

shinogi-zukuri, iori-mune, normal *mihaba*, relative thick *kasane*, deep and conspicous *sakizori*, *chū-kissaki*. The *jigane* is a standing-out *itame* partially mixed with *nagare* and *masame*. *Ji-nie* and *chikei* appear and the steel is blackish. The *hamon* and the *bōshi* can be seen on the *oshigata*. There are *tobiyaki*, *ashi*, *yō*, *kinsuji*, *sunagashi* and plentiful of *nie*, whereas the latter accumulate to conspicious *mura-nie* in places. On both sides a *bōhi* with *kake-nagashi* is applied. The *nakago* is almost *ubu* (only a little *machi-okuri* and re-worked tip), had originally a *ha-agari kurijiri* which tended to a pronounced *katayama-jiri*, the *yasurime* are shallow *katte-sagari* and there are three *mekugi-ana*. There is a signature chiselled centrally on the tang. (Note: There are many works of that smith which show a clearly visible *shirake-utsuri*.)

This *wakizashi* of Fujishima Tomoshige dates into the early Muromachi period, or to be more precise around Ōei (1394-1428). The Fujishima school has its origins in Echizen province but later a moving to Kaga took place. As a reference point for this moving serves an extant *wakizashi* with the signature „Gashū Fujishima Tomoshige" (賀州藤島友重) and the dating „Ōei jūrokunen" (応永十六年, 1409). With other words, at the beginning of the Muromachi period the school worked already from Kaga province.

One of the earliest extant blades of a Fujishima Tomoshige is the *jūyō-bijutsuhin tachi* with a *niji-mei* which is preserved in the Atsuta-jingū in Nagoya. It is dated into the transitional period between Kamakura and Nanbokuchō and shows a *hamon* which bases on *ko-gunome* and which is interpreted in the style of the Shikkake school. Such early works are very rare and most of the rather old Tomoshige blades do not date earlier than the late Nanbokuchō period. But the extant works are considerably more numerous from the Muromachi to the Edo period and although the workmanship is basically kept, the quality decreases noticeably over the time.

The *kantei* blade has a normal *mihaba*, a relative thick *kasane*, a conspicious *sakizori* and a *chū-kissaki*, so we can date it into the early Muromachi period. The *jigane* of the Tomoshige lineage is a standing-out *itame* mixed with *masame-nagare*. The steel is blackish and a *shirake-utsuri* appears. But early works from the early Muromachi period show often a dense *ko-itame*, a relative bright *jigane* and no *shirake-utsuri* but a *midare-utsuri* similar to Bizen-*mono*.

The *hamon* is like here an irregular *koshi-no-hiraita midare* mixed with *togariba* and *yahazu*-like claws (*tsuno-ha*, 角刃). But there also exist as mentioned works in Shikkake style with a connected *ko-gunome*. The interpretation in angular *gunome* mixed with *togariba* and *yahazu* reminds of Ōei Nobukuni (応永信国) but there are also works in *suguha*. In any case, plentiful of *nie* and *sunagashi* appear. The *bōshi* is *nie*-loaden too and shows conspicious *hakikake*. Such a *koshi-no-hiraita gunome* with *togariba* which are connected by *midare* is also typical for the Tomoshige lineage.

In general it is said that Tomoshige mixed the Bizen, the Mino and the Yamato tradition and already the „*Honchō-kaji-kō*" (本朝鍛冶考) writes: „works with hard to tell stylistic origins".

Around Ōei, the Tomoshige lineage applied a *ha-agari kurijiri* or a pronounced *katayamagata-jiri*. The *yasurime* are shallow *katte-sagari* and the *yoji-mei* „Fujishima Tomoshige" is chiselled at *katana*, *wakizashi* and *tantō* on the *sashi-omote* side centrally under the *mekugi-ana*. But from time to time we find blades like this where the signature runs over the *ubu-mekugi-ana*.

Most participants got all characteristics right and bade *atari* on Fujishima Tomoshige. But there were also some who went for Yukimitsu (行光) and Kiyomitsu (清光) who were also Fujishima smiths of the early Muromachi period. Their workmanship is similar and so bids on them were this time counted as *atari* too. But it has to be mentioned that the *kantei* blade displays a textbook *deki* for Fujishima Tomoshige and there are only few works of such early Yukimitsu and Kiyomitsu extant. So it is rather not recommended to bid on these two in such a case.

There were also some few bids on Uda Kunimune (宇多国宗). The Uda school was as the Fujishima school active in northern Japan (i.e. they are classified as so-called „*Hokkoku-mono*" or „*Hokuriku-mono*"). So their steel is blackish and shows mostly a clearly visible *shirake-utsuri* too. Also the *midareba* can be similar at the Uda school and from this point of view, such bids are understandable. But mostly the Uda school applied a *suguha* with shallow *notare* or a *notare*-based *hamon* mixed with *gunome*. Also they applied characteristically roundish and brightly flashing *ha-nie*. And in addition, the Uda school made tangs with a *kurijiri*.

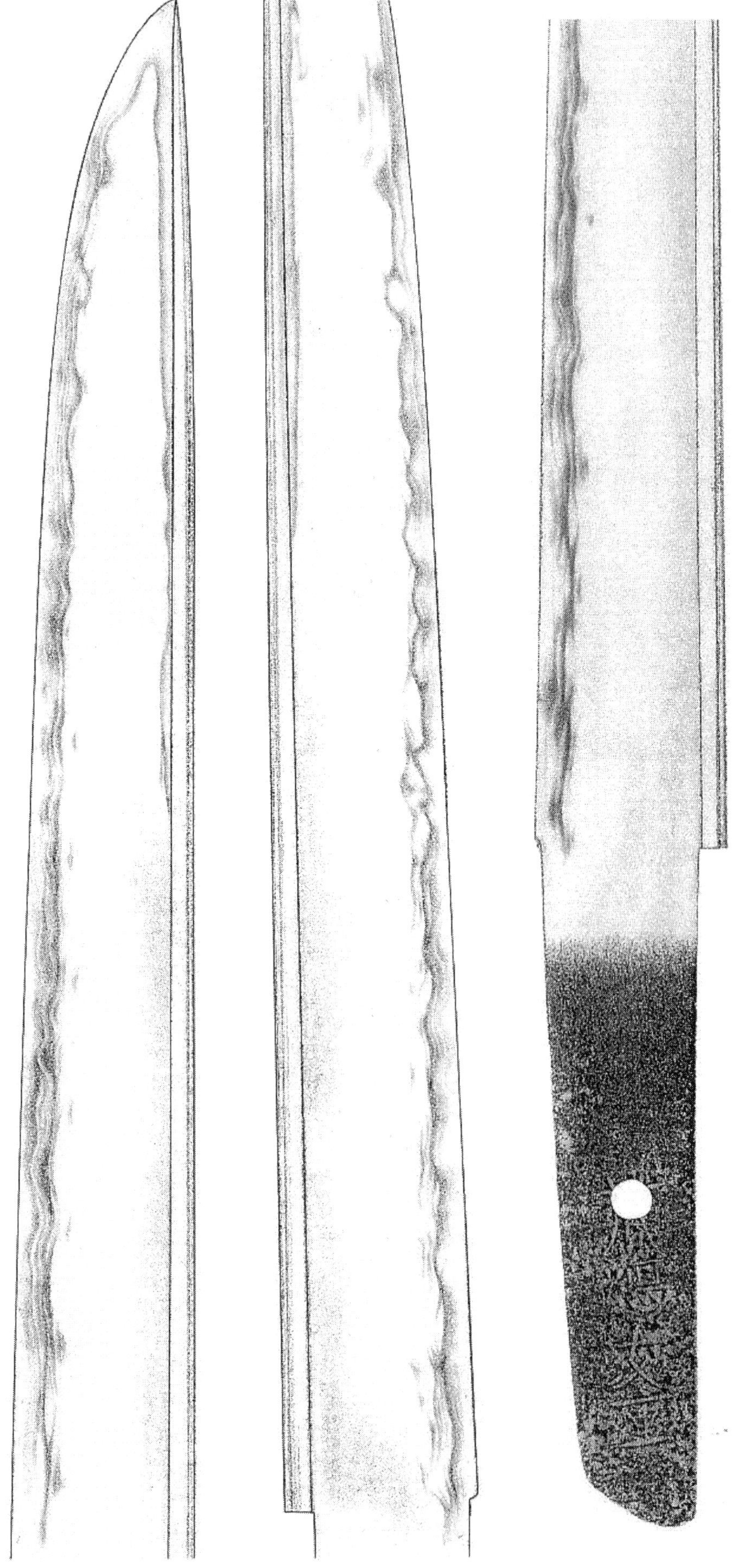

169.636k *tantō*
mei: Fujishima Tomoshige (藤嶋友重)

nagasa 25,76 cm	*uchizori*
moto-haba 2,5 cm	*moto-kasane* 0,6 cm
nakago-nagasa 10,15 cm	only a little *nakago-sori*

hira-zukuri, *mitsu-mune*, relative slender *mihaba*, strong *uchizori*, scarce *fukura*. The *jigane* is a standing-out *itame* mixed with *mokume*. *Ji-nie*, *chikei* and a *shirake-utsuri* appear. The steel is blackish. The *hamon* and the *bōshi* can be seen on the *oshigata*. In addition plentiful of *hotsure*, *ko-nie*, *sunagashi* and *kinsuji*. The *nakago* is *ubu*, has a pronounced *ha-agari kurijiri* in *katayamagata* shape, shallow *katte-sagari yasurime* and one *mekugi-ana* which runs through the uppermost character of the signature. The *mei* is chiselled centrally on the *sashi-omote* side.

The blade has a rather slender *mihaba*, a strong *uchizori* and scarce *fukura* and so we can date it into the Muromachi period. Early Tomoshige works from the early Muromachi period and before show a dense *ko-itame*, a relative bright *jigane* and sometimes a *midare-utsuri* similar to Bizen-*mono*. But mostly the *kitae* is a standing-out *itame* (mixed with some *nagare*), the steel is blackish and a *shirake-utsuri* appears.

Older Tomoshige works are for example the dated *jūyō-bijutsuhin tachi* from Nagoya´s Atsuta-jingū which bears a *niji-mei*. It is dated into the transitional period between Kamakura and Nanbokuchō. But such early works are very rare for this lineage because the vast majority of all blades extant today are from the late Nanbokuchō and subsequent Muromachi period. There were several generations active, even until the Edo period, but the Muromachi-period smiths display a very similar workmanship and so they form quasi an individual group within the Fujishima lineage.

Old sword documents describe the Tomoshige workmanship quite different. We find for example entries which mention a *gunome-chō* with *midare* in the style of Nobukuni (信国), a *deki* in angular *gunome* with *togariba*, a *koshi-no-hiraita gunome* with *togari*, or a *yahazuba* which shows *togari* too. But also a *suguha* was applied and in most cases plentiful of *sunagashi* and *hakikake* appear in the *bōshi* which run parallel to the *ha*.

There are normal dimensioned or *sunnobi-tantō* which show a *hamon* with connected *ko-gunome* and a *habuchi* with plentiful of *hotsure*, *nie* and *sunagashi*. The *kantei* blade is such a case. The mentioned *tachi* of the Atsuta-jingū has a normal *mihaba* and a *hamon* in *ko-gunome-chō* which reminds of the Shikkake school and also the *kantei* blade reminds at a glance of Shikkake Norinaga (尻懸則長). And when we combine this with the *ha-agari kurijiri* or pronounced *katayamagata-jiri*, then it is possible to nail the bid down to Fujishima Tomoshige. Well, threre are different theories on the origins of Tomoshige. Some say he came from the school of Rai Kunitoshi (来国俊) or Kashū Sanekage (加州真景) and also a Yamato background is assumed. Works like the *kantei* blade speak strongly in favour of the latter approach (and also that there are relative many works in *kanmuri-otoshi-zukuri* extant).

As different as the workmanship, as different is the *bōshi*, but in most cases plentiful of *hakikake* are seen and the *kaeri* runs back in a pointed manner. Somtimes the *kaeri* runs back wide along the *mune*. The tip of the tang is a *ha-agari kurijiri* which tends to a *katayamagata-jiri*, the *yasurime* are shallow *katte-sagari* and the signature is in the case of *hira-zukuri tantō* interpreted as *yoji-mei* „Fujishima Tomoshige" centrally on the *omote-side*.

Most bids were on Tomoshige but besides of *atari* and *dōzen*, some went also for Etchū Norishige (則重) or the mentioned Kashū Sanekage. This is quite understandable because Tomoshige´s roots are in the northern provinces (*hokkoku*, 北国) too and therefore a local influence, so to speak with Norishige and Sanekage as „pioneers“, can´t be denied. But maybe the *uchizori* was mistaken as *takenoko-sori* and this was the reason for a bid on Norishige. But his *itame-mokume* structure is larger and stands more out. And the plentiful of *ji-nie* and the thick *chikei* which follow the forging structure appear as so-called „*matsukawa-hada*“ (松皮肌). Also the *hamon* would show more and thicker *nie*, the *kaeri* would not be that long and the tip of the tang a *kurijiri*.

There is a *jūyō-bunkazai tantō* extant by Sanekage which is dated Jōji seven (貞治, 1367). That means he was mainly active during the heyday of the Nanbokuchō period. Accordingly, his *tantō* and *hira-zukuri wakizashi* have a wide *mihaba*, are *sunnobi*, have a thin *kasane* and shallow *sori*. There are no *tantō* in standard length with *uchizori* which would come close to the *kantei* blade. Also his *nie* would be more prominent and his tip of the tang has a regular and not so pronounced *ha-agari kurijiri*.

Ise

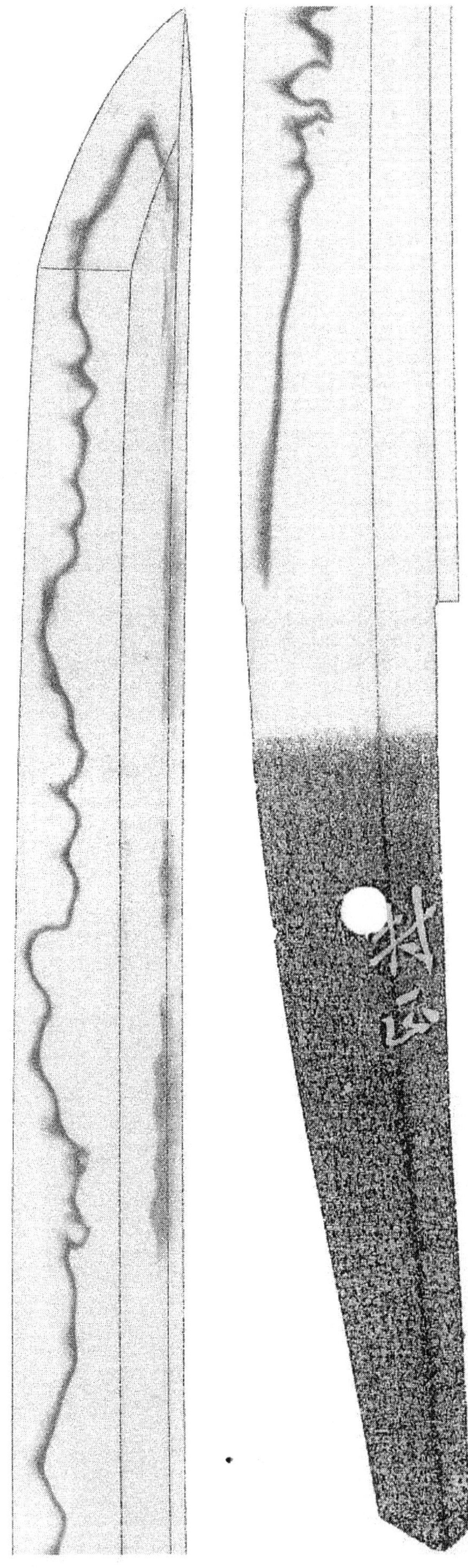
村正

170.645 *katana*
mei: Muramasa (村正)
nagasa 62,3cm, *sori* 1,5 cm, *shinogi-zukuri*, *iori-mune*

ji: *ko-itame* which appears on the *ura* side partially as *itame*, in addition *ji-nie* and a little *shirake-utsuri*
hamon: *yakidashi* which turns into a mix of *gunome*, *ko-gunome*, *togariba* and angular *gunome*, the *hamon* bases in general on a *midareba* whose valleys drop repeatedly deeply, in adition *ashi* and *ko-nie*, the *nioiguchi* is rather subdued and there is a discontinuous *muneyaki* which starts with the *kaeri* of the *bōshi*
bōshi: small dimensioned *midare-komi* with a *ko-maru-kaeri* on the *omote* side and a more roundish *kaeri* on the *ura* side, some *hakikake* appear on both sides

This is a compact *katana* with *sakizori* which measures just a little bit over two *shaku*. That means it is a *katate-uchi* which can be straightforward dated in the middle Muromachi period around Bunki (文亀, 1501-1504), Eishō (永正, 1504-1521) and Daiei (大永, 1521-1528). Noticeable are the *shirake-utsuri*, the slightly blackish steel and the *yakidashi*. Other characteristic features are the vivid *gunome* with *togariba* and angular elements and the partially *hako-midare*-like *midare* protrusions. Also very conspicious is the long and discontinuous *muneyaki* and that the *yakiba* drops down deeply towards the *ha* in some areas. When we combine all these elements with the fact that the *hamon* is identical on both sides and has a subdued *nioiguchi*, it should not be too hard to arrive at Sengo Muramasa.

But some focused on the *yakidashi* and went for Kunisuke (国助) and other Ōsaka-*shintō* smiths. But the *sugata* had to be beared in mind because it rules out early Edo and also the *jiba* of a *shintō* blade would be more bright than of a Sue-*kotō* work.

Incidentally, the blade was once owned by Prince Arisugawa no Miya Taruhito (有栖川宮熾仁, 1835-1895), who was in command of the Imperial Japanese Army during the Boshin War (戊辰戦争, 1868-1869). From the Arisugawa line of the imperial family it came into the possession of the Takamatsu no Miya line (高松宮) which presented it eventually to the NBTHK.

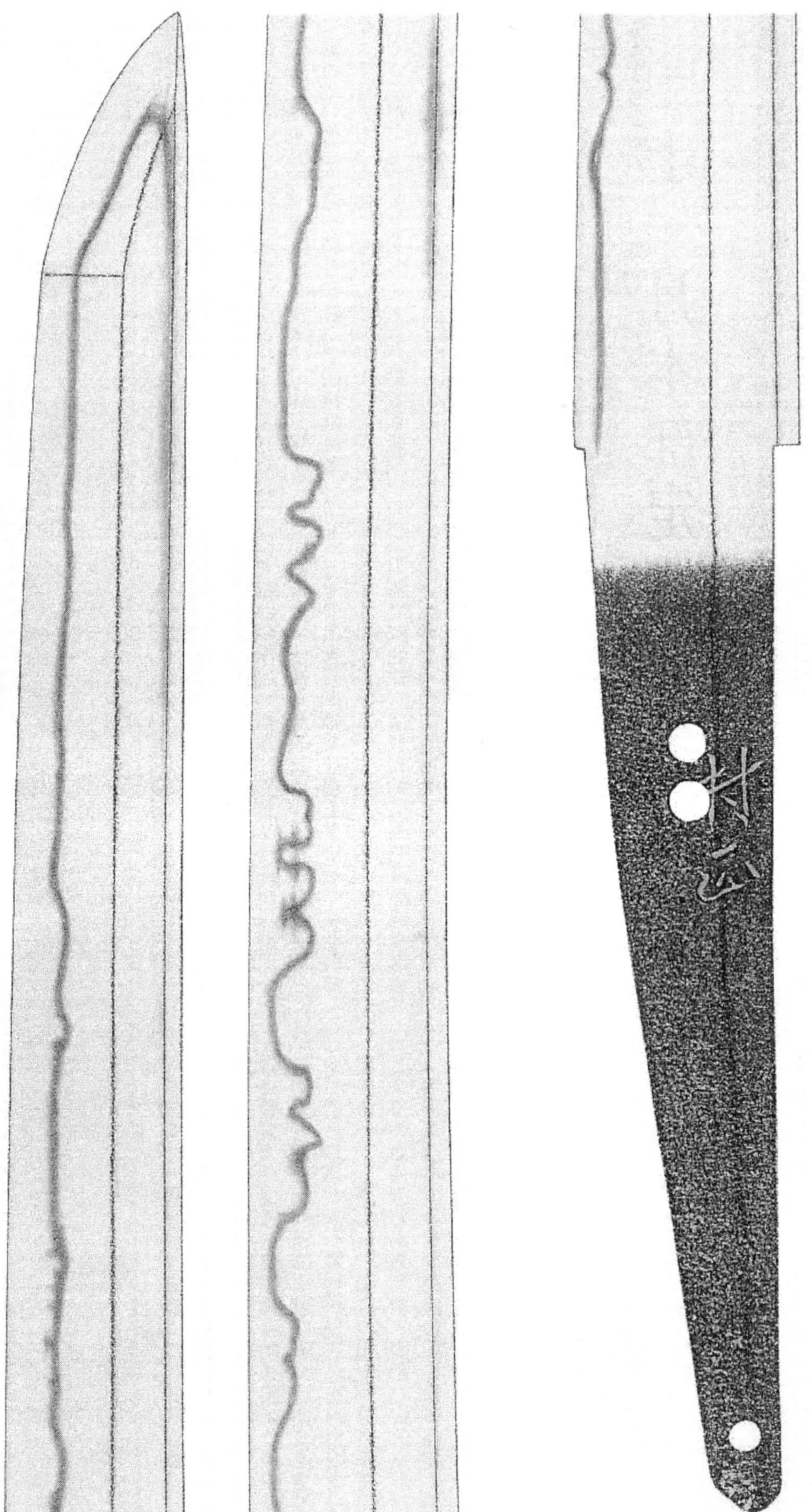

171.599 *katana*
mei: Muramasa (村正)
nagasa 68,2 cm, *sori* 1,2 cm, *shinogi-zukuri, iori-mune*

ji: rather standing-out *itame-hada, ji-nie*, the steel is a little blackish
hamon: *sugu-yakidashi* which turns into a *gunome* with some *togari* and angular *hako-midare* along the lower half and a *suguha* mixed with *ko-notare*, *ko-gunome* and some partial knobs along the upper half, the *hamon* is identical on both sides, in addition *ko-nie*, fine *sunagashi* and *muneyaki* appear, the *nioiguchi* is rather subdued
bōshi: shallow *notare-komi* with a *ko-maru kaeri* which connects with the *mune-yaki*

There is *funbari* and so we can assume that the blade is *ubu* or almost *ubu*. The *nagasa* is not that long, the blade has no noticeable taper, scarce *hira-niku*, a *sakizori* and a slightly elongated *chū-kissaki*, and so we have a typical *katana-sugata* of the Daiei (1521-1521), Kyōroku (1521-1532) and Tenbun eras (1532-1555). Also typical for that time is a *hamon* which appears conspiciously different along the upper and the lower half. And characteristical for Muramasa is especially the lower half with its *gunome* and *togari* which are connected by *notare*, the angular *hako-midare*-like elements, the *yakidashi* and the subdued *nioiguchi*. Also the identical interpretation of the *hamon* on both sides of the blade is very typical for this smith.

All these elements were well grasped by the participants and accordingly the vast majority went *atari* for Muramasa at the very first round. But some bade also on Magoroku Kanemoto (孫六兼元), Kanesada (兼定, No-Sada) or Sue-Seki. Well, there are some similarities in workmanship but contrary to them, Muramasa did not apply a conspicious *shirake-utsuri* and his steel is a little blackish.

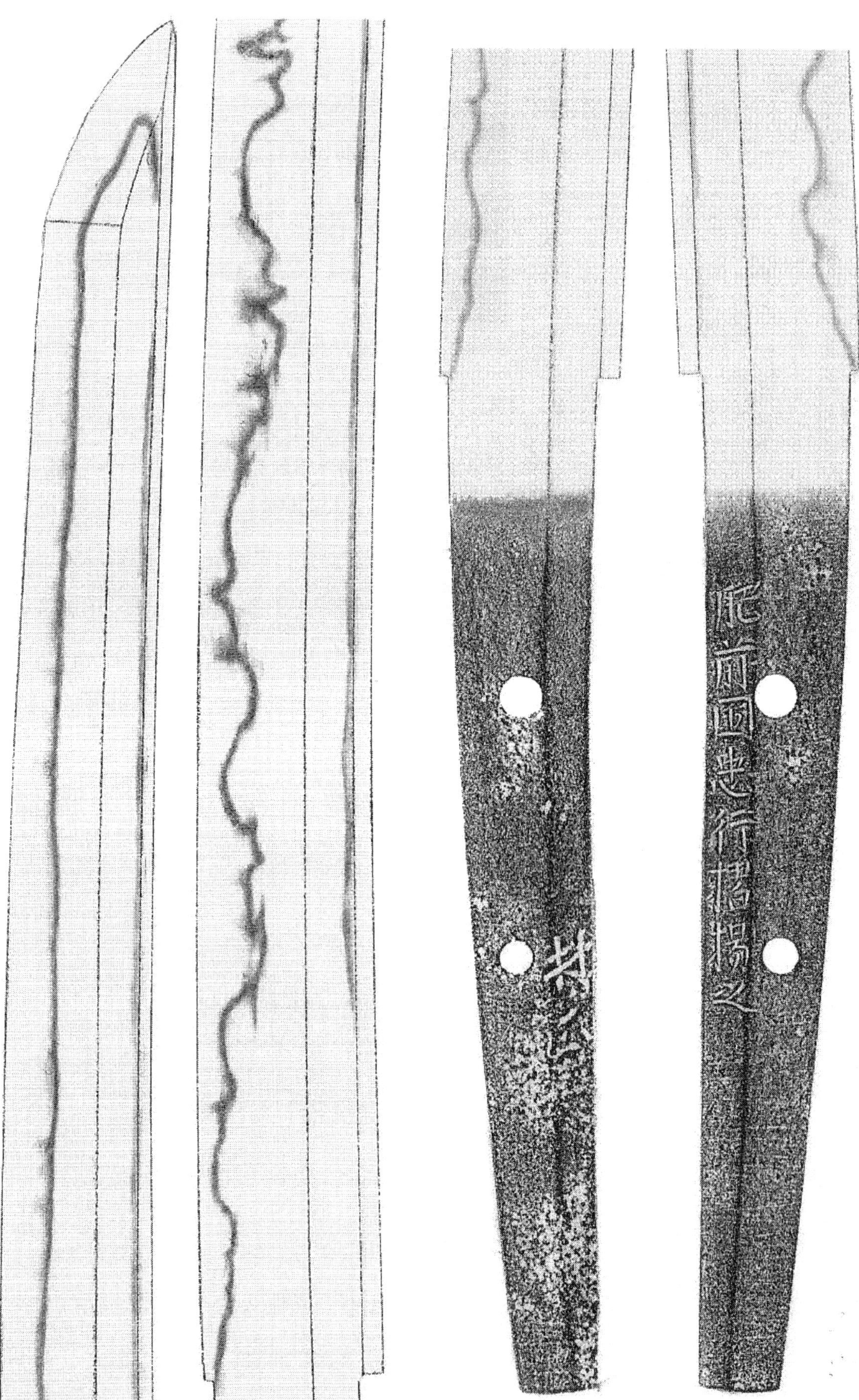

172.655k *katana*
mei: Hizen no Kuni Tadayuki suriage kore (肥前国忠行摺揚之, „shortened by Hizen Tadayuki“)
Muramasa (村正)
nagasa 69,0 cm *sori* 2,27 cm
moto-haba 2,65 cm *saki-haba* 1,9 cm
moto-kasane 0,6 cm *saki-kasane* 0,4
kissaki-nagasa 3,3 cm *nakago-nagasa* 16,82 cm
only very little *nakago-sori*

shinogi-zukuri, *iori-mune*, normal *mihaba*, noticeable taper, *sakizori*, *chū-kissaki*. The *jigane* is a somewhat standing-out *itame* mixed with *nagare* and *ji-nie*. The steel is blackish but shows also *shirake* in places. The *hamon* and the *bōshi* can be seen on the *oshigata*. In addition, there are *tobiyaki*, the valleys drop down towards the *ha*, the *hamon* is identical on both sides, and the *nioiguchi* is rather subdued and shows *nie* and *sunagashi*. The *nakago* is a bit *suriage* (whereas the original tang tapered in a peculiar manner towards an *iriyamagata-jiri*, had a *kaku-mune* and a rounded-off cutting-edge side). It has two *mekugi-ana* and bears on the *sashi-omote* at the *ubu-mekugi-ana* and towards the *nakago-mune* a *niji-mei*. The *ura* side bears under the *habaki* area and towards the *mune* the signature of the smith who carried out the shortening.

The blade has a normal *mihaba*, tapers noticeably, has a *sakizori* and ends in a *chū-kissaki*, that means we can date it into the Muromachi period. A transmission says that Muramasa had studied in Kyōto under Heianjō Nagayoshi (平安城長吉). We find some similarities in their workmaships but Nagayoshi forged primarily a fine and bright *jigane* in dense *itame* which is typical for Kyō-*mono*. In contrast, Muramasa´s *itame* stands out, the steel is blackish and no entire *shirake-utsuri* but only some isolated *shirake* appears.

The *hamon* of the *kantei* blade is in the upper half a *suguha* and in the lower half a *midareba*. Such a characteristic is typical for Sue-*kotō* and also seen the other way round, i.e. *midareba* on top and *suguha* towards the bottom. The *midareba* of this Muramasa bases on a *notare* and shows mixed-in *gunome* and *togari*, whereas the valleys in between drop conspiciously down to the *ha*. Also the *notare* tends to be angular in places and the *hamon* is identically interpreted on both sides. This too was mentioned in the description of the *kantei* and so it should not be too hard to arrive at Muramasa.

The tang of Muramasa is a tapering *tanagobara* with an *iriyamagata-jiri* (or can also show a *kurijiri* or *ha-agari kurijiri*). His *yasurime* are *katte-sagari* and the signature is chiselled on the *sashi-omote* towards the *nakago-mune*. All this – except the *tanagobara* which is lost due to the shortening – is found on this blade and accordingly almost all bidṣ were *atari* on Muramasa. But some *dōzen* bids were also found on Masashige (正重). Masashige worked in a very similar style to Muramasa but his *jihada* stands more out, the *ha-nie* are a hint stronger and there appear thick *nie*, *nie-kuzure* and more conspicious *kinsuji* and *sunagashi*. Also his back of the tang is round. So when there are no other hints seen which would speak for Masashige, one should go for Muramasa at such a *kantei*.

But besides of that there were also some who bade on Fujishima Tomoshige (藤島友重). The Tomoshige smiths too were active during the Muromachi period and in one of the more distant provinces. Their *jigane* is an *itame* mixed with *nagare* and the *jigane* is blackish. The *hamon* has also a subdued *nioiguchi* and so a bid on this school is quite understandable. But on the other hand, a clearly visible *shirake-utsuri* appears on Tomoshige works and the *hamon* consists of a vivid mix of *kosho-no-hiraita midare*, *togariba*, *yahazuba* and angular elements, of a connected *ko-gunome* in Shikkake-manner, or an angular *gunome* mixed with *togariba*. In addition, the *ha-nie* are more conspicious and turn also into *sunagashi* and *hakikake* within the *bōshi*.

Incidentally, such a largely protruding angular *hako-midare* like seen on this blade is quite rare.

Ô shû

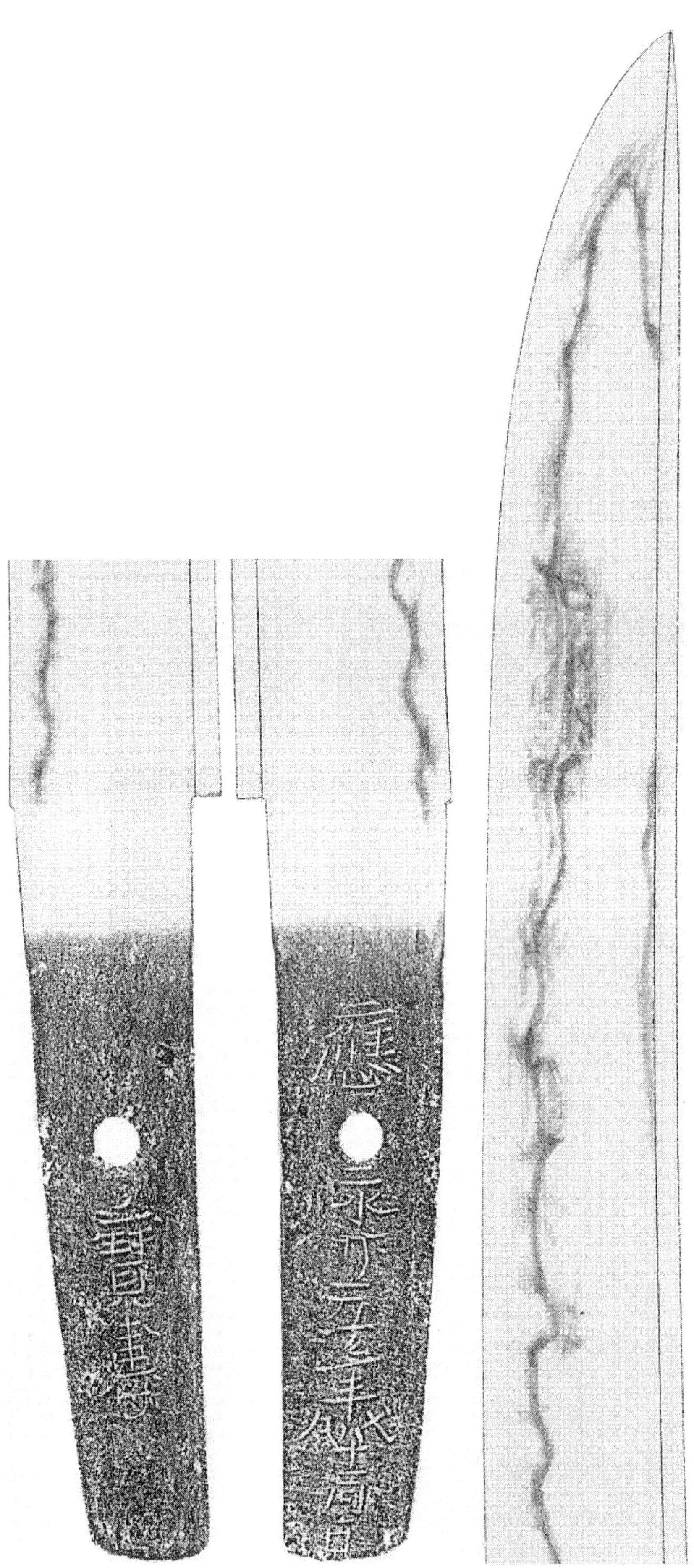

173.658 *wakizashi*

mei: Hōju (宝寿) [Note: The characters are signed in the old fashion: 寶壽]
Ōei nijūgonen tsuchinoe-inu jūichigatsu-hi (応永廿五年戊戌十一月日, „a day in the eleventh month Ōei 25 [= 1418], year of the dog")

nagasa 35,1 cm, *sori* 0,6 cm, *hira-zukuri*, *iori-mune*

ji: dense *itame* mixed with smaller and larger *mokume*, the *jihada* appears also as *ayasugi* in places and stands out finely, in addition plentiful of *ji-nie* and many *chikei*, the *jigane* is blackish

hamon: wide and *nie*-loaden *ko-notare* mixed with *gunome*, *nie-ashi*, some *nie-kuzure*, *sunagashi*, fine *hotsure*, *uchinoke*, *yubashiri* and long *muneyaki*

bōshi: *notare-komi* with a somewhat pointed *ko-maru-kaeri* with *hakikake*, the *kaeri* runs for a while parallel to the *mune*

The old sword documents list smiths for the northern Ōshū region basically from the Heian period onwards, whereas they are mostly attributed either to the Mōgusa (舞草) or the Gassan school (月山). However, the vast majority of the extant Ōshū-*mono* dates not earlier than the Nanbokuchō period and regarding signed specimen which would date back that early, only works of the Hōju lineage from the Kamakura period are extant. The Hōju group was active in Ōshū´s Hiraizumi (平泉) and successive smiths worked until the Muromachi period. The oldest extant Hōju blade is a *jūyō-bunkazai tachi* with a *niji-mei* which is dated into the middle Kamakura period. It is preserved in the Seikadō Bunko Art Museum (静嘉堂文庫). Regarding date signatures, the oldest one is from the Shōchū era (正中, 1324-1326). The *ō-dachi* with the *mei* „Hōju" which is preserved in the Mitake-jinja (御嶽神社) is dated around Kenmu (建武, 1334-1338). But from the Muromachi period onwards, extant date signatures increase and like the *kantei* blade we know quite some from the Ōei era (応永, 1394-1428), or to be more precise from the fifth, sixth, twelfth, 14th, 22nd and 25th year of that period (1398, 1399, 1405, 1415 and 1418).

This blade is rather long for its *mihaba* and has a shallow *sori* and so it might look like Nanbokuchō-period work at a glance. Well, *ubu* and unaltered *hira-zukuri sunnobi* blades with a thick *kasane* are anyway difficult to date but they were mostly produced by Bizen and Sōshū smiths from the Ōei era. Thus let´s narrow down the production time around Ōei and turn towards the *jigane*. It appears as *itame* mixed with larger and smaller *mokume* and tends to *ayasugi* in places. This is typical for Gassan and Hōju.

The Hōju-*hamon* is either a *suguha* or a *midareba*. In the case of a *midareba* we see a densely arranged mix of *ko-midare*, *ko-chōji* and *ko-gunome*. The rather subdued *nioiguchi* shows *hotsure* and *sunagashi* interwoven with the *hada* and the entire hardening looks rather rustic. But this blade shows a wide, more flamboyant than usual *yakiba* with a wide *nioiguchi* and plentiful of *ko-nie*. But the horizontal *hataraki* like *sunagashi* and *hotsure* are as mentioned interwoven with the *hada* and so the *hamon* is nevertheless typical for Hōju.

There are generally not often Hōju blades provided for a *kantei* and so many participants were somehwat insecure. Some recognized the *Hokkoku* characteristics like a blackish standing-out *ji* and a *bōshi* with *hakikake* and went so for Uda (宇多). Others focused on the partially connected *mokume-hada* and went for Shitahara (下原). And others bade on the basis of the *hamon* and the *bōshi* on Seki-*mono* from the transitional time between *kotō* and *shintō*. Others in turn went round by round along the Tōsandō (the main road which connected the Kinai era with the northern provinces) and ended eventually up in Ōshū. By the way, this blade is an heirloom of Echigo´s Murakami branch (村上) of the Naito family (内藤).

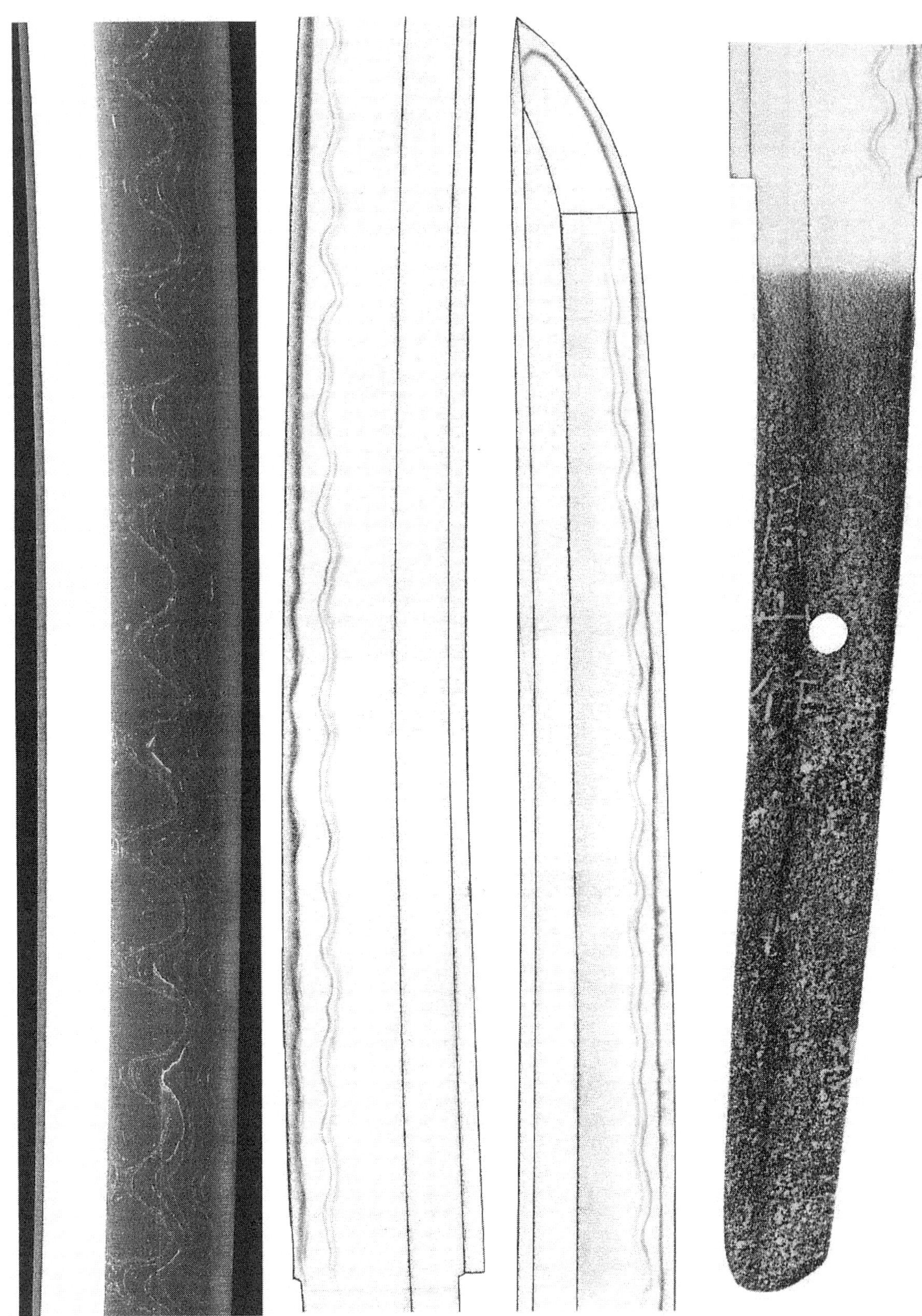

174.605k *tachi*
mei: Gassan saku (月山作)
nagasa 77,27 cm *sori* 2,73 cm
moto-haba 2,32 cm *saki-haba* 2,0 cm
moto-kasane 0,8 cm *saki-kasane* 0,4 cm
kissaki-nagasa 3,4 cm *nakago-nagasa* 19,7 cm
nakago-sori 0,28 cm

shinogi-zukuri, *iori-mune*, wide *mihaba*, high *shinogi*, thick *kasane*, deep *sori*, elongated *chū-kissaki*. The *jigane* shows the typical forging structure of that school and stands out all over the blade. In addition *ji-nie* and *chikei* appear. The steel is blackish and there is a *jifu-utsuri* running parallel to the forging structure. The *hamon* and the *bōshi* can be seen on the *oshigata*. The *nioiguchi* is subdued and blurry and shows *ko-nie* and *nie* which intertwine with the *hada* and appear as *sunagashi*. The *nakago* is *ubu*, has a *ha-agari kurijiri*, *katte-sagari yasruime* and one *mekugi-ana*. There is a *sanji-mei* on the *haki-omote* besides of the *mekugi-ana* and towards the *nakago-mune*.

Well, from the shape and the *deki* this *kantei* blade can be straightforward identified as Gassan work from the early Muromachi period and not much later. There are some few older Gassan blades which can be dated back to the late Nanbokuchō period. For example a *jūyō-bijutsuhin tachi* with the *niji-mei* „Gassan" and the date signature „Jōji 2" (貞治, 1363) which is preserved in Dewa´s Sanzan-jinja (三山神社). There exists another work from the Gassan school which is signed „Gunshō" (軍勝) and bears a date signature of the Jōji era (1362-1368). But most of the extant *kotō* Gassan blades are from the middle Muromachi period and such old ones as the aforementioned are very rare.

Very conspicious on the *kantei* blade – which is also seen on the foto and the *oshigata* – is the peculiar forging structure which appears as continuous wavy pattern from the base to the tip. Towards the valleys of these waves, *uzumaki*-like *mokume* whirlpools appear. Such a *hada* is called *„ayasugi-hada*" and this is the most typical characteristic of the Gassan school.

At *kotō* Gassan works, the *ayasugi-hada* stands mostly out all over the blade. The steel is blackish as we are in the northern provinces and there appears also a clearly visible *shirake-utsuri*. The *shirake-utsuri* of most of the other schools appears faintly but at the Gassan school, it is as clearly visible. However, there are blades where the *shirake-utsuri* stands more out towards the *mune* and gets weaker towards the *ha*. And so the *jigane* of such *kotō*-period Gassan works gets a colourful appearance.

The *hamon* of the Gassan school bases mostly on a rather narrow *suguha* which is similar to the Naminohira or Kongōbei school. But the *habuchi* tends with the intertwining of the *ayasugi-hada* to *ko-notare*. The *ha-hada* stands mostly out and *nie* and *sunagashi* appear. The *nioiguchi* is all over the blade subdued and dull and is besides of the rustic *ji* another typical characteristic of the Gassan school. The *bōshi* is mostly *sugu* with a *ko-maru-kaeri*.

As mentioned, this *kantei* blade can be dated at the latest into the early Muromachi period. The oldest extant Gassan-*tachi* – and the even older Hōju works (for example the *jūyō-tōken tachi* which is dated with the Eiwa era [永和, 1375-1379] and the *jūyō-bunkazai tachi* from the Seikadō Bunkō Art Museum from the middle Kamakura period) – have often a longer *nagasa*, a wider *mihaba*, a thicker *kasane* and a deeper *sori* (which increases again towards the tip) than contemporary works from the major schools. In short, old Ōshū-*mono* can show a magnificent *sugata*.

The tip of the tang of Gassan blades is mostly a *kurijiri* and the *yasurime* are *katte-sagari*. The signature is mostly executed as *niji-mei* „Gassan" or like at the *kantei* blade as *sanji-mei* with the supplement „saku". But we also know longer *naga-mei* like „Ushū-jūnin Gassan Chikanori" (羽州住人月山近則) and some accompanying date signatures.

Allmost all bids this time were *atari* on Gassan but some went for an individual smith like Chikanori, Hiroyasu (寛安) oder Masanobu (正信). Well, *kotō*-period Gassan works show all quite the same *deki* but Chikanori forged also a dense and fine *itame* in combination with a bright *jigane* and a *midare-utsuri*. His *hamon* is in *nie-deki* and shows *gunome* arranged in pairs so the entire interpretation reminds at a glance of Sue-Bizen. So he is rather an unique smith of his school and it is therefore assumed that he maintained some contact with Bizen smiths.

But there were also some few bids on Hōju which were counted as *dōzen*. It has to be mentioned that old Ōshū-*mono* show many similarities but the *jigane* of Hōju works is mostly not such a prominent *ayasugi-hada* like seen on the *kantei* blade. It appears rather as *itame* with large undulating *masame* areas and stands even more out. But the clearly visible *shirake-utsuri* and the differently coloured *jifu* areas can be similar to Gassan-*mono*. The Hōju *hamon* bases on *suguha* with shallow *notare* and shows mixed-in *ko-midare* and *ko-chōji*. The *habuchi* is wide and appears often as continuous *hotsure* all over the blade. The *nioiguchi* is subdued and there are plentiful of *sunagashi*. So all in all Hōju works appear even more rustic than contemporary Gassan works.

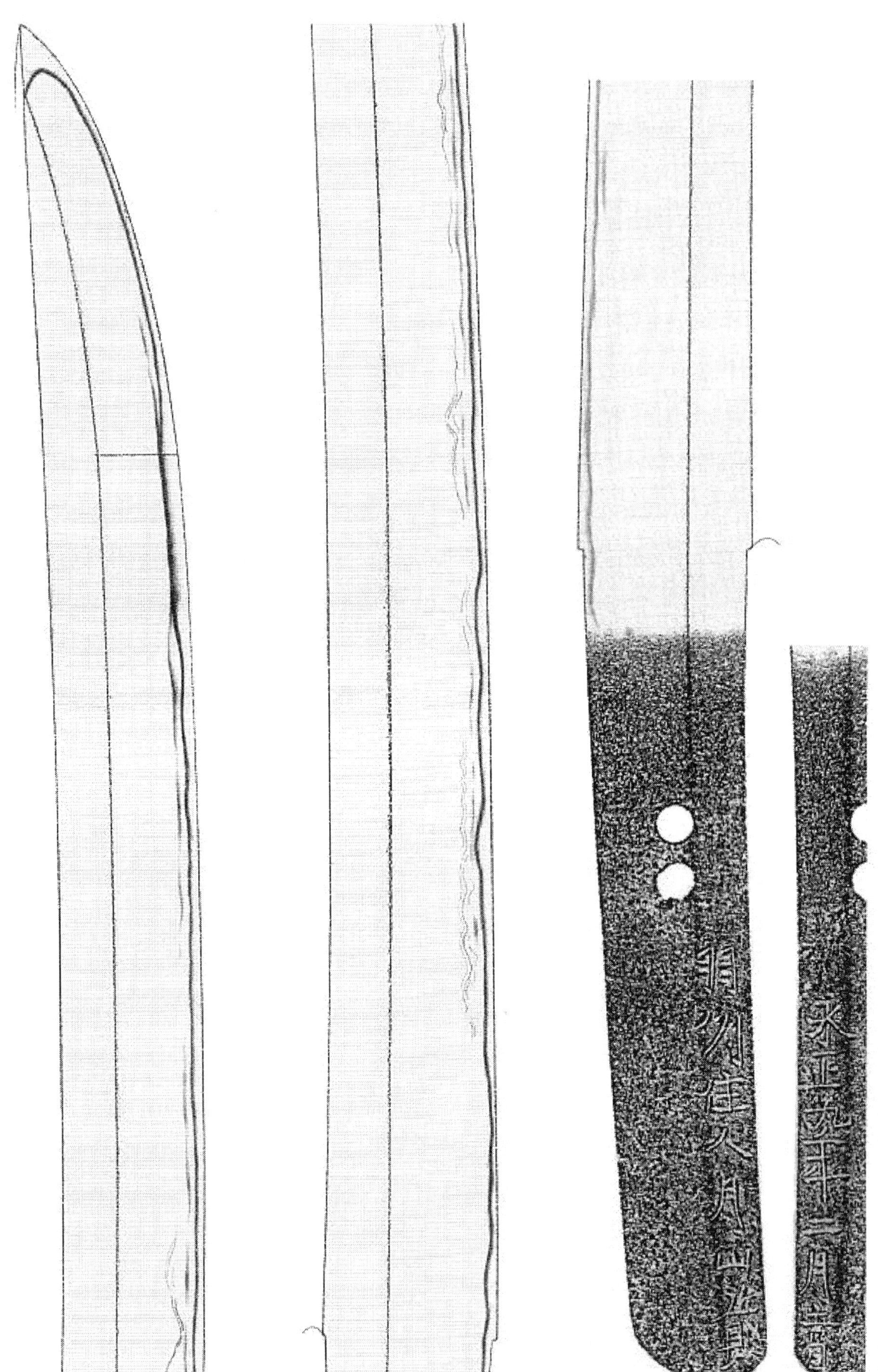

175.665k *wakizashi*

mei: Ushū-jūnin Gassan Chikanori (羽州住人月山近則)

Eishō kyūnen nigatsu kichijitsu (永正九年二月吉日, „a lucky day in the second month Eishō nine [1512]“)

nagasa 58,33 cm *sori* 1,52 cm *moto-haba* 2,9 cm *sakihaba* 2,3 cm
moto-kasane 0,45 cm *saki-kasane* 0,35 cm *kissaki-nagasa* 7,4 cm *nakago-nagasa* 14,24 cm
nakago-sori 0,2 cm

shinogi-zukuri, *maru-mune*, normal *mihaba*, no noticeable taper, high *shinogi*, relativ thin *kasane*, *sakizori*, *ō-kissaki*. The *jigane* is an *itame* mixed with plentiful of *nagare* whereas the *nagare* appears in a quite wavy manner in places. This is a characteristical feature of this school. The *hada* stands rather out, there is *ji-nie*, *chikei*, a *shirake-utsuri* and the steel is blackish. The conspiciously narrow *hamon* and the *bōshi* can be seen on the *oshigata*. In addition *nijūba*, *yubashiri* and *ko-ashi* appear. The *nioiguchi* is bright, compact and shows *ko-nie*. The *nakago* is *ubu*, has a *kurijiri* which tends to *ha-agari*, shows *katte-sagari yasurime* and two *mekugi-ana*. There is a *naga-mei* on the *sashi-omote* side below of the *mekugi-ana* and towards the back of the tang. The date signature of the *ura* side starts somewhat lower. (Note: The smiths of this school applied mostly a subdued *nioiguchi*.)

The blade measures 58,33 cm and comes so under the category of a *wakizashi*. Such short blades shortly under 2 *shaku* (~ 60,6 cm) with a normal *mihaba*, only a little tapering and *sakizori* were popular around the Eishō era (永正, 1504-1521) and intended for a single-handed use (*katate-uchi*). When we combine this with the *maru-mune* than we have as a starting point a provincial, i.e. not a mainline work of the Muromachi period.

Gassan Chikanori was one of the most outstanding Gassan smiths of his time. He often forged blades with a dense *ko-itame* and a *gunome* in *ko-nie-deki* whose elements are grouped in pairs. The *jiba* is bright and clear and reminds rather of contemporary Sue-Bizen works than of northern *Hokkoku-mono*. But this blade is made in the traditional Gassan style which means – for the Muromachi period – a typical *ayasugi-hada*. Well, the Muromachi-period Gassan *ayasugi* can appear as large waves or like here more unobtrusive and mixed into *itame*. But the *jihada* is in any case standing out and the steel is blackish and shows a *shirake-utsuri*. The *hamon* of the Gassan school bases mostly (like here) on *suguha* whereas the *yakiba* is rather narrow compared to the *mihaba* of the blade. A *suguha* is anyway typical for a provincial work of that time. The Gassan-*suguha* is hardened in *ko-nie-deki* and the *nie* intertwine along the *habuchi* with the *ayasugi-hada* which makes the *hamon* appear as *ko-notare*. *Hamon* and *nioiguchi* are subdued but not here. The *kantei* blade of Chikanori has a bright and compact *nioiguchi* with *nijūba* and *yubashiri* and is much more refined than other Gassan works of that time. The *bōshi* of the Gassan school is mostly a *suguha* with a *ko-maru-kaeri*. The tang has a *kurijiri* and *katte-sagari yasurime* and many blades are just signed with „Gassan“ (月山) or „Gassan saku“ (月山作).

But there are some individually signed Gassan *naga-mei* known like here „Ushū-jūnin Gassan Chikanori“ or for example „Gassan Masanobu saku“ (月山正信作) or „Gassan Toshiyasu saku“ (月山利安作). Often such *naga-mei* comes along with a date signature. Most of the participants bade *atari* on Gassan Chikanobu but some went also for other Muromachi-period Gassan smiths like Munetsugu (宗次) or just for Gassan. As the workmanship is rather close, all bids which mentioned somehow Gassan in combination with the Muromachi period were counted as *atari*. But relative many thought that it is a work of the Muromachi-period Naminohira school. Usually when a Gassan work is provided for *kantei* and a bid is submitted on Naminohira, it is counted as *dōzen*. However, when you see a classical *ayasugi* you should always better go for Gassan but the *kantei* blade shows also *itame* and besides of *higaki-yasurime*, some Muromachi-period Naminohira smiths applied also *katte-sagari yasurime*. And so in this special case, bids on Muromachi-Naminohira were counted as *atari* too. Incidentally, it is thought that the spreading of the forging in *ayasugi-hada* of the Gassan school is connected to the *shugendō* mountain ascetism. The Gassan smiths workd close to the foot of the holy mountain Gassan of the same name. They climbed Mt. Gassan for religous purifying rituals and the like and were well known for travelling throughout the entire country. So it is likely that they brought their forging techniques even down to Satsuma were it was adopted by the local Naminohira smiths. But historical references are rare and further studies are necessary to clarify this matter.

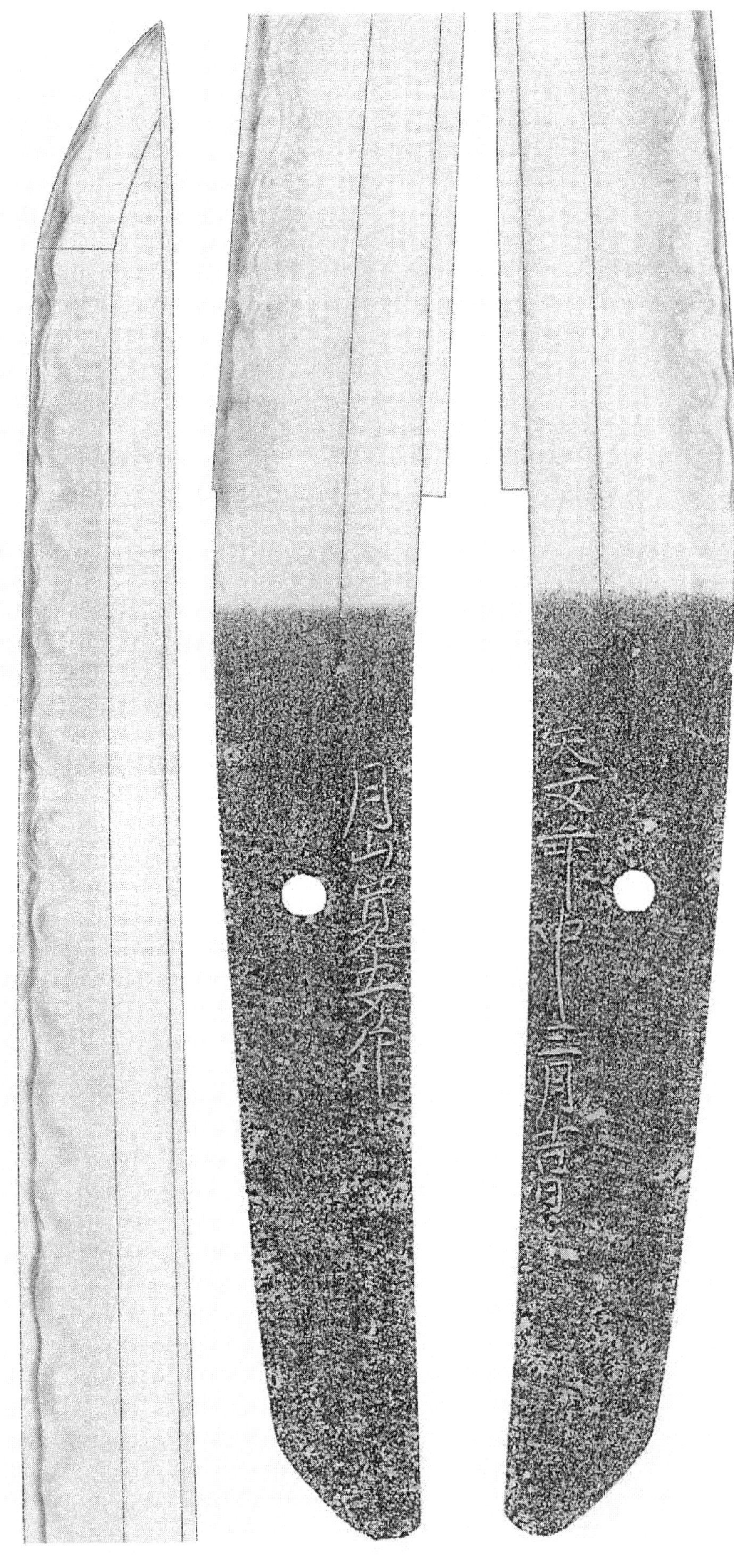

176.592 *katana*

mei: Gassan Hiroyasu saku (月山寛安作)
Tenbun nenchū sangatsu kichijitsu (天文年中三月吉日, „on a lucky day in the third month during the Tenbun era [1532-1555]")

nagasa 69,5 cm, *sori* 1,8 cm, *shinogi-zukuri*, *iori-mune*

ji: rather standing out *ayasugi-hada* with *ji-nie* and blackish *chikei*-like elements, a *shirake-utsuri* appears parallel to the forging structure, the steel itself is blackish too

hamon: *suguha-chō* mixed with *ko-notare* and *ko-chōji* in *ko-nie-deki*, in addition *ashi*, fine *sunagashi*, some *hotsure* and *uchinoke*, the *nioiguchi* is rather subdued

bōshi: slightly *midare-komi* which ends almost in *yakitsume*

If you take a look at the blade first of all the forging structure catches the eye. It appears as continuous waves from the base to the tip whereas the valleys show some *mokume* areas. The *jihada* stands out and the steel is blackish. So all in all we have the typical characteristics of the Gassan school and an *ayasugi-hada* is therefore also called „Gassan-*hada*". The *hamon* bases on *suguha* but the waves of the *jihada* force it into a *ko-notare*-like appearance. Also we see *hotsure* and *uchinoke*. The *nioiguchi* is subdued and the entire *jiba* lacks clarity and brightness. Thus this is a typically rustic work of that school and all bade *atari* on Gassan.

It is said that Hiroyasu went westwards and settled eventually either in Hyūga or in Satsuma province. There are *meikan* entries which list signatures like „Nisshū-jū Hiroyasu saku" (日州住寛安作) and „Naminohira Hiroyasu" (波平寛安) which support this handed down transmission, whereas his artistic period is generally quoted with Eiroku (永禄, 1558-1570). This blade is dated with Tenbun, that means it dates back to the time when he was still active in Dewa province and this makes this *katana* a very precious reference piece for that smith.

Chixuzen

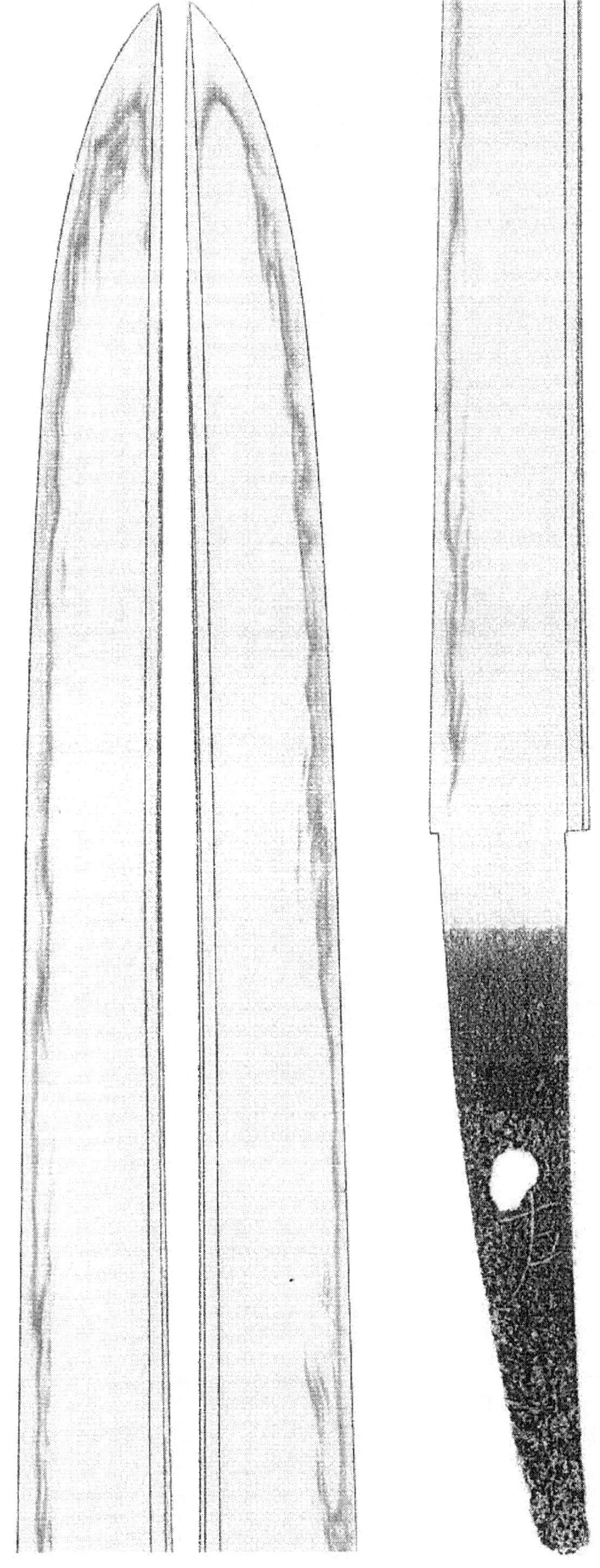

177.666 *tantō*
mei: Sa (左)
nagasa 23,0 cm, only a little *sori*, *hira-zukuri*, *mitsu-mune*

ji: dense *ko-itame* mixed with *mokume*, in addition plentiful of *ji-nie*, much *chikei* and a *nie-utsuri*
hamon: *suguha-chō* with a tendency to shallow *ko-notare*, also some *ko-gunome* appear in places, in addition *ko-ashi*, *hotsure*, *yubashiri*, *kinsuji*, *sunagashi* and plentiful of *ko-nie*
bōshi: *suguha-chō* with a long *kaeri*, the *omote* side shows along the pointed *kaeri* also *yubashiri*, *nie-kuzure*, many *hakikake* and *kinsuji*, the *ura* side appears as *ko-maru-kaeri* with fine *hakikake*

Sa, also called „Samonji" (左文字) or „Ō-Sa" (大左), was according to transmission the grandson of Sairen (西蓮) and the son of Jitsu´a (実阿). He broke with the so-far handed-down classical Kyūshū style and adopted new techniques and interpretations. This change took place somewhere between the second year of Ryakuō (暦応, 1339) and the first year of Kan´ō (観応, 1350). At the January meeting 2009 namely a Samonji blade was presented which is dated Ryakuō two and which shows still the Kyūshū-typical *suguha*. This *tantō* can be dated to the transitional period before he established his own style. Together with earlier works it is quite rustic. The *kantei* blade in turn shows a considerably finer and beautifully forged *jigane*. Also the *hamon*, which shows a slight approach of *notare* and *ko-gunome*, is much brighter and clearer as seen on his earlier interpretations. We also recognize a trend towards more *hataraki* like *yubashiri* and *sunagashi*. In short, this piece can be dated right before he perfected his later style. The *bōshi* is not yet the later pointed *jizō*-like *bōshi* with the long *kaeri*.

The small dimensions of this *tantō* leaded some astray at the *kantei*. But especially Samonji, Kaneuji (兼氏) and Chōgi (長義) made still during the Nanbokuchō period many smaller *tantō* when most of the other smiths had changed to wide *sunnobi-tantō*. In the case of Samonji, these *tantō* have a thin *kasane* and scarce *fukura* and this applies to the *kantei* blade too. So if you know these pecularities, it was easy to nail the bid down to Samonji. But at a glance, the *tantō* looks like a Kamakura-period work of Shintōgo Kunimitsu (新藤五国光) or the Awataguchi school.

Samonji was ever since listed as student of Masamunes (正宗) but in recent years and based on similarities in workmanship, more and more the theory got accepted that he came somewhere from the vicinity of Rai Kunimitsu (来国光). The NBTHK owns namely a *tantō* of Rai Kunimitsu which is apart from the *sugata* and in terms of *jiba* and *hataraki* very similar to this one. I think that this blade should be provided for a *kantei* in the next future and think, that Samonji oriented towars Rai Kunimitsu at a certain point of his career but moved on and adopted the elements of the great Sōshū masters. That means he applied more *nie* in general and *nie*-based *hataraki* as *kinsuji* and *sunagashi*.

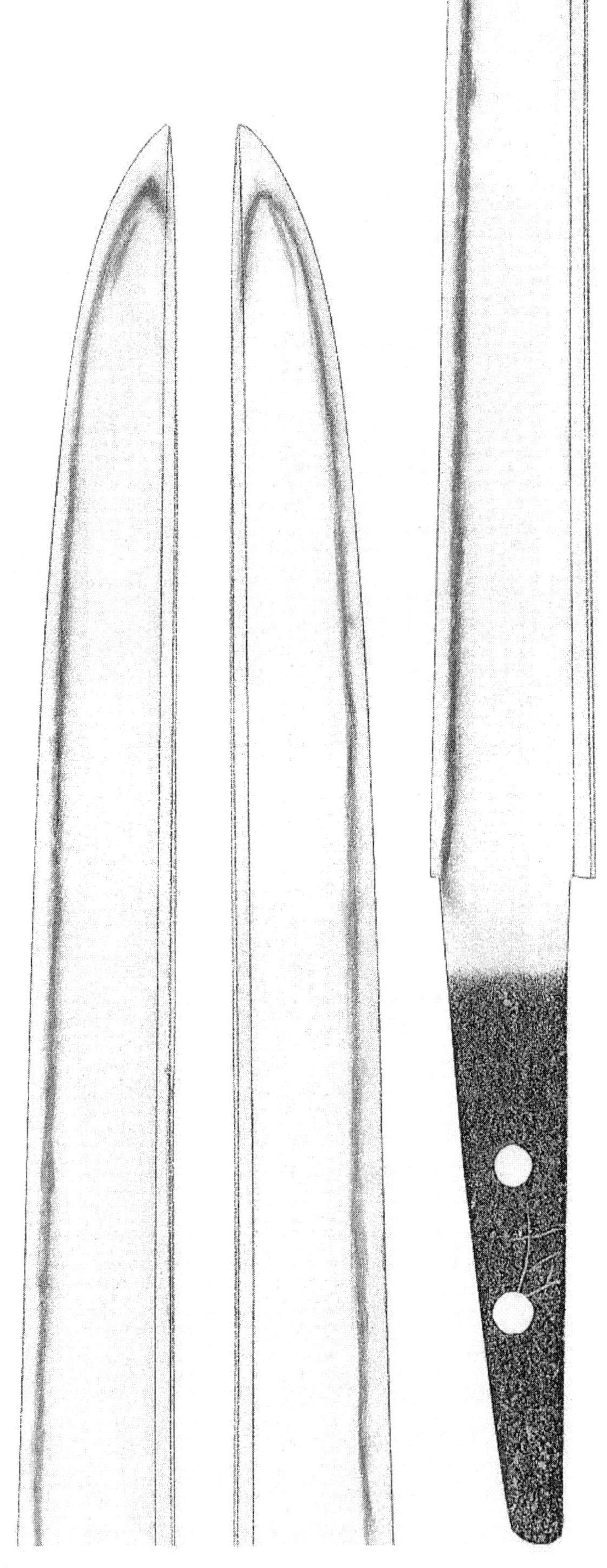

178.640 *tantō*
mei: Sa (左)
nagasa 22,4 cm, only a little *sori*, *hira-zukuri*, *mitsu-mune*

ji: *itame* mixed with *mokume*, in addition *ji-nie* and a *shirake-utsuri*
hamon: *chū-suguha* with some *ko-ashi*, the hardening is in *nioi-deki* with *ko-nie*
bōshi: on both sides *sugu* with *nijūba* and a pointed and long *ko-maru-kaeri*, the *ura* shows also some *kuichigaiba*

This is a *tantō* of Samonji (左文字). It is small dimensioned but has a thin *kasane* and a little *sori* whereupon we can date it nevertheless into the Nanbokuchō period. Known for such smaller *tantō* shapes during that time were namely Samonji, Shizu Kaneuji (志津兼氏) and Chōgi (長義).

Generally Samonji's *jigane* looks „wet", his *hamon* bases on a *midare* and the rather wide *bōshi* has a pointed and long *kaeri*. The *kantei* blade is somewhat calm and differs from his usual workmanship. There exists a dated Samonji *tantō* from the second year of Ryakuō (暦応, 1339) which is rather calm too and one from the first year of Kan'ō (観応, 1350) from his student Yukihiro (行弘) which shows the fully developed and vivid Samonji interpretation. Therefore it is assumed that his style change took place somewhere within these ten years.

By the way, the Kan'ō era (1350-1352) was representative for the unrests of the Nanbokuchō period, a time, when Ashikaga Takauji (足利尊氏, 1305-1358), his brother Ashikaga Tadayoshi (足利直義, 1306-1358) and Kō Moronao (高師直, ?-1351) were antagonists. So this time of change would theoretically support also the change of the forging style of Samonji.

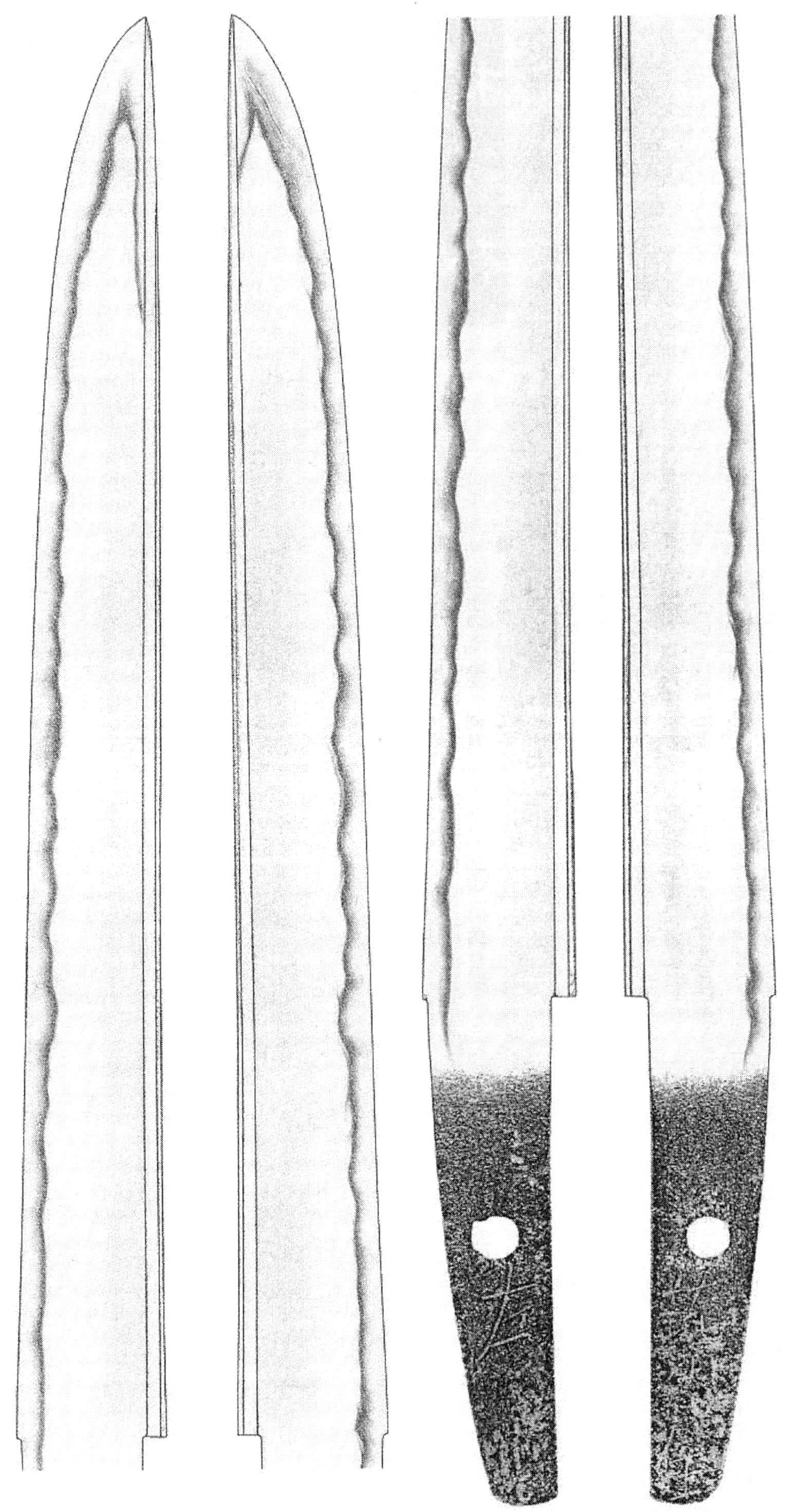

179.592k *tantō*
mei: Chikushū-jū – Sa (筑州住・左)

nagasa 21,25 cm	only a little *sori*
motohaba 2,0 cm	*moto-kasane* 0,5 cm
nakago-nagasa 7,58 cm	very little *nakago-sori*

hira-zukuri, *mitsu-mune*, normal *mihaba*, thin *kasane*, a little *sori*, scarce *fukura*, altogether rather a small *tantō-sugata*. The *jigane* is altogether quite densely forged and appears as *itame* mixed with *mokume*. Plentiful of *ji-nie*, fine *chikei* and a *nie-utsuri* appear. The steel is clear. The *hamon* and the *bōshi* can be seen on the *oshigata*. In addition *ko-ashi*, plentiful of *ko-nie*, *kinsuji* and *sunagashi*. The *nioiguchi* is wide, bright and clear and gets more compact in the *kaeri*. The *nakago* is *ubu*, has a *ha-agari kurijiri*, *ō-sujikai yasurime* and one *mekugi-ana*. The signature is divided-up on the two sides of the tang. These parts are executed with a fine chisel and positioned under the *mekugi-ana*, whereas the *omote* part is arranged centrally and the *ura* part more towards the *nakago-mune*.

During the heyday of the Nanbokuchō period there were three master smiths who continued to produce small dimensioned *tantō*, namely Shizu Saburō Kaneuji (志津三郎兼氏), Chōgi (長義) and Sa. When we compare Chōgi and Sa we see that the former was active from about Jōwa (貞和, 1345-1350) to Kōryaku (康暦, 1379-1381), that means around the distinctive Enbun (延文, 1356-1361) and Jōji eras (貞治, 1362-1368). This was namely the time when the characteristically wide *sunnobi-tantō* or *hira-zukuri ko-wakizashi* respectively were made in masses. From Sa we know date signatures of the fifth year of Kenmu (建武, 1334) – on a *saiha* – and two from the second year of Ryakuō (暦応, 1339). That means he was more active in the early Nanbokuchō period and was not so affected by the increase in size like Chōgi. In short, his *tantō* are rather small dimensioned, have a slender *mihaba*, a thin *kasane*, a little *sori* and scarce *fukura*, that means they show the peculiar „sharp" *tantō* shape and this is one of the most important characteristics of Sa.

The shortest extant Sa *tantō* measures 21,0 cm. It is designated as *jūyō-bijutsuhin* and was once a heirloom of the Kuroda family (黒田). The biggest one was so far the *jūyō-bunkazai* with a *nagasa* of 25,4 cm. But there is a slightly shortened *tantō* with a *nagasa* of 24,6 cm with *tokubetsu-jūyō* papers which would measure 25,7 cm when in original length. But then another *tantō* of Sa with an *ubu-nakago* was discovered which has a *nagasa* of 27,4 cm. This is at the moment the biggest *tantō* of this smith.

Tantō from the early artistic period of Sa, i.e. the ones made around Kōryaku, show an *itame* with *nagare* and *masame*, a blackish *jigane* with *shirake-utsuri* and a *hoso-suguha* with a subdued *nioiguchi*. This corresponds more or less with the classical Ko-Kyūshū style. But Sa broke off from that style and started to forge finer blades with a bright and clear *jigane*. The latter appears accordingly as fine and densely forged *ko-itame* with plentiful of *ji-nie* and fine *chikei*. The steel is no longer that rustic as Ko-Kyūshū-*mono*. Often he also applied a *nie-utsuri*. These blades show sometimes a *suguha* or a *suguha* which tends to *notare*, but mostly a *notare-chō* mixed with *ko-gunome*, plentiful of *ko-nie*, fine *kinsuji* and *sunagashi* and a wide but bright and clear *nioiguchi*. The *bōshi* is a *midare-komi* with a pointed, *jizō*-like and long *kaeri*. A peculiarity of Sa´s *bōshi* is that the *habuchi* of the *kaeri* is more compact than the *habuchi* of the actual *hamon*. And another typical characteristic of that smith is a pronounced *yakikomi* over the *ha-machi*.

The old transmissions say that Sa was a student of Masamune (正宗). But in recent years more and more the theory gained ground that his *tantō* have much more in common with Yamashiro-*mono* like for example of Rai Kunimitsu (来国光) or Rai Kunitsugu (来国次). The similarity is first and foremost seen in the *jigane*, the finely forged *jihada*, the way the *chikei* appear and the *nie-utsuri*. Contrary to Masamune and his fine *hotsure*, *yubashiri*, the highly *nie*-loaden *ha* and the plentiful of *kinsuji*, *sunagashi* and *inazuma* (thus the typical *midare* of the great Sōshū masters), there are no such conspicious *hotsure* and *yubashiri* at Sa. Also the line of the *nioiguchi* is more even and the *kinsuji* and *sunagashi* are mostly finer and not that prominent. And there is also the blueish colour of the steel, the whitish *hamon* and the clear *jiba* with a *mizukage* which is both seen on Sa and on Rai *tantō*. However, similarities in style were already recognized in earlier times because the „*Kaifun-ki*" (触紛記) for example writes on Sa: „deeply blueish colour like at Kyō-*mono*, the *yakiba* is similar to Sadamune (貞宗) but by trend somewhat smaller."

Only very few *tantō* of Sa have *horimono*. Sometimes a *koshibi* or *gomabashi* are engraved but elaborate *horimono* are unknown. The *nakago-jiri* on Sa-*tantō* is a *kurijiri* or a *ha-agari kurijiri*. The *yasurime* are *ō-sujikai*. The signature is often interpreted in the way that the relative large character for „Sa" (左) is chiselled on the *sashi-omote* side centrally and below of the *mekugi-ana*, and the part „Chikushū-jū" (筑州住) on the *ura-side* and more towards the back of the tang. But some blades are just signed with „Sa" and others with the whole *mei* „Chikushū-jū Sa" on one side.

As this *tantō* is a textbook example for this smith, almost all bids were *atari* on Sa.

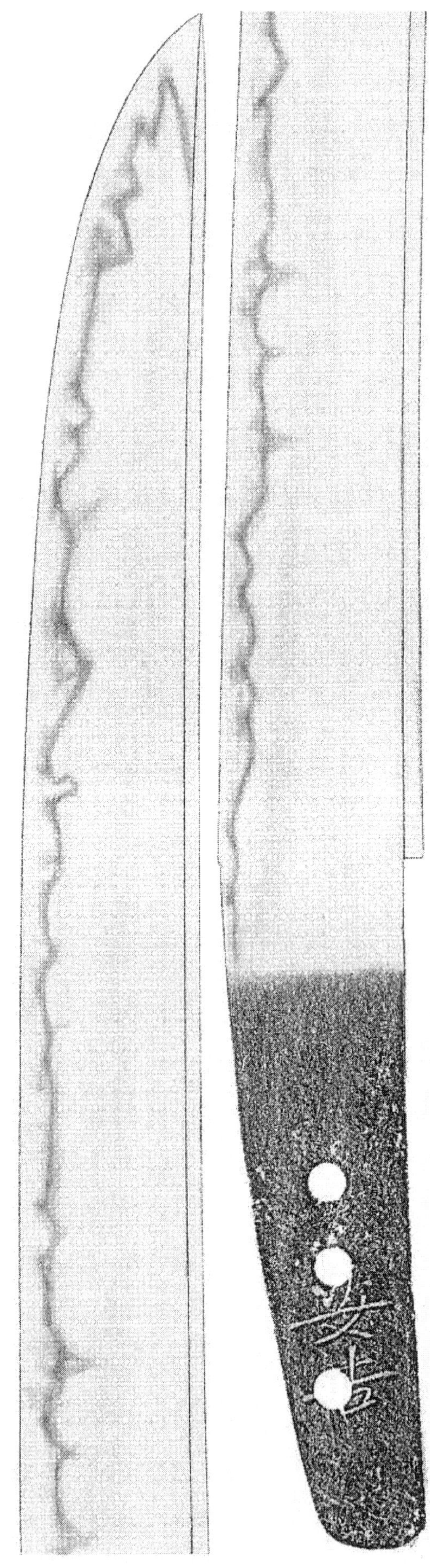

180.658 *tantō*
mei: Yasuyoshi (安吉)
nagasa 30,1 cm, *sori* 0,3 cm, *hira-zukuri*, *iori-mune*

ji: standing-out *itame* mixed with *mokume*, fine *ji-nie*, many *chikei*, in addition a *bō-utsuri* which starts from the *machi* and runs parallel to the *ha*, at the *fukura* this *utsuri* gets wider and turns into a *shirake-utsuri*, the *jigane* is somewhat blackish
hamon: *ko-notare-chō* mixed with *ko-gunome*, *gunome* which tend to *togari*, *ko-ashi* and long *sunagashi*, the hardening is in *nioi-deki* with *ko-nie*
bōshi: pointed *midare-komi* with a long *kaeri*

Yasuyoshi was according to transmission the son of Chikuzen´s Ō-Sa (大左). There exist date signatures from the twelfth (1357) and 17th year of Shōhei (正平, 1362) on a *jūyō-bunkazai* and a *jūyō-bijutsuhin tantō* respectively. The latter bears the signature „Chōshū-jū Yasuyoshi" (長州住安吉), what shows that Yasuyoshi had moved at the latest around that time from Chikuzen to Nagato (= Chōshū). This *tantō* here dates around the same time, that means according to the counting of the Northern Dynasty around Enbun (延文, 1356-1361) and Jōji (貞治, 1362-1368). It shows well the then typical characteristics which are large dimensioned *sunnobi-tantō* in *hira-zukuri* with a wide *mihaba* and a shallow *sori*.

Yasuyoshi belonged to the Sa school but forged a standing-out *itame* mixed with *nagare* and a *shirake-utsuri* in the sense of Kyūshū-*mono*. He also applied a *bō-utsuri* right above the *yakiba* and a *gunome*-based *hamon* in *nioi-deki* which reminds of the Bizen tradition. This *tantō* has rather few *nagare* but the *jigane* is strong and blackish and speaks for Kyūshū. Also the *bōshi* and the interpretation of the *hamon* and *nioiguchi* are very typical for Yasuyoshi so that we have here rather a textbook example of that smith. The *bōshi* namely appears as *midare-komi* with a *jizō*-like *kaeri* which leans towards the *ha*, an interpretation, which is very typical for Ō-Sa.

All the characteristic features were well recognized and almost half of the participants went right at the first round *atari* for Yasuyoshi. But many bade also on contemporary Bizen smiths like Kanemitsu (兼光) or Tomomitsu (倫光). This is understandable because the *tantō* does not show the usual *nagare* and such a *nioi-deki hamon* with a pointed *bōshi* and a *bō-utsuri* is sometimes also seen at Kanemitsu and Tomomitsu. But the arrangement of the *hamon* is different from Bizen. At the latter, it would base either on *notare* or *gunome* and in the case of the former, some calm *koshi-no-hiraita* elements would be mixed in. And in the case of a *gunome-chō* we would find some angular and *kataochi-gunome*.

Incidentally, the blade shows some *togari* elements which look like as if they would „fume" out into the *ji*. This characteristic is often seen at Yasuyoshi and so you should take a good note of these elements. By the way, the *tantō* was a heirloom of the Owari-Tokugawa family.

Bungo

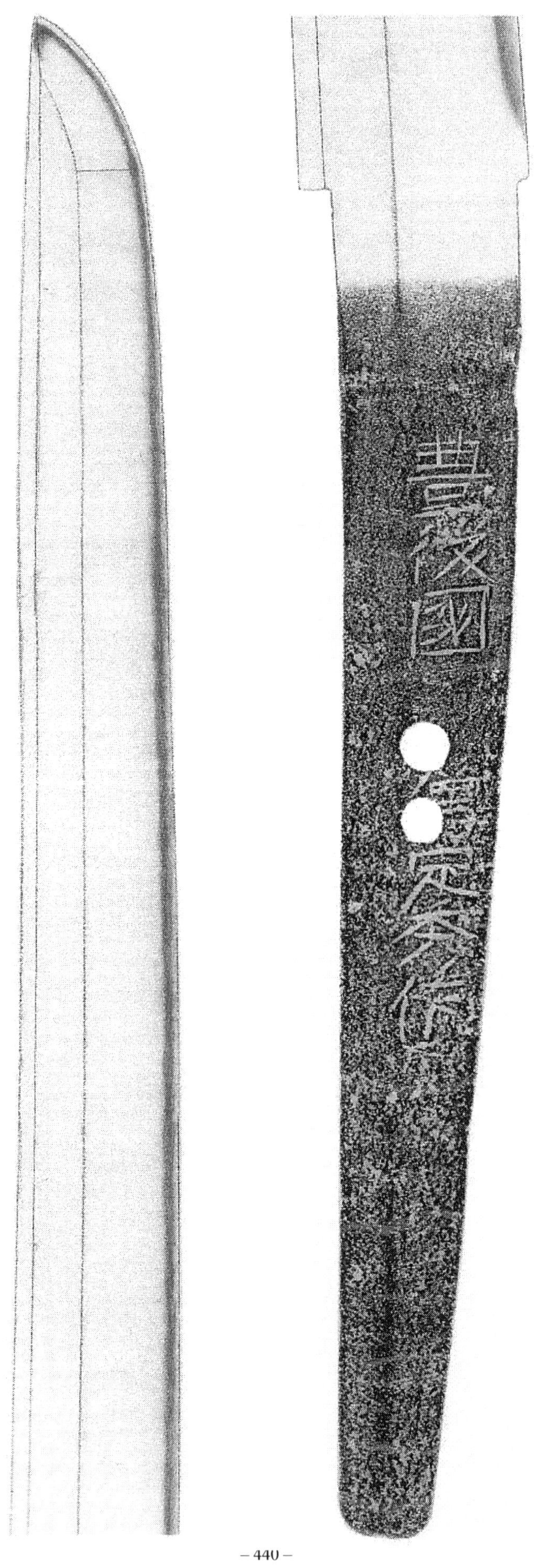
豊後國

181.649 *tachi*
mei: Bungo no Kuni Sō Sadahide saku (豊後国宗定秀作)
nagasa 78,5 cm, *sori* 2,6 cm, *shinogi-zukuri*, *iori-mune*

ji: dense *ko-itame* mixed with *nagare*, fine *ji-nie* and a *shirake-utsuri*
hamon: *yaki-otoshi*, later a *hoso-suguha-chō* mixed with *ko-midare*, *ko-gunome* and *ko-chōji*, in addition some *hotsure* and small *yubashiri*, the *nioiguchi* is entirely subdued and misty
bōshi: very narrow *notare-komi* with a *ko-maru-kaeri*

This is one of the few extant *zaimei* blades of Bungo Sadahide. It is designated as *jūyō-bijutsuhin* and comes from the collection of Suzuki Kajō (鈴木嘉定). Regarding the shape, we have a textbook example of a late Heian, early Kamakura period *tachi-sugata*, that means a slender *mihaba*, a *ko-kissaki* and a deep *koshizori* which bends down towards the tip and *funbari*. The *jigane* is also very typical for Sadahide. It is densely forged and looks „wet", a feature which is common for Kyūshū blades and therefore also called „*Kyūshū-gane*" (九州鉄). This and the *yaki-otoshi* identify the blade apart from the shape as early Kyūshū-*mono* from the beginning Kamakura period too and so we can nail down the bid on Sadahide, Yukihira (行平) or Ko-Naminohira (古波平).

Sadahide was according to transmission a student of Yukihira and so he worked in a rather close style. But in direct comparison, Yukuhira´s blades show a little more *tobiyaki* and Sadahide applied more often (mostly simple) *horimono*. However, Sadahide and Yukihira belong to the best old Kyūshū smiths and this blade is one of the most outstanding extant works of Sadahide.

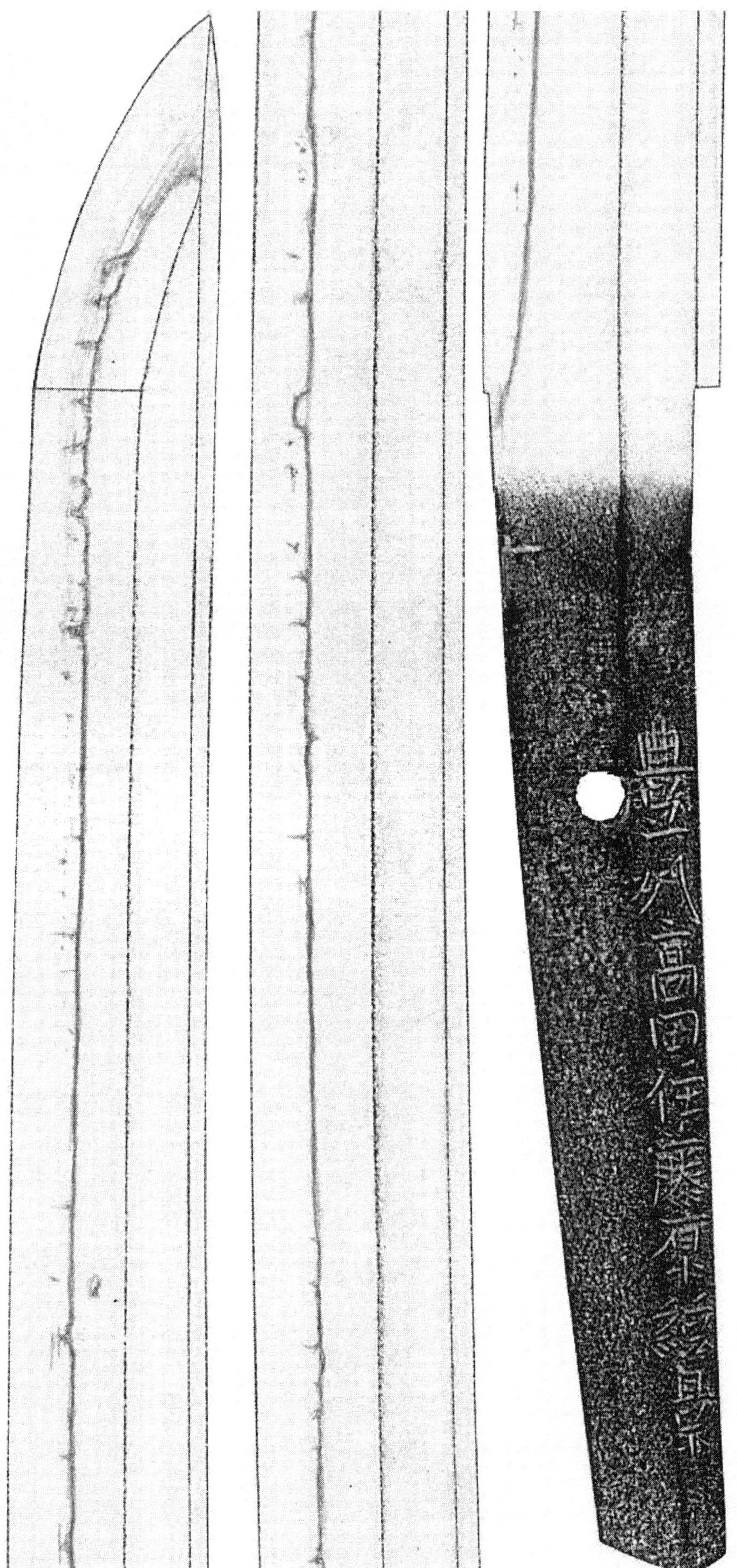
豊後国高田住藤原

182.655 *katana*
mei: Hōshū Takada-jū Fujiwara Munekage (豊州高田住藤原統景)
nagasa 71,4 cm, *sori* 1,7 cm, *shinogi-zukuri*, *iori-mune*

ji: dense *ko-itame* with *ji-nie* and a *shirake-utsuri*
hamon: *hiro-suguha*, partially mixed with some angular *gunome*-like elements, in addition *ashi* and *yō*, the *nioiguchi* is compact and shows *ko-nie*
bōshi: on both sides *sugu* wich tends to *yakitsume* and which shows angulary arranged *ashi* and *yō*

This is a *katana* of the Takada smith Munekage who was active around the end of the Muromachi period. The blade has a wide *mihaba* and an *ō-kissaki*, that means it looks large and magnificent and because of this shape and the *suguha-hamon*, many were too early at the *kantei* and went for the Aoe school. However, this is not an *ō-suriage* Nanbokuchō shape from the Enbun (延文, 1356-1361) and Jōji eras (貞治, 1362-1368) but an *ubu uchigatana-sugata* with *funbari* and *sakizori*, that means we are definitely in the late Muromachi period.

In the case of the Aoe school we would expect a finely standing-out *itame* mixed with *mokume* and *chikei* which appears as typical *chirimen-hada*. Also the steel would blueish black. Here we have a dense *ko-itame* which does not show any of the aforementioned characteristics and also does not reach the quality of an Aoe-*jigane*. In addition, there is no Aoe-typical *dan-utsuri* but a faint *shirake-utsuri*. Well, the *hamon* is as mentioned a *suguha* which is similar to Aoe but the *ha* is not so bright and clear and does not show the same *hataraki*. We see here namely the small pointed *ashi* and *yō* which are often described as „like scratched with a needle into the *ha*“. This is a very typical characteristic of Takada works.

Some got the time right but went for the Sue-Bizen mainline and smiths like Genbei no Jō Sukesada (源兵衛尉祐定). In that case, the *jigane* would also appear as *jigane* but with finer *chikei* and a much brighter *ji-nie*. And furthermore, the *jihada* would be finer and better forged and the *hamon* would show larger *nie*, *ashi* and *yō*.

Takada smiths of the late Muromachi period like Nagamori (長盛) or Shizunori (鎮教) made blades with a typically wide *mihaba*, no noticeable taper, a *chū-kissaki* and a conspicious *sakizori*. But at smiths like Munekage who was active somewhat later and towards the end of the Muromachi period, we often find an even larger *sugata* which is a precursor of the Keichō-*shintō* shape. [Translators note: Munekage is dated into the Bunroku era (文禄, 1592-1596).]

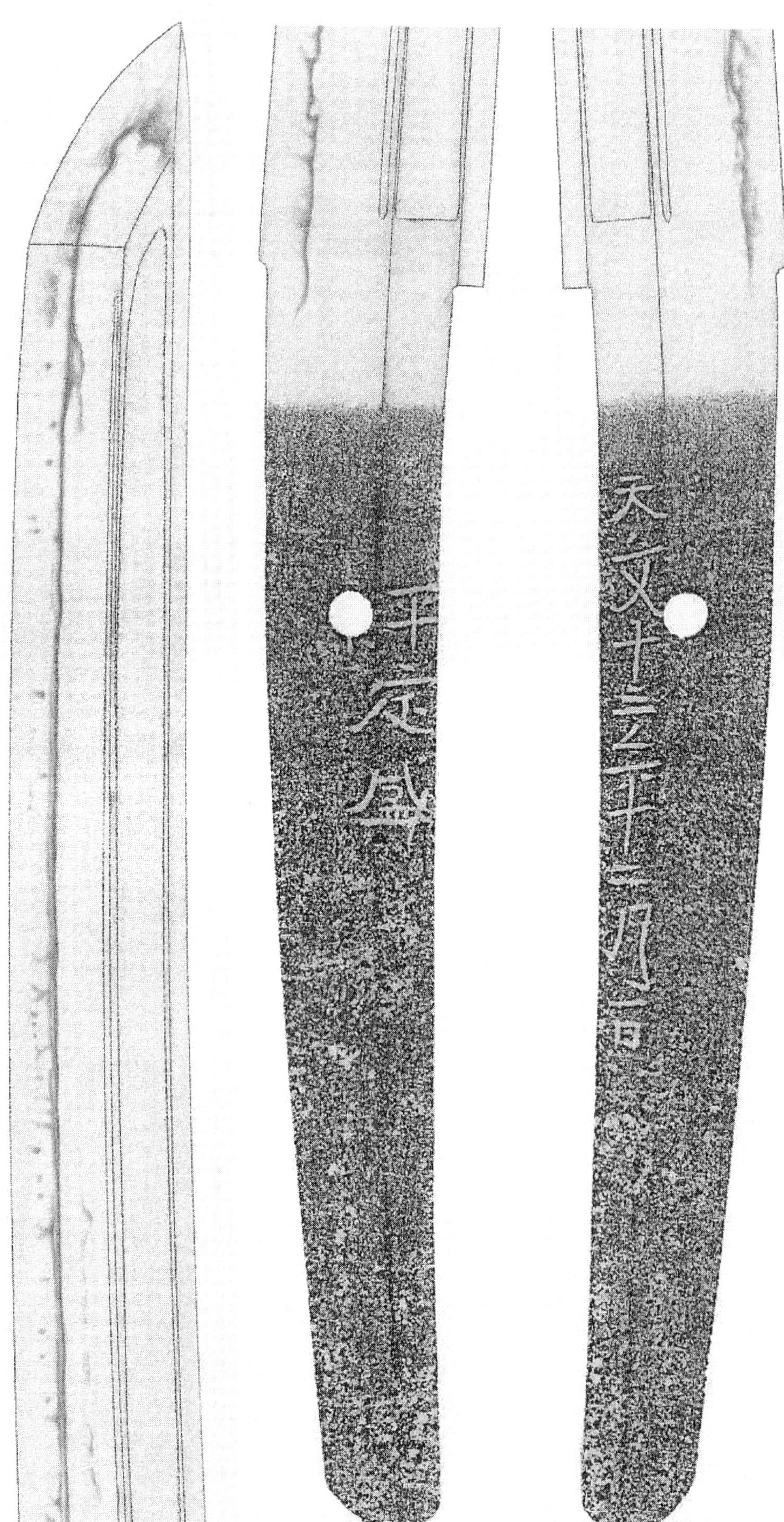
平定盛
天文十三年十二月日

183.592 *katana*

mei: Taira Sadamori (平定盛)
Tenbun jūsannen nigatsu ichinichi (天文十三年二月一日, „first day in the second month Tenbun 13 [= 1544]")

nagasa 70,9 cm, *sori* 3,3 cm, *shinogi-zukuri*, *iori-mune*

ji: standing-out *itame* mixed with *mokume* and *nagare*, *ji-nie*, *chikei*, there is a faint *shirake-utsuri* along the lower half of the blade

hamon: *hiro-suguha* mixed *ko-gunome* and *ko-chōji*, in addition *ko-ashi* and many *yō*, the *nioiguchi* is compact and shows *ko-nie*, some *nijūba* and small *yubashiri*

bōshi: *sugu* with some *midare* towards the *ko-maru-kaeri*, also *hakikake*

horimono: on both sides a *bōhi* with *soebi* whereas the *bōhi* ends with a *kaku-dome* and the *soebi* with a *maru-dome*

The Takada school (高田) of Bungo province was founded during the Nanbokuchō period by Tomoyuki (友行) and Tokiyuki (時行). The school was quite successful and flourished throughout the entire Muromachi and Edo period, whereas the *shintō* smiths are classified as „Fujiwara-Takada" (藤原高田). The latter name goes back to the signature because with the Edo period, most of the Takada smiths started to sign with the clan name „Fujiwara". On the other hand, the *kotō*-period Takada smiths signed mostly with „Taira" (平) and so they are also called „Taira-Takada" (平高田). Anyway, many of the Takada smiths used either the character „Mori" (盛) or „Shizu" (鎮) in their names.

The workmanship of the school experienced several phases and is quite varied. First a *gunome*-based *midareba* was applied which was more and more given up in favor of a *suguha*. The *suguha* was changed to a *notare*, followed by a *koshi-no-hiraita gunome* in Sue-Bizen style and also a *hitatsura*. Works in *suguha* show a characteristically compact *nioiguchi* and „hard" looking *ko-ashi* and *yō*. The latter *hataraki* are also circumscribed as „like if they were scratched into the *ha* with a needle". The *kantei* blade shows them very well and also the typically strong *sakizori* of then Takada-*mono*. The latter is namely more pronounced than at contemporary schools.

Unfortunately, Takada blades are not so often presented for *kantei* and so only half of the participants got the answer right. Some went because of the *suguha* for Osafune Kiyomitsu (清光) but his *nioiguchi* is not that compact and his *ashi* and *yō* do not point right-angled towards the *ha* but slant also towards the tip.

Hugo

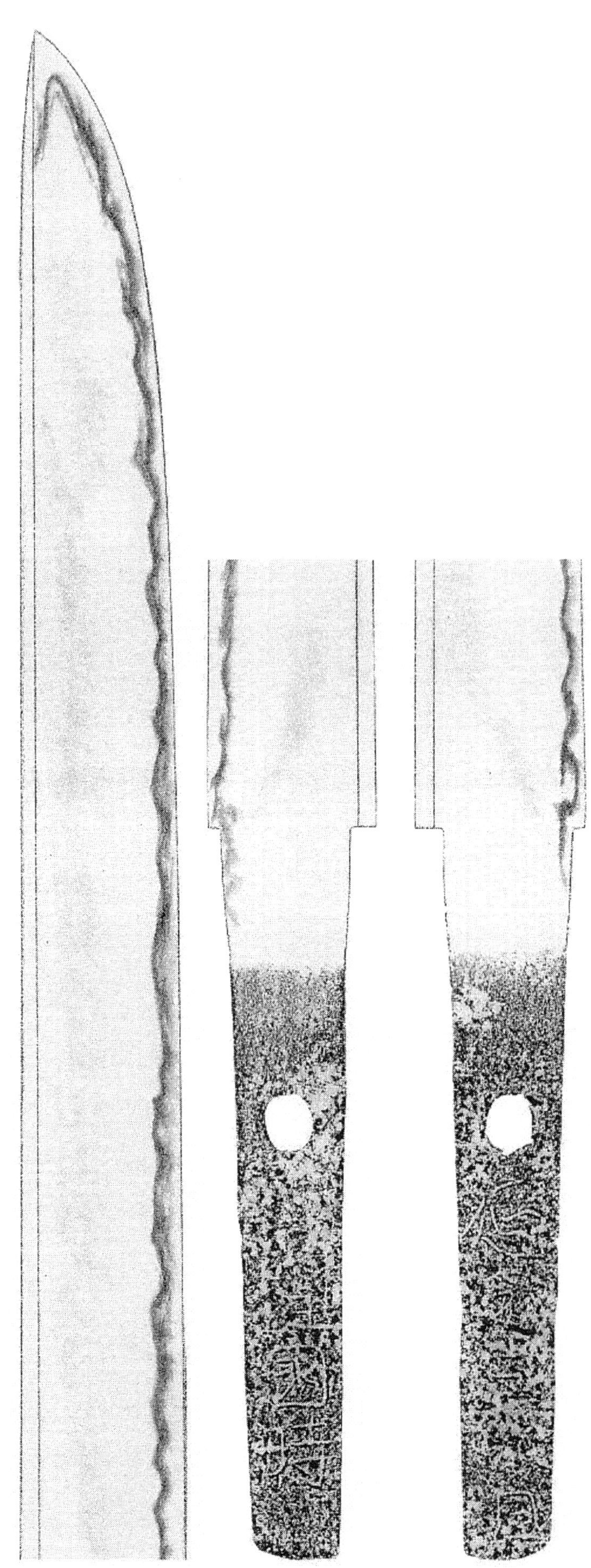

184.635 *tantō*
mei: Kikuchi-jū Kunitoki (菊池住国時)
Engen ... hi (延元···日, Engen = 1336-1340)
nagasa 24,2 cm, *muzori*, *hira-zukuri*, *iori-mune*

ji: rather densely forged but standing-out *ko-itame-hada*, partially some *nagare* and *masame* and an *utsuri* which tends to *shirake*
hamon: shallow *notare* mixed with *ko-gunome*, in addition some fine *sunagashi* and *kinsuji* and plentiful of *ko-nie*
bōshi: on the *omote* side *sugu* with a narrowing *ko-maru-kaeri*, on the *ura* side also *sugu* with a standard *ko-maru-kaeri*

Unfortunately the date signature is almost entire illegible, but the era can be read and so this is anyway one of the very few extant signed and dated works of Enju Kunitoki. The blade is relative wide, has almost no *sori*, and altogether a rather stout and robust shape. Such a *tantō-sugata* was typical for the end of the Kamakura era up to Kenmu (建武, 1334-1338). After that era, the *tantō* got constantly larger and wider, the *kasane* became thinner and the *sori* increased. The climax of this development was during the Enbun (延文, 1356-1361) and Jōji eras (貞治, 1362-1368).

The *kitae* is a rather dense *ko-itame* and the *hamon* a *ko-notare* mixed with *ko-gunome* and plentiful of *ko-nie*. Accordigly, rather few went straightforward to Enju but for the Rai school. But the blade was the most difficult one at this *kantei* session. At a glance, yes, it looks like a Rai work, but one had to recognize the *nijūba* along the *bōshi* of the *ura* side. When you combine this with the *masame-nagare*, you have the typical characteristics of the Enju school. There is namely not such a *masame* at Rai blades and also such *hotsure* and *sunagashi* are not seen.

Regarding the Enju school, it is hard to name an individual smith because their workmaship is very similar. But as a hint and judging from the quantity of extant works, it has to be mentioned that there are hardly any *tantō* of Kunimura (国村) and Kuninobu (国信) extant but some by Kunisuke (国資) and Kuniyoshi (国吉).

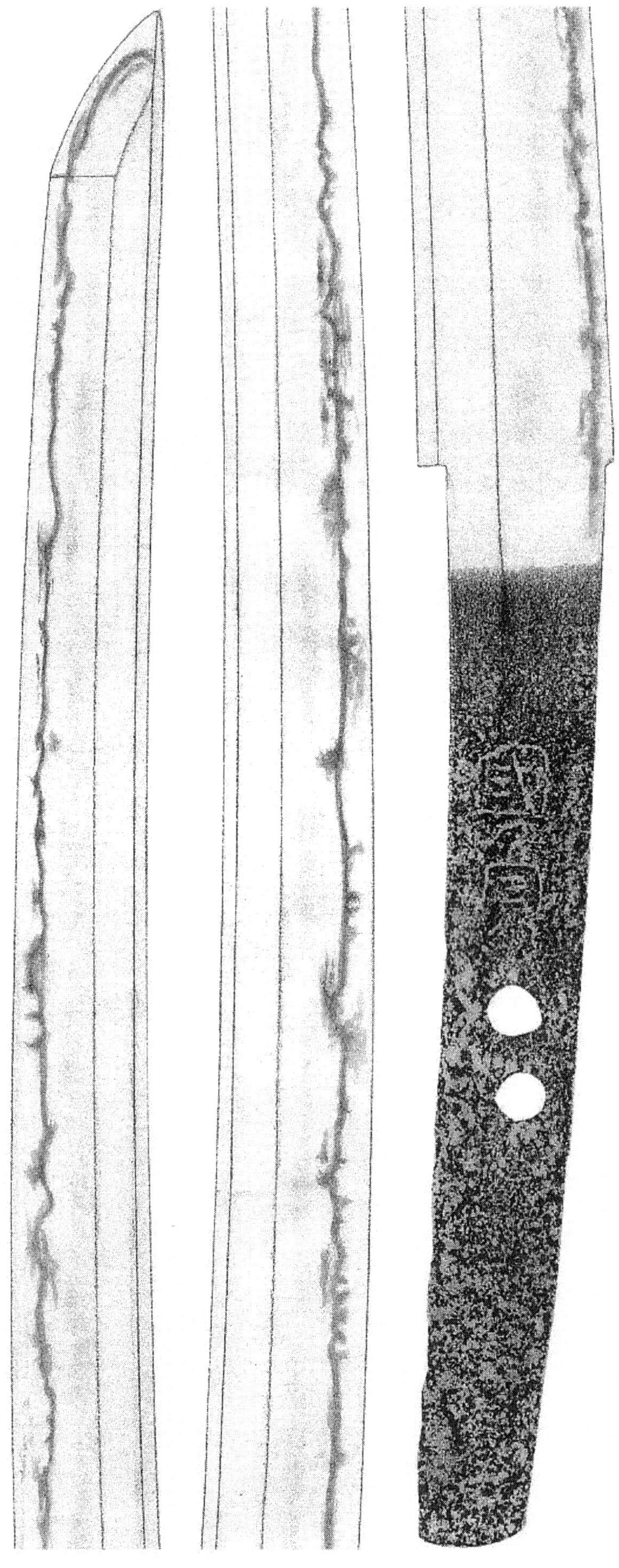

185.625 *tachi*
mei: Kunisuke (国資) [Enju]
nagasa 67,6 cm, *sori* 3,03 cm, *shinogi-zukuri*, *iori-mune*

ji: *ko-itame* mixed with *mokume* which tends all over the *haki-omote* to *nagare*, in addition *ji-nie*, fine *chikei*, and a *shirake-utsuri*
hamon: *suguha-chō* which tends somewhat to *notare* and mixed with *ko-chōji* and *ko-gunome*, in addition *ashi*, *yō*, *ko-nie*, fine *kinsuji*, *sunagashi*, and *yubashiri* as *yubashiri*-like *tobiyaki* which appear parallel to the *yakigashira*, also a *nijūba* appears in places
bōshi: shallow *notare* with a *kuichigai-ba* on the *haki-omote*, on both sides a *nie-kuzure* appears towards the tip which turns partially into a *nijūba* on the *ura* side

The blade has a relative slender *mihaba*, tapers noticeably, has a deep *sori* and ends in a compact *ko-kissaki*. The *sori* does not bend down towards the tip but appears as regular *toriizori* and so most of the participants bade on Rai Kunitoshi (来国俊) and Rai Kunimitsu (来国光). Well, the *kantei* blade has quite a bright *jiba* for the Enju school and also the outstanding quality speaks at a glance for the Rai school. So this might be the reason for the bids, combined with the elegant *sugata* which would speak for Rai Kunitoshi and the *midareba* which would speak for Rai Kunimitsu.

The *jigane* does not show much tendency towards *masame* as we would expect it for the Enju school and interestingly, the *haki-omote* is finely forged and the *ura* side tends rather to a somewhat rougher *nagare*. Such a characteristic is known from some Rai works and the conspicious *yubashiri*-like *tobiyaki* which turn into a discontinuous *nijūba* in places might be interpreted in the favor of Rai Kunimitsu. So this blade shows clearly that the Enju school is a Rai offshoot. However, the *utsuri* is not a *nie-utsuri* and the *nie* of the *hamon* and *habuchi* are not uniform. Also typical for Enju are the vivid *ashi* and *yō* and the *bōshi* in *nie-kuzure* and *nijūba*.

Most of the Enju smiths worked in a very similar style and so it was enough to bid on Enju in general. But incidentally, mostly the signed blades of Kunisuke show such a varied and bright *hamon* and they testify to his great skill. Some went directly for Kunimura (国村) and Kunitoki (国時). In general it might be said that Kunimura´s blade are usually longer and his *jigane* tends more to stand out. And Kunitoki´s *hamon* in turn bases mostly on a plain *suguha* with rather few *hataraki*.

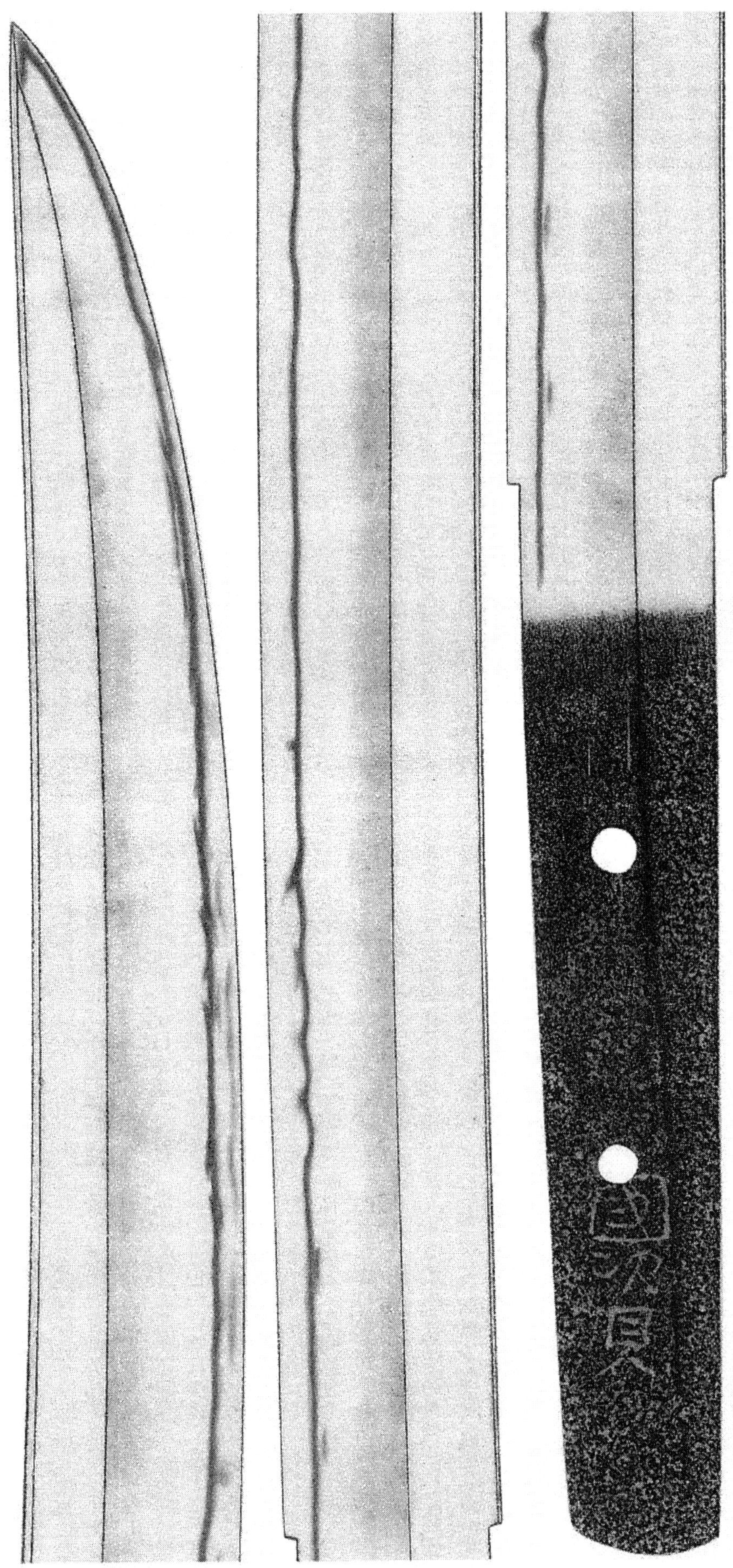

186.609 *naginata-naoshi wakizashi*
mei: Kunisuke (国資) [Enju]
nagasa 54,8 cm, *sori* 1,5 cm, *naginata-naoshi-zukuri, iori-mune*

ji: *itame* mixed with *mokume* which tends strongly to *nagare* towards the *ha* and turns almost into a pure *masame*, in addition *ji-nie*, fine *chikei* and a *nie-utsuri*
hamon: based on *suguha* with partial shallow *notare* and mixed with *ko-gunome*, some few *ko-ashi*, the tight and bright *nioiguchi* shows *ko-nie*, some *hotsure*, fine *kinsuji* and *sunagashi*
bōshi: *sugu-chō*, the *omote* shows a kind of *ko-maru-kaeri* and the *ura* side is quite pointed, but *hakikake* are seen on both sides
horimono: there are traces of a thin *hi* parallel to the *shinogi*, namely seen on the upper half of the *omote* side and on the middle section of the *ura* side´s *nakago*

There is no *funbari* at the *base* and so we can assume that the blade is shortened. The *shinogi* is rather high and the *kasane* noticeably thin. The blade shows also a *sakizori* but scarce *fukura* and so we have a typical *naginata-naoshi* shape. And when we take into consideration the course of the *bōshi* with the pointed *kaeri* we can guess that this blade had once an old-fashioned, classical *naginata* shape. The *kitae* is excellent and finely forged and the *nie-utsuri* is clearly visible. And with the calm *hamon* in *ko-nie-deki*, the bright *nioiguchi* with the few *Kyō-saka-ashi* along the base, first of all the Rai school comes into mind. But the very strong *masame-nagare* towards the *ha* and the appearance of the *nie-utsuri* which reaches somewhat down to the *ha* too, we see some characteristics which do not match with Rai works. Also the *nioiguchi* is quite compact and the *nie* therein are not so strong, and there are in general rather few *hataraki* within the *ha*. In addition, the *nioiguchi* lacks the clarity of Rai-*mono* but is not dull and so we can nail the attribution eventually down to Enju.

Well, the smiths of the Enju school worked in a very similar style and so it was enough to bid on Enju. But when you want to use this attribution as a starting point for a direct *kantei*, than it might be said that within the Enju school most blades in this *tsukuri-komi* are known from Kunisuke and that his works are those who can eventually compete with the quality of Rai-*mono*. So a bid on him is in this case the most appropriate one among all Enju smiths.

Besides of Enju and Rai there were relative many bids on Yamato-*mono*. When we trace back the origins of the Enju school we will find a connection to the Yamato tradition but if it was really a Yamato work, then we would expect more horizontal *hataraki* focussing around the *habuchi*. Well, Kunisuke applied here and there *hotsure* and *uchinoke* and so the *yakiba* is more vivid than some other Enju works. So a bid on Yamato is not that off.

Incidentally, the signature of the *kantei* blade is chiselled contrary to regular *naginata* on the *haki-ura* side. But Kunitoki signed sometimes also on the opposite than usual side of the tang.

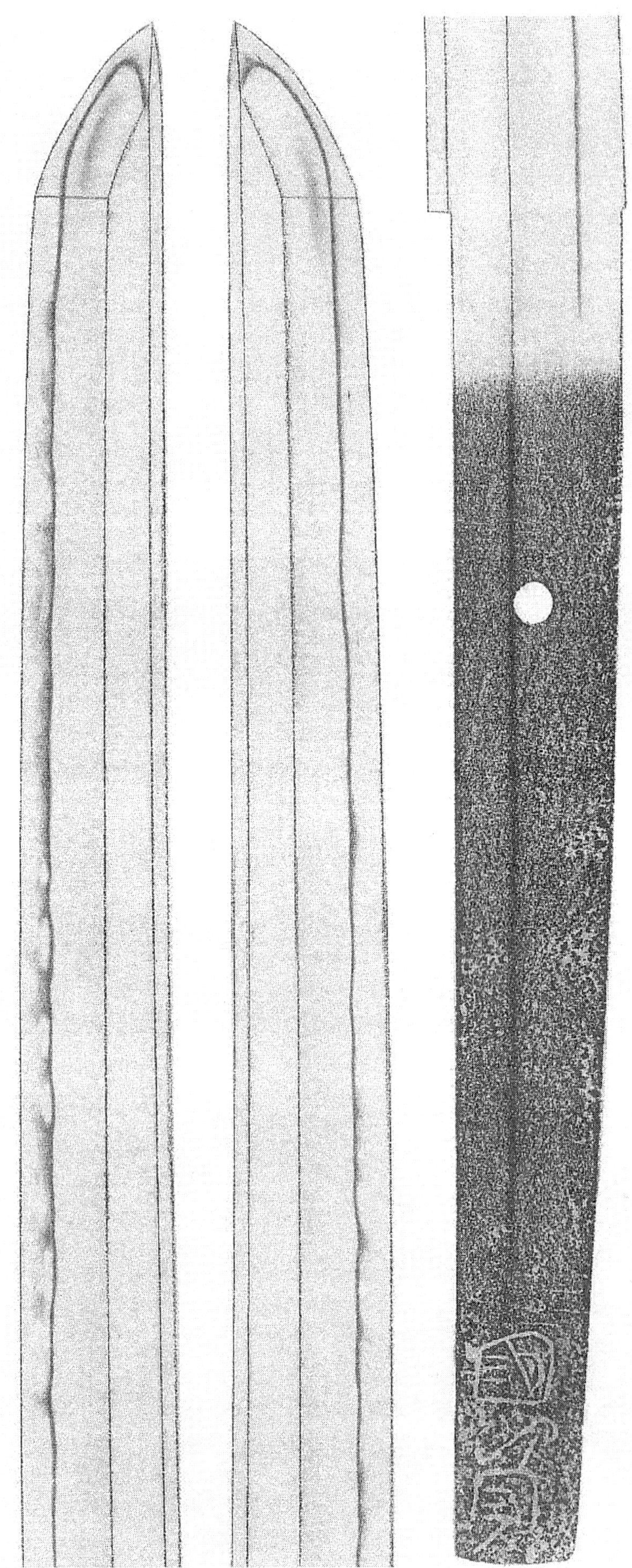

187.604 *tachi*
mei: Kunisuke (国資) [Enju]
nagasa 67,60 cm, *sori* 1,33 cm, *shinogi-zukuri, iori-mune*

ji: fine and densely forged *ko-itame-hada*, plentiful of *ji-nie*, faint *utsuri*
hamon: *chū-suguha* mixed with some *ko-gunome*, in addition *ko-ashi*, *ko-nie* and *nijūba*
bōshi: *sugu* with a *maru-kaeri* and *nijūba*

This *tachi* is a work of Enju Kunisuke. The Enju school is an offshoot of Yamashiro´s Rai school and moved with its founder Kunimura (国村) during the end of the Kamakura or early Nanbokuchō period to Higo province on Kyūshū where successive smiths like Kunitoki (国時), Kunisuke, Kuniyasu (国泰) and Kuninobu (国信) were flourishing. Like the Rai school many Enju smiths used the character for „Kuni" and from the point of view of quality, Kunisuke was closest to Rai.

The *kantei* blade has a slender and elegant *sugata*, the *jigane* is excellent and finely forged and the *hamon* is a *suguha* in *ko-nie-deki*. It does not show the common Enju workmanship with conspicious *masame* and a whitish *ji* but a refined *suguha* and so it is no wonder that many went for Rai-*mono* at the *kantei*.

But when we examine the blade more closely we see that the *habuchi* is too tight for Rai and that the *nioiguchi* is not so bright. Also the *hataraki* within the *ha* are inferior to the Rai school. In addition, the *kaeri* is a bit too round and short for Rai and such a *nijūba* within the *bōshi* is a often seen on Enju works.

But not all Enju smiths showed these characteristics so clearly. Kuniyasu for example made often quite *nie*-loaden blades and Kunimura forged often long and slender classical *tachi* with a *ko-kissaki*. So for the final bid we have to go back to the undertanding that the quality does not reach Rai but is close and that Kunisuke was the Enju smith which came closest to the Rai originals. And voila, it is quite safe to bid on Enju Kunisuke.

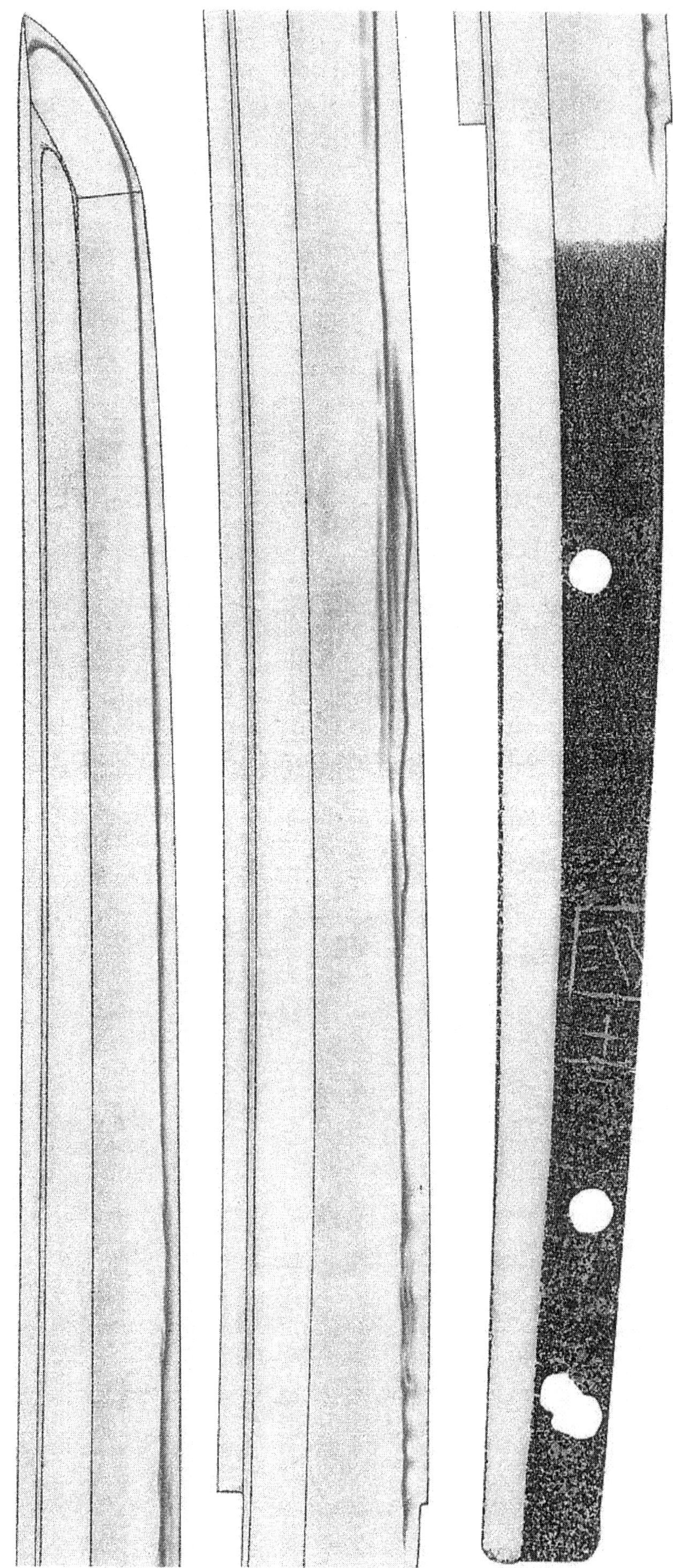

188.623 *tachi*
mei: Kuniyoshi (国吉) [Enju]
nagasa 75,5 cm, *sori* 2,1 cm, *shinogi-zukuri*, *iori-mune*

ji: dense *itame-hada* mixed with *mokume* and *nagare*, in addition *jifu*-like areas, plentiful of *ji-nie*, fine *chikei*, and a kind of *shirake-usuri*

hamon: *suguha-chō* which tends to a shallow *ko-notare* along the lower half, there are conspicious *nijūba* in the valleys of this *ko-notare*, also we see *ko-midare*, *ko-ashi* and plentiful of *ko-nie*, the latter are somewhat stronger in places and also *hotsure* and *kuichigaiba* appear which make the *hamon* appear partially frayed and dull

bōshi: *sugu* with a *ko-maru-kaeri* on the *haki-omote* side and *yakitsume* with only a little *kaeri* on the *ura* side

horimono: on both sides a *bōhi* which runs with *kake-nagashi* into the tang

The scarce *funbari* along the base let us assume that the blade is shortened but with the remaining *toriizori* we have nevertheless an elegant *tachi-sugata*. The *kitae* is a dense *itame* with plentiful of *ji-nie* and the *hamon* bases on *suguha* and is full of *ko-nie*. This *deki* reminds of Rai at a glance and because of the slender *sugata* and the *ko-kissaki* there were many who went for Rai Kunitoshi (来国俊).

Well, the *kitae* shows some *masame* which differs from the usual *masame* of the Enju school and the *jiba* is clear and so a bid on the Rai school is quite unterstandable. However, there is no *nie-utsuri* but a kind of *shirake-utsuri* and the *nie* of the *habuchi* are inhomogenous in strength and some parts of the *hamon* are unclear and dull. So we have to realize that this is not a Rai-*mono* but a work from a school which is close to Rai and thus we arrive at Enju.

In addition, there are conspicious *nijūba* along the valleys of the *notare* which appear along the lower half of the blade. Such *nijūba* are typical for Enju. The *kitae* shows some *jifu* and the *kaeri* is short, also two features of that school.

Most got that right and bade on Enju. However, the blade does not show peculiar features which would allow us a straightforward attribution to an individual smith and so a bid on Enju was enough to receive *atari*. But many went for Kunimura (国村) and Kuniyasu (国泰). Kunimura´s blades are mostly somewhat longer, taper, and end in a *ko-kissaki*, that means they show a rather classic and elegant *sugata*. Kuniyasu on the other hand applied more *ko-nie* which also tend to conspicious *ara-nie* in places. That means when one arrived at Kunimura because of the rather elegant *sugata* of the blade and at Kuniyasu because of the *nie*, than this was a very good *kantei*.

Satsuma

189.670 *tachi*
mei: Naminohira Yasutsugu (波平安次)
nagasa 72,3 cm, *sori* 2,4 cm, *shinogi-zukuri*, *iori-mune*

ji: standing-out *itame* which tends strongly to *masame-nagare*, partially also mixed with *mokume*, in addition *ji-nie*, *chikei* and a *shirake-utsuri*
hamon: *hoso-suguha* with some *ko-gunome* and *ko-notare*, in addition *ko-nie*, *kinsuji*, *sunagashi* and *hotsure*, the *nioiguchi* is subdued and rather dull
bōshi: *sugu* with *yakitsume*, whereas the *omote* side tends to *kuzure*

Let us first address the shape. We see a not that wide *shinogi-ji*, a high *shinogi* and a thick *kasane*, that means despite the rather narrow *shinogi-ji*, we can put the blade somewhere in the vicinity of the Yamato tradition. The *sugata* is generally slender and the *jigane* appears as *itame* with a strong tendency to *masame* and has the characteristical „sticky" appearance which brings us with the rather subdued *hoso-suguha* to Ko-Kyūshū. Well, the smiths of the Ko-Naminohira school worked all in quite the same style and so a bid just on Ko-Naminohira was enough.

Also active in Kyūshū were Sairen (西蓮) and Jitsu´a (実阿) from Chikuzen and Yukihira (行平) from Bungo. Bids on them were counted as *dōzen*. Jitsu´a is known within the group of Kyūshū-*mono* for his relative wide *mihaba* and Yukihira forged rather a fine *ko-itame* than a normal *itame*. So this blade would most likely be attributed somewhere in the vicinity of Sairen.

But some went also directly for Yamato and bade on Kanenaga (包永) or the Taima (当麻), Hoshō (保昌) or Shikkake school (尻懸). Well, Kanenaga´s works have quite a refined *jiba* and not such a standing-out *hada*. At Taima, the *nie* would be stronger and more conspicious and a tendency towards Sōshū gould be grasped. From the Hoshō school we would expect a pure ore even more *masame* and noticeable *hotsure*. And at the Shikkake school, the *hamon* would be different and appear namely as connected *ko-gunome*.

Made in the USA
Middletown, DE
05 September 2024

60381137R00258